The Microsoft Office 365 Bible

The Complete and Easy-To-Follow Guide to Master the 9 Most In-Demand Microsoft Programs

Secret Tips & Shortcuts to Stand Out from the Crowd and Impress Your Boss

Max Clark

Table of Contents

★ A GIFT FOR YOU (DOWNLOAD IT) ★

SCAN THE QR CODE BELOW AND GET

- **The top 30 Excel interview questions and answers**
- **The top 5 mistakes everybody makes when using Excel**
- **The #1 secret I used to quickly improve my skills**

Microsoft Excel

Introduction

Excel is a database-like spreadsheet program. Large volumes of data may be organized and analyzed quickly and simply by using the individual cells in the spreadsheet. Using columns and rows, Excel allows you to store data in a logically ordered manner. Allows for the presentation of extensive data sets in an easy-to-understand manner. The corporate world's most used spreadsheet program is Microsoft Excel. All professions use Excel regularly: bankers, accountants, business analysts, marketers, scientists, or entrepreneurs. To remain competitive in today's global marketplace, all businesses must constantly adapt and innovate. Implementing training and development programs for staff is one method to keep on top of the newest technology and maximize revenue. Employers may safeguard their most important assets by ensuring their employees get ongoing training and growth opportunities.

A company's best workers desire to be stretched and work hard to maintain their leadership position. Employers may reduce employee turnover and the danger of losing their best employees to the competition by offering them the ongoing education they require to be productive as they aspire to be. This educational instruction often includes Microsoft Excel for Business. What is the purpose of Excel? Excel permits users to organize, analyze, & assess mathematical data, enabling managers & senior executives to make significant options that might directly impact the firm. They can better communicate their data to senior management if they are schooled in sophisticated Excel functionalities. It's also a must-have ability for those aiming to get to the top of their respective organizations. Both individuals and employers may profit from learning advanced Excel. Let's take a closer look at the benefits of using Excel as part of a company's regular staff training program.

After reading this guide, you'll get a firm grasp of the fundamentals of Excel, including what it is, how it works, the most useful functions, and formulae. To progress in your work, you must keep learning and improving your abilities. There are certain important abilities that advanced Excel emphasizes, and these talents may be put to good use in every position within a firm. After learning this guide, you must be able to: Visualize, modify, and assess the data. Improve the productivity of your workflow, projects, financial predictions, and budgets by developing equations that may help you collect more data. Provide senior management with an easy-to-understand collection of facts to analyze current projects or conditions at the organization. Create spreadsheets that make it easier to enter data and show it more meaningfully. The ability to decipher information in spreadsheets and from third-party providers and customers. Help the company by being capable of unraveling more complex data and finding solutions to its difficulties. Complicated financial and inventory records must be kept in order and balanced. Work with multiple departments and activities to develop tracking systems considering the diverse workflows involved.

So, it would help if you started this amazing journey of learning from basic to advanced features of excel that can help you grow in your professional and personal life.

Chapter 1: Getting Started With Microsoft Excel

Information may be stored, sorted, and analyzed with the help of Excel, a spreadsheet tool. Excel's tremendous features aren't only for experts; despite popular belief, anybody can learn to utilize them to their advantage. Excel simplifies working with many kinds of data, whether you're maintaining a budget, arranging a learning log, or making an invoice.

Microsoft Office Overview (Versions of Excel)

From 1985 up till now, there have been thirty versions of MS Excel. Most users use Excel 2016, Excel 2019, Excel 2021, or Excel 365. Excel has undergone major revisions with each release, and there are still notable differences between the Windows and Mac versions. The most recent version of Excel is what you should use to learn the program rather than an older version. The reason behind this is discussed in this chapter.

Excel 365

Excel 365 will live forever. Instead of a 3-year upgrade cycle, 365 adds new features with every edition.

Microsoft established "update channels" for Office 365 because corporate customers don't want continual change. Large corporations may choose six-monthly updates. This gave a tested "semi-annual" version in Jan and Jul. The Smart Method updates its books whenever Office 365 adds new functionality. In February 2022, Microsoft issued the sixth edition containing the Jan 2022 update. Only The Smart Method updates its products this way.

Excel 365 has gained numerous great features since 2019, but nothing compares to July 2020's Dynamic Arrays and functions. This change isn't minor. Excel's engine was rewritten to support dynamic arrays. Automatic Data Analysis & Natural Language Queries debuted in 2021. Expanded linked data types.

In Excel 365, many older functions behave differently, and array-aware functions have substituted several old favorites. LOOKUP replaces VLOOKUP.

Excel 365's new dynamic array feature surpassed Excel 2019. Dynamic arrays are incompatible with using Excel 2019 & will cause current (Excel 365) files to not operate in outdated versions. Excel 2021 has no trouble with dynamic arrays.

Excel 365 would be the newest, finest, and most capable Excel version & costs a small monthly fee.

Excel 2021

Many critics said Excel 2021 wouldn't exist, but they were incorrect again.

It's odd to offer another "perpetual license" edition of Office alongside Excel 365. Microsoft has adopted the SaaS model, where software is leased and not sold. Some buyers still favor the "buy once, use forever" strategy.

Many pundits believe Excel 2021 is the final perpetually licensed version. Excel 2021 is already far behind Excel 365, with connected data types, automated analysis, & Natural Language inquiries only accessible to Excel 365 customers. Some additional innovations are introduced to Excel 2021. Excel 2021 included dynamic arrays and related capabilities.

Excel 2019

Many critics believe Excel 2019 is the final perpetual license edition. Excel 2019 is already far behind Excel 365, with dynamic arrays only accessible to Excel 365 customers. No new additions have been introduced to Excel 2019.

All versions of Excel 2019 have Power Query, Power Pivot, & Power Maps (3D Maps). These high-level OLAP tools let Excel examine "big data" and execute "contemporary data analysis" on any version. "Power" tools have developed since MS Excel 2019 was published, providing more "power" capabilities accessible solely to Excel 365 customers.

Excel 2016 and Excel 2016 for the Office 365 Members

There were two major ways in which Excel 2016 diverged from earlier versions of the program:

While there are significant differences between the Mac & Windows versions, both are referred to as "Excel 2016." (Previous versions utilized different year numbers to avoid confusion).

If you subscribed to Office 365, you got updates automatically over the internet, which made the copy of "Excel 2016" different from the version used by those who didn't pay for the service.

For example, we had to constantly update our Excel 2016 book to accommodate both Excel 2016 & Excel 2016 for Office 365 users, making this a challenging Excel edition to provide instructional materials. The two diverged during the product's lifespan.

The Smart Method breathed a sigh of relief when subsequent releases clearly distinguished between Excel 2019 & Excel 365.

Excel 2016 & Excel 365 for Windows

As with Excel 2016, MS has started rolling out incremental improvements to the program's functionality via the internet rather than waiting until a major version update is issued. Users who purchased the boxed retail edition of Excel were left with a completely different version of the program than those who subscribed to Office 365, who had access to all the new features.

Excel 2016 for Mac

Microsoft decided to finally unify the Excel names for both Windows and Mac in 2016 with MS Excel 2016. However, the iOS operating system's unique user interface still separates these apps from one another.

Excel 2013 (Windows)

Excel 2013 included the Slicers, Flash Fill features, & 50 new functions; however, it was only available for Windows systems.

Excel 2011 (Mac)

The 2011 version of Excel is Mac-exclusive. Excel for Mac no longer shared its name with its Windows equivalent since this was the final version.

This was version 13 of Excel for Mac, much as Windows' Excel 2010; however, because of fear of the number 13, Excel 2011 was renamed version 14.

Excel 2010 (Windows)

Microsoft Excel 2010 is exclusive to Windows PCs. The new features it debuted were the multi-threaded support, sparklines, the ability to personalize the Ribbon, and a hidden "backstage" view. Because 13 is an unlucky number, Microsoft decided to bypass version 13 instead of labeling Excel 2010 as version 14.

Excel 2008 (Mac)

Excel 2008 had only been made available on computers manufactured by Apple.

Excel 2007 (Windows)

The 2007 version of Excel is exclusive to Windows PCs.

Excel 2007 was a major improvement over past versions, including new features like the Ribbon interface and a new file format that replaced the old.xls and xlsm files. With this update, Excel files gained the capacity to contain over one million rows (up from the previous maximum of 16,384) & received significant security upgrades. The Excel charting tools have also been upgraded significantly.

Even though surveys at the time indicated that most users disapproved of the Ribbon, Microsoft stuck with it, and now, those same people wouldn't want to return.

Excel 2004 (Mac)

Excel 2004 was made available only on Macs.

Excel 2003 (Windows)

The "Windows, Menus, Icons, Pointer" ('WIMP') user interface, which was used in earlier versions of Excel, was retired in Excel 2003. There were drop-down menus & icons up top that you'd recognize if you used it.

Tables were introduced in Excel 2003 and were further enhanced in subsequent versions.

Older Windows version (2002, 2000, 97, 95, 4.0, 3.0, 2.0)

Previous versions of Excel may be traced back to 1987 with the introduction of Excel 2.0. Excel's most recognizable features have been around for quite some time.

1992 saw the introduction of Excel 4.0, which included the initial version of the now-standard AutoFill feature.

Excel 5.0 was published in 1993, and it was then that VBA and Macros first appeared. As a result of VBA's adaptability, Excel was a prime target for macro infections until the release of Excel 2007, which introduced new file formats with enhanced protection.

Excel 97 introduced the Office Assistant "Clippy," but most workers found it very irritating. Excel 2002 had it turned off by default, while Excel 2007 got rid of it altogether.

Older Mac version (2001, 2000, 98, 5, 4, 3, 2, 1)

Microsoft had a spreadsheet software called Multiplan that ran on MS-DOS & other console operating systems before Excel was even published; nevertheless, this is a little-known fact.

Excel 2, first released for the Mac, was ported to Windows in the initial version of Excel.

Microsoft's Excel 2019 on Windows & Excel 2019 on Mac go by the same name, and this isn't the first time they've done so; in 2000, Excel was made available for both Windows and Mac under the same moniker.

OS/2 Version (2.2,2.3,3)

In 1985, Microsoft and IBM collaborated to create OS/2, an operating system. There were 3 editions of Excel for OS/2 before IBM completely took it over in 1992.

Excel User Interface

Microsoft Excel users' interface is not limited to the grid pattern of columns and rows described within Excel Spreadsheets.

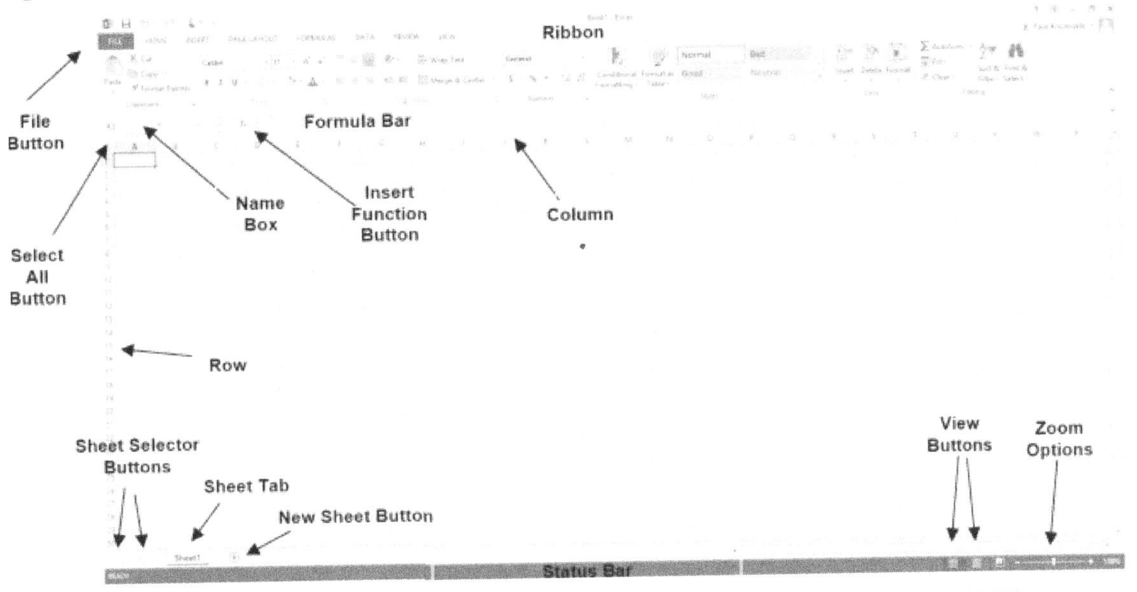

Interface Element	Description
Ribbon Tabs	Ribbon Tab is a tab that organizes commands by topic
The Ribbon	Commands underneath the Tabs
Ribbon Groups	Grouping of related commands
Dialog Box Launcher	Opens a dialog box that includes additional commands
Quick Access Toolbar	One click accesses to any frequently used command
Name Box	Displays cell location and can be used to navigate to a cell location
Select All Button	Selects all the cells in a worksheet
Formula Bar	View, enter, or edit cell contents
Insert Function Button	Displays Insert Function dialog box
Scroll Bars	Used to navigate up, down, left & right
Zoom Slider	Zoom into an area of the worksheet
View Buttons	Switch between Normal, Page Layout and Page Break Preview views
Worksheet tabs	Tabs used to select individual worksheets
The Workspace	The area inside of the columns and rows used in Excel
Columns	Columns use letters
Rows	Rows use numbers

Ribbon Overview

- **Home** - Standardized layout with access to standard features, common organization methods, and more.
- **Insert** - Use this section to enter various tables, figures, charts, hyperlinks, and other textual objects.
- **Page Layout** - Regarding Drawing Object Themes, Scaling, Page Setup, Sheet Options, & Layout
- **Formula** - The Insert Function, Formula Auditing, Range Name, & Calculations Options
- **Data** - Data Tools, Filter/sort, and Outlining are all Database Options.
- **Review** - To Edit, Comment, Safeguard, and Keep Track of Changes
- **View** - Indicators for Views, Hide/Show, Zoom, Window Controls, & Macros in a Worksheet

Excel Workbook

Workbooks are the common name for Excel files. In Excel, a new workbook must be created for each new project. Excel 2016 provides several entry points for beginning work on a worksheet.

You may start from scratch when making a new workbook, or you can use one of several available templates.

Creating a blank workbook

Here are the procedures you need to take to create a brand new, empty workbook in Microsoft Excel:

Start by going to the File menu, which will open the Excel Backstage window.

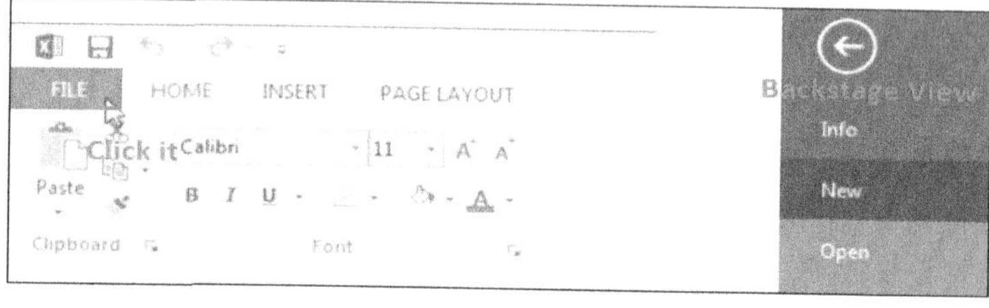

Followed by clicking New, followed by Blank workbook.

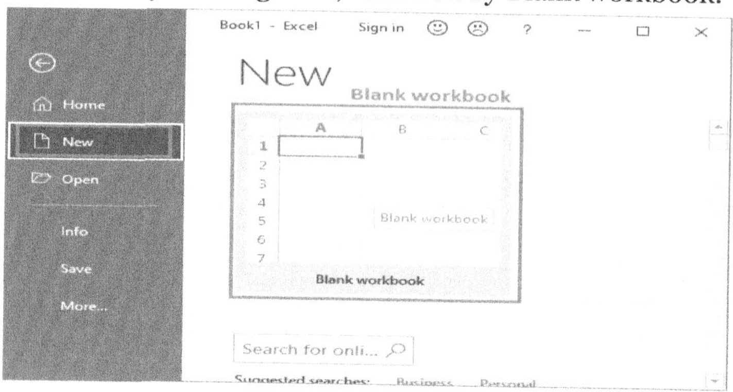

Here, a brand-new, empty spreadsheet will be generated automatically.

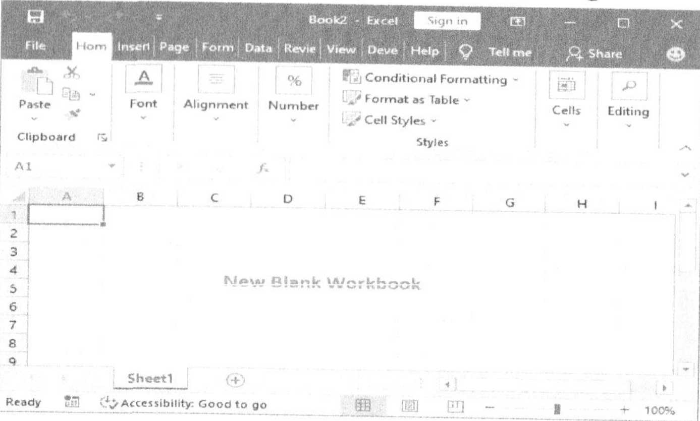

Open your existing workbook

You won't only be making new workbooks but also opening ones that have been saved. Data may already be present in an existing worksheet. It may be opened either in its native format or in Microsoft Excel. Just do what's written down here:

From the File menu, choose Backstage view, and then click Open.

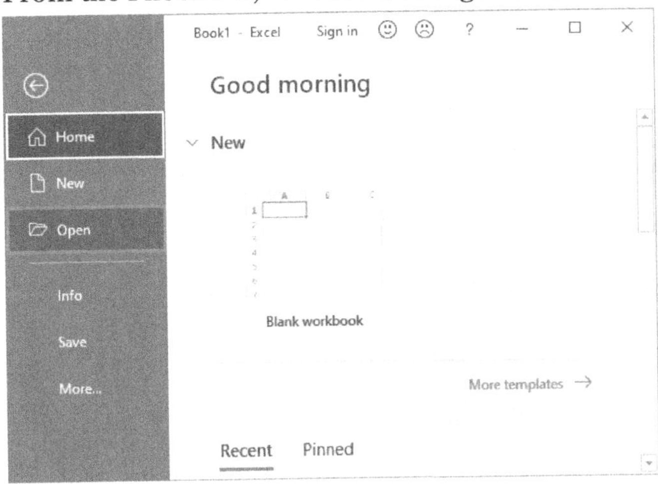

You can now use Microsoft Excel to access previously saved files from your local hard drives or your cloud storage space (OneDrive) under the "Recent" tab.

Opening an existing file from your local storage

Click your Browse option to choose an already-existing file from your computer.

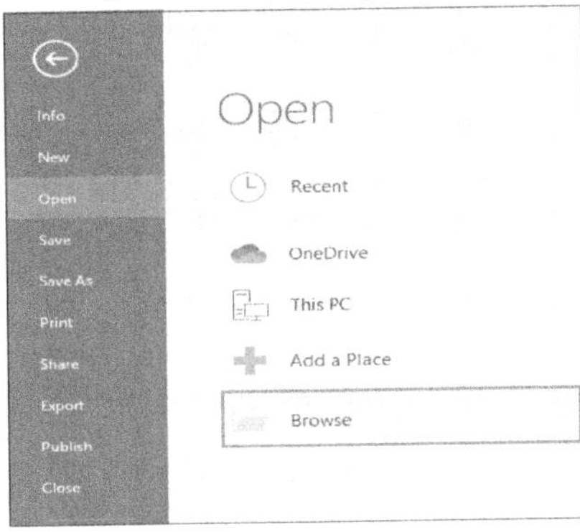

The Open box will pop up, and you may access your computer's local storage. Find the file you want to open, then press the Open button.

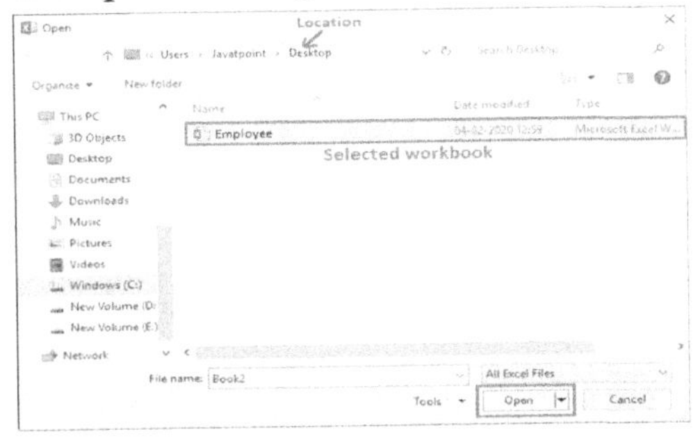

The Employee worksheet, found on the Desktop, has been opened.

Opening your files from your cloud storage

Follow these procedures to access your Excel file from a cloud service like OneDrive:

To access your OneDrive cloud storage from Excel backstage area, follow these steps:

If you haven't already, sign in to the OneDrive account.

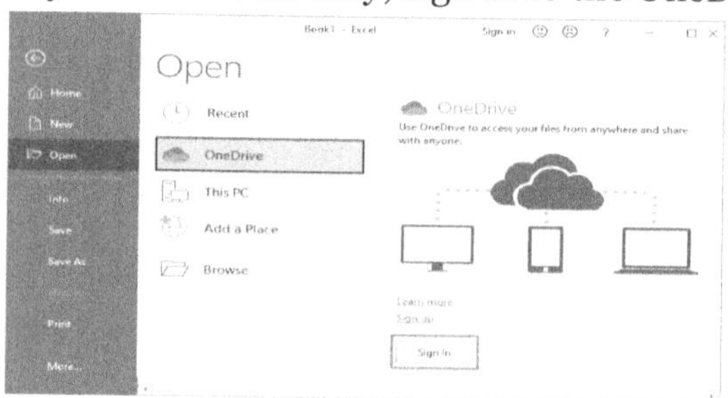

Now, access the existing file saved on the cloud storage.

You may save time by looking through your recently used workbooks instead of searching for the one you're looking for if you've opened it in the last few days.

Opening your existing files from the Recent files

In Excel, a Recent folder is available in the program's settings. It remembers recently seeing documents in a cache. Follow these instructions to access the included Excel file:

Click Open in Excel's backstage area, then locate the file you wish to open in Recent.

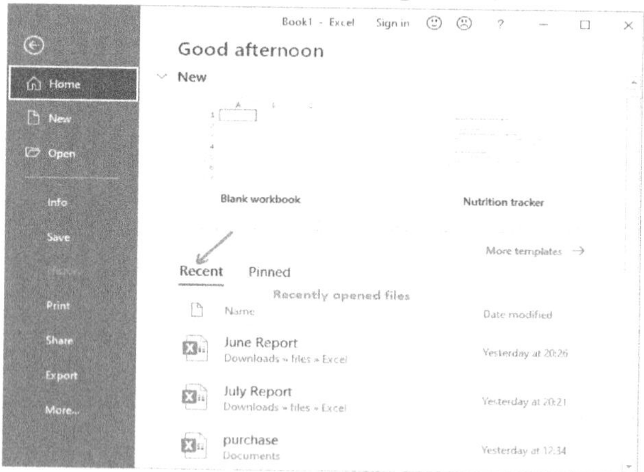

Pin your workbook

If you use the same worksheet often, you may "pin" it to your Backstage view so you can easily retrieve it.The first step is to open the "Backstage" window by clicking the "Open" button. Your revised workbooks are set in stone.

Second, you need to move the cursor over the desired spreadsheet before you can pin it. In the new window, a pin icon will appear next to the worksheet. Follow the on-screen instructions and choose the pin.

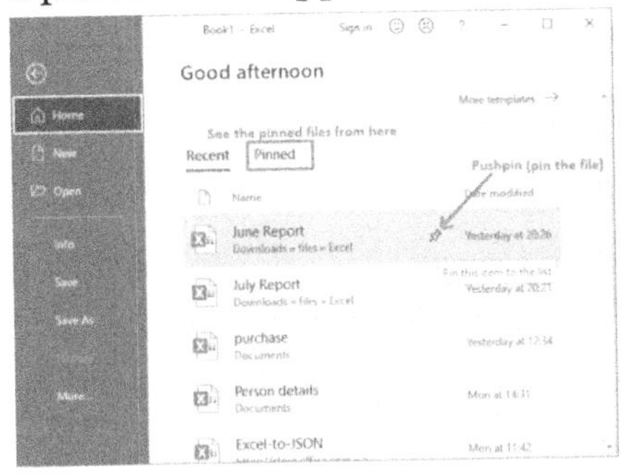

The workbook may be retrieved via the Recent Workbook or even the Pinned tab. Simply re-click the pushpin button to remove the workbook from the pinboard.

Compatibility mode

You may be working with a version of Excel many years old, like Excel 2003 and Excel 2000, and you have some files from that version lying around. Those worksheets need your attention and modification sometimes. The Compatibility view will be activated automatically when you open a file of this kind.

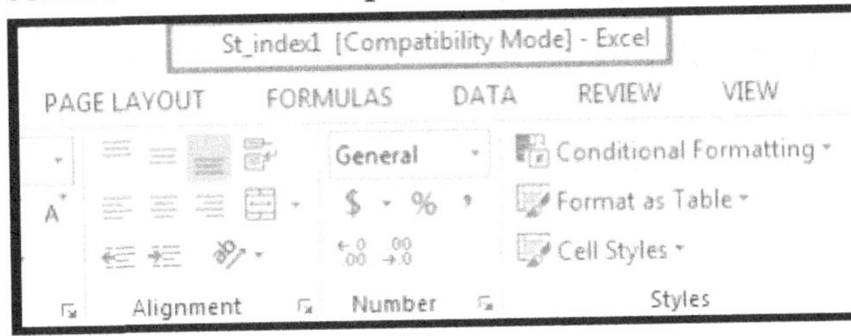

When you switch to compatibility mode, certain functions may be disabled. If a file was originally produced in Excel 2003, for instance, then just the tabs and instructions from that version of Excel will be accessible. As a result, you can only utilize the functions in the software that generated the worksheet.

To leave Compatibility mode, you must update the worksheet to the most updated version type. It's recommended to keep the worksheet in Compatibility mode if you're collaborating with people who are still using an older version of Excel.

For converting your workbook

You may convert the worksheet to the format used by the most recent version of Excel if you want to use all the enhancements in that program. For instance, update a workbook from an earlier version to the Current format.

If you want to open an older Excel file, follow these procedures.

1. Select the Information panel on the left side of the Excel Backstage screen.

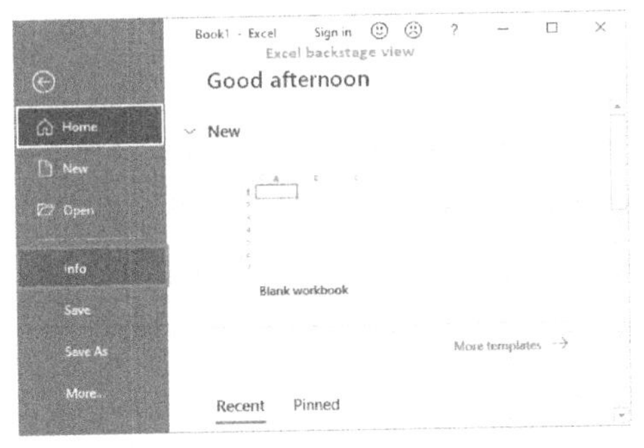

To do this, go to your Help menu, choose to Check for Issue, and then select Check Compatibility.

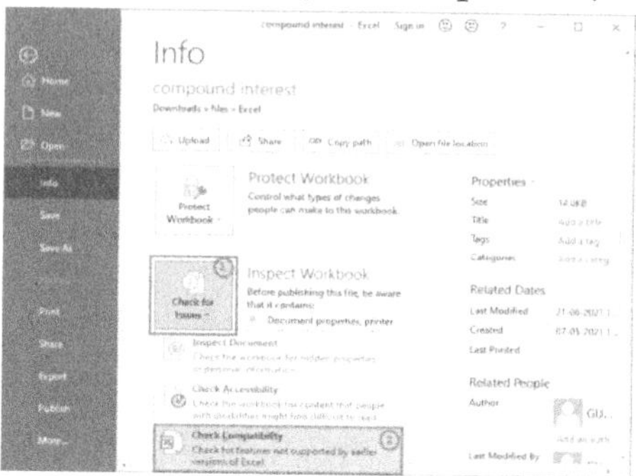

Compatibility issues with the current file will appear here. Click OK after selecting an Excel version.

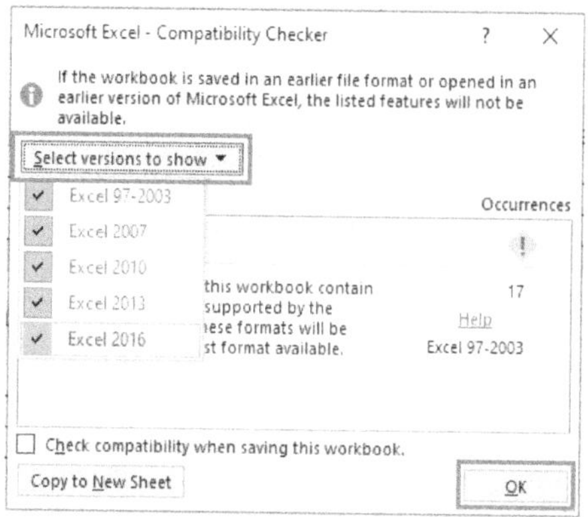

Open Save As. Choose where to store the workbook, name the presentation file, then click Save.

Your workbook will be updated.

Saving & Sharing Workbooks

When you create your new Excel worksheet, you'll need to save it so you may change it later. You may save Excel files locally, as in earlier versions. Excel 2016 and later versions save workbooks to OneDrive, unlike prior versions.

Excel can export & share workbooks.

Save & Save As

Save & Save As is Excel's file-saving option. These solutions are similar yet have key distinctions.

- **Save:** Save is used to save changes while creating or editing a worksheet. This is your main command.
- The first time you save a file, you must choose a location and a name. Click Save to save this with a similar location and name. Ctrl+S works too.
- **Save As:** This command duplicates the original worksheet. You must change the copy's name and location when using Save As.

Steps for saving your workbook

You must save your workbook when you start your new project or alter an existing one. Saving frequently prevents lost work.

1. Open your Quick Access Toolbars and choose Save.

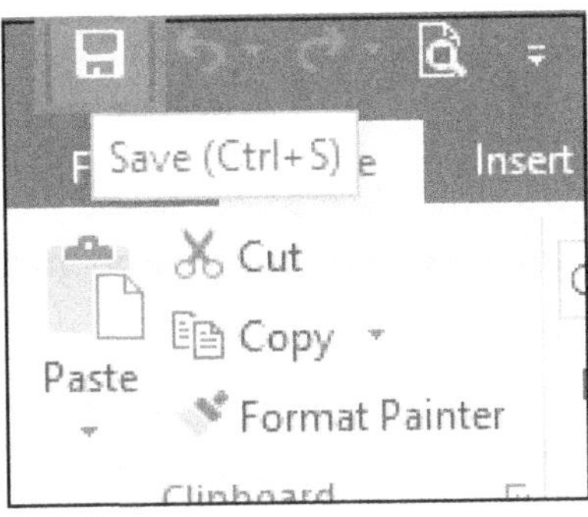

2. The Save As window appears in Backstage when saving a file for the first time. Choose a location and rename your file.

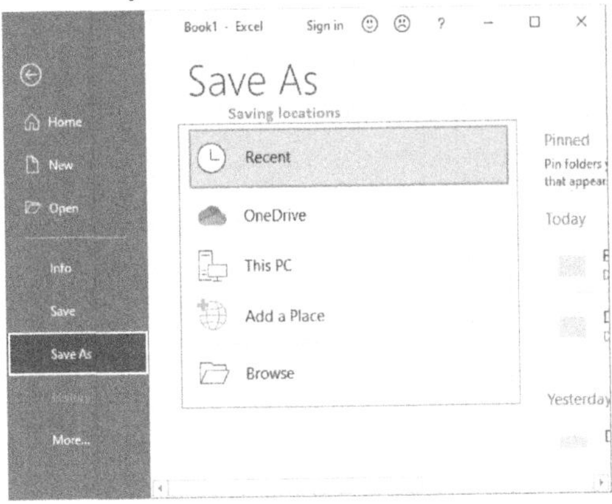

3. Click Browse to save the worksheet. Click OneDrive to save the file there.

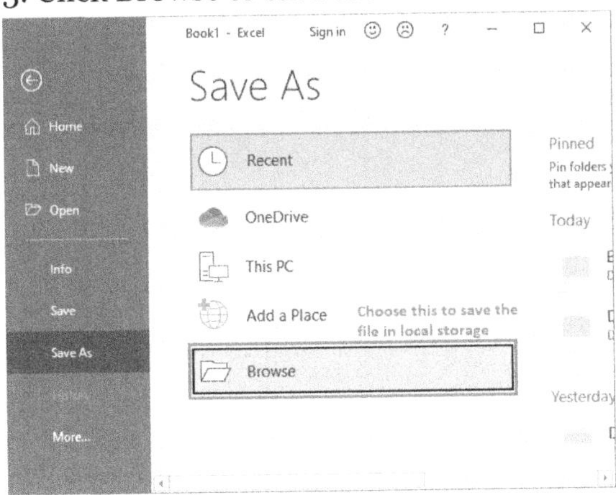

The Save As dialogue box will appear at this point. Your workbook will be saved in a local storage area. To save the worksheet, type in the file name and click Save.

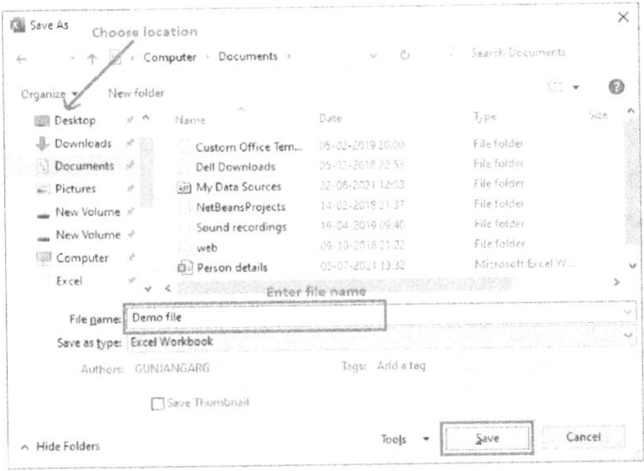

A copy of the spreadsheet will be stored. A Save command (Ctrl + S) may be used again to save your modifications to the worksheet as you make them.

Using your Save for making a copy

Create a duplicate of the workbook to save a new version while maintaining the original. If you had a file called "Sales Data," for example, you might save this as "Sales Data-2" so that we can modify the new file & still refer to the original.
Select a Save As button within the Backstage view of the currently open file. If you are doing this 1st time, just choose a location to save your data & give this a new filename.

Auto Recover

While working in an Excel spreadsheet, it automatically saves it to a temporary folder. Excel Auto Recover lets you recover a file if you've forgotten to save your modifications or if your Excel crashes.

Using Auto Recover

1. Open the Latest version of Excel. The Document Recovery window will appear if any previous file versions have been auto saved.
2. Click on a file to open it. You'll get the workbook back.

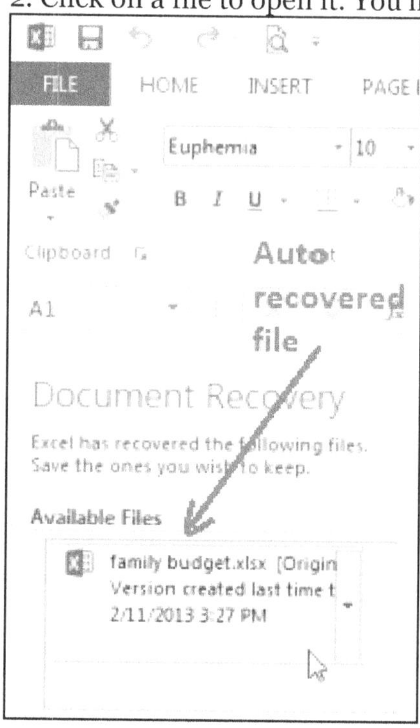

Using the Backstage view, you may go through all your AutoSaved files to find the one we're looking for. Look at the Help menu, then choose to Recover Unsaved Workbooks. You may configure the needed auto-recovery option from this point on.

Exporting Workbooks

Excel files are saved in the.xlsx file format by default. A PDF and Excel 97-2003 workbook may be appropriate in certain situations. Excel allows us to export your workbook in several file formats.

Exporting your workbook as a PDF file

A PDF file might be very useful if you want to share your workbook with someone who doesn't have Adobe Acrobat installed on their computer. Your workbook may be viewed but not edited by recipients using a PDF. To open the Backstage view, first, click the File tab. Export, then choose the option to create PDF/XPS.

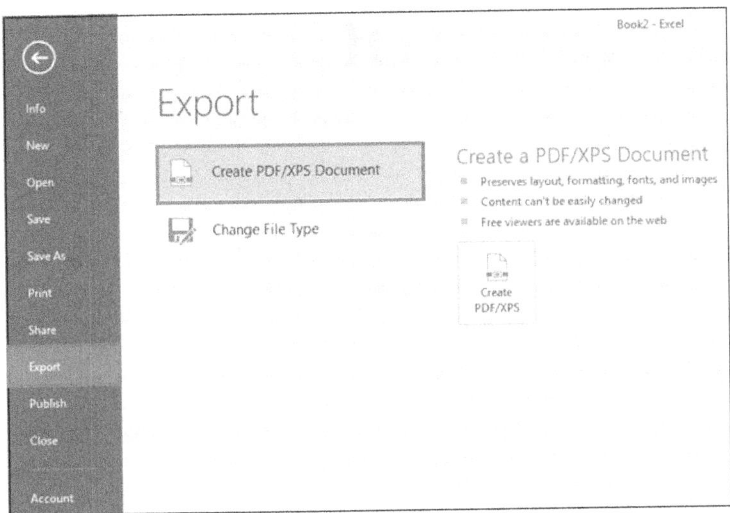

You'll see the Save As dialogue box open. Enter the file name you want to save and click the Publish button.

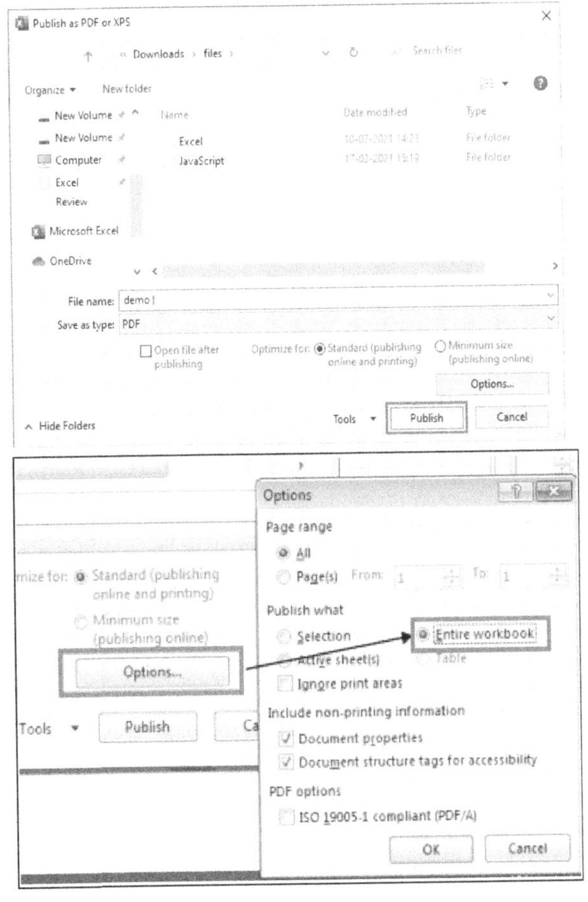

Exporting your workbook into some other file types

If you need to share your worksheet with someone using an earlier version of Excel, you may want to consider exporting it as Excel 97-2003 Workbook or a. If you require a plain-text workbook edition, you may use a CSV file instead.

To open the Backstage view, choose File from the View menu.

Click Export, then choose a different kind of file from the drop-down menu that appears.

Click Save As after choosing a popular file format.

A dialogue window called Save As will pop up. Click Save after deciding where to save the workbook and giving it a filename.

Chapter 2: Basic Features Of Excel

In this chapter, you will learn some basic features of excel including spreadsheets, understanding of rows and columns, conditional formatting, other users the features, feature excel and how you can import and export data in your excel file.

Understanding Excel Spreadsheet

There is at least one worksheet in each workbook. It would help if you created several worksheets to better arrange your workbook and make finding things easier when working with a sizable amount of data. You may also group worksheets to apply data to several worksheets at once.

Rename worksheet

One Sheet1 worksheet comes with a modern Excel workbook when you create it. The name of a worksheet may be altered to describe more accurately what's on it.

Right-click each worksheet you want to rename, then choose the worksheet menu.

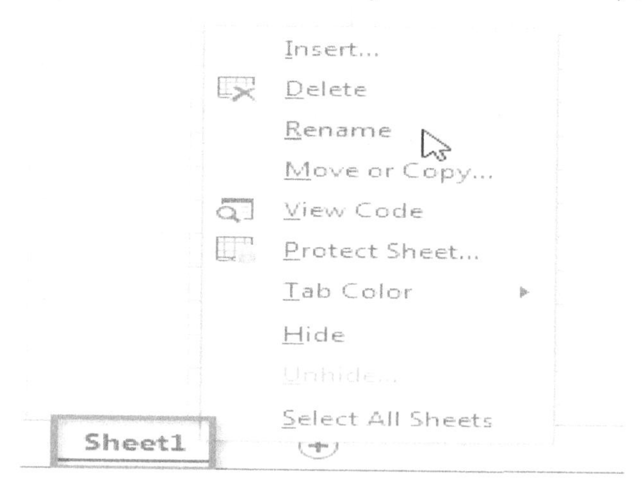

Name the worksheet you wish to use in the appropriate field.

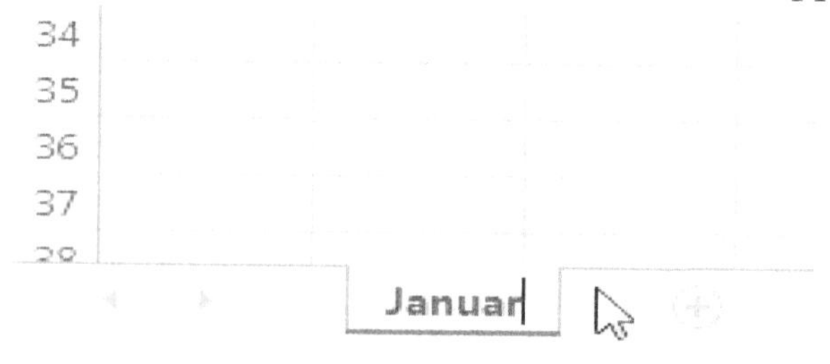

Press Enter or use your computer and mouse to travel outside your worksheet. The name of the spreadsheet would be modified.

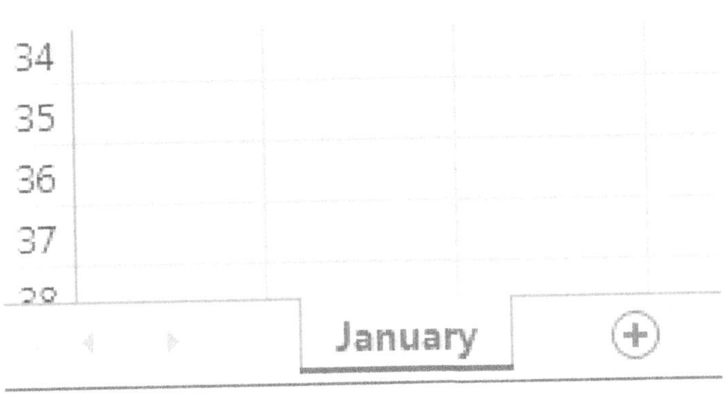

Insert a new worksheet

Click your new sheet key when you find it.

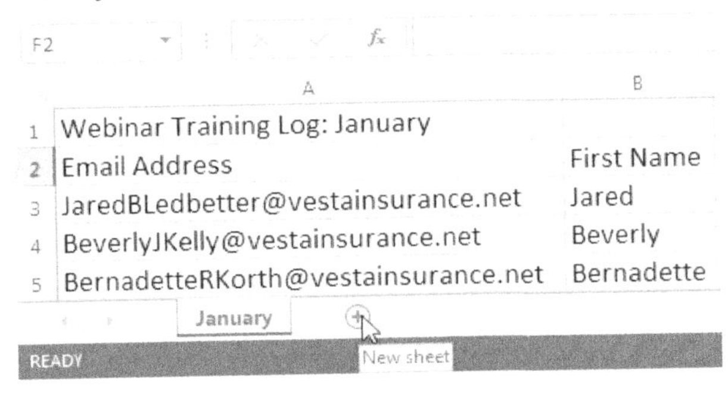

The screen would display a fresh, empty worksheet.

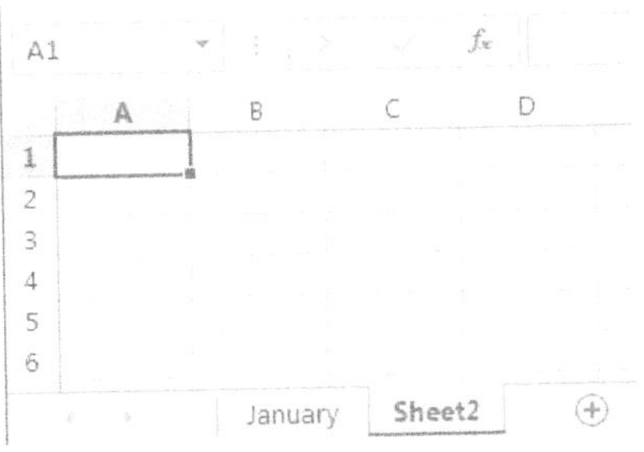

Go to Backstage preview, touch Options, and choose the appropriate number of worksheets for each new workbook to change the default workbook count.

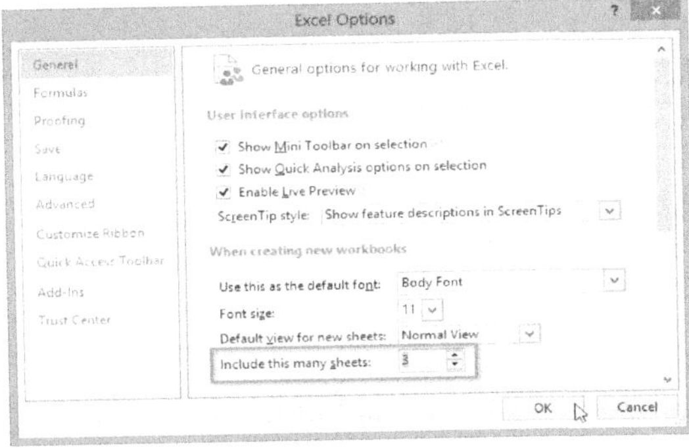

Delete worksheet

When you right-click on a worksheet you want to get rid of, you'll get an option to Delete it.

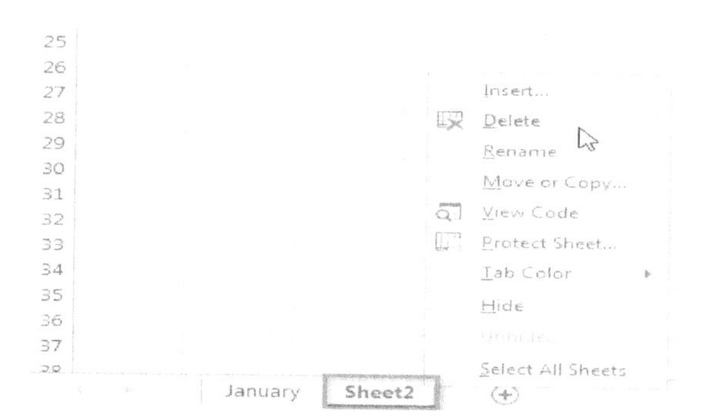

The worksheet on your spreadsheet will be removed.

When you right-click on a worksheet, you can choose Protect sheet from the worksheet menu to keep it from being edited or destroyed.

Copy worksheet

The contents of one worksheet may be copied to another using Excel's help.

Right-click the worksheet you want to copy and choose "Move or Transfer" from the worksheet menu.

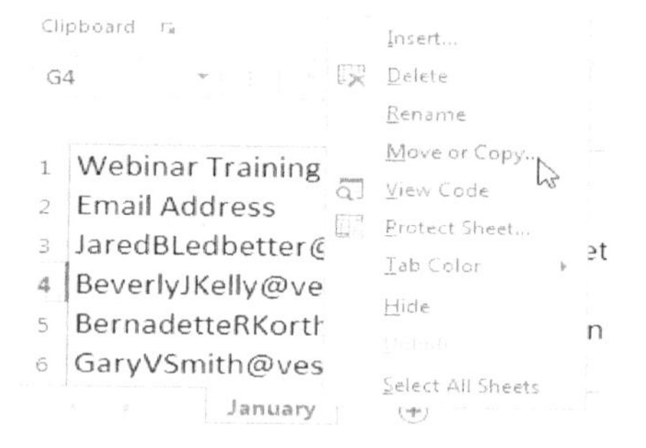

The "Move / Copy" dialogue box would display. Specify the location of your sheet in this field. The worksheet will be moved to the right of the present one (move toward the end).

Please click OK after selecting "Create a copy" from the drop-down menu."

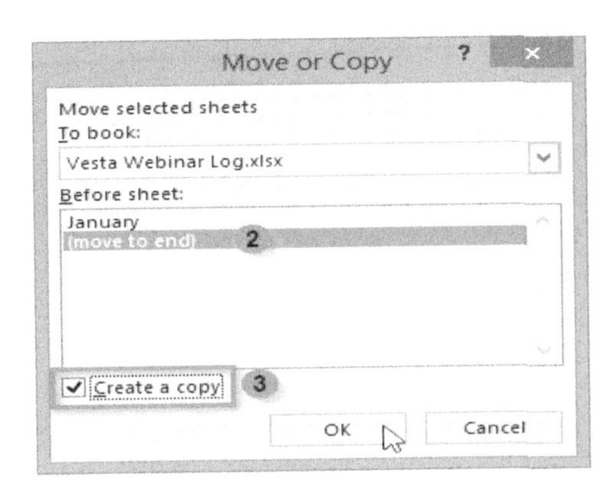

It will be possible to duplicate the worksheet. Your scenario's clone would have the same name & version number as the original worksheet since you copied it from a January worksheet (2). This month's data came from the January (1) worksheet and was carried over to the January (2) worksheet.

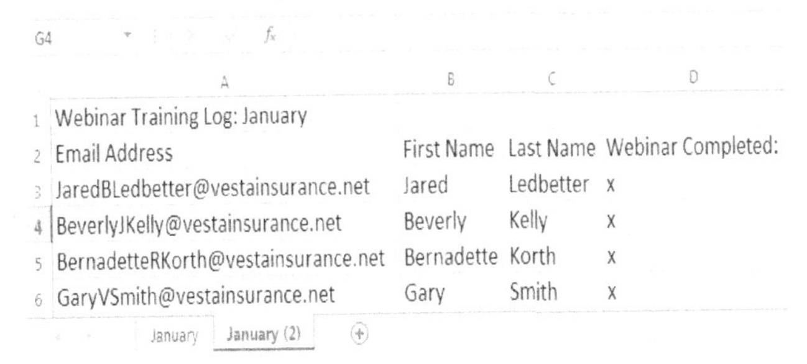

	A	B	C	D
1	Webinar Training Log: January			
2	Email Address	First Name	Last Name	Webinar Completed:
3	JaredBLedbetter@vestainsurance.net	Jared	Ledbetter	x
4	BeverlyJKelly@vestainsurance.net	Beverly	Kelly	x
5	BernadetteRKorth@vestainsurance.net	Bernadette	Korth	x
6	GaryVSmith@vestainsurance.net	Gary	Smith	x

It is also possible to copy a worksheet from one workbook to another. The book drop-down menu allows you to choose from any accessible workbook.

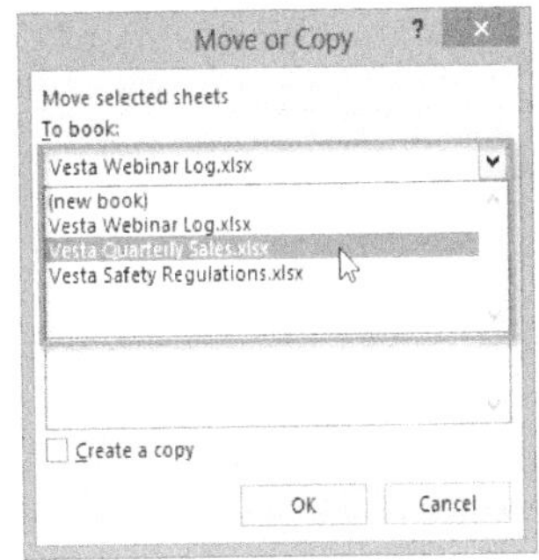

Move worksheet

You may have to swap out worksheets to rearrange the spreadsheet. Select the worksheet you'd want to edit. You may see the cursor change into a little worksheet icon. Keep an eye out for a little black arrow once you've kept your cursor on the target region.

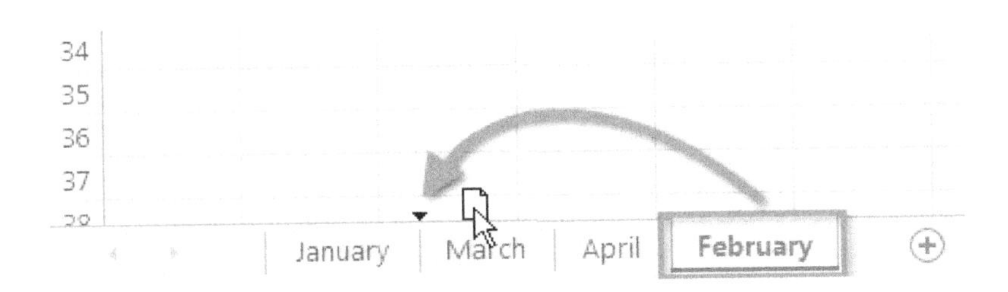

Release the mouse button. The worksheet has been moved to a new location.

Change the worksheet tab color

Change the color of a worksheet page to better organize your worksheets and make your workbook more user-friendly. After right-clicking on a worksheet tab, hover your mouse over the Tab color. The screen would show a color selection option. Pick a color that you like. As you move your mouse over different options, a sample of the most recent worksheet tab color will show. An example of this is Red.

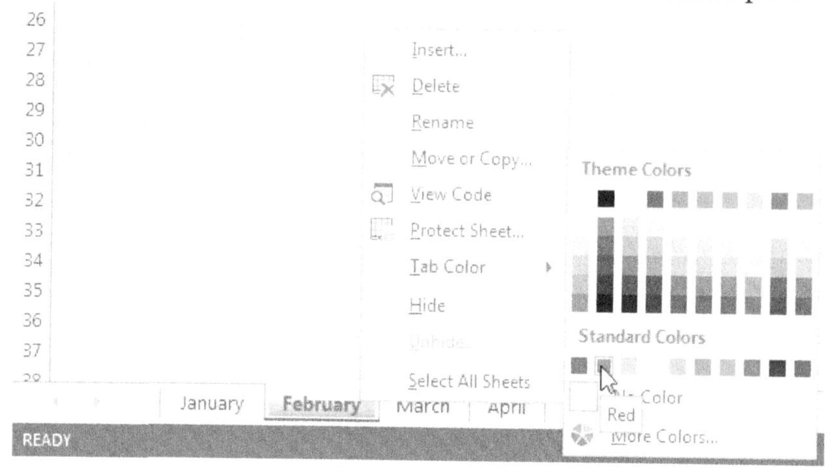

The tabs' color will be changed on the worksheet.

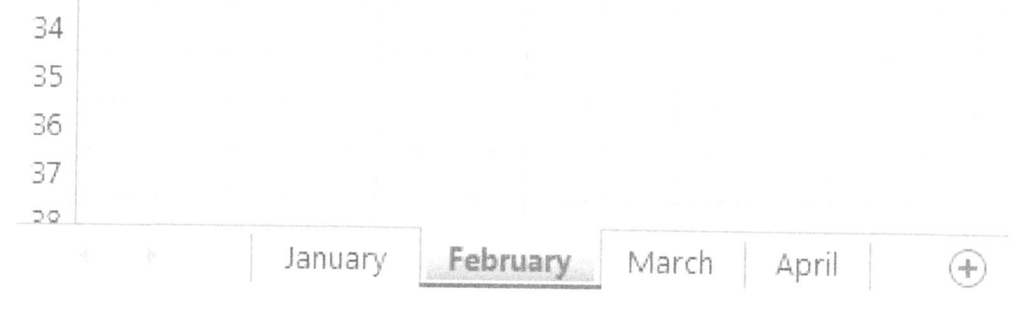

When you choose a worksheet, you'll see that the worksheet tab's color has faded dramatically. You can notice how the color changes if you choose another worksheet.

Switching between worksheets

Clicking the tab will take you to a different worksheet. If your workbook is large, you may find this time-consuming since you will have to search through each tab individually. Using the lower-left corner of the screen's scroll arrows to navigate instead is better.

There will be an appearance of a dialogue box with a list of all the sheets in the workbook in it. Once you've done that, double-click the sheet you wish to go to.

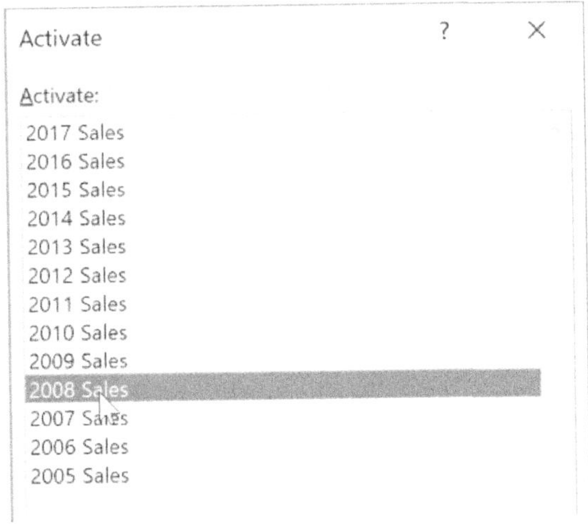

Grouping and ungrouping worksheets

You may work on one worksheet at a time, or you can work on many worksheets at once. It's possible to create a collection of worksheets by mixing worksheets. Changing one worksheet affects the other worksheets in the same category.

Grouping worksheets

In this instance, employees are required to be taught every three months. Because of this, you will create a separate worksheet category for them. Adding an employee's name to a spreadsheet will show up on all worksheets in the group.

Make sure you choose the first worksheet when adding a new worksheet to a category.

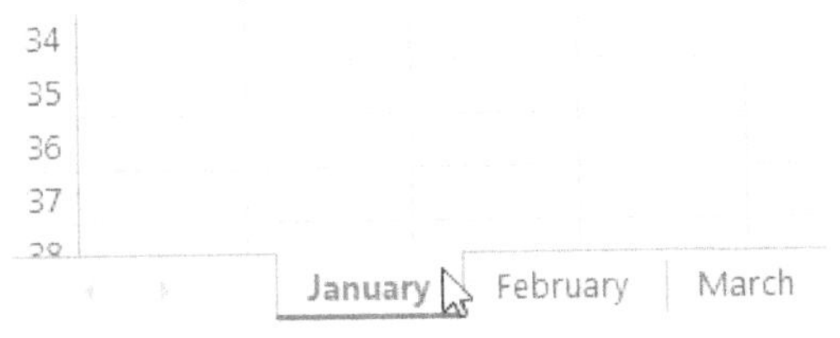

The Ctrl key on your keyboard should be held down.

From the drop-down menu, choose the next worksheet for the group. Select as many worksheets as you need to arrange before you stop.

The Ctrl key may be released. Groups have been created for your worksheets.

Once you've categorized the worksheets into a category, you may browse the worksheets in that category. Changes to one worksheet would be mirrored in the other worksheets for the group. If you want a worksheet that isn't a part of the community, you'll have to ungroup everything.

Ungrouping all worksheets

Right clicking a worksheet and selecting Un-group from the context menu will bring up the worksheet menu, from which you may choose sheets to print.

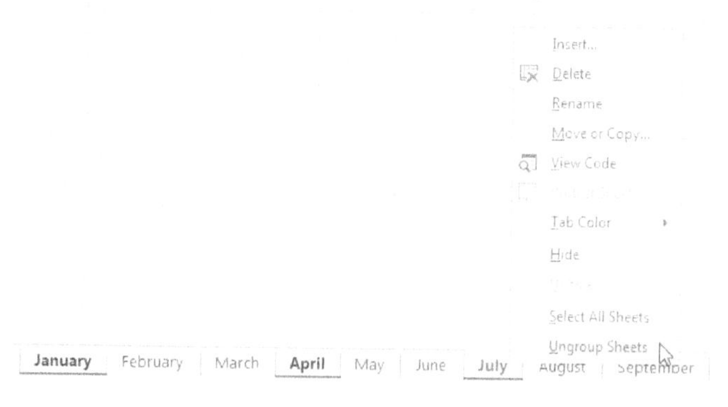

Groups of worksheets would be created. Instead, you may ungroup the worksheets by clicking on one of them.

Ungrouped and grouped worksheets are available. Group your January and March worksheets if you're following along with the scenario. Add fresh content to the January worksheet and compare it to the March worksheet.

Page Layout view

Open the worksheet in the Page Layout view to examine your layout modifications.
Page Layout may be accessed by clicking on the command in the right-bottom corner of your worksheet.

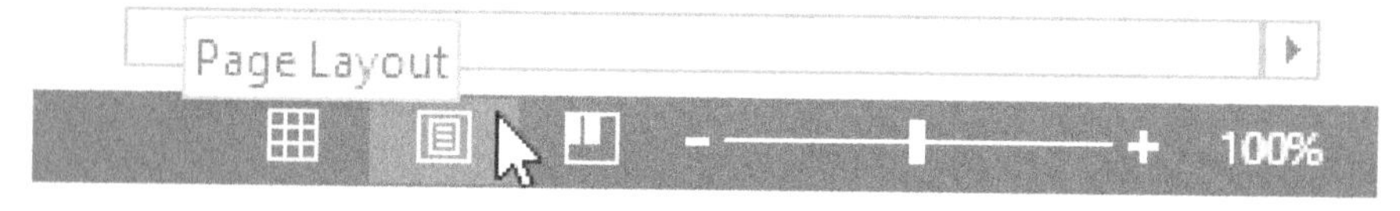

Page Orientation

Excel supports two-page landscapes and portraits. Horizontal landscape, vertical portrait. The portrait is preferable for rows and the landscape for columns. When there are more rows than columns, portrait orientation works best.

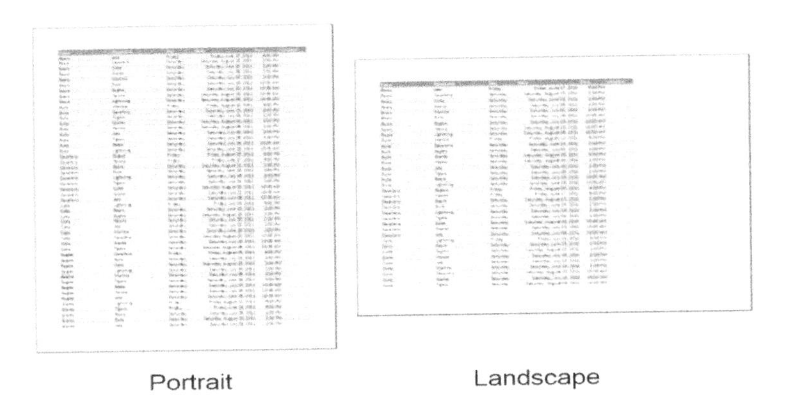

To change page orientation

- Select the Page Layout tab from the Ribbon.
- The Orientation drop-down box lets you choose between landscape and portrait.

Team	Opponent	Day	Date	Time
Bears	Jets	Friday	Friday, June 17, 2011	6:00 PM
Bears	Cavaliers	Saturday	############	2:00 PM
Bears	Colts	Saturday	############	2:00 PM
Bears	Giants	Saturday	############	2:00 PM
Bears	Marlins	Saturday	############	2:00 PM
Bears	Bulls	Saturday	Saturday, July 16, 2011	#####
Bears	Eagles	Saturday	############	#####
Bears	Hawks	Saturday	############	#####
Bears	Lightning	Saturday	############	#####
Bulls	Marlins	Friday	############	6:00 PM
Bulls	Cavaliers	Saturday	############	2:00 PM
Bulls	Eagles	Saturday	############	2:00 PM
Bulls	Giants	Saturday	############	2:00 PM
Bulls	Hawks	Saturday	############	2:00 PM
Bulls	Jets	Saturday	############	2:00 PM

- The page orientation of the workbook will be changed.

To format page margins

It's the space between the text and the page's margin. A one-inch space between the material on the page's boundaries and the default setting for every workbook. If your data doesn't fit on the page, you may need to adjust the margins. Excel has a variety of pre-set margin sizes from which you may choose.

- You may do this by clicking on the Page Layout menu on the Ribbon and selecting the Margins option.
- The margin size may be selected from the drop-down list. Narrow is an option to include more content on the page.

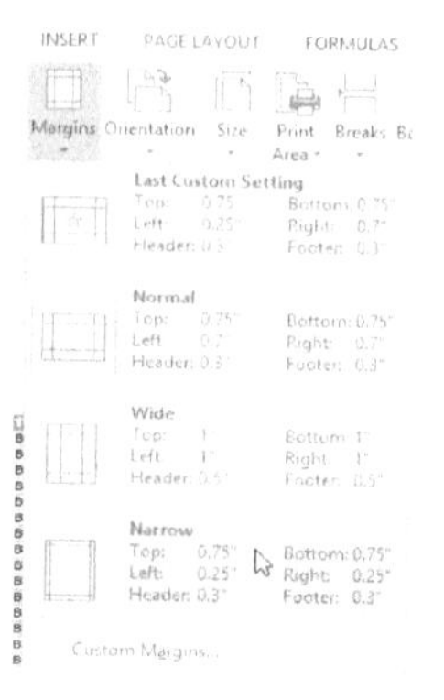

- In this case, the margins would be resized to fit your new selection.

To use custom margins

The Page Setup dialogue box in Excel lets you choose the margin size.

- On the Page Layout tab, choose the Margins option and click OK. Custom Margins may be selected from the drop-down menu.

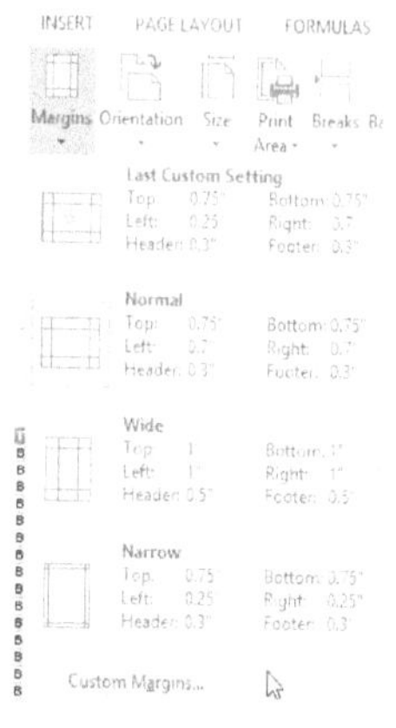

- Is there going to be a Page Setup dialogue box?
- To see your changes, click OK at the bottom of the window.

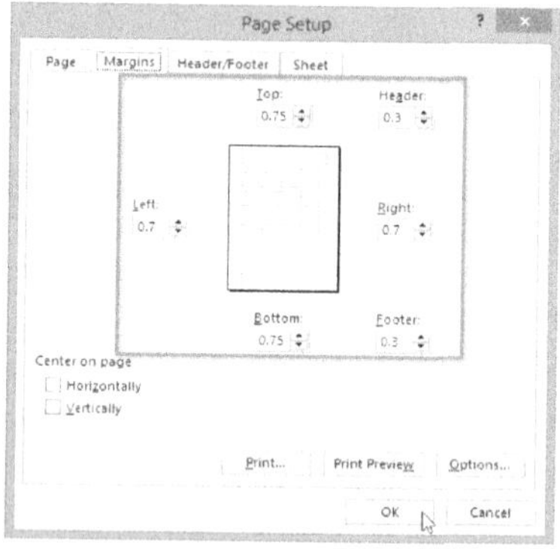

The margins of the notepad will be resized.

To include Print Titles

Make sure the title headings are included on each page of your worksheet. The title headings appearing on the first page of a printed workbook would be confusing. Print Titles instructions let you choose which rows and columns appear on each page.

- Page Layout ➔ Print Layout ➔ Print Titles.

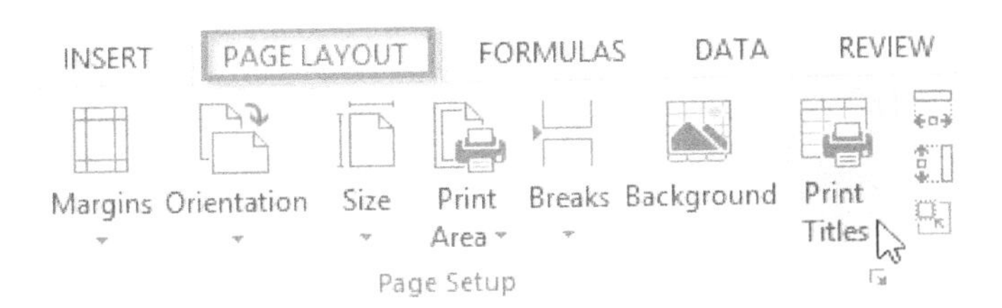

You may now make modifications to your page via Page Setup. Each page may have the same rows and columns from here on out. In our situation, a row will be repeated.

Next, pick the Collapse Dialogs option to see rows to repeat at the top.

The page Setup dialogue box is collapsed, and the mouse cursor is replaced with a selection arrow. Select the rows you want to repeat so that each printed page has the same row. Let's look at the first row.

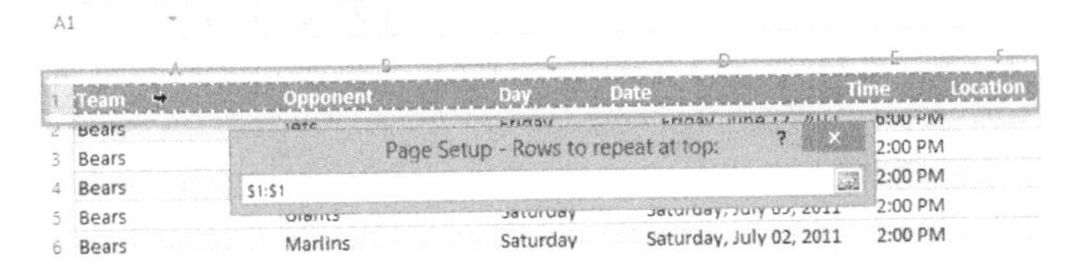

Row one will be inserted into the Rows for repeating at the top field. The "Collapse Dialog" should be reactivated.

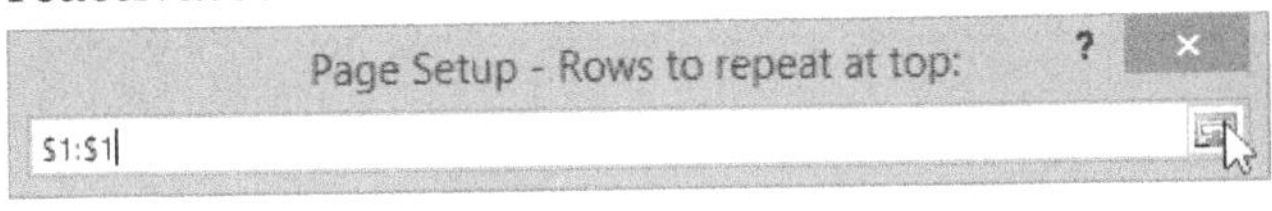

The Page Setup dialogue box may be enlarged by clicking on the arrows. To confirm your decision, press the OK button. Row 1 will be on top of every page.

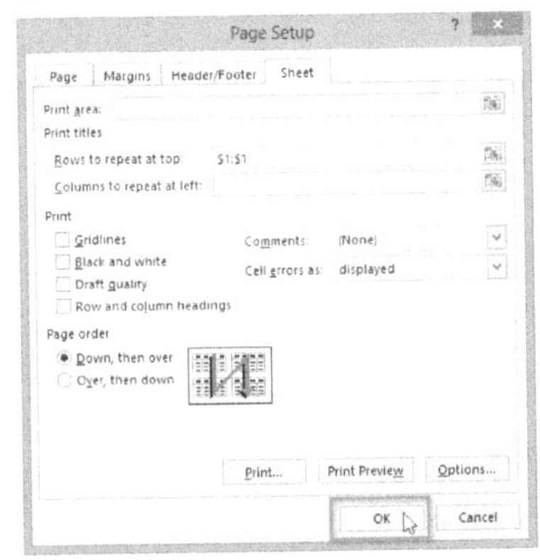

To insert a page break

Adding a page break to your worksheet lets you print different portions. Page breaks are vertical and horizontal. Page breaks divide columns and rows. Here's a horizontal page split.

Here is the Page Break command. It's in Page Break mode.

Choose the check box below where you want the page break to appear. After row 28, pick a page break (in this case, 29).

	A	B	C	D	E
19	Bulls	Lightning	Saturday	Saturday, June 18, 2011	10:00 AM
20	Cavaliers	Eagles	Friday	Friday, August 05, 2011	6:00 PM
21	Cavaliers	Hawks	Friday	Friday, June 17, 2011	6:00 PM
22	Cavaliers	Bears	Saturday	Saturday, August 13, 2011	2:00 PM
23	Cavaliers	Bulls	Saturday	Saturday, June 25, 2011	2:00 PM
24	Cavaliers	Lightning	Saturday	Saturday, July 16, 2011	2:00 PM
25	Cavaliers	Tigers	Saturday	Saturday, July 02, 2011	2:00 PM
26	Cavaliers	Colts	Saturday	Saturday, August 20, 2011	10:00 AM
27	Cavaliers	Giants	Saturday	Saturday, July 23, 2011	10:00 AM
28	Cavaliers	Jets	Saturday	Saturday, July 09, 2011	10:00 AM
29	Colts	Lightning	Friday	Friday, July 01, 2011	6:00 PM
30	Colts	Bears	Saturday	Saturday, June 25, 2011	2:00 PM
31	Colts	Eagles	Saturday	Saturday, August 13, 2011	2:00 PM
32	Colts	Hawks	Saturday	Saturday, July 30, 2011	2:00 PM
33	Colts	Jets	Saturday	Saturday, July 23, 2011	2:00 PM
34	Colts	Marlins	Saturday	Saturday, June 18, 2011	2:00 PM
35	Colts	Cavaliers	Saturday	Saturday, August 20, 2011	10:00 AM

Click Page Layout on the Ribbon and pick Breaks.

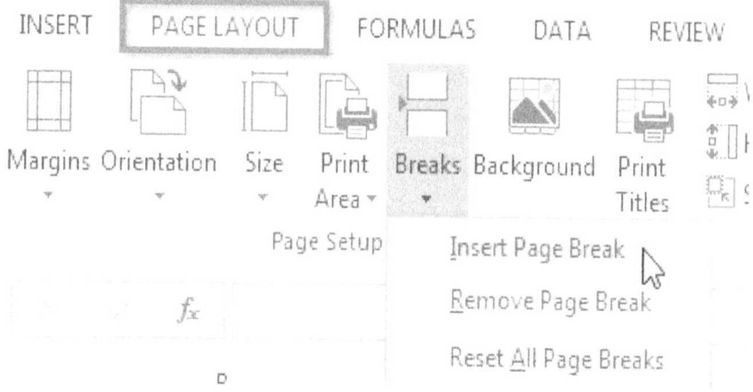

Place the dark blue page break bar.

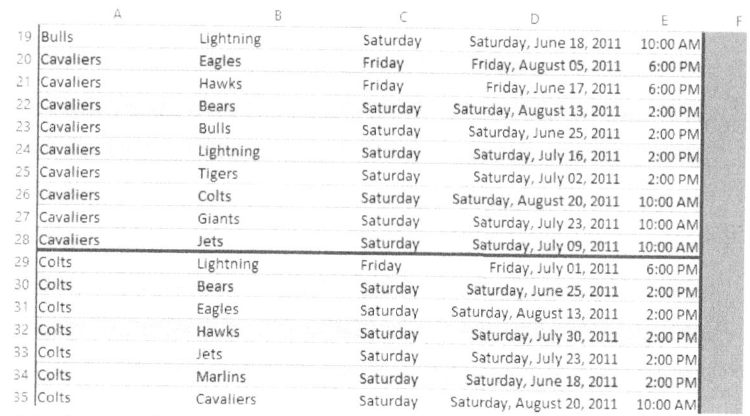

	A	B	C	D	E
19	Bulls	Lightning	Saturday	Saturday, June 18, 2011	10:00 AM
20	Cavaliers	Eagles	Friday	Friday, August 05, 2011	6:00 PM
21	Cavaliers	Hawks	Friday	Friday, June 17, 2011	6:00 PM
22	Cavaliers	Bears	Saturday	Saturday, August 13, 2011	2:00 PM
23	Cavaliers	Bulls	Saturday	Saturday, June 25, 2011	2:00 PM
24	Cavaliers	Lightning	Saturday	Saturday, July 16, 2011	2:00 PM
25	Cavaliers	Tigers	Saturday	Saturday, July 02, 2011	2:00 PM
26	Cavaliers	Colts	Saturday	Saturday, August 20, 2011	10:00 AM
27	Cavaliers	Giants	Saturday	Saturday, July 23, 2011	10:00 AM
28	Cavaliers	Jets	Saturday	Saturday, July 09, 2011	10:00 AM
29	Colts	Lightning	Friday	Friday, July 01, 2011	6:00 PM
30	Colts	Bears	Saturday	Saturday, June 25, 2011	2:00 PM
31	Colts	Eagles	Saturday	Saturday, August 13, 2011	2:00 PM
32	Colts	Hawks	Saturday	Saturday, July 30, 2011	2:00 PM
33	Colts	Jets	Saturday	Saturday, July 23, 2011	2:00 PM
34	Colts	Marlins	Saturday	Saturday, June 18, 2011	2:00 PM
35	Colts	Cavaliers	Saturday	Saturday, August 20, 2011	10:00 AM

Solid grey lines represent extra page breaks, whereas dashed grey lines indicate automatic page breaks in Normal mode.

To insert headers and footers

Headers & footers improve worksheet readability and presentation. The worksheet's header and footer are shown in the top and bottom margins. Headers and footers often include page numbers, dates, and workbook names.

The Page Layout command is near the bottom of Excel. Page Layout mode displays the worksheet.

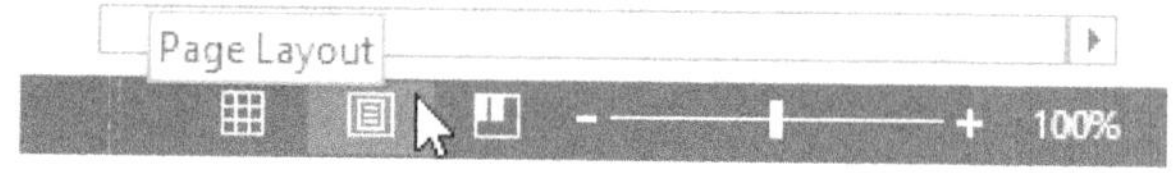

Choose a new header or footer. This page's footer will change.

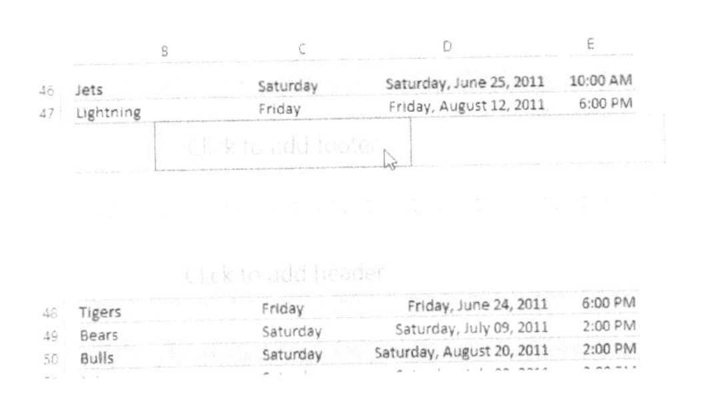

- Your Ribbon will display a new tab titled Header & Footer Tools. Commands that contain dates, page numbers, & workbook names may be found here. Page numbers will be added to this sample.

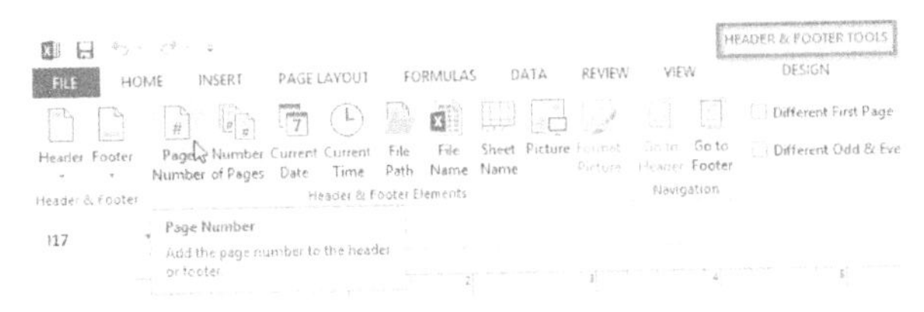

- The page numbers will be added to the footer automatically.

Adding New Rows and Columns

Organize your spreadsheet by adding and deleting columns and rows.

Inserting or deleting a column

Use the Home Insert (Sheet Columns) option to add or remove sheet columns.
Alternatively, by clicking the column's header, you may pick Insert or Delete from the context menu.

Inserting or deleting a row

If you want to add or remove sheet rows, you may select a cell in the row and then go to Home ➔ Insert ➔ Add or Remove Sheet Rows.
Alternatively, you may pick Insert or Delete from the context menu by right-clicking on the row number.

Formatting options

When you enter a new column or row after selecting one with formatting, the formatting is copied. If you do not want to format, choose Insert Options after inserting and pick one of these options:

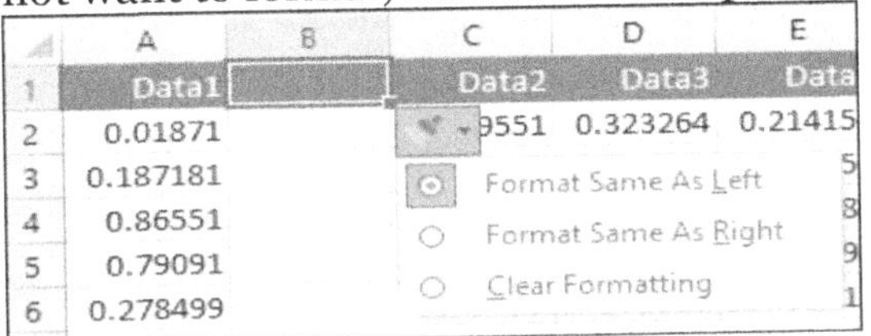

If the Add Options button is still not visible, click on File ➔ Options ➔ Advanced and check the Cut, copy, and paste group.

Conditional Formatting & Data Filters

Conditional formatting using Excel highlights cells based on their value.

Highlighting Cells Rules

To highlight cells greater than a value, execute the following steps.

1. Select the range A1: A10

	A	B
1	14	
2	6	
3	39	
4	43	
5	2	
6	95	
7	5	
8	11	
9	86	
10	57	
11		

2. Click the Conditional Formatting within the Styles category on the home tab.

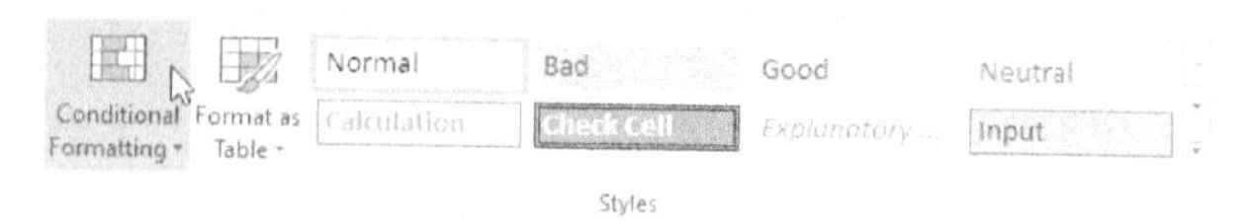

3. Then, choose Greater Than from the Cells Rules menu.

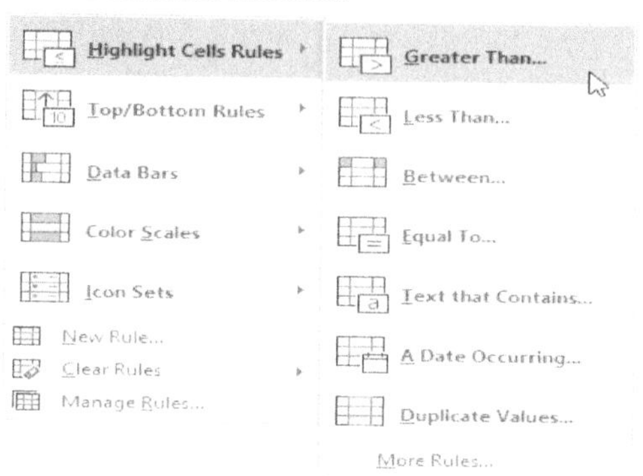

4. Enter that value and choose a style to format the number 80.

Greater Than

Format cells that are GREATER THAN:

80 with Light Red Fill with Dark Red Text

OK Cancel

Select "OK."

5. Result. Cells that are bigger than 80 are marked as such in Excel.

	A	B
1	14	
2	6	
3	39	
4	43	
5	2	
6	95	
7	5	
8	11	
9	86	
10	57	
11		

6. Change cell A1's value to 81.

Excel has automatically changed cell A1's format.

	A	B
1	81	
2	6	
3	39	
4	43	
5	2	
6	95	
7	5	
8	11	
9	86	
10	57	
11		

Clear Rules

Execute the following procedures to remove a conditional formatting rule.

The A1: A10 range should be selected.

	A	B
1	81	
2	6	
3	39	
4	43	
5	2	
6	95	
7	5	
8	11	
9	86	
10	57	
11		

2. Click on Conditional Formatting within the Styles category on your home tab.

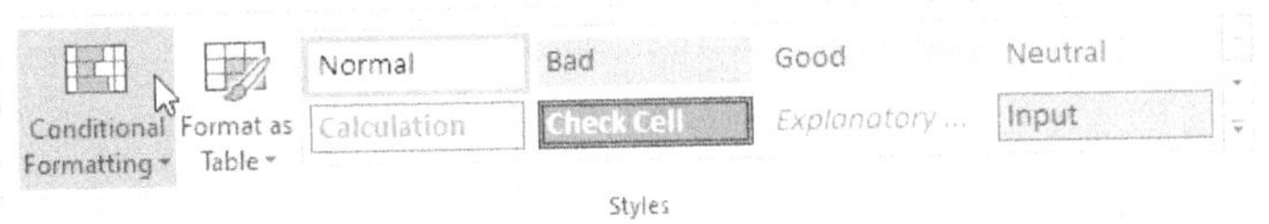

You may also clear the rules from your selected cells by clicking Clear Rules.

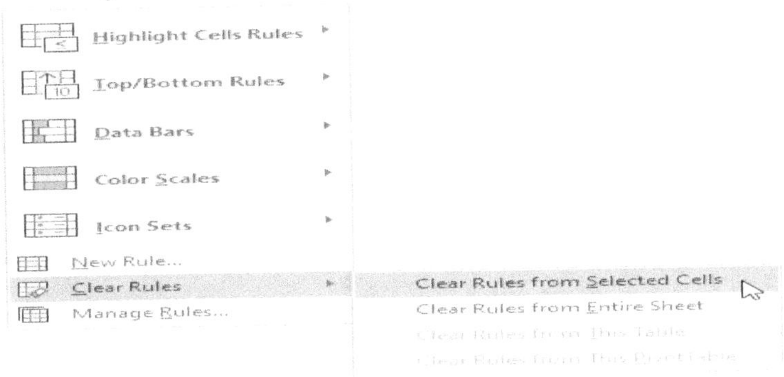

Top/Bottom

Follow these procedures to draw attention to particularly noteworthy cells.

The A1: A10 range should be selected.

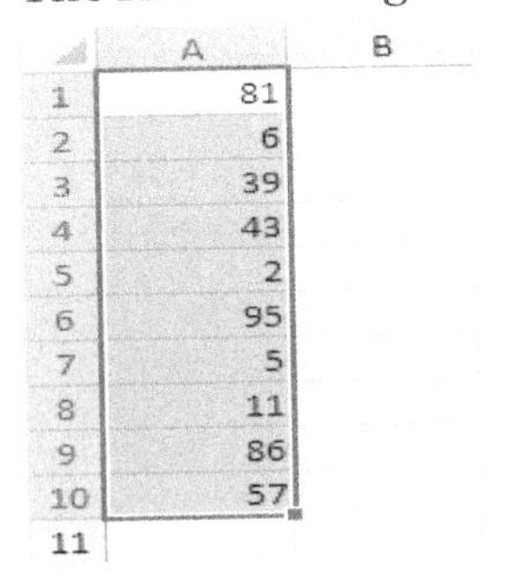

Click on the Conditional Formatting within the Styles category on your home tab.

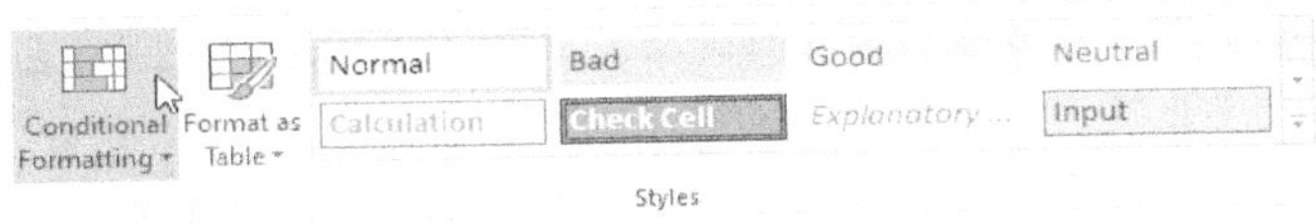

Select Above Average, Top/Bottom Rules.

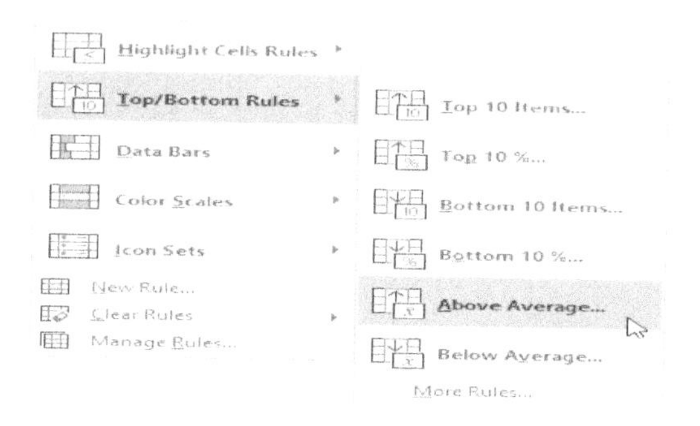

Select your formatting style.

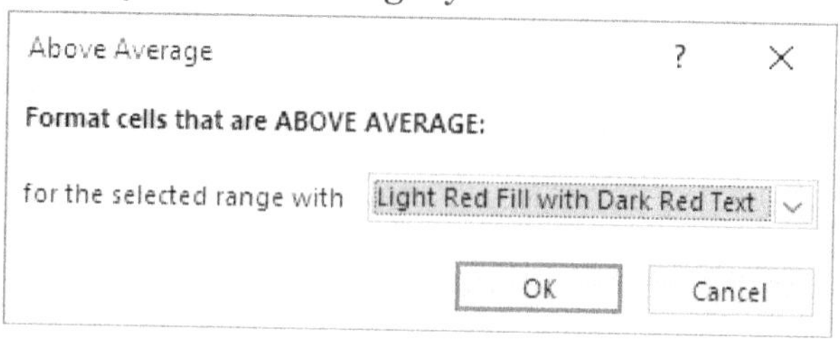

Press OK.

Result. Excel calculates the average (42.5), and the cells over this average are formatted.

	A	B
1	81	
2	6	
3	39	
4	43	
5	2	
6	95	
7	5	
8	11	
9	86	
10	57	
11		

Conditional Formatting using Formulas

To enhance your Excel skills, use a formula to determine which cells should be formatted. Formulas of Conditional formatting must respond to FALSE & TRUE.

Choose the A 1: E 5 range.

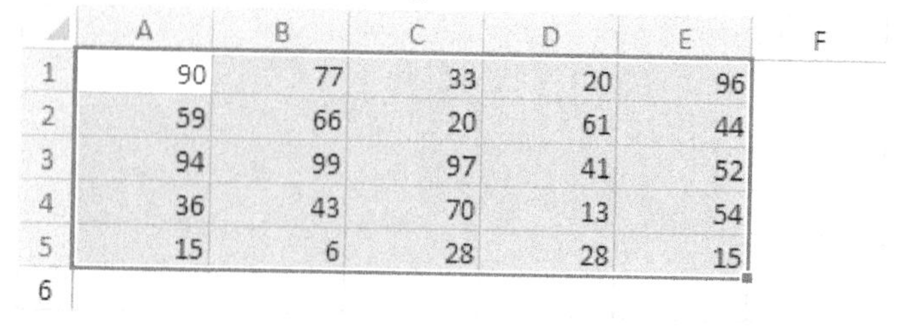

	A	B	C	D	E	F
1	90	77	33	20	96	
2	59	66	20	61	44	
3	94	99	97	41	52	
4	36	43	70	13	54	
5	15	6	28	28	15	
6						

On your home tab, go to the Styles section and choose Conditional Formatting.

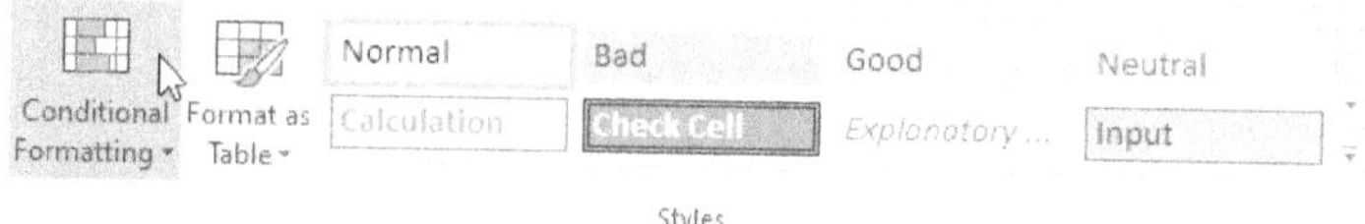

Select "New Rule."

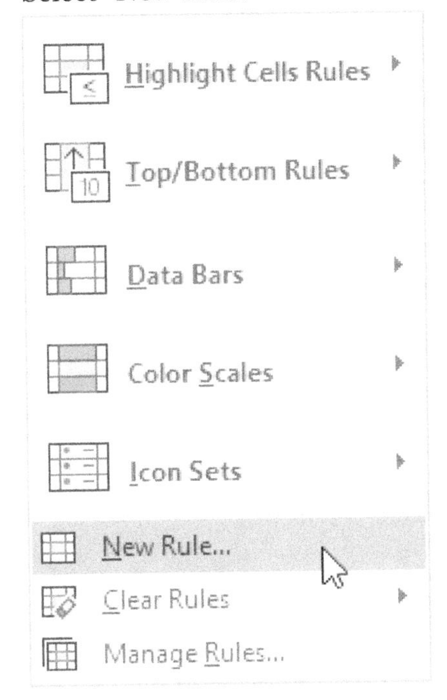

To choose which cells for formatting, click on "Use a formula."
Now Type = ISODD into the formula (A 1)
Then Click on OK after selecting one formatting option.

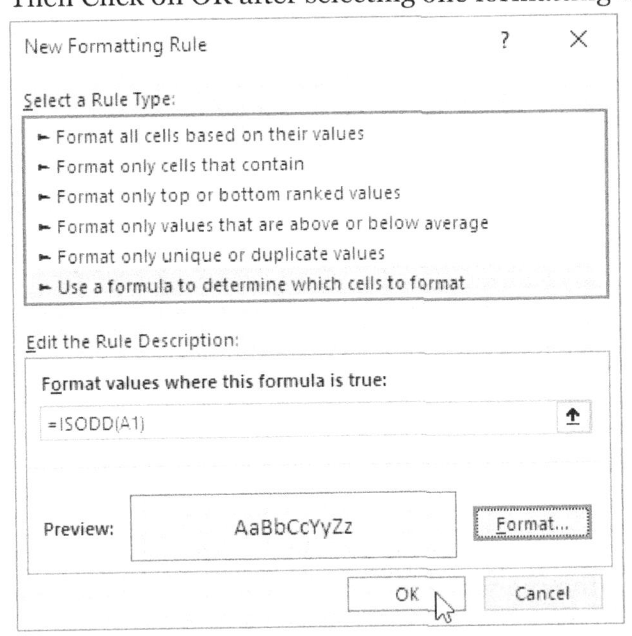

Result. Each odd number is highlighted in Excel.

	A	B	C	D	E	F
1	90	77	33	20	96	
2	59	66	20	61	44	
3	94	99	97	41	52	
4	36	43	70	13	54	
5	15	6	28	28	15	
6						

Explanation: Always write your formula for the upper-left cell in the specified range. The formula is automatically copied to the other cells by Excel. As a consequence, cell A2 has the formula = ISODD (A2), & the same holds for the cs A 3 forward.

Here's another illustration.

Choose the A2: D7 range.

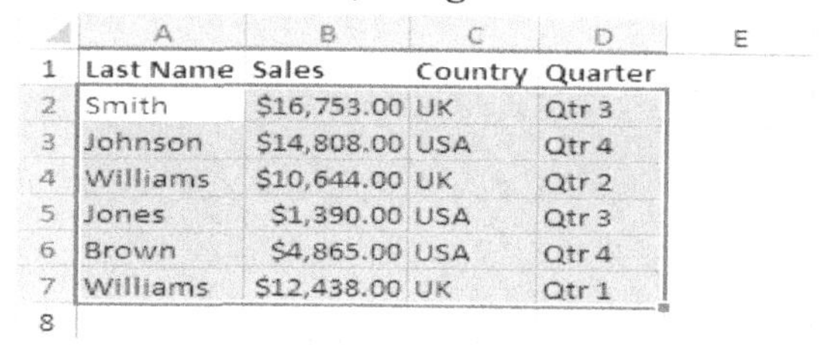

	A	B	C	D	E
1	Last Name	Sales	Country	Quarter	
2	Smith	$16,753.00	UK	Qtr 3	
3	Johnson	$14,808.00	USA	Qtr 4	
4	Williams	$10,644.00	UK	Qtr 2	
5	Jones	$1,390.00	USA	Qtr 3	
6	Brown	$4,865.00	USA	Qtr 4	
7	Williams	$12,438.00	UK	Qtr 1	
8					

Follow steps 2-4 again.
Type =$C2="USA" in the formula box.
After choosing a formatting option, click OK.

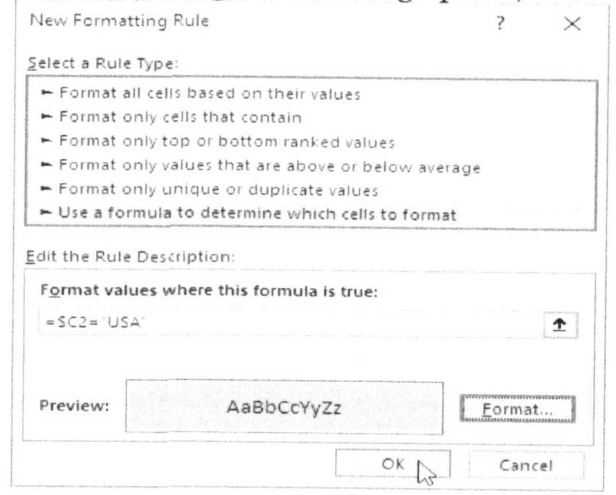

Result. Excel shows all USA orders in bold.

	A	B	C	D	E
1	Last Name	Sales	Country	Quarter	
2	Smith	$16,753.00	UK	Qtr 3	
3	**Johnson**	**$14,808.00**	**USA**	**Qtr 4**	
4	Williams	$10,644.00	UK	Qtr 2	
5	**Jones**	**$1,390.00**	**USA**	**Qtr 3**	
6	**Brown**	**$4,865.00**	**USA**	**Qtr 4**	
7	Williams	$12,438.00	UK	Qtr 1	
8					

Adding a $ sign in front of a column letter ($C2) corrected the reference to column C. Consequently, the formula =$C2="USA" is also present in cells B 2, C 2, and D 2, as well as cells A 3, B 3, C 3, and D3.

Data filter

Use Excel filtering to see entries that fulfill a certain set of conditions.
A data set may be accessed by selecting a single cell and clicking on it.
Select Filter from the Filter & Sort group on your Data tab.

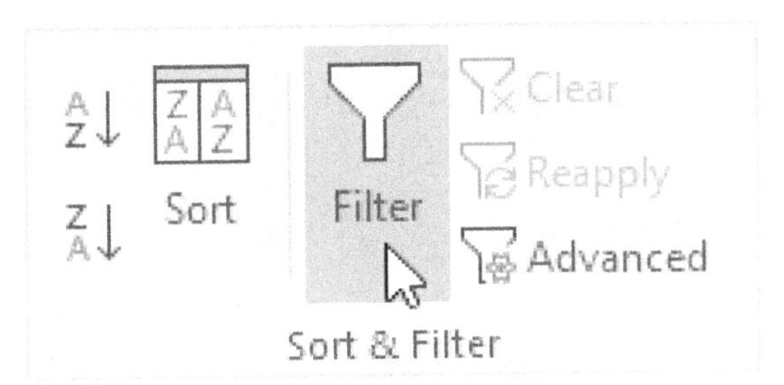

The column headings have arrows in them.

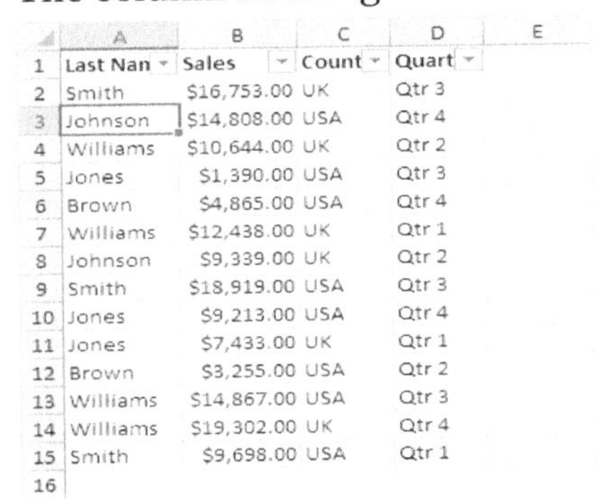

	A	B	C	D	E
1	Last Nan	Sales	Count	Quart	
2	Smith	$16,753.00	UK	Qtr 3	
3	Johnson	$14,808.00	USA	Qtr 4	
4	Williams	$10,644.00	UK	Qtr 2	
5	Jones	$1,390.00	USA	Qtr 3	
6	Brown	$4,865.00	USA	Qtr 4	
7	Williams	$12,438.00	UK	Qtr 1	
8	Johnson	$9,339.00	UK	Qtr 2	
9	Smith	$18,919.00	USA	Qtr 3	
10	Jones	$9,213.00	USA	Qtr 4	
11	Jones	$7,433.00	UK	Qtr 1	
12	Brown	$3,255.00	USA	Qtr 2	
13	Williams	$14,867.00	USA	Qtr 3	
14	Williams	$19,302.00	UK	Qtr 4	
15	Smith	$9,698.00	USA	Qtr 1	
16					

Select your country by clicking the arrow beside it.

Clear all your checkboxes by clicking Select All, then selecting the USA from the drop-down menu.

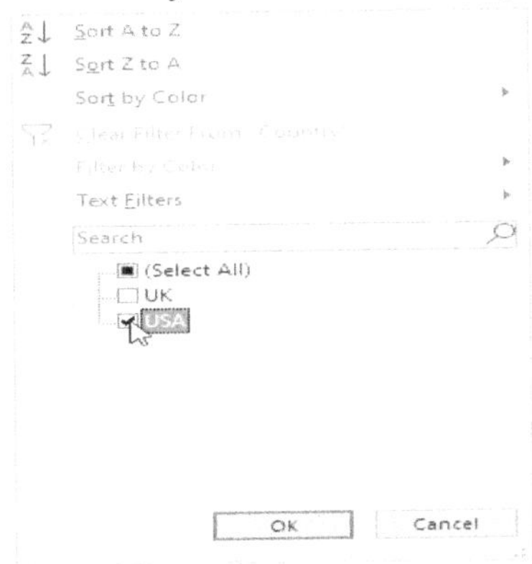

Select "OK."

Result. Excel only shows data from the United States.

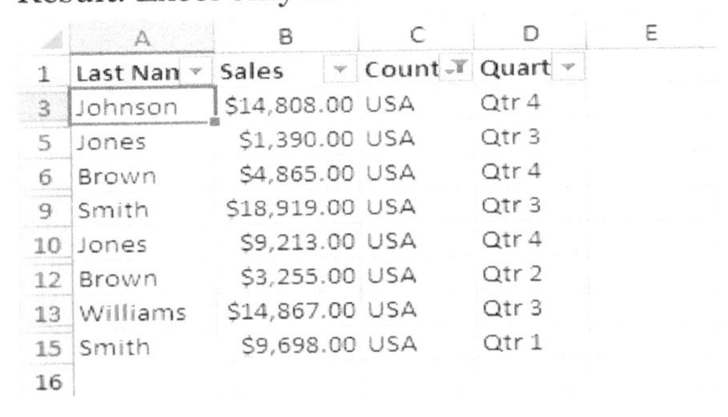

	A	B	C	D	E
1	Last Nan	Sales	Count	Quart	
3	Johnson	$14,808.00	USA	Qtr 4	
5	Jones	$1,390.00	USA	Qtr 3	
6	Brown	$4,865.00	USA	Qtr 4	
9	Smith	$18,919.00	USA	Qtr 3	
10	Jones	$9,213.00	USA	Qtr 4	
12	Brown	$3,255.00	USA	Qtr 2	
13	Williams	$14,867.00	USA	Qtr 3	
15	Smith	$9,698.00	USA	Qtr 1	
16					

Click on the arrow beside Quarter to bring up the context menu.

When you're done, click Select All to remove all the checkboxes, then select the checkbox beside Qtr 4.

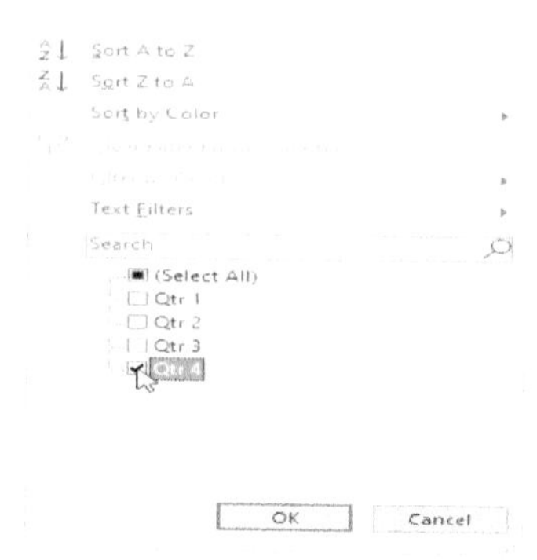

Click the OK button.

Results. Excel only displays sales within the United States into the fourth quarter.

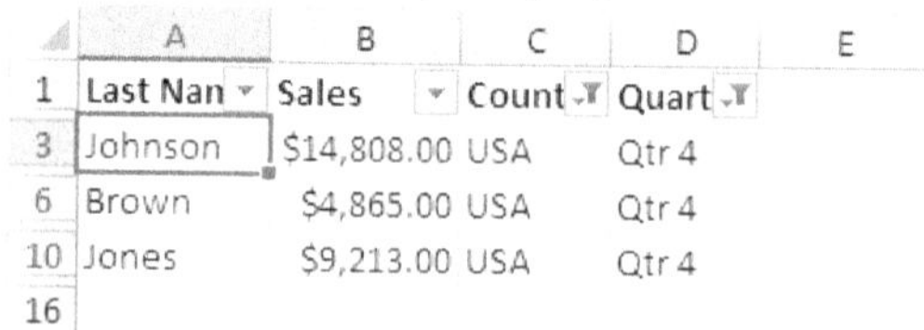

	A	B	C	D	E
1	Last Nan	Sales	Count	Quart	
3	Johnson	$14,808.00	USA	Qtr 4	
6	Brown	$4,865.00	USA	Qtr 4	
10	Jones	$9,213.00	USA	Qtr 4	
16					

Click Clear within Sort & Filter on your Data tab to remove the filter. To remove the arrows and the filter, click Filter.

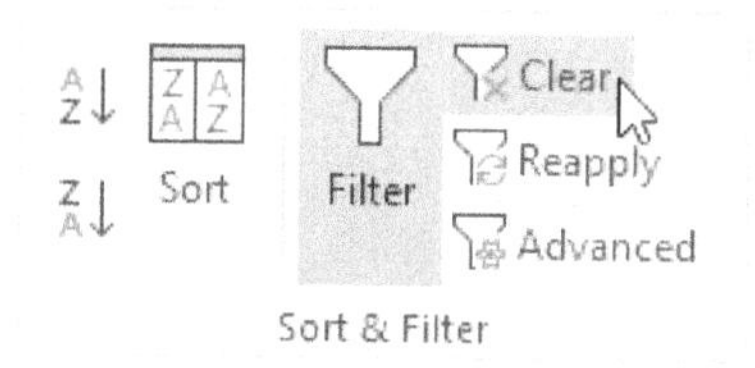

Excel data may be more quickly filtered.

Select the cell in the table by clicking on it.

	A	B	C	D	E
1	Last Name	Sales	Country	Quarter	
2	Smith	$16,753.00	UK	Qtr 3	
3	Johnson	$14,808.00	USA	Qtr 4	
4	Williams	$10,644.00	UK	Qtr 2	
5	Jones	$1,390.00	USA	Qtr 3	
6	Brown	$4,865.00	USA	Qtr 4	
7	Williams	$12,438.00	UK	Qtr 1	
8	Johnson	$9,339.00	UK	Qtr 2	
9	Smith	$18,919.00	USA	Qtr 3	
10	Jones	$9,213.00	USA	Qtr 4	
11	Jones	$7,433.00	UK	Qtr 1	
12	Brown	$3,255.00	USA	Qtr 2	
13	Williams	$14,867.00	USA	Qtr 3	
14	Williams	$19,302.00	UK	Qtr 4	
15	Smith	$9,698.00	USA	Qtr 1	
16					

Then, right-click and choose Filter, select Filter the Selected Cell's Value, and click OK.

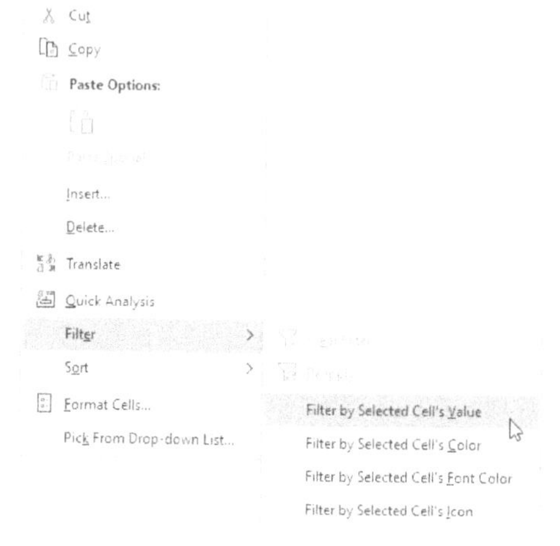

Result. Excel shows data from the United States.

	A	B	C	D	E
1	Last Nan	Sales	Count	Quart	
3	Johnson	$14,808.00	USA	Qtr 4	
5	Jones	$1,390.00	USA	Qtr 3	
6	Brown	$4,865.00	USA	Qtr 4	
9	Smith	$18,919.00	USA	Qtr 3	
10	Jones	$9,213.00	USA	Qtr 4	
12	Brown	$3,255.00	USA	Qtr 2	
13	Williams	$14,867.00	USA	Qtr 3	
15	Smith	$9,698.00	USA	Qtr 1	
16					

Cursor & Dragging

A Fill Handle is a strong Excel autofill feature in the current cell's bottom right corner. It copies values down the column or fills a string of numbers, dates, messages, formulae, or a similar sequence to a specified number of cells. The mouse cursor transforms from the white cross towards the black plus sign over the fill handle. Click & hold your handle to move between cells. When you remove the mouse button, all dragged cells are auto-filled.

Fill handle saves time and prevents human error (like typos).

Using the AutoFill with Excel

Excel's autofill function is accessible through the fill handle. It's like copy-and-paste, but much more. Fill handle isn't the only technique to utilize autofill.

First, choose a cell's range, beginning with the cell holding the data to be duplicated. Ctrl+D to copy, Ctrl+R to fill right.

Fill Button - Click the 'Fill' button within the Editing category of the 'Home' tab to get the fill command. Down, Up, Left, Right, Series, Justify, Across Worksheets, & Flash Fill is available.

Double-click the Fill handle to autofill a column. Double-click the fill handle to swiftly fill down the column if the next cell has data. If your data collection contains blank cells, this will fill in an adjacent blank cell.

Duplicate Data with Fill Handle

The fill handle copies cell content to multiple cells. Using the fill handle, you may effortlessly copy text, numbers, formulae, etc.

Simply choose the cell(s) you wish to copy & drag the fill handle in either direction. It rapidly fills dragged-over cells with specified cell data.

C2 fx 20%

	A	B	C	D	E
1	**Agent**	**Sales**	**Commission**		
2	Ben	2000	20%		
3	Rick	3000			
4	James	6500			
5	Van	1200			
6	Nick	6522			
7	Pen	3120			
8	Wen	3200			
9	Wyett	2800			
10					
11					

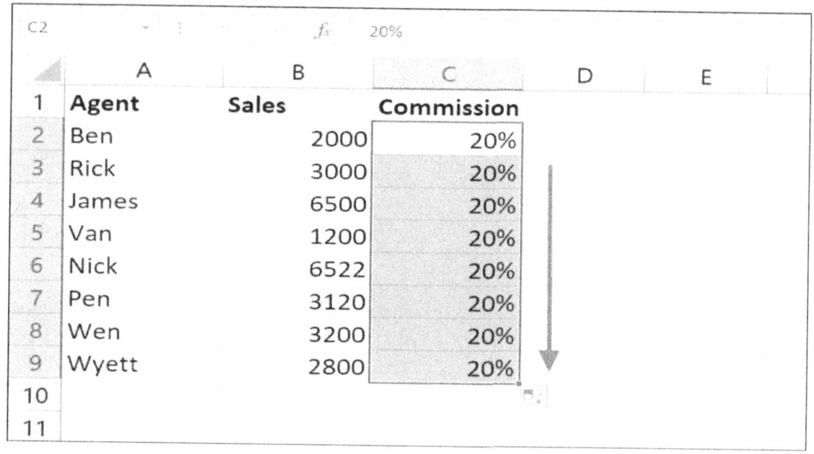

	A	B	C	D	E
1	**Agent**	**Sales**	**Commission**		
2	Ben	2000	20%		
3	Rick	3000	20%		
4	James	6500	20%		
5	Van	1200	20%		
6	Nick	6522	20%		
7	Pen	3120	20%		
8	Wen	3200	20%		
9	Wyett	2800	20%		
10					
11					

Double-clicking on your fill handle in cell C2 will fill this column till C9 since data is in B9.

Autofill Options

When you drag a fill handle, it identifies data patterns & fills your list while giving you choices.

After dragging your fill handle (or double-clicking) and filling the list, the 'Auto Fill Options' icon appears in the bottom right corner.

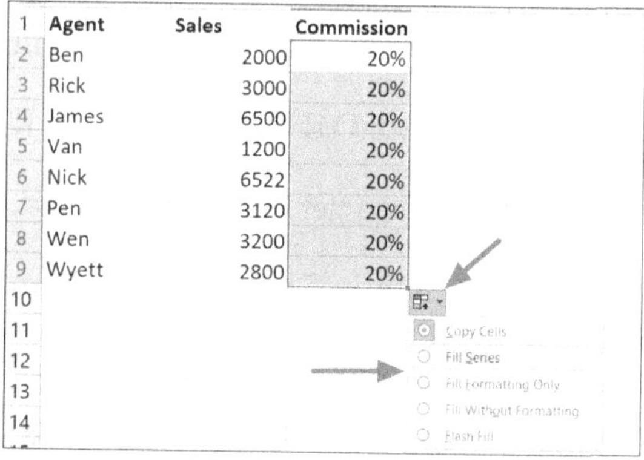

1	**Agent**	**Sales**	**Commission**
2	Ben	2000	20%
3	Rick	3000	20%
4	James	6500	20%
5	Van	1200	20%
6	Nick	6522	20%
7	Pen	3120	20%
8	Wen	3200	20%
9	Wyett	2800	20%

Depending on the data, clicking this symbol gives you the following options:

- **Copy cells** – This will duplicate the first cell throughout the list of cells you've chosen.
- **Fill series** – Fill the chosen cells with a sequence or set of values, starting with the original cell value, using the option
- **Fill formatting** – However, this one does not include any data in the given range.
- **Filling Without formatting** – Fills the chosen range with the beginning cell's data, but not with the formatting
- **Flash fill** – This option uses data patterns to populate a list of items. As an illustration, the Flash fill feature inside the example below fills in the list by identifying 2000 as 20%, assuming 3000 as 30%, and assuming 6500 as 65%.

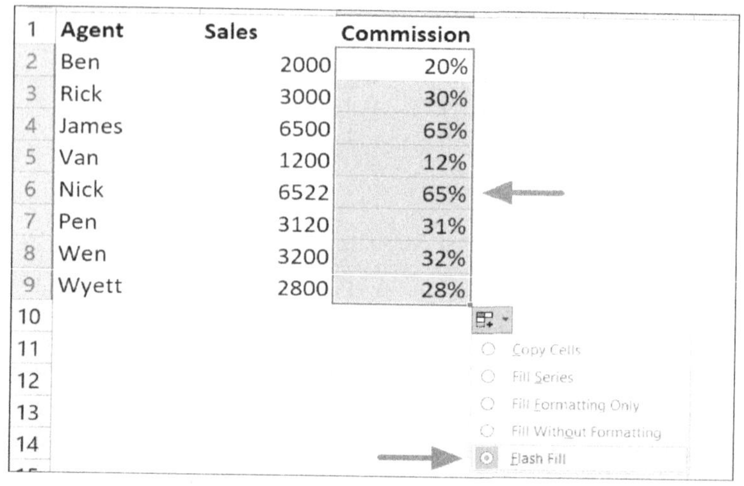

1	**Agent**	**Sales**	**Commission**
2	Ben	2000	20%
3	Rick	3000	30%
4	James	6500	65%
5	Van	1200	12%
6	Nick	6522	65%
7	Pen	3120	31%
8	Wen	3200	32%
9	Wyett	2800	28%

Autofill Text Value with Fill Handle

Excel fill handle autocompletes a list by duplicating the starting cell's text contents (s). It can also identify day names, month names, & other text sequences. Abbreviated or complete names of months, weekdays, etc.

First, put month abbreviations or complete names in the first field, then utilize your fill handle for filling additional cells.

Weekdays

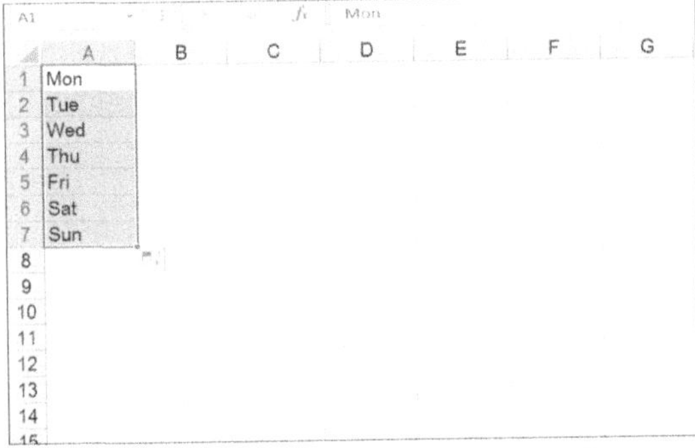

The fill handle may also autocomplete number-based text. First, type text in one cell, then use the fill handle to fill others.

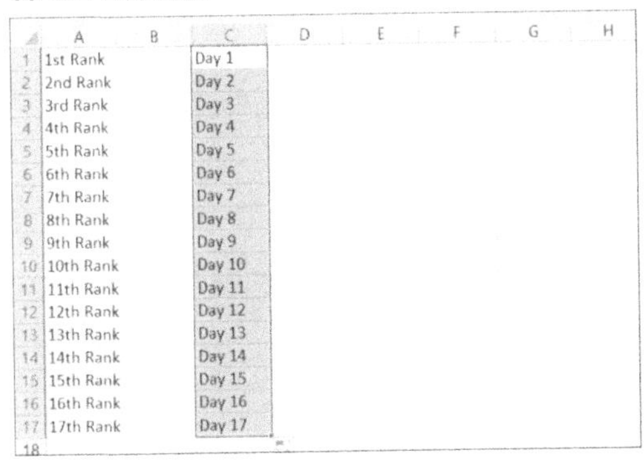

Autofill Numbers with Fill Handle

The fill handle creates a number sequence. It might be odd, even, or 1-increment numbers, etc.

Select almost 2 numbers to create a pattern for the first two cells, then drag the fill handle.

Excel copies the same number if you pick one cell containing a number & drag it down since there isn't any pattern inside one number.

Enter "2" in B1 and "4" in B2. Select B1 and B2 and slide the AutoFill handle lower to get even numbers.

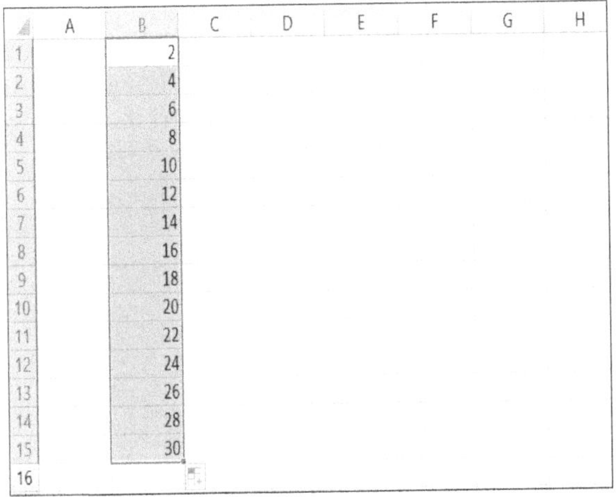

When you choose 'Auto Fill Choices,' the following options appear:

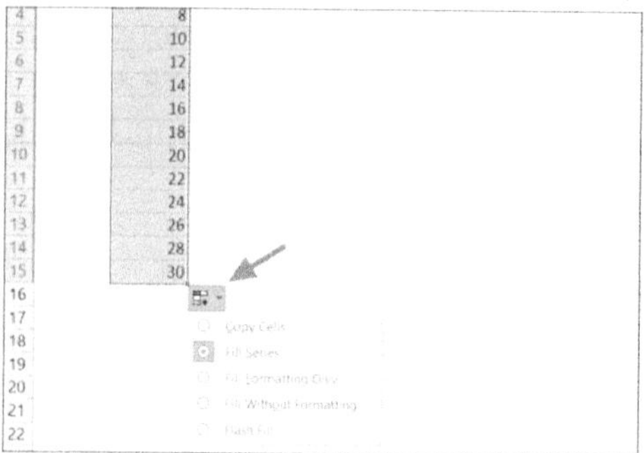

Instead of dragging with the left mouse button, use the right mouse button. When you release it, other alternatives will appear, as seen below.

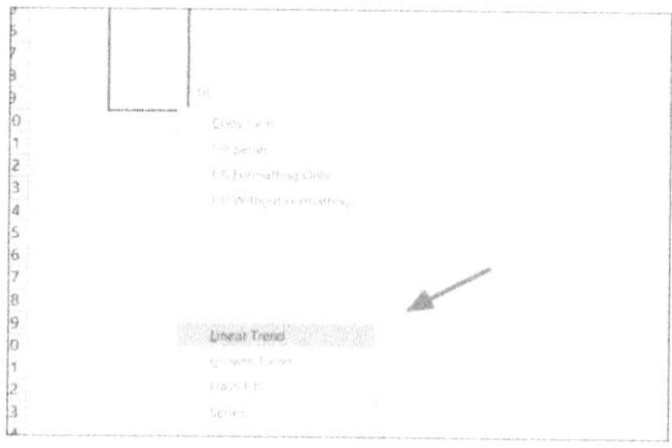

You've covered the first four & flash-fill possibilities; now, let's look at the others.
Linear Trend options – Excel makes a straight-line chart with linear numbers.
Growth Trend options – Excel uses the initial data to calculate an exponential growth series.
Series option – This opens the Series dialogue with advanced settings.

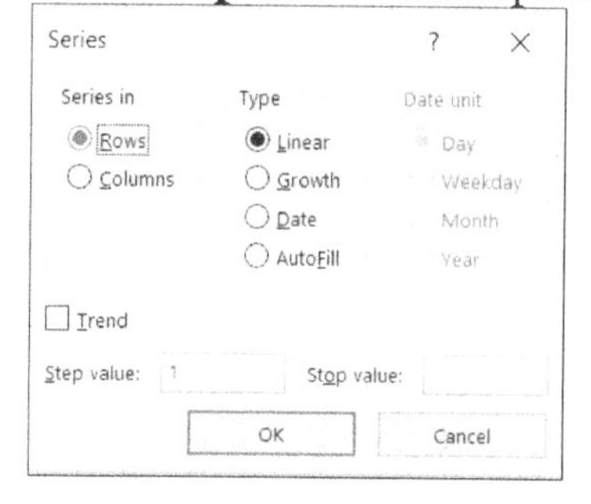

Copying Formulas with Fill Handles

It is like copying numbers along a column or auto-fill a succession of values when you copy a formula.

Drag your fill handle from one cell to another to duplicate the formula in those other cells. Whenever you copy a formula, it will immediately update to reflect the new location of the cell where you pasted it.

Using the fill handle, copy the formula from cell B1 to B10.

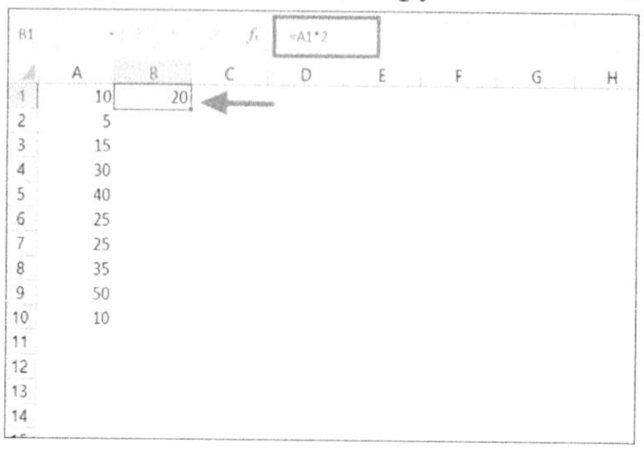

When a cell is next to another, the formula automatically adapts.

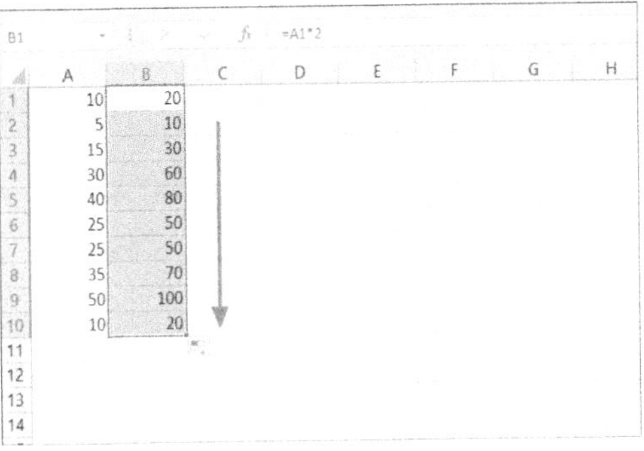

You'll get results for all the rows.

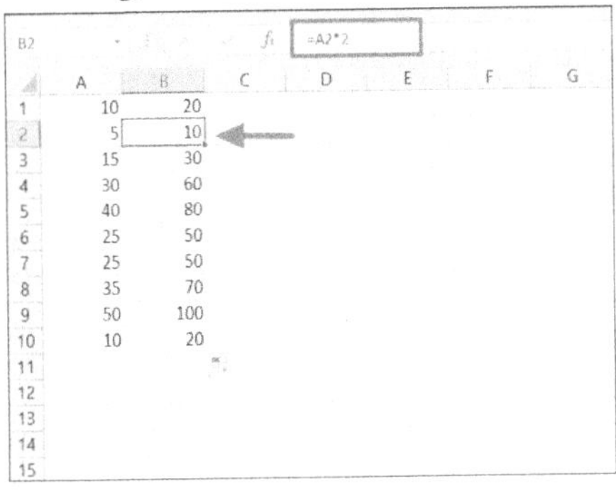

Autofill Dates with Fill Handle

Enter your dates within the first cell of a range in either format, which Excel recognizes to automatically fill within dates in the rest of the cells in the range.

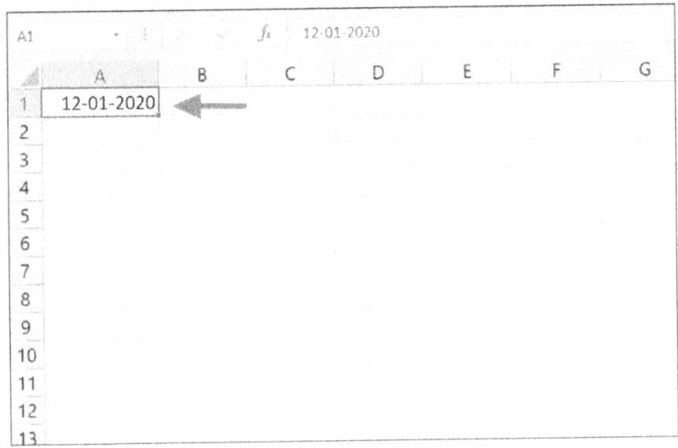

Drag your fill handle downwards to a cell where you'd like the date to finish, and then release it to release the date.

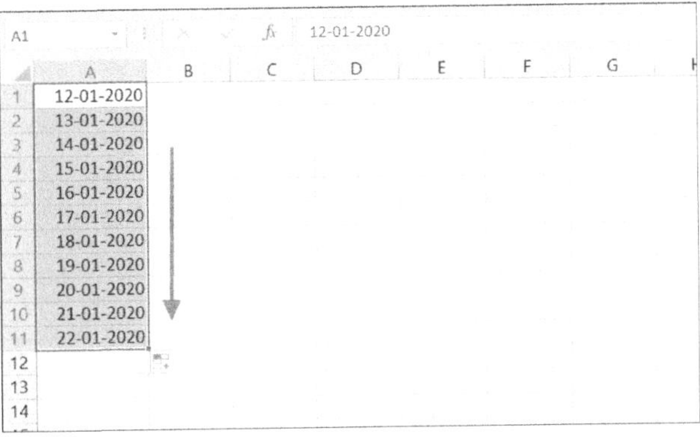

For dates, extra AutoFill choices appear when you select the "Auto Fill Options" icon just at the end of an auto-filled range, as shown in the following illustration.

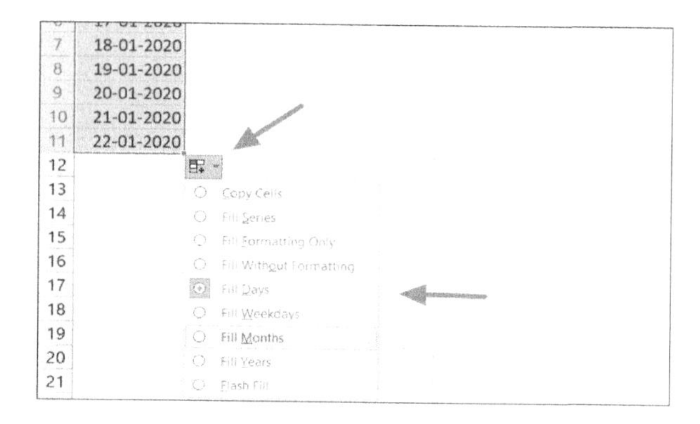

Along with the five pre-existing choices, you'll find four more advanced date selections in this section:

Fill Days – This adds one more day to the list by incrementing the value by one.

Fill Weekdays – Only weekdays are included in the lists, eliminating Saturdays and Sundays.

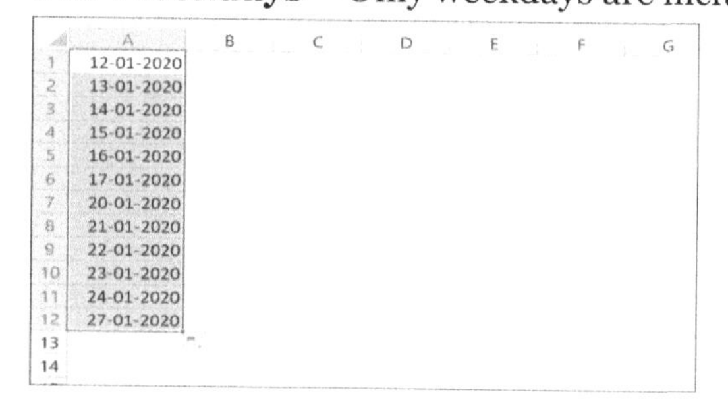

Fill Months – While the day stays constant in all cells, the option fills your list with months that increase sequentially.

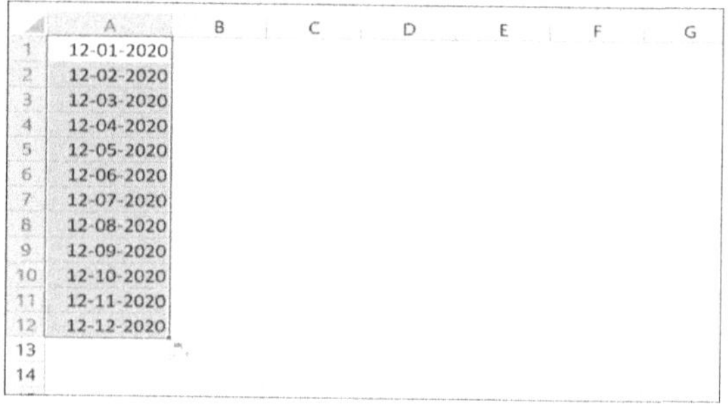

Fill Years – These years are added one at a time while day & month stay static.

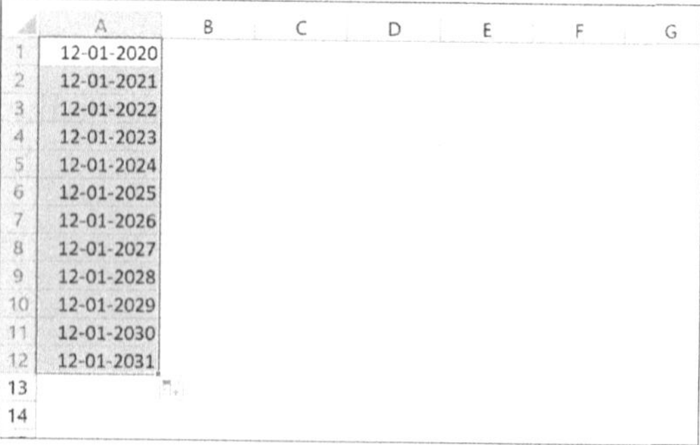

Creating the Custom Lists for Your Autofilling Data

Lists don't always have to be organized in the same manner. You can use Excel's built-in lists to arrange data in these situations. Fill handles may be used to populate cells from the custom list.

Select 'File' from the menu and then 'Options'.

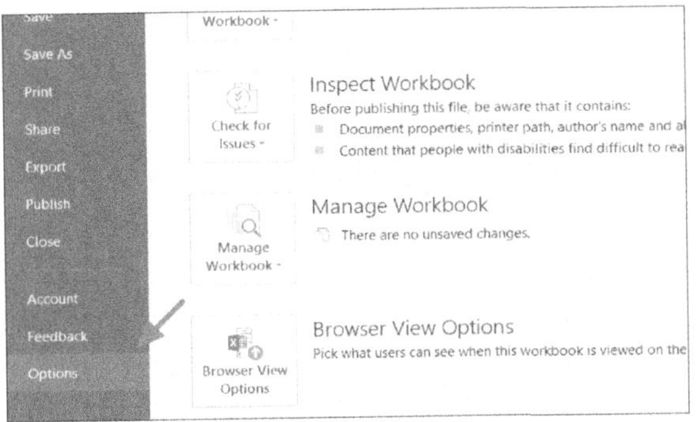

The "Edit Custom Lists." button may be found under the "General" section within the right pane by selecting "Advanced" within the left panel.

To go to the Custom List dialogue box, click on the button.

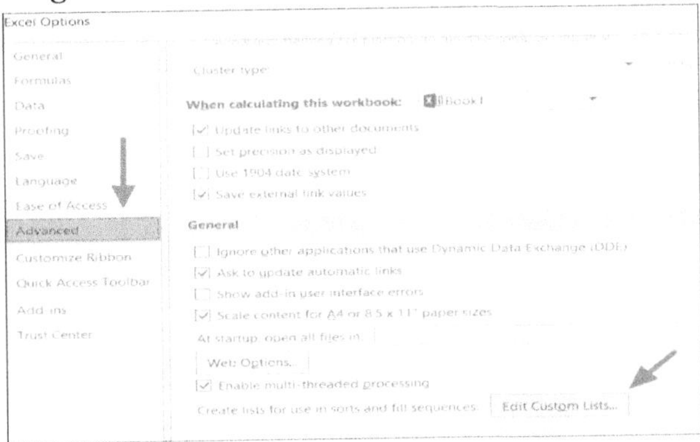

Right-clicking on "Advanced" in the left-hand panel brings up a menu containing the "Edit Custom Lists." button. To access your Custom Lists dialogue, click the button.

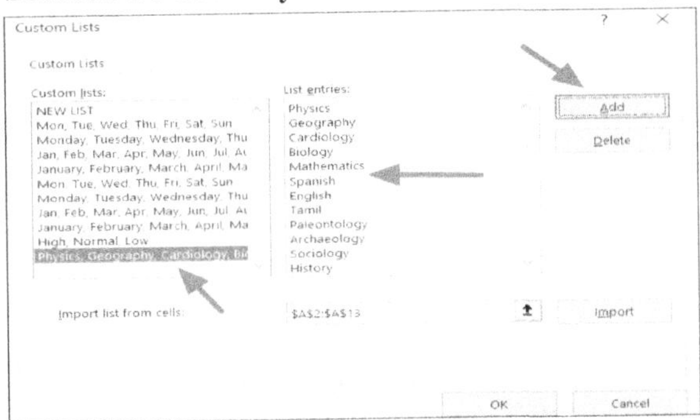

Select the cell where you want your list and enter the 1st item of the custom list, then save your list.

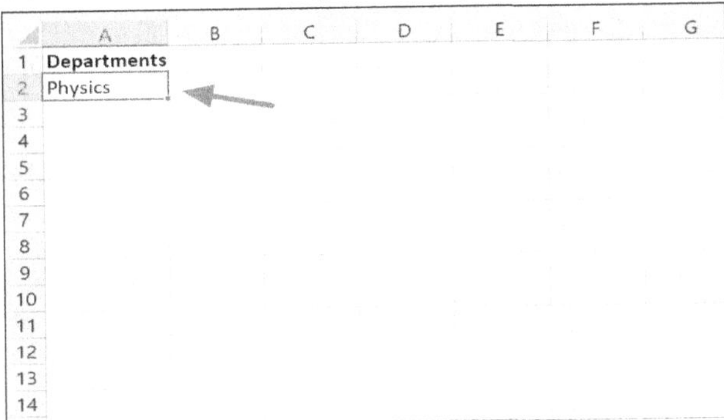

Once you've dragged the fill handle, the custom list of values will be used to auto-fill the cells.

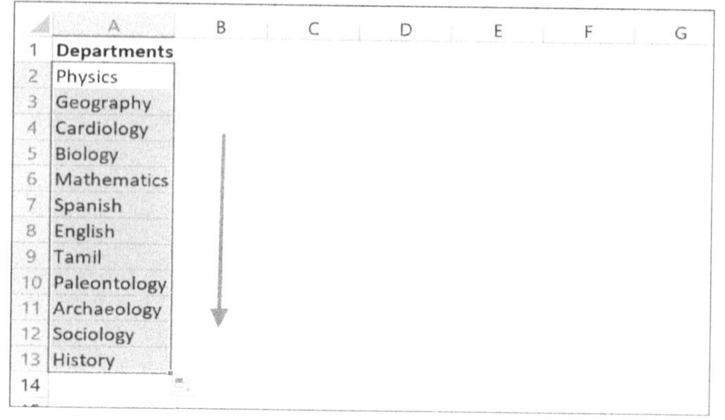

Disable or Enable your AutoFill Options in Excel

In Excel, if your fill handle isn't functioning, you may activate the Autofill functionality on the Excel options: Other options may be found by clicking on the "File" tab & then selecting "Options".

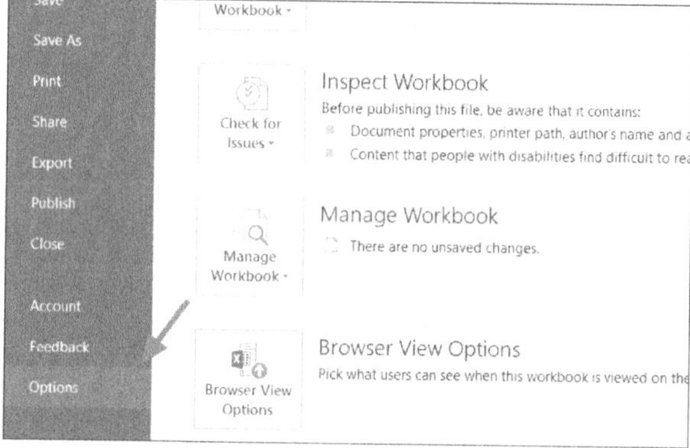

Activate the fill handle & cell drag and drop by selecting 'Advanced' in Excel & checking the 'Editing Options' option. This will allow Excel's fill handle.

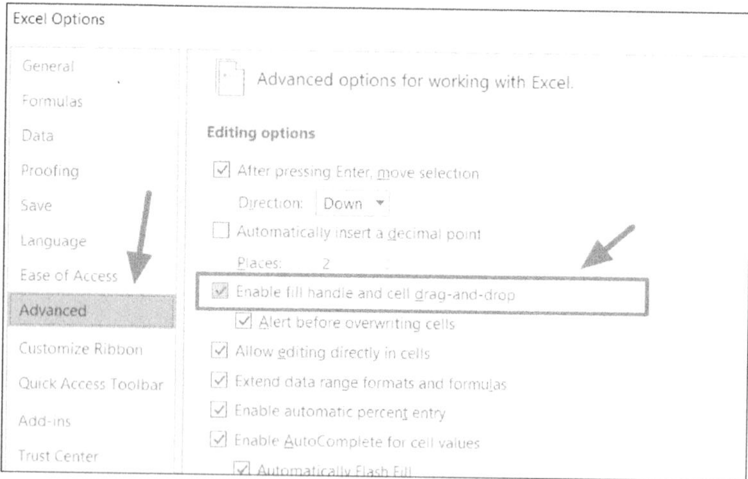

Then click on 'OK' to exit this dialogue box, and you're done.

Import / Export Data

In addition to the standard.xslx format, Excel can export and import various other file formats. A separate file type may be required if your saving data will be shared with other applications, such as a database.

Export Data

A CSV or a text file may be used to move data from Excel to different software, such as another spreadsheet application.

Go to the Files tabs.

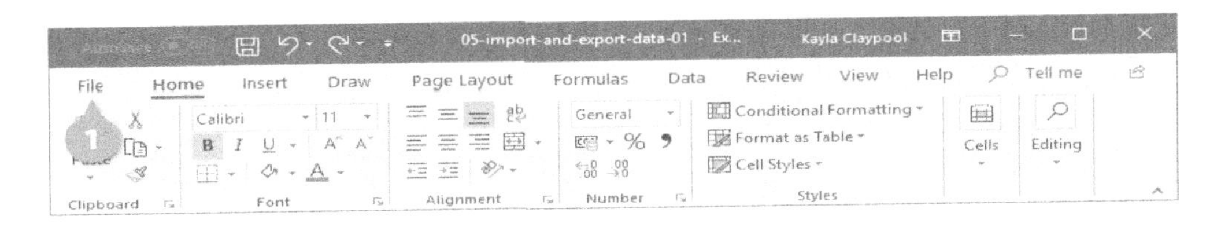

Click the Export from your menu on the left.
Click your Change File Format button.
To pick a file type, click on Other File Types.
Text (Tab delimited): A tab will be used to separate every cell data.
CSV (Comma delimited): A comma will be used to denote the end of each row of information in the table.
Formatted Texts (space delimited): A space will be used to separate the data in each cell.
Save as some other File Type: When you Save As dialogue box pops up, choose a new file type.
The file you choose will depend on the software that will use the exported data.
Click on Save As.

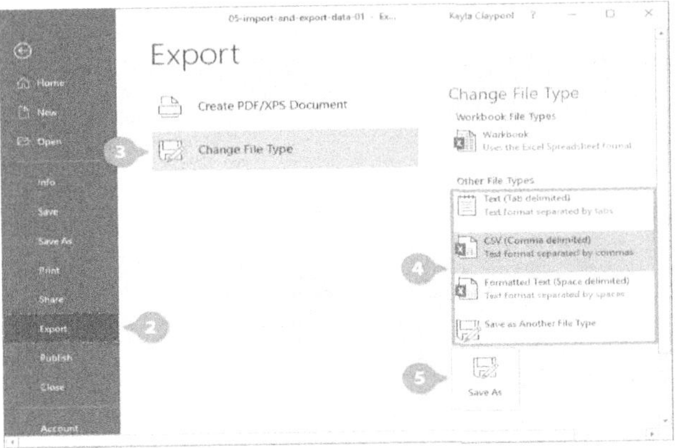

Select some location where you want to store your document.
Save your work.

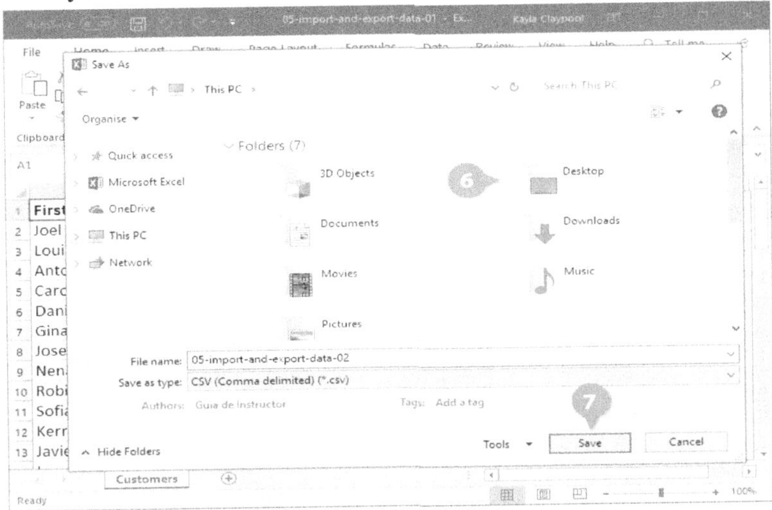

You'll see a warning that a portion of the workbook's functionality will be lost when you do this.
Click on Yes.

Import Data

External data sources, such as other databases, files, & web pages, may be imported into Excel.

- On the Ribbon, choose the Data tab.
- The Get Data button may be accessed by clicking on it.

Certain data sources need specific security access, & the connecting procedure might be complicated. For assistance, contact the technical support team at your company.

- Select a File from the drop-down menu.
- Select from CSV/Text.

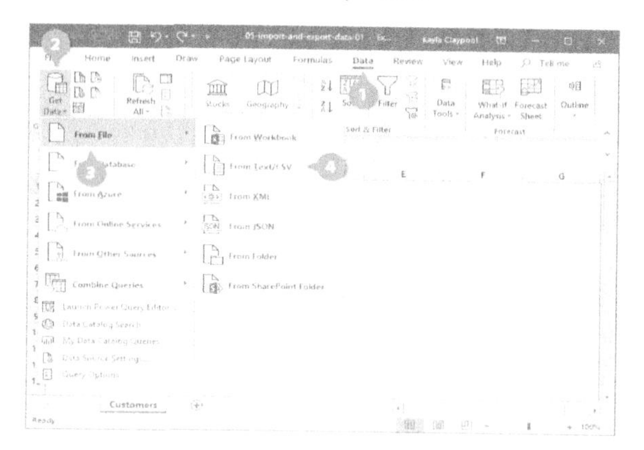

To import data from an external source, pick one of the Get External Data choices within Get the External Data groups instead.
Import the file you desire by clicking on the file's name.
Import your file by clicking on the Import button.
If a security warning displays when importing external data stating that a connection to an external source may not be secure, click OK.

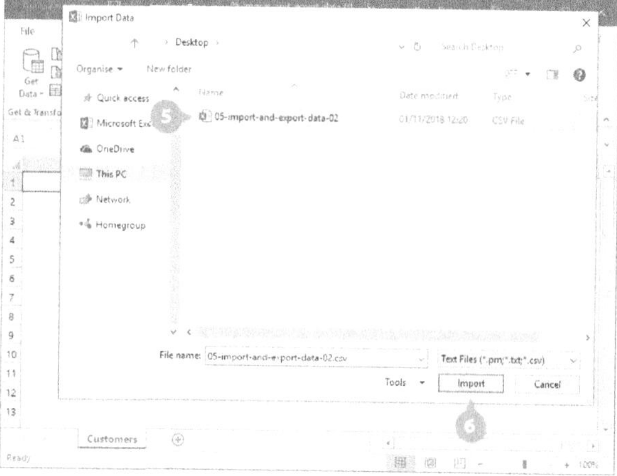

Make sure the preview is accurate.
The delimiter has been defined since you indicated that commas split the data. This option allows you to make any necessary adjustments.
Click on Load.

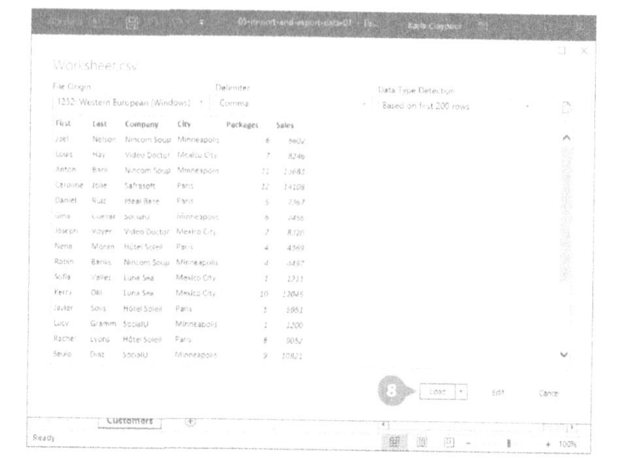

Chapter 3: Advanced Features Of Excel

Learners must know Excel formulae before doing financial research. Microsoft Excel is a standard data-processing program. Microsoft's spreadsheet tool is popular among investment bankers and financial analysts for data analysis, modeling, and presentation. This book contains an overview and collection of Excel functions.

Basic Terms in Excel

In Excel, formulas and functions are used for computations.

Formulas

Excel formulas operate for a cell count or just a single cell. = A 1 + A 2 + A 3 finds A1-A3 values.

Functions

Functions in Excel are pre-defined formulae. By giving them human-friendly names, they do away with the time-consuming manual involvement of formulae. Such as (A1:A3) = SUM. The function totals the values from A1 through A3.

Five Time-Saving Excel Data Insertion Methods

There are five distinct methods for using basic Excel formulae when examining the outcomes. Every strategy offers a unique set of advantages. Therefore, let's go over those tactics before discussing the important formulae so that you may begin working on your preferred procedure immediately.

Simple insertion: Typing the formula in a cell

Simple Excel formulae may be inserted by putting a single formula into the cells or utilizing the formula bar. The Excel feature name is usually followed by one equal sign at the start of the operation.

Excel is ingenious because a pop-up feature hint appears when you write the function phrase. From this selection, you will choose your choice. But refrain from pressing the Enter key. Instead, use the Tab key to start adding more options. Otherwise, you can get an incorrect name error that appears as "#NAME?" Simply pick that cell and finish the role in your formula bar to fix it.

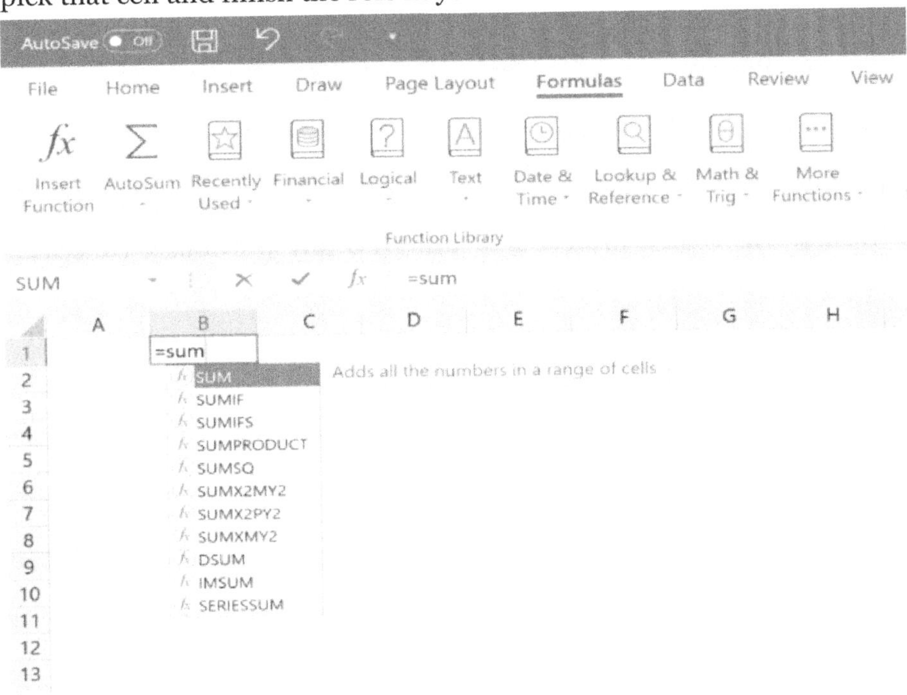

Using the Insert Function Options from your Formulas Tab

You need an Excel Insert Feature dialogue box to fully use the function insertion's potential. To accomplish this, choose Insert Function from the first option on your Formula tab. You may find many of the responsibilities you'll need in your conversation box to complete the financial report.

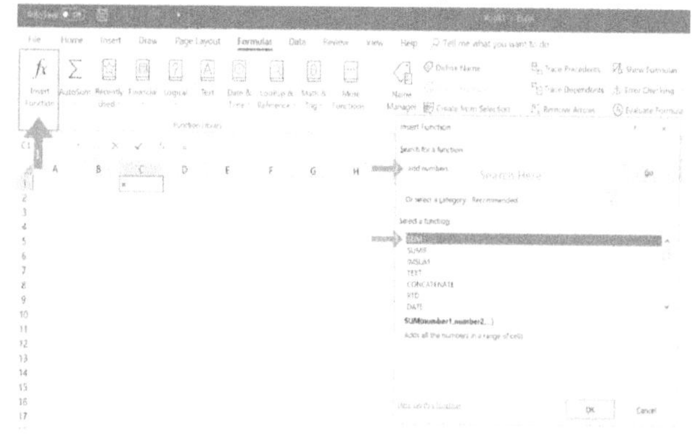

Selecting the Formula among the Groups from Formula Tab

This option is for those who like quick access to their favorite features. To reach that menu, choose the Formulas tab and your preferred category. Click to see a sub-menu with a list of these features. Then, you may make your chosen selection. If your preferred category isn't shown on the page, go to More Functions and check; it's hidden there.

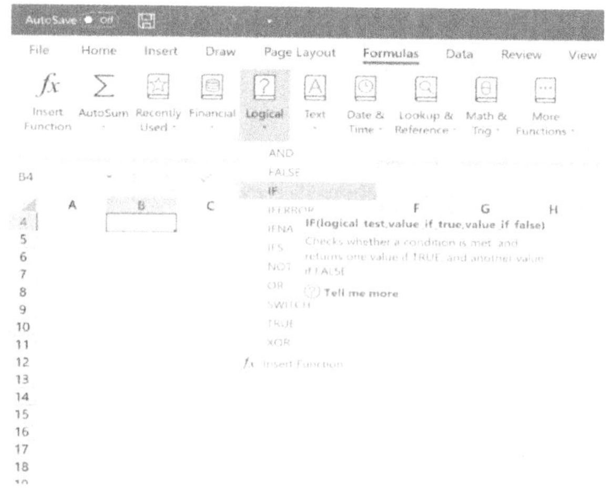

Using an AutoSum Option

For routine and easy chores, AutoSum is the preferred choice. Therefore, choose the home tab and click the AutoSum button in the upper-right corner. Then click the caret to bring up any previously concealed formulae. This option is also available in your Formulas tab following the Insert Function.

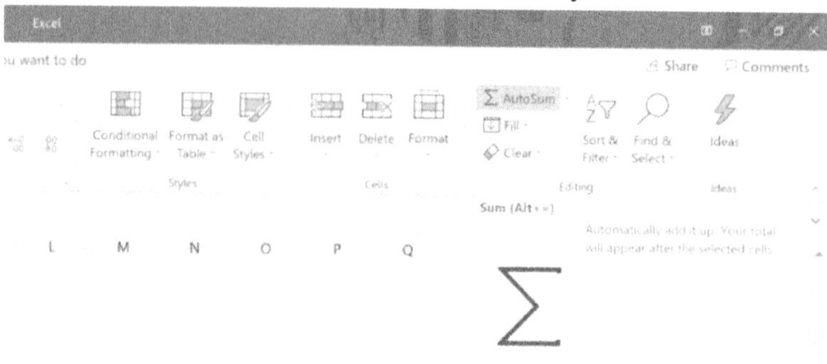

Quick Insert: Using Recently Utilized Tabs

If inputting the most often used formula again seems laborious, try using the Currently Used option instead. It is the third menu option under AutoSum on the Formulas tab.

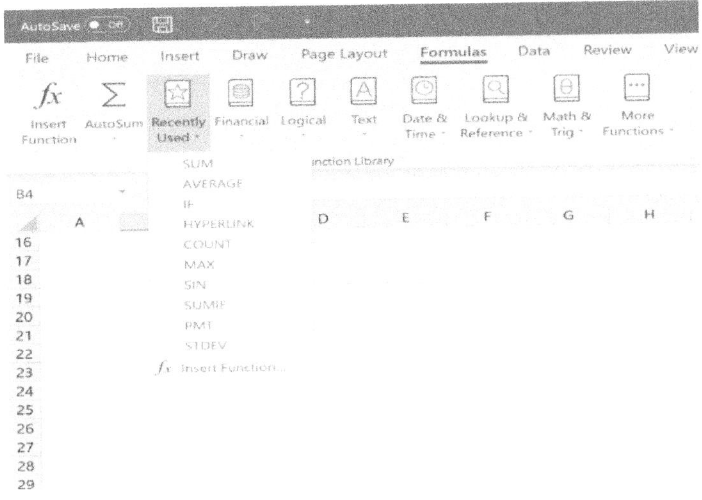

Seven Excel Formulas for the Workflow

Since you can now input and apply your favorite formulae properly, let's start by looking at some fundamental Excel functions.

1. SUM

The first Excel calculation you may learn is the SUM function. Normally, values from the specified settings' selected rows or columns are aggregated.

= *SUM* (**number 1**, *[number 2], ...)*

Examples:

= *SUM (B 2: G 2)* – A basic selection that sums all values of a single row.

= *SUM (A 2: A 8)* – A basic selection that sums all values of a single column.

= *SUM (A 2: A 7, A 9, A 12: A 15)* – A complex collection which sums values of range A2-A7, skips A 8, adds A 9, jumps A 10 & A 11, then ultimateladdsdd from A 12-A 15.

= *SUM (A 2: A 8) / 20* – Demonstrates you can turn the function into a formula.

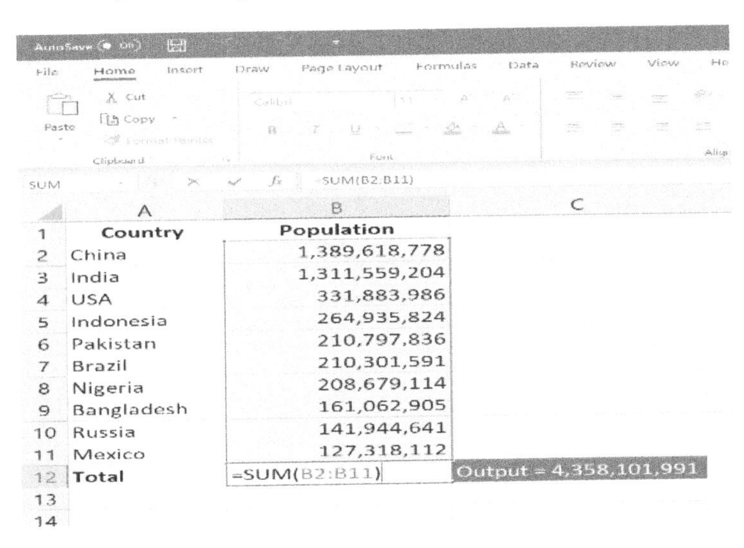

	A	B	C
1	Country	Population	
2	China	1,389,618,778	
3	India	1,311,559,204	
4	USA	331,883,986	
5	Indonesia	264,935,824	
6	Pakistan	210,797,836	
7	Brazil	210,301,591	
8	Nigeria	208,679,114	
9	Bangladesh	161,062,905	
10	Russia	141,944,641	
11	Mexico	127,318,112	
12	Total	=SUM(B2:B11)	Output = 4,358,101,991
13			
14			

2. AVERAGE

Simple averages of the results should be considered while utilizing the AVERAGE function, much like the total number of owners within the given shareholding pool.

= *AVERAGE* (**number 1**, *[number 2], ...)*

Example:

= *AVERAGE (B 2: B 11)* – Demonstrates an average and alike (SUM (B 2: B 11) / 10)

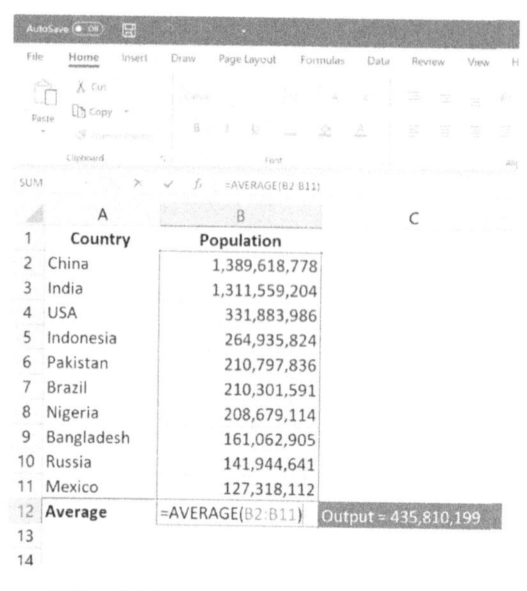

	A	B	C
1	Country	Population	
2	China	1,389,618,778	
3	India	1,311,559,204	
4	USA	331,883,986	
5	Indonesia	264,935,824	
6	Pakistan	210,797,836	
7	Brazil	210,301,591	
8	Nigeria	208,679,114	
9	Bangladesh	161,062,905	
10	Russia	141,944,641	
11	Mexico	127,318,112	
12	Average	=AVERAGE(B2:B11)	Output = 435,810,199
13			
14			

3. COUNT

A collection of cells with solely numerical values is counted using the COUNT feature.

= *COUNT* (**value 1, [value 2], ...**)

Example:

COUNT (A: A) – enters a total for all numerical values in column A. To count rows, however, you need to change a range in the calculation.

COUNT (A 1: C 1) – Now, it could count the rows.

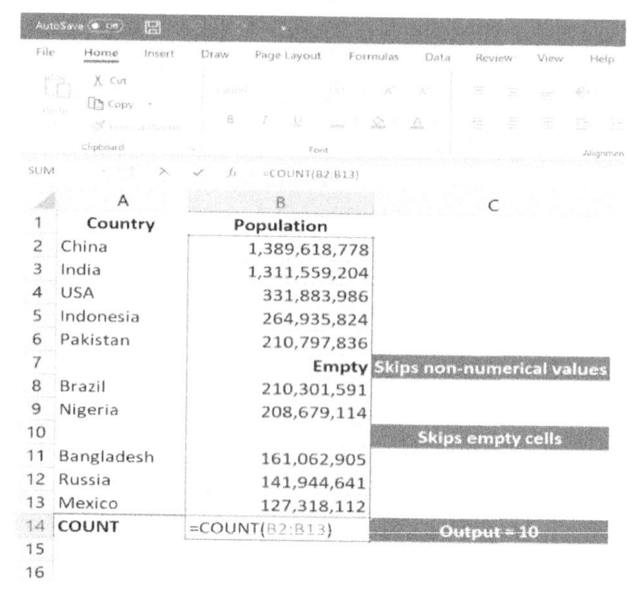

	A	B	C
1	Country	Population	
2	China	1,389,618,778	
3	India	1,311,559,204	
4	USA	331,883,986	
5	Indonesia	264,935,824	
6	Pakistan	210,797,836	
7		Empty	Skips non-numerical values
8	Brazil	210,301,591	
9	Nigeria	208,679,114	
10			Skips empty cells
11	Bangladesh	161,062,905	
12	Russia	141,944,641	
13	Mexico	127,318,112	
14	COUNT	=COUNT(B2:B13)	Output = 10
15			
16			

4. COUNTY

All cells within a rage are counted using COUNTA's COUNT feature, for example. However, regardless of cell type, it does count all cells. Unlike COUNT, which exclusively saves numeric data, it often counts dates, days, sequences, logical values, errors, void strings, and text.

*=COUNTA (***value 1, [value 2], ...***)*

Example:

COUNTA (C 2: C 13) - The C column's rows 2 through 13 are tallied regardless of the sort. However, unlike COUNT, a comparable method cannot count rows. You'll need to change the range between the brackets; for example, COUNTA (C 2: H 2) would count columns in the C and H categories.

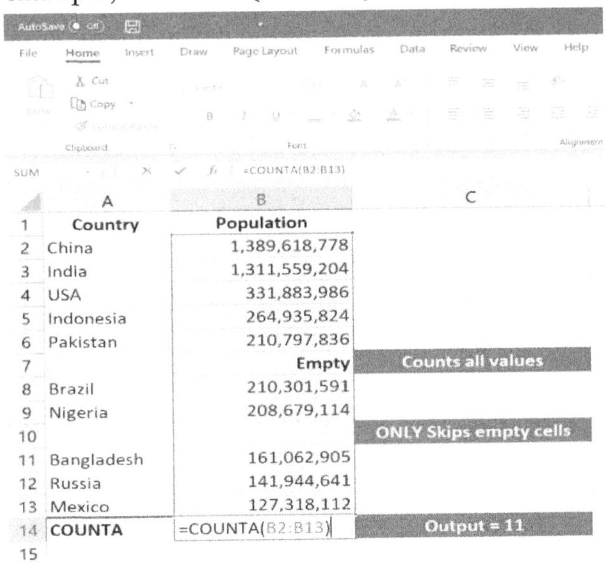

=COUNTA(B2:B13)

	A	B	C
1	Country	Population	
2	China	1,389,618,778	
3	India	1,311,559,204	
4	USA	331,883,986	
5	Indonesia	264,935,824	
6	Pakistan	210,797,836	
7		Empty	Counts all values
8	Brazil	210,301,591	
9	Nigeria	208,679,114	
10			ONLY Skips empty cells
11	Bangladesh	161,062,905	
12	Russia	141,944,641	
13	Mexico	127,318,112	
14	COUNTA	=COUNTA(B2:B13)	Output = 11
15			

5. IF

This function may also be used to sort the data according to criteria. The IF formula's advantage is that it enables the usage of formulae and functions.

=IF (**logical test, [value_if_false] [value_if_true],**)

Example:

=IF (C 2<D 3, 'TRUE,' 'FALSE') – It determines if C 3 is lower than D 3 in terms of value. Your cell value should stay TRUE if your reasoning is correct or false.

=IF (SUM (C 1: C 10)➔SUM (D 1: D 10), SUM (C 1: C 10), SUM (D 1: D 10)) – IF logic situation that is challenging. It initially adds up C 1–C10 and D 1–D10 before comparing the numbers. A cell's value becomes equal to a sum of C 1-C10 when the total of C1-C10 surpasses the sum of D 1-D10. Otherwise, it is the sum of C1 through C10.

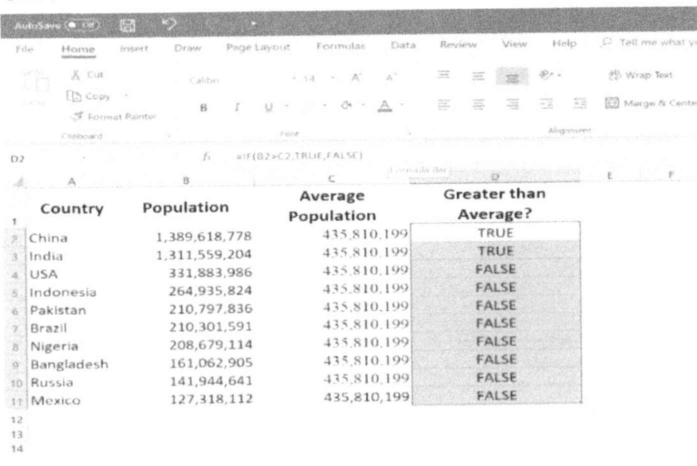

=IF(B2>C2,TRUE,FALSE)

	A	B	C	D
1	Country	Population	Average Population	Greater than Average?
2	China	1,389,618,778	435,810,199	TRUE
3	India	1,311,559,204	435,810,199	TRUE
4	USA	331,883,986	435,810,199	FALSE
5	Indonesia	264,935,824	435,810,199	FALSE
6	Pakistan	210,797,836	435,810,199	FALSE
7	Brazil	210,301,591	435,810,199	FALSE
8	Nigeria	208,679,114	435,810,199	FALSE
9	Bangladesh	161,062,905	435,810,199	FALSE
10	Russia	141,944,641	435,810,199	FALSE
11	Mexico	127,318,112	435,810,199	FALSE
12				
13				
14				

6. TRIM

Thanks to the TRIM function, unruly spaces won't lead to problems in your routines. It denotes the absence of open places. TRIM only affects a single cell, unlike many other activities that could affect a group of cells. Its disadvantage is that it duplicates information in a spreadsheet.

*=TRIM (***text***)*

Example:

TRIM (A 2) – Deletes any empty spaces from the values in cell A-2.

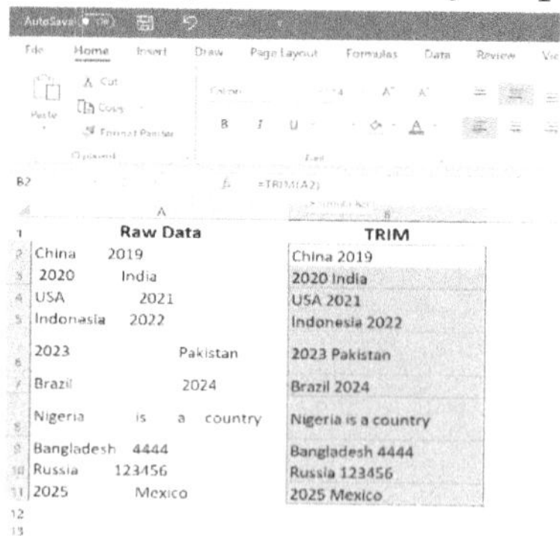

	A	B
1	Raw Data	TRIM
2	China 2019	China 2019
3	2020 India	2020 India
4	USA 2021	USA 2021
5	Indonesia 2022	Indonesia 2022
6	2023 Pakistan	2023 Pakistan
7	Brazil 2024	Brazil 2024
8	Nigeria is a country	Nigeria is a country
9	Bangladesh 4444	Bangladesh 4444
10	Russia 123456	Russia 123456
11	2025 Mexico	2025 Mexico

7. MAX and MIN

Finding the highest and lowest values within a group of data is made easier with the help of the MAX and MIN functions.

*=MIN (***number 1***, [number 2], ...)*

Example:

=MIN (B 2: C 11) – The minimal number is determined between the B column from B 2 and C column from C 2 to 11 in all columns, B & C.

*=MAX (***number 1***, [number 2], ...)*

Example:

=MAX (B 2: C 11) – The greatest number among B column from B 2 and C column from C 2 to 11 row is considered for both columns B & C.

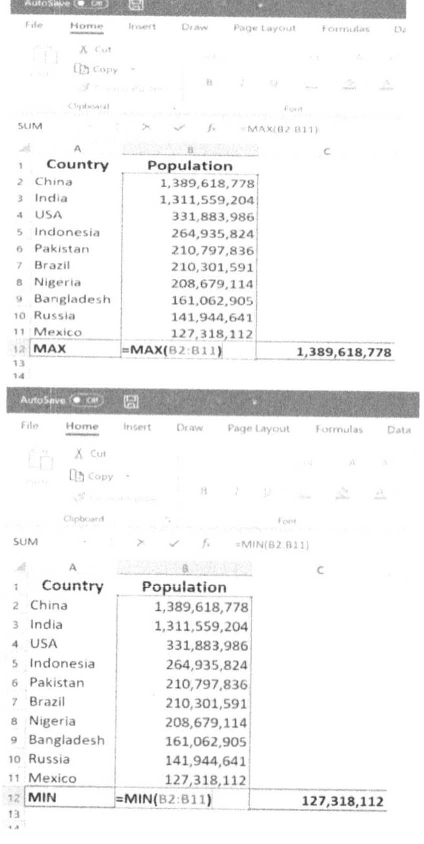

=MAX(B2:B11)

	A	B	C
1	Country	Population	
2	China	1,389,618,778	
3	India	1,311,559,204	
4	USA	331,883,986	
5	Indonesia	264,935,824	
6	Pakistan	210,797,836	
7	Brazil	210,301,591	
8	Nigeria	208,679,114	
9	Bangladesh	161,062,905	
10	Russia	141,944,641	
11	Mexico	127,318,112	
12	MAX	=MAX(B2:B11)	1,389,618,778

=MIN(B2:B11)

	A	B	C
1	Country	Population	
2	China	1,389,618,778	
3	India	1,311,559,204	
4	USA	331,883,986	
5	Indonesia	264,935,824	
6	Pakistan	210,797,836	
7	Brazil	210,301,591	
8	Nigeria	208,679,114	
9	Bangladesh	161,062,905	
10	Russia	141,944,641	
11	Mexico	127,318,112	
12	MIN	=MIN(B2:B11)	127,318,112

Advanced Formulas in Excel

You have practiced some basic Excel formulas; Let's get into some advanced formulas in Excel.

1. WORKDAY.INTL

Use WORKDAY.INTL to estimate a project's completion date.

It's more flexible than WORKDAY, which assumed weekends were always Sunday and Saturday. You may pick different weekends or construct your list.

WORKDAY.INTL Arguments

WORKDAY.INTL requires 2 parameters and allows 2 more.

- **start_date:** the date on which the computation begins
- **days:** beginning and ending dates are counted as complete days
- **weekend: (optional)** working days are indicated with a special code
- **holidays: (optional)** calendar days that are not in use

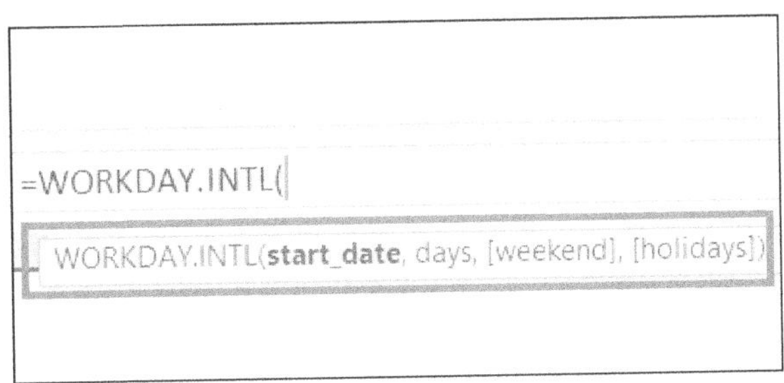

Notes regarding WORKDAY.INTL

The WORKDAY.INTL function may be used in a variety of ways:

Start Date

- The first digit of the current date will be omitted, leaving just the integer
- A time and date, for example, will be disregarded if entered.
- For best results, choose a day that falls on a workday.

Days

We're going to round down the number of days to the nearest integer.

A number might be positive, negative, or zero to indicate forward or backward movement. A zero indicates a return to the beginning date.

Weekend

In this case, it's not required. Non-working days are Sunday and Saturday if they are not included.

To begin, let's have a look at this issue:

- Choose a choice from the drop-down menu
- A 7-digit array with one non-functional character and zero functioning characters may also be created.

Holidays

- In this case, it's not required. There are no specific non-working days if calendar dates are excluded.

Project End Date

The WORKDAY.INTL function may be used to compute the end date of a project in this example. Like WORKDAY, but with the ability to choose the days off.

As an example:

- Begin with the WORKDAY arguments. Start date & days for INTL.
- Then comes the Christmas shopping.

- Finally, non-working days would be designated.

Start with Basics

Two pieces of information are necessary to get started with WORKDAY.INTL function's basic features:

How long will it take to complete the task?

Now it's WORKDAY!

INTL will figure out when the required amount of time has passed from the start date to arrive at the actual working date.

You begin on Thursday, Dec 10th (cell C 8), and your project will be completed in two days, as shown in the screenshot (cell C10).

Cell C12 has the following WORKDAY.INTL formula:

=WORKDAY.INTL (C8, C10)

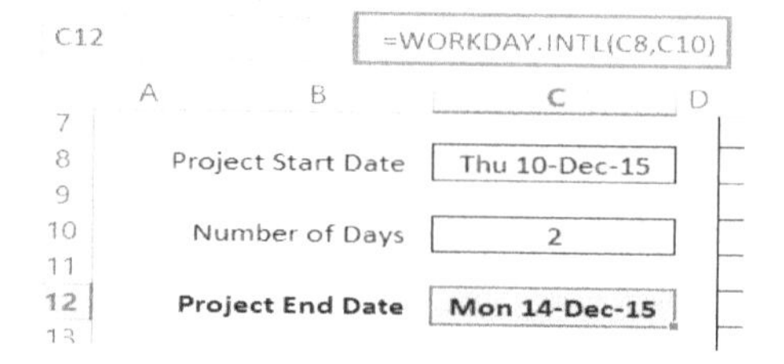

Check your Calculation

See the following table to see why December 14th was chosen.

Thursdays and Fridays are dedicated to working on the project (2 days).

It thinks you don't work on Saturdays or Sundays since you didn't indicate them.

The following working day was Monday, Dec 14th; that is the formula's outcome.

Date	Work?	Project Day
Thu 10-Dec-15	1	1
Fri 11-Dec-15	1	2
Sat 12-Dec-15	0	
Sun 13-Dec-15	0	
Mon 14-Dec-15	1	
Tue 15-Dec-15	1	

Adjust your End Date

Instead of the following business day, you'd want to know when the job is expected to be done. So, you deduct one from the number of days within the calculation to get the desired result.

=WORKDAY.INTL (C8, C10-1)

That makes Friday, December 11, the end date for the project.

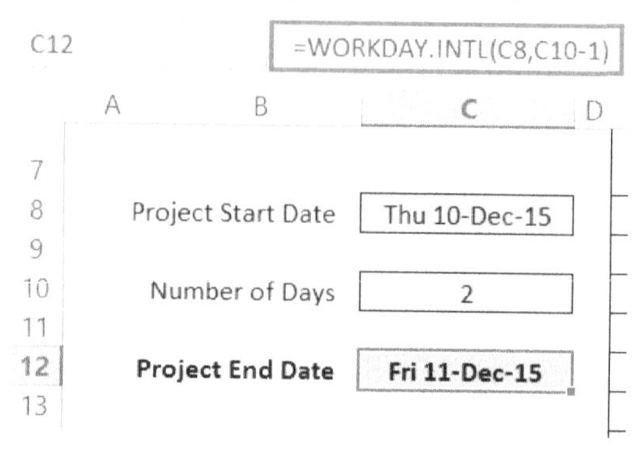

Exclude Holidays

Like the earlier WORKDAY function, you may omit holidays from WORKDAY.INTL.

Adding or removing dates is trivial in a named Excel table. In the image below, tblHol's date column is the Holiday List.

Enter a List of Holidays

Date	Holiday
26-Nov-2015	Thanksgiving
25-Dec-2015	Christmas
26-Dec-2015	Boxing Day
1-Jan-2016	New Year's Day

You'll use the function's fourth parameter to omit holidays from date computations.

=WORKDAY.INTL (C8,C10-1,tblHol[Date])

With this change, a project that started on December 24 will expire on December 28.

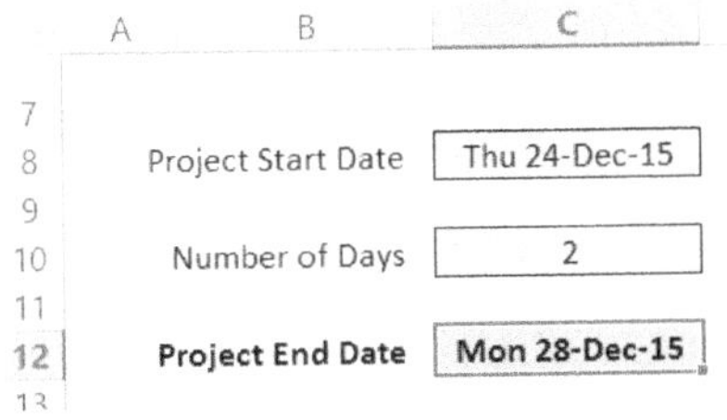

Here's a table containing working days and orange-highlighted holidays.

Date	Work?	Project Day
Thu 24-Dec-15	1	1
Fri 25-Dec-15	0	
Sat 26-Dec-15	0	
Sun 27-Dec-15	0	
Mon 28-Dec-15	1	2
Tue 29-Dec-15	1	

Specify your Non-Working Days

If you don't say, WORKDAY. INTL ignores weekends (non-working days) automatically. You may pick other days as weekends using either method:

- choose from the list
- 1 & 0 string

Select from the Drop-Down List

Selecting from a drop-down list of alternatives makes it much simpler to designate weekend days. The list will immediately display when you begin the function with the third parameter.

If you don't see the list, use Alt + Down Arrow to bring it up.

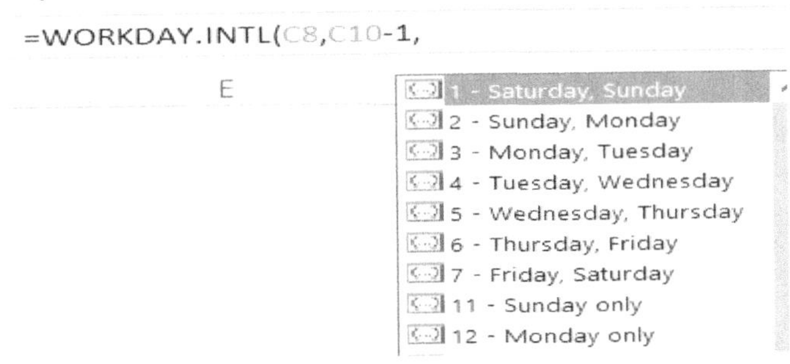

Option 2 - Sunday, Monday – shifts the project deadline to Tuesday, Dec 29th.

=WORKDAY.INTL(C8, C101,2, tblHol[Da)

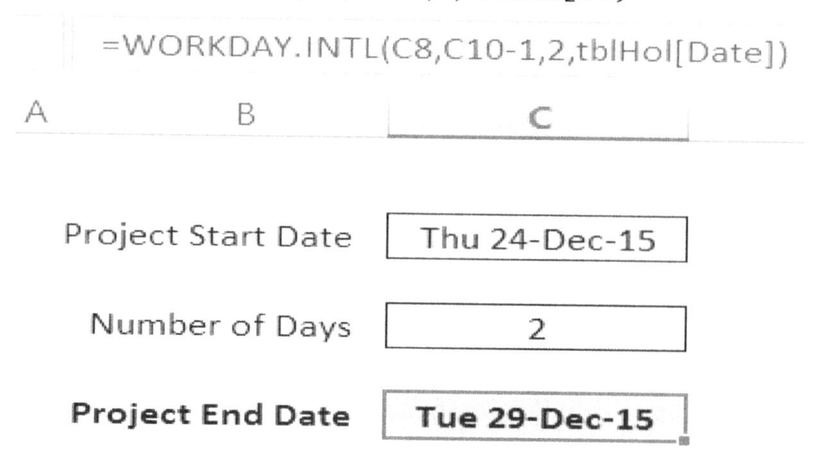

Create Non-Working Days String

Create your string if none of the drop-down selections are what you're looking for. Weekdays are represented by the first seven numbers of the string.

- Workdays are marked with a zero.
- For non-working days, use a 1.

Just use string 0101011 if you just work on Mondays, Wednesdays, and Fridays.

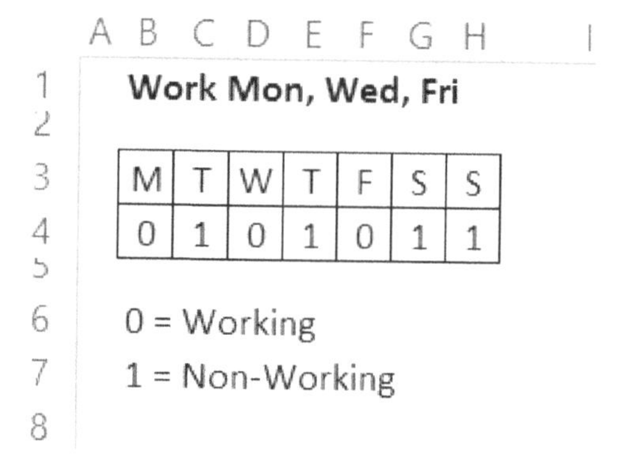

You'll modify the start date to Wednesday, December 23rd, a working day in our new calendar. Below is the amended formula with a 7-digit string within double quotation marks in the third parameter.
=WORKDAY.INTL (C8,C10-1,"0101011",tblHol[Date])

As a result of these modifications, the deadline has been moved forward to Monday, Dec 28th.

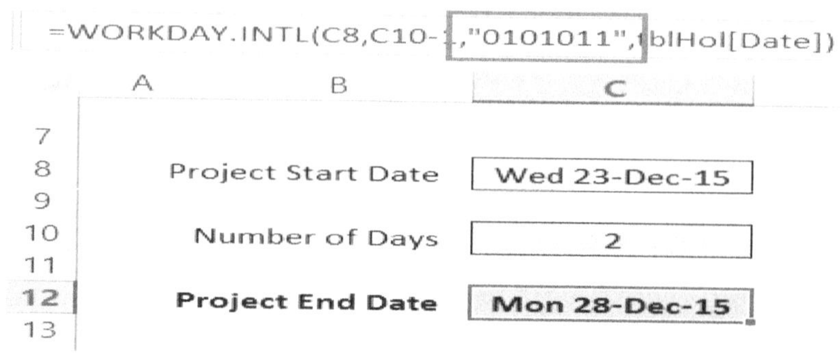

Calculate Non-Working String

A table like the one below might make it simpler to pick non-working days. Use an X to indicate days off from work and an IF formula that displays 0 or 1 in every row.

=IF (K8="x",1,0)

A CONCATENATE formula is used to condense the string into its final form:

= CONCATENATE (M8, M9, M10, M11, M12, M13, M14)

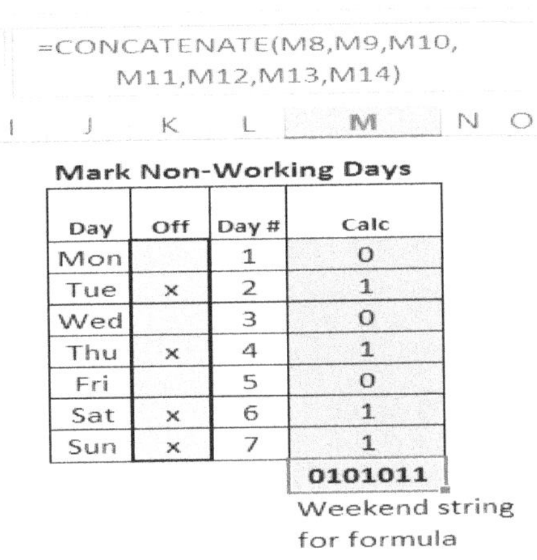

=CONCATENATE(M8,M9,M10,
M11,M12,M13,M14)

I	J	K	L	M	N	O

Mark Non-Working Days

Day	Off	Day #	Calc
Mon		1	0
Tue	x	2	1
Wed		3	0
Thu	x	4	1
Fri		5	0
Sat	x	6	1
Sun	x	7	1
			0101011

Weekend string
for formula

Use that cell as the 3rd parameter within WORKDAY.INTL calculation.

=WORKDAY.INTL (C 8, C 10-1, M 15, tblHol [Date])

Your calculation columns might be concealed to prevent individuals from mucking up formulae.

Nth Weekdays of the Month (WORKDAY.INTL)

The DAY AT WORK. Using the INTL function along with one customized string of the nonworking days, one may get the Nth weekday of the month.

Excel's WORKDAY.INTL function may be utilized to discover the Nth weekday into a given month and year. Thanksgiving in Canada is honored on the 2nd Monday in Oct, so check the calendar to see when it falls this year.

Examples: Thanksgiving Day USA - Nth Weekday of the Month

In the United States, for example, Thanksgiving falls on the fourth Thursday of November.

The following formula, seen in cell C10 of the image below, may be used to determine the date of Thanksgiving:

=WORKDAY.INTL (DATE (C4, D5, 0), C7, "1110111")

There is one working day (Thursday) within a 7-digit string for non-working days.

Because of this, the actual Thanksgiving date is the fourth Thursday of November.

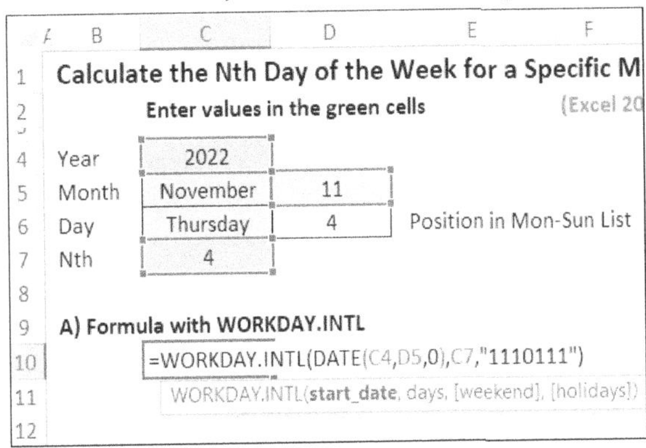

	A	B	C	D	E	F
1		**Calculate the Nth Day of the Week for a Specific M**				
2			**Enter values in the green cells**			(Excel 20
3						
4		Year	2022			
5		Month	November	11		
6		Day	Thursday	4	Position in Mon-Sun List	
7		Nth	4			
8						
9		**A) Formula with WORKDAY.INTL**				
10			=WORKDAY.INTL(DATE(C4,D5,0),C7,"1110111")			
11			WORKDAY.INTL(**start_date**, days, [weekend], [holidays])			
12						

2. RANDBETWEEN Function

Based on the input values, the RANDBETWEEN function outputs a random number. Every time the worksheet is accessed or edited, this feature is activated.

The following parameters are used when using the RANDBETWEEN function:

Down: This is the least integer in the set that the function may return (Mandatory Function).

Peak The greatest integer the function may produce in the set (Mandatory Function).

Application of RANDBETWEEN Function

Let's examine the table below to see how the RANDBETWEEN function is used.

fx =RANDBETWEEN(A2, B2)

	A	B	C	D
1	Bottom	Top	Result	
2	2	3	3	
3	3	10	4	
4	120	300	205	
5	32	121	102	

The table above uses the RANDBETWEEN method (A2, B2).

The worksheet's outcome varies when the equations in the table are repeated, as seen below.

fx =RANDBETWEEN(A2, B2)

	A	B	C	D
1	Bottom	Top	Result	
2	2	3	2	
3	3	10	8	
4	120	300	181	
5	32	121	87	

RANDBETWEEN has a few considerations.

When tabulated or changed, RANDBETWEEN returns a new value.

Enter the RANDBETWEEN function in the formula bar and press F9 to change the model into its output. Choose a cell, enter RANDBETWEEN, then press Ctrl + Enter.

3. TRANSPOSE

TRANSPOSE flips a spectrum or array. Vertical and horizontal ranges are transformed.
TRANSPOSE has one parameter. =Transpose (array)
Select blank cells. Ensure the chosen cells' numbers match the original set.

- In the selected blanks cells, type =**TRANSPOSE**

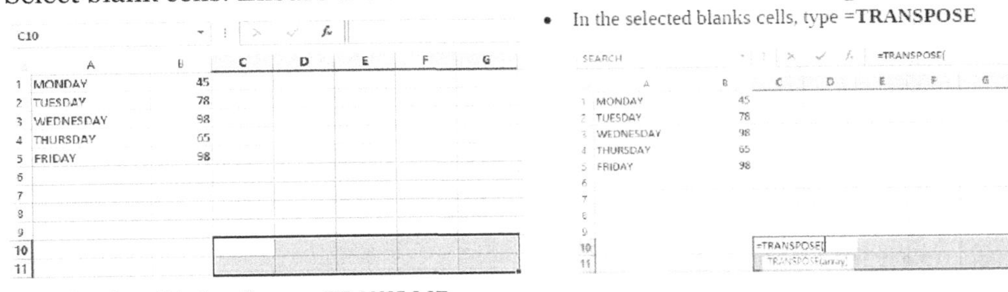

Transpose cells in their native environment.

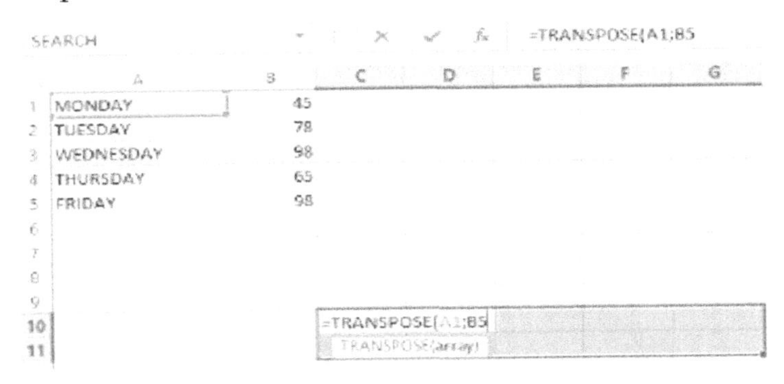

CTRL+SHIF+ENTER transposes the cell range.

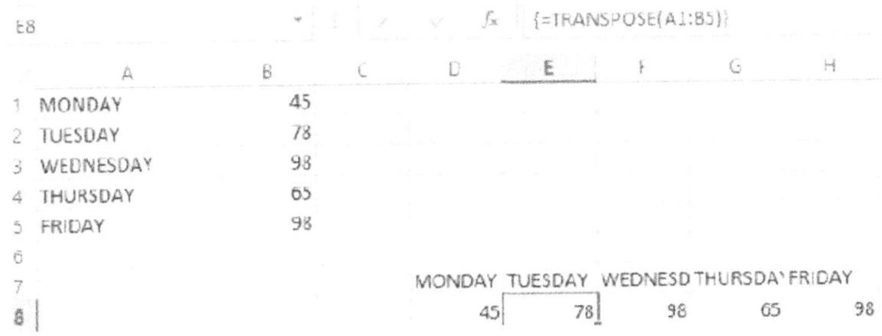

E8 {=TRANSPOSE(A1:B5)}

	A	B	C	D	E	F	G	H
1	MONDAY	45						
2	TUESDAY	78						
3	WEDNESDAY	98						
4	THURSDAY	65						
5	FRIDAY	98						
6								
7				MONDAY	TUESDAY	WEDNESD	THURSDA'	FRIDAY
8				45	78	98	65	98

4. COUNTBLANK

Excel's STATISTICAL functions include COUNTBLANK[1]. COUNTBLANK counts a range's empty cells. The function may highlight or count empty cells in financial analysis.

Formula

=COUNTBLANK (range)

Where:

Range defines which cells to count as blank.

For COUNTBLANK:

- This function doesn't count text, numbers, mistakes, etc.
- Empty formulas ("") are counted. COUNTBLANK counts a cell as blank if it contains a blank text string and formula that yields one.
- Zero-filled cells aren't counted as blank.

Using COUNTBLANK Function within Excel?

COUNTBLANK can be used in a worksheet cell's formula. Consider an example to learn the function's applications.

COUNTBLANK Example

This method uses conditional formatting to count empty cells.

Consider the following data:

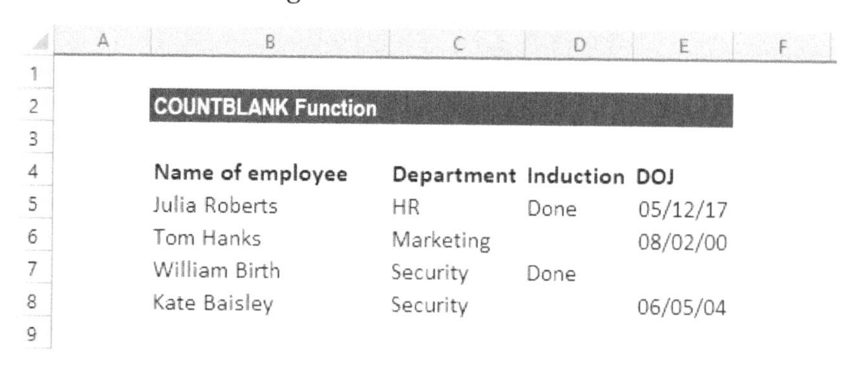

	A	B	C	D	E	F
1						
2		COUNTBLANK Function				
3						
4		Name of employee	Department	Induction	DOJ	
5		Julia Roberts	HR	Done	05/12/17	
6		Tom Hanks	Marketing		08/02/00	
7		William Birth	Security	Done		
8		Kate Baisley	Security		06/05/04	
9						

=COUNTBLANK (A2:D5) counts empty rows.

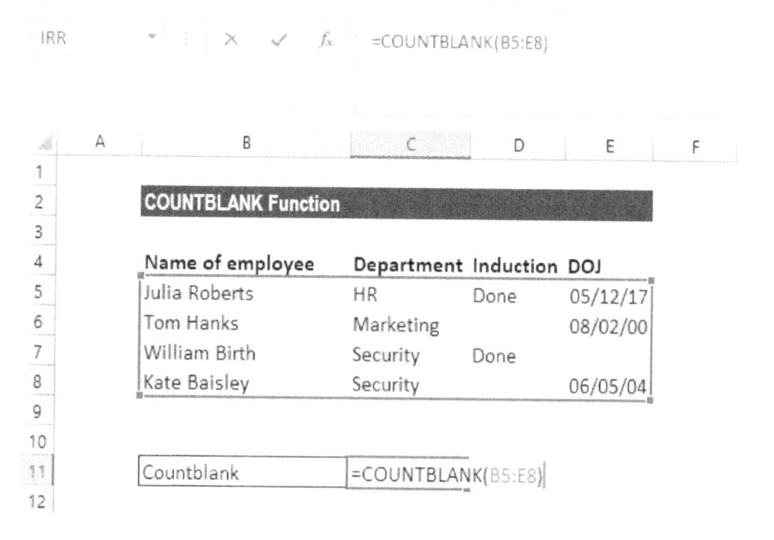

IRR =COUNTBLANK(B5:E8)

	A	B	C	D	E	F
1						
2		COUNTBLANK Function				
3						
4		Name of employee	Department	Induction	DOJ	
5		Julia Roberts	HR	Done	05/12/17	
6		Tom Hanks	Marketing		08/02/00	
7		William Birth	Security	Done		
8		Kate Baisley	Security		06/05/04	
9						
10						
11		Countblank	=COUNTBLANK(B5:E8)			
12						

Results:

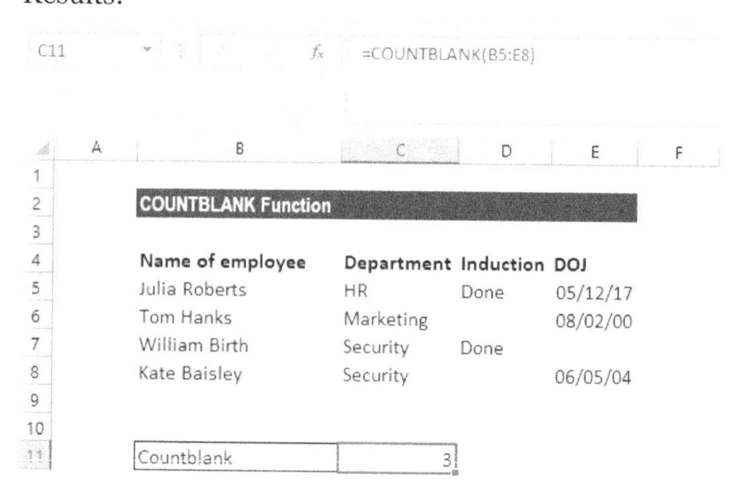

C11 =COUNTBLANK(B5:E8)

	A	B	C	D	E	F
1						
2		COUNTBLANK Function				
3						
4		Name of employee	Department	Induction	DOJ	
5		Julia Roberts	HR	Done	05/12/17	
6		Tom Hanks	Marketing		08/02/00	
7		William Birth	Security	Done		
8		Kate Baisley	Security		06/05/04	
9						
10						
11		Countblank	3			

Using conditional formatting and COUNTBLANK, you may highlight rows containing empty cells. Select the required range, then apply COUNTBLANK() conditional formatting. This highlights all Blank cells in the range.

5. VLOOKUP

The VLOOKUP function looks up data within the 1st column of a dataset/table and returns equal data from a separate column in the same row.

VLOOKUP uses these parameters:

=VLOOKUP (col_index_num, table_array, lookup_value, [range_lookup])

- **Look-up_value (Required argument):** The value to look for in the table's or dataset's first column.
- **Table_array (Required argument):** the data array that the lookup value may search within the column's left-hand part.
- **Col_index_num (Needed argument):** The returned corresponding statistics are listed in the table as column numbers or integers.
- **Range_lookup (optional argument):** Whether VLOOK can discover an exact match or a good match depends on this piece of code. Either TRUE or FALSE determines the statement's value. The next highest value is returned if a suitable match cannot be found. FALSE indicates an exact match, and #N/A is returned as an error if none is discovered.

The steps listed below may be used to utilize this function to get the value of yam within the table above:

- Choose an empty cell, then type your lookup value method, that is, the cell containing the desired data. The lookup cell in this instance is A12, which has the formula Yam =VLOOKUP (A12)

=VLOOKUP(A12

	A	B	C	D	E	F	G
1	GOOD TABLE						
2							
3							
4	FRUIT	IN STOCK	PRICE $				
5	Grapes	Yes	23				
6	Yam	Yes	54				
7	Bananas	No	78				
8	Orange	Yes	54				
9							
10							
11	FRUIT	PRICE					
12	YAM	=VLOOKUP(A12					
13		VLOOKUP(lookup_value, table_array, col_index_num, [range_lookup])					

6. HLOOKUP

The HLOOKUP function, which stands for "horizontal lookup," is a device for retrieving a value or a piece of information from the top row of a table array or dataset and returning it together with another row's given value or item in the same column.

The HLOOKUP function uses the following inputs to conduct its job.

(Lookup value, table array, row index number, [range lookup]) = HLOOKUP

Follow the instructions below to calculate your overall Joy in Mathematics score.

Select a blank cell, then enter the lookup value or the cell containing the data to be looked for.

- The lookup cell in this instance is B1, which contains the name. Pleasure; =HLOOKUP (B1

× ✓ fx =HLOOKUP(B1

	A	B	C	D	E	F	G
1	STUDENT SCORES	JOY	LOVETH	JOHN	ADE X		
2	MATHEMATICS	59	45	68	98		
3	ENGLISH	69	78	43	76		
4	ECONOMICS	34	56	65	89		
5	PHE	23	89	24	97		
6							
7	THE TOTAL SCORE OF JOY IN MATHEMATICS	=HLOOKUP(B1					
8		HLOOKUP(lookup_value, table_array, row_index_num, [range_lookup])					

Finally, by selecting TRUE or FALSE, you may inform Excel whether you're looking for an exact or a great fit. = HLOOKUP (B1, A1:E5,3, FALSE) or =HLOOKUP (B1, A1:E5,3, TRUE)

× ✓ fx =HLOOKUP(B1, A1:E5,2, FALSE)

	A	B	C	D	E	F	G
1	STUDENT SCORES	JOY	LOVETH	JOHN	ADE X		
2	MATHEMATICS	59	45	68	98		
3	ENGLISH	69	78	43	76		
4	ECONOMICS	34	56	65	89		
5	PHE	23	89	24	97		
6							
7	THE TOTAL SCORE OF JOY IN MATHEMATICS	=HLOOKUP(B1, A1:E5,2, FALSE)					
8		HLOOKUP(lookup_value, table_array, row_index_num, [range_lookup])					

Chapter 4: Excel Tables

This chapter covers Excel table fundamentals. This book creates a multi-sheet file for Jan. weather data in 2 cities. Most employees must organize, manage, and report outcomes.

This chapter's Figure shows a full workbook. This workbook contains three pages. The first worksheet depicts Portland, Maine's January weather. The 2nd page displays Jan's weather in Portland, Oregon, which is different. The third sheet adds a weekly column to Portland, Oregon results for subtotaling.

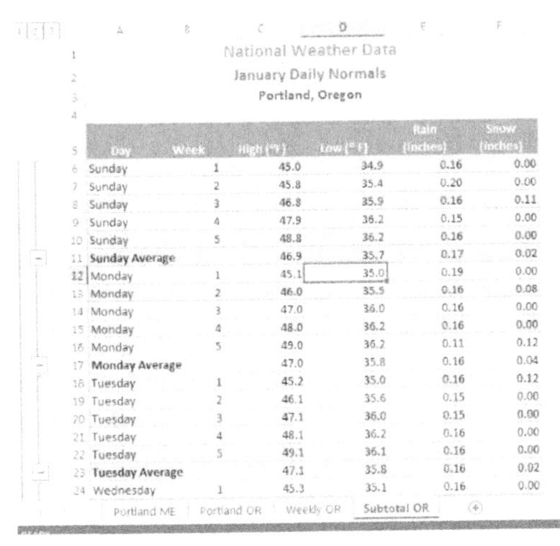

National Weather Data
January Daily Normals
Portland, Oregon

Day	Week	High (°F)	Low (°F)	Rain (inches)	Snow (inches)
Sunday	1	45.0	34.9	0.16	0.00
Sunday	2	45.8	35.4	0.20	0.00
Sunday	3	46.8	35.9	0.16	0.11
Sunday	4	47.9	36.2	0.15	0.00
Sunday	5	48.8	36.2	0.16	0.00
Sunday Average		46.9	35.7	0.17	0.02
Monday	1	45.1	35.0	0.19	0.00
Monday	2	46.0	35.5	0.16	0.08
Monday	3	47.0	36.0	0.16	0.00
Monday	4	48.0	36.2	0.16	0.00
Monday	5	49.0	36.2	0.11	0.12
Monday Average		47.0	35.8	0.16	0.04
Tuesday	1	45.2	35.0	0.16	0.12
Tuesday	2	46.1	35.6	0.15	0.00
Tuesday	3	47.1	36.0	0.15	0.00
Tuesday	4	48.1	36.2	0.16	0.00
Tuesday	5	49.1	36.1	0.16	0.00
Tuesday Average		47.1	35.8	0.16	0.02
Wednesday	1	45.3	35.1	0.16	0.00

Portland ME | Portland OR | Weekly OR | Subtotal OR

Creating the Table

A correctly set up table with a lengthy list or column helps present data. When entering data from scratch, follow these rules:

Use adjacent columns and rows to coordinate data.

Start your table at the top-left corner and proceed down.

Skipping rows and columns "spacings out" info. (Rows and columns may be enlarged and aligned to create white space between features.)

Set aside a column on the table's left for row headers.

Just above your table's rows, put the column titles.

Table titles should be placed above column heads in a row (s).

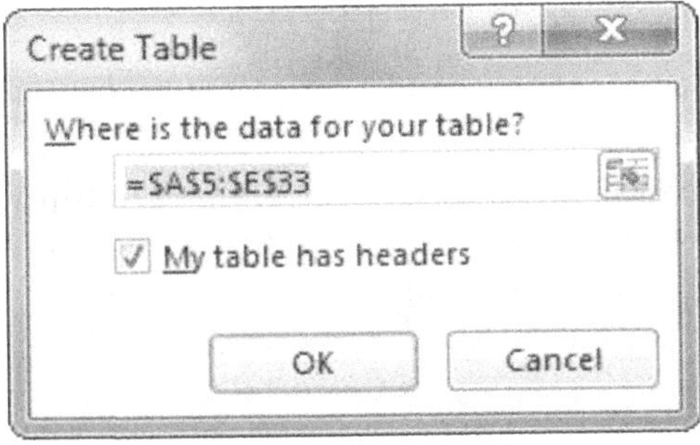

Following these recommendations will guarantee that the table's types, filters, totals, and subtotals provide desired results. You'll need these rules for a National Weather Portland M E worksheet. Now, your data is in rows and columns. The Upper left is now A5, and Row5 names are beneath column headers. After setting up your data, you're pleased to alter it in Excel. Open (CH5 Data) and save it as National Weather CH5.

A5 in Portland-ME.

On the Insert tab, click Table.

The figure appears onscreen.

Troublemaker
My table contains the headers" Okay.
Reload A5.
Adjust column widths to view row5 headers with filter arrows. Your table's filter arrows display as down-arrow buttons in row 5. You'll discover how to filter & sort data later in the chapter.
Your spreadsheet should resemble Figure.

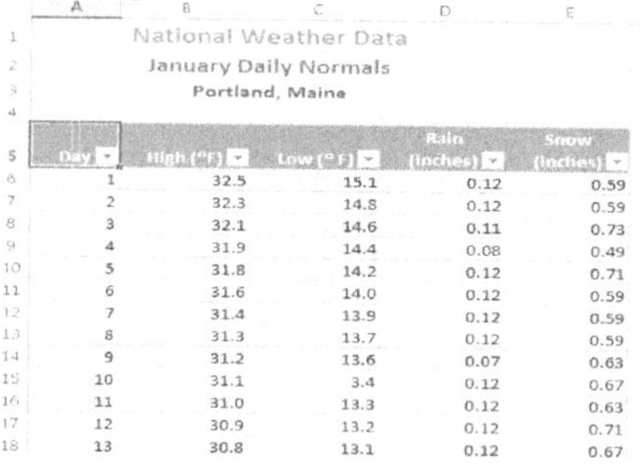

National Weather Data
January Daily Normals
Portland, Maine

Day	High (°F)	Low (°F)	Rain (inches)	Snow (inches)
1	32.5	15.1	0.12	0.59
2	32.3	14.8	0.12	0.59
3	32.1	14.6	0.11	0.73
4	31.9	14.4	0.08	0.49
5	31.8	14.2	0.12	0.71
6	31.6	14.0	0.12	0.59
7	31.4	13.9	0.12	0.59
8	31.3	13.7	0.12	0.59
9	31.2	13.6	0.07	0.63
10	31.1	3.4	0.12	0.67
11	31.0	13.3	0.12	0.63
12	30.9	13.2	0.12	0.71
13	30.8	13.1	0.12	0.67

Table Tool Design appears when you click within the table. This ribbon tab allows update, style, and application table features.

Follow these steps:

- Choose A5 or Portland.
- Insert tab, Table button.
- My table contains the headers" Okay.
- Reload A5.
- Adjust column widths to view row5 titles and filter arrows.

Creating the Table

- Select the top left cell in the data.
- Click the Table button under the Insert tab.
- The "My table contains headers" checkbox should be selected. Choose the OK option.
- Click once more on the top-left cell.
- Adjust the column widths to view all the headers with the filter arrows.

Formatting Tables

There are several formatting options for the Excel table. Pre-installed table styles come in Light, Medium, and Dark color options. Below are also included many table designs.

Table Style Options

Table Style	Description
Header Row	Top row of the table that includes column headings
Total Row	Row added to the bottom that applies column summary calculations
First Column	Formatting added to the left-most column in the table
Last Column	Formatting added to the right-most column in the table
Banded Rows	Alternating rows of color added to make it easier to see rows of data
Banded Columns	Alternating columns of color added to make it easier to see columns of data
Filter Button	Button that appears at the top of each column that lists options for sorting and filtering

In the steps that follow, you'll format both of your Portland weather tables as follows:

1. Locate the Portland file in your open file (ME sheet).

2. On the Table Tool Design tab, click the Further button in the Table Style group.

A selection of table kinds will show up, as seen in the figure below.

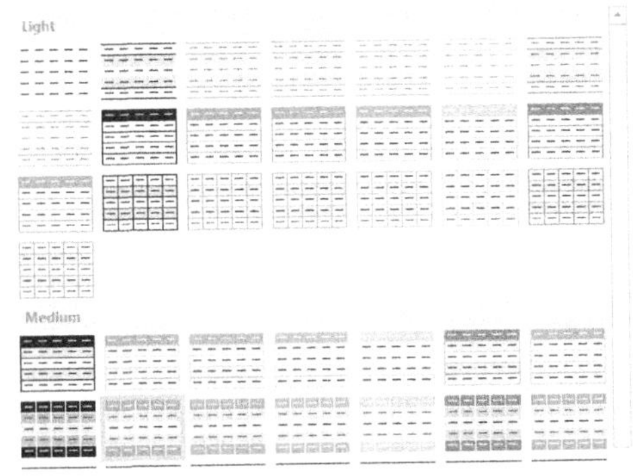

3. Select Table Styles Medium 7 from the Medium Section of the Table Style collection.
4. On the Ribbon, choose Banded Rows under the Table Styles Option category.

The color-contrasting line would disappear. Reading the data in the table has gotten more difficult.

5. Try out one of the many Table Styles options. Once finished, just choose the Banded Rows, Header Row, and Filter Button, as shown in the figure below.

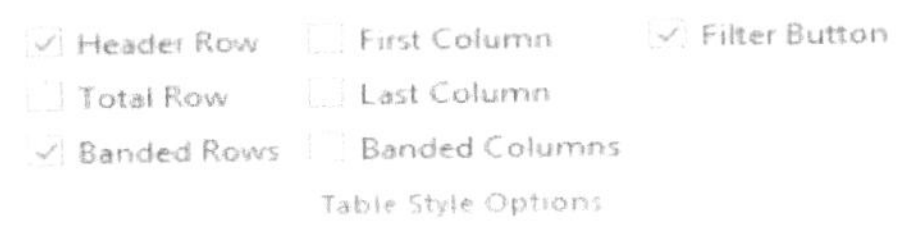

Adding Data to your Tables

You'll need to update an Excel table over time. You'll update your Excel table with fresh data. In the blank area, data will be inserted. The easiest technique is to place data in the table's first blank row. The table's data will be sorted. If you wish to include data in the table's middle, insert a blank row and fill it in. Both Portland, Ma,ine and Portland, Oregon should get the final 3 days of the month. Below are the steps.

Drop-down menu: Portland, Maine worksheet.

Choose A34 (a left-most cell underneath your last row within the table).

Details below:

Maine data Portland

Day	**High (°F)**	**Low (°F)**	*Rain (inches)*	*Snow (inches)*
29	31.4	13.3	0.12	0.59
30	31.6	3.4	0.08	0.47
31	31.7	13.5	0.12	0.63

Banded rows formatting continues when extra columns are added.

- Drop-down menu: worksheet or Portland.
- Choose A34 (a left-most cell underneath your last row within the table). Details below:

Table Portland, Oregon detail

Day	High (°F)	Low (°F)	*Rain (inches)*	*Snow (inches)*
29	48.8	36.2	0.16	0
30	49.0	36.2	0.11	0.32
31	49.1	36.1	0.16	0

Finding & Editing Data

You'll need to rectify table data mistakes. Visually scanning a table for mistakes is time-consuming and tiring. Excel's Find command helps. Start at the top of your table and go down to ensure all data is covered.

You know that 3.40 degrees were recorded wrongly in Portland, Maine. It was 13.40. Follow these procedures to fix this.

Portland, Maine.

- Press CTRL+HOME to reach the top of your sheet.
- Home ➔ Find & Edit Group ➔ Find.
- 3.40, then Find Next.

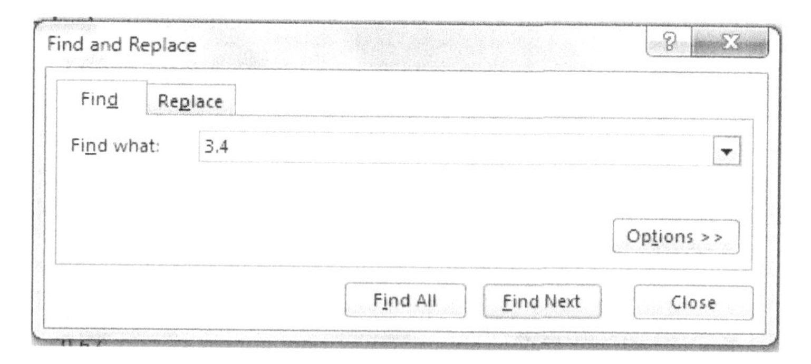

Find/Replace

- Click to close the window.
- Day 10's Low column should be 13.4.
- Look for.32 Snow on your Portland, Oregon sheet. Set 0.12 On day 3, check for the error.

Finding & Replacing Data

- Home ➔ Find & Choose ➔ Find.
- Then click Find Next.
- Click Search Next to continue.
- Change files after closing the window.

Freeze Rows & Columns

When users freeze windows, columns and rows in their table stay visible while they click. If the spreadsheet's initial row has column labels, they should freeze each row to keep them visible as they scroll. That'd be good if you could keep column heads apparent when scrolling over weather data.

To freeze headings:

- Click A6's leftmost cell underneath the heading lines.
- Select View from the ribbon.
- Freeze Panes twice.
- When you scroll your sheet, headers remain at the end.

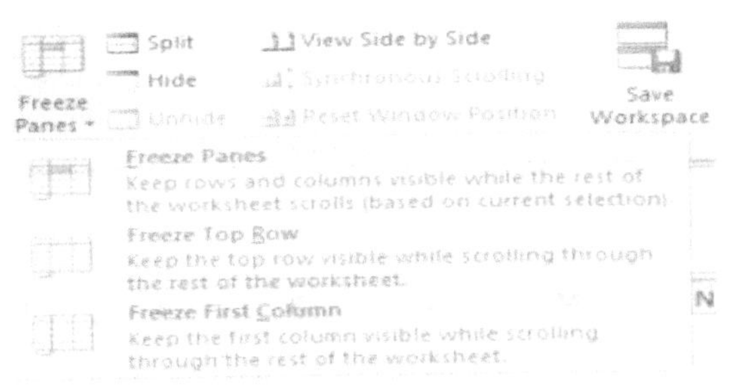

Click the View tab to unfreeze headers.

Unfreeze panes.

Simple Sort

Tables may be sorted alphabetically, numerically, or in other ways. Sorting orders table data by one or more columns. The table below gives sort orders for each column.

Table Sort Options

Sort Order	Text	Numbers	Dates
Ascending	Alphabetical (A to Z)	Smallest-Largest	Chronological (oldest-newest)
		Lowest-Highest	
Descending	Reverse Alphabetical (Z to A)	Largest-Smallest	Reverse Chronological (newest-oldest)
		Highest-Lowest	

If you want to discover which day in January in Portland, Maine, received the most snow, sort the Snow column in descending order.

Click the filter. In Portland M E, click Snow's down arrow (inches).

Click a choice. Pick ZA. Largest-smallest. The figure shows more.

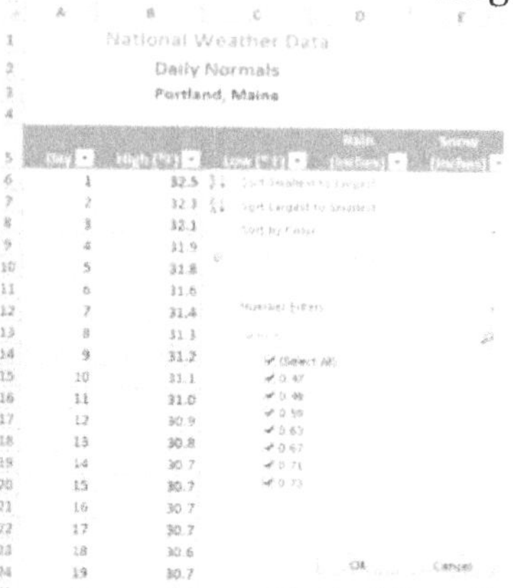

National Weather Data

Daily Normals

Portland, Maine

Day	High (°F)
1	32.5
2	32.3
3	32.1
4	31.9
5	31.8
6	31.6
7	31.4
8	31.3
9	31.2
10	31.1
11	31.0
12	30.9
13	30.8
14	30.7
15	30.7
16	30.7
17	30.7
18	30.6
19	30.7

If you make an error, you'll notice that January 3rd (row 6) had 0.73" of snow. In the snow section, a filter arrow changes to a downward arrow, signifying declining order (largest-smallest).

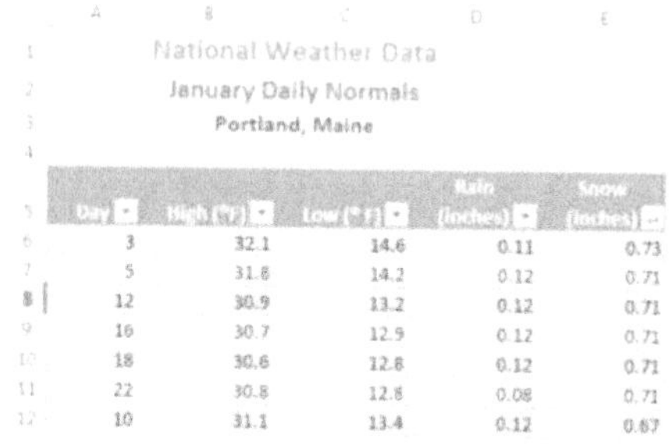

National Weather Data

January Daily Normals

Portland, Maine

Day	High (°F)	Low (°F)	Rain (inches)	Snow (inches)
3	32.1	14.6	0.11	0.73
5	31.8	14.2	0.12	0.71
12	30.9	13.2	0.12	0.71
16	30.7	12.9	0.12	0.71
18	30.6	12.8	0.12	0.71
22	30.8	12.8	0.08	0.71
10	31.1	13.4	0.12	0.67

To find Oregon's snowiest day, sort a Portland sheet. Check your answers using the chart below.

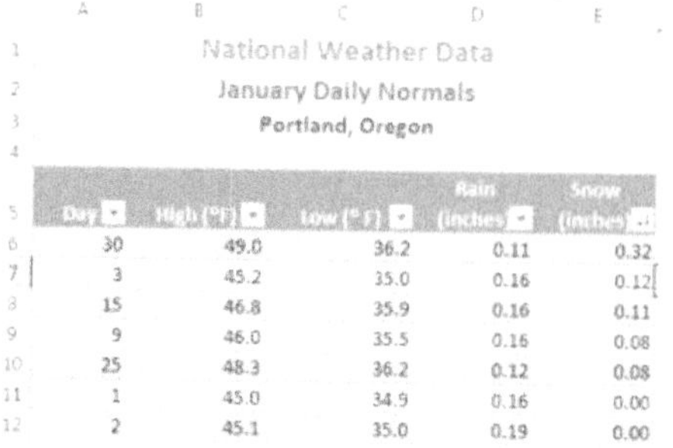

National Weather Data

January Daily Normals

Portland, Oregon

Day	High (°F)	Low (°F)	Rain (inches)	Snow (inches)
30	49.0	36.2	0.11	0.32
3	45.2	35.0	0.16	0.12
15	46.8	35.9	0.16	0.11
9	46.0	35.5	0.16	0.08
25	48.3	36.2	0.12	0.08
1	45.0	34.9	0.16	0.00
2	45.1	35.0	0.19	0.00

Sorting the Column

Click the filter. To sort, click the header arrow.

Choose AZ or ZA from the drop-down menu to sort that column.

Multi-Level Sort

You may need to filter the table by many columns for optimal data interpretation. If you were looking at several loan categories from multiple bank offices, you'd need to filter by loan form and bank officer's name. If you have a list student'sts' high school grades, you want to sort them by student name and grade level (first-year student, sophomore, junior, senior) so grades are consecutive.

Let's look at Oregon's snow days and see how chilly they were.

Press a table cell on your sheet or Portland.

In the ribbon, click Data and Sort.
Column: Snow.
Order by Largest-Smallest.
Click Add Levels in a dialogue box to add a second level type.
Click Low (°F) for a Column in new, now by lines.
Order a comparable row by Smallest-Largest. Below is a dialogue box.

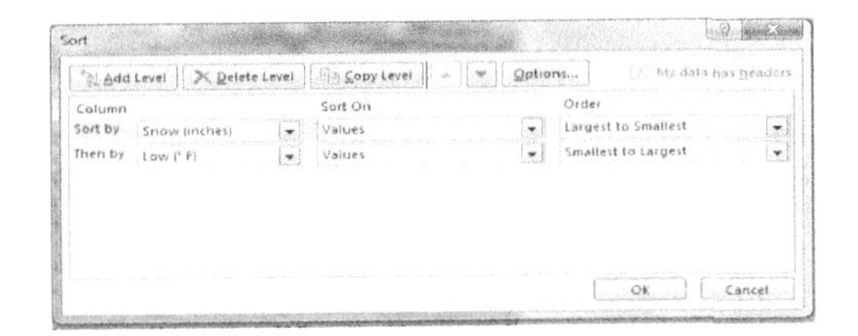

Okay. Your table type should look like the one below. From Day9's low of 35.50 to Day25's low of 36.20, 0.08" of snow falls. The lowest score was first. The selection arrows on sorted columns have been changed to show how effectively they're sorted.

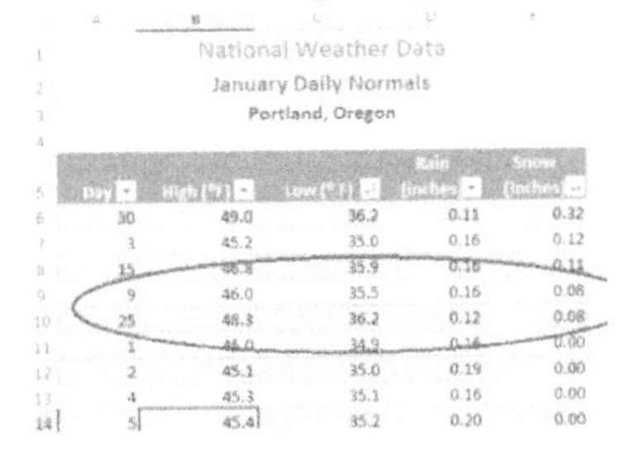

National Weather Data
January Daily Normals
Portland, Oregon

Day	High (°F)	Low (°F)	Rain (inches)	Snow (inches)
30	49.0	36.2	0.11	0.32
3	45.2	35.0	0.16	0.12
15	[illegible]	35.9	[illegible]	0.11
9	46.0	35.5	0.16	0.08
25	48.3	36.2	0.12	0.08
1	44.0	34.9	[illegible]	0.00
2	45.1	35.0	0.19	0.00
4	45.3	35.1	0.16	0.00
5	45.4	35.2	0.20	0.00

Custom Sorts

In certain cases, you choose "conventional" data order: highest-lowest quantities, alphabetical words, etc. Sorting daily data this way makes little sense. Friday, Monday, Thursday, Tuesday, Saturday, Sunday, and Wednesday are alphabetically sorted. This request isn't profitable. Alphabetizing a year's months is also confusing. Is there a high-low or low-high sum that seems reasonable? (Great puzzle!)

You've added a weekday column to your weather information and updated it Sunday through Saturday. This sheet enables everyone to examine Portland, Oregon's weekly weather trends. Let's organize the sheet by Week or Day.

- Drop-down menu: Weekly worksheet.
- Insert A5 table.
- Sort on the ribbon's Data tab.
- Column: Week.
- Order by Smallest-Largest.
- To add a second level sort, click Add Level in a dialogue box's top-right corner.
- Choose Day from Column inside new, So by lines.
- Choose Custom List from Order. Below will appear on the screen.

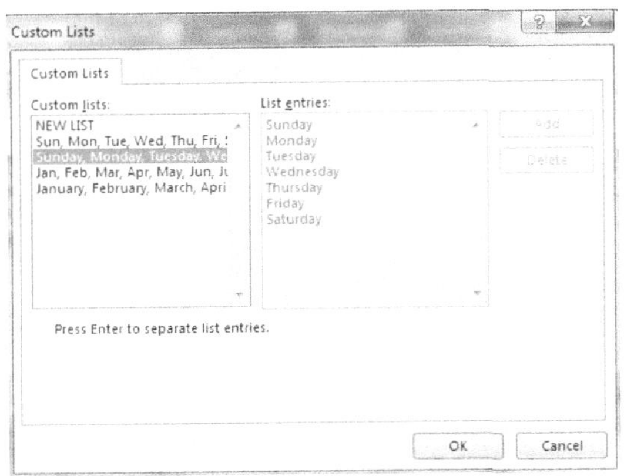

Choose Sunday, Monday, Tuesday, etc., in a dialogue box's Custom list. Choose written days of the week, not acronyms.

After clicking OK, the Sort box should look like this:

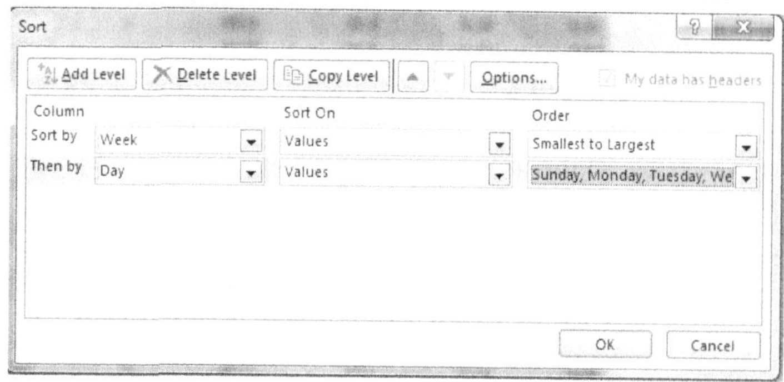

OK again. Below is a sorted table. Week-by-week data is grouped by day.

Save it.

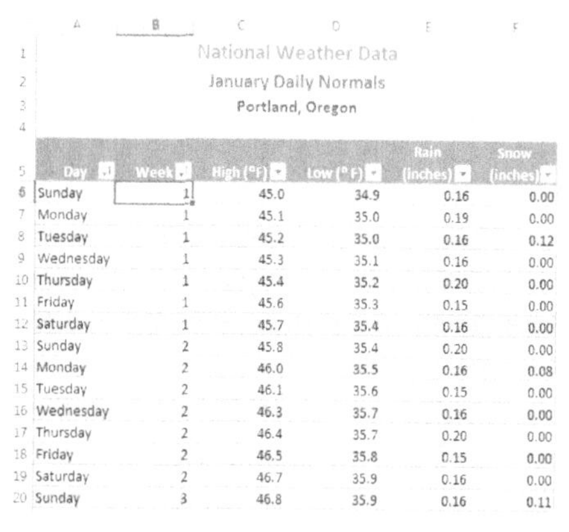

National Weather Data
January Daily Normals
Portland, Oregon

Day	Week	High (°F)	Low (°F)	Rain (inches)	Snow (inches)
Sunday	1	45.0	34.9	0.16	0.00
Monday	1	45.1	35.0	0.19	0.00
Tuesday	1	45.2	35.0	0.16	0.12
Wednesday	1	45.3	35.1	0.16	0.00
Thursday	1	45.4	35.2	0.20	0.00
Friday	1	45.6	35.3	0.15	0.00
Saturday	1	45.7	35.4	0.16	0.00
Sunday	2	45.8	35.4	0.20	0.00
Monday	2	46.0	35.5	0.16	0.08
Tuesday	2	46.1	35.6	0.15	0.00
Wednesday	2	46.3	35.7	0.16	0.00
Thursday	2	46.4	35.7	0.20	0.00
Friday	2	46.5	35.8	0.15	0.00
Saturday	2	46.7	35.9	0.16	0.00
Sunday	3	46.8	35.9	0.16	0.11

How to build Pivot Tables (basic commands)

Excel's pivot tables are strong. A pivot table helps you analyze huge, comprehensive data sets.

213 records & 6 fields make up our dataset. Amount, Date, ID, Category, and Country.

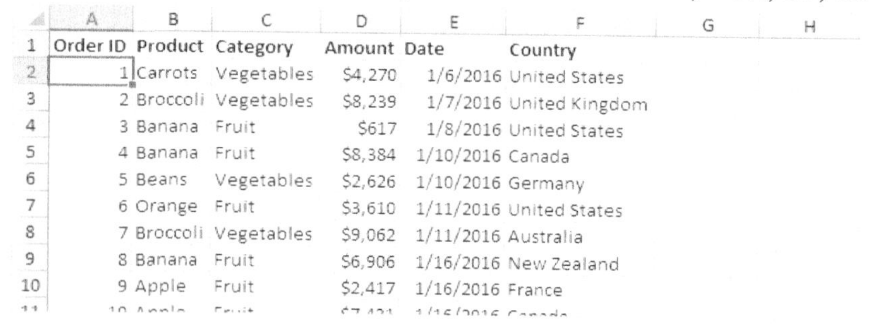

Order ID	Product	Category	Amount	Date	Country
1	Carrots	Vegetables	$4,270	1/6/2016	United States
2	Broccoli	Vegetables	$8,239	1/7/2016	United Kingdom
3	Banana	Fruit	$617	1/8/2016	United States
4	Banana	Fruit	$8,384	1/10/2016	Canada
5	Beans	Vegetables	$2,626	1/10/2016	Germany
6	Orange	Fruit	$3,610	1/11/2016	United States
7	Broccoli	Vegetables	$9,062	1/11/2016	Australia
8	Banana	Fruit	$6,906	1/16/2016	New Zealand
9	Apple	Fruit	$2,417	1/16/2016	France

Insert your Pivot Table

Steps for inserting a pivot table.

1. Select a data set cell.
2. Click PivotTable under Insert > Tables.
   - This box appears. Excel auto-selects data. The new pivot table defaults to New Worksheet.

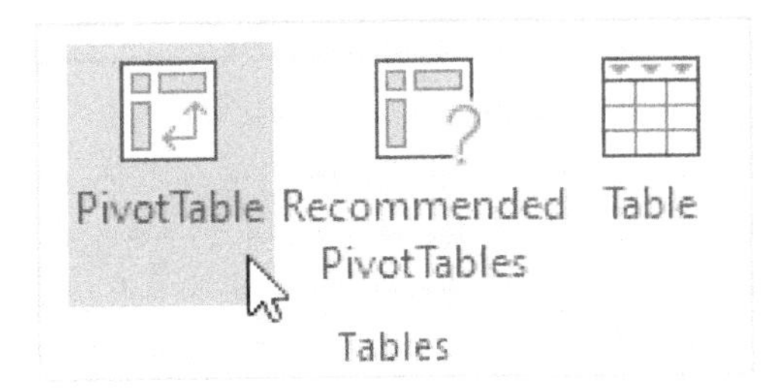

- Clink on, OK

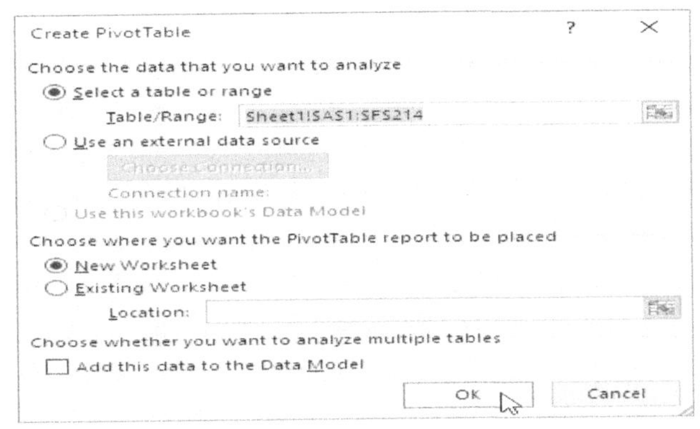

Drag fields

PivotTable Fields opens. Drag the following fields to determine every product's export total.

1. Add Product to Rows.
2. Add the amount to values.
3. Country to Filters.

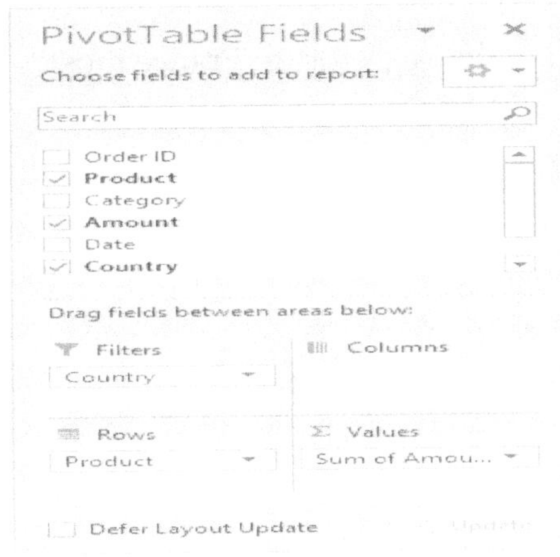

The table pivot is below. You export mostly bananas. Pivot tables are that simple.

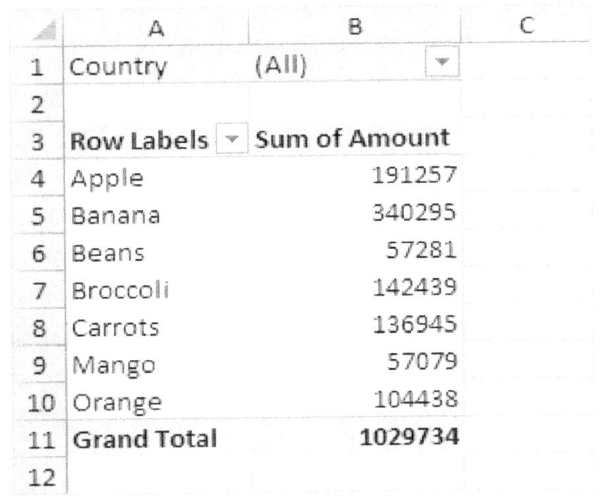

	A	B	C
1	Country	(All)	
2			
3	**Row Labels**	**Sum of Amount**	
4	Apple	191257	
5	Banana	340295	
6	Beans	57281	
7	Broccoli	142439	
8	Carrots	136945	
9	Mango	57079	
10	Orange	104438	
11	**Grand Total**	**1029734**	
12			

Sort

Sort your pivot table to put Banana first.

1. Click a Sum of Amount cell.
2. Click Sort, Largest to Smallest.

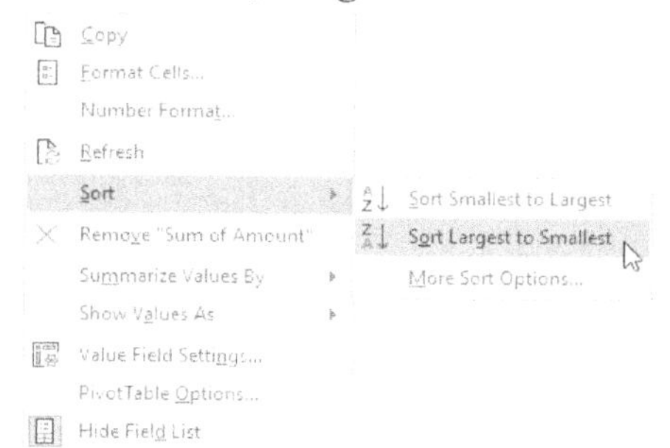

Result.

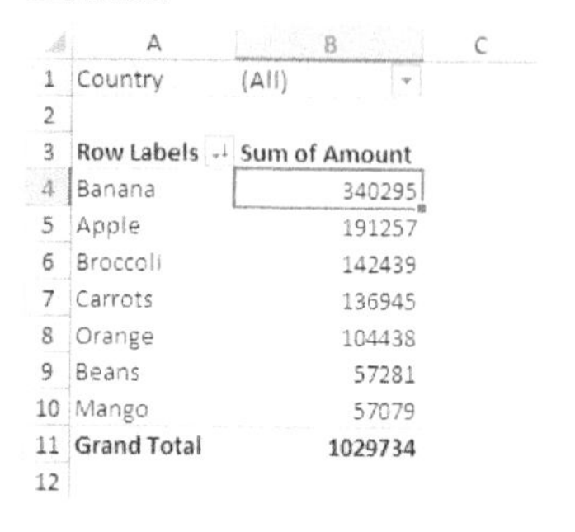

	A	B
1	Country	(All)
2		
3	Row Labels	Sum of Amount
4	Banana	340295
5	Apple	191257
6	Broccoli	142439
7	Carrots	136945
8	Orange	104438
9	Beans	57281
10	Mango	57079
11	Grand Total	1029734
12		

Filter

You can filter your pivot table per Country since you added it to Filters. What do we export to France most?

1. Click your France filter.

Result. France's top import is apples.

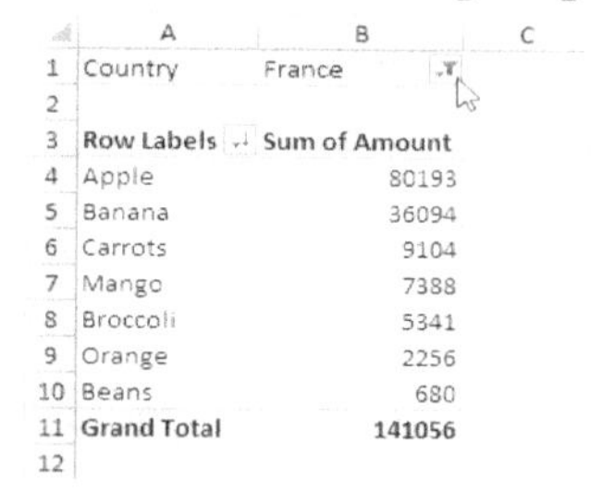

	A	B
1	Country	France
2		
3	Row Labels	Sum of Amount
4	Apple	80193
5	Banana	36094
6	Carrots	9104
7	Mango	7388
8	Broccoli	5341
9	Orange	2256
10	Beans	680
11	Grand Total	141056
12		

Change Summary Calculations

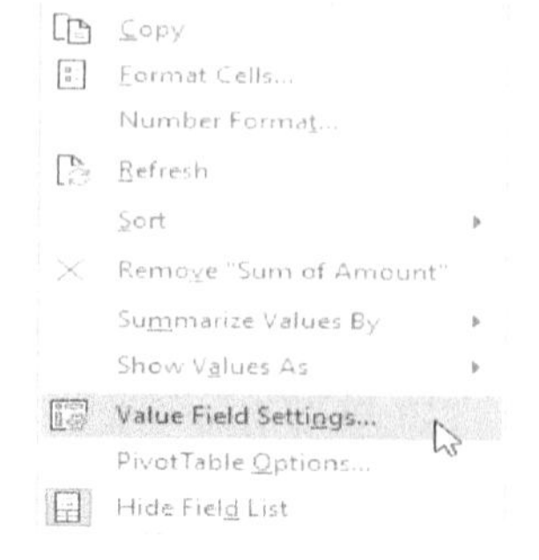

Excel sums or counts data by default. Follow these procedures to update your calculations.

1. Click a Sum of Amount cell.
2. Right-click Value Field Settings.
3. Choose a computation. Click Count.

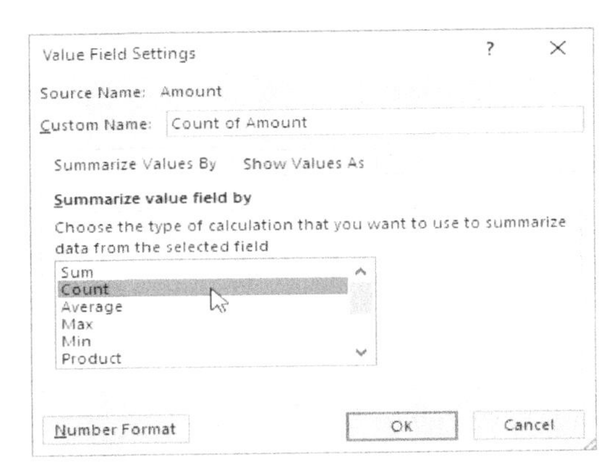

4. Click on OK.

The third step is to decide on the kind of computation to be used. Count, for instance, is an example.

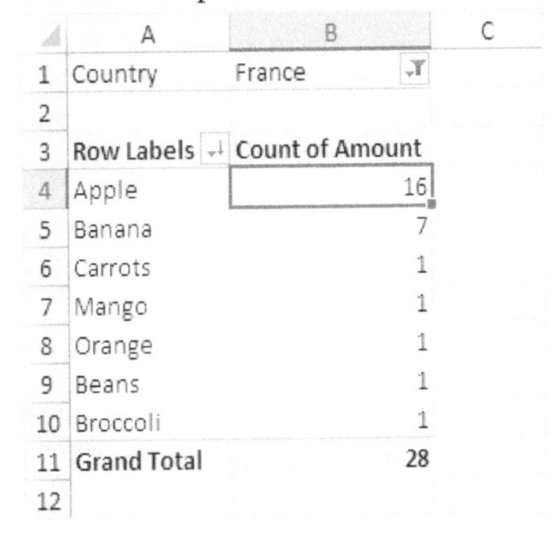

	A	B	C
1	Country	France	
2			
3	**Row Labels**	**Count of Amount**	
4	Apple	16	
5	Banana	7	
6	Carrots	1	
7	Mango	1	
8	Orange	1	
9	Beans	1	
10	Broccoli	1	
11	**Grand Total**	**28**	
12			

Two-dimensional Pivot Tables

With the Columns & Rows areas, you may build the two-dimensional pivot tables by dragging a field. Make use of the convenience of a pivot table by doing so first. To find out how much of each commodity was shipped to each nation, move the following fields around.

1. The Rows location is surrounded by farmland.
2. An additional column for products.
3. To the Values box, add the Amount field.
4. The category field has been added to the Filters section.

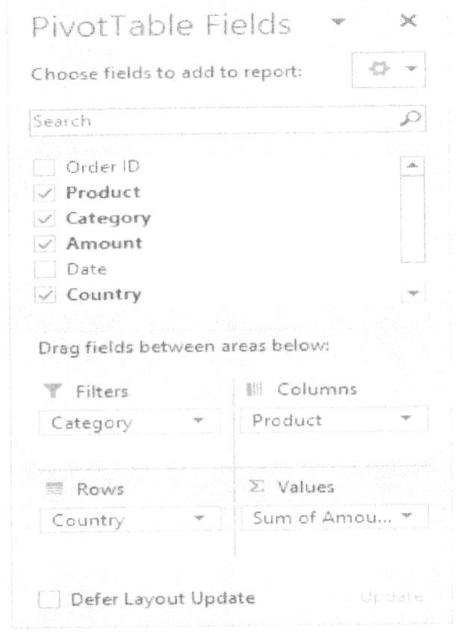

A two-dimensional pivot table is shown below.

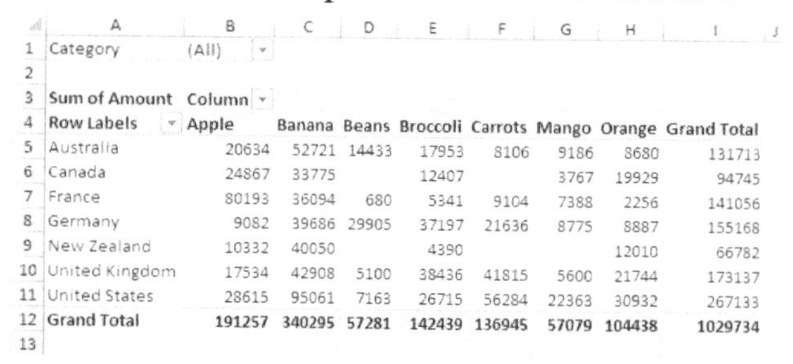

Category (All)

Sum of Amount	Column							
Row Labels	Apple	Banana	Beans	Broccoli	Carrots	Mango	Orange	Grand Total
Australia	20634	52721	14433	17953	8106	9186	8680	131713
Canada	24867	33775		12407		3767	19929	94745
France	80193	36094	680	5341	9104	7388	2256	141056
Germany	9082	39686	29905	37197	21636	8775	8887	155168
New Zealand	10332	40050		4390			12010	66782
United Kingdom	17534	42908	5100	38436	41815	5600	21744	173137
United States	28615	95061	7163	26715	56284	22363	30932	267133
Grand Total	**191257**	**340295**	**57281**	**142439**	**136945**	**57079**	**104438**	**1029734**

The best way to compare these figures is to build your pivot chart & add a filter. This may be a phase too much for you at this point, but it demonstrates to you one of the numerous strong pivot table capabilities that Excel has to offer.

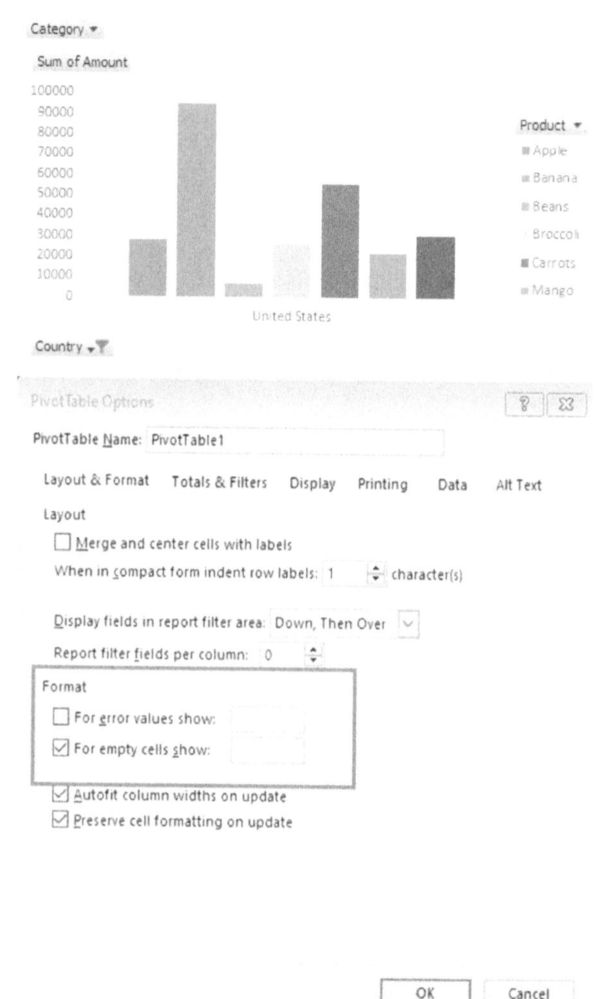

Chapter 5: Charts & Graphs

Charts & graphs help you comprehend outcomes by visualizing numbers. These terms are different despite being regularly interchanged. Graphs are the easiest way to visually depict numbers over time. Charts are more sophisticated since they help compare data sets. Charts are more attractive than diagrams since they don't employ x- and y-axes.

In reports, charts & graphs are used to show management, customers, or team members' progress or results. You can construct a chart or graph to illustrate any statistical data, saving you time searching through spreadsheets to uncover links and trends.

Excel makes it simple to create charts & graphs, especially when you keep the data in your Excel Workbook. Excel provides various pre-made chart & graph types from which to pick.

Tired of Those Static Spreadsheets?

Microsoft Excel wasn't designed to manage tasks. Examine Excel vs. Smartsheet's work management, accessibility, collaboration, visibility, and integrations.

When to Make Charts & Graphs

Excel's chart and graph library let you graphically present findings. It's important to choose a chart style that tells the narrative you want your data to tell. Vector graphics should be used to improve charts and graphs. Microsoft Excel 2016 has 5 chart types:

Column Charts: Column charts are extensively used to analyze data or divide one component into numerous parts (for instance, multiple genres or products). Excel's 7-column chart formats are clustered, staggered, 100% stacked, 3D stacked, 3D clustered, and 3D 100% stacked. Choose the best visualization for your findings.

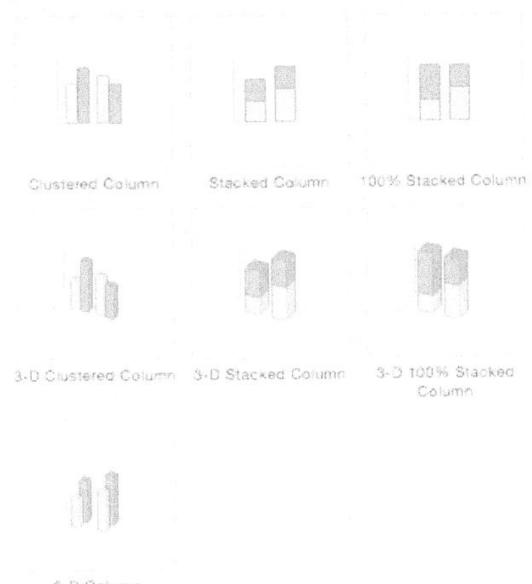

Bar Chart: Bars in a bar chart are horizontal, whereas columns are vertical. Bar charts and column charts may be used equally, while some prefer column charts for visualizing negative numbers on a y-axis.

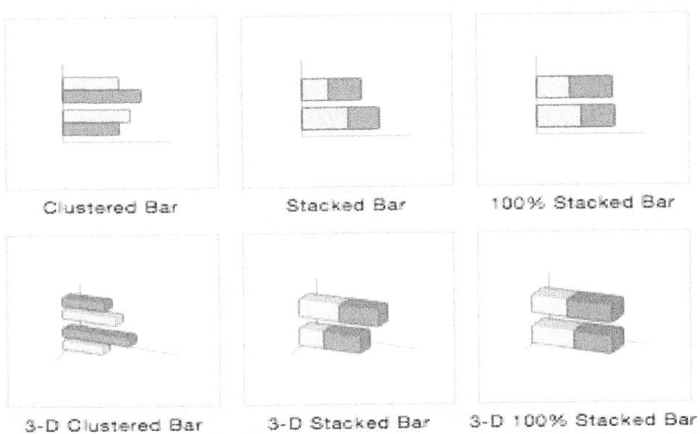

Pie Charts: Pie charts measure the proportion of the entire (many data values). A pie crust represents each concept, showing proportions. There are approximately five pie charts: pie, pie (which splits a pie in half to show subcategory proportions), a bar of the pie, 3D pies, and doughnut.

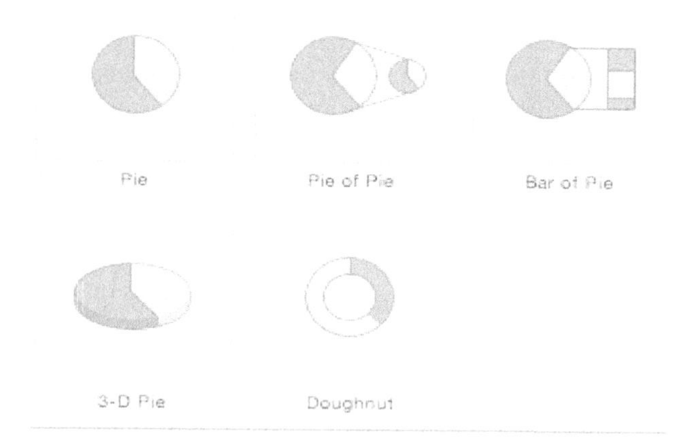

Line Charts: Line charts show temporal patterns instead of static data points. The lines connect every data point, showing whether values improved or fell over time. 7-line chart versions include line, 100% stacked line, stacked line, line with markers, stacked line with markers, & 3D line.

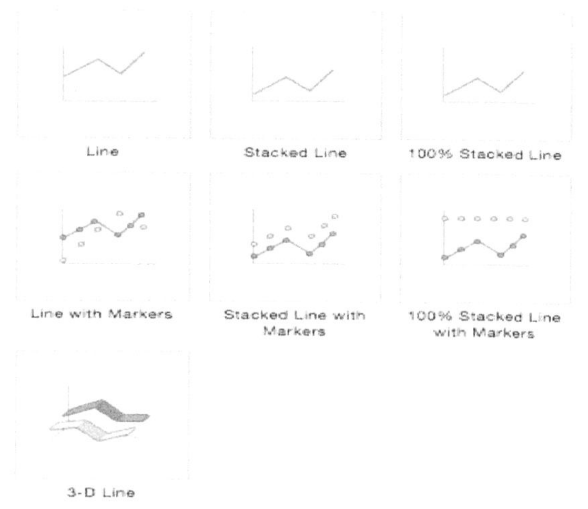

Scatter Charts: Scattered charts show the relationship between variables. They assist show development over time like line diagrams. (Correlation) Bubble charts are scattered. Seven scatter chart options include smooth lines & markers, straight lines, bubbles, and 3D bubbles.

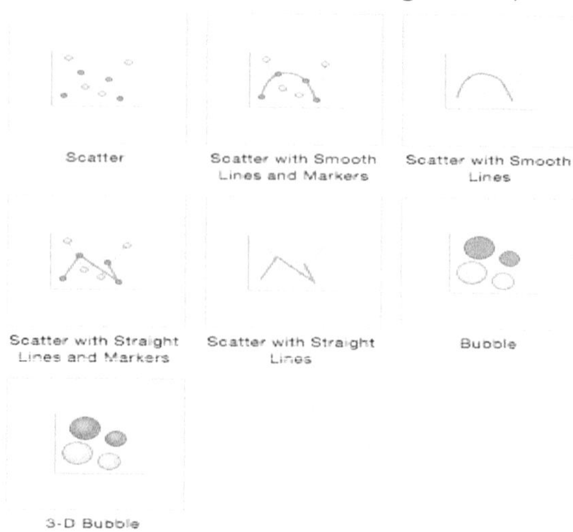

In addition, there are 4 minor divisions. These graphs are more case-specific:

Area charts: These charts, like line charts, show value fluctuations over time. Since the area beneath each line is solid, area charts illustrate transitions across numerous variables. 6 areas include area, 100% stacked area, 3D area, and 3D 100% stacked area.

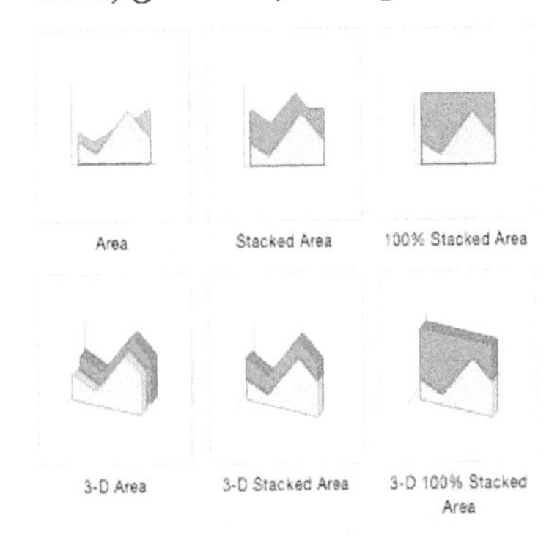

Stock: This graphic shows a stock's high, low, and closing prices in financial reports and by investors. You may utilize a value range (or predicted value range) and its precise value in every circumstance.

Open-high-low-close, volume-high-low-close, high-low-close, & volume-open-high-low-close are chart options.

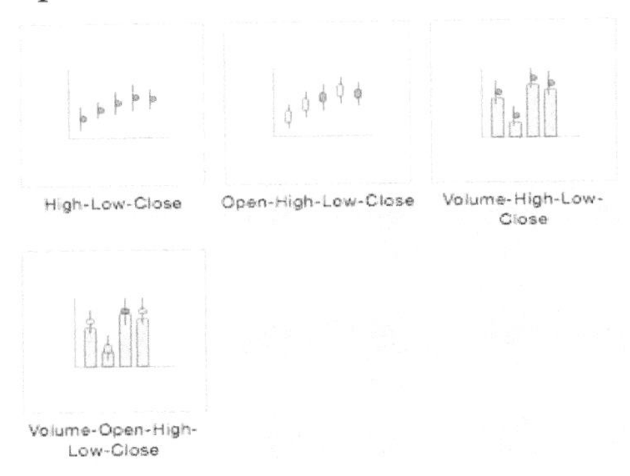

Surface: This surface chart displays data in 3D. Wide data sets with more than 2 variables and data sets with groups benefit from the extra plane. Surface charts may be hard to comprehend, so ensure your audience is comfortable. Wireframe 3D surface, contour, and wireframe contour are all available.

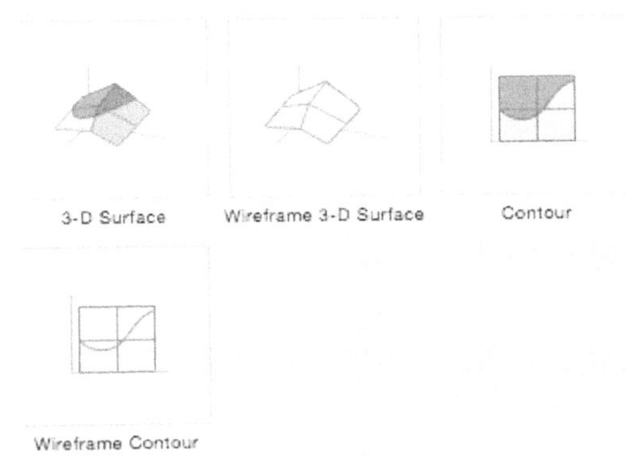

Radar: A radar map compares many variables. All variables start at the center. The key to utilizing a radar chart is comparing all elements; they're often used to compare items or personnel. Charts might be radar, radar with marks, or filled radar.

The waterfall chart displays positive and negative gains over time using column graphs. You may download a tutorial to help easily create a waterfall map in Excel.

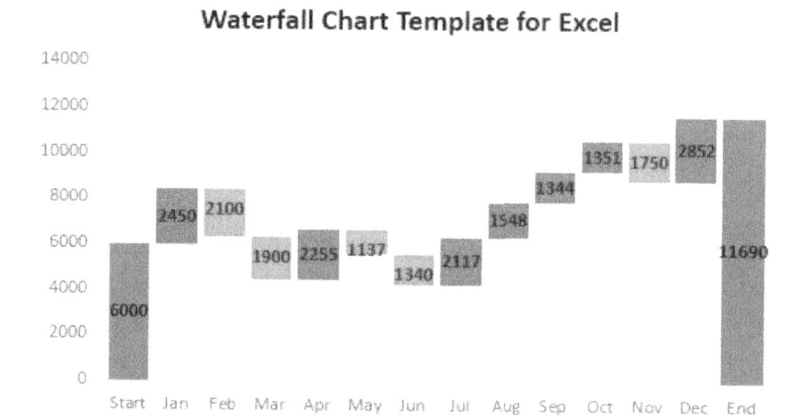

Top Five Excel Chart & Graph Tips

Excel has many styles, and stylistic presets to enhance table appearance and readability but utilizing them doesn't ensure the best results. These 5 recommended practices will make your chart & graph as easy and useful as feasible.

Clean It Up: Diagrams with multiple colors and text are confusing and don't stick out. Remove distractions so viewers may focus on your point.

Select the Most Appropriate Themes: Consider the audience, topic, or chart's main goal when picking a theme. Try out several models but choose one that fits your requirements.

Use Text Carefully: Maps and graphs are visual, although the text may be included (like axis labels or titles). Be succinct, clear, and thoughtful about each document's orientation (it's not comfortable to switch heads to read text on the x-axis, for example).

Place Elements Carefully: Place names, tales, symbols, and other graphics carefully. They may enhance the graph.

Before making the chart, sort your data: People don't filter their data or eliminate duplicates until they make a map, which might lead to inaccuracies.

How You Can Chart Data Within Excel

You must first provide Excel with some data to work with before you can construct an Excel chart or graph. With this chapter, you'll discover how to chart data in Excel 2016.

Step1: Enter Data in a Worksheet

- Excel File → New Workbook.
- Input data for a graph or map. In this situation, you're comparing 2013-2017 goods. Number all columns and rows. You may then create charts and graphs using basic axis markings.

	A	B	C	D	E	F
1	Product	2013	2014	2015	2016	2017
2	Product A	$18,580	$49,225	$16,326	$10,017	$26,134
3	Product B	$78,970	$82,262	$48,640	$48,640	$48,640
4	Product C	$24,236	$131,390	$79,022	$71,009	$81,474
5	Product D	$16,730	$19,730	$12,109	$11,355	$17,686
6	Product E	$35,358	$42,685	$20,893	$16,065	$21,388
7						

Step2: Select any Range to make a Chart and Graph from the Workbook Data

- By highlighting the data cells, you want to include in the graph.
- After highlighting a cell, pick a chart form.

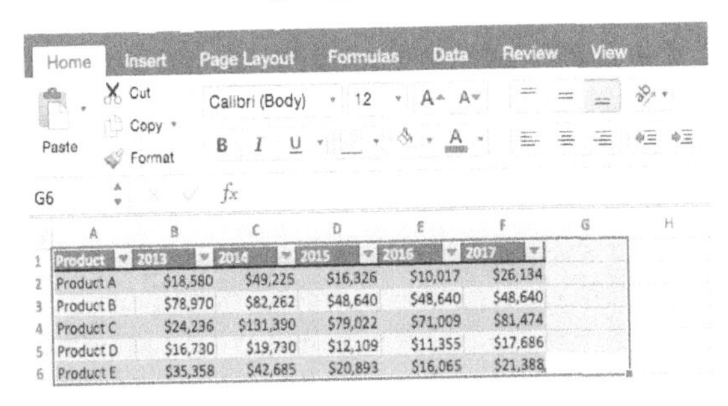

	A	B	C	D	E	F
1	Product	2013	2014	2015	2016	2017
2	Product A	$18,580	$49,225	$16,326	$10,017	$26,134
3	Product B	$78,970	$82,262	$48,640	$48,640	$48,640
4	Product C	$24,236	$131,390	$79,022	$71,009	$81,474
5	Product D	$16,730	$19,730	$12,109	$11,355	$17,686
6	Product E	$35,358	$42,685	$20,893	$16,065	$21,388

This chapter covers building a chart (clustered column) in Excel.

How You Can Make Your Chart Through Excel

After entering data and selecting a cell set, choose a chart form. The following example creates a chart (clustered column) using prior data.

Step1: Select the Chart Type

Click Insert until your data is outlined in Workbook. The toolbar's middle has various chart options. You may pick a different Recommended Chart by using the drop-down choices.

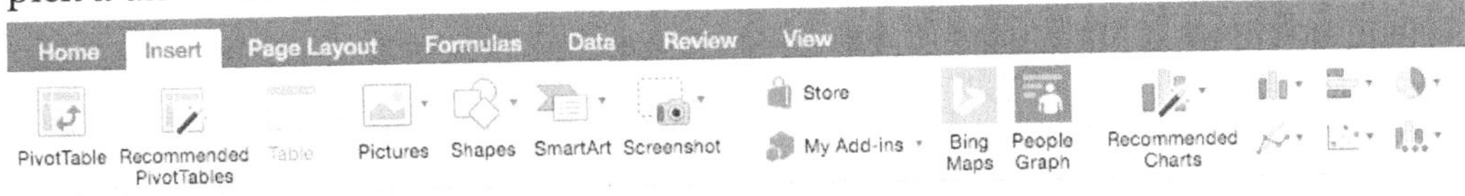

Step2: Create Your desired Chart

Insert ➔ Column Chart ➔ Clustered Column.

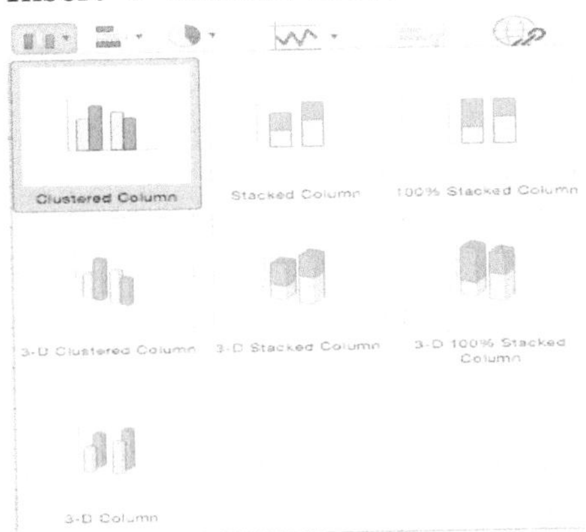

Using your data, Excel can create a cluster chart column. The chart will be in the center.

Double-click a Chart Title and input a tag. "Product Profit 2013-2017" describes this graph.

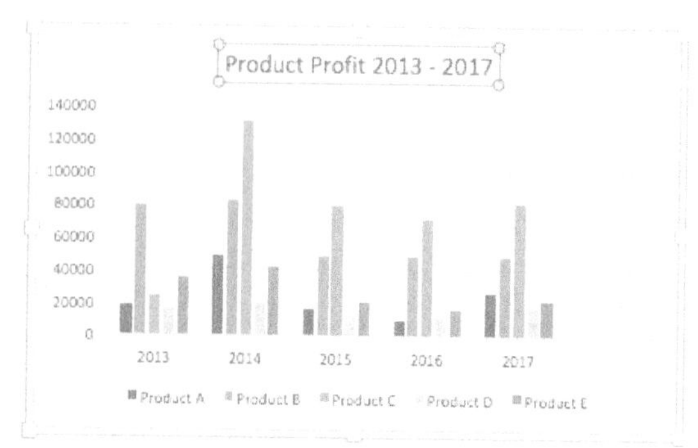

This chart will guide a walkthrough. Download the chart to continue.

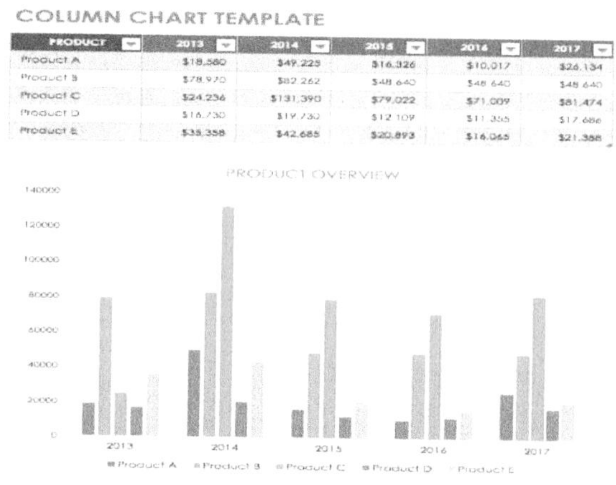

COLUMN CHART TEMPLATE

PRODUCT	2013	2014	2015	2016	2017
Product A	$18,580	$49,225	$16,326	$10,017	$26,134
Product B	$78,970	$82,262	$48,640	$48,640	$48,640
Product C	$24,236	$131,390	$79,022	$71,009	$81,474
Product D	$16,730	$19,730	$12,109	$11,355	$17,686
Product E	$35,358	$42,685	$20,893	$16,065	$21,388

Cart Design & Format are toolbar components for making chart adjustments. By default, Excel applies a predefined style, layout, and format to charts & graphs; you may alter them using tabs. Then you'll see Chart Design choices.

Step3: Add the Chart Elements

Adding chart components to a graph or chart may clarify or add significance. Choose a chart element from the top-left Add Chart Feature drop-down menu (below your home tab).

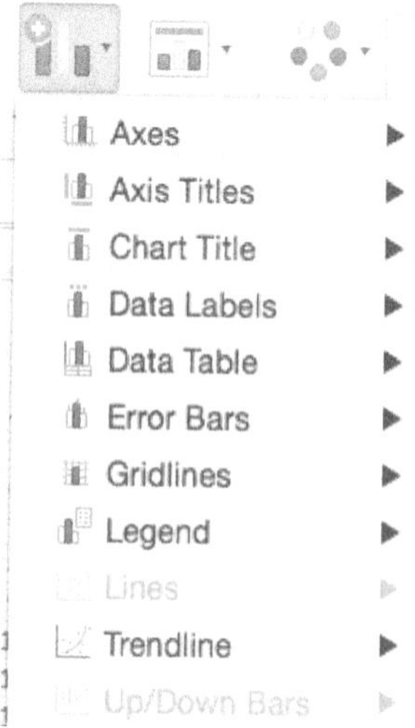

To Hide or Display Axes:

Choose axes. Excel will automatically grab column and row headers from your selected cell set to display horizontal and vertical axes (check Primary Horizontal & Primary Vertical under Axes).

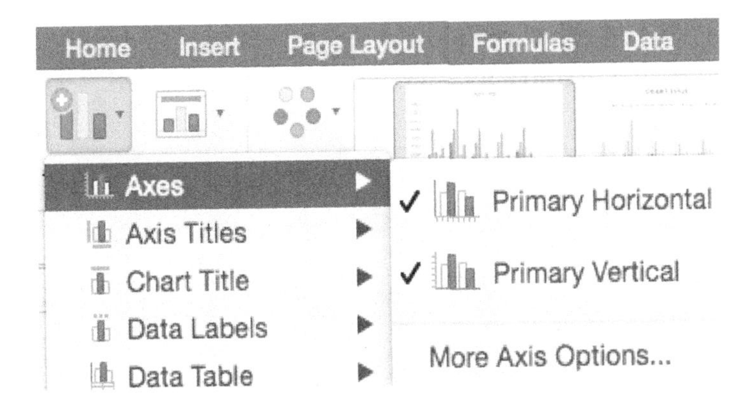

Uncheck these to remove the chart's view axis. Selecting Primary Horizontal removes the years from the horizontal axis.

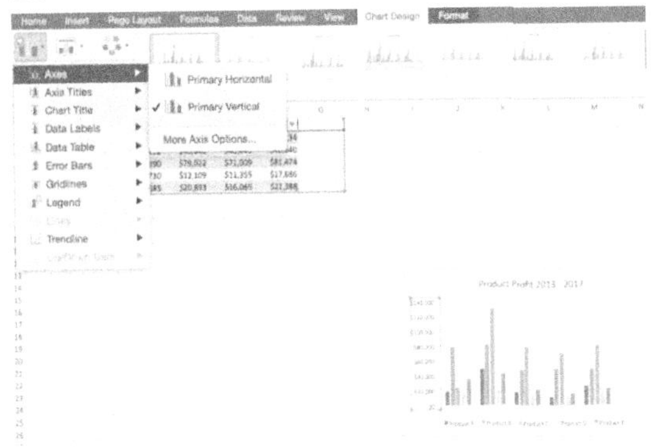

More Axis Choices... displays a window with more formatting & text choices, such as identifiers, numbers, tick marks, or altering text color & height.

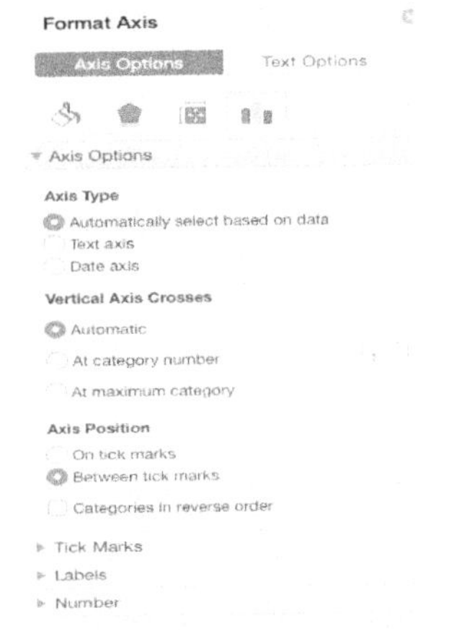

To Add the Axis Titles:

After selecting Add Chart Element, choose Axis Title. Since Excel doesn't automatically assign axis names, Primary Horizontal or Primary Vertical are unregulated.

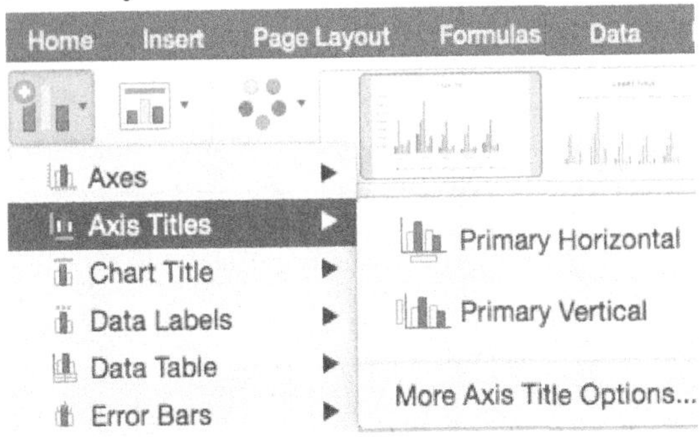

Pressing Primary Horizontal & Primary Vertical on the map generates axis names. Both were pushed. Title axis. You added "Year" and "Profit."

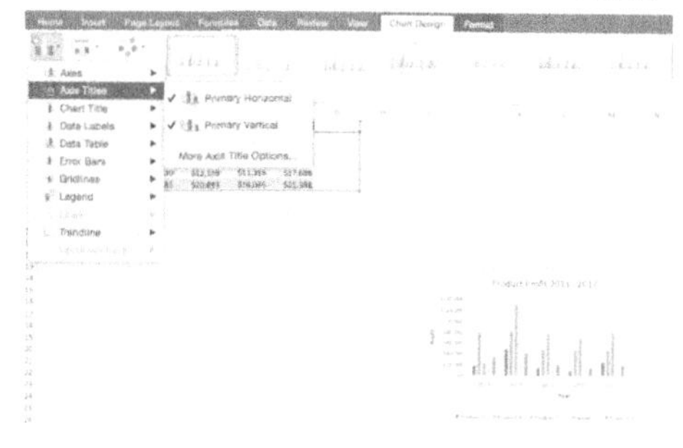

To Move or Remove Chart Title:

Add Chart Elements drop-down menu: Chart Title. None, Above the Chart, Focused Overlay, & Further Title Choices.

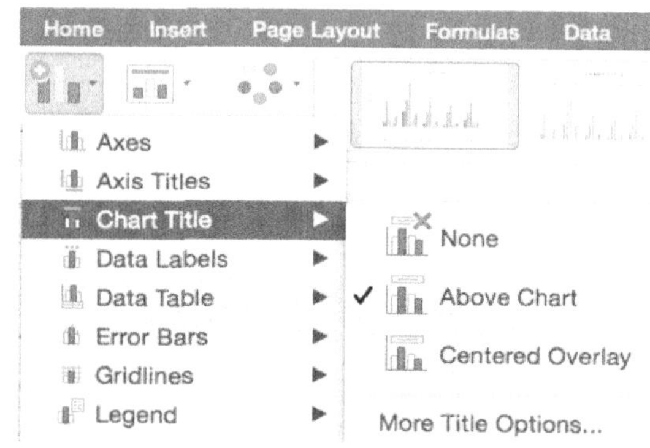

Selecting None deletes the chart title.

Click the Above Chart to add a title. Excel may automatically add a chart's title above it.

Choose Centered Overlay to center the chart's title. Be careful not to obscure data or clutter the graph with your title (like in this example below).

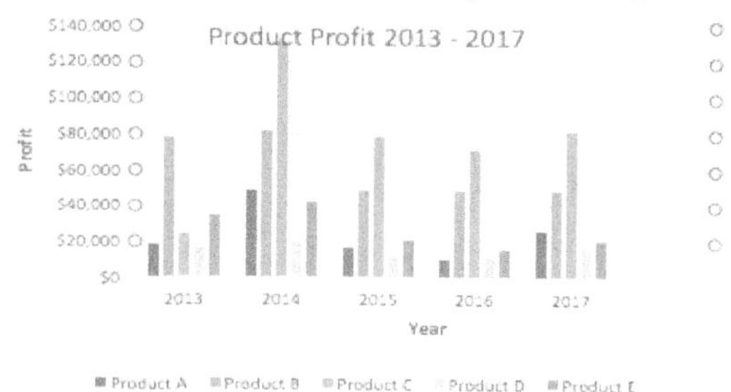

To Add the Data Labels:

Add Chart Elements ➔ Data Labels. There are 6 data labels: Inside End, Outside End, Inside Base, & More Label titles.

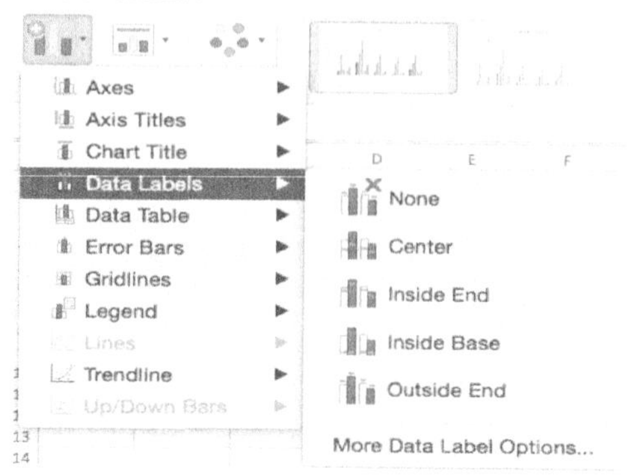

The 4 placement options give each computed data point a distinctive mark. Choose one. This adjustment may be handy if you have few details or plenty of chart space. The graphic (clumped column) would seem overloaded with data labels. So does picking the Center data label.

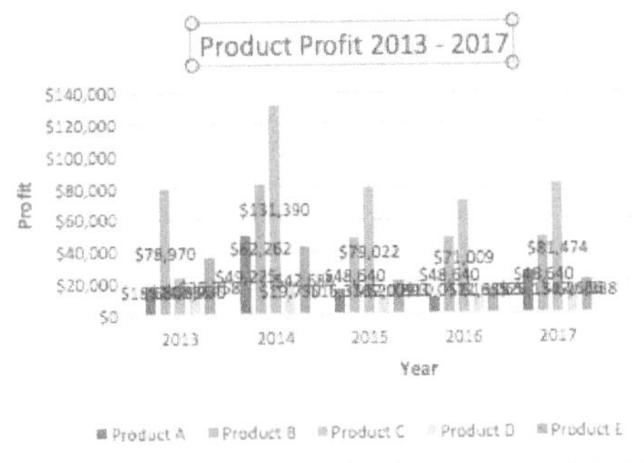

To Add the Data Table:

Add Chart Elements ➔ Data Table. Further Data Table Choices offers 3 pre-formatted alternatives and an enlarged menu.

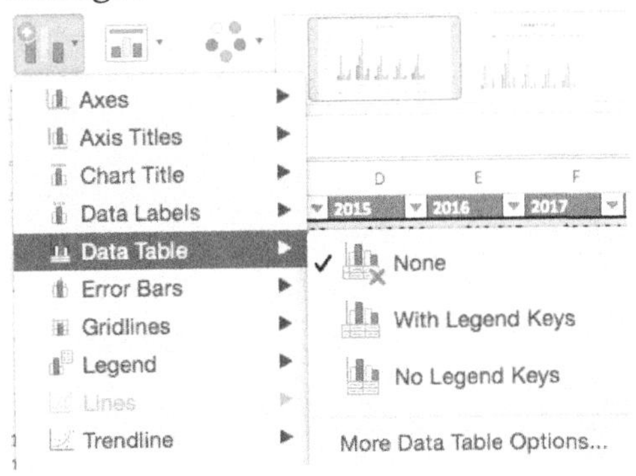

None is the default value, so data tables aren't repeated in charts.

Legend Keys displays a data table underneath the list. The legend is color-coded.

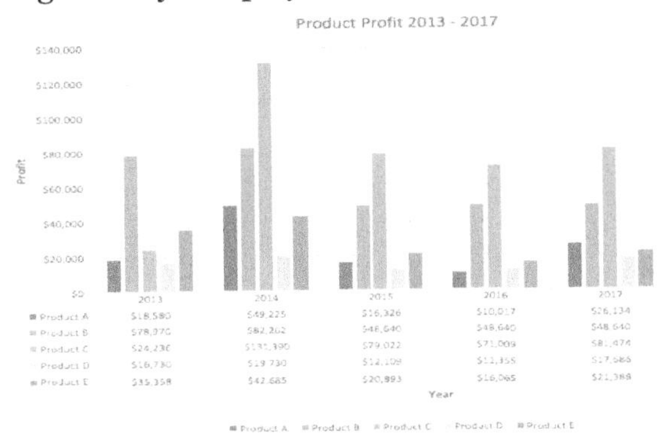

No Legend Keys charts typically have a data table without a legend.

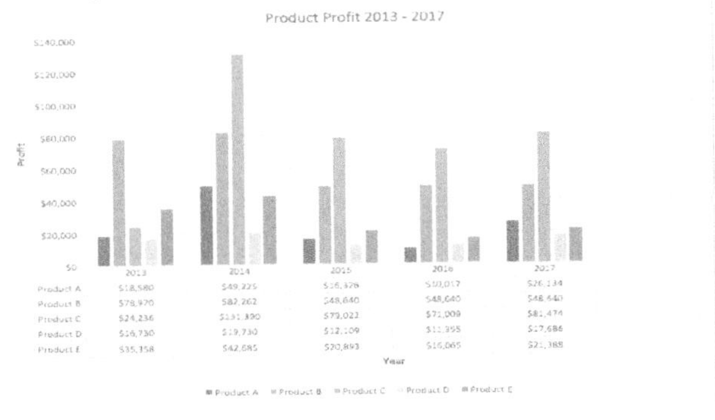

If you need to add a data table, enlarge your chart. Click a corner to scale your chart.

To Add the Error Bars:

Add Chart Elements ➔ Error Bars. None (default), 5% (Percentage), Standard Error, & Standard Deviation. Inaccuracy bars show the probable error in reported results using conventional formulae.

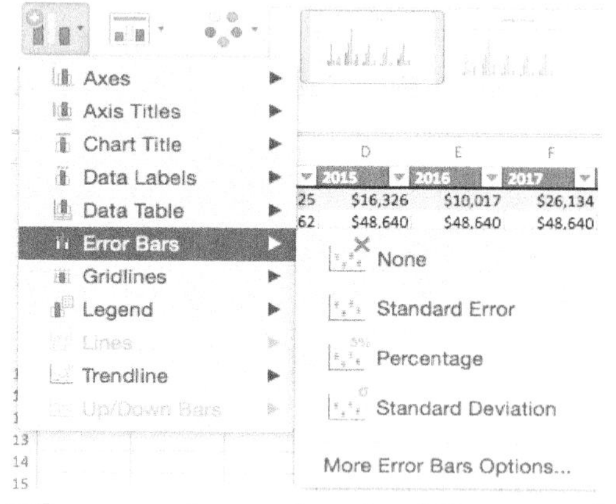

When you choose Standard Errors, a chart appears.

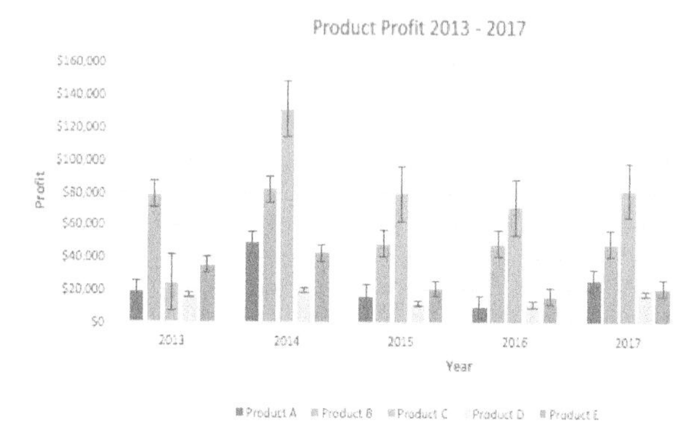

To Add the Gridlines:

Add Chart Elements & Gridlines adds gridlines to a chart. Prime Major Horizontal, Prime Major Vertical, Prime Minor Horizontal, & Prime Minor Vertical. Excel adds a horizontal gridline to column tables.

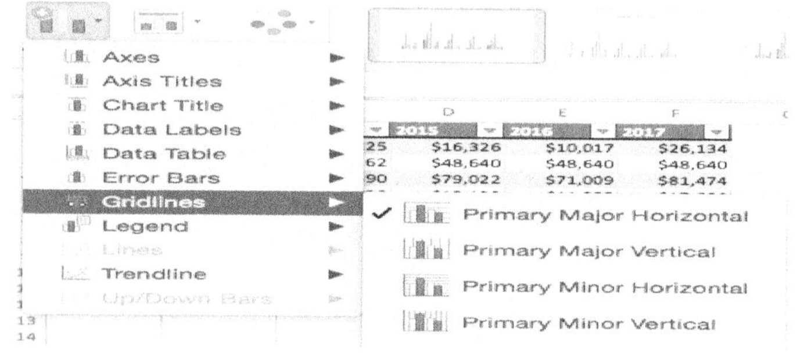

You may choose as many gridlines as you wish using the options. Here's your chart with all 4 gridlines chosen.

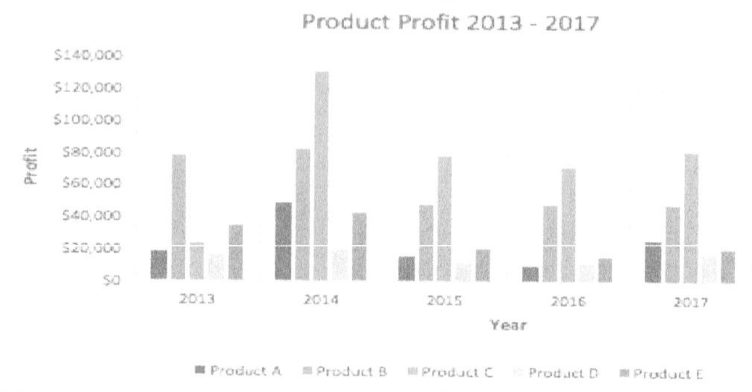

To Add the Legend:

Add Chart Elements ➔ Legend. Contrary to Legend Preferences, there are 5 legend placement options: None, Correct, Top, Left, and Bottom.

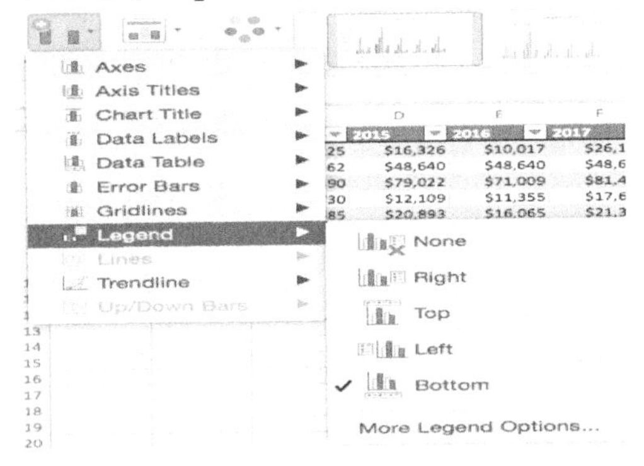

The legend's placement depends on the chart's type and format. Choose the best graph option. This is how your chart appears when you press the Right legend.

Clustered column charts don't support lines (clustered). In certain chart categories, you should add lines by selecting the correct answer (e.g., goal, average, comparison, etc.).

To Add the Trendline:

Add Chart Elements ➔ Trendline. There are 5 options: None (default), Linear Forecast, Linear, Exponential, and Moving Average. Use the correct data-collection instrument. Choose Linear.

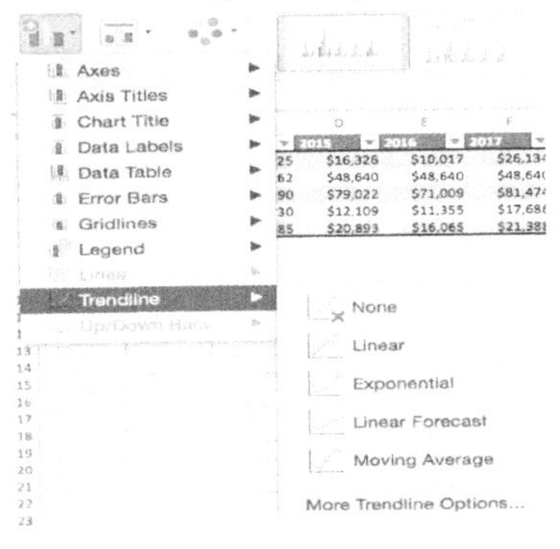

Excel gives trendlines for 5 distinct items when compared over time. Click a product's blue OK button to construct linear trendlines.

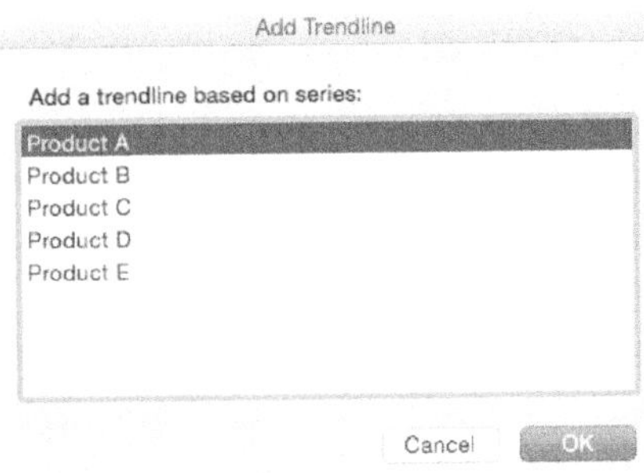

Now your chart will show Product A's linear growth with dotted trendlines. Excel's legend has Linear (A Product) applied.

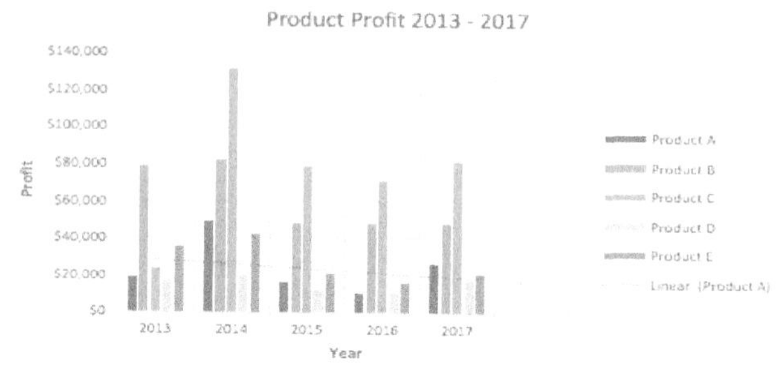

Double-click trendlines to reveal trendline equations. Format Trendlines may appear on the right. Check the box below. Display equation on chart. The chart now shows the equation.

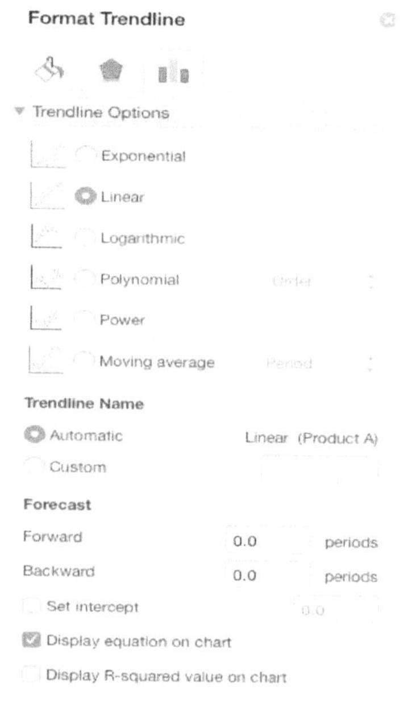

Each chart characteristic may have as many trendlines as desired. Here's a graphic showing A&C's trendlines.

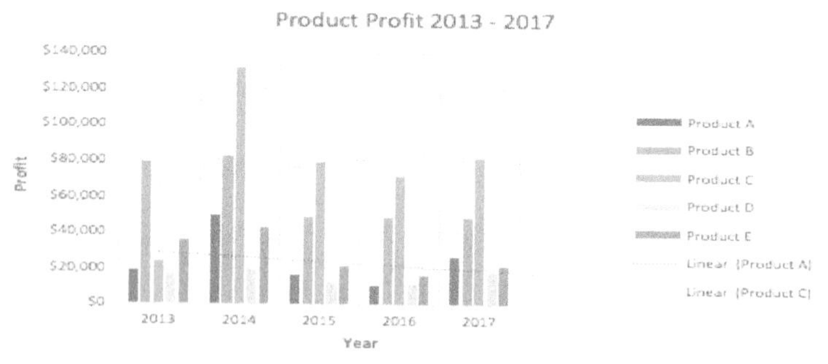

Up/Down Bars can't be used in column charts, but they may be used in line charts to show data point climbs and drops.

Step4: Adjust a Quick Layout

Quick Layout is the toolbar's second drop-down option that lets you arrange chart components (legend, titles, clusters, etc.).

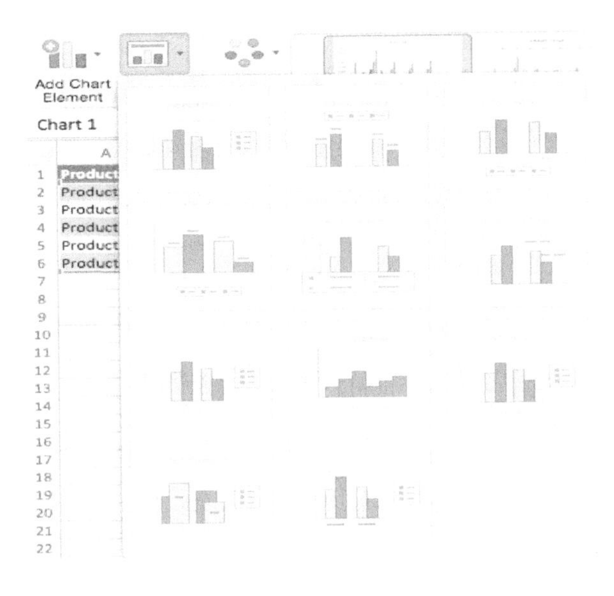

Eleven layouts are available. Hover over each option for a description, then choose it.

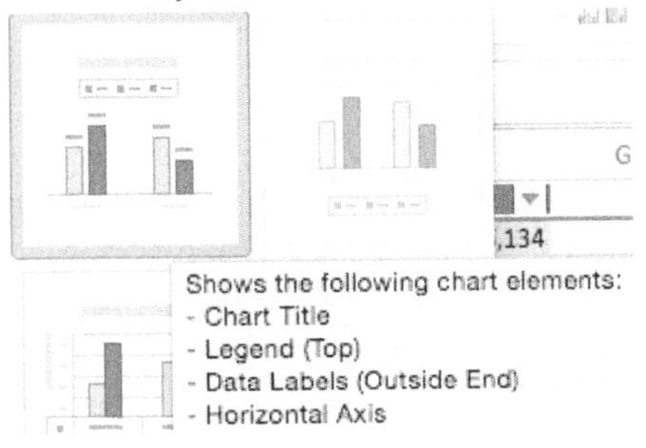

Shows the following chart elements:
- Chart Title
- Legend (Top)
- Data Labels (Outside End)
- Horizontal Axis

Step5: Change the Colors

In the toolbar, choose Colors. Choose the finest color scheme (these may be aesthetic and complement the colors & theme of your brand).

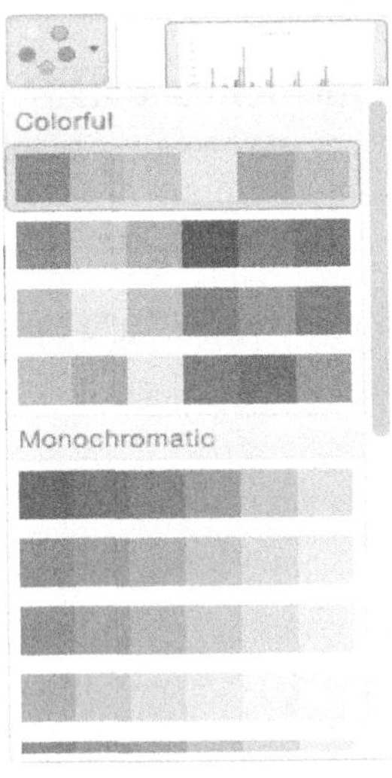

Step6: Change the Style

Charts employ 14 forms (cluster column). The chart defaults to Style 1, but you may change it. Click the photo bar's right arrow for more options.

Step7: Switch Column/Row

To rotate the axis, click Switch Row/Column. If you have more than 2 variables, switching axes isn't intuitive.

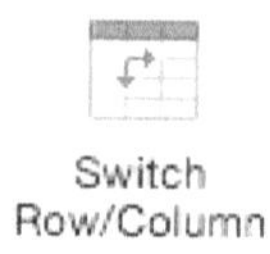

Switching column and row reverses the product and year (profit remains on your y-axis). The graph is now arranged by product (not by year), and the legend is color-coded (not-product). To avoid confusion, change Series to Years in legend.

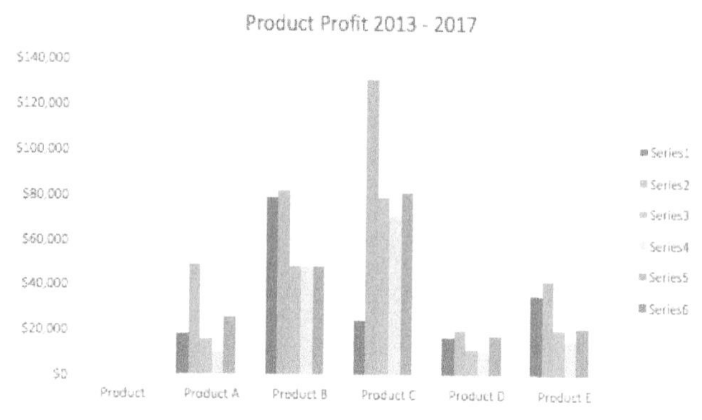

Step8: Select the Data

Click Select Data on your toolbar to change the file context.

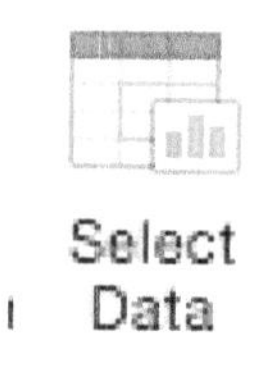

Wide-swinging doors. When you're done, click Ok. The table would automatically reflect the newest data.

Step9: Change the Chart Type

Change the chart type.

Here you may change Excel's 9 chart kinds. Check that the data fits your chart format.

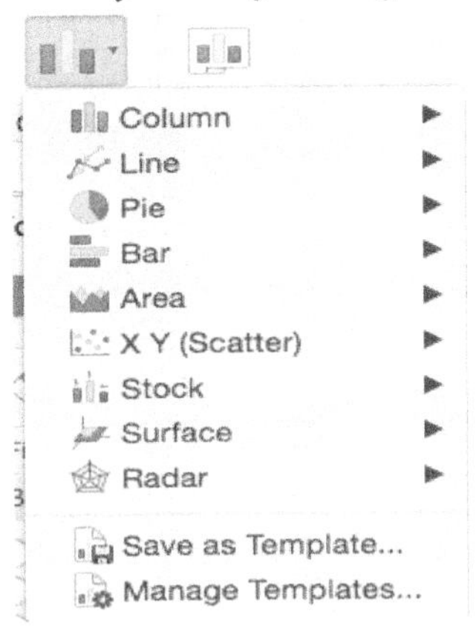

Save the chart as a template by clicking Save as...

You'll be prompted to name your design. Excel can construct model folders for rapid organization. To save, click Save.

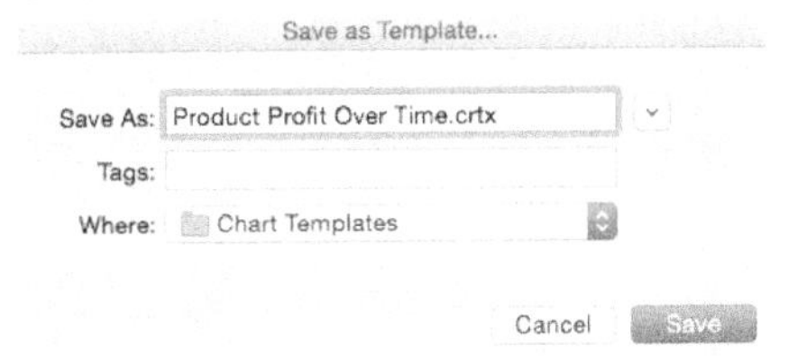

Step10: Move the Chart

Click Move Chart in the rightmost toolbar.

You may place the chart in a conversation box. You may use this map to create a new layer or as an object in another sheet. Press blue OK to continue.

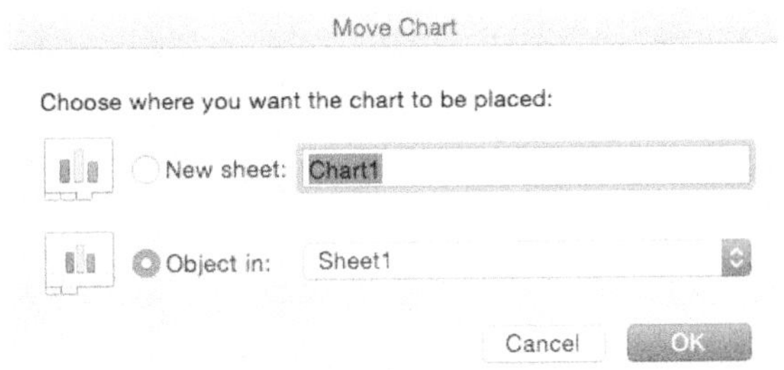

Step11: Change the Formatting

The Format tab lets you change the colors, size, design, fill, and orientation of chart components and text and insert objects. To construct a brand map, click Format and use a shortcut (images, colors, etc.).

Choose the chart feature to update from the toolbar's drop-down menu.

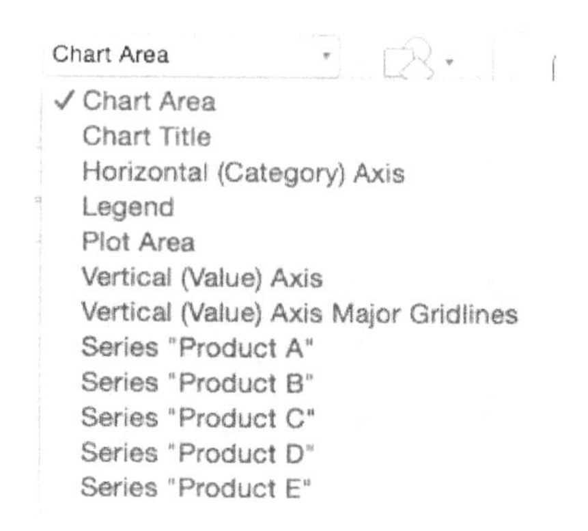

Step12: Delete the Chart

To remove a chart, select it and hit Delete.

How can you make the Graph using Excel?

Excel groups graph into chart categories because graphs and charts are distinct. Follow these instructions to create a graph or chart.

To make a graph with workbook data, select a range

Highlight cells with the data, you want on the graph.
Illuminate the grayed-out cell spectrum.

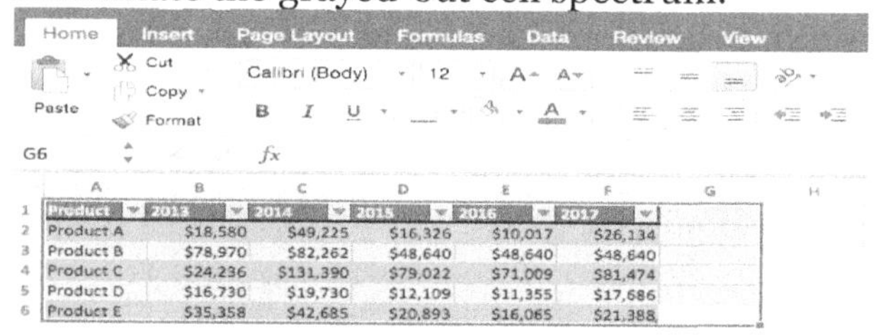

Product	2013	2014	2015	2016	2017
Product A	$18,580	$49,225	$16,326	$10,017	$26,134
Product B	$78,970	$82,262	$48,640	$48,640	$48,640
Product C	$24,236	$131,390	$79,022	$71,009	$81,474
Product D	$16,730	$19,730	$12,109	$11,355	$17,686
Product E	$35,358	$42,685	$20,893	$16,065	$21,388

After outlining, pick a graph (Excel refers to a chart). Insert tab, Recommended Charts. Choose a graph type.

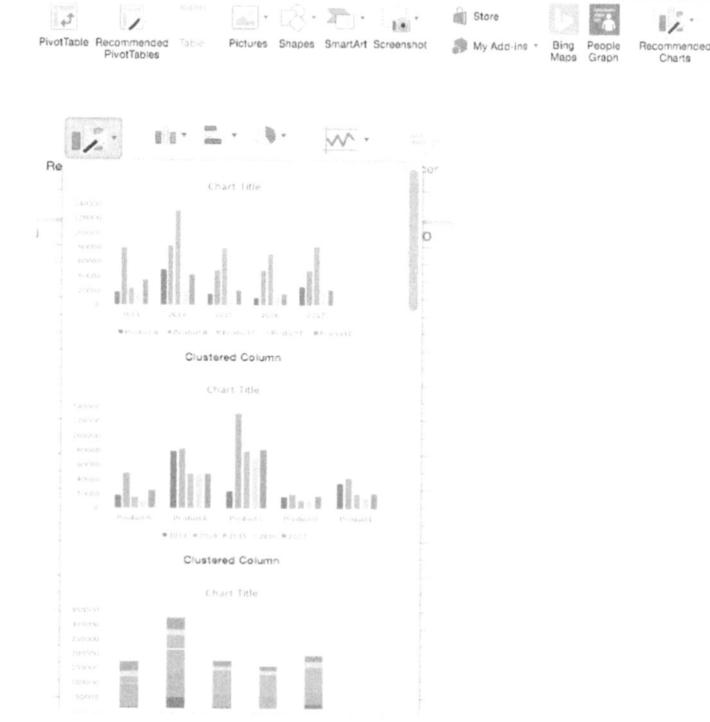

The graph appears onscreen. Repeat the preceding steps to customize your graph. All graph-making routines are the same.

Chapter 6: Data Management Techniques

In this chapter, you will learn about multiple data management techniques including data validation and rules to validate your data, data formatting,g and consolidation, and, data analysis.

Data Validation & Rules

Excel's Data Validation tool helps users input reliable data. Data validation limits what may be input in a cell and provides guidelines.

Create a Validation Rule

- Decide which cells you'd want to verify.
- Go to the Data tab by clicking on it.
- Click on the button Data Validation.

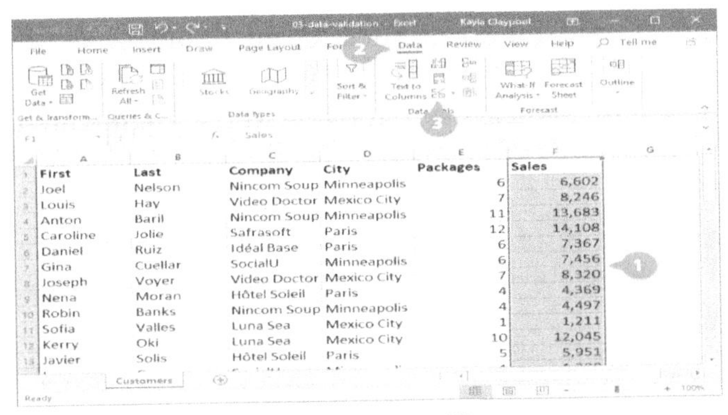

- A selection of options will appear.
- Choice the form of data that you command to let in.

Any value: Not validation criteria were applied.
Whole number: Allows any number between 0 and the specified minimum/maximum.
Decimals and percentages may be input as decimals within the defined limitations.
List: Select a value from the drop-down menu. Users may choose from a list by clicking on the list arrow in the cell.
Date: Permits a specific date if it's not outside the specified range.
Time: Permits a certain amount of time if it's not exceeded.
Text length: Permits a specified number of characters to be entered.
Custom: A formula might be entered to compute what is permitted in the cell.

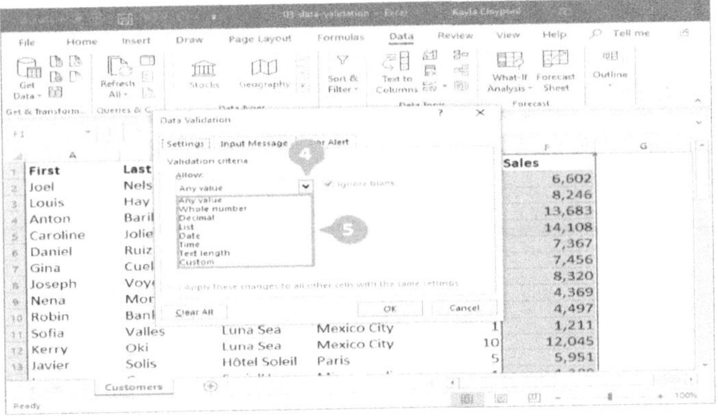

Give specifics on how the data will be validated.

Depending on the Allow option chosen, the validation choices will be different.

Then press the OK button.

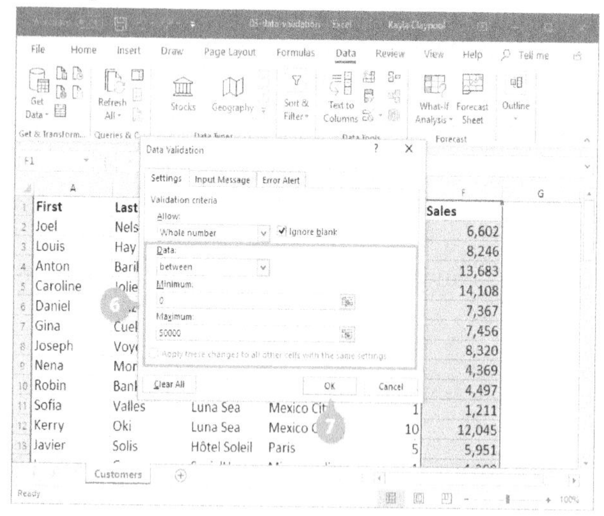

Set cell data validation (s). Excel prevents invalid data entering and displays a notification about the restricted cell.

To discover verified data inside a worksheet, select Find & Choose and choose Data Validation. Highlighted verified cells.

Add Input & Error Messages

Set Excel to show a notification when a cell or range is chosen to prevent data validation errors. These notifications help when others input data into your spreadsheet. Invalid data might trigger an error message.

- Select the cells in which you wish to see an input message.
- Go to the Data tab by clicking on it.
- Click on the Data Validation button.
- Input Message is on the left-hand side.
- Input a message here.

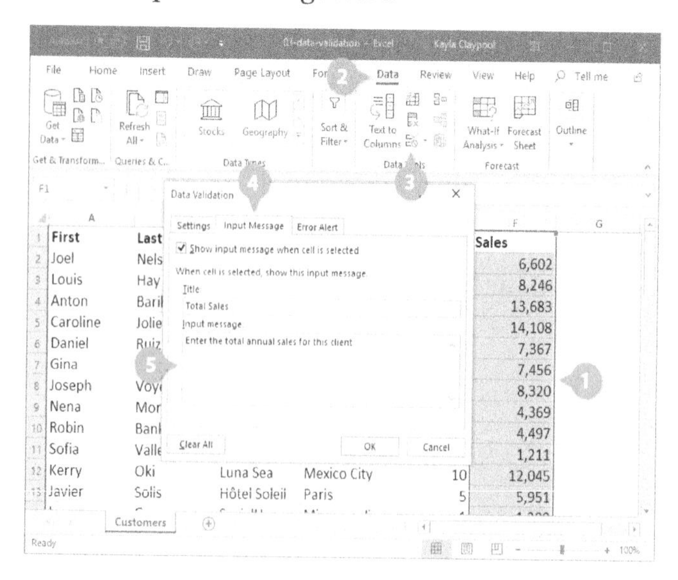

Look at the Error Alert section.

Select the kind of error message that should be shown to the user.

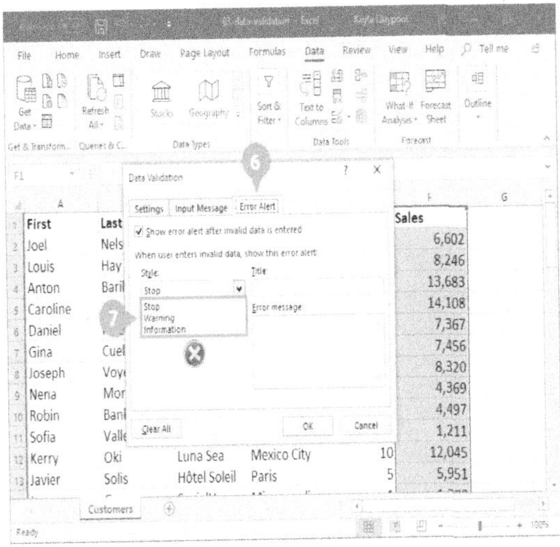

Stop: Prevents the entry of incorrect data into a cell by a user.

Warning: The user can accept an invalid input, change it, or cancel the process.

Information: Users are given the option of either clicking OK to approve the incorrect input or clicking Cancel to get it removed.

- Enter a warning message in the field.
- Then press the OK button.
- Select any cell containing a text you need to enter.

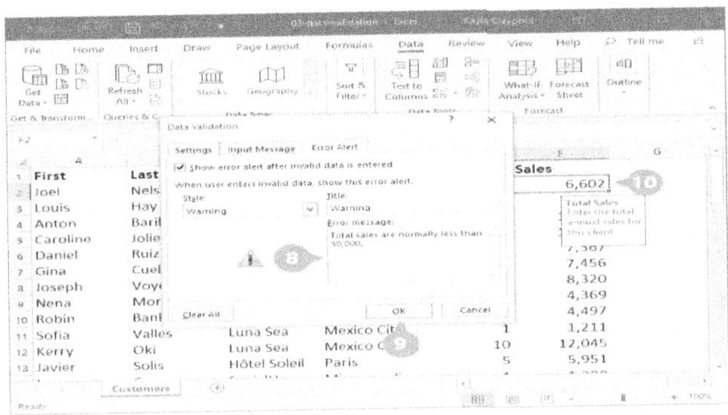

Selecting a cell within range now creates a pop-up with the range's title and message. The custom warning message is shown if an incorrect value is entered.

Rules

You must develop data-validation criteria in Excel since inputting data is so boring. Data validation rules are essential. A data-validation rule specifies what may be entered in a cell.

Here's what to type when you choose a cell with a rule. An error message appears if you input data improperly.

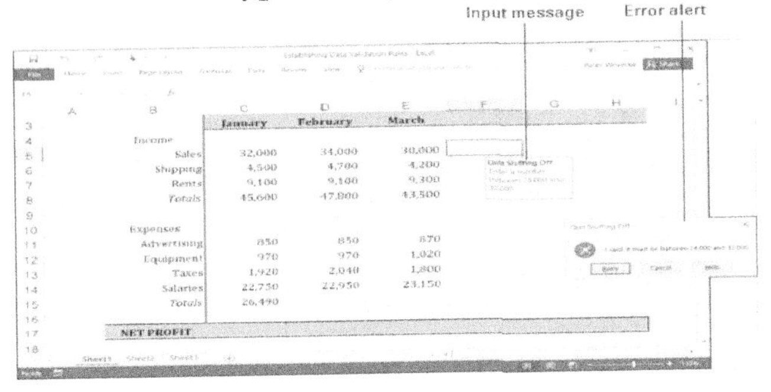

A data-validation rule in action.

Data validation procedures prevent careless data input and that uncomfortable sensation during tedious tasks. In a date cell, you may need dates.

In a text-entry cell, you may pick an element from a list. In numeric cells, you may set a range. The table lists data-validation categories.

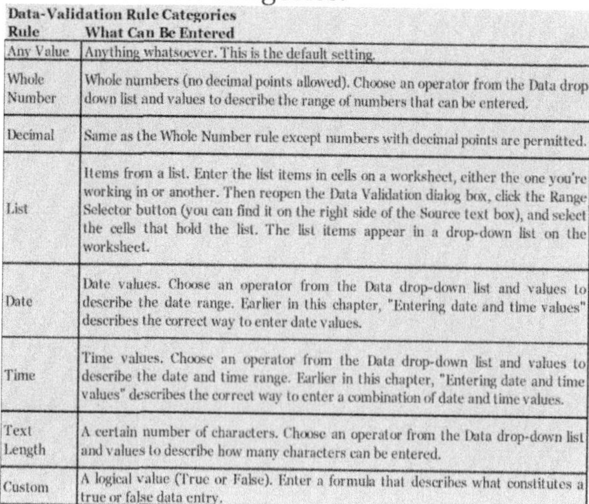

Data-Validation Rule Categories

Rule	What Can Be Entered
Any Value	Anything whatsoever. This is the default setting.
Whole Number	Whole numbers (no decimal points allowed). Choose an operator from the Data drop-down list and values to describe the range of numbers that can be entered.
Decimal	Same as the Whole Number rule except numbers with decimal points are permitted.
List	Items from a list. Enter the list items in cells on a worksheet, either the one you're working in or another. Then reopen the Data Validation dialog box, click the Range Selector button (you can find it on the right side of the Source text box), and select the cells that hold the list. The list items appear in a drop-down list on the worksheet.
Date	Date values. Choose an operator from the Data drop-down list and values to describe the date range. Earlier in this chapter, "Entering date and time values" describes the correct way to enter date values.
Time	Time values. Choose an operator from the Data drop-down list and values to describe the date and time range. Earlier in this chapter, "Entering date and time values" describes the correct way to enter a combination of date and time values.
Text Length	A certain number of characters. Choose an operator from the Data drop-down list and values to describe how many characters can be entered.
Custom	A logical value (True or False). Enter a formula that describes what constitutes a true or false data entry.

Set a data-validation rule using these steps.

- Choose the needed cells.
- Click Data Validation under Data.
- Data Validation dialogue box Settings tab.

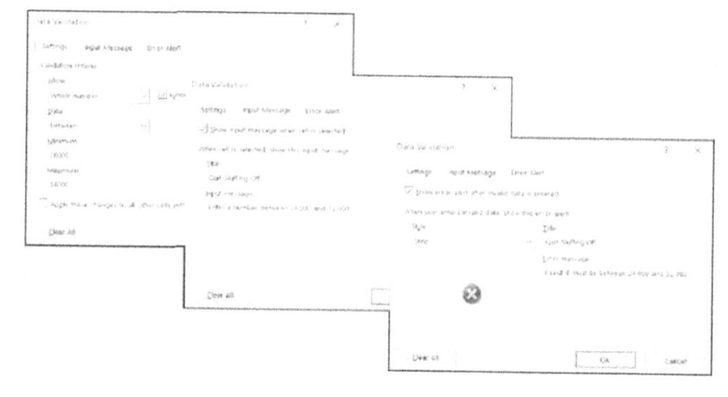

The Data Validation dialogue box's Settings tab.

- Use the Allow drop-down menu to choose the rule type you wish to apply.
- Specify the rule's parameters here.
- For each rule category, the criterion is different. The table explains how to input the criteria for each rule type. The worksheet's cells may be referenced by clicking on them. To do so, you may either choose them straight or select the Ranges Selector button & select them.
- Enter a title and a message in the Input Message field.
- For example, "Quit Slacking Off" is prominently displayed on the page. The title has been bolded out. Tell us more about the kind of data you chose for the cell(s).
- A warning message may be added to the Message Alert dialogue box by using the Error Alert tab's style, title, and message fields.

- The stop was selected within the error message given before. The message shows next to the symbol, and the title that enters appears across the top of the dialogue box to the left.
- Right-click to accept.
- Remove data-validation rules by selecting the cells, going to the Data tab, and clicking Data Validation, then on the Settings tab of the Data Validation dialogue box, clicking Clear All, and then clicking OK.

Data Formatting & Consolidation

You may use Data Consolidation to combine data from many worksheets into a single expert worksheet. If you have a lot of different spreadsheets or workbooks, you may use the Data Consolidation feature to combine all the information into a single spreadsheet.

Data Consolidation may be challenging to deal with, but don't give up. Data Consolidation is a powerful tool that may help you rapidly and effectively analyze and display your data. Good groundwork is the key to accomplishment, no matter how frightening the screen may seem at first.

Using this example, you'll learn from one of your Excel experts how to organize the data before summarizing it to make your findings more comprehensible.

The following is what you'll be looking at:

- Workbook consolidation by merging data from numerous worksheets.
- In a new worksheet, merging the data from numerous spreadsheets into a single summary

Versions 2007 and later Excel versions are all compatible with the steps below. This advice might not function if you use Excel 2003 or an earlier program version.

Multiple worksheets in the same workbook may have their data combined using

In this example, you can see how much you spent on tea, coffee, & milk over the last three years. One year's worth of data is divided into quarters and kept on a single worksheet every quarter in one workbook.

It is possible to construct an annual or quarterly "Consolidated Summary" that shows all your expenses in one place. It doesn't matter whether the columns and rows are arranged similarly. Excel can take care of it. Amazing!

Year 1 worksheet

	A	B	C	D	E
1		Quarter 1	Quarter 2	Quarter 3	Quarter 4
2	Coffee	£ 2,128	£ 3,526	£ 5,372	£ 9,378
3	Tea	£ 1,633		£ 5,392	£ 1,730
4	Milk	£ 4,837		£ 3,082	£ 5,272

Year 1 | Year 2 | Year 3 | Consolidated Summary

Year 2 worksheet

8		Quarter 1	Quarter 2	Quarter 3	Quarter 4
9	Coffee	£ 2,944	£ 3,528	£ 7,822	£ 8,464
10	Milk	£ 8,227		£ 9,462	£ 2,748
11					

Year 1 | Year 2 | Year 3 | Consolidated Summary

Year 3 worksheet

7		Quarter 4	Quarter 3	Quarter 1
8	Coffee	£ 9,664	£ 7,123	£ 2,643
9	Tea	£ 7,356	£ 2,865	£ 6,092
10	Milk	£ 6,787	£ 1,595	£ 8,356
11				

Year 1 | Year 2 | Year 3 | Consolidated Summary

Columns & rows are arranged differently in Years 1, 2, & 3, as seen in the table. For example, in Year two, there is no tea, and in Year Three, there isn't any Quarter Two & the Quarters aren't in sequence. Consolidated ranges need not be the same dimension in each worksheet; the number of columns or rows may vary from one worksheet to the next. You may create a summary sheet by condensing all the data. What a fantastic discovery!

Consolidation step:

Use an active worksheet or generate a new one if required as your master worksheet before using the Data Consolidation tool. A new title for the worksheet is 'Consolidated Summary.

Ensure the upper-left cell in the region where the aggregated data will be shown is selected.

To see the Consolidate dialogue, choose Data ➔ Consolidate on the Ribbon.

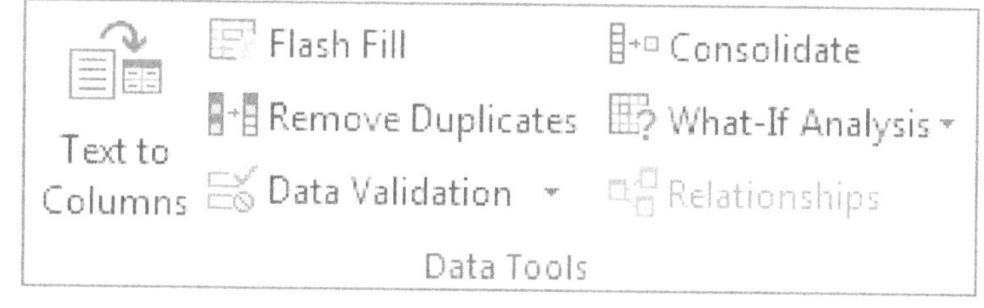

Excel will aggregate the data using the summary function you provide in the Function box. Eleven functions are available, as you can see in the drop-down menu. You'll use the Sum function since you'll add the numbers in your dataset.

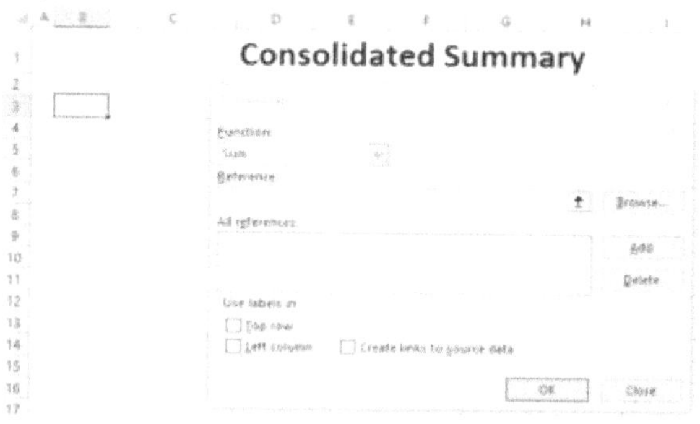

You may add the first piece of data to a consolidation dialogue by selecting it within the Reference area & then dragging the data (containing column and row headers) over to the Sheet tab and clicking the Add button.

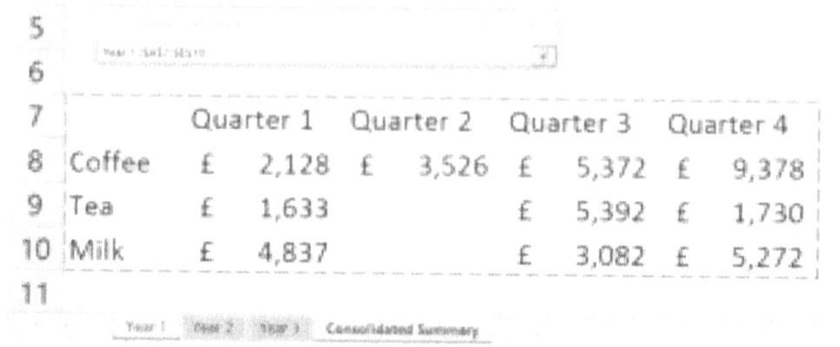

7		Quarter 1	Quarter 2	Quarter 3	Quarter 4
8	Coffee	£ 2,128	£ 3,526	£ 5,372	£ 9,378
9	Tea	£ 1,633		£ 5,392	£ 1,730
10	Milk	£ 4,837		£ 3,082	£ 5,272
11					

You may keep doing this until you have all your information listed under "References," such as "Year 2" & "Year 3," by selecting the following page and then selecting the data on it with your mouse.

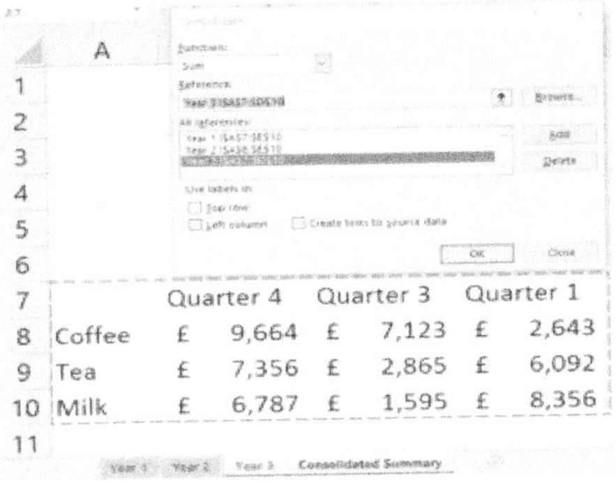

To get the most out of the Consolidation process, you may name the ranges before you begin the procedure. Consolidation may be done by pressing F3 within the Reference field and selecting the range from the Paste Name dialogue box if you have named each range.

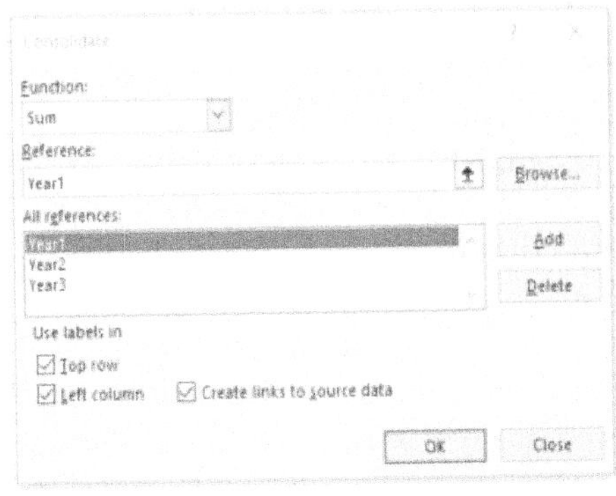

Select the checkboxes under Use tags in the top row, left column, & to show where the labels are contained in the source ranges. Quarter1, Quarter2, etc., are shown in the top row, whereas the products listed in the left column are, for example, coffee, tea, and milk.
What's the difference between automatic and manual updates? Select the Create connections to original data tick box if you want Excel to update the consolidation table automatically as the source data changes. If this option is unchecked, you may still manually update your consolidation.

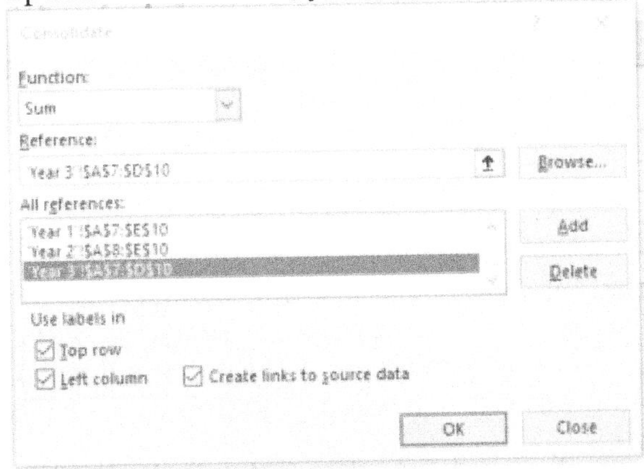

Excel creates a new page for you to use as the master worksheet when you click OK (Consolidated Summary).

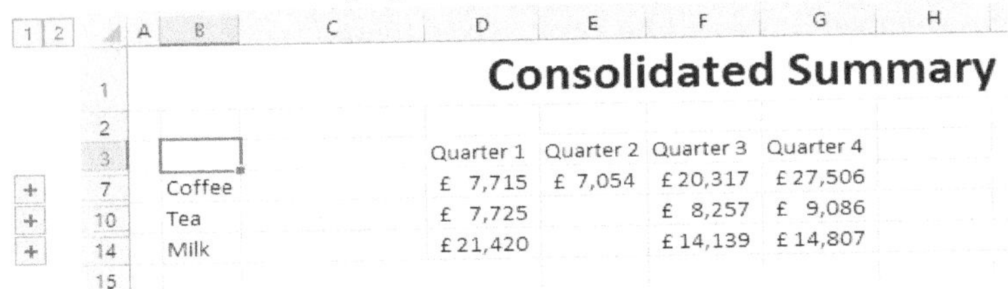

You'll see something new in the Excel spreadsheet that you haven't seen before. To show and conceal data, utilize the grouping tools on the left side of the screen. Rows 7, 10, and 14 all have plus signs next to them. In this case, the cells are components of a collapsing group. When you click the + symbol, you'll see a line that connects all rows to the left:

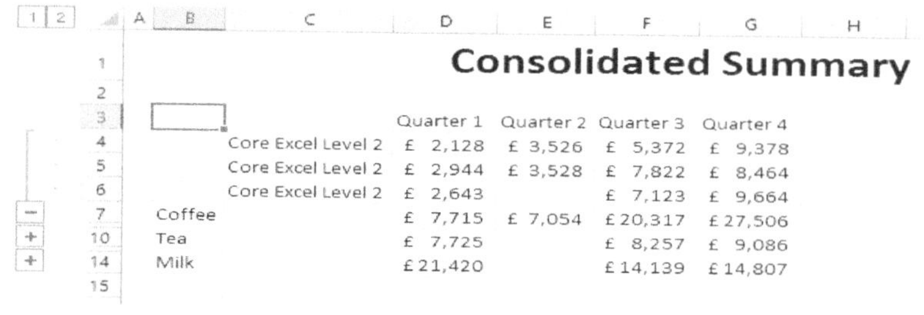

Consolidated Summary

Row	B	C	D	E	F	G
3			Quarter 1	Quarter 2	Quarter 3	Quarter 4
4		Core Excel Level 2	£ 2,128	£ 3,526	£ 5,372	£ 9,378
5		Core Excel Level 2	£ 2,944	£ 3,528	£ 7,822	£ 8,464
6		Core Excel Level 2	£ 2,643		£ 7,123	£ 9,664
7	Coffee		£ 7,715	£ 7,054	£ 20,317	£ 27,506
10	Tea		£ 7,725		£ 8,257	£ 9,086
14	Milk		£ 21,420		£ 14,139	£ 14,807

Column C of data indicates the workbook name (Column C) that includes the data. If you don't want to see this column, just right-click on it and choose Hide. This merely conceals the column so you can still access the data if needed.

Copying the worksheets to a new workbook

Once again, having everything planned out ahead of time will be beneficial.

As you'll see, several entries in your Consolidated Summary aren't useful. Because range C4: C6 displays just the workbook's title, it's difficult to tell where the numbers in the range D4: G6 originate. You should consider separating all worksheets into independent workbooks before applying data consolidation if the source data is included on the summary page. To help you out, here are some instructions.

You will copy your selected worksheet into some new workbook; now, select from your book drop-down categories. Select a Create the copy box. Because you're creating a new workbook, there are no worksheets within Before sheet lists before which you can insert a copied worksheet. This will be the only worksheet within the new workbook.

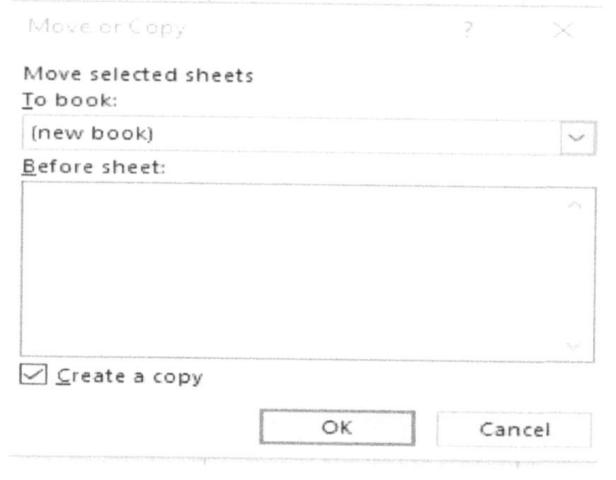

Click Yes. The worksheet gets copied into a new workbook created for this purpose. The worksheet will be removed from the original workbook if you want to relocate it. Save the current workbook as "Year 1.xls" after copying a worksheet. Workbooks for years two and three should be called Year 2.xls (for the second year) & Year 3.xls (for the third year), accordingly. As laborious as this may be at first, it will pay off in the long run!

Join numerous workbooks together into a single new one.

To aggregate several open workbooks, make sure they are all open.

Keep your master worksheet in an empty spreadsheet or create a new one if needed. Worksheet "Consolidate Summary" has been changed to "Consolidate Summary" and saved as Summary.xls in the new workbook.

Ensure the upper-left cell in the region where the aggregated data will be shown is selected.

Data > Consolidate on the Ribbon and may be accessed by clicking the Consolidate button.

The only difference is that you pick data ranges from separate workbooks instead of distinct worksheets, as you did in the previous example.

When you select OK, Excel creates a new master worksheet with all the data you entered (Consolidated Summary).

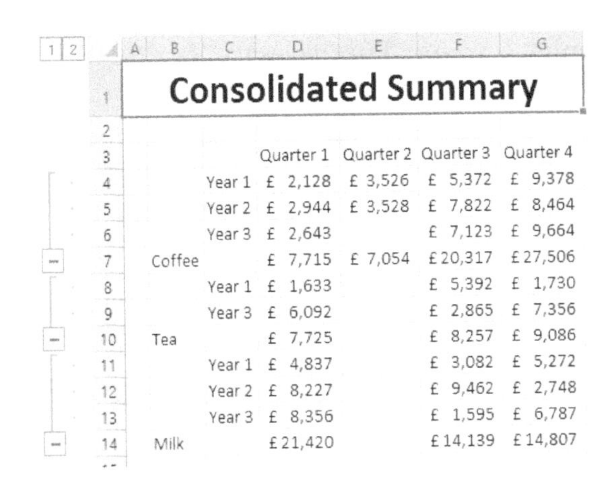

Consolidated Summary

		Quarter 1	Quarter 2	Quarter 3	Quarter 4
	Year 1	£ 2,128	£ 3,526	£ 5,372	£ 9,378
	Year 2	£ 2,944	£ 3,528	£ 7,822	£ 8,464
	Year 3	£ 2,643		£ 7,123	£ 9,664
Coffee		£ 7,715	£ 7,054	£ 20,317	£ 27,506
	Year 1	£ 1,633		£ 5,392	£ 1,730
	Year 3	£ 6,092		£ 2,865	£ 7,356
Tea		£ 7,725		£ 8,257	£ 9,086
	Year 1	£ 4,837		£ 3,082	£ 5,272
	Year 2	£ 8,227		£ 9,462	£ 2,748
	Year 3	£ 8,356		£ 1,595	£ 6,787
Milk		£ 21,420		£ 14,139	£ 14,807

Column C now displays the name of a workbook that contains your data, which is more useful than the previous example.

How to Analyze Data in Excel

In every field, people utilize Microsoft Excel as a standard piece of software. Some excel with crucial tables and histograms, while others stick to pie charts & conditional formatting as their primary tools.

Excel may be used for data analysis, but it can also be used as a canvas for artistic expression. Microsoft Excel and its usefulness will be examined in depth in this session. This lesson will go through the many tips and tactics for analyzing Excel analytics data. Excel data analysis techniques will also be discussed.

We'll go through several Excel analytics capabilities to better understand how to analyze data in Excel, functions, and best practices.

Making the Pivot Table a Best Friend

You can quickly and easily summarize massive volumes of data using a pivot tool. One of Excel's most useful tools is identifying and analyzing dataset trends.

It's easy to see trends in a tiny dataset. However, the sheer size of the datasets necessitates more work to uncover any trends. To sum up large amounts of data in just a few minutes utilizing a pivot table is a big benefit. An example of data analysis can be found using a dataset of regions and the number of sales. A breakdown of sales by region might help you figure out what's going wrong in a particular location and what you can do to fix it. You may quickly and easily build an excel report and save it for future use using a pivot table.

Using a Pivot Table, you may average, sum, or count data from another spreadsheet or table in Excel. Using this tool, you can organize and display data rapidly, which is useful for swiftly producing reports.

The spreadsheet you've put up may be copied and pasted into Excel or Google Docs (simply click File ➔ Make one Copy) if you need to use it in another program.

You will find information on a fictitious company's customers in the spreadsheet. For rapid analysis, we may use a pivot table to aggregate this data to view the total transactions per firm and evaluate purchases across various organizations.

Using the Pivot table, you may reorganize a table with several data in it so that you can only see the information that is relevant to you.

If you're using a Mac or PC, you may pick the whole dataset and choose "Data" ➔ "Pivot Table" from the drop-down menu. A table should open in a new tab when you press that.

Data Set

b) When you have the table next to you, you may drag & drop your Row Labels, Column Labels, & Report Filter.

- Your table's top row is occupied with column labels (for example, Company Name, Date, Month)
- For example, dates, months, and your company's name are good candidates for row labels that run the length of your table on the left side.

- Data that you want to be analyzed is entered here (for example, Revenue, Purchases)
- Refine your findings using the Report Filter. About anything goes here

The data in your reports may be easily organized using pivot tables. Alternatively, you may make a copy inside Google App (File ➔ Make a Copy) by copying and pasting the data.

Analyzing Data Set with Excel

Using Excel, you can quickly generate various graphs, including line & column charts, or even add micrographs to your spreadsheet.

Table styles, PivotTables, fast totals, & conditional formatting are all options. When working with enormous datasets in Excel, there are a few easy principles to remember:

- Identify the cells containing the information in which you are interested.
- To quickly analyze your chosen data, click your Quick Analysis icon picture button (or enter CRTL + Q).
- The Quick Analysis Lens icon is available while viewing selected data.
- Select a tab from the Quick Analysis gallery. For example, you may use Charts to display your data on a graph.
- Choose from one of the choices or point to any of them to get a preview.
- It is possible to note that the possibilities available to you aren't always identical. In many cases, this is because the selections in your worksheet vary according to the kind of data you've chosen.

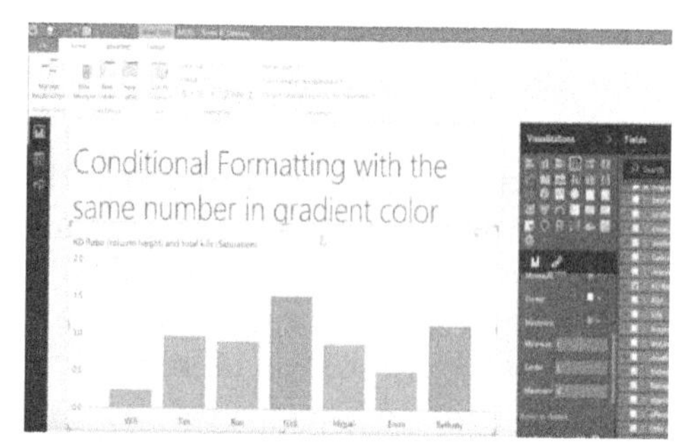

You may want to discover which Excel analysis option is appropriate for you to grasp the best technique to analyze data in Excel. Here, we summarize a few of the most popular solutions.

- **Formatting:** Data bars & colors may be added to your data to make it easier to see what you're looking at. With this, you may instantly view the highest and lowest figures.
- **Charts:** Excel provides various charts depending on the data you've chosen to work with. If you can't find the chart you're looking for, click More Charts to explore more options.
- **Totals:** It is possible to determine the totals for each row and column. Running Total, as an example, inserts a total that increases as new items are added to your data. To show more possibilities, utilize the small black arrows to the right & left of the current selection.
- **Tables:** Filtering and sorting your data is a breeze using tables. More is the option if you don't find the table format you desire.
- **Sparklines:** It is possible to display small graphs, called sparklines, alongside your raw data. Trends may be seen thanks to these tools quickly.

Tips & Tricks

If you know how to play the game, data analysis in MS Excel may be a lot of fun.

Following are some tips on how you can use Excel to evaluate data.

Data Cleaning

One of Excel's most fundamental tasks, data cleaning, is made easier with several helpful tips and tactics. With the help of Power Query, you may master how to do the same thing in Excel. Excel 2016 has a function called Power Query, which is also available as an Add-in for Excel. Your data may be extracted, transformed, and loaded with only a few clicks.

Convert text numbers to numeric formats

When importing data from a non-Excel source, numbers may be imported as text in certain cases. A green popup within the cell's upper-left corner will appear to let you know that an error has occurred.

You may easily convert the values in the range to numbers by selecting 'Convert to a number from the tooltip choices, depending on the number of the range's values.

Excel will take a few extra seconds to complete the conversion if you've over 1000 values.

Using Text-to-Columns and the procedures below, you may convert these values to numeric format:

- You'll need to choose the range of numbers you want to convert.
- Select Data → Text to Columns from the menu bar.
- Once you've selected Delimited, click Next.
- Click Next after clearing all the delimiter checks (see the image below for a visual guide).
- Text-Columns-Checkboxes

Select General & click on the Finish

If you have many numbers to convert, this trick will save you a lot of time. Converting columns in Power Query is as simple as clicking on a column header and right-clicking.

- Then, click on the Change Type option to make the necessary adjustments.
- then choose the type of number you desire (such as a Whole Number or Decimal)
- Power-Query-Datatype

Data Analysis

With Excel analytics, data analysis is simplified and expedited. Here are some pointers for the workplace:

- Excel tables may be used to create auto-expanding ranges. Excel Tables are one of Excel's most underutilized capabilities. Excel's tables include several useful features that make it easier to get things done. The following are only a few of these features:
- Formula It is possible to automatically have a formula duplicated to the remainder of a table after you input it.
- Adding more entries to the table by typing them below or to the right will cause it to expand automatically.
- Your headers will be displayed no matter where you are on the table.
- The sum of a row may be calculated automatically by using the appropriate formula.
- As part of a calculation, you may use Excel tables. Like dropdown lists, formulas that rely on tables will automatically be updated as new entries are added to those tables.

- Create a graphic using data from Excel Tables: Excel Tables may also be used to update charts automatically. There is no requirement to manually update data sources with Excel Tables, as seen in the example.

Data Visualization

Sparklines, a visualization tool of MS Excel, enable you to rapidly view the general trend of a group of information. Mini graphs called sparklines may be found within cells. You may wish to depict the average monthly revenue a team of salespeople generates.

Follow these procedures to make the sparklines:

- Decide on the data range you want to plot. To create a sparkline, go to Insert ➔ Sparklines ➔ Sparkline Type. I'm going to use Lines as an example for the time being.
- Select a range by clicking on the button. After selecting the range from the Excel button, press Enter & click OK to locate the sparklines' position. Determine how much space is required to accommodate the data source. There must be six rows in each position of a sparkline if your data source provides six rows.

You might attempt the following to format the sparkline:

For changing the color of markers:

- Sparkline Tools may be accessed by clicking on a cell in the sparkline.
- To alter the color of a certain marker, go to the Sparkline tool menu and choose the marker from the drop-down menu.

Example: High points are in green, low points are in red, and the rest are blue. Example:

For changing the width of your lines:

- Sparkline Tools may be accessed by clicking on a cell in the sparkline.
- To modify the width of a Sparkline line, go to the Sparkline Color ➔ Weight within the Sparkline tools contextual menu.

Excel 2013's Quick Analysis tool was a big time-saver when it was first launched. When you use this functionality, you may easily produce many types of graphs and charts with a single button click.

If you're using Excel 2013 or later, you'll see a new button in the lower-right corner of your chosen range called the Quick Analysis Excel Button.

If you choose "Quick Analysis," the following choices will appear:

- Sparklines
- Formatting
- Totals
- Charts
- Tables

After selecting an option, Excel will provide a view of the potential outcomes based on your data.

- If you go to charts and click over the Quick Analysis icon, you may rapidly construct the graph.
- The average value for every column may be rapidly inserted by selecting Totals and then inserting a row:
- You may easily insert Sparklines by clicking on Sparklines: See how simple it is to do a variety of visualizations and analyses with the Quick Analysis feature.

Data Reporting

Excel analytics data reporting demands more than accounting expertise; it also necessitates a complete understanding of Excel's features and the capability to improve the report's aesthetic appeal.

- Before making any changes to the Excel spreadsheet, disable Auto Refresh. Making changes to a worksheet will prevent the table from updating.
- Refresh the Xls Report Designer Tasks Pane and choose "Switch auto-refresh off" from the Refresh icon.
- The new row should be inserted into the layout by selecting a cell below where you wish to place it.
- Then, right-click and pick Insert ➔ Table Row Above from the context menu. Make careful to utilize the Table Delete methods like the Insert operations above when removing columns or rows.
- Select a cell within the table area of a column or row you wish to remove, and then press the delete key. After that, right-click and choose
- Delete from the context menu, after which you may choose between deleting Table Columns & Table Rows.
- Delete any columns or rows that aren't required. To make the table refresh faster, you should remove any unnecessary cells from its layout.

Here, you've just scratched the surface of what Excel can do. Using Excel analytics, you may play around with complicated data visualizations or arrange divergent statistics to uncover the endless variety of Excel features. Being proficient with Excel is an asset if you're interested in working in data analytics.

Chapter 7: Excel Macro & VBA

Visual Basic for Applications (VBA) Macros allows users to develop their functions in Excel and automate repetitive manual chores. In addition, Microsoft Windows Application Programming Interface (API) may be accessed using VBA (API). Customizing toolbars, menus, dialogue boxes, and forms is one of the most common applications of this tool.

Use the form below to obtain instant access to our Excel VBA cheat sheet, which includes an overview of the most important codes & terminology, macros, and best practices.

Creating VBA Macros

The user must first create the Module file before they can begin coding. Several macros may be found in a single module file. Insert ➔ Module should be used to build a brand-new module. The properties panel in the bottom left quadrant of your editor allows the user to give this module a name. To add a new module, start typing its name and enter.

Naming VBA Macros

To begin, the macro should be assigned a distinctive name. This macro's name can't be confused with the names of any other macros or Excel properties, functions, or tools. To activate a macro, the user must type in the macro name.

In the editor's code window, write Sub name() and hit "enter" to create a macro name. Fill your window with the macro's general format by pressing Enter. CFI Macro, for example, may be named by typing in the command "Sub cfiMacro()" and pressing enter. Just a few lines underneath the "Sub," your VBA Editor would automatically add an "End Sub" line.

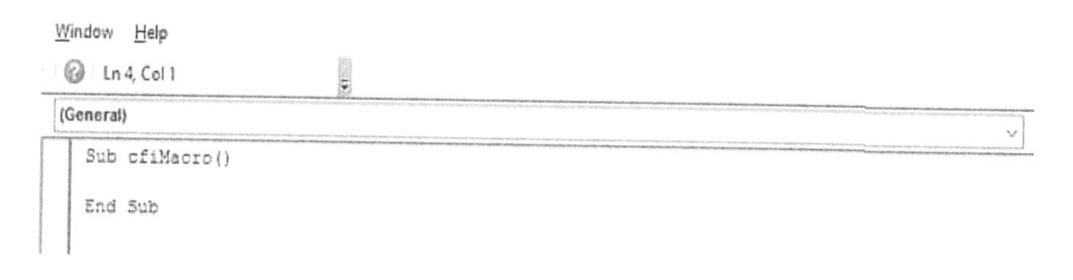

It is important to remember that function, VBA macro, or variable names should be written in lowercase if there are only one or two words and in uppercase for every additional work. VBA names are often not allowed to include spaces.

There are two words in CFI Macro; hence it should be spelled as "cfiMacro." It is significant to remember that these are only suggestions for best practices and are not legally required to be followed.

Sub Naming into VBA

The beginning of the macro code is shown by the Sub Name() line. The End Sub serves as a marker for the conclusion of the paragraph.

If the user decides to, he or she might create a new Sub Name () line beneath the first End Sub and construct a second macro. Excel will automatically draw a line between the two macros when you run this.

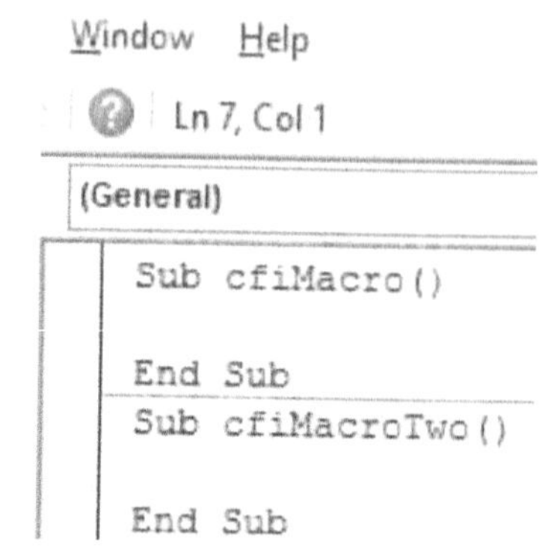

An Excel macro's fundamental structure looks like this.
The next stage is to specify the parameters the user will utilize in the code before diving into actual process coding.

Enabling Macros

To enable macros is to execute or run a macro in a certain file to reduce the time it takes to do the same task again.
Click the "allow all macros" checkbox in the "trust center" of the File tab's "settings" button to make macros available.
When a macro-enabled worksheet is opened, there is a chance that problems may be encountered.
As a result, macros from external sources are disabled in Excel because of security concerns.**Enabling Macros into Excel**
When activating macros, the user is primarily responsible for determining the scope of the permissions granted. Partial, full, or nil consent may be granted (no permission).
Excel macros may be activated by following the following steps:

- Click "options" within the File menu.
- You'll find the "trust center settings" option within the Excel options dialogue box.

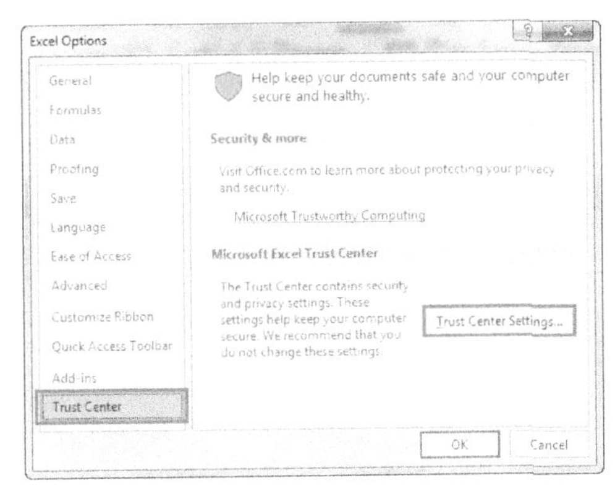

For "macro settings," choose how much access to provide. The user has the choice of selecting among the following alternatives (shown in the following graphic) based on their specific needs:

- No alerts are sent when "Disable all macros without notification" is selected.
- Using the "Disable all macros with notice" command, you may get alerts that all macros in the current file have been deactivated.
- Only digitally signed macros may be used when "Disable all macros excluding digitally signed macros" is selected.
- The command "Enable all macros" allows you to execute whatever macro you choose.
- The specified macro parameters may be applied by clicking "OK."

It's important to note that the option "allow all macros" only appears if the source can be trusted.

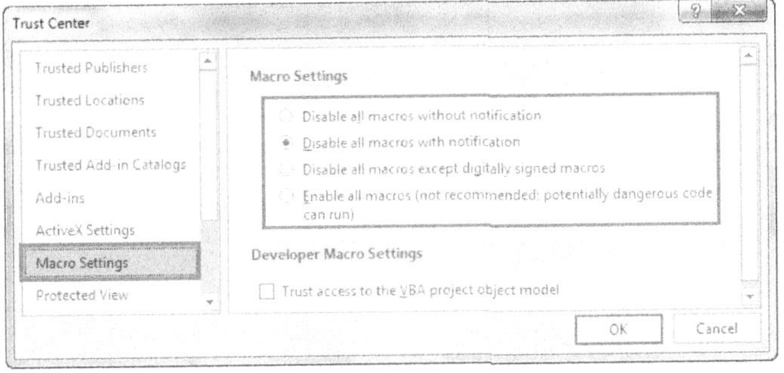

Select "Allow all controls without limits and without prompting" in the "ActiveX settings" option under "trust center settings."

To enable macros, ActiveX controls must be active. The purpose of macros necessitates certain controls.

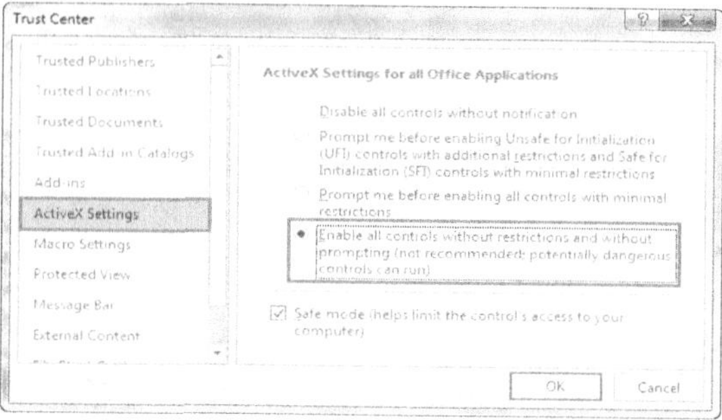

Enabling Macro Files Permanently

To use a VBA or macro content in a file acquired from a reputable source, the macros must be activated in the file. In some situations, the macros are permanently activated to save time.

Excel macros may be permanently enabled by following these steps:

- In the File menu, choose "options."

This option may be found in the "Excel Options" dialogue box under the "trust center" section.

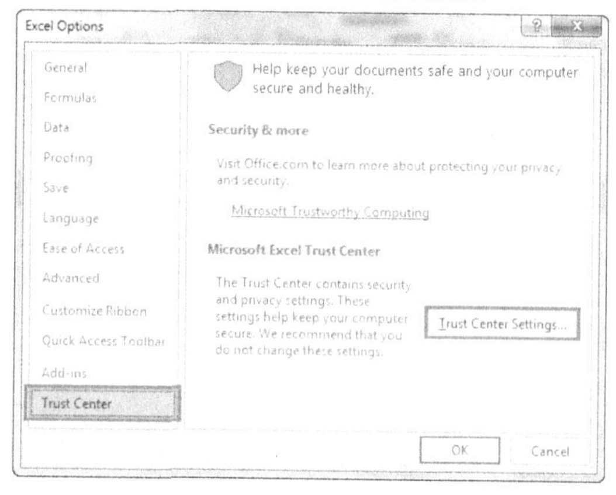

Step 3: Choose "Enable all macros" within the "macro settings" tab. The specified macro parameters may be applied by clicking "OK."

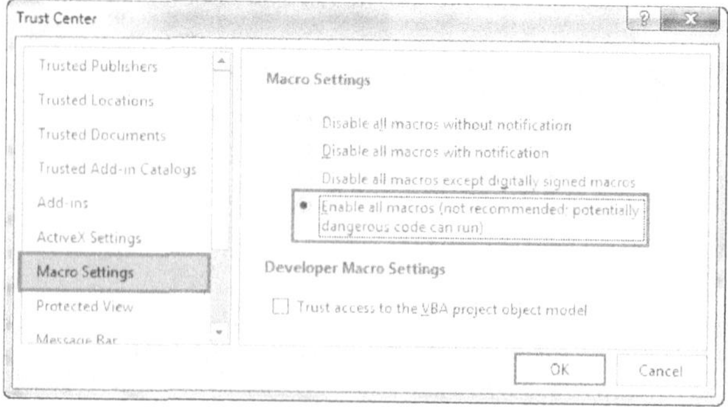

Alerts When Activating Macros

To use macros, the following things must be kept in mind:

- Save the file as a "macro-enabled workbook" if it contains VBA code. The VBA code is not saved when a file is saved with a different extension; hence, macros are not enabled.

- Enabling all macros has the effect of automatically running all macros. Macros from both trustworthy and untrusted sources may be enabled, which is a risk.
- To deactivate all macros with no indication, there is no explanation for why they are not functioning. If you want to see the warnings, pick the "disable all notification macros" option.

Automate Recurring Tasks with VBA

One irritating thing is that very few people know that VBA programming allows you to automate incredibly repetitious processes.

Modifying a code is easy no matter what operation you try to automate. Breaking the code down line-by-line reveals how easy it is.

Here are some examples of how VBA coding might simplify your life.

To utilize VBA code in Excel, ensure that the Developer option is enabled in the application. Make sure you check the "Developer" checkbox in the Ribbon & Toolbar section of Excel's preferences before you can use it. To access Macros, go to the Developer tab and choose it.

While it is possible to record macros, editing the code is required to "generalize" them so that they may be used again, such as 100 times in a row.

In Microsoft Visuals Basic for Applications, you can simply copy & paste the code & save the changed macro by clicking Macros➔ Edit.

How can you Delete any Other Row?

Excel users sit for hours at a time, meticulously erasing every row.

You may erase one row at a time, then hit F4 to delete the next row you'd want to remove.

Excel's F4 shortcut allows you to repeat the previous action you took, but if you want to erase every other row, it will take a long time.

Suppose we wish to remove every single row in Spreadsheet 1000 times. The following is the code that we employ:

```
Sub Delete_Rows()

Dim i As Integer

For i = 1 To 1000
    ActiveCell.Offset(1, 0).Rows("1:1").EntireRow.Select
    Selection.Delete Shift:=xlUp
Next i

End Sub
```

Note that when executing the code, Excel's active cell should be placed in the upper left-hand corner or a single cell just above the cell you wish to begin removing.

Make a backup before using macros since this code will remove every row for the following 1000 times without regard to context.

Let's dissect this. The macro's name is Delete Rows. You create a new integer I and place it in a loop from one to ten thousand.

You remove the row one row underneath our current row in each of these loops.

After the first iteration is completed, it is repeated 999 times. In each cycle, variable I am raised by one step. After the macro is finished, you will have erased every row for thousand rows.

There may be times when this macro isn't enough for your needs. Instead of 1000, enter the desired number.

Instead of deleting every nth row, what if you wanted to do so? ActiveCell needs a "2" instead of a "1". Add the value of each row to offset(1, 0) so that you may remove them one by one.

This situation instructs Excel to shift 1 downward and 0 horizontally. Every third or fourth row may be deleted by replacing the number 1 with 2 or 3.

Notice that the integer is misaligned by one with the nth row you wish to remove. Be cautious. It's important to remember that removing every other row also deletes the row after it.

To see it yourself, create a simple Excel spreadsheet with a few numbers and play about it to notice that every second, third, etc., the number would be deleted.

How can you Delete any Other Column?

Excel's additional columns may now be deleted using the following code:

```
Sub Delete_Columns()

Dim i As Integer

For i = 1 To 20
    ActiveCell.Offset(0, 1).Columns("A:A").EntireColumn.Select
    Selection.Delete Shift:=xlToLeft
Next i

End Sub
```

They're all the same notions. We decided to limit the loop to 20 repetitions this time around. Moving a single column to the right is now possible as opposed to the previous option of (1,0). As a bonus, the loop's final code uses x1ToLeft rather than x1Up.

Remember that you may alter the number of times this code iterates by altering the value of i. In addition, you may eliminate every third or fourth column, for example, by changing the parameter (0, 1) to, say, (0, 2) or (0, 3), respectively.

The number within the parameter is one fewer than the number of columns you would eliminate. 1 will remove all the columns in the second row; 2 will remove all the columns in the third row; and so on.

VBA code can be used to start filling a column using Excel with many values, such as 100,000.

Have you ever had to enter 100000 entries into an Excel spreadsheet?

You can keep counting by dragging a column down, but it takes a long time.

Only if you're filling with an adjoining column that has already been filled may you double-click the bottom-right section of a cell. Make any code that will begin counting from 1,2,3 up to 100,000. While Excel 2007 can only support 64000 rows, newer Excel versions allow you to create as many rows or columns as you like if the computer has enough RAM.

```
Sub Counting()
    ActiveCell.FormulaR1C1 = "1"
    ActiveCell.Offset(1, 0).Range("A1").Select
    ActiveCell.FormulaR1C1 = "2"
    ActiveCell.Offset(-1, 0).Range("A1:A2").Select
    Selection.AutoFill Destination:=ActiveCell.Range("A1:A100000"), Type:
        xlFillDefault
End Sub
```

What is the purpose of this VBA program? As a result, you currently have one column that goes from 1 up to 100000, filling the cells below us with "1," "2," and "3," respectively.

A new number or a different method of counting to 100000 is possible by changing the value you enter. Any desired value can be substituted for the default value of 1000000. To count in multiples of three, simply substitute "3" and "6" for "1" and "2," respectively.

Alternatively, you may write it in a simpler way like this:

```
Sub Counting()

For i = 1 To 100000
    Cells(i, 1).Value = i
Next i

End Sub
```

If you keep looping, the counter will keep going up by one.

To increase by 2s instead of 1s, replace I with I+I * 1; however, remember that this will necessitate a slight modification to the code.

If you want to measure in various steps, you can adjust the number I get multiplied by. To count in multiples of 4, use I + I * 3, for example.

Data Entry Form with VBA

A user form is used to input the data into an Excel database and then updated using VBA code in an Excel workbook. I've constructed a user form that includes the following fields: Id, Name, Email, Phone, Gender, Location, and Remarks. The following chapter displays the user form design. How to automate your project with VBA is explained in full in the following steps.

How do you create an Excel Workbook Data Entry User form? Let's look and find out!

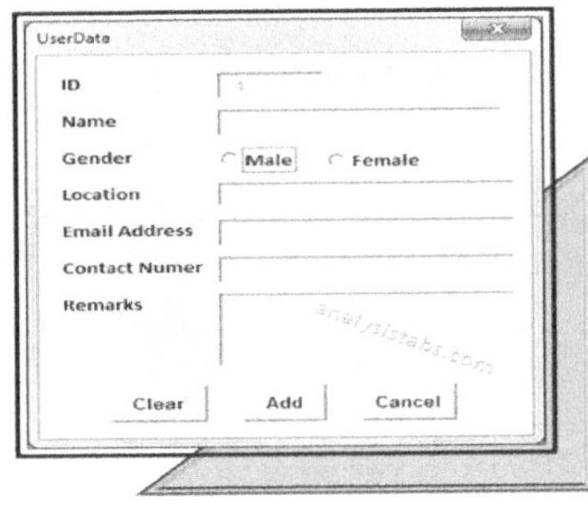

The KEY stages to creating this Data Entry Userform:

- In this example, you'll walk through how to build a data input user form throughout Excel using VBA.
- Let's elaborate on the procedure of creating such a Data entry user form. To write many procedures, you will use the following method.
- You'll employ several variables and objects as part of your routines.
- Step 2: Disable auto-update and events on the screen: Screen flickering and application events are temporarily disabled. In the initial stages of the procedure, you can use this.
- Creating a user form is the third step. Use your insert menu for adding the user form. Use the toolbox to add the necessary controls to the user form.
- Step 4: Develop a field validation procedure: The user must provide us with the correct data format. Your Data Worksheet must be validated before being updated. We begin the procedure when the user clicks on the "Add" button. In other words, whenever a user enters data, you check together all fields (Textboxes & radiobuttons) for validity.
- To find the last row, you need to write a function. A new function (fn LastRow) has been created to discover the last row within the data Worksheet and update data using a user form.
- A mechanism for erasing user form fields should be developed in Step 6. Data Worksheet columns A through G will be cleared using the technique (Clear DataSheet).
- To keep your spreadsheet up to date, follow these Create steps. Add or edit data in the Data Worksheet using a procedure (cmdAdd Click).

- Step 8: Create a procedure to remove the user from memory: CommandCancel Click can be used to quit a user form. To remove the user form, click on the 'cancel' button in the window's top right corner.
- Screen updates and events can now be enabled: Let's restart the application's screen updates and events. After the procedure, you can use this.

Designing Data Entry Userform:

In the next section, you'll examine your Data Entry UserForm project's control properties & values.

Control	Property	Value
UserForm	Name	frmData
	Caption	UserData
Label	Name	lblId
	Caption	ID
Label	Name	lblName
	Caption	Name
Label	Name	lblGender
	Caption	Gender
Label	Name	lblEAddr
	Caption	Email Address
Label	Name	lblCNum
	Caption	Contact Numer
Label	Name	lblRemarks
	Caption	Remarks
OptionButton	Name	obMale
	Caption	Male
	GroupNmae	g1
OptionButton	Name	obFMale
	Caption	FeMale
	GroupNmae	g1
TextBox	Name	txtId
	Enabled	FALSE
TextBox	Name	txtName
TextBox	Name	txtLocation
TextBox	Name	txtEAddr
TextBox	Name	txtCNum
TextBox	Name	txtRemarks
	MultiLine	TRUE
CommandButton	Name	cmdClear
	Caption	Clear
CommandButton	Name	cmdAdd
	Caption	Add
CommandButton	Name	cmdCancel
	Caption	Cancel

This is the Data Entry UserForm style that Was created. The form will take on the appearance shown below if all the control's properties and values are altered in the manner described above.

Code and Explanation:

Initialize global variables that will be used throughout the project.

```
'Variable declaration
Dim txtId, txtName, GenderValue, txtLocation, txtCNum, txtEAddr, txtRemarks
Dim iCnt As Integer
```

Disable the Screen Updating & Disable Events to prevent screen flickering and popups from interrupting your work.

```
With Application
    .ScreenUpdating = False
    .EnableEvents = False
End With
```

Add controls from the Toolbox to the user form to create a user form. Seven Labels, 2 Radio buttons, 6 Textboxes, and 3 CommandButtons will be used in this project. Use the design elements of the Data input user form to develop your user form.

A method for field validation must be developed in Step 4.

Before updating our Data Worksheet, you must ensure that the data is correct. As a result, you must collect data in the right format from the user. When the people click on the "Add" button, you begin the procedure. In other words, whenever a user enters data, you check all fields (radio buttons & Textboxes) for validity.

```
'Variable Declaration
Dim BlnVal As Boolean

 ' Check all the data(except remarks field) has entered are not on the userform
Sub Data_Validation()
      If txtName = "" Then
         MsgBox "Enter Name!", vbInformation, "Name"
         Exit Sub
      ElseIf frmData.obMale = False And frmData.obFMale = False Then
         MsgBox "Select Gender!", vbInformation, "Gender"
         Exit Sub
      ElseIf txtLocation = "" Then
         MsgBox "Enter Location!", vbInformation, "Location"
         Exit Sub
     ElseIf txtEAddr = "" Then
         MsgBox "Enter Address!", vbInformation, "Email Address"
         Exit Sub
     ElseIf txtCNum = "" Then
         MsgBox "Enter Contact Number!", vbInformation, "Contact Number"
         Exit Sub
     Else
         BlnVal = 1
     End If
End Sub
```

The function to discover the final row is the fifth step.

You may get the final row in a Data Worksheet using this function code below. Alternatively, you may supply the name of a sheet into the method as an argument to have it return the last row of that sheet.

```
'In this example we are finding the last Row of specified Sheet
Function fn_LastRow(ByVal Sht As Worksheet)

    Dim lastRow As Long
    lastRow = Sht.Cells.SpecialCells(xlLastCell).Row
    lRow = Sht.Cells.SpecialCells(xlLastCell).Row
    Do While Application.CountA(Sht.Rows(lRow)) = 0 And lRow <> 1
        lRow = lRow - 1
    Loop
    fn_LastRow = lRow
End Function
```

Step 1: Design a mechanism for erasing user form fields.

To clear your Userform fields, use the following code. Such a feature helps when you need to change more than 1 record at a time. The UserForm is ready for new data when you add a new record to a worksheet, then clear the data fields.

```
'Clearing data fields of userform
Private Sub cmdClear_Click()
   Application.ScreenUpdating = False
      txtId.Text = ""
      txtName.Text = ""
      obMale.Value = True
      txtLocation = ""
      txtEAddr = ""
      txtCNum = ""
      txtRemarks = ""
   Application.ScreenUpdating = True
End Sub
```

Step 2: Create a procedure to update data to the Worksheet.

Here is the code to add or update data to the Worksheet.

```
Sub cmdAdd_Click()
    On Error GoTo ErrOccured
    'Boolean Value
    BlnVal = 0

    'Data Validation
    Call Data_Validation

    'Check validation of all fields are completed are not
    If BlnVal = 0 Then Exit Sub

    'TurnOff screen updating
    With Application
        .ScreenUpdating = False
        .EnableEvents = False
    End With

    'Variable declaration
    Dim txtId, txtName, GenderValue, txtLocation, txtCNum, txtEAddr, txtRemarks
    Dim iCnt As Integer

    'find next available row to update data in the data worksheet
    iCnt = fn_LastRow(Sheets("Data")) + 1

    'Find Gender value
    If frmData.obMale = True Then
      GenderValue = "Male"
    Else
      GenderValue = "Female"
    End If

    'Update userform data to the Data Worksheet
    With Sheets("Data")
        .Cells(iCnt, 1) = iCnt - 1
        .Cells(iCnt, 2) = frmData.txtName
        .Cells(iCnt, 3) = GenderValue
        .Cells(iCnt, 4) = frmData.txtLocation.Value
        .Cells(iCnt, 5) = frmData.txtEAddr
        .Cells(iCnt, 6) = frmData.txtCNum
        .Cells(iCnt, 7) = frmData.txtRemarks

        'Diplay headers on the first row of Data Worksheet
        If .Range("A1") = "" Then
            .Cells(1, 1) = "Id"
            .Cells(1, 2) = "Name"
            .Cells(1, 3) = "Gender"
            .Cells(1, 4) = "Location"
            .Cells(1, 5) = "Email Addres"
            .Cells(1, 6) = "Contact Number"
            .Cells(1, 7) = "Remarks"

            'Formatiing Data
            .Columns("A:G").Columns.AutoFit
            .Range("A1:G1").Font.Bold = True
            .Range("A1:G1").LineStyle = xlDash

        End If
    End With

    'Display next available Id number on the Userform
    'Variable declaration
    Dim IdVal As Integer

    'Finding last row in the Data Sheet
    IdVal = fn_LastRow(Sheets("Data"))

    'Update next available id on the userform
    frmData.txtId = IdVal

ErrOccured:
    'TurnOn screen updating
    Application.ScreenUpdating = True
    Application.EnableEvents = True

End Sub
```

A process to empty the user form is needed in step 6.

Here is your code to leave from the user form. You may also click on the upper right corner of a user interface.

```
'Exit from the Userform
Private Sub cmdCancel_Click()
   Unload Me
End Sub
```

Ending the project by enabling or turning on Screen Update & Events.

```
With Application
   .ScreenUpdating = True
   .EnableEvents = True
End With
```

Final VBA's Module Code (Macro):

These instructions are for creating a Data Entry UserForm project, as shown below. Add your following code to a Userform(FrmData) by double-clicking it.

```
'Variable Declaration
Dim BlnVal As Boolean

Private Sub UserForm_Initialize()
   'Variable declaration
   Dim IdVal As Integer

   'Finding last row in the Data Sheet
   IdVal = fn_LastRow(Sheets("Data"))

   'Update next available id on the userform
   frmData.txtId = IdVal
End Sub
Sub cmdAdd_Click()
   On Error GoTo ErrOccured
   'Boolean Value
   BlnVal = 0

   'Data Validation
   Call Data_Validation

   'Check validation of all fields are completed are not
   If BlnVal = 0 Then Exit Sub

   'TurnOff screen updating
   With Application
      .ScreenUpdating = False
      .EnableEvents = False
   End With
```

```
'Variable declaration
Dim txtId, txtName, GenderValue, txtLocation, txtCNum, txtEAddr, txtRemarks
Dim iCnt As Integer

'find next available row to update data in the data worksheet
iCnt = fn_LastRow(Sheets("Data")) + 1

'Find Gender value
If frmData.obMale = True Then
  GenderValue = "Male"
Else
  GenderValue = "Female"
End If

'Update userform data to the Data Worksheet
With Sheets("Data")
   .Cells(iCnt, 1) = iCnt - 1
   .Cells(iCnt, 2) = frmData.txtName
   .Cells(iCnt, 3) = GenderValue
   .Cells(iCnt, 4) = frmData.txtLocation.Value
   .Cells(iCnt, 5) = frmData.txtEAddr
   .Cells(iCnt, 6) = frmData.txtCNum
   .Cells(iCnt, 7) = frmData.txtRemarks


   'Diplay headers on the first row of Data Worksheet
   If .Range("A1") = "" Then
      .Cells(1, 1) = "Id"
      .Cells(1, 2) = "Name"
      .Cells(1, 3) = "Gender"
      .Cells(1, 4) = "Location"
      .Cells(1, 5) = "Email Addres"
      .Cells(1, 6) = "Contact Number"
      .Cells(1, 7) = "Remarks"

      'Formatiing Data
      .Columns("A:G").Columns.AutoFit
      .Range("A1:G1").Font.Bold = True
      .Range("A1:G1").LineStyle = xlDash

   End If
End With
```

```
'Display next available Id number on the Userform
'Variable declaration
    Dim IdVal As Integer

    'Finding last row in the Data Sheet
    IdVal = fn_LastRow(Sheets("Data"))

    'Update next available id on the userform
    frmData.txtId = IdVal
ErrOccured:
    'TurnOn screen updating
    Application.ScreenUpdating = True
    Application .EnableEvents = True

End Sub

'In this example we are finding the last Row of specified Sheet
Function fn_LastRow(ByVal Sht As Worksheet)

    Dim lastRow As Long
    lastRow = Sht.Cells.SpecialCells(xlLastCell).Row
    lRow = Sht.Cells.SpecialCells(xlLastCell).Row
    Do While Application.CountA(Sht.Rows(lRow)) = 0 And lRow <> 1
        lRow = lRow - 1
    Loop
    fn_LastRow = lRow

End Function

'Exit from the Userform
Private Sub cmdCancel_Click()
    Unload Me
End Sub

' Check all the data(except remarks field) has entered are not on the userform
Sub Data_Validation()
    If txtName = "" Then
        MsgBox "Enter Name!", vbInformation, "Name"
        Exit Sub
    ElseIf frmData.obMale = False And frmData.obFMale = False Then
        MsgBox "Select Gender!", vbInformation, "Gender"
        Exit Sub
    ElseIf txtLocation = "" Then
        MsgBox "Enter Location!", vbInformation, "Location"
        Exit Sub
    ElseIf txtEAddr = "" Then
        MsgBox "Enter Address!", vbInformation, "Email Address"
        Exit Sub
    ElseIf txtCNum = "" Then
        MsgBox "Enter Contact Number!", vbInformation, "Contact Number"
        Exit Sub
    Else
        BlnVal = 1
    End If
End Sub
```

```
'Clearing data fields of userform
Private Sub cmdClear_Click()
  Application.ScreenUpdating = False
    txtId.Text = ""
    txtName.Text = ""
    obMale.Value = True
    txtLocation = ""
    txtEAddr = ""
    txtCNum = ""
    txtRemarks = ""
  Application.ScreenUpdating = True
End Sub
```

Add the below code for your newly created module, which you can access using the Insert Module menu item.

```
'Here is the code to Show Data Entry UserForm
Sub Oval2_Click()
  frmData.Show
End Sub
'To clear data columns data on Data Worksheet
Sub Clear_DataSheet()
  Sheets("Data").Columns("A:G").Clear
End Sub
```

Worksheet Data Entry UserForm Displayed:
A 'Data Entry User Form' may be created following these steps.

- Selecting insert from the drawings group in the insert menu may insert whatever form you choose.
- It's simple: Right-click a shape and choose "assign macro."
- Click OK after selecting 'Oval2 Click' from the list of potential macro names.
- Navigate now to the Developers section.
- The Controls group should be unchecked to disable Design Mode.
- Return to the shape and choose your Data Entry UserForm by clicking the produced shape in the current Workbook's Worksheet.

Instructions for Executing the Procedure:

You may examine the code in the attached file and then run it. Using the code to build a new workbook and then testing it is also possible. To put the code above into action, follow these steps.

- Press Alt+F11 to bring up the VBA Editor window.
- Using the Insert menu, create a new module.
- Paste the given instructions into the new module.
- You may access your Data Entry UserForm by pressing the F5 key on your keyboard or selecting 'Show Data Entry UserForm!' from the Data Worksheet.

Conclusion

Excel is the industry standard for database programs often used for data input, budgeting, and money management. Like every other piece of software, Microsoft Excel has its flaws. Once you've purchased a certificate, consider the upsides and downsides to determine if Excel is the right choice for you. One of the most fundamental uses for MS Excel is for data organizing and collecting.

Information may be organized by kind of data and then quickly sorted into tidy columns and rows. Although it may be difficult to observe a large amount of data in its raw form, the program's resources allow users to create presentations in which the data is evaluated and added to graphs, charts, or tables for better visualization and interpretation.

Excel's ability to organize huge amounts of data into logical, well-organized spreadsheets and graphs is one of its most crucial characteristics. Data that has been organized makes it much easier to read and analyze, especially when it is utilized to create charts and other visual data interpretations.

Excel does calculations on numbers in a fraction of a second, making it far easier to perform bulk computations using Excel than using a calculator. Depending on one's familiarity with Excel and level of expertise working with the program, formulas and computations may be utilized to efficiently calculate simple and complex equations by using huge volumes of data. There are several entry-level positions for which excel is a necessary ability, like Personal Assistant, Admin Aide, Bookkeeper/Project Manager, and so on. You should take Excel if you want a better chance of getting a job; thus, it makes sense to do so!

Excel is a must-have tool for every company, and it's no surprise it's so popular. You will never run out of things to learn with Excel, no matter how much experience you have. Excel will never tire you, and you'll be thrilled by its strength and what you discover about it regularly.

Speeding efficiency and making employees more effective when dealing with big data and computations are critical to Excel's success. Excel's more advanced functions help you finish your tasks and analyze your data more rapidly when you understand the program better. Makes it possible to keep teammates updated on data, which may help simplify workflows.

Advanced Excel skills will also help you speed up your computations. Repetitive computations consume a lot of time, particularly when you double-check the work. Complex computations may be performed using Excel's more powerful features. Using computer software to execute the computations saves more time for other duties and ensures that you get correct data the first time, making it a win-win situation for everyone involved.

The advantages do not stop here; begin using Microsoft Excel and educate yourself on your own.

Microsoft Word

Introduction

In an era where digital documentation has become a cornerstone of personal and professional communication, mastering word processing software is more than just a desirable skill—it's a necessity. Microsoft Word, a flagship product of Microsoft Office Suite, stands as one of the most popular and powerful word-processing tools in the market. Its intuitive interface, combined with a wide array of features, makes it an indispensable tool for individuals and businesses alike.

This comprehensive guide aims to traverse the expansive landscape of Microsoft Word, catering to both novices finding their footing and seasoned users aspiring to attain a deeper understanding of this robust application. From the rudimentary tasks of creating, saving, and navigating documents to the more nuanced functionalities like formatting, referencing, and collaborating in real-time, this book aims to provide a well-rounded insight into what makes Microsoft Word a go-to choice for many.

The sequential chapters are meticulously crafted to ensure a gradual and coherent learning curve. We start with the basics, acquaint you with the installation process and setting preferences, and give a tour of the Word interface. As we progress, the chapters delve into more complex topics, including advanced text tools, document layout customization, working with visual elements, and mastering long documents. Each chapter not only elucidates the functionalities but also illustrates how to leverage these features to improve your documentation efforts, thereby going beyond mere feature location.

Furthermore, this guide aims to address common, specific tasks users often wish to accomplish, coupled with best practices to optimize their workflow. Whether it's creating a structured document, inserting images, or collaborating with others, you'll find step-by-step instructions to navigate these tasks proficiently.

While screenshots have been included to provide a clearer understanding of complex topics, the emphasis remains on explaining the practical application of features, ensuring you can effectively apply what you learn in real-world scenarios.

With a blend of fundamental principles and advanced techniques, this book is geared towards empowering you to use Microsoft Word with confidence and competence, irrespective of your level of expertise. As you turn the pages, you'll uncover the multitude of features that make Microsoft Word a remarkable word-processing tool and, hopefully, discover new ways to make it an asset in your personal or professional ventures.

Chapter 1:Getting Started With Words

Embarking on the journey of discovering Microsoft Word is akin to unlocking a new world of digital documentation possibilities. Whether you are a student typing your thesis, a professional writing technical reports, or an author breathing life into a story, Microsoft Word is your companion.

This chapter is your doorstep to becoming adept at this indispensable tool, ensuring your footing is firm as you delve deeper into the various features of **MICROSOFT WORD.** The sections that follow will guide you through the initial steps of installing Microsoft Word, acquainting you with the interface, and familiarizing you with key terminology that will become part of your daily lexicon as you navigate through Microsoft Word.

This book covers various versions of Microsoft Word, including Office 365, Word 2016, Word 2019, and Word 2021, making sure many different users find it useful in the pages that follow.

Getting Microsoft Word

Stepping into Microsoft Word requires getting the right version of the software. Today, Microsoft Office 365 offers different plans suited for students, professionals, or home users. These plans give you access to Word and other helpful tools like PowerPoint and Excel. Some plans even include extra services like Teams and SharePoint.

To get Microsoft Office and make sure it's a good deal, I've gathered a list of places where you can find some attractive offers.

Free Access to Microsoft Word

For nearly three decades, Microsoft Office has been synonymous with professional document processing. Although traditionally a paid software, the advent of Microsoft 365 brought forth a subscription model. However, fret not, for there are options to access Microsoft Word and other Office applications for free, albeit with some limitations.

Microsoft 365 offers a variety of apps like Word, Excel, and PowerPoint, which are essential for different tasks. You can try these apps for free or get them through educational offers. Let's discuss how you can access Microsoft 365 apps.

Free Trial

Microsoft 365 gives you a chance to try out their apps for a month without any cost. However, you'll need to provide your credit card information and remember to cancel the subscription before the trial ends to avoid charges for a full year's subscription.

Educational Access

If you're a student or educator, you can access Microsoft 365 Education for free using your school email address. This offer includes Word, Excel, PowerPoint, OneNote, and additional classroom tools. Even after graduating, you can continue to use these apps at a discounted rate as long as you have a valid school email address.

Online Access

You can use Microsoft Office apps like Word, Excel, and PowerPoint for free online without any installation. Just visit Microsoft365.com, and you can edit and share documents using these apps on your devices through a web browser.

Limitations For Free Versions

The free versions of these apps offer basic functionalities. If you require more extensive functionality, you might want to think about purchasing a subscription plan. Also, the free versions are accessible only online, so you'll need a stable internet connection to use them.

There are different ways to access Microsoft 365 apps either for free or at a discounted rate, especially if you are associated with an educational institution. This makes it flexible for various users to make the most out of these essential productivity tools.

Installing and Setting Preferences

Before you begin the installation process, ensure you've selected the right version of Microsoft Word or Microsoft 365 (the suite that includes Word) compatible with your operating system (OS). Go to the official Microsoft website to buy and download the program right away.

Compatibility Check

Check the system requirements on the Microsoft website to ensure your computer is compatible with the software version you intend to install.

Installation

For Windows:

1. Go to the Microsoft 365 homepage [https://www.microsoft.com/en-us/microsoft-365/buy/microsoft-365], sign in with your Microsoft account, and download the installer.
2. Sign in and follow the on-screen instructions to download the installer.
3. Locate and run the installer, then follow the prompts to complete the installation.

For Mac:

1. Follow steps 1 and 2 above.
2. Once downloaded, locate and double-click the Microsoft Office installer.pkg file.
3. Follow the on-screen instructions, entering your Mac login password when prompted to complete the installation.
4. License Agreement: Review the software license agreement and click "Continue". Select "Agree" to agree to the terms of the software license agreement.
5. Installation Preferences: Choose how you want to install Microsoft 365 and click "Continue." You can review the disk space requirements or change your install location if necessary.
6. Install: Click "Install". If prompted, click "Install Software" after entering your Mac login password.
7. Completion: Once the installation is complete, click "Close" to finish the installation process.

Setting Up

Upon successful installation, launch Microsoft Word. You'll be prompted to sign in with your Microsoft account. After signing in, you can now set your preferences.

1. Navigating to Preferences: Click on "Word" on the menu bar at the top, then select "Preferences."
2. General Preferences: Here, you can set your User Information, customize the Ribbon and Quick Access Toolbar, and more.
3. Proofing Options: Set your spelling and grammar-checking preferences.
4. Save Options: Set auto-recovery intervals, default file locations, and other save options to safeguard your work.

This comprehensive setup ensures that Microsoft Word is tailored to your liking, making your document creation process smooth and personalized.

The Word Interface: A Tour

Starting with Microsoft Word is easy. All it takes is launching the software. When you do, you'll see the Start Screen. This is where you can pick what you want to do next. You can start a new document, choose a template if you need a specific layout, or open a file you worked on before.

To begin writing, just select a blank document. This will take you to the main part of Word, where all the tools and features are. It's designed to be easy to use, so you can focus on writing and getting your ideas down.

Exploring the Word Environment

The modern iterations of Word, including the versions spanning from Word 2016 to the recent Word 2023, feature a sleek and functional interface comprising of the Ribbon, the Quick Access Toolbar, and the Backstage view, among other elements.

The Ribbon

The Ribbon in Microsoft Word is like a control center where you'll find all the tools you need to work on your document. It's placed at the top of the screen for easy access.

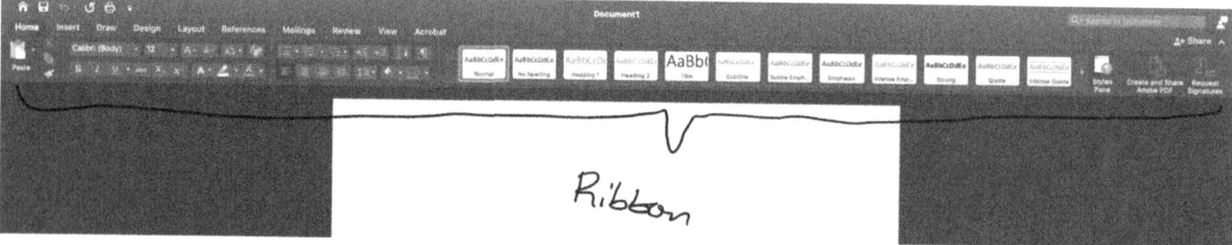

Here's a breakdown of what you'll find in the Ribbon:

1. **Tabs:** There are several tabs within the Ribbon, including Home, Insert, Design, and Layout. Every tab focuses on a distinct component of document editing or formatting.
2. **Groups:** Under each tab, there are groups of related tools. For example, under the Home tab, you'll find groups like Font, Paragraph, and Styles, which help with text formatting.
3. **Commands:** Inside these groups are the actual tools or commands you'll use, like Bold, Italic, Align Left, and others for text formatting.
4. **Dialog Box Launcher:** Some groups have a small arrow in the bottom-right corner called the Dialog Box Launcher. If you click it, a box with more options will open up for more detailed adjustments.
5. **Contextual Tabs:** Sometimes, extra tabs will appear on the Ribbon depending on what you're doing. For example, if you insert a table, you'll see extra tabs with tools just for working with tables.
6. **Quick Access Toolbar:** Although not part of the Ribbon, right above it is the Quick Access Toolbar,

where you can keep shortcuts to tools you use often.

The Ribbon is designed to make it easy to find and use all the different tools Word offers. It's a smart way of keeping the screen uncluttered while still having everything you need close by.

Customizing the Ribbon

For a more personalized interface, Word allows you to customize the Ribbon. You can add, remove, or rearrange tabs and commands to better align with your workflow. By right-clicking on the Ribbon and selecting '**Customize the Ribbon**,' a dialog box opens up where you can make your desired modifications, facilitating a more convenient and efficient work environment.

Quick Access Toolbar

Above the Ribbon lies the Quick Access Toolbar (QAT), a space dedicated to frequently used commands. Regardless of the tab currently displayed on the Ribbon, the commands on the QAT remain accessible, saving you time and effort. You can easily customize the QAT by adding buttons representing commands of your choice.

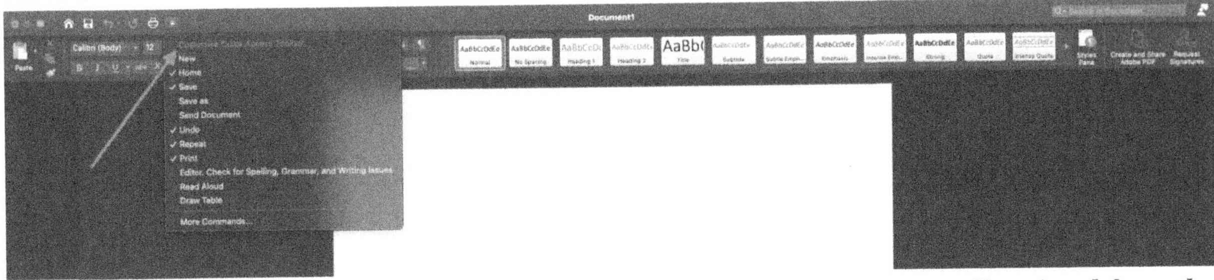

To modify the QAT, right-click on it, select '**Customize Quick Access Toolbar**,' and from the dialog box, choose the commands you wish to add or remove.

Backstage View

Clicking on the '**File**' tab on the Ribbon sends you to the Backstage view—a hub for managing your documents. Here, you can save, open, print, and share documents or explore Microsoft Word's settings to tweak the software to your liking.

Understanding Document Views and Zooming Options

Microsoft Word offers a number of viewing options to suit your needs better. Whether it's the default Print Layout view, the Web Layout view for online publishing, or the Read Mode for distraction-free reading, switching between these views is straightforward.

Additionally, the zoom control slider at the bottom-right corner of the Word window allows you to zoom in and out of your document. This enhances readability and user experience.

As you play around with the Word interface, getting to know its cool features and customization tricks, you'll find yourself getting the hang of this software.

Key Terminologies

As we dive deeper into Microsoft Word, it's important to get familiar with the language used to describe various features and functionalities of the software. Like learning the basics of any new language, getting accustomed to Microsoft Word's terminology will empower you to use the software more effectively and make the most out of its vast capabilities.

In this section, we'll crack some common and perhaps some not-so-common terms you might encounter while navigating through Microsoft Word. From the very basics, like what a '**Document**' or '**Ribbon**' is, to more advanced and lesser-known terms like '**Kerning**' or '**Gutter Margin**,' we'll shed light on these terminologies to ensure you have a clear understanding as you explore Microsoft Word.

This will not only make it easier for you to follow along with the rest of the guide but also empower you to communicate more effectively with others when discussing Word-related tasks or issues.

So, let's get started and demystify these terms!

Common Terminologies

1. **Document:** A file created within Microsoft Word containing text, images, tables, and other elements.
2. **Ribbon:** The tabbed toolbar area is present in Microsoft Word, housing groups of commands and tools.
3. Quick Access Toolbar: A customizable toolbar with a set of commands that is not dependent on the ribbon tab that is being displayed.
4. **Backstage View:** Accessed by clicking on the 'File' tab, it houses commands for managing documents, including saving, opening, and printing.
5. **Cursor/Insertion Point:** The position of the following characters that you will input on the keyboard.
6. **Spell Check:** A feature that checks the spelling of words.
7. **Grammar Check:** A tool for checking the grammar of the text.
8. **Thesaurus:** A tool to look up synonyms and antonyms of a word.
9. **Clipboard:** A temporary storage area for text or objects that you cut or copy.
10. **Macro:** A set of commands and instructions combined into a single command to do a task automatically.
11. **Template:** A pre-designed document that you can use to quickly generate a new document.

Uncommon Terminologies

1. Widow/Orphan Control: A feature that keeps single paragraph lines from showing on a different page than the rest of the paragraph.
2. Gutter Margin: While printing, extra space is added to the binding side of a page.
3. Kerning: The modification of the space between specific letters in a word.
4. Leading: The space between lines of text.
5. Drop Cap: A large capital letter at the beginning of a paragraph, typically used in publishing.
6. Endnote: A note placed at the end of a document or section, usually used for citation purposes.
7. Field: A placeholder for potentially changing data, such as dates or page numbers.
8. Mail Merge: A tool for generating multiple documents, like letters or labels, from a single template and a structured data source.
9. Watermark: A faint design created in certain papers during manufacturing that can be seen when held up to the light and usually identifies the manufacturer.
10. Workgroup: A group of individuals working on a project that requires close communication and multiple documents sharing and editing.

These terms cover both the basic and more nuanced aspects of Microsoft Word. Understanding them will provide a solid foundation for mastering the software and enhancing your word-processing skills.

Chapter 2: Essential Document Tasks

Understanding the essentials of document management is pivotal for anyone keen on mastering Microsoft Word. These fundamental tasks serve as the foundation for all subsequent functionalities. They include creating, saving, and opening documents, as well as navigating and viewing documents. The mastery of these tasks facilitates a seamless experience as you draft, edit, and share your documents.

Creating, Saving, and Opening Documents

Starting a new project in Microsoft Word begins with creating a new document. This document can either be blank or created from a template. When you launch Word, the Start Screen appears, presenting you with these options.

Choosing '**Blank Documen**t' will lead you to a new workspace where you can begin typing immediately. On the other hand, selecting a template allows you to work with a pre-structured document, which could be beneficial for specific tasks or projects.

Templates provide a predefined layout and formatting, saving time and ensuring consistency across similar documents.

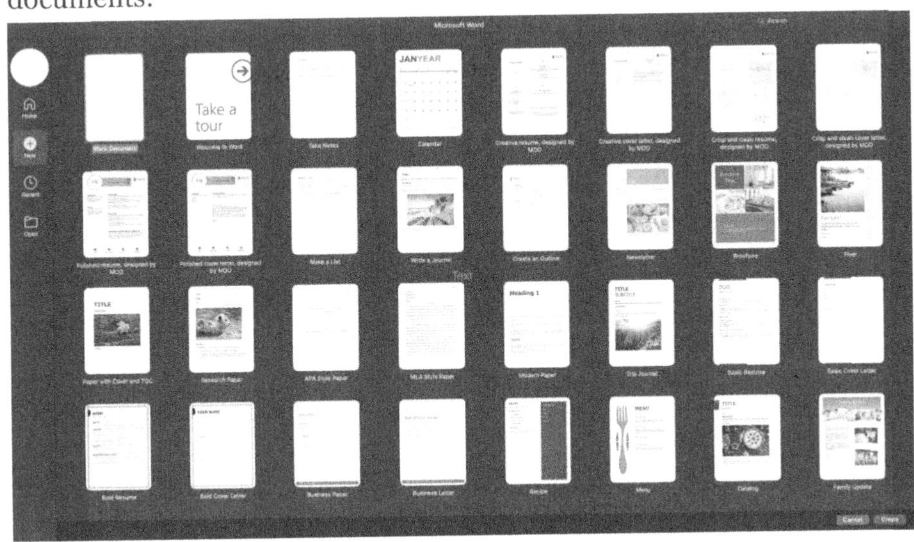

Saving your work frequently is a smart practice to avoid losing your progress due to unforeseen events like a computer crash or power outage. To save a document for the first time, you would navigate to the **'File'** tab, click **'Save As**,' and then browse to your preferred location to save the document.

In subsequent saves, you can simply click **'Save'** to update the document. Word also provides an AutoSave feature, which is available when working with OneDrive or SharePoint. This feature automatically saves your document as you work, ensuring that the latest version of your document is always saved online.

Revisiting a document in Word is a simple process. You would navigate to the **'File'** tab, select **'Open**,' and then browse to the location of your document to open it. Word also maintains a list of recently accessed documents, which can be found under the **'Open'** tab. This list provides a quick way to reopen documents you've worked on recently without having to browse through your file directories.

Additionally, if you've saved your document to OneDrive or SharePoint, you can access it from any device, provided you're logged into your Microsoft account.

Navigating and Viewing Documents

Efficiently moving through and viewing your document is essential to a smooth and productive workflow. Microsoft Word, being a robust word processing tool, is equipped with various features and tools designed to help in document navigation and viewing.

Here, we will take a look at some of these critical features, which not only improve your navigation experience but also provide various viewing options to cater to different tasks and preferences.

Navigation Pane

The Navigation Pane is a handy feature that facilitates quick movement through your document, especially when working with long or complex documents. Formerly known as the Document Map in Word 2007, the Navigation Pane has evolved to become a central navigation hub within Word.

If you have applied heading styles to your document, these headings will appear in the Navigation Pane, allowing for direct access to different sections of your document. By simply clicking on a heading within the pane, you can instantly jump to that section in your document.

This feature is particularly useful when working with documents that have a well-defined structure with multiple headings and subheadings.

Navigation Shortcuts

Word is equipped with a variety of keyboard shortcuts designed to speed up document navigation. For instance, pressing **Ctrl+F** opens the Navigation Pane, which also houses a search functionality allowing you to quickly find and jump to specific text within your document.

Other useful navigation shortcuts include **Ctrl+G**, which opens the '**Go To**' dialog, allowing you to jump to a specific page, section, or line, and **Ctrl+Z** and **Ctrl+Y**, which undo and redo the last action, respectively.

Document Views

Depending on the task at hand, Word offers different document views to provide the most conducive environment for your work. The Print Layout view, for instance, provides a realistic preview of how your document will appear when printed, including all formatting, columns, and page breaks.

On the other hand, the Web Layout view displays your document as it would appear on a webpage, which is useful when preparing documents for online publishing.

Other viewing options include Draft View, which presents a simplified layout for editing text, and Outline View, which shows the document outline structure, allowing for easy organization and reorganization of content.

Zooming

Sometimes, being able to zoom in for a closer look at text or images or zoom out for a broader view of the document layout can be invaluable. The zoom control slider located at the bottom-right corner of the Word window allows for easy zoom adjustments.

Alternatively, you can use the View tab on the Ribbon to specify a particular zoom level or choose a zoom option, such as Page Width or Text Width, that automatically adjusts the zoom level based on the window size.

Keyboard Shortcuts for Navigation

Keyboard shortcuts are a quick way to navigate through your document. They provide a means to move from page to page, line to line, or even character to character with speed and precision. For instance, using the arrow keys allows for character-by-character or line-by-line navigation, while **Ctrl+arrow** keys enable word-by-word or paragraph-by-paragraph movement.

Page Up and Page Down keys facilitate moving a screen up or down, and **Ctrl+Home** and **Ctrl+End** provide quick access to the beginning and end of the document, respectively.

The proficiency in navigating and viewing your document significantly impacts the ease with which you can work within Microsoft Word. Being able to quickly jump to different sections, view your document in various layouts, or swiftly find specific text improves your efficiency and the overall quality of your work.

As you become accustomed to these essential document tasks, you lay a solid foundation for a proficient use of Microsoft Word, opening doors to explore the plethora of features it offers.

Chapter 3: Working with Text

Unleashing the full potential of Microsoft Word begins with mastering the art of working with text. As a powerful word processor, Microsoft Word offers an array of tools and features designed to help you input, edit, and manipulate text effortlessly.

In this chapter, you will learn about the various functionalities that will help you work with texts better in Microsoft Word.

Inserting Text in Microsoft Word

Inserting text in a new document in Microsoft Word is a straightforward process. Here's how you can go about it:

- Launch Microsoft Word from the Start menu by locating and clicking on its icon.
- Click on the option for a blank document.
- Upon opening, In the text space beneath the ribbon, you'll see a blinking cursor or insertion point, ready for text input.
- Start typing, and the words will appear in the text area.
- To change the position of the blinking cursor or insertion point, use the Tab, Enter, or spacebar keys.

Deleting Text in Word

Deleting text in Word is simple and can be done in various ways:

- Position the cursor to the left of the text you wish to delete, then press the Delete key.
- Position the cursor next to the text, then hit the Backspace key.
- Select the text to delete and type over it with new text, or press either the Backspace or Delete keys.

Selecting Text in Microsoft Word

Selecting text is easy. Follow these steps:

- Place the cursor next to the desired text, left-click and hold, then drag it over the text.
- Release the mouse button to complete the selection.

Handy Shortcuts:

- Double-click within a word to select it.
- Triple-click within a paragraph to select it.
- To select the entire document, go to the Home tab, click on Select in the Editing group, and choose Select All, or press CTRL + A.

Highlighting Text in Microsoft Word

Highlighting text is a powerful tool for drawing attention to essential information. Here's how to go about it:

- Select the text you want to highlight.
- Go to the Home tab.
- In the Font group, choose the Text Highlight Color option.
- Choose the highlight color you want to use from the drop-down menu.

Changing Font Color in Microsoft Word

Changing the color of your text can help differentiate or emphasize text in your document. Follow these steps:

- Select the text whose color you wish to change.
- Go to the Home tab.
- In the Font group, click on the Font Color button (represented by an underlined "A").

- Pick a color from the theme colors and standard colors, or click on More Colors if you need a custom color.

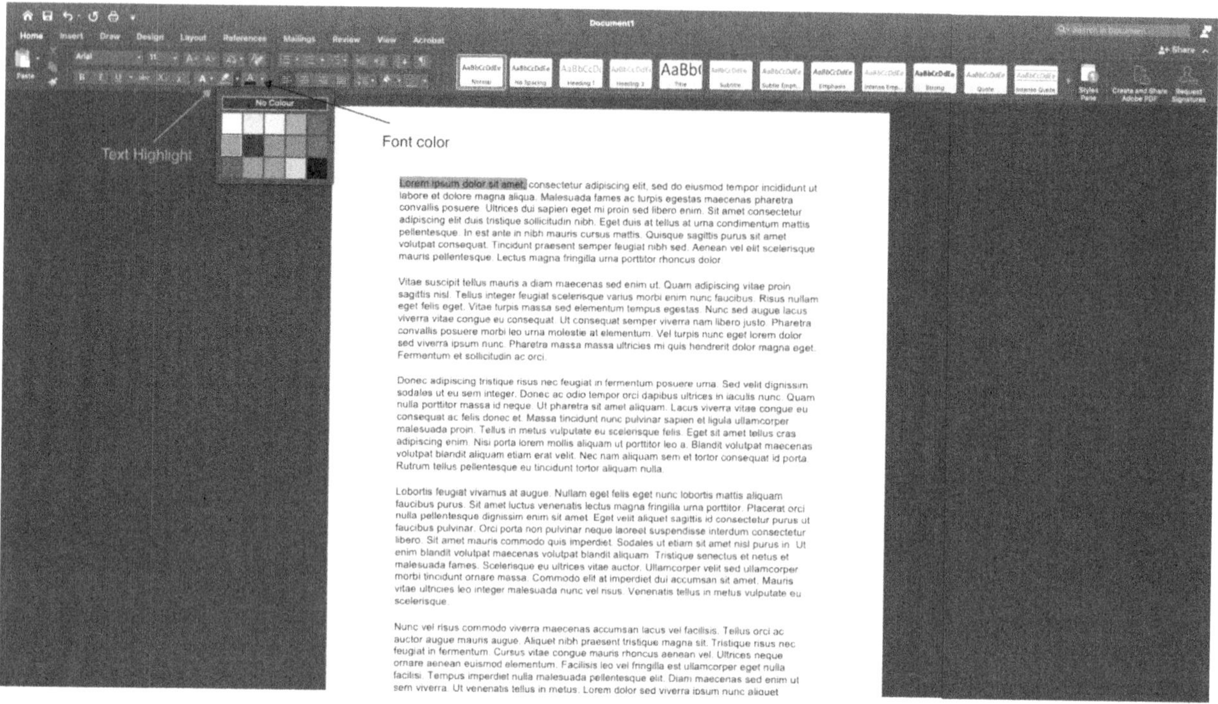

Adjusting Font Size in Microsoft Word

Adjusting the font size is crucial for readability and aesthetics. Here's how to go about it:

- Select the text you want to resize.
- Go to the Home tab.
- In the Font group, use the Font Size drop-down menu to select a new size, type the size you want, and press Enter.

Copying and Pasting Text in Microsoft Word

Copying and pasting text is made easy with these steps:

Option 1:

- Select the desired text.
- Go to the Home tab and click on the Copy command.
- Position the cursor at the desired paste location.
- On the Home tab, select the Paste command.

Option 2:

- Select the text you want to copy.
- Right-click the mouse while the cursor is over the selected text and choose "Copy."
- Position the cursor where you want to paste the copied text.
- Right-click the mouse again and select the "Paste" option.

Saving Your Document in Microsoft Word

Saving your document is essential for future reference and modifications. Microsoft Word provides two main options: "Save" and "Save As."

Using the "Save" Option

"Save" allows you to save changes to an already saved document.

- Click on the "File" tab in the upper left corner of the screen.

- Select "Save" from the menu.

If it's a new document, you will be prompted to select the document's location and name via the "Save As" dialogue box.

Using the "Save As" Option

"Save As" allows you to save a copy of your document with a different name, location, or file format.

- Click on the "File" tab in the upper left corner of the screen.
- Select "Save As" from the menu.
- Choose the place where you wish to save the document.
- In the "File name" field, enter the desired name for your document.
- Choose the relevant file format from the drop-down option (e.g., .txt, .pdf, or .docx).
- Click the "Save" button.

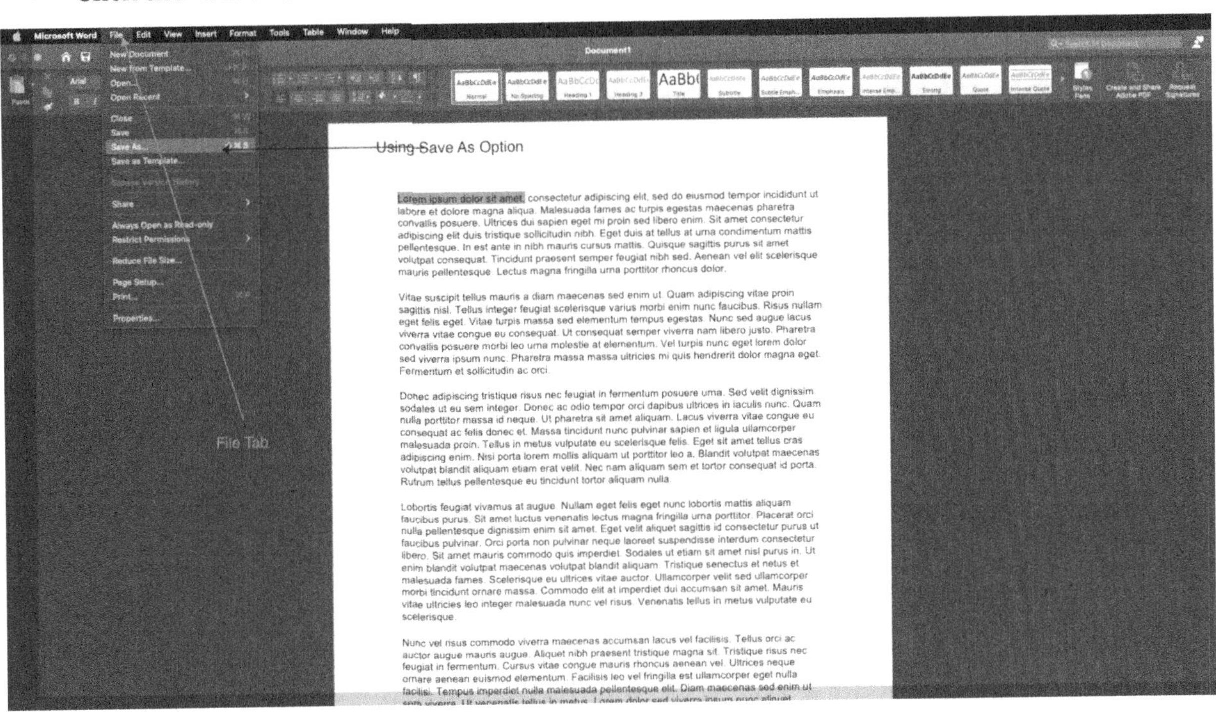

Using the Shortcut Option

To save a document quickly, press the Ctrl and S keys together. This will open the 'Save As' dialog box, allowing you to name your document and choose where to save it.

Correcting Errors in Microsoft Word

Word provides real-time feedback on grammatical, spelling, and contextual errors in your document with different types of underlines: green for grammar, red for spelling, and blue for contextual.

To correct errors, follow these steps:

- Hover your cursor over the text you want to correct.
- Right-click your mouse.
- A list of suggestions will be displayed.
- Select the correct word by clicking on it.

Checking the Word Count in a Word Document

Word automatically tracks your word and page count, displaying the information on the status bar. Here's how to check your word count:

- Open the document and go to the bottom-left corner for the total number of pages and word count.
- To find out the word count of a given paragraph or line, select it, and Word will reveal the word count

of that paragraph or line as well as the total word count.

Formatting Text in Microsoft Word

Formatting text involves changing its appearance, alignment, indentations, and spacing. You can easily format text using the tools available under the Home tab in the ribbon. Use the Font group for changing the font type, size, color, and other character formatting.

Use the Paragraph group for paragraph formatting like alignment, line spacing, and indentations.

Manually Adding Page Breaks in MS Word

To start a new page, you can either rely on automatic page breaks or manually insert one.

- Set your cursor to the point where you want the current page to finish and the new one to begin.
- Navigate to the "Insert" tab.
- Select "Page Break."

Deleting a Page Break from a Word Document

To remove a page break, follow these steps:

- Locate the Paragraph group in the Home tab.
- Click on the Show/Hide button to display every formatting mark, including page breaks.
- Double-click on the desired page break to select it.
- Push the Delete key on your keyboard to remove the page break.

Chapter 4: Basic Text Formatting

Formatting text might seem tedious, but it's crucial for making nice-looking documents. Microsoft Word has several ways to format text that help you organize things and make it easier to read.

In this chapter, we'll learn about fonts, paragraph alignment, spacing between lines and paragraphs, and lists with bullets and numbers.

Fonts are a big deal because they set the mood and make text easier to read. Getting your paragraphs lined up neatly and with the correct spacing keeps things structured so readers can understand what they are reading. Lists with bullets or numbers help break down complicated chunks of text into bite-sized pieces.

In this chapter, we will take a look at different font styles in Microsoft Word, how paragraphs can be aligned and spaced, and when to use lists. These basic parts of text formatting lay the groundwork for more advanced things later, so you can make pro-looking docs that look good.

By mixing theory and hands-on tips, the goal here is to give you a solid base in Microsoft Word's text formatting tools, and this will set you up for diving into the more complex formatting things down the road.

Fonts, Sizes, and Attributes

Fonts are important. They're the characters - letters, numbers, symbols - styled and sized differently. Your choice of font will change how readable your text is and what kind of feel it gives off.

Serif fonts like Times New Roman are mostly categorized as formal or traditional and suitable for professional or academic texts.

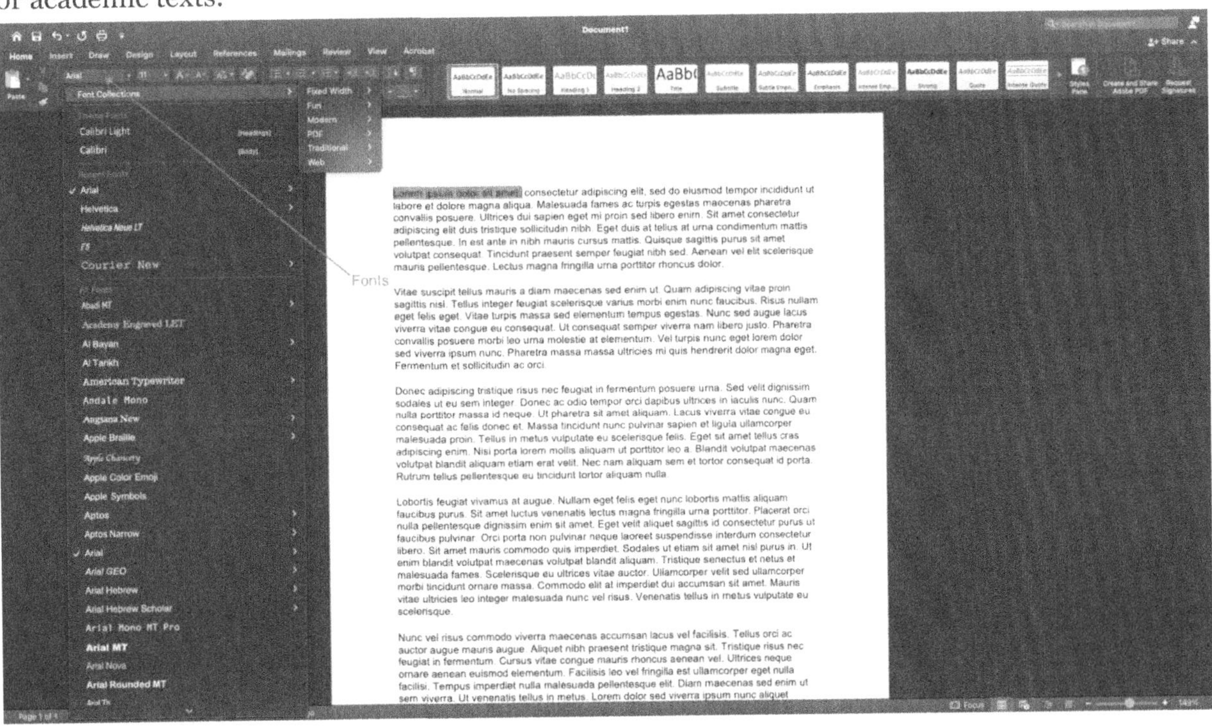

Types of Fonts

The primary font types are Serif, Sans-serif, Script, and Decorative.

- To aid in letter identification and the flow of horizontal reading, serif fonts contain tiny lines or accents at the ends of each character.
- Sans-serif fonts lack these embellishments, offering a clean, modern appearance.
- Script fonts mimic handwriting or calligraphy, suitable for invitations or artistic texts.
- Due to their strong visual impact, decorative fonts with unique characteristics are reserved for special

occasions or headings.

Font Families: Common font families like Times New Roman, Arial, and Courier New provide a range of styles and weights, ensuring consistency and versatility across your text.

Changing Font Type

- Navigate to the Home tab on the Ribbon.
- To access a list of available fonts, click the font drop-down menu in the Font group.
- Scroll through and select the desired font. Your text will change accordingly.

Adjusting Font Size

- Under the Home tab in the Font group, you'll find the Font Size box.
- Type the desired size, or use the drop-down menu to select a size.
- Alternatively, use the Increase Font Size or Decrease Font Size buttons for incremental adjustments.

Text Attributes

- Enhance text by applying attributes like Bold, Italic, or Underline to emphasize or differentiate text.
- Use Strikethrough to indicate removed text, Superscript for exponentials or references, and Subscript for chemical formulas or footnotes.
- Explore Text Effects and Typography options for a creative touch. Apply shadows, reflections, ligatures, stylistic sets, or other enhancements to add visual interest and improve aesthetics.

These attributes and font options in Microsoft Word allow for a plethora of formatting possibilities, enabling you to convey information effectively and aesthetically.

Paragraph Alignment and Spacing

Alignment determines the appearance and orientation of the text in your document. Microsoft Word offers four types of alignment:

1. **Left Alignment (Ctrl + L):** Aligns the text along the left margin, and it's the standard for most document types.
2. **Center Alignment (Ctrl + E):** Centers text in between the margins is often used for titles, headings, or special document sections.
3. **Right Alignment (Ctrl + R):** Aligns the text along the right margin, used in certain formal documents like cover letters for contact information.
4. **Justify Alignment (Ctrl + J):** Spreads the text across the width of the column, creating a clean, book-like appearance.

To change paragraph alignment:

- Navigate to the Home tab.
- Locate the Paragraph group.
- Click on the desired alignment option.

Line and Paragraph Spacing

Spacing is crucial for readability and aesthetics. Word allows you to adjust both line spacing and paragraph spacing.

1. Line Spacing: The vertical separation of text lines.

- **Single (1.0):** Standard spacing.
- **1.5 Lines:** One and a half times single spacing.
- **Double (2.0):** Twice the standard spacing.

2. Paragraph Spacing: The vertical space before and after paragraphs.

- Adjust by inputting the desired point size or using the up/down arrows.

To adjust spacing:

- Right-click within the paragraph.
- Select Paragraph to open the Paragraph dialog box.
- Under Spacing, adjust as needed and click OK.

Indentation

Indentation sets the margin for paragraphs, distinguishing them from other text blocks. There are three types of indents:

- **First Line Indent:** The first line of the paragraph is the only one that is indented.
- **Hanging Indent:** Except for the first, every line is indented.
- **Left/Right Indent:** The whole paragraph is moved either to the left or to the right.

To adjust indentation:

- Use the Indent markers on the ruler.
- Or, right-click, select Paragraph, and adjust under Indentation.

Using Lists: Bullets and Numbering

Lists are effective for organizing information. For unordered lists, use bullets, and for stages or sequences, use numbers.

1. Creating a Bulleted or Numbered List:
   - Click the Bullets or Numbering icon in the Paragraph group on the Home tab.
   - Or, start a line with "1." or a "*," Word will auto-format the list.

2. Customizing Lists:
   - Right-click the list.
   - Modify the bullet character, number format, or indent level.

3. Multi-Level Lists:
   - Utilize for outlining or hierarchical information.
   - Choose a style from the library or define a new multi-level list on the Home tab.

4. List Levels:
   - Promote or demote list levels using the Tab key or Shift + Tab.

5. Continuing or Restarting Numbering:
   - Right-click a list item.
   - Select Continue Numbering or Restart at 1.

Microsoft Word's rich formatting options provide the tools necessary to structure and emphasize text, ensuring clear, effective communication within your documents.

Using Lists: Bullets and Numbering

Creating lists is fundamental to organizing and presenting information in a document. Here's a more detailed step-by-step process for creating bulleted or numbered lists in Microsoft Word:

1. Initiating Lists:
   - Highlight the text you want to list.
   - Navigate to the Home tab.
   - In the Paragraph group, click on the Bullets icon for a bulleted list or the Numbering icon for a numbered list.
   - Alternatively, you can start typing on a new line with "1." for a numbered list or a "-" for a bulleted list, then press the Spacebar or the Tab key, and Word will auto-format the text into a list.

2. Keyboard Shortcuts:
   - Use Ctrl + Shift + L to toggle bullet points on and off quickly.

- For numbered lists, after typing "1." followed by a space, Word will automatically start a numbered list.

Formatting Lists

Customizing the appearance of lists can make your document more engaging and easier to read. Here are steps to format your lists:

1. Customize Bullets or Numbers:
   - Right-click on any bullet or number in your list.
   - Select "Define New Bullet" or "Define New Number Format" from the context menu.
   - Customize the bullet symbol, number style, font, or color as desired and click OK.

2. Adjust List Levels:
   - Place your cursor on the line you wish to adjust.
   - To create a sub-item, indent the item to the right by using the Increase List Level button or the Tab key.
   - Use the Decrease List Level button or press Shift + Tab to outdent the item to the left.

Nested Lists

Nested or multilevel lists help display hierarchical or sequential information.

1. Creating Nested Lists:
   - Start with a regular list.
   - Place your cursor at the start of the line where you wish to create the sublist.
   - Press the Tab key to indent the line and create a sublist item.
   - To return to the main list level, press Shift + Tab.

2. Customizing Nested Lists:
   - Highlight the nested list.
   - Right-click and choose "Adjust List Indents."
   - Customize the indent level, text distance, and other settings as desired.

3. Managing Nested List Levels:

Use the Increase/Decrease List Level buttons in the Paragraph group on the Home tab or the Tab and Shift + Tab keyboard shortcuts to move between list levels.

These detailed instructions should help you create, format, and manage lists, contributing to the organization and readability of your documents.

Chapter 5: Advanced Text Tools

In the last few chapters, we looked at some of the basic and intermediate text tools in Microsoft Word. Now, we're moving into the more advanced parts of Word that let you get creative and take your documents to the next level. This is where we go from just typing words on a page to crafting polished, professional documents.

This chapter focuses on the Find, Replace and Go To features. These let you quickly navigate through your document to make changes and edits. We'll also talk about spelling/grammar check and AutoCorrect; these help catch and fix common errors. They seem simple, but using them well can boost your editing speed. Together, all these tools help you smooth out your documents and fix any issues.

The goal here is to give you an environment where you can easily create flawless documents and reports. With some hands-on practice, you'll learn how to master these advanced Word tools. This takes your editing skills up a notch so you can efficiently turn out professionally polished documents. This chapter will guide you through the ins and outs of these features. By the end, you'll have the knowledge to take your Word skills to an advanced level.

Find, Replace, and Go To

Searching through long Word documents can feel like finding a needle in a haystack. Features like Find, Replace, and Go To tools make jumping around and editing text easy.

These powerful tools, akin to a wizard's spell, help you effortlessly transit through the tapestry of text in extensive documents, locate the needles in the haystack, substitute phrases, and easily leap across pages to specified sections.

Using the Find Function

- The Find feature in Word is like a magical portal to any word or phrase you need to locate in your document. Go to the Home tab and click Find, or use the keyboard shortcut Ctrl + F to make the dialog box appear instantly.
- In the dialog box, type the text you seek, and watch as Microsoft Word illuminates the occurrences within the document, making them stand out amidst the sea of words.
- To get more advanced options, click on 'More' to discover a chest of advanced options. You will gain access to features like matching cases or whole words to refine your search to the epitome of precision.

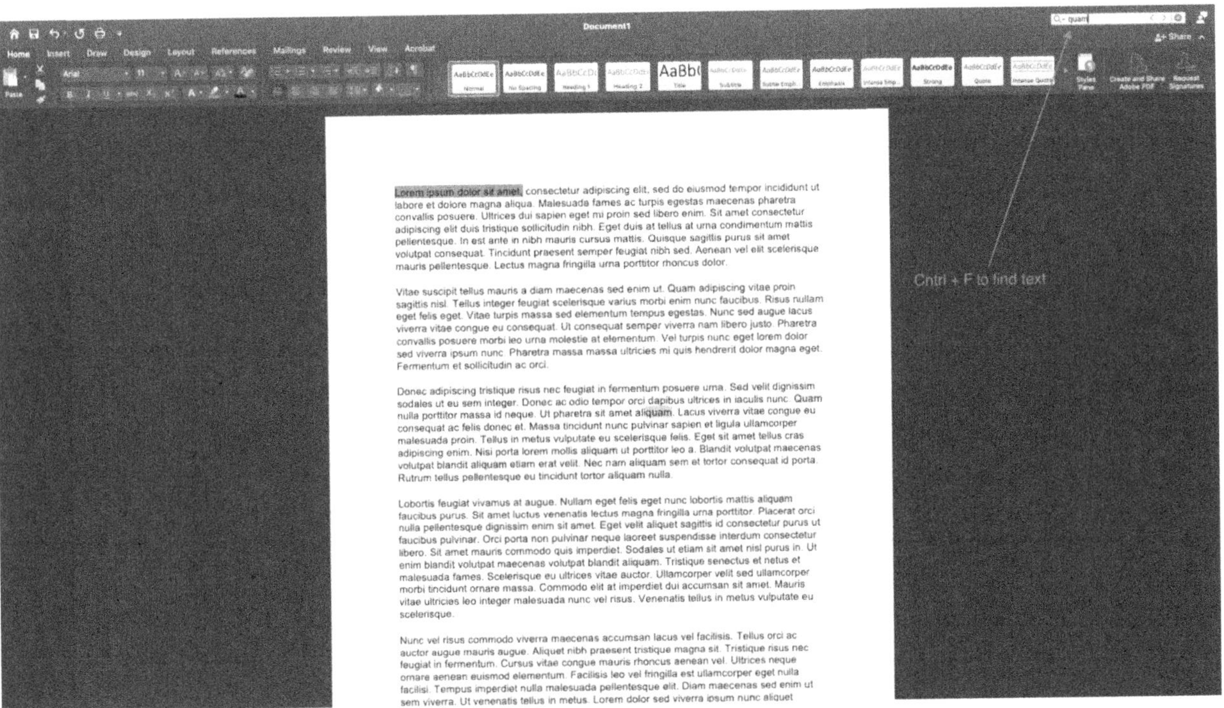

This is much better than trying to locate something just by scrolling through the document manually.

Using the Replace Function

- To use the Replace feature, go to the Home tab and click Replace. Or you can press Ctrl + H to bring it up.
- When the box pops up, type in the words or phrases you want to change and what you want to change it to. Then, hit Replace to change one instance at a time. Or, if you want to change every case simultaneously, hit Replace All instead.
- Under More, you can use some extra options, like finding text with specific formatting to replace. It opens up different editing methods that you might not think of normally.

Using the Go-To Function

- Leap through the pages and lines with the 'Go To' function. Access this portal by navigating to the 'Home' tab, clicking on 'Find,' then selecting 'Go To,' or simply pressing Ctrl + G.
- In the dialog box, whisper the page or line number to jump to, and click 'Go To' to teleport instantly.
- This function is your winged steed, carrying you swiftly across the vast expanses of your document, saving invaluable time in the process.

Practical Applications

The Find, Replace, and Go To features in Word are very helpful when you have a document full of problems. Instead of manually fixing the same typos repeatedly, you can use Find and Replace to fix them all at once like magic.

When working with a lengthy document, 'Go To' makes it easy to zip right to the section you need, saving you a lot of time compared to endless scrolling.

Spell Check, Grammar Check, and AutoCorrect

These handy tools - spell check, grammar check, and autocorrect - can improve your documents by catching spelling mistakes, grammar problems and typos. Since they work automatically, they speed up editing a lot, which makes Word super helpful for school and work.

Using Spell Check and Grammar Check

- **Access:** Navigate to the 'Review' tab and select 'Spelling & Grammar' to initiate the checks. Microsoft Word begins the checking process from the cursor's location, identifying spelling and grammar errors and suggesting corrections in a navigation pane.
- **Review & Apply Corrections:** Engage with the suggested corrections by clicking on them or add words to the dictionary if they are flagged incorrectly. This interactive process ensures your document adheres to the desired linguistic standards.
- **Customization:** Delve into the settings by navigating to 'File,' then 'Options,' and selecting 'Proofing' to toggle features like checking grammar with spelling, which provides a more tailored reviewing experience.

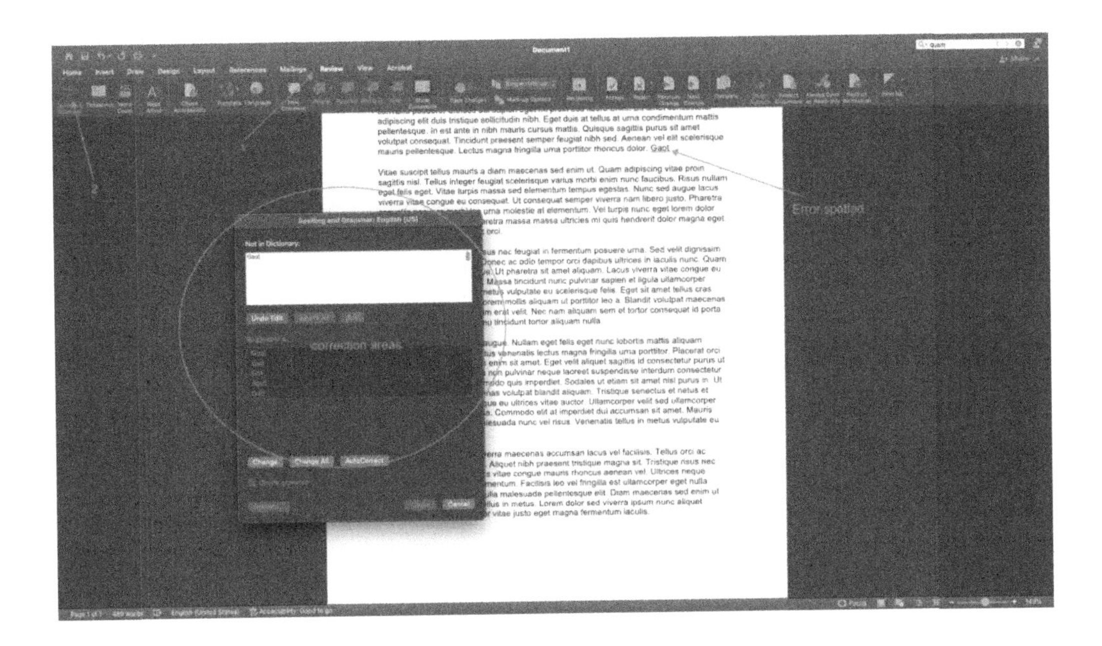

Using AutoCorrect

- **Access:** To access AutoCorrect, click the 'File' tab, select 'Options,' click the 'Proofing' tab, and then click the 'AutoCorrect Options' button.
- **Functionality:** AutoCorrect is not merely a typo corrector; it's a powerful tool that automates routine formatting and capitalization functions alongside correcting common spelling errors.
- **Customization:** Within the AutoCorrect options window, you can add or modify new entries to tailor the AutoCorrect behavior to your preferences. This customization is helpful for making Word work better for how you type and the mistakes you tend to make.

Chapter 6: Page And Document Layout

Getting the layout of your document right is important for making pieces that look professional and polished, whether they're simple docs, complex reports, or publications you want to print out. How you present your content matters almost as much as the actual content, and a document that's laid out well can grab the reader's attention, make things easier to understand, and give off a sense of professionalism and purpose.

This chapter will get into the basics and more detailed parts of page and document layout using Microsoft Word, a tool used everywhere in work and school settings.

Margins, Orientation, and Paper Size

This section talks about some critical things in Microsoft Word that affect how your document looks: the margins, which is the blank space around the edges; orientation, which is whether you set it up vertically or horizontally; and paper size, which is the page's dimensions.

Setting up these basics right makes a big difference in making your Word document look decent and easy to read.

By going through the steps here, you'll learn how to tweak these features so your Microsoft Word documents look professional and things don't get all jammed together. It's like building the foundation before you put up the walls and roof when you're building a house.

Margins

Margins are important for making documents look good. They're like the empty spaces around the edges of the page that help frame the words nicely. Margins ensure the text doesn't look crammed or spilled over the edges. They also give you space to bind documents together or hold the pages without covering words, and here's a quick rundown on how to change margins in Word to get what you want:

Custom margins:

- You can customize the margins if the presets are not what you want.
- First, go to the margins menu and click Custom Margins. This opens the Page Setup box.
- Here, you can enter your own numbers for the top, bottom, left, and right margins. You can also set the gutter margin, which is good for bound documents.
- Under Preview, you can apply the margins to the whole document or just from that point on.
- Once you've put in the margins you want, hit OK, and it'll change your document.

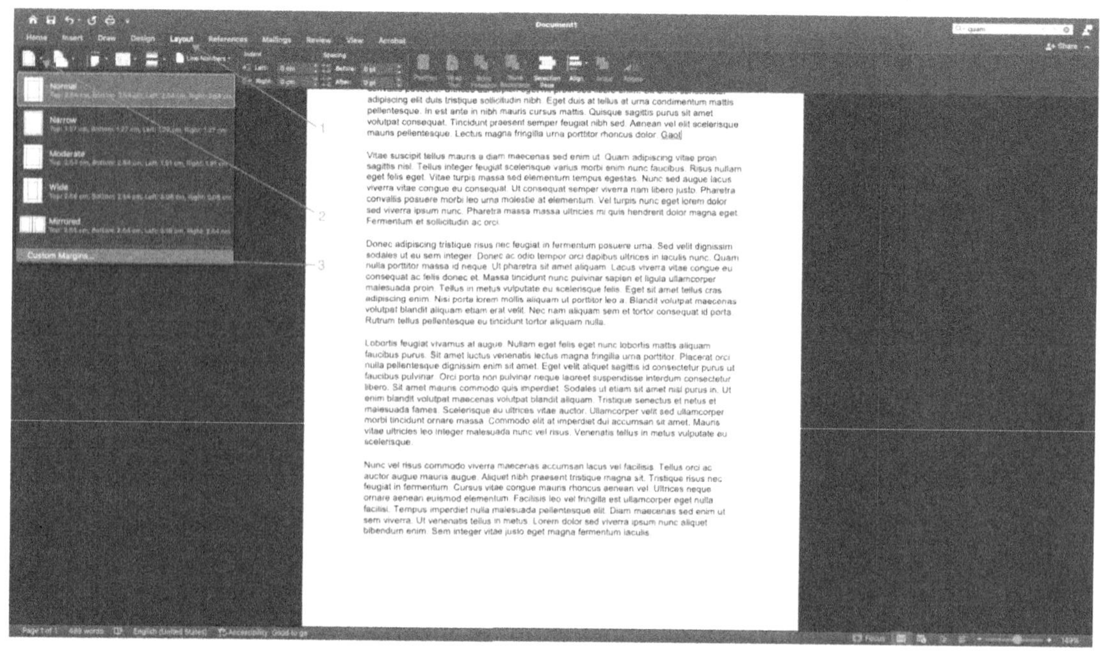

Reviewing and Adjusting Margins:

- Review your document and ensure the new margins fit the content and layout.
- If not, go back and tweak the settings until you get the layout you want.

Knowing how to adjust margins in Word is important for making professional-looking documents. Whether using the defaults or customizing your own, getting a handle on margins gives you more control over how readable your document is.

Orientation

Orientation in laying out stuff on a page refers to which way the content is shown - either taller than wide (portrait) or wider than tall (landscape).

Portrait works better for letters or documents that are mainly text since it's easier to read texts that flow down the page. Also, landscape is good when you need more horizontal space for wide charts, tables, images, etc or if you're designing a brochure or pamphlet.

Accessing Orientation Settings:

- First, open the document you want to change.
- Go to the Layout or Page Layout tab.
- In the Page Setup group, locate the Orientation button.

Selecting Orientation:

- Click Orientation
- A dropdown shows up with Portrait and Landscape.
- Pick Portrait for a vertical layout - it's the default for most documents since it works well for many documents.
- Choose Landscape if you need more width for visuals, tables, etc.

Applying the Selected Orientation:

- Changing your document's orientation in Word is pretty straightforward. Choose between the portrait and landscape orientations. The document will rearrange itself automatically when you do that.
- After, review the document and ensure the new orientation makes sense for the content and what you're trying to do with the document.
- Sometimes, you need to tweak things like the margins or columns to make it fit better.

Orientation matters because it impacts how people take in your information while reading your document. So, think carefully about which orientation best suits your content and goals.

Paper Size

Choosing the right paper size is important for your document layout. It decides how big your pages are, which affects where all the words and pictures go. Microsoft Word gives you standard sizes like letters, Legal, A4, and everything for regular documents. However, you can also make custom sizes if you need something specific.

Whether printing a document or just putting it online, getting the paper size right matters.

Here's more about dealing with settings for that in Word.

Accessing Paper Size Settings:

- Open the document your document in Microsoft Word.
- Navigate to the ribbon menu at the top and click on the Layout tab.
- You will see several options for page setup, and somewhere in the Page Setup section, you'll see a button labeled Size.

Selecting Standard Paper Size:

- After choosing the size, a list will pop up with some standard paper sizes.
- Hover over each one to see a tooltip with the size of the paper.
- Select the size that suits you best- as soon as you click it, your document will resize automatically.

Reviewing and Adjusting Paper Size:

- First, review your document and ensure your new paper size works for the content and layout.
- If it doesn't seem right, adjust the paper size settings until you get the layout you want.

Creating and Saving Custom Paper Size Presets:

- If there's a specific custom paper size you use a lot, consider making a preset for it so you can access it easily later.
- Follow the steps for customizing the paper size, and once you have the size you want, give it a name and save it.

Knowing how to pick and customize paper sizes in Word is important for making professional, nicely formatted documents.

Columns, Breaks, and Hyphenation

Mastering page layout in Word is more than just margins or paper size. You have to understand columns, breaks, and hyphens to make things organized, readable and look good. This section explains these elements so you can use Word better.

Making columns can help if there's a lot of text, like in newspapers. Here's how to set them up:

Getting to Column Settings

- Open your Word doc.
- Go to the Layout tab at the top.
- Find and click the Columns button in the Page Setup group.

Choosing Column Layouts

- A menu will pop up with predefined column layouts.
- Hover over each one to preview it.
- Select the layout that works for your document.

Customizing Columns

- Click on additional Columns at the bottom of the drop-down menu if none of the options work.
- A dialog box will come up where you can customize the number and width of columns.
- Choose how many columns width spacing, and decide if you want lines between.
- Click OK to apply the settings to your document.

Breaks

Breaks in Microsoft Word are important for controlling how text flows in your document. They let you manage things between pages, columns, or sections. Breaks help give your document a good structure and make it look good. Here's a deep dive on working with breaks:

Accessing Break Options

- Open Word and the document you wish to change.
- Click on the Layout tab to change the ribbon.
- Locate and choose the Breaks button from the Page Setup group.

Inserting Breaks

- A menu will appear with different break types that you can insert.
- Choose the type you want - for instance, a Page Break to start a new page or a Column break to move text to the next column.
- The new break will be updated in the document.

Understanding Break Types

- **Page Break:** This type transitions text to the start of a new page, which is good for when you want to start a new chapter or section on a fresh page.

- **Column Break:** If your document has columns, a column break moves the text to the start of the next column.
- **Text Wrapping Breaks:** These breaks help text flow around images or shapes in Word docs. It makes things look neat and easy to read.
- **Continuous Section Breaks:** On the same page, new sections begin after this break. They're good for changing the number of columns without a new page, which is nice in docs with different columns on one page.
- **Even and Odd Page Breaks:** These start new sections on the next even or odd page. It is helpful if you want specific layouts for even and odd pages, like in books.

Practical Applications of Breaks

- Breaks can separate chapters, so each one starts on a new or even/odd page, depending on what you want.
- Text Wrapping Breaks help when there are a lot of graphics to keep things clean.
- Continuous Section Breaks allow different column layouts on the same page, so your document looks neat and structured.

Using breaks in Word will help make your documents look professional.

Hyphenation

Hyphens in Word help make text look neat and consistent by splitting words at the end of lines when needed. This prevents awkward spacing between words and makes the layout look clean and organized.

Here's a guide to working with hyphens in your document:

Automatic Hyphenation:

- Open your document and go to the Layout tab at the top.
- Locate the Hyphenation button in the Page Setup group.
- Click Hyphenation and select Automatic from the menu.
- Word will automatically analyze the text and hyphenate where needed to improve word spacing and alignment.

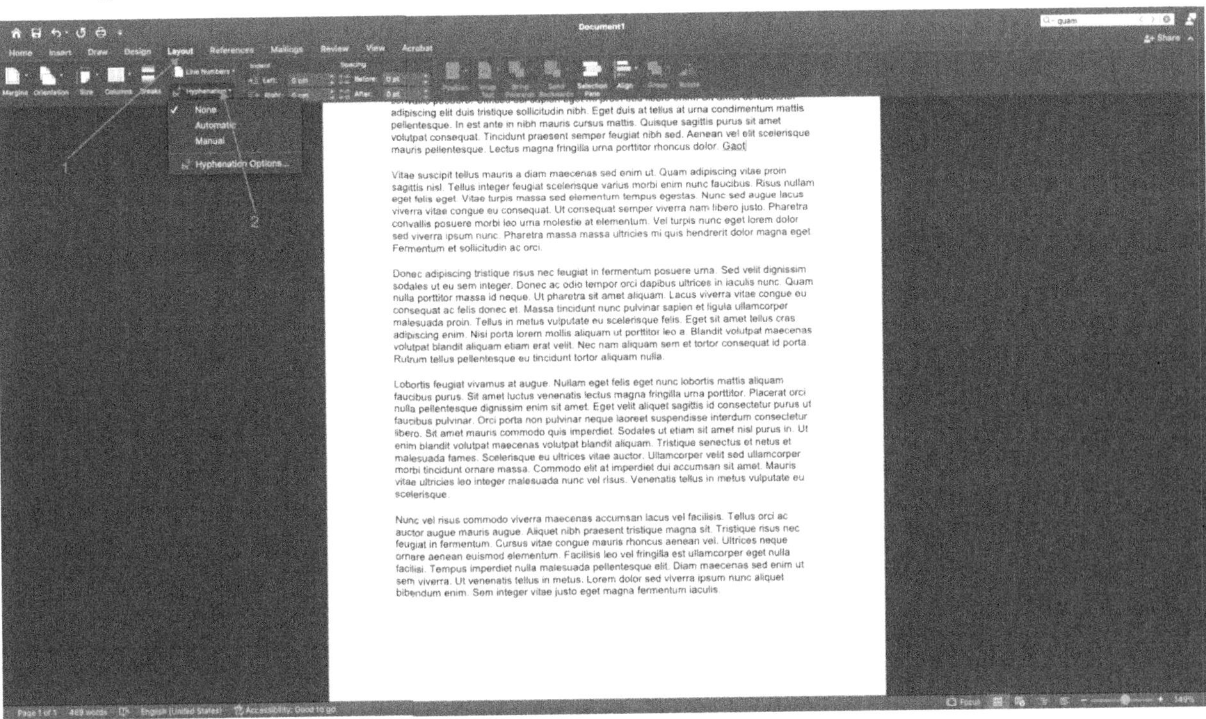

Manual Hyphenation:

- Make sure your document has text in it.

- Go to the Layout tab at the top menu.
- Click Hyphenation and choose Manual from the menu.
- A dialog box will pop up showing suggested hyphen words at the end of lines.
- You can review the suggestions and accept or reject individual hyphens, so you control where words split.

Hyphenation Options:

- For more control, after clicking Hyphenation, choose Hyphenation Options.
- When you open the options for hyphenation in Word, a dialog box will pop up. Here, you can tweak settings like how much space Microsoft Word should leave at the end of a line before splitting a word in half or the maximum number of lines in a row it can split words across.
- Adjust the settings however you like, then click OK to save them.

Disabling Hyphenation:

If you don't want to use hyphenation, go to the Layout tab, click Hyphenation, and choose None from the menu to turn it off completely.

Hyphenation has some handy real-world uses. It can make your document look much nicer, especially if you have long words or narrow columns of text. You can also hyphenate words manually, which is handy when you need total control over which words get split and where they split - like in academic work or professional documents where formatting has to be just right.

Once you have figured out the hyphenation settings in Microsoft Word, you'll be way ahead of the game in making structured and fantastic documents.

Chapter 7: Styles And Themes

This chapter explains how to use Styles and Themes in Word to make your documents look professional and consistent.

Styles let you save formatting, like fonts, spacing, etc., as reusable elements so you can quickly apply the same look over and over. Also, themes take it up a notch by coordinating all the fonts, colors, effects, and more across your whole document. Both are game changers for making documents look polished and cutting down on repetitive formatting work.

If you want your Microsoft Word documents to look like they were professionally designed, you have to learn these tools. Styles and Themes will save you a ton of time manually formatting, plus they help different parts of your document flow together visually.

Applying and Modifying Styles

Styles are essential when it comes to formatting documents. They let you keep everything uniform and professional across your text. Styles bundle up formatting into one command, so you can be consistent without all the work.

Microsoft Word gives you some ready-made styles for headings, subheads, body text etc. However, styles can do way more than that. You don't just have to use the defaults—you can modify them or customize your own styles for exactly what you need.

Understanding Styles

Microsoft Word's styles are like templates for formatting text. They let you save elements like font, size, color, alignment spacing, and indentation all in one preset package. The styles make it easy to keep your document looking consistent and professional.

Microsoft Word comes with default styles like Normal, Heading 1, and Heading 2 to handle different needs and manage the styles. Click the little arrow in the Styles section on the Home tab, and it will open.

The pane shows all the styles available so you can select your choice. With the Styles Pane, you can tweak the styles or browse for the perfect one to format your text. It makes the whole process smooth and simple.

Applying Styles

- Applying styles is straightforward in Word. Go to the Home tab and select the styles group where the most used styles, like bold, italic, etc., are located.
- Alternatively, the Styles Pane provides a more detailed view and management of styles, allowing for more fine-grained control over style application.
- The Home tab styles and Quick Styles sets will let you restyle your document fast. It contains a collection of style sets that can be applied with a single click, providing a quick way to overhaul the document's formatting.

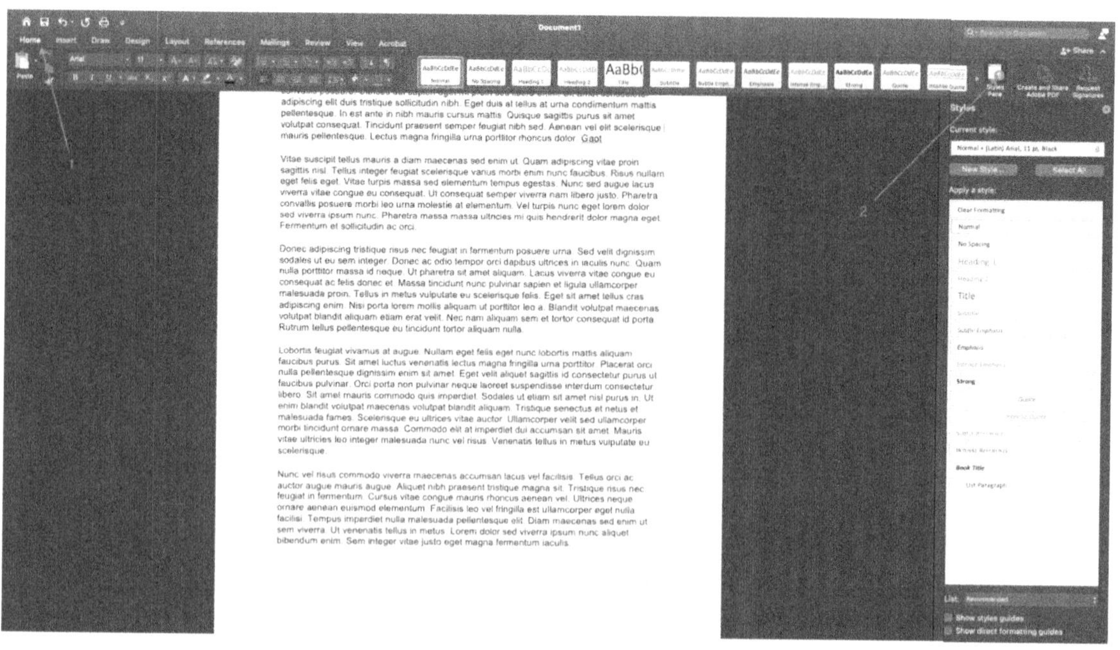

Modifying Existing Styles

- If you want to change a style you've already made, right-click on it in the ribbon or Styles Panel and click Modify. This will bring up the Modify Style box.
- In the Modify Style dialog box, you can modify the style however you want - font, size, color alignment, and all kinds of formatting.
- When you change a style, it automatically changes the formatting for all the text you already styled that way and makes it easy to make big changes without touching each part individually.

Creating New Styles

- Making a new style is easy. Click the New Style button in the Styles Pane or choose Create a Style from the Styles group on the Home tab.
- You can start with formatting that's already there or do it from scratch. Give your style a name, pick the formatting you want, and click OK.
- The new style will show up in the Styles Pane, so you can use it on text just like the built-in ones.

Style Sets

Style Sets are collections of styles designed to work together to make a document look good. They help ensure headings, subheadings, and body text all go together nicely so the document looks organized and pleasant to view.

Also, Microsoft Word lets you create custom Style sets and save them so you can quickly use the same styles in different documents. This is helpful when you're working on a set of related documents that are supposed to look the same - it makes it easy to keep everything uniform.

With Style Sets, Microsoft Word makes it much easier to get a consistent look across documents, saving time and making your documents look more professional.

Organizing and Managing Styles

- Styles can be shared between documents or people by importing and exporting them. This keeps things consistent when working on multiple files or with others.
- Getting rid of styles you no longer need declutters the Styles Pan, making it easier to find and use what's left.
- The styles you use often can be dragged to the top of the pane for quicker clicking.

Selecting and Customizing Themes

Themes in Microsoft Word are another excellent way to make your documents look good. It is like an easy way to match everything - the colors, fonts, effects, etc. Hence, if you want to give your Word document a makeover, playing around with themes is the way to go. It is like picking an outfit, except for your document.

You can pick something professional, elegant, fun - whatever fits the vibe you're going for. And just like outfits, you can customize the pieces.

Themes save you time from having to format everything piece by piece. Just pick your theme and let it work its magic!

Understanding Themes

Themes in Word are like picking out an outfit for your document - they set the look and feel with colors, fonts, and other effects. It's an easy way to get a coordinated visual style on every page.

To apply a theme, click on any theme of choice under the Design tab, and everything changes instantly.

Applying Themes

You are not stuck with the built-in themes. You can customize the colors by trying out different hues on the color palette until you find ones that fit the vibe you want. Fonts and effects can also be tweaked so the theme really represents your document's purpose or your brand's style.

Customizing Themes

Basically, themes are an easy way to get a polished, unified look across your whole document. To customize a theme, start with a preset and then customize it to perfection. Your document will look like you spent hours sweating the formatting details, even though applying a theme takes just a click.

Theme Fonts and Effects

Themes let you dive deeper into the stylistic world by customizing the fonts and effects to match your narrative or brand. Each font has its own personality, so picking the right one can majorly boost how nice your document looks and reads. Little effects here and there also add some sophistication to help your document stand out.

Saving and Reusing Themes

Saving your carefully crafted theme is like locking away a treasure chest of style. Why keep it confined to one document when it could make other documents look great, too? Set it as a default theme, and use it for every new Word document that you create.

Switching or Removing Themes

As your document evolves, your needs may change, and the theme no longer fits. No problem! Going back to default is easy, so your document can always carry a look that matches its content.

Choosing and tweaking themes isn't just about looks but also about finding your document's visual identity. Follow the steps, tips, and best practices here, and you'll not only master styles and themes but unlock serious time-saving potential, too. Using these tools means a consistent, eye-catching presentation that will give your documents a unique personality that makes them stand out.

Chapter 8: Visual Elements

Visual elements can break boring walls of text and get ideas across better. They give your eyes a break and make your documents more interesting and easier to understand.

Microsoft Word has several tools for inserting images, shapes, SmartArt graphics, WordArt, text boxes, drop caps, and pull quotes. Using these elements properly can call attention to critical points, show concepts, and make your documents look presentable.

This chapter will discuss how to use all these visual tools. We'll go through inserting and editing images, creating diagrams with SmartArt, making text boxes, making initial caps look artsy, and designing quotes to highlight important texts.

Inserting and Editing Images

Visual elements can break boring walls of text and get ideas across better. They give your eyes a break and make your documents more interesting and easier to understand.

Inserting Images

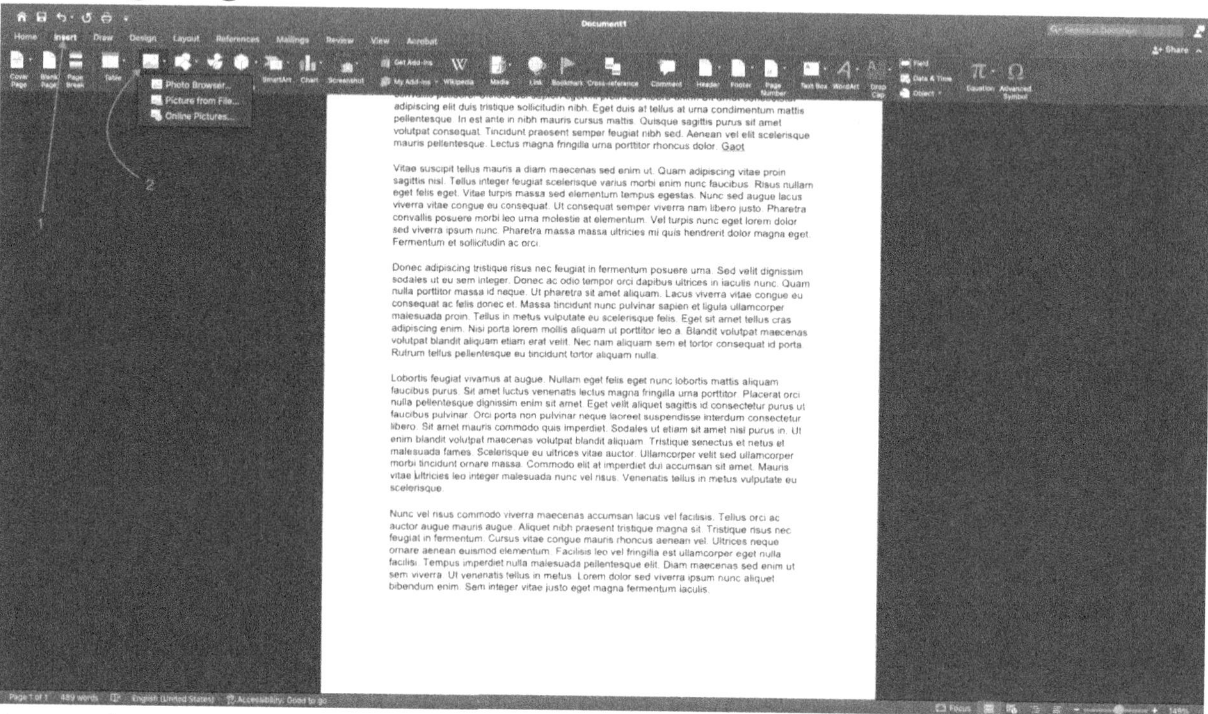

Accessing the Insert Tab

- Launch Microsoft Word and open the document you intend to modify.
- Go to the Insert tab on the Ribbon.

Inserting Images from Your Computer

- To use a picture already on your computer, click the Pictures button under the Text or Illustrations group.
- A window will open for you to browse your files and find the right photo. Choose the one you want and click Insert.

Inserting Online Images

- If you don't already have the picture, you can get one from the internet.
- Click Online Pictures in the text or illustration group.
- Input a search term to look for an image or paste in a link if you have one. Pick the image and click Insert again to add it.

It's easy to add images to your Word document. The Insert tab has everything you need to insert images from your computer or the web.

Editing Images

Once you can insert an image into a Word document, you get access to several tools to edit the image so it fits your document's look.

Here's a deeper look at the process:

Selecting the Image

- Click the image to select it, and this activates the Picture Tools on the Ribbon.

Accessing Picture Tools

- When you select the pic, the Picture Tools Format tab shows up on the Ribbon, giving you a ton of editing options.

Resizing and Cropping

- Use the handles around the image to change it to the desired size.
- To crop, hit the Crop button in the Size group, then drag the crop handles and press enter to apply.

Rotating

- Use the circular rotate arrow above the image to rotate it to the desired angle.

Applying Effects

- In the Picture Tools Format tab, explore the Picture Styles group to put predefined styles on the image or customize its look with borders, effects etc.

Adjusting Image Layout

- Also, in the Picture Tools Format tab, in the Arrange group, you can edit the image position, alignment and text wrapping so it fits nicely in your document's layout.

Color Correction

- You can also adjust the image's color, brightness, contrast etc., in the Adjust group. The Adjust group under the Picture Tools Format tab lets you edit images' brightness, contrast and color. You can use the Corrections menu to access presets for brightness/contrast and sharpening/softening - just hover over each option to preview it before clicking to apply.

Shapes, SmartArt, and WordArt

Unleashing the visual potential of your document is effortlessly achievable with Microsoft Word's trio of graphical tools: Shapes, SmartArt, and WordArt. Here's how to navigate through each:

Shapes

Navigate to the "Insert" tab, click on "Shapes," and you're presented with a medley of shapes ready to grace your document.

As you sketch the shape on your document, the "Drawing Tools Format" tab springs to life, ready to assist you in molding its appearance to your liking.

- **Adding More Shapes:** If the initial assortment of shapes leaves you yearning for more, fear not. While working with SmartArt graphics, you can easily add more shapes by clicking on an existing shape or clicking "Add Shape After" or "Add Shape Before" based on where you want the new shape to be relative to the selected shape.
- **Aligning Shapes:** Use the alignment options to ensure your shapes are in perfect harmony. Select the shapes you want to align, then under the "Shape Format" or "Drawing Tools > Format" tab, find the "Arrange" group and click "Align".

SmartArt

SmartArt graphics are visual portrayals of your information and ideas. They come in various layouts, each tailored for different types of information representation like organization charts, Venn diagrams, or simply enhancing a bulleted list.

With a click on "Insert" and then "SmartArt," a world of diagrammatic expression unveils itself. The "SmartArt Tools" tabs are your companion in customizing your SmartArt graphic to encapsulate your intended message.

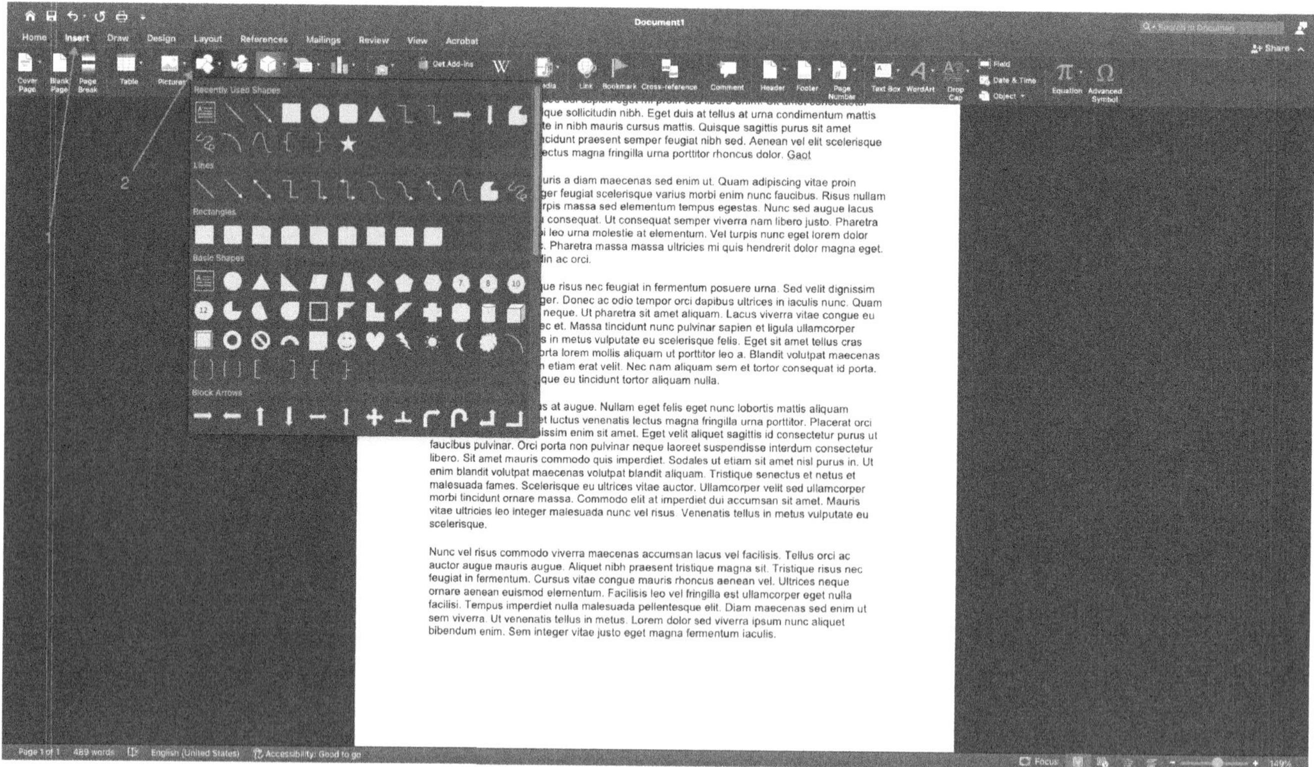

WordArt

Embark on a textual adventure by going to the "Insert" tab, clicking on "WordArt," choosing a style, and typing away. The "Drawing Tools Format" tab awaits your command to customize the text to your aesthetic preference.

- **Extending WordArt Possibilities:** You're not limited to short text; entire sentences and even paragraphs can be transformed into WordArt. Additionally, existing text can be converted to WordArt, and symbols can be included as WordArt text.

- **Transforming WordArt:** Change the shape of your WordArt by selecting it, then navigating to "Shape Format" or "Drawing Tools Format > Text Effects." Choose "Transform" and select the effect you desire. You can also rotate or flip your WordArt to achieve your desired look.

This section equips you with the knowledge to experiment and express your ideas visually in your document, opening avenues for a more engaging and visually pleasing reader experience.

Text Boxes, Drop Caps, and Pull Quotes

Text boxes, drop caps, and pull quotes in Word help make your documents look better. Text boxes let you add extra effects wherever you want. Drop caps make the first letter of paragraphs big and fancy.

Pull quotes highlight important parts of what you're saying. Using all these elements makes your paper nice to look at, not just read.

Text Boxes

Text boxes let you add extra text or notes to your documents, framing your words neatly. Here's how to use them:

- **Making a Text Box:** Go to Insert, click Text Box, and pick a style you like. If you want to make your own, select Draw Text Box and sketch a box on your document.
- **Customizing Your Box:** Once you've added a text box, head to Drawing Tools Format to change the color, border, and other looks of your text box. Add your text and adjust the font and size as you want.
- **Positioning Your Box:** Drag your text box wherever you want on the page and resize it by pulling the circle handle or rotating it around with the circular arrow at the top.

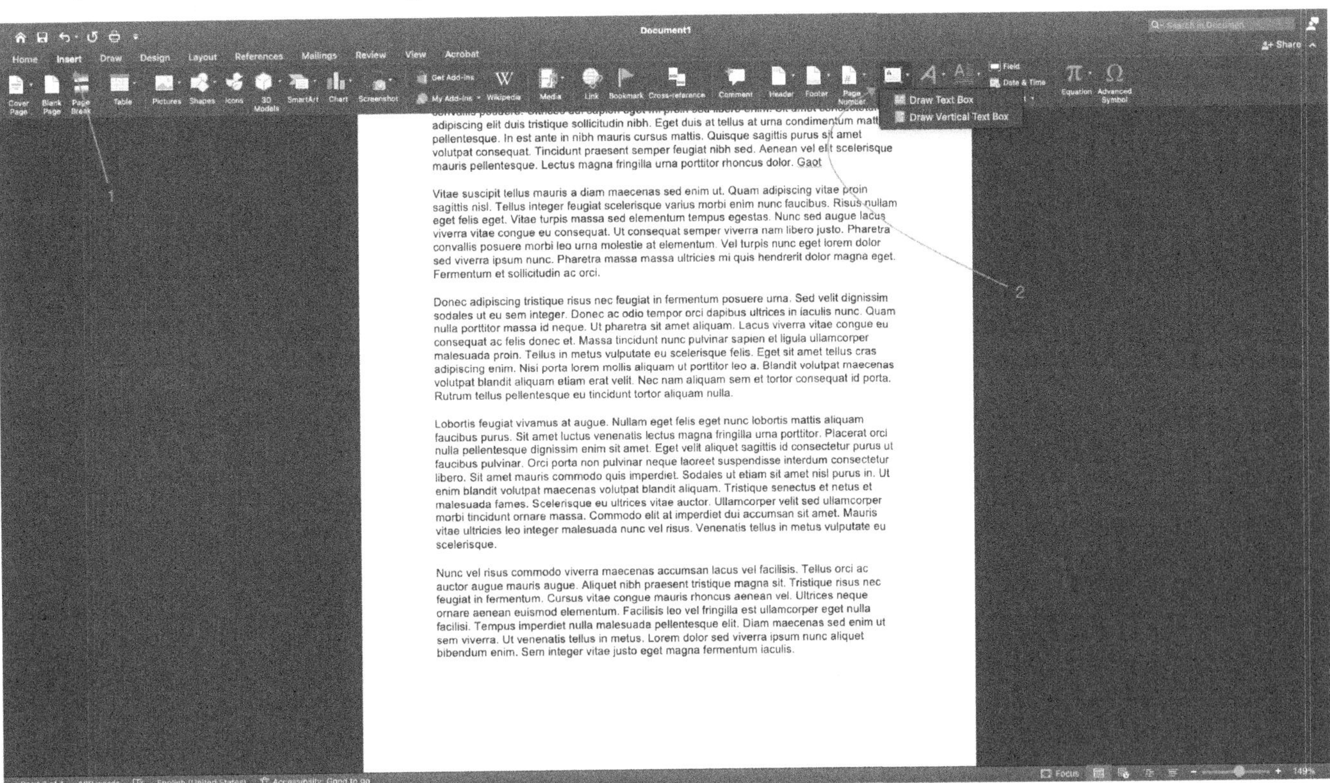

Drop Caps

Drop caps are a timeless approach to starting a new section or chapter. You kick things off with a fancy, big initial letter that grabs the reader's attention right away.

- **Creating a Drop Cap:** Click where you want it to go and hit the Insert tab. Select Drop Cap and pick from three styles - 'Dropped,' In margin,' or explore 'Drop Cap Options' to customize it more.

- **Customization:** You can make your drop cap unique by playing with different font colors, background colors, or even drop shadows if you want something distinct. There are a ton of settings to match the style of your document or just stand out.
- **Aesthetic Appeal:** Drop caps let you capture that fancy old manuscript feel by tweaking the settings to your formatting taste.

Pull Quotes

Pull quotes can be a tool to highlight text, making it stand out and emphasizing key points.

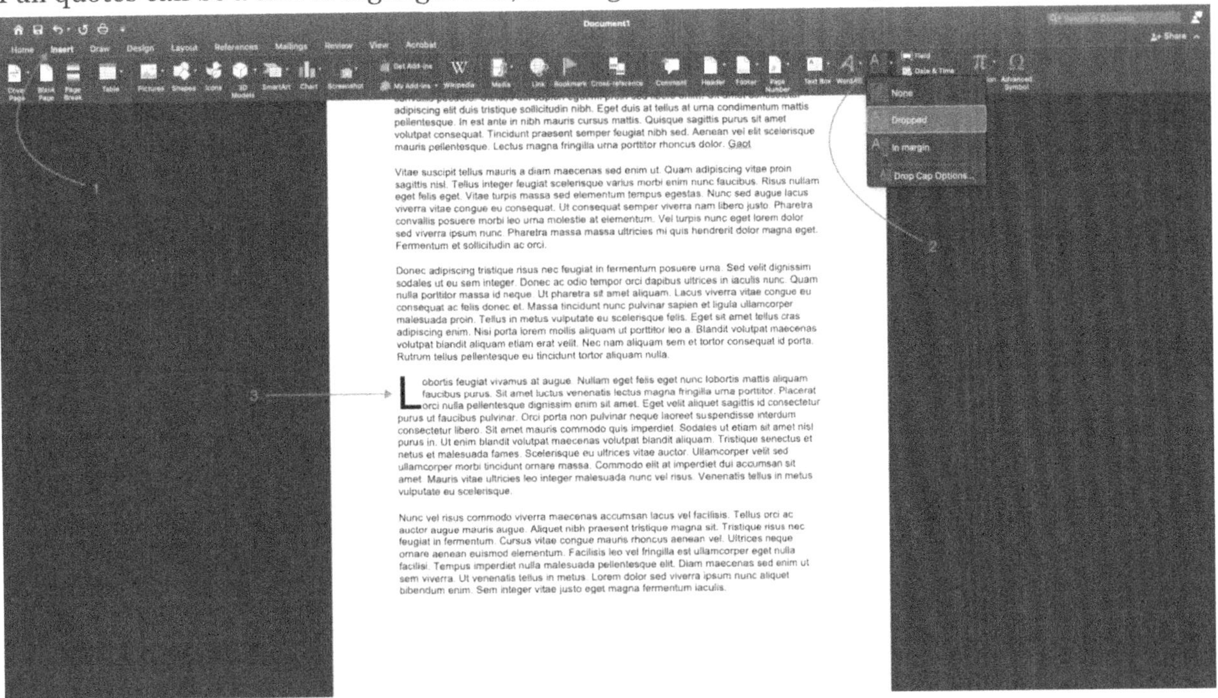

- **Creating a Pull Quote:** Highlight the desired text, go to the "Insert" tab, click on "Text Box," and choose a style. You can also create your own and position it accordingly. This technique visually breaks up texts and directs attention to specific content.
- **Positioning and Formatting:** When positioning and formatting your pull quote, you have two options: place it either to the side of the document or in line with the text. Make sure there is space for the text box by adjusting the document's indentation if needed. Customize the appearance of the text box by experimenting with font sizes and colors in order to achieve your desired emphasis.

By adding these elements to your documents using the methods described above, you will boost the appearance of your document.

Chapter 9: Tables And Charts

Tables play a role in presenting data in an organized, clear and effective way. They provide frameworks where information can be arranged in rows and columns, making it easy to navigate and understand. On the other hand, charts offer a representation of data, allowing you to quickly identify trends, make comparisons and gain insights at a glance.

Both tables and charts are important elements in Microsoft Word as they will help you to portray data accurately. In this chapter, we will explore the intricacies of creating, modifying and formatting tables using Microsoft Word.

Creating Tables

Accessing Table Creation Tools:

- Open Microsoft Word. Select the document you want to work on.
- Go to the "Insert" tab located in the menu.

Methods for Creating Tables

- **Insert Table:** Click on tables in the tables group, and choose the number of rows and columns for your table. You can also draw it manually.
- **Draw Table:** Select the "Draw Table" command. Manually draw your table specifying the desired number of rows and columns.
- **Quick Tables:** Use the "Quick Tables" option. This provides a range of preformatted tables for you to choose from.
- **Importing Tables:** You can also import tables from sources such as Excel. This will allow you to integrate data into your Word document.

Modifying Tables

Adjusting Rows and Columns

- You can add rows and columns based on your needs.
- Customize the layout by merging or splitting cells.

Sorting and Organizing Data

- Simplify your analysis by sorting the data within the table.

Resizing

- Tailor the table to fit your document layout by adjusting the column width and row height.

Formatting Tables

Applying Table Styles

- Give your table a consistent look by using predefined styles. You can even create custom styles to suit your preferences. Modify borders, shading, text formatting, paragraph formatting and other properties for an appearance.

Displaying Gridlines

- Make your work easier by activating gridlines. They provide a view while you're working on the table, making it easier to make adjustments.

Table Style Options

- Improve the formatting of your table with options such as Header Row, Total Row, Banded Rows, First Column, Last Column and Banded Columns. This ensures that your table aligns with the theme and purpose of your document.

Modifying Table Styles

- Make changes to table styles and properties. This way, all tables using a style will be updated accordingly. It helps maintain consistency throughout your document.

Inserting and Customizing Charts

Charts serve as a visual lexicon, translating numerical data into graphical insights. They distill complex data into a form that's easy to understand, enabling the viewer to grasp trends, comparisons, and patterns at a glance.

Commonly deployed charts include bar charts, pie charts, and line charts, each offering a unique lens through which to interpret data.

Inserting Charts

Initiating the journey of chart creation in Microsoft Word is a straightforward process:

- Position your cursor where you desire the chart to be placed.
- Navigate to the "Insert" tab on the ribbon.
- Click on "Chart" in the "Illustrations" group, which will usher you into the "Insert Chart" dialogue box.
- Here, you're presented with a plethora of chart types. Select one that resonates with your data's narrative. For example, pie charts represent part-whole relationships, bar charts are used for comparisons, and line charts show patterns over time.
- Upon selection, a subtype option appears where applicable—for example, 3-D variations for pie or bar charts.
- Click "OK" to close the dialogue box, and voila, your chart is inserted with a spreadsheet to input your data.
- Populate the spreadsheet with your data, which will dynamically reflect in the chart.

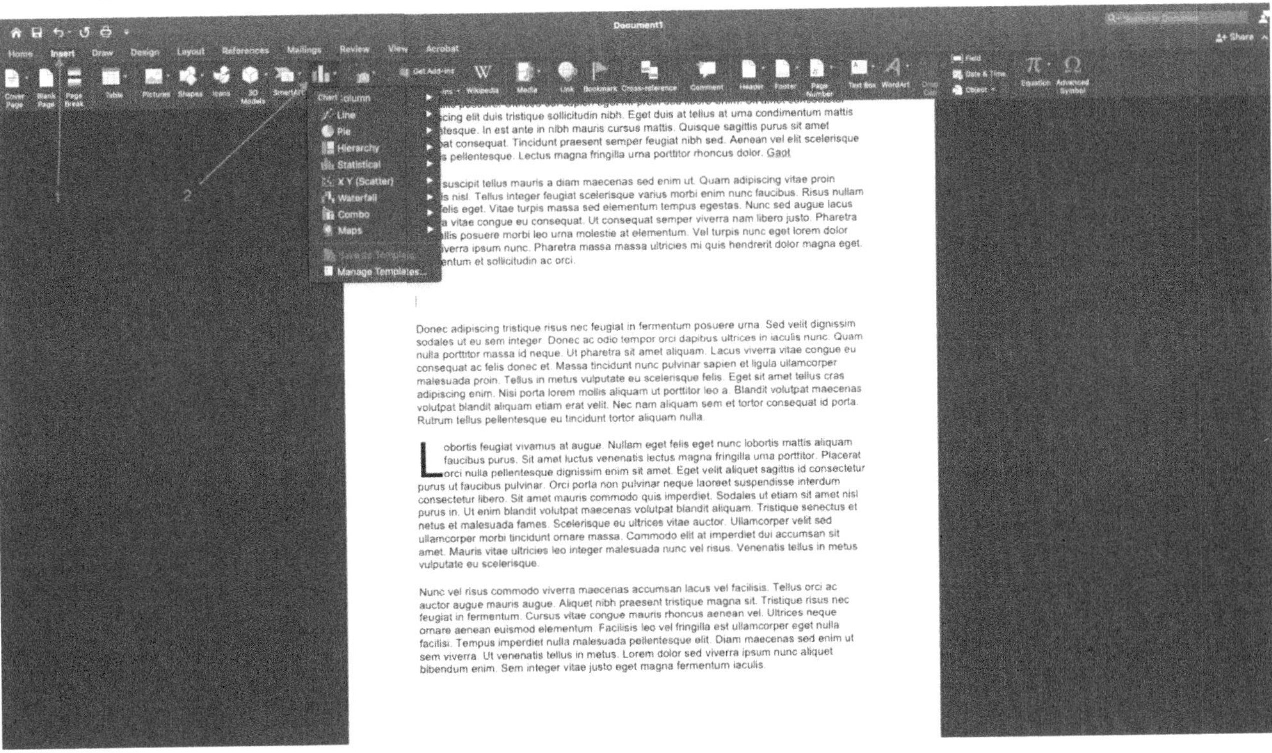

Customizing Charts

Once your chart is embedded within your document, the journey of customization begins, allowing you to tailor the visual aesthetics and data representation to your liking:

- Click on your chart to activate the "Chart Tools," comprising the "Design" and "Format" tabs.
- Explore the "Chart Styles" group in the "Design" tab to swiftly alter the color and style of your chart.

Dive into the "Chart Layouts" group to tweak the chart title, axis titles, legend, and more.

- The "Format" tab is your playground for refining the chart elements' appearance. Here, you can modify chart elements' fill, outline, and effects.
- For more advanced customization, the "Chart Elements" and "Chart Filters" buttons beside your chart offer a myriad of options to show, hide, or format various elements and data points.

Managing Charts

Management of your charts is crucial for maintaining their relevance and accuracy as your document evolves:

- To resize or move your chart, simply click and drag the edges or the whole chart, respectively.
- Updating the chart data is as simple as performing a right-click on the chart and choosing "Edit Data." This brings up the spreadsheet for you to amend the data.
- If your data is extensive or subject to frequent updates, consider creating your chart in Excel and copying it to Word. This way, you can link the chart to the original Excel file, ensuring it stays updated with the latest data.

Through the prism of charts, your document will embody a visually engaging character and a profound clarity in data-driven storytelling. The tools and techniques shared above pave the way for you to harness the power of charts in articulating data effectively and aesthetically in Microsoft Word.

Chapter 10: References And Research Tools

In the world of professional writing, it is crucial to maintain authenticity and conduct research. Achieving this requires referencing using effective research tools. This section serves as an introduction to the features of Microsoft Word that can assist you in streamlining your referencing and research processes.

You will learn about footnotes, endnotes and citations, which play a role in acknowledging your sources and providing insights. Additionally, you will discover how to create bibliographies and manage your sources efficiently.

Footnotes, Endnotes, and Citations

The location of footnotes and endnotes within a document is the main difference between them. Footnotes are found at the bottom of the page, while endnotes are located at the end of a complete document or sometimes at the end of a chapter.

Footnotes are best used when providing a small amount of supplemental material, ensuring the reader sees it. Endnotes are preferable when there is a significant amount of supplemental material.

Inserting Footnotes and Endnotes

Navigating to the "References" tab:

- In a Microsoft Word document, navigate to the References > Footnotes on the main ribbon.

Using the "Insert Footnote" and "Insert Endnote" commands:

- Type your note in the recently created footnote or endnote after selecting Insert Footnote or Insert Endnote as necessary.

Inputting text for footnotes and endnotes:

- Once the footnote or endnote is inserted, type the relevant text into the provided space.

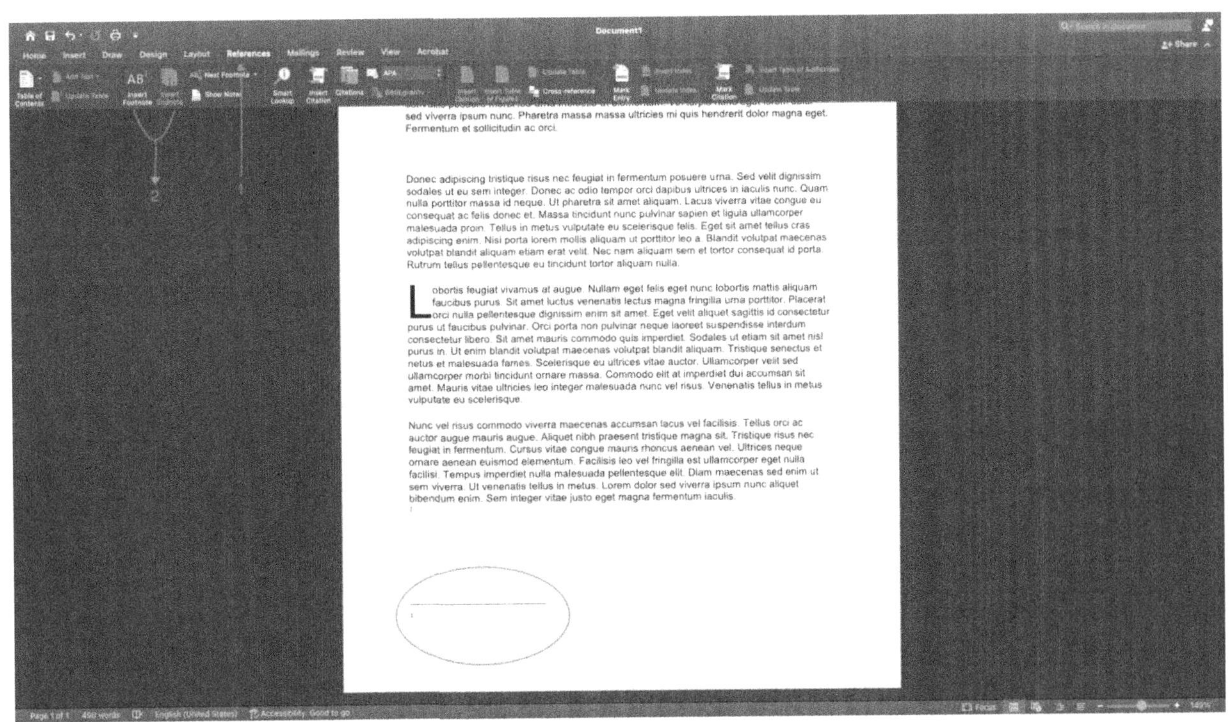

Editing and Formatting Footnotes and Endnotes

Accessing and using the Note Options dialog box

- Right-click on the footnote or endnote.

- From the popup menu, click Note Options...".
- In the dialogue box that appears for Footnotes and Endnotes, you can make any changes.

Customizing the numbering format, layout, and appearance:

- Go to the References tab.
- In the Footnotes section, click on the arrow located in the right corner.
- By doing this, a window with your formatting options will open.

Citations

Citations play a role in professional writing as they serve as acknowledgments to the sources used. They not only give credit to the authors but also allow readers to trace the source of the information provided.

There are different citation styles that are widely used in professional settings, including APA, MLA and Chicago. Each style has its rules and guidelines for creating citations and bibliographies.

Citation Styles

The different citation styles—APA, MLA, and Chicago—each have unique formatting guidelines tailored for specific types of writing.

- APA (American Psychological Association): Primarily used in the social sciences, the APA style places emphasis on the author and date of publication, helping readers quickly trace the source material.
- **MLA (Modern Language Association):** Favoured in humanities, MLA focuses on the author and page number, facilitating a detailed exploration of the source.
- **Chicago:** Known for its versatility, the Chicago style offers two systems: the Notes-Bibliography System, used in literature, history, and the arts, providing full bibliographic details in footnotes or endnotes along with a bibliography, and the Author-Date System, mirroring the APA style, used within the physical, natural, and social sciences.

Each style has distinct rules governing the formatting of citations and reference entries, enabling coherent, traceable scholarly communication within and across various disciplines.

Inserting Citation

Using the "Insert Citation" command

- Navigate to References > Insert Citation in a Microsoft Word document, then either add a new source or select an existing one.

Selecting or adding a new source

- To add a new source, click Add New Source, and in the Create Source dialog box, select the type of source you want to use.

Adding page numbers or other details to citations

- To add details like page numbers, select Citation Options, then Edit Citation.

Creating Bibliographies and Works Cited

The integrity of academic or professional writing is often underscored by the transparency in source attribution through bibliographies or works cited pages. Microsoft Word facilitates this through its "Bibliography" and "Manage Sources" commands.

Using the "Bibliography" command

- To generate a bibliography or works cited page in Microsoft Word, you can use the "Bibliography" command. To access this command, navigate to the References tab. Click on the Bibliography button. A dropdown menu will appear, providing you with formatted bibliography styles to choose from. You also have the option to insert a bibliography without any formatting or header.

Selecting a format style

- Before creating your bibliography, it's important to select the citation style for your document. To do this, go to References > Style. Choose a citation style such as APA, MLA or Chicago. Once you've selected a style, your bibliography or works cited page will be automatically formatted accordingly.

Updating the bibliography as new sources are added:

- Remember that as you add citations to your document, it's crucial to update your bibliography. To do this, simply click anywhere in the existing bibliography. Select Update Citations and Bibliography under the References > Bibliography tab. This will ensure that your bibliography reflects any source information you've added.

Managing Sources

When it comes to creating professional papers, it is essential to handle your sources in order to maintain credibility and follow proper citation guidelines. Microsoft Word's "Manage Sources" feature is a tool that simplifies the process of organizing, editing and formatting citations seamlessly.

Using the "Manage Sources" command

To manage your sources in Microsoft Word, you can use the "Manage Sources" command. This feature allows you to organize and handle the sources used in your document efficiently. To access it, go to the "References" tab, then click on "Citations & Bibliography " and select "Manage Sources."

Editing, deleting, or adding new sources

In the Source Manager, you have options for editing, deleting or adding sources. To modify or remove a source, simply choose it. Click on the Edit" or "Delete" button. If you want to add a source, click on the "button and provide all the necessary information in the dialog box that appears.

Organizing sources for ease of use

The Source Manager offers an interface to help you organize your sources effectively. It presents both a Current List of sources for your document and a Master List of sources that can be reused in documents. You can also search for sources using keywords or other criteria within the Source Manager. This promotes efficiency and makes managing your sources easier.

Using the Research Pane and Thesaurus

To produce well-researched and eloquently articulated documents, writers often require robust tools to explore synonyms or delve into broader research directly within their word processing environment. Microsoft Word caters to these needs through the Research Pane and Thesaurus features.

The Research Pane facilitates quick access to a plethora of reference materials, while the Thesaurus helps with enriching vocabulary by providing synonyms and antonyms.

Accessing and Using the Research Pane

Navigating to the "Review" tab:

- To start using the Research Pane, first navigate to the "Review" tab on the ribbon at the top of Microsoft Word.

Using the "Research" command to open the Research Pane:

The "Research" command has changed over different versions of Word:

- In Word 2010 and earlier versions, click Review > Research to open the Research Pane.
- In Word 2016, you can access the Research task pane by pressing Alt + Click on the word you want to research.
- In more recent versions, the Research Pane has been replaced by the "Researcher" tool. Click "Researcher" in the "Research" area of the ribbon after selecting the "References" tab.

Conducting searches and accessing various reference materials:

- Once the Research Pane or Researcher tool is open, type a term into the search box to begin exploring various reference materials. Review the relevant topics and sources that appear, facilitating a deeper understanding of the subject matter.

Using the Thesaurus

Accessing the thesaurus via the "Thesaurus" command:

- To access the thesaurus, highlight the word you wish to look up, navigate to the Review tab on the ribbon, and click the Thesaurus button.

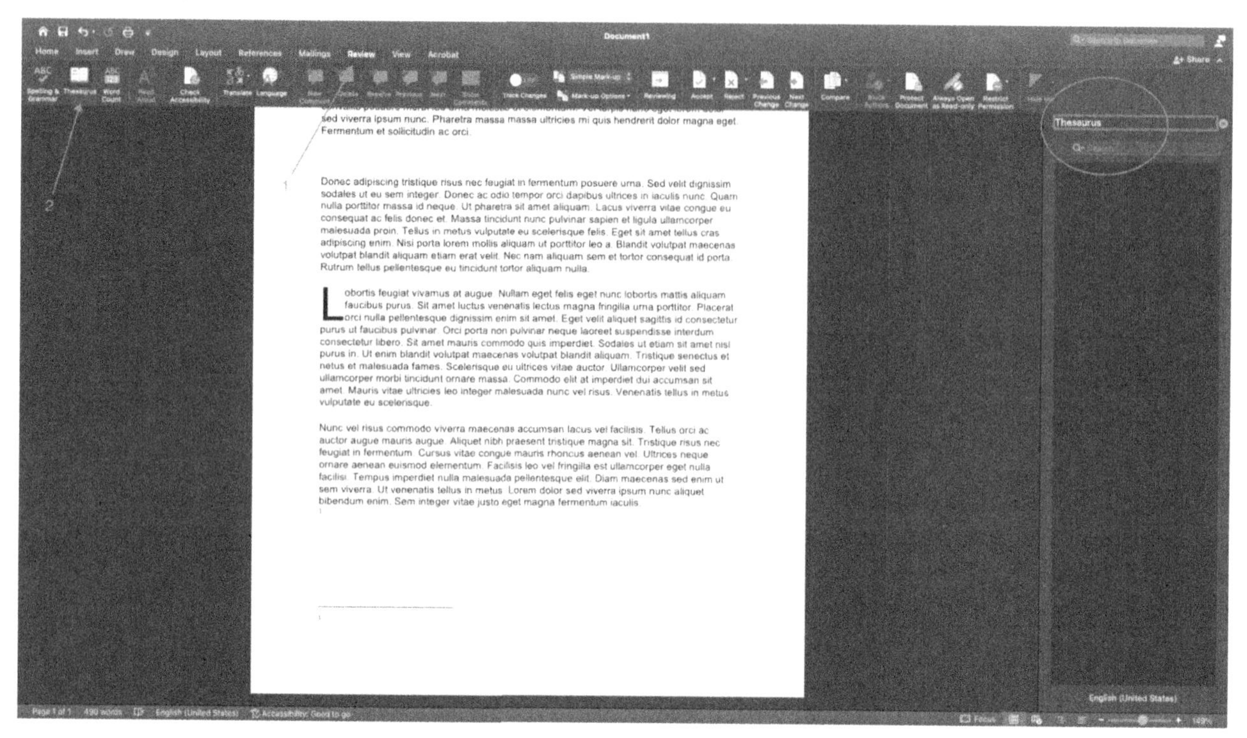

Searching for synonyms and antonyms:

- With the thesaurus open, you can view a list of synonyms and antonyms for the selected word. This feature assists in finding alternative words with the same or opposite meanings, enriching your vocabulary.

Inserting or copying results into your document:

- If you find a suitable synonym or antonym, point to the word, click the down arrow, then click Insert to replace the selected word in your document with the new word from the thesaurus. Alternatively, you can copy the word to your clipboard and paste it wherever needed in your document.

Chapter 11: Long Documents Mastery

Understanding the complexities of formatting and arranging documents is essential for people engaged in writing tasks, such as creating manuals, books or dissertations. It guarantees that the document is easily navigable, maintains an appearance and allows for referencing. In this chapter, we will explore the elements that contribute to becoming adept at managing documents.

Building a Table of Contents and Index

An organized Table of Contents (TOC) and index are crucial components for effectively managing lengthy documents. The TOC serves as a roadmap providing an overview of the document structure, while the Index acts as a guide to terms and topics covered.

Mastering the creation and maintenance of these elements not only improves the professionalism and accessibility of your document it also improves the reader's experience by enabling easy navigation and quick referencing.

The Importance of a Table of Contents and Index

- **Easy Navigation:** A Table of Contents (TOC) and Index make it simple for readers to navigate the document, helping them in locating the desired information easily.
- **Professional Presentation:** They contribute to an appearance showcasing an organized document.
- **Time-saving:** TOC and Index enable referencing, saving time for both the writer and the reader.

Creating a Table of Contents

- **Using Heading Styles:** Using heading styles to differentiate between sections, sub-sections, and other levels of content will automatically generate the TOC.
- **Formatting the TOC:** Ensure that you keep the TOC up to date as you work on your document.
- **Customizing the TOC:** Personalize the Table of Contents to match your document's structure by adding or removing levels or adjusting its appearance.

Building an Index

- **Creating an Index:** Begin by marking terms and phrases that should be included in the index, ensuring indexing.
- **Updating the Index:** Once you have marked all text, generate the index. Remember to update it as changes are made to your document.
- **Customizing and Formatting the Index:** Apply formatting styles that meet your document's requirements and customize the index accordingly.

Document Sections and Master Documents

When dealing with documents, adopting a method that ensures the document is structured user, user-friendly and effectively managed is crucial. This is where the concepts of Document Sections and Master Documents come into action. Document Sections enable the formatting and segmentation of content within a document, facilitating the creation of a layout.

On the other hand, Master Documents serve as a hub for housing smaller subdocuments in a structured manner. This proves beneficial when overseeing documents or projects involving authors.

Working with Document Sections

- Sections are helpful for controlling the flow and formatting of a document.

- You can insert section breaks to separate different parts. That way, you can format each section differently if you want.
- Sections also let you customize the headers and footers in specific parts of your document.

Understanding Master Documents

- Master documents are great for lengthy papers or reports. They let you break the document into smaller subdocuments, which is way more manageable.
- You make a master document first, then add the subdocs to it. The master doc stays in control, but you can work on the subdocs individually.
- You can edit and format the sub docs separately from the master and from each other. So, master documents make it easy to organize and manage long, complex documents.

Bookmarks and Hyperlinks

In Microsoft Word, ensuring navigation through lengthy documents is crucial to providing a pleasant reading experience. There are two methods at your disposal to improve navigability: Bookmarks and Hyperlinks. Bookmarks act as markers, allowing both authors and readers to jump to parts within a document quickly.

On the other hand, hyperlinks create pathways to resources, whether they are within the document or external, on the web. By mastering these tools, you can greatly improve the accessibility and professionalism of your documents.

Using Bookmarks

Bookmarks are incredibly useful for improving the ease of navigation in documents, enabling you to jump to relevant sections without having to search through numerous pages of content.

Creating Bookmarks

1. **Purpose:** Bookmarks are essential for marking specific locations within a document that you may need to return to frequently. They are particularly useful in lengthy documents where navigating to particular points can become cumbersome.
2. **Procedure:** In most word processors like Microsoft Word:

a. Place the cursor where you want to insert a bookmark.
b. Go to the 'Insert' tab.
c. Click on 'Bookmark' in the Links group.
d. Enter a name for your bookmark, and click 'Add.'

Navigating with Bookmarks:

1. **Ease of Access:** Once bookmarks are set up, they provide a convenient way to navigate through the document. They are like digital shortcuts to designated locations.
2. **Usage:** To navigate using bookmarks:

a. Go to the 'Insert' tab.
b. Click on 'Bookmark'.
c. A list of bookmarks will appear; select the one you want to go to and click 'Go To.'

Editing and Managing Bookmarks:

- **Modifying:** Over time, as your document evolves, you may need to edit or remove bookmarks.
- **Management:** Managing your bookmarks effectively includes renaming, deleting, or repositioning them as necessary. The process is similar to creating bookmarks; you'll find these options in the same 'Bookmark' dialogue box.

Incorporating Hyperlinks

Hyperlinks play a role by connecting different pieces of information together. Whether it is within a document or across sources, hyperlinks act as bridges that expand the scope of your content. They provide readers with a way to explore topics, references or additional resources with just a simple click.

Inserting Hyperlinks

Hyperlinks provide a way to link to external documents, web pages, or other sections within the document, serving as a bridge to additional resources or information.

1. **Procedure**: To insert a hyperlink:
    a. Highlight the text or select the image you want to link.
    b. Right-click and choose "Hyperlink," or select "Hyperlink" from the "Insert" menu.
    c. Enter the link in the address field or browse to select a document, and click 'OK.'
2. **Purpose**: Hyperlinks offer a means to connect with documents, web pages or other sections within the document. They act as a bridge to access resources or information.
3. **Procedure**: To add a hyperlink;
    a. Select the desired text or image you wish to link.
    b. Right. Choose 'Hyperlink' or navigate to the 'Insert' tab and click on 'Hyperlink.'
    c. Enter the link in the address field. Use the browsing option to select a document, then click 'OK.'

Editing and Removing Hyperlinks:

- To make changes to hyperlinks, you can follow a process. Right-click on the hyperlink.
- Choose the option to either edit the URL or remove the hyperlink altogether.

Linking to External Documents and Web Pages:

- Adding links to resources can greatly improve your document by allowing readers to explore topics in depth.
- It is important to ensure that these links are relevant, accurate and up-to-date to maintain your document's integrity and usefulness.

Chapter 12: Reviewing And Collaboration

In today's fast-paced world, it is crucial to have efficient methods for reviewing and working together on documents. Whether you're collaborating with others seeking feedback or making revisions, the tools and techniques discussed in this chapter are essential.

This final chapter explores the features of Track Changes and Comments, delves into Document Protection and Restrictions, and highlights the nature of Sharing and Engaging in Real Time Collaboration.

Track Changes and Comments

When it comes to reviewing and editing documents, Microsoft Word offers tools called Track Changes and Comments. These tools not only help with organizing the reviewing process but also encourage collaboration by allowing multiple people to give feedback on a document in real-time.

Track Changes

Enabling Track Changes marks every addition, deletion, or formatting alteration, making it straightforward to visualize what changes have been made and by whom.

1. Enabling Track Changes:
   a. Navigate to the 'Review' tab on the ribbon and select 'Track Changes' to activate this feature.
   b. Once enabled, every textual or formatting change will be recorded and highlighted.
2. Identifying Changes:
   a. All text insertions, deletions, and formatting alterations are distinctly marked, with different colors representing different authors.
3. Finalizing Changes:
   a. Review the tracked changes, accepting or rejecting them individually or collectively, to finalize the document.

Comments

You can use comments to annotate a document, whether it's for giving feedback, asking questions or clarifying content. To make a comment, just select "New Comment" from the "Review" tab once you have highlighted the text you wish to comment on.

1. Navigating Comments:
   a. In order to easily navigate through comments, you will find them displayed in the margin and connected to the text.
   b. Use the 'Previous' and 'Next' buttons found in the 'Comments group under the 'Review' tab to navigate between comments in your document.
2. Managing Comments:
   a. To effectively manage comments, you have the option to reply to them, mark them as done, or delete them. This encourages collaboration and facilitates addressing all feedback provided by collaborators.

Document Protection and Restrictions

With sharing documents just a click away, it's incredibly important to protect your documents from unauthorized access or changes. Microsoft Word offers features for safeguarding your documents and controlling who can access them.

Implementing Document Protection

In Microsoft Word, there is a feature called document protection that allows you to limit access or editing capabilities for a document.

To access the protection features, go to File > Info > Protect Document.

Two primary ways to protect a document are:

1. Password Protection:
    a. Encrypt your document with a password by selecting "Encrypt with Password."
    b. Set up a password with a mix of digits, symbols, and capital and lowercase characters.
2. Confirm your password by retyping it and saving your document for the password settings to apply.
3. Restricted Access:
    a. Control permissions for individuals by selecting "Restrict Permission by People." Then "Restricted Access."
    b. In the Permissions dialog box, assign desired access levels for each user.

Allowing Restricted Editing

Microsoft Word gives you the ability to designate sections of a document where you can permit edits while keeping the rest of it protected.

- To do this, go to the Review tab. Click on "Restrict Editing" in the Protect group.
- In the Editing restrictions area, check the box that says "Allow this type of editing in the document," and from there, choose "No changes (Read only)" from the list of editing options.
- Then, choose the section of the document that you wish to allow revisions on. This could be a block of paragraphs, a heading, a sentence or even just a single word.
- Under Exceptions, you have two choices: you can. Allow anyone who opens the document to edit that selected part or specify individuals who are allowed to make changes.
- To enforce this protection, click on "Yes" and then select "Start Enforcing Protection" under Start Enforcement.
- Additionally, if desired, you can assign a password so that those who know it can remove the protection and work on the document. Alternatively, you can encrypt the document so that authorized owners can remove this protection.

Sharing and Collaborating in Real-Time

In today's work environment, collaborating in real-time and easily sharing documents is no longer just a luxury but a necessity. Microsoft Word, which has long been a go-to tool for document processing, has adapted to meet these needs.

Real-Time Collaboration:

- Take advantage of the Share feature in Microsoft Word to invite others to collaborate on a document in time.
- When a document is shared, multiple users can work on it simultaneously using co-authoring. All changes made by each user will appear instantly.
- To make collaboration smoother, colored flags are used to indicate which sections of the document each author is currently working on.

Sharing Documents

- To share documents, you can. Send them via email. Create a shareable link using Microsoft Word. To do this, click on the "Share" option. Go to File > Share in Microsoft Word.
- If your document is not saved on OneDrive, you will be asked to upload it before sharing.
- Alternatively, you can right-click on the file in OneDrive. Select "OneDrive > Share" to share it with others.

Collaboration Platforms

There are collaboration platforms that work seamlessly with Microsoft Word to facilitate real-time collaboration and document sharing.

- **Microsoft 365:** It is a suite of cloud-based applications that includes Microsoft Word and other tools, allowing for collaboration and file sharing.
- **SpiraTeam:** This platform provides Application Lifecycle Management and integrates with Microsoft

Word, enhancing the nature of document creation and editing.

- **HighQ:** Designed specifically to streamline legal processes, HighQ integrates with Microsoft Word for seamless document collaboration.
- **Visual Planning:** An effective resource management, scheduling and planning software that also has integration capabilities with Microsoft Word for collaborating on documents.

In addition to these integrations, collaborative environments like Google Docs and Microsoft SharePoint can be used in conjunction with Microsoft Word for real-time document editing and sharing.

Conclusion

As we come to the end of this book, we have explored the world of creating, managing and collaborating on documents. From learning the basics of structuring documents to mastering the art of editing, in time, our journey has been enlightening. Throughout our exploration, we have explored the process of creating organized and easily navigable documents that serve not only as a repository of information but also as interactive platforms for collective intellectual engagement.

The explanations on the significance and process of crafting a Table of Contents and a comprehensive Index highlight the importance of documentation. Additionally, our exploration into Document Sections and Master Documents has opened up avenues for managing documentation with professionalism and ease.

As we progressed through each chapter, we unraveled the importance of reviewing and collaborative editing in today's fast-paced world. The tools and techniques discussed, such as Track Changes and real-time collaboration, not only optimize the reviewing process but also foster a culture of collective input and seamless teamwork. Our discussion on document protection also emphasized the need to safeguard property while encouraging engagement.

Moreover, our expedition into bookmarks, hyperlinks and day collaborative platforms revealed the potential offered by current document processing software. It demonstrated how, with the tools and knowledge, creating and managing documents could go beyond boundaries. This allows for an interactive approach to handling written materials.

The integration of platforms showcased a seamless combination of Microsoft Word with other modern technologies. This pushes document creation to become an effort that aligns with the era.

As the digital landscape continues to evolve, the skills and techniques explained in this guide establish a foundation for those seeking excellence in document management and collaborative editing. The knowledge gained here not only improves efficiency but also significantly contributes to fostering collaboration in professional environments.

Overall, this book serves as a guiding light for individuals and professionals aspiring to master the art of document management in today's workspace. It is a source of knowledge for navigating the intricate yet rewarding world of collaborating on document creation and editing.

Microsoft PowerPoint

Introduction: The Power Of PowerPoint

In a world where we want to communicate better, Microsoft's PowerPoint helps a lot. It's more than just a basic application. It's a platform where you can create and refine your ideas and messages to captivate and engage your audience deeply, both emotionally and intellectually. In this exploration of PowerPoint's extensive capabilities, we'll see how it can transform ordinary presentations, making them engaging, informative, and memorable.

PowerPoint is a versatile tool for everyone. It helps share ideas easily with its user-friendly design and many features, making visual storytelling accessible to people with different levels of experience.

In the modern world of today where it's hard for people to stay focused for long, PowerPoint is a powerful tool. It maintains the audience's interest during a presentation. It's like a platform where you can turn plain ideas into multimedia shows, using pictures, videos, and sounds to create a captivating experience that touches people's emotions.

PowerPoint serves as more than a mere medium for transmitting information; rather, it functions as a comprehensive framework for constructing coherent and persuasive narratives. Whether the aim is to present an innovative business proposal, deliver an educational lecture, or advocate for a new idea, this platform provides the necessary tools for organizing content clearly and persuasively.

Furthermore, PowerPoint isn't just for one person. It helps people work together and connect. Many people can work on a presentation together, and their creative ideas come together to make digital slides. And the best part is, they can share it online with people all over the world.

As we explore PowerPoint, we'll understand how it works, its role in making presentations interesting, and using data for more effective messages.

Whether you're experienced at presenting or just starting out, PowerPoint is here for you. It's a tool that can make your messages powerful and engaging. With some knowledge and creativity, you can improve your communication skills and inspire others. In this detailed guide, we'll learn how to use PowerPoint effectively. Becoming skilled at this software is a valuable goal for anyone looking to communicate better.

Chapter 1:Getting Started With PowerPoint

Introduction to the Interface

PowerPoint helps you combine visuals and stories to connect with your audience. By understanding the subtle details and techniques, you'll be able to craft visual compositions that leave a lasting impact on your audience.

PowerPoint might seem a bit tricky at first, but as you check it out, you'll discover many ways to create and arrange your stuff.

When you open PowerPoint, you see a blank page where you can start being creative. You have tools like text, shapes, and images to use and create your story. There's a ribbon with tabs and commands that helps you design and organize your work.

Slide Master keeps your presentation style consistent. Slide Sorter View shows all slides at once, making it easy to arrange. It helps your ideas flow smoothly.

PowerPoint's transitions and animations make your presentation more interesting. They add excitement and variety. Just like arranging your points and pictures in a specific order matters, these effects help keep things engaging.

We'll look into slide layouts, master slides, and themes. These details define how your presentation looks. We'll also explore how to add images, videos, and sound to engage your audience's senses.

As we go through the interface, we'll learn the secrets of making things look good, using fonts, and choosing colors. With each step, you will get better at using this tool, making presentations that touch people's minds and hearts.

Setting Up Preferences

PowerPoint helps you to tell your story. With its tools for text, images, and shapes, you're in control of your artistic vision.

Accessing the Preferences Menu: At the top, the "File" tab provides access to the preferences menu. When you click on it and then choose "Options" or "Preferences," you can change lots of things to fit your needs.

General Preferences: This section allows you to configure essential parameters such as language preferences, proofing options, and startup settings. Choose your preferred language to ensure that your messages resonate fluently, and adapt the software's behavior to your workflow, whether it's launching PowerPoint directly into a blank page or displaying recently viewed documents.

Save Preferences: Save preferences in PowerPoint let you choose where and how your files are saved. Set AutoSave to keep your work safe from unexpected interruptions.

Advanced Preferences: Customize how PowerPoint handles cut-and-paste operations, configure editing options to suit your style, and set your mouse and touchpad preferences for seamless navigation.

Preferences for Proofreading: Take good care of the words in your presentation. Set up spelling and grammar checks, and choose your language preferences for proofreading. This makes sure your story is well-written and accurate.

Customize the Ribbon: This feature lets you choose and arrange your favorite commands on the Ribbon. It's like customizing your toolbox to fit how you work.

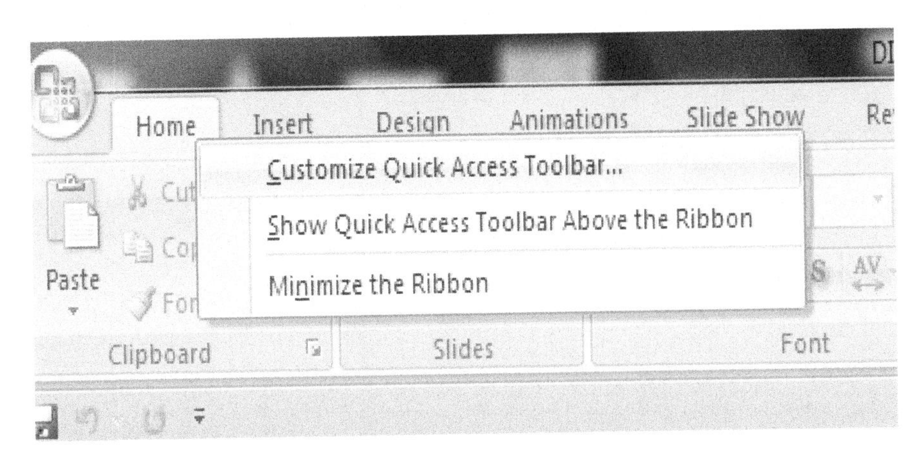

Add-Ins: PowerPoint's Add-Ins enable you to integrate additional features and functionalities that are tailored to your needs. Enhance your creativity with these extensions.

Trust Center: The Trust Center preferences provide you with the means to safeguard your PowerPoint presentations from potential threats, such as malicious macros and unsafe content.

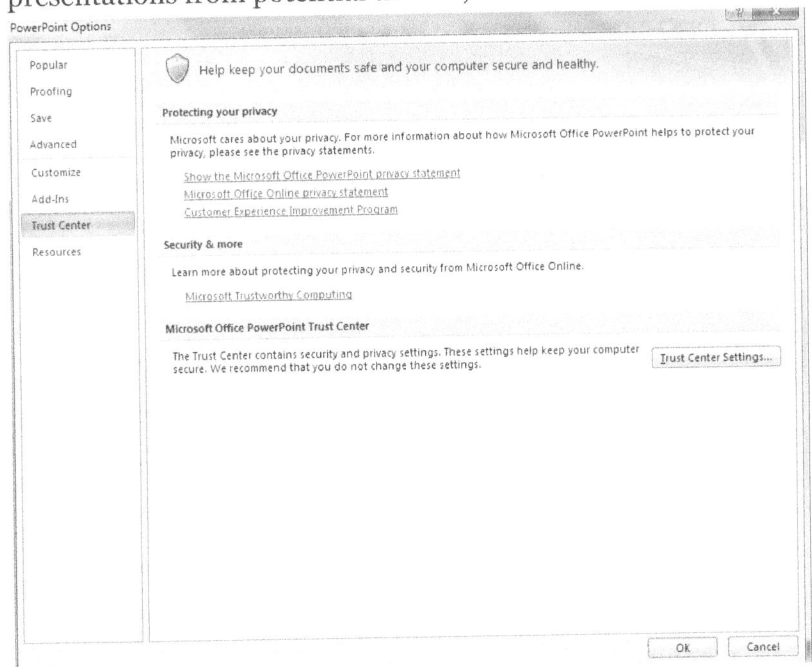

As we finish up, think of each setting as a piece in your creation. You have control, and with these options, you can make presentations that are well-spoken, polished, and accurate. Your choices will bring your PowerPoint work to life, making it something people won't forget.

Creating, Opening, and Saving Presentations

In PowerPoint, ideas are brought to life, stories are told, and messages are conveyed with elegance. In this visual guide, we will go through the essential steps involved in creating, opening, and saving presentations.

Presentation Creation

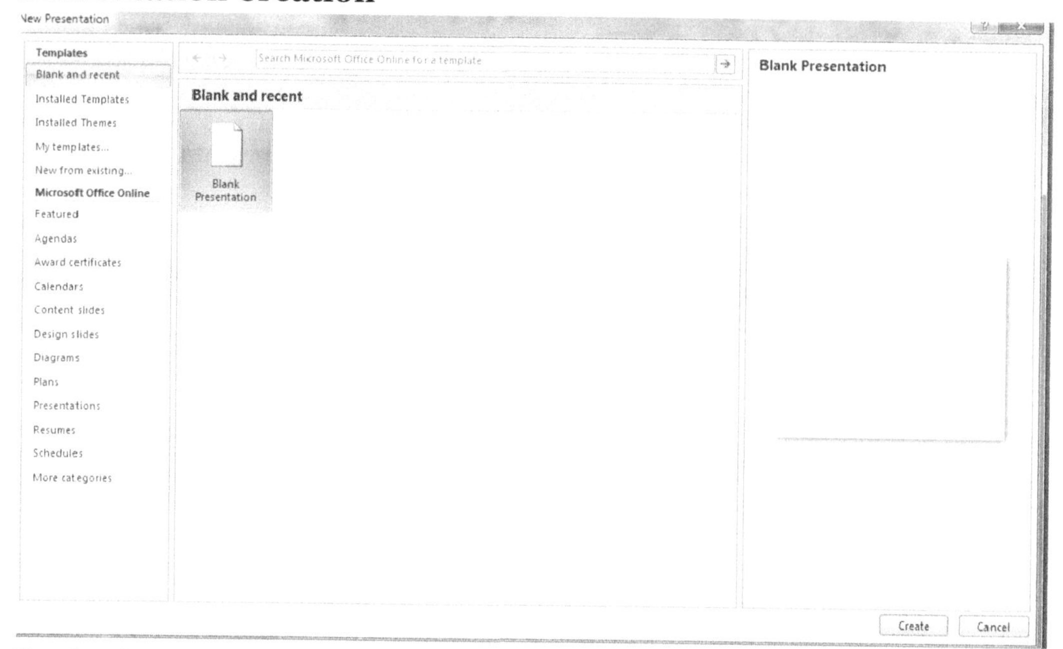

Beginning a Presentation: To create a new presentation, launch PowerPoint and click the "New" button, or press Ctrl + N (Windows) or Cmd + N (Mac). You will be presented with numerous template options to jumpstart your creativity.

Choosing a Template: Templates serve as the basis for the design of your presentation. Choose from the available templates based on your desired content and design. If you prefer full creative control, you can also begin with a blank presentation.

Opening to a Presentation

Accessing Recent Presentations: To access a presentation you worked on recently, click "File" and then "Open." A list of recent presentations will be displayed. Click on the file you wish to open, or navigate to it on your computer.

Opening from one-drive: If your presentation is stored on a cloud service such as OneDrive or SharePoint, you can directly access it by clicking "Open" and navigating to the cloud location.

How to Save a Presentation?

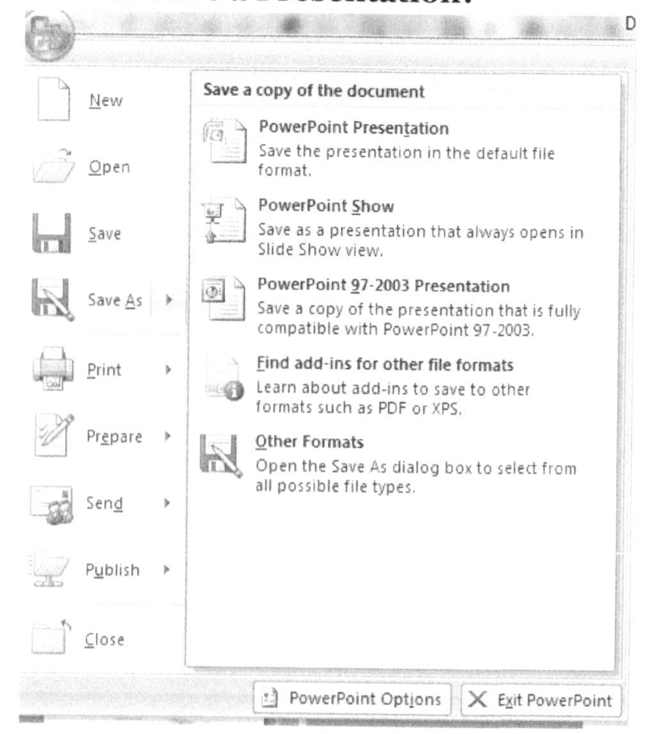

Regularly saving your work is an absolute necessity. Click "File" and then "Save" or "Save As." If this is a new presentation, you will be prompted to name and select a location for the file. If an existing presentation is stored locally, changes will be automatically saved. Click "Save a Copy" to create a new version if the file is stored in the cloud.

Selecting a File Format: When saving, you can select the file format that best meets your needs. PowerPoint's default format is "PPTX", but you can also save it in "PDF" for sharing or "PPSX" for a slideshow format.

Saving to OneDrive or SharePoint: You can save your presentation directly to OneDrive or SharePoint for universal accessibility. This facilitates remote access and collaboration.

Your workspace in PowerPoint is where you create, and every click and choice matters. Opening and saving your presentations carefully keeps your work safe, letting you impress your audience with your storytelling skills. Whether it's a business proposal or a compelling story, these simple steps open up a world of PowerPoint possibilities.

Ribbon and Tabs

PowerPoint's Ribbon is like a control center with lots of buttons and tools that help you create your presentation. It's divided into different tabs, each with its own set of options. Let's examine the Ribbon and its different tabs.

The Home Tab

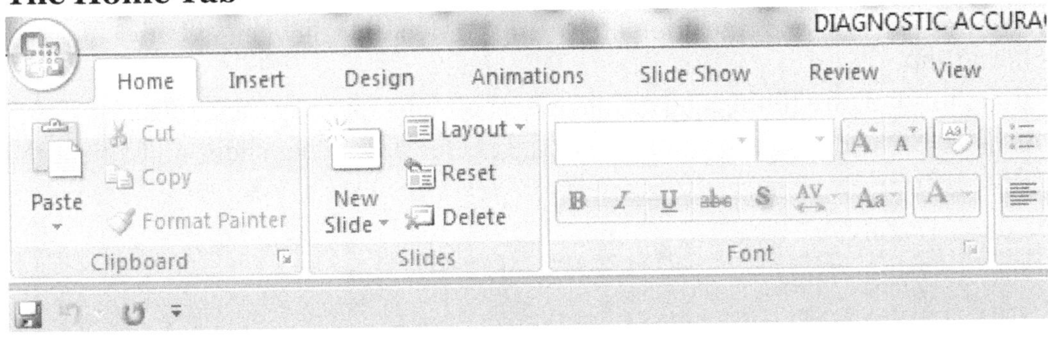

Clipboard: The Clipboard group contains essential commands such as Cut, Copy, and Paste, allowing you to effortlessly manage your content.

Slides: Control the structure of your presentation using the Slides group's options for adding, deleting, and rearranging slides.

Font: Customize your text with Font options, including font style, size, and color, in the Font group.

Paragraph: Using the Paragraph group, adjust text alignment, spacing, and bullet points.

Drawing: Use the Drawing group to add shapes, lines, and other drawing elements to your slides.

The Insert Tab

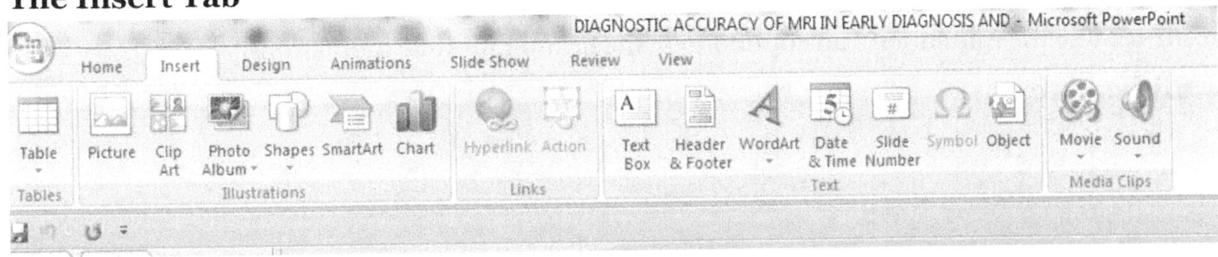

Tables: In the Tables group, you can insert and format tables for data or layout purposes.

Pictures: Use the Pictures option to embed images and graphics into your presentation.

Shapes: Access a variety of shapes and connectors to enhance your presentation slides in the Shapes group.

Charts: Create data-driven visuals such as graphs and charts using the Charts group.

Text: Use the Text group to insert text boxes, WordArt, and other textual elements.

The Design Tab

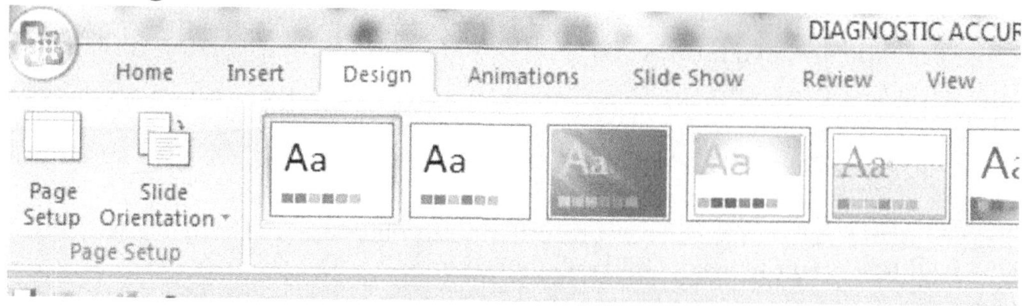

Themes: Within the Themes section, apply professionally designed themes to your presentation to alter its visual style.

Variants: Choose complementary color schemes and font sets for your selected theme in the Variants section.

Slide Size: Within the Customize section, adjust the dimensions of your slides for various outputs, such as widescreen and standard.

Background: Using the Background group, you can modify slide backgrounds and add design elements.

The Transitions Tab

Transition Effects: Choose from a variety of transition effects to add dynamic movement between slides in the Transition to This Slide group.

Timing: Use the Timing group to configure timing and advancement options for your transitions.

Advance Slide: In the Advance Slide group, you can specify triggers for advancing slides and adjust the duration of transitions.

The Animations Tab

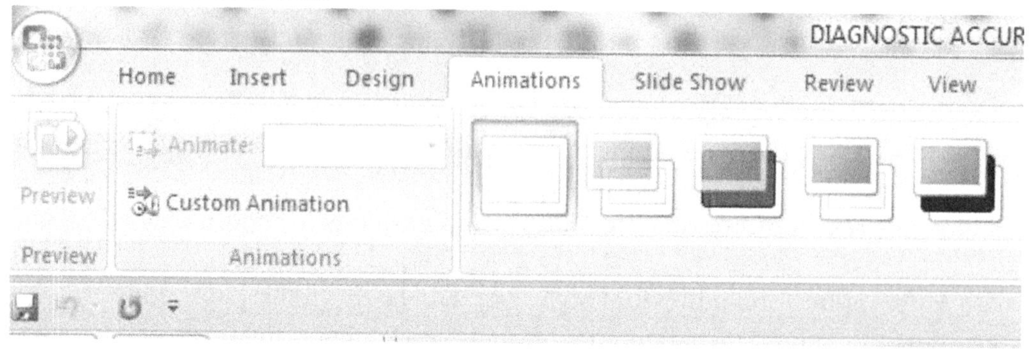

Animation Effects: Apply entrance, emphasis, and exit animations to slide objects in the Animation group using the Animation Effects option.

Animation Pane: Use the Animation Pane option to manage and fine-tune animations.

The Show Slides Tab

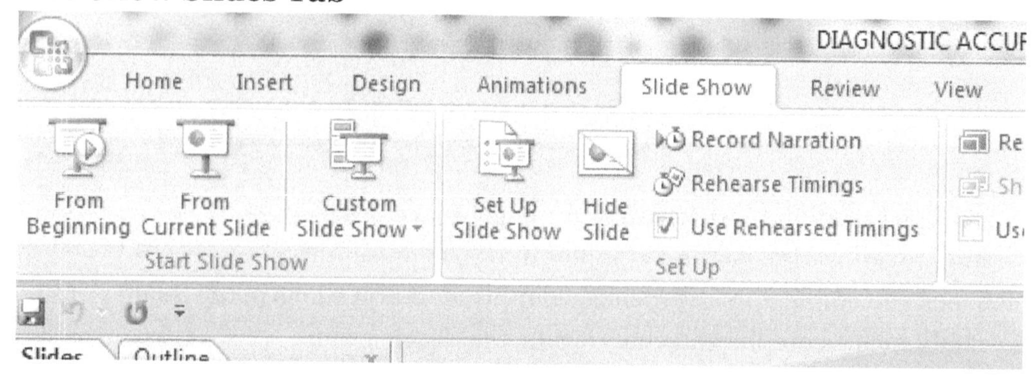

Start Slide Show: Using the Start Slide Show group, you can start your presentation from the current slide or the beginning.
Monitors: Configure how your presentation appears on various displays using the Monitors group.
Set Up: Customize settings for the slide show, including looping and narration, in the Setup section.

The Review Tab

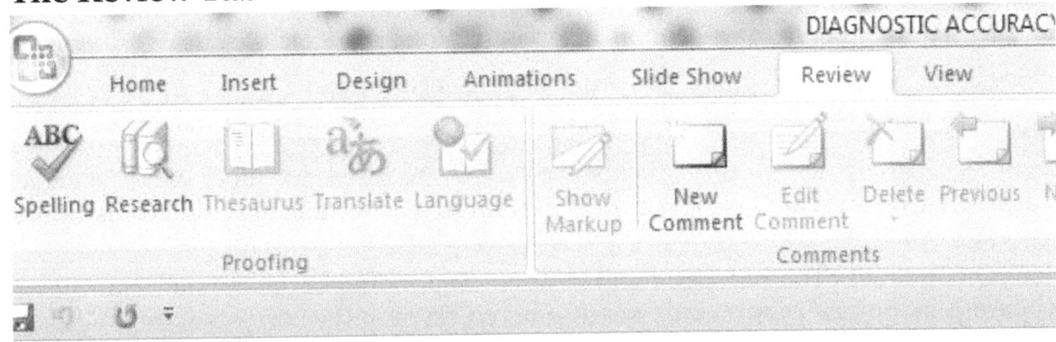

Proofing: Access options for spelling and grammar checking as well as translation in the Proofing group.
Comments: Collaborate with others through the addition and management of comments in the Comments group.
Compare: Compare and merge different versions of a presentation using the Compare group.

The View Tab

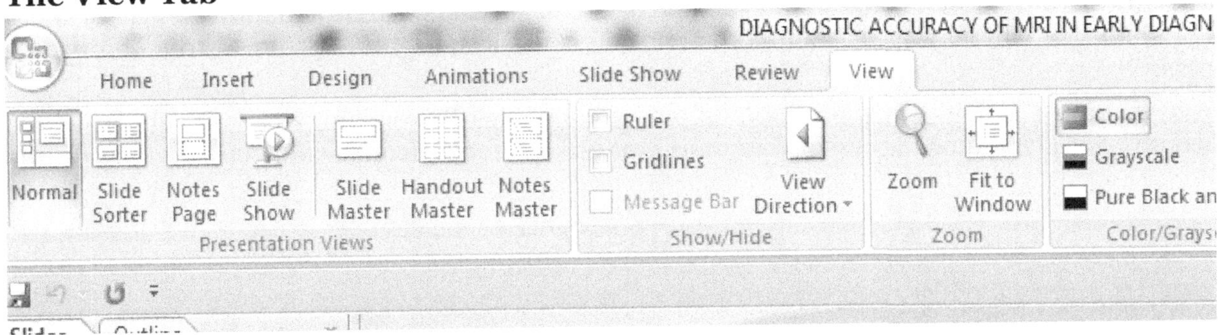

Presentation Views: Use the Presentation Views group to toggle between various presentation views, such as Normal, Slide Sorter, and Reading View.
Show/Hide: Toggles the visibility of gridlines, rulers, and other Show/Hide group elements.
Zoom: In the Zoom group, adjust the zoom level for precise editing.

As you go through these Ribbon tabs, remember each one has lots of commands to make your presentation better. Use the Ribbon and its tabs to guide you as you create an interesting experience for your audience, whether you're telling stories or giving persuasive talks.

Quick Access Toolbar

The Quick Access Toolbar is a small, customizable center with all your favorite tools. By using the Quick Access Toolbar, we can see how this simple thing can really make working in PowerPoint better.

Customization and placement

Adding Commands: The Quick Access Toolbar can be completely personalized. Any tool or command on the Ribbon may be added to the Quick Access Toolbar by performing a right-click and choosing "Add to Quick Access Toolbar."
Placement Options: The default position for the Quick Access Toolbar is above the Ribbon. However, you can also position it below the Ribbon or on the left side of the application window, based on your preferences and available screen space.

Popular Commands

Save: The "Save" icon is a popular choice for the Quick Access Toolbar because it ensures that your work is always safe. It allows you to easily save your presentation.

Undo and Redo: The "Undo" and "Redo" arrows provide a shortcut for undoing and redoing actions without using menus.

Slide Show: Add the "Start From Beginning" or "Start From Current Slide" icons to the Quick Access Toolbar to start your presentation immediately.

New Slide: Include the "New Slide" icon to add a new slide to your presentation quickly.

Customized Efficiency

Customizable Effectiveness: The Quick Access Toolbar can be modified to meet your specific requirements. Include frequently used commands, whether they pertain to text formatting, slide transitions, or design elements.

Keyboard Shortcuts: Each Quick Access Toolbar command has a corresponding keyboard shortcut. When you press "Alt" on the keyboard, the toolbar's commands are numbered. Typing the corresponding number activates the command, which improves your productivity.

Export and Import Configuration

You can export your Quick Access Toolbar settings to a file if you frequently switch between computers or collaborate with others. You can bring this file to another computer, making sure everything looks the same wherever you work.

Contextual Significance

Context-aware Commands: The Quick Access Toolbar adapts to the current situation. When working with images or shapes, it will display relevant commands such as "Rotate" and "Group," streamlining the creative process.

The Quick Access Toolbar is like your go-to tool, helping you manage PowerPoint easily. It's designed for what you need and gives you quick access to the tools you use the most. It makes navigating PowerPoint simple.

Chapter 2: Slide Basics: Creation And Design

Adding, Duplicating, and Deleting Slides

In PowerPoint, the key is to organize your content well. It's like making your presentation tell a clear and tidy story. Explore easy techniques to make your presentation organized and straightforward.

Adding Slides

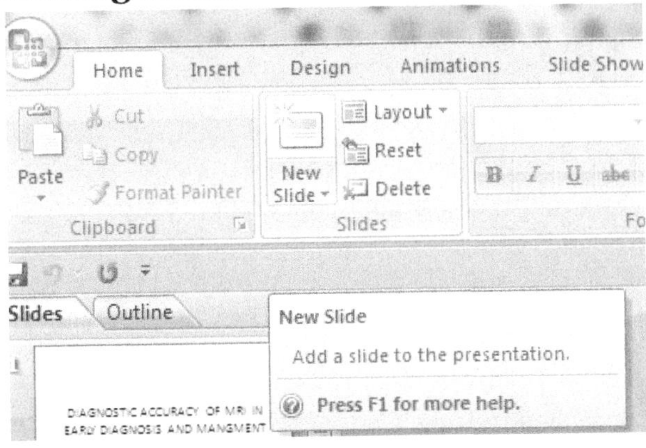

New Slide Button: The most straightforward method for incorporating a new slide into your presentation involves selecting the "New Slide" button situated within the Slides group on the Home tab. The software provides a variety of slide layouts for users to select from.

Keyboard Shortcut: Additionally, users have the option to employ a keyboard shortcut to expedite the process of inserting a new slide at their present location. On Windows, this can be achieved by simultaneously pressing the Ctrl and M keys, while on Mac, the combination of Cmd and M keys is utilized for the same purpose.

Slide Layout: When incorporating a new slide into your presentation, it is advisable to carefully deliberate on the specific content you intend to include. Various layouts are specifically designed for titles, bullet points, images, and other elements. The option that best suits your needs should be selected.

Duplicating Slides

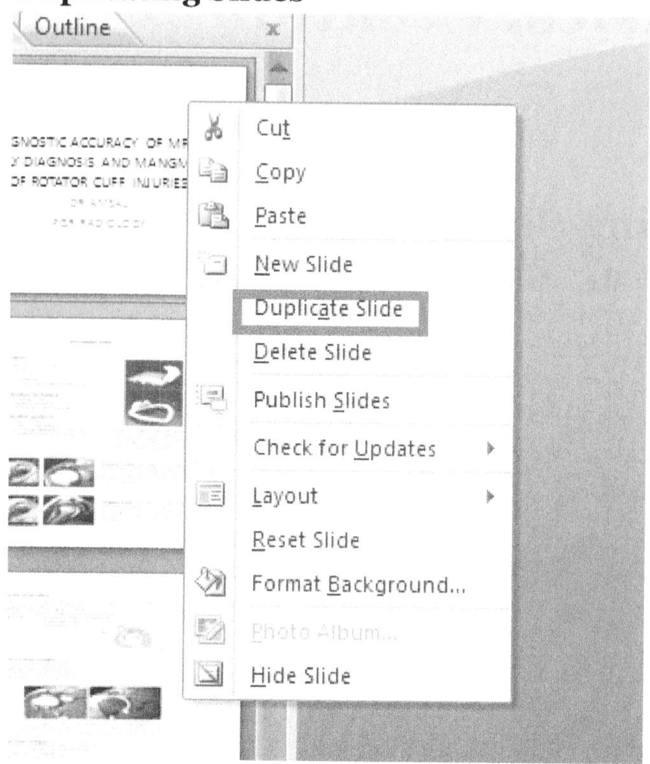

Right-Click Duplicate: To replicate a slide, users can perform a right-click action on the desired slide located in either the Slide Pane on the left-hand side or the Slide Sorter View accessible through the View tab. Following this, users should opt for the "Duplicate Slide" option from the available menu.

Ctrl + Drag: In Slide Sorter View, it is possible to duplicate a slide by simultaneously holding the Ctrl key (Windows) or Cmd key (Mac) and dragging the slide to a different position.

Deleting Slides

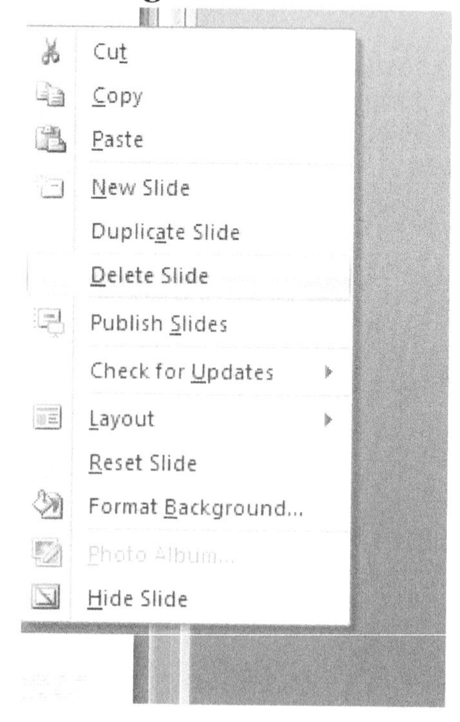

Right-Click Delete: To remove a slide from a presentation, the user can utilize the right-click function by clicking on the desired slide in either the Slide Pane or Slide Sorter View. From the context menu that appears, the user should select the option labeled "Delete Slide." The deletion will require confirmation from the user.

Keyboard Shortcut: A potential alternative approach involves the selection of the desired slide followed by the utilization of the Delete key on the keyboard to execute the deletion action.

Rearranging Slides

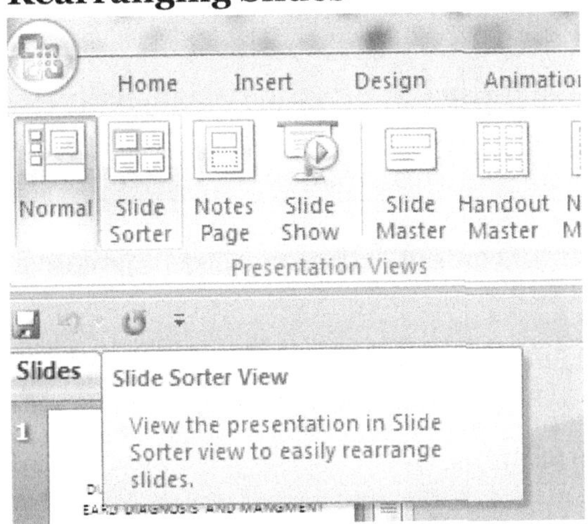

Drag and Drop: The process of rearranging slides in Slide Sorter View involves a simple drag and drop action, where users can click on a slide and move it to a different position. This feature enables users to effectively manage the progression of their presentation without interruptions or disruptions.

Cut and Paste: The process of relocating a slide can be accomplished by coosing the cut function (Ctrl + X or Cmd + X) to remove the slide from its current position, followed by the paste function (Ctrl + V or Cmd + V) to insert it into a new location.

Slide Sorter View: The Slide Sorter View, which can be accessed from the View tab, offers a visual representation of the presentation, allowing for easy rearrangement of slides.

Adding, copying, and deleting slides are important methods to shape your presentation's story. Think of each slide as an important piece. Using these methods helps you put together ideas that capture the audience's attention and leave a strong impression.

Slide Layouts and Themes

Slide layouts and themes help make your presentation look great. Let's explore how to use slide layouts and themes to design your presentation and make it interesting, like composing a captivating symphony.

Slide Layouts

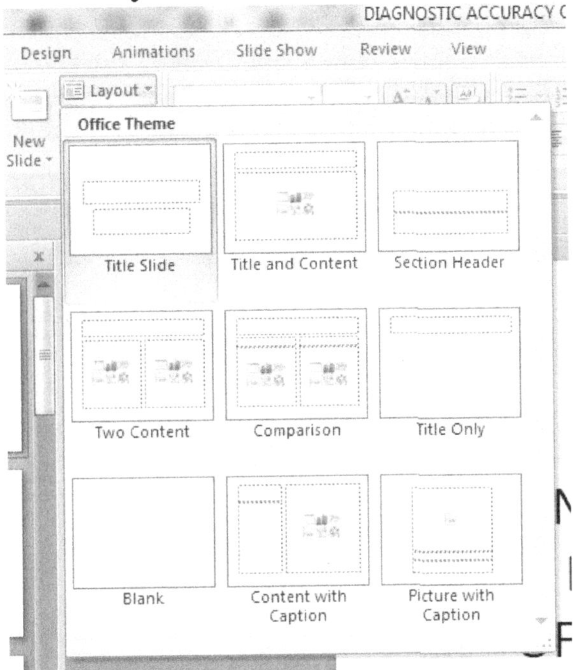

Accessing Slide Layouts: When you create a new slide (or right-click an existing slide and select "Layout"), a gallery of slide layouts is displayed. Each design is tailored to accommodate particular types of content, including titles, bullet points, images, and charts.

Title Slide: The Title Slide layout provides space for a captivating title and a subtitle, making it ideal for beginning a presentation. It establishes the tone for your story.

Content Slide: The Content Slide provides a combination of textual and visual information. It is appropriate for presenting data in a structured format.

Two-Content Slide: This layout allows you to display two content blocks side-by-side, facilitating comparisons or dual narratives.

Blank Slide: The Blank Slide gives you a clean slate with no set areas for content, letting you be fully creative. It's great for big pictures and your own designs.

Section Header Slide: Use Section Header Slides to introduce new sections within your presentation, thereby creating a clear and organized structure.

Title and Content Slide: Comparable to the Content Slide, this format includes a title but provides greater placement flexibility for content. It is excellent for multimedia presentations.

Themes

Selecting Themes: Themes are like the style for your presentation. They help set the overall feel. You can access them via the Design tab. Select a motif that complements your content and audience.

Variants: Themes provide variants with various color palettes and font combinations. These variations are accessible via the Design tab's "Themes" group.

Customization: Although themes provide a cohesive design foundation, you can further customize them by modifying their colors, fonts, and background styles to meet your particular branding or design needs.

Slide Master: The Slide Master allows for global design modifications to your presentation. Obtain it through the View tab. Adjust your slide's fonts, colors, and placeholders to maintain uniformity.

Background Styles: Themes typically include background styles that enhance the aesthetic appeal of your slides. Try out several formats to find the one that best fits your material.

Content and Consistency

Consistency: By choosing a cohesive combination of slide layouts and themes, you ensure visual consistency throughout your entire presentation. This consistency facilitates audience comprehension and participation.

Content Hierarchy: Establishing a Content Hierarchy Using slide layouts, you can arrange titles, subtitles, bullet points, and images to optimize the flow of information.

Audience Engagement: A well-chosen theme can captivate your audience and elicit the desired emotional response, thereby enhancing your presentation's overall impact.

Slide layouts and themes in PowerPoint help organize and design your ideas, making them visually appealing to your audience. You can choose the right combination of layouts and themes to create a unique presentation.

Slide Transitions

Slide transitions guide the way from one part of your presentation to the next. You can control how your presentation moves smoothly and impressively. Let's delve into slide transitions to discover how they can improve the storytelling in your PowerPoint presentation.

Accessing Slide Transitions

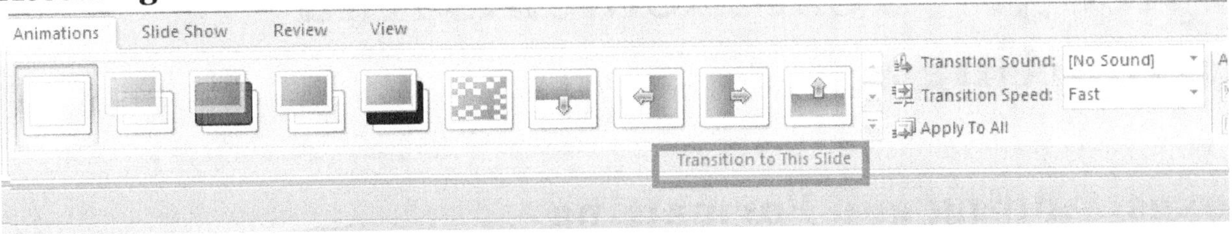

Tab Transition: Navigate to the "Transition" tab on the PowerPoint ribbon to access slide transitions. This page contains a gallery of transition effects.

Applying Transitions: Select the slide to which you wish to apply a transition, and then click on the desired transition effect. In the Timing group, you can also specify the duration of the transition.

Enhancing Visual Flow

Professionalism: Slide transitions lend your presentation an air of professionalism by smoothly guiding the audience through the content. Avoid using too many flashy transitions because they can be distracting.

Consistency: Maintain a uniform transition style throughout your presentation to create a unified visual experience. Use comparable transitions for related sections or content.

Preview: Before finalizing your transitions, use the "Preview" button located on the Transition tab. This allows you to visualize how your presentation's transitions will appear.

Types of transitions

Subtle Transitions: Subtle transitions, such as "Fade" and "Crossfade," offer a gentle transition between slides. They are suited for the majority of presentations.

Exciting Transitions: Consider "Zoom" and "Slide Left" for transitions that add flair to presentations.

Dynamic Transitions: "Cube," "Cover," and "Uncover" transitions can create dramatic effects for impactful moments or key reveals.

Content-Specific Transitions: Align your transitions with the text. For example, "Wipe" transitions are effective when introducing lists and bullet points.

Timing and Control

Duration: Adjust the transition duration in seconds or milliseconds to control the speed of the transition effect. Longer durations result in slower transitions, whereas shorter durations produce more rapid transitions.

Advance Options: Customize the rate at which each slide advances. You have the option of selecting "On Mouse Click," "After," or "Automatically." Timing and sequence are crucial to your narrative.

Sound Effects

Sound Accompaniment: Some transitions can be enhanced with the addition of sound effects. In the "Transition Sound" drop-down menu of the Timing group, you can assign a sound to a transition.

Hints and Tips

Relevance: Ensure that the transitions you choose are pertinent to your content. They should contribute to your message, not detract from it.

Consider Your Audience: Remember who you are speaking to. Transitions should facilitate comprehension and interest, rather than confuse or divert.

Storytelling: Utilize transitions when narrating your story. Timing and selection should correspond to the tempo of your story.

Slide transitions are the choreography of your PowerPoint presentation, leading the audience through the visual movements of your narrative. Transitions can be used to improve the flow and impact of a presentation. With careful selection and timing, it elevates your PowerPoint performance to one that is captivating and memorable.

Chapter 3: Text Elements And Formatting

Text Boxes: Adding and Formatting

Text boxes in PowerPoint are like your writing tools, where you can put your thoughts and ideas onto your slides. They're flexible and help you express your ideas clearly and beautifully. Let's learn how to add and style text boxes to turn plain words into an interesting and engaging story.

Including Text Box

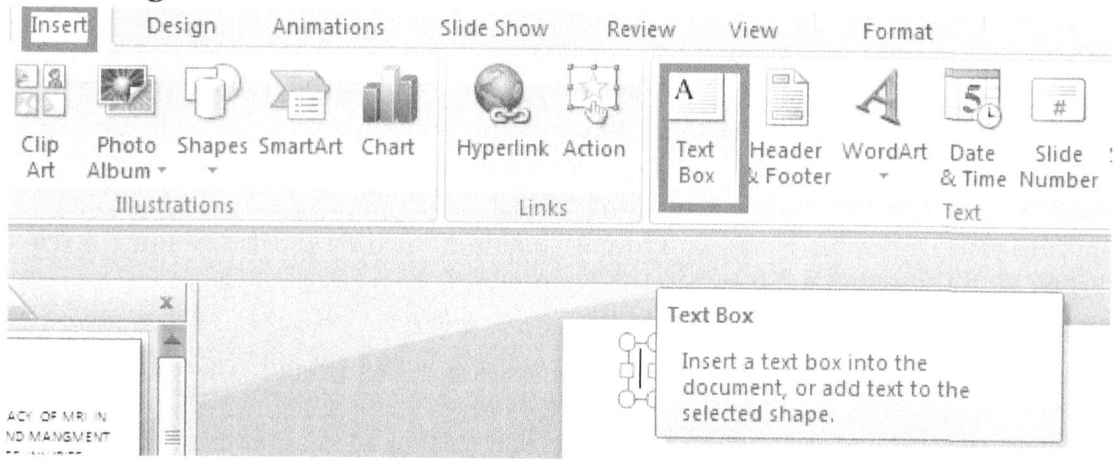

Insert Tab: Navigate to the "Insert" tab on the PowerPoint ribbon to add a text box.

Text Box: Select "Text Box" from the menu. Your mouse pointer will become a crosshair.

Click and Drag: Click on the slide where you want to insert the text box and drag it to create a rectangle that will determine the size of the text box.

Typing: Once the text box has been created, start typing your text. PowerPoint adjusts the text size automatically to fit within the box.

Resize and Reposition Text Boxes

Selection: Click the text box's border to select it. Then, you can resize it by dragging the corner or side handles.

Moving: To move a text box on the slide, click and drag it to the desired spot.

Text Box Formatting

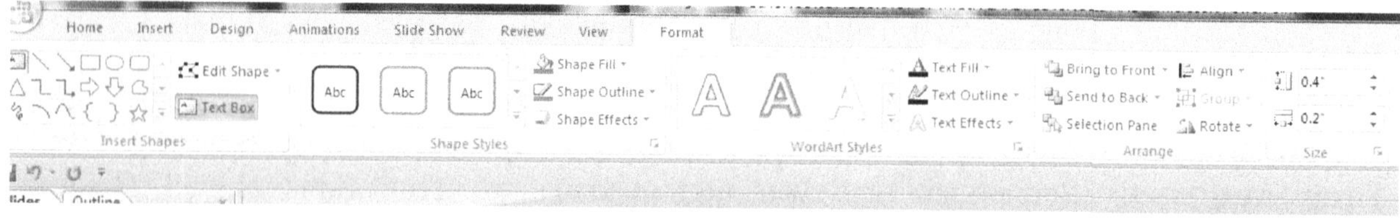

Text Formatting: To format text, select the text within the text box. Using the options on the "Home" tab, you can modify font styles, size, color, and alignment.

Fill and Outline: Modify the background color and outline of the text box using the "Format Shape" option on the "Format" tab.

Shape Effects: From the "Format" tab, apply various effects such as shadows, reflections, and bevels to your text box.

Text Box Designs and Alternatives

AutoFit Text: PowerPoint automatically adjusts text size to fit within a text box when AutoFit Text is enabled. In the Format Shape pane, you can also manually adjust text size and enable or disable AutoFit options.

Word Wrap: PowerPoint text boxes have word wrap enabled by default, allowing text to flow automatically to the next line when it reaches the box's edge.

Margins and Indentation: Fine-tune text positioning within the text box by adjusting margins and indentation.

Linking Text-Boxes

Overflowing Text: When you have more text than fits in a single text box, a small handle appears at the bottom right corner of the box, indicating overflow.

Linking Boxes: To continue overflowing text in another text box on a different slide, click on the handle and then click on the slide where the linked text box should appear.

Best Methods

Clarity and Brevity: Keep your writing concise and clear. Utilize bulleted or numbered lists to improve readability.

Consistency: Maintain consistent font styles and text box formatting throughout your presentation for a professional appearance.

Visual Balance: Ensure that your text boxes are appropriately sized and positioned to maintain a visually appealing and balanced composition.

Text boxes in PowerPoint carry your words. When used well and styled carefully, they turn plain text into a visually interesting story. Use these tools to make presentations that captivate, inform, and inspire your audience.

Fonts, Styles, and Alignment

Choosing fonts, styles, and alignment in PowerPoint is like picking the right tools for a job. It sets the mood, expresses feelings, and makes things easy to understand. Learn how to use these features to make your presentations look good and convincing.

Selecting Fonts

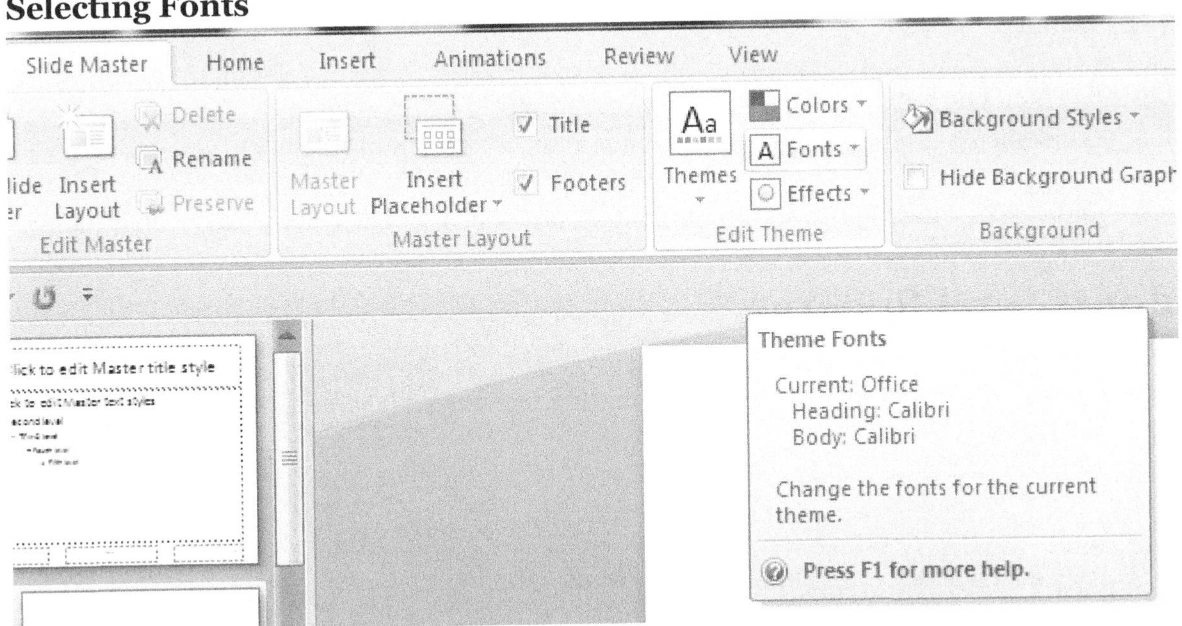

Font Selection: Click the text you'd like to format, then navigate to the "Home" tab on the PowerPoint ribbon. Here, you can select fonts from the Font group's dropdown menu.

Font Themes: PowerPoint includes font themes that work well together, ensuring that your design is consistent. Use the "Design" tab to access these themes.

Font Styles

Bold, Italics, and Underline: Using the bold, italic, and underline options in the Font group on the "Home" tab, you can emphasize your text.

Font Size: Adjust the size of your text using the font size dropdown menu or by entering the desired size manually. It is essential to ensure readability at various viewing distances.

Font Color: Experiment with various font colors to create visual contrast or to complement your brand's color palette. This option is also available in the Font group.

Line Spacing and Alignment

Alignment: You can control text alignment using the alignment buttons in the Paragraph group on the "Home" tab. Left, center, right, or justified alignment options are available.

Line Spacing: Using the "Line Spacing" options in the Paragraph group, you can adjust the space between lines in your text. This can improve readability and visual attractiveness.

Boxes for Text and SmartArt

Text Boxes: Text boxes can be positioned anywhere on a slide, permitting flexible text placement and formatting. They can be formatted similarly to standard text.

SmartArt: When presenting complex information, you should consider using SmartArt graphics. These pre-designed layouts provide an aesthetically pleasing method for organizing and displaying text.

Textual Coherence

Slide Master: Use the Slide Master to ensure text formatting consistency across all slides. It is accessible via the "View" tab.

Design Templates: Utilize PowerPoint's design templates for a consistent, professional look that includes predefined fonts and formatting.

Best Methods

Legibility: Prioritize readability over aesthetics. Ensure that the fonts and sizes you choose are legible, especially from a distance.

Consistency: Maintain consistency in font selection, size, and style throughout your entire presentation. This contributes to an elegant and professional appearance.

Whitespace: Allow sufficient whitespace in your design to prevent text from appearing crowded. Correct spacing improves readability.

Hierarchy: Use font styles, sizes, and colors to establish a distinct hierarchy of information. The titles, subtitles, and body text should be visually distinct from one another.

Alignment: Align text elements intentionally to guide the audience's eye and establish a sense of order in your slides.

Typography quietly guides your PowerPoint, setting its pace and mood. Use fonts, styles, and alignment to make your message not just heard but also seen and felt.

Lists, Indents, and Spacing

Lists, indents, and spacing give structure and order to your content in PowerPoint presentations. Similar to arranging elements in a well-organized manner, these formatting techniques help create clear and engaging presentations.

Creating Bulleted and Numbered Lists

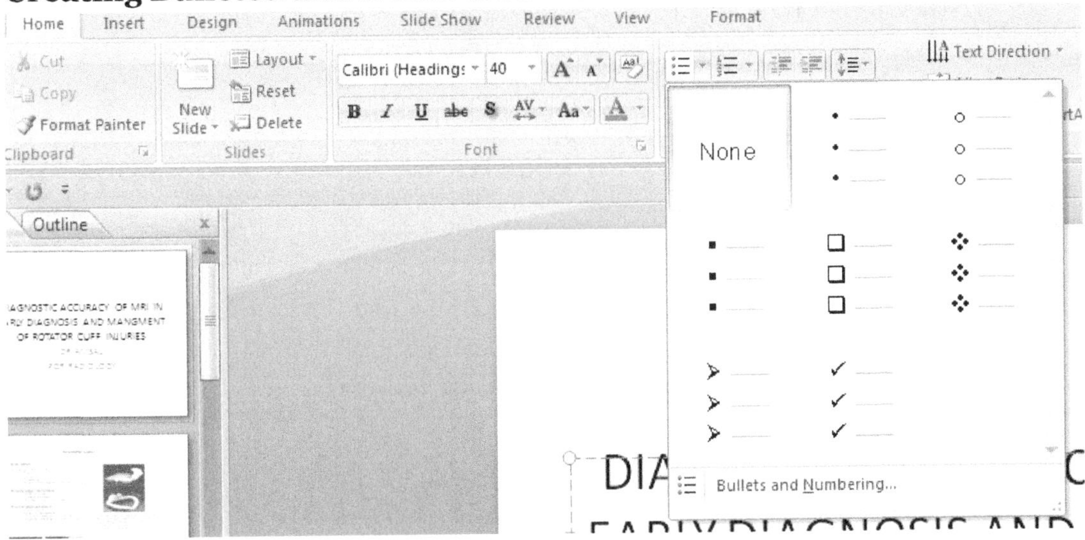

Bullet Points: Begin by highlighting the text you wish to transform into a bulleted list. Use the "Bullets" button on the "Home" tab to apply bullet points to the selected text.

Numbered Lists: Follow the same steps for creating numbered lists, but click the "Numbering" button instead. This is especially helpful for steps, sequences, and ordered data.

Customizing Bullet Points and Numbers

Bullet Styles: There are several bullet styles available in PowerPoint. Selecting "Bullets and Numbering" from the menu after selecting the arrow next to "Bullets" or "Numbering" will modify the bullet style.

Custom Bullet Points: If you have specific bullet points in mind, you can create custom bullet characters by selecting "Define New Bullet" from the "Bullets and Numbering" dialogue box.

Indentation and Outdentation

Indentation: To create sub-points or nested lists, use the Increase Indent button on the "Home" tab's Paragraph group. This right justifies the text.

Outdentation: Select the indented text and click the Decrease Indent button to reverse the indentation. This is useful when you wish to return to the list's main level.

Spacing and Line Breaks

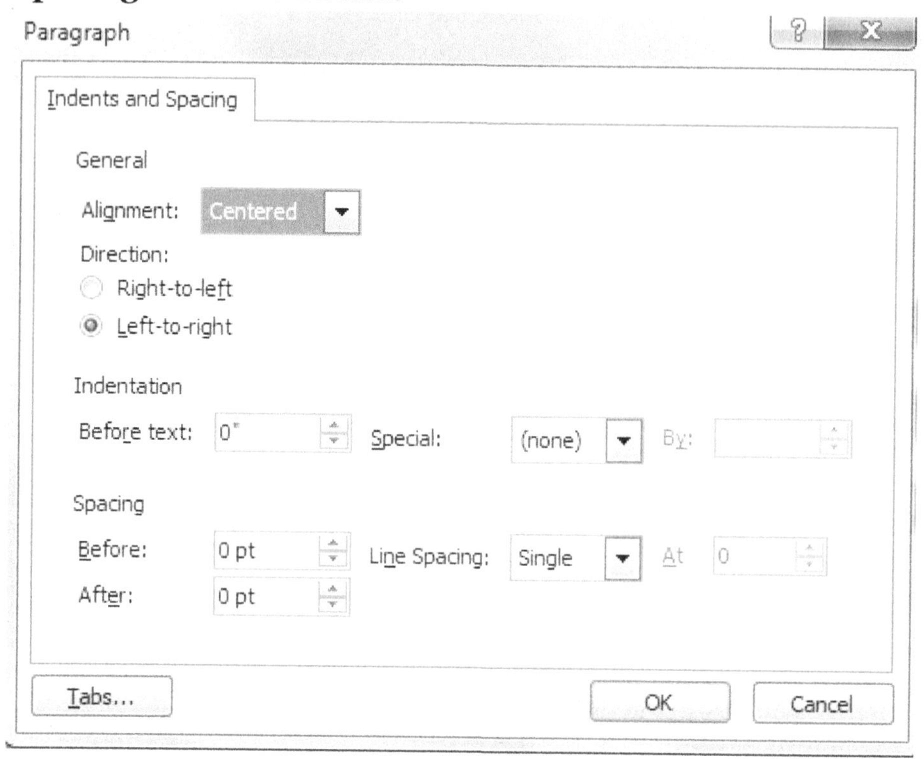

Line Spacing: Adjust the distance between lines in a list by selecting the text and modifying the line spacing in the Paragraph group.

Paragraph Spacing: In the Paragraph dialog box, you can adjust the line spacing before and after paragraphs. This helps refine the structure of your lists.

Nested Lists and Subpoints

Creating Nested Lists: To create nested lists, use the Increase Indent button to indent the items beneath the main point. This results in a hierarchical organization.

Different Bullet Styles: To visually differentiate between main points and subpoints, you can use different bullet styles. Customize these formats through the "Bullets and Numbering" dialog.

Best Practices

Clarity: Use lists to simplify and enhance the readability of complex information. Ensure that each point is succinct and pertinent.

Consistency: Maintain consistent list formatting throughout the entirety of your presentation. This includes the use of bullets, indents, and spacing.

Hierarchy: Create a hierarchical structure by using indentation for subpoints. This assists your audience in comprehending the relationships between various points.

Visual Balance: Pay close attention to the visual equilibrium of your lists. Avoid lengthy lists that could overwhelm your audience.

The rhythm and structure of your PowerPoint presentation are determined by the use of lists, indents, and spacing. You can guide your audience through your content with precision and clarity using these formatting techniques.

Chapter 4: Visual Elements: Graphics, Images, And Shapes

Inserting and Modifying Images

In PowerPoint presentations, pictures make your story more interesting. Let's discover how to insert and adjust images in PowerPoint, an essential skill for creating an effective and engaging presentation.

Inserting Images

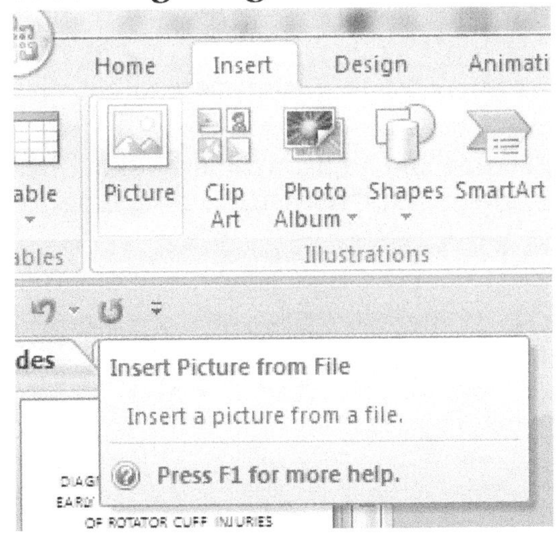

Insert Tab: To incorporate an image into a PowerPoint presentation, navigate to the "Insert" tab located on the ribbon.

Image: Selecting the "Picture" option will launch a dialogue box from which you can navigate to the desired online or local source of the image.

Drag and Drop: An alternative approach entails the straightforward act of dragging and dropping an image file onto your slide from your computer or a web browser.

Modifying Images

Resizing: To resize an image, select it with your mouse and then manipulate the corner handles to the inward or outward direction. Hold the Shift key while dragging to preserve the aspect ratio of the image.

Cropping: To crop an image, click the "Crop" button located on the Format tab after selecting the image. Press Enter after adjusting the cropping handles to specify the desired area.

Rotation: To rotate an image, select it and manipulate the rotate handle located at the top of the interface. Additionally, you can right-click the image, select "Rotate," and then enter the desired rotation angle.

Image Styles: Shadows, reflections, and outlines are among the image styles accessible via the Format application. Experimentally utilize these to improve the aesthetic quality of your photographs.

Alignment and Positioning of Images

Alignment: To align images with the slide or other objects, utilize the alignment options located on the Format tab. This ensures that the composition is visually balanced.

Positioning: Right-click an image, select "Format Picture," and navigate to the Size & Properties tab to precisely position it. In this field, precise position and size values can be specified.

Image Transparency

Adjusting Transparency: To increase the transparency of an image, navigate to the Format tab, select it, and use the Transparency slider. This may result in visually appealing overlay effects.

Aesthetic Effects

Artistic Effects: Artistic effects can be accessed through the Format tab, where users can apply a variety of filters and styles to their images to impart them with a distinct visual identity.

Alternating Images

Image Replacement: Right-click an image and select "Change Picture" to replace it while preserving its dimensions and orientation. By selecting a new image, the current one will be replaced.

Ideal Procedures

Significance: Opt for images that are in direct alignment with your content and serve to bolster your message. Avoid using irrelevant or distracting visuals.

Quality: To guarantee clarity and sharpness, prioritize images with high resolution, particularly when intending to project your presentation onto a sizable screen.

Consistency: Maintaining a consistent visual style, including alignment, size, and effects, for your images will help you create a polished and cohesive presentation.

Accessibility: To guarantee that all audiences can comprehend your content, ensure accessibility by including alternative text (alt text) for images.

Images bring depth and meaning to your content in PowerPoint. By adding and adjusting images skillfully, you create a collection of visuals that deeply resonates with the audience. Use visual storytelling in PowerPoint to make your presentations vibrant and captivating.

Using Shapes and SmartArt

Shapes and SmartArt help you make PowerPoint slides look good. These versatile tools let you creatively and clearly share ideas, concepts, and relationships. Discover how to use shapes and SmartArt in PowerPoint to create a solid visual foundation for your storytelling.

Inserting Shapes

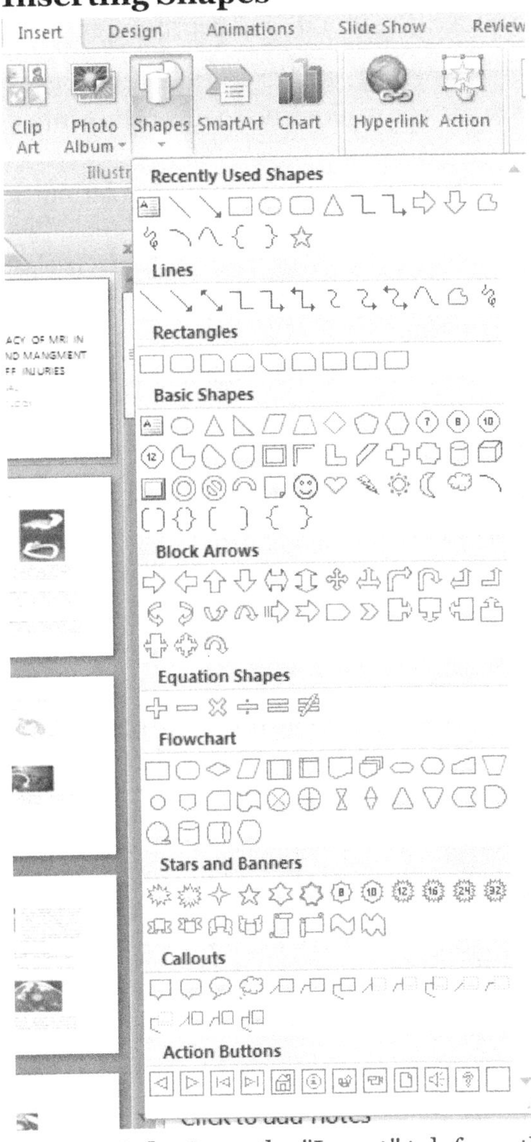

Insert Tab: Open the "Insert" tab from the PowerPoint ribbon to incorporate a shape into your presentation.

Shapes: A variety of shape categories, including rectangles, circles, arrows, and more, can be accessed by clicking the "Shapes" button.

Drawing a Shape: Click the slide containing the desired shape to begin drawing it. Release the mouse button after dragging to generate the shape. Additionally, to preserve proportions, you may hold down the Shift key while dragging.

Shape Alteration

Resizing and Rotating: To access the resizing handles, one must first select a shape. To resize the shape, drag these handles. Utilize the rotation handle (depicted in green) located at the top to rotate a shape. Additionally, the option to "Rotate" and "Edit Points" is accessible by right-clicking the shape.

Filling and Outlining: Alternate fill colors and outlines are both viable methods of personalization for shapes. Accessed via the Format tab, these options are labeled "Shape Fill" and "Shape Outline."

Shape Effects: Change the appearance of your shapes by utilizing the Format tab to apply a variety of effects, including reflections, shadows, and three-dimensional formats.

Shape Distribution and Alignment

Alignment: The process of aligning multiple shapes on the slide involves selecting them, navigating to the Format tab, and utilizing the "Distribute" and "Align" options.

Inserting SmartArt

SmartArt: Select "SmartArt" from the "Insert" menu to incorporate SmartArt into your presentation.

Choose a SmartArt Graphic: A gallery containing SmartArt graphics will be displayed after you select one. Choose the one that aligns most closely with your information or idea. Press "OK" to incorporate it.

SmartArt Editing

Text Entry: Clicking a shape or text box and commencing to type are the steps required to insert text into a SmartArt graphic. Pasting text from outside sources is another option.

Adding and Deleting Shapes: SmartArt graphics are modifiable through the addition and deletion of shapes. Right-click on an existing shape and choose "Add Shape" to create a new one Press "Delete" after selecting the desired shape to removc it.

Repositioning and Resizing: Clicking on a SmartArt image to select it enables repositioning and resizing. Apply the resizing handles to modify their size or drag them to relocate them.

Changing SmartArt Style: Altering the Visual Presentation of Your Graphic: In the Design tab, investigate various SmartArt styles to modify their appearance.

Optimized Methods

Clarity: Improve the clarity of your message by incorporating shapes and SmartArt. Your content ought to be complemented by visual elements rather than detract from it.

Consistency: To achieve a visually unified appearance, ensure that your presentation adheres to a consistent set of guidelines regarding color, style, and alignment.

Simplicity: Keep your slides uncluttered by avoiding the use of SmartArt or shapes. Prudently employ these components to exemplify fundamental ideas.

PowerPoint's artistic tools, SmartArt and shapes, enable you to visually enhance the clarity and originality of your presentations. By skillfully using these elements, you can transform complex concepts into engaging visuals, creating a dynamic canvas that captivates your audience.

Image and Graphic Effects

Image and graphic effects in PowerPoint are like tools that make your slides stand out. They add depth, draw attention to important parts, and give your presentation a unique touch. Let's explore how to use these effects to enhance your storytelling and make your visuals like a canvas for your ideas.

Applying Image Effects

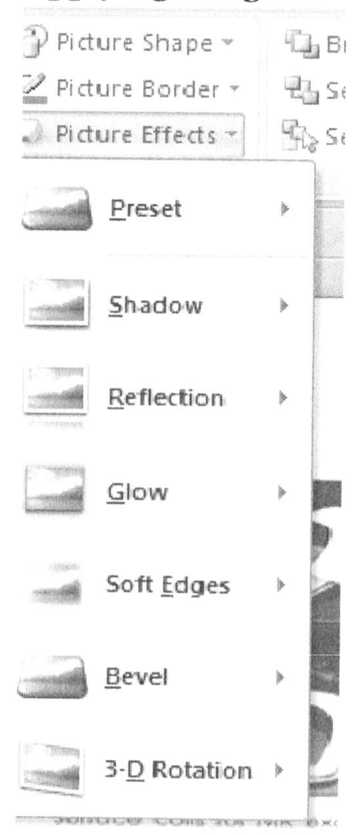

Select the Image: Select the desired image to apply effects to by clicking on it.

Format Tab: To access the "Format" tab in PowerPoint, proceed to that section after the image has been selected.

Image Effects: You will discover an assortment of image effects under the "Format" tab. These include, among other things, presets for shadows, reflections, and glows.

Effect Personalization: To access comprehensive customization options for individual effects, navigate to the "Picture Effects" dropdown menu. Configurable parameters include transparency, distance, and size.

Using Graphic Effects

Opt for the Graphic: Text boxes, shapes, or SmartArt graphics are examples of graphic elements that can be selected.

Format Tab: Access the "Format" tab to modify the selected element with a variety of graphic effects.

Artistic Effects: Explore a variety of artistic effects accessible through the "Artistic Effects" dropdown menu, which can convert your graphic element into various artistic styles.

Combining Effects

Layering Effects: Integrate numerous effects into a layered effect. One can augment an image with a distinct visual impact, for instance, by incorporating a glow and a shadow effect.

Reordering Effects: Right-click the image or graphic, select "Format Picture" or "Format Shape," and navigate to the "Effects" tab to rearrange the effects. You can reorder effects in this section.

Ideal Methods

Subtlety: Use effects carefully in PowerPoint. Flashy effects can distract from your message. Aim for a subtle approach that enhances instead of overwhelming.

Consistency: Maintaining consistency in the implementation of effects across the entirety of your presentation will assist in establishing a unified visual aesthetic.

Pertainingness: Make sure the effects you choose match your content and make it more meaningful. In a narrative, effects should serve a specific purpose.

Aspects of the Audience: Bear in mind your intended audience. Effects must not hinder the understanding or availability of all viewers.

Artistic stokes, images, and graphic effects make your visuals compelling in presentations. Using these effects skillfully adds depth, meaning, and creativity to your slides, captivating the audience with a visually engaging story. Mastering the art of enhancing visuals in PowerPoint can boost the impact and creativity of your presentations.

Chapter 5: Tables, Charts, And Data Visualization

Inserting and Formatting Tables

Tables are the structured ensembles utilized within PowerPoint presentations to effectively and precisely present data and information. Learn the proficiency required to insert and format tables in PowerPoint, where the systematic arrangement of data plays a critical role in creating an engaging and enlightening discussion.

Table Insertion

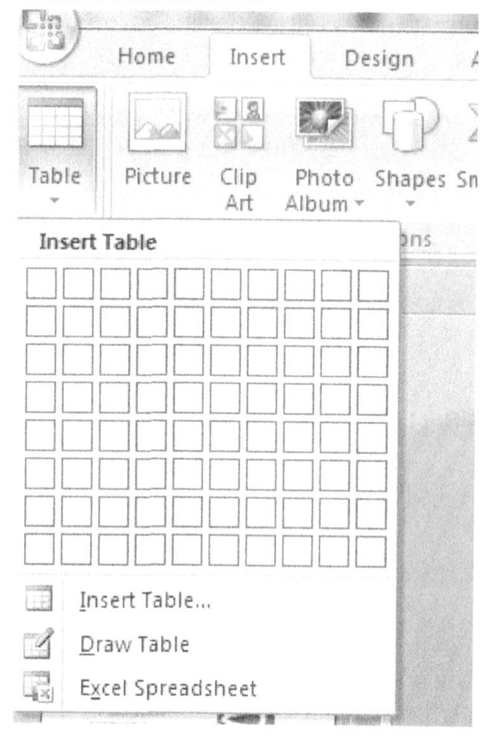

Insert Tab: Go to the "Insert" tab located on the PowerPoint ribbon to incorporate a table into a slide.

Table: When prompted for a grid, select the "Table" option. The required number of columns and rows for the table can be modified by hovering over the grid.

Insert Table: By selecting the "Insert Table" alternative and entering the required number of rows and columns in the resulting dialogue box, it is also possible to insert a table.

Formatting Tables

Table Styles: Various table styles are accessible through the "Design" tab on the PowerPoint ribbon once the table has been inserted. The table's overall appearance and formatting are determined by these styles.

Tabular Borders and Shading: In the "Format" tab, select the table or individual cells and utilize the "Borders" and "Shading" options to modify the table's borders and shading.

Text Formatting: To apply formatting to text contained in table cells, select the text and use the available font and text formatting options from the "Home" tab.

Adding and Deleting Rows and Columns

Row or Column Insertion: To insert a row or column, right-click the row or column to which you wish to add the new one and select "Insert." Columns accept inserts to the left or right, while rows accept entries above or below.

Deletion of Columns or Rows: A column or row can be deleted by right-clicking on it and choosing "Delete." After a dialog box appears, validate your selection.

Cells Merging and Splitting

Merging Cells: To merge cells in a table, right-click on the desired cells and select "Merge Cells." For combining cells for special formatting or to generate header cells, this is useful.

Cell Splitting: To perform cell splitting, right-click the merged cell and select "Split Cells." Columns and rows into which the cell is to be divided can be specified.

Optimized Methods

Simplicity: Maintain uncluttered and simple tables. Prevent them from becoming overloaded with formatting or data.

Clarity: To aid the audience in comprehending the content of the table, use headers that are both clear and concise for columns and rows.

Alignment: For visual appeal and consistency, align text and data within the table.

Consistency: For a professional appearance, maintain a consistent visual style for your tables throughout your presentation.

Tables in PowerPoint are like organized containers for accurate and clear data presentation. Skillfully adding and formatting tables can make your information well-organized and turn raw data into a visually appealing and informative story. Mastering the skill of presenting data in PowerPoint enhances the precision and impact of your presentations.

Creating and Customizing Charts

Charts help explain complex data in PowerPoint presentations. They make it easier for people to quickly understand trends, comparisons, and insights. Let's learn about creating and customizing PowerPoint charts. This is important for making persuasive and informative presentations where showing data in a visual way is really important.

Chart Insertion

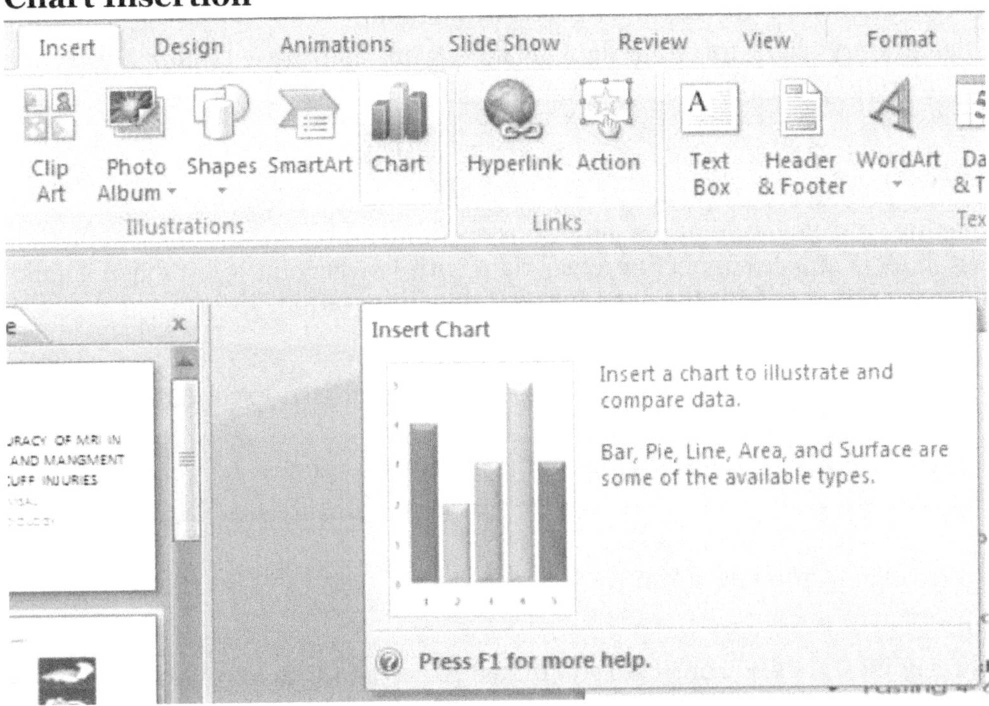

Tap Insert Tab: Navigate to the "Insert" tab on the PowerPoint ribbon to incorporate a chart into a slide.

Chart: The Insert Chart dialog box will appear when you click on the "Chart" option.

Options for Chart Types: You can pick from different types of charts, like bar, column, pie, line, and more. Choose the one in which your data fits most effectively.

Data Source: Select the Excel-like worksheet and input or paste the data into it. Labels should be placed in the first row and categories should be in the first column to ensure that your data is neatly organized.

Insert: To incorporate the chart into your slide, click "OK" after entering your data.

Customizing Charts

Chart Styles: Apply various color schemes and styles to your chart using the "Chart Styles" button once the chart has been inserted.

Chart Elements: To access the "Chart Elements" button (plus icon), click the chart. This permits the modification of elements.

Formatting Data Series: To change the format of a specific data series, click on the points or series of data in the chart. You may then modify colors, line styles, and more through the "Format" tab.

Chart Title: Replace the placeholder text with the desired title to add a title to your chart. The appearance and font of the title can be modified with the "Format" tab.

Data Labels: Choose "Add Data Labels" with a right-click on the data series. Use this to give your chart data labels. In the "Format" tab, you may also modify their visual appearance.

Change Chart Type

Altering Chart Types: To modify the type of a chart that you have already created, execute the following steps: right-click the chart, select "Change Chart Type," and then opt for an alternative chart style.

Data Editing: In the Excel-like worksheet that is connected to your chart, you can continue to modify your data. Adjustments will be reflected in the chart automatically.

Optimized Methods

Simplicity: Make sure your charts are easy to understand and only show the most important information. Cease superfluous information and disorder.

Clarity: To make your charts easy to understand, use labels, titles, and data points that are easy to read.

Color Choices: Be careful with the colors you use and make sure they can be read by everyone. Strategically apply color to emphasize critical information.

Consistency: For a polished presentation, use the same chart style throughout.

Charts in PowerPoint act as visual storytellers for your data, making your narrative clearer and more impactful. Skillfully turning raw data into compelling visual insights through well-designed and customized charts can captivate your audience.

Linking Excel Data

Up-to-date data is crucial for keeping your PowerPoint presentations accurate and relevant. You can do this by bringing Excel data into your slides. Explore connecting Excel data with PowerPoint to establish a solid foundation for reliable and persuasive presentations through dynamic data integration.

Excel Object Insertion

Insert Tab: Navigate to the "Insert" tab on the PowerPoint ribbon to incorporate Excel data into your presentation.

Object: Clicking the "Object" option will cause the Insert Object dialogue box to open.

Create from File: Navigate to your Excel file and select "Create from file". Ensure the "Link" option is enabled in the "Checkbox."

Insert: Click "Insert" to add the Excel object to PowerPoint.

Linked Excel Data Update

Edit Data: Double-click the PowerPoint slide Excel object to edit linked Excel data. The Excel workbook that is linked is loaded.

Data Update: Revisions or revisions to the data should be implemented in Excel. Protect the Excel spreadsheet.

Refresh Link: Right-click the Excel object in your PowerPoint presentation to return there. Select "Update Link" to reload the information contained in the linked Excel file.

Advantages of Linking Excel Data

Real-Time Updates: By linking Excel data to PowerPoint, the presentation is guaranteed to incorporate the latest information, eliminating the need for manual updates.

Data Consistency: By utilizing linked data, it is possible to ensure that multiple presentations that utilize the same Excel source maintain consistency.

Efficiency: Excel users are more comfortable editing and updating data.

Considerations

Locations: Store your PowerPoint and Excel files on a shared drive or in the cloud.

Data Security: If the linked Excel data contains sensitive information, consider data security and access permissions.

Compliance: Verify that the versions of PowerPoint and Excel are compatible to guarantee that linking and updating will proceed without difficulty.

Maintaining dynamic, accurate, and dependable presentations requires the skill of linking Excel data to PowerPoint. You provide your audience with the most pertinent insights by establishing a correlation between your presentation and Excel data, which guarantees that the information is current and consistent. One can enhance the credibility and dependability of their presentations by dynamic data integration in PowerPoint.

Chapter 6: Animations And Advanced Transitions

Custom Animations: Entrance, Emphasis, and Exit

Custom animations breathe life into PowerPoint slides, making them more engaging and impactful. They allow you to control how elements appear, emphasizing important details and turning your slides into dynamic storytelling tools.

Using Custom Animations

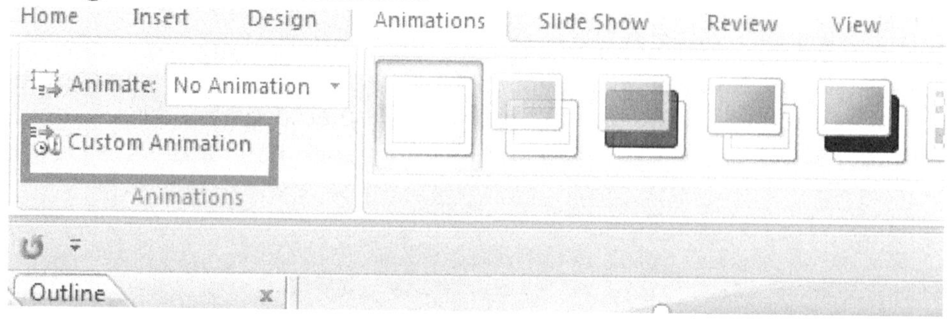

Select a Subject: Select the object to be animated (e.g., text box, image, shape) as a starting point.

Animations Tab: To access animation options, navigate to the "Animations" tab on the PowerPoint ribbon.

Add Animation: Choose "Add Animation" from the drop-down menu to choose an animation effect category. These consist of Entrance, Emphasis, and Exit, among others.

Choose an Animation: Select a particular animation effect from the resulting submenu. PowerPoint provides an extensive collection of animations, including "Fade," "Fly-In," and "Grow & Turn," among others.

Preview: Click "Play" in the Animation pane to preview. By doing so, one can visualize the animation as it would appear on the slide.

Animation Effects Personalization

Animation Pane: To access advanced animation options, click the "Animation Pane" button located on the Animations tab to open the Animation pane. Within this pane, every animation on the current slide is displayed.

Effect Options: The "Effect Options" dropdown in the Animation pane provides additional customization options for animations that have been applied. Options differ following the animation effect selected.

Duration and Delay: Modify the duration and delay of the animation by selecting it in the Animation pane and selecting "Timing" from the drop-down menu. Timing details can be specified in this section.

Entrance, Emphasis, and Exit Animations

Entrance Animations: Objects are rendered on the slide via these animations. Select effects such as "Appear," "Fade In," or "Fly-In" to regulate how elements enter the scene.

Emphasis Animations: Particular objects or text are highlighted with emphasis animations. Important details can be emphasized using effects such as "Color Pulse," "Spin," or "Grow."

Exit animations: Choose how elements leave the slide. Options like 'Fade Out,' 'Fly Out,' and 'Disappear' control how elements disappear

Triggers and Sequences of Animation

Animation Sequences: Arrange animations in the Animation pane to modify their sequence. As required, reorder animations by dragging and dropping them.

Animation Triggers: Set animation triggers to create interactive presentations. This makes animations happen when you hover over or click on specific objects.

Ideal Procedures

Subtlety: Use animations carefully and purposefully. Too many or flashy animations can take away from your message and be distracting.

Consistency: For a professional appearance, keep the timing and animation style of your presentation constant.

Relevance: Make sure that the animations you use add to your content and help people understand it. Rather than overpowering your message, they need to support it.

Custom animations in PowerPoint bring life to your slides. By using these animations thoughtfully, you can control how elements enter, exit, and stand out, creating a presentation that is engaging and impactful. Following animation principles in PowerPoint adds energy and purpose to your slides.

Motion Paths

In PowerPoint, motion paths are like the tracks that objects follow when you're giving a presentation. They make objects rotate, zoom, and move, adding energy and engagement to your slides. You can use these animations to control how things move on the screen, making your storytelling more exciting.

Implementation of Motion Paths

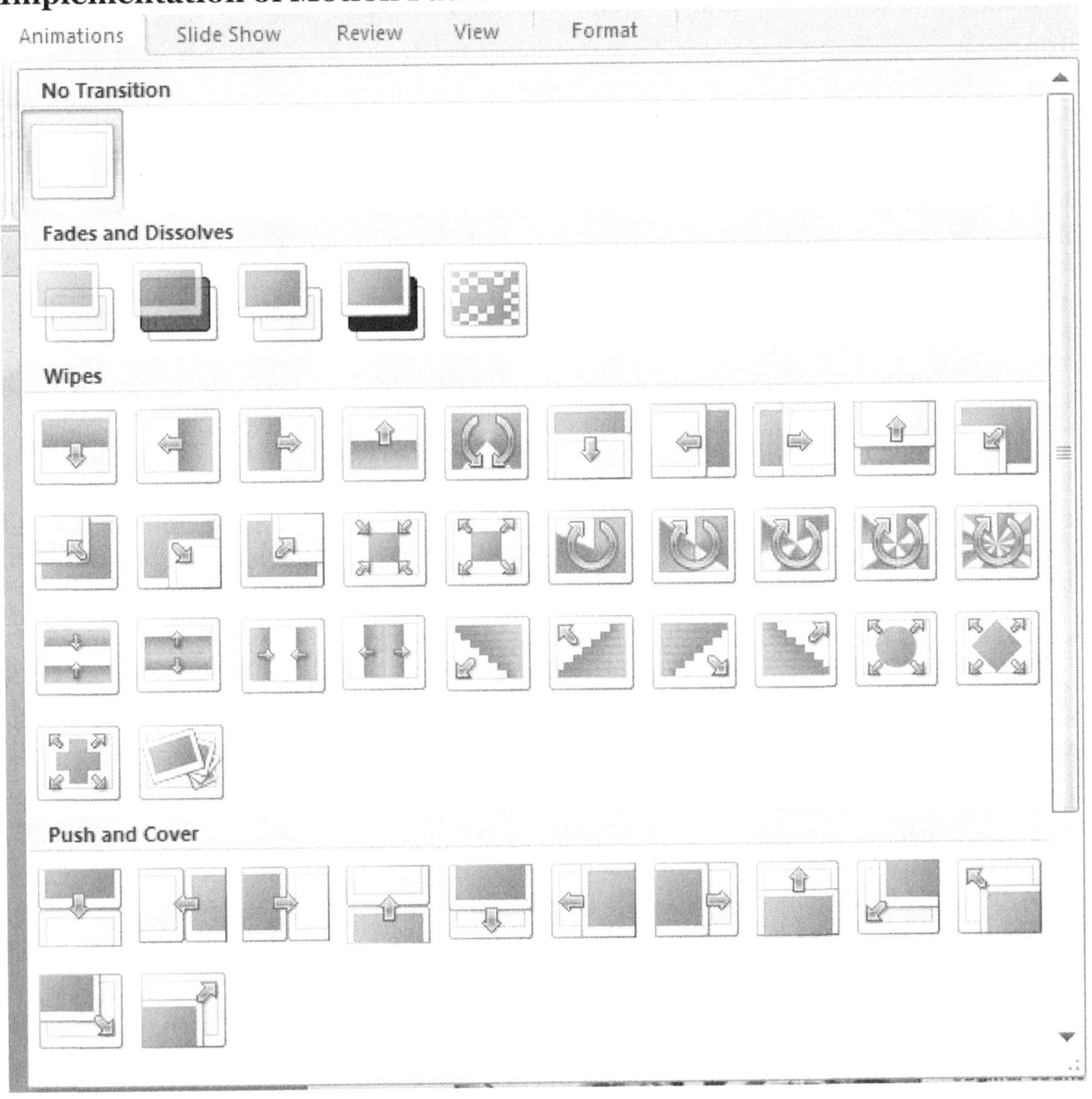

Select an Object: To commence, choose the object (such as a text box, shape, or image) that you intend to animate using a motion path.

Animations Tab: To access animation options, navigate to the "Animations" tab on the PowerPoint ribbon.

Add Animation: Click "Add Animation" and select "More Motion Paths" from the "Motion Paths" category.

Choose a Path: An interface comprising preset motion paths, including loops, lines, and curves, will be presented in a dialog box. Select the appropriate path for your animation requirements, then click "OK."

Personalized Motion Paths

Customizable Motion Path Options: The "Effect Options" dropdown menu in the Animation pane provides the means to modify a motion path once it has been applied. Additional options may consist of the starting and ending points, directions, and more.

Modifying the Path: To access adjustment handles, click on the path itself (represented by the dashed line). Slide these handles to modify the trajectory and refine the motion.

Duration and Delay: Modify the duration and delay of the animation by selecting it in the Animation pane and selecting "Timing" from the drop-down menu. Timing details can be specified in this section.

Combining Effects and Multiple Motion Paths

Multiple Paths: Complex animations can be generated by applying multiple motion paths to the same object. A curve-moving object, for instance, may subsequently undergo a spin as it traverses an alternate path.

Integrating Effects: Incorporate additional intricacy and depth into your animations by combining motion paths with other animation effects, such as entrance or emphasis animations.

Animation Triggers

Animation Triggers: Establish animation triggers to add interactivity to your presentation. Triggers facilitate the initiation of animations in response to the selection of particular objects through clicking and augmenting user engagement.

Ideal Procedures

Intentional Motion: Use motion paths to enhance your story and highlight important points. Be mindful not to use too many animations that could be distracting.

Flowing Realistic Motion Paths: Create smooth and natural motion paths on your slides. Avoid abrupt or strong movements for a more polished presentation.

Timing: Ensure that animations correspond with the rhythm of your speech or narrative by paying close attention to timing and pacing.

Consistency: For a polished and professional appearance, maintain a consistent animation style and timing throughout your presentation.

Think of PowerPoint motion paths as the way elements move on your slides. Using these animations well helps you control how things move, making your presentation more interesting and impactful. Understanding motion in PowerPoint will turn your slides into dynamic stages for your story.

Linking Animations and Triggering Events

In PowerPoint, connecting animations and triggering events is important to make your slides interactive and interesting. These techniques let you control how animations work when people interact with your presentation, like clicking or moving the slides.

Configuring Animations to Trigger Events

Select an Object: To commence, make a selection of the object that will be animated in response to a trigger event (e.g., text box, image, shape).

Animations Tab: To access animation options, navigate to the "Animations" tab on the PowerPoint ribbon.

Incorporate Animation: Select an animation effect category (e.g., Entrance, Emphasis, Exit) via the "Add Animation" dropdown menu.

Determine the Animation: Select a particular animation effect from the resulting submenu. An event will serve as the trigger for this effect.

Animation Pane: From the Animations tab, select the "Animation Pane" button to access the Animation pane. Within this pane, every animation on the current slide is displayed.

Timing and Trigger: Select the animation in the Animation pane to associate it with a trigger event. Select an event to trigger using the "Trigger" dropdown menu on the Animations tab (for instance, "On Click of" an object or "On Mouse Click"). If necessary, you may also specify a delay.

Event Triggers for Interactive Animations

On Click: When the presenter clicks on the object, animations that are set to "On Click" play.

Upon Mouse Click: This trigger is triggered whenever, during the presentation, the presenter clicks on any location on the slide.

On Mouse Over: "On Mouse Over" animations occur when the presenter hovers over the object.

Slide Transition: Animations can be configured to commence upon the slide transitioning to the current slide.

Numerous Triggers and Animations

Multiple Animations: You can give the same object more than one animation, which lets you make effects that are layered or happen in a certain order and are triggered by different events.

Trigger Combinations: Complex interactions can be generated by combining multiple trigger events. For instance, "On Click" and "On Mouse Over" animations can occur simultaneously on an object.

Ideal Procedures

Clarity: Make sure that the actions and interactive parts are clear and easily understood by the people you're presenting to.

Consistency: Keep the interactive animations' style and timing uniform for a more professional look and feel.

Testing: Make sure your interactive animations function properly before presenting them.

Using PowerPoint's linked animations and triggers, you can turn your slides into interactive experiences that engage your audience with a dynamic story. Applying these methods allows you to create animations that respond to user actions. Adding interactivity to PowerPoint transforms your slides into immersive experiences, encouraging audience engagement and exploration.

Chapter 7: Multimedia Integration

Inserting Videos and Sound

Videos and audio are components of PowerPoint presentations that effectively animate the content, interacting with the visual and auditory senses of the audience. You can communicate information and generate dynamic, memorable experiences with the help of these multimedia components.

Inserting Videos

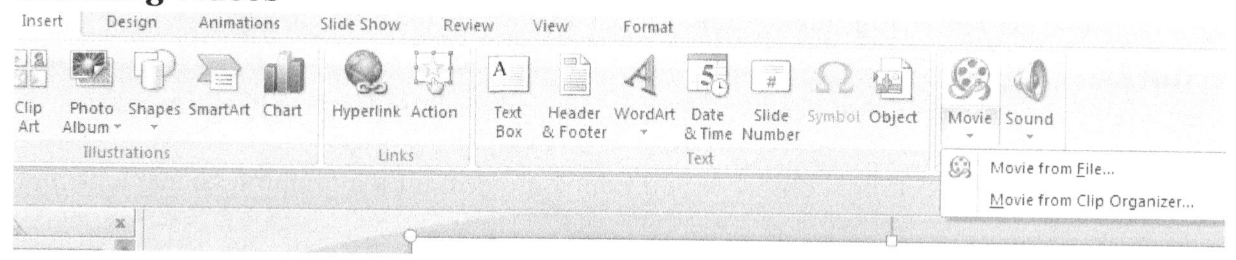

Insert Tab: Use the PowerPoint ribbon's "Insert" tab to add a video.

Video: To upload a video from your computer or the Internet, select the "Video" option. You may choose to embed the video or link to it.

Browse and Select: Navigate through your computer to locate the video file that you wish to embed. If linking, provide the URL of the video on the web.

Insert: Select "Insert" to include the clip in your presentation. It is then repositionable and resizable as necessary.

Playback Options for Videos

Controls for Playback: The "Playback" tab will appear on the PowerPoint ribbon once the video has been selected. Utilize this tab to adjust playback settings such as volume, play, and pause.

Autoplay: Upon displaying the slide, you have the option of setting the video to begin automatically or manually by clicking.

Looping: Enable looping to allow the video to play indefinitely until stopped manually.

Adding Sound

Insert Tab: Navigate to the "Insert" tab on the PowerPoint ribbon to add sound to a slide that you have created using PowerPoint.

Audio: To import audio from your computer or online sources, select the "Audio" option. You may choose to link to the audio or embed it.

Browse and Select: Navigate through your computer to locate the audio file that you wish to embed. Provide the audio's online URL if linking.

Insert: Select "Insert" to include the sound file in your presentation. It is then repositionable and resizable as necessary.

Playback Options for Sound

Controls for Playback: The "Playback" tab will appear on the PowerPoint ribbon once the audio file has been selected. Utilize this tab to adjust playback settings such as volume, play, and pause.

Autoplay: The audio can be configured to begin playing automatically upon the slide's display, or it can be activated manually through a click.

Looping: Enable looping to have the audio play indefinitely until stopped manually.

Ideal Procedures

Content Relevance: Enhance your speech with sounds and visuals to grab your audience's attention. Make sure the multimedia you include relates to what you're talking about.

Quality: Opt for media files of superior quality to ensure crisp and vivid visuals and audio. Perform playback tests beforehand to prevent technical issues.

File Size: When you embed media, keep file size in mind because big files can slow down your presentation. As required, compress audio and video.

Accessibility: To enhance usability, videos should be accompanied by transcripts or captions, and crucial information should not be conveyed solely through sound.

PowerPoint videos and audio are the components that enhance the memorability and immersion of your slides by adding dimension and depth. Through adeptly integrating and regulating multimedia components, one can craft presentations that are both dynamic and captivating, effectively evoking a response from the audience's senses. By incorporating multimedia storytelling into PowerPoint, your slides will transform into immersive canvases that facilitate the progression of your narrative.

Video and Audio Playback Options

Essential for delivering a seamless and engaging PowerPoint presentation experience is the ability to regulate video and audio playback. By utilizing these playback options, you can precisely adjust the behavior of audio and video files on your slides, thereby guaranteeing that your multimedia components augment your message.

Options for Playing Videos

Video Playback Controls: The "Playback" tab of the PowerPoint ribbon becomes accessible to video playback controls when a video is inserted into PowerPoint. The following describes how to use them:

Play/Pause: To initiate video playback, click the "Play" button. It transitions to a "Pause" button during playback, enabling the user to temporarily halt the video.

Volume: Utilize the volume slider to modify the volume of the video. The video can be muted through the use of the speaker icon.

Rewind: The "Rewind" button returns the user to the video's beginning.

Full Screen: To extend the video to the entire slide, click the full-screen button. To disable full-screen mode, press and hold the "Esc" key.

Playback Options: The "Playback Options" dropdown menu contains options such as "Loop until stopped" and "Start automatically" that allow the user to regulate the video's start and end times.

Playback Options for Audio

Playback Controls: The "Playback" tab of the PowerPoint ribbon provides controls for the playback of audio that is inserted into the presentation. The following describes how to utilize these controls:

Play/Pause: To play music, click the "Play" button. It changes to a "Pause" button during playback, enabling the user to pause the audio at any moment.

Volume: Utilize the volume slider to modify the volume of the audio. To silence the audio, simply click the speaker icon.

Playback Options: The "Playback Options" dropdown menu contains options such as "Loop until stopped" and "Start automatically" that allow the user to regulate how the audio file begins and ends.

Hide During Show: The "Hide During Show" checkbox allows you to control whether or not the audio icon is displayed while the presentation is being given.

Sophisticated Multimedia Controls

Incorporate Animation Triggers: Generate interactive presentations by integrating multimedia components with animation triggers. For instance, a button can be configured to initiate video playback upon being clicked.

Custom Timing: Align the timing of audio and video playback with the duration of your presentation. Adjust the duration and start times with precision using the Animation Pane.

Syncing Audio with Animation: You can sync audio with certain animation events to make sure that sound effects or narration go perfectly with what's happening on the screen.

Ideal Procedures

Content Relevance: Strictly adhere to the message of your presentation and augment its impact by incorporating multimedia elements, such as audio or video, that are directly pertinent to it.

Quality and File Size: To guarantee sound and visual clarity, utilize media files of superior quality. Large files should be compressed to prevent performance issues.

Testing: Always test the playback of video and audio before your presentation so that there are no technical problems.

Accessibility: To make your presentation accessible to all viewers, you should provide captions or transcripts for any multimedia content that you include.

Managing video and audio playback in PowerPoint involves coordinating multimedia elements for a cohesive and captivating experience. By skillfully using these playback options, you can ensure that multimedia content enhances your message and engages the audience.

Recording Slideshow with Narration

With PowerPoint, you can record a slideshow with narration, offering a powerful way to deliver a dynamic presentation remotely or on-demand. Narration adds a personal touch, allowing you to guide the audience through the material using your voice.

Making a Slideshow Narration Video

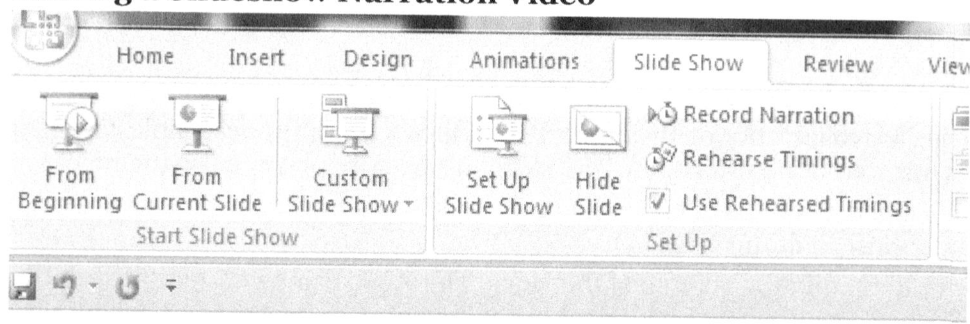

Slide Show Tab: Go to the "Slide Show" tab on the PowerPoint ribbon to start. This tab grants users access to the essential tools required to create a presentation recording.

Slide Show Recording: Click the "Record Slide Show" button to begin recording.

Commence Recording: Select one of the following recording options:

Commence at the Outset: Commence the recording of your presentation from the initial slide.

Commence from the Present Slide: Commence the recording process from the slide that is presently being selected.

Controls for Recording: During the recording process, the lower-left corner of the screen will contain controls for recording. These controls facilitate slide navigation and provide command over the recording process.

Slide Navigation: To navigate between slides, use the arrows.

Pause: Temporarily pause the recording.

Stop: Save the recording after it has concluded.

Narration: Deliver the narration by speaking into the microphone as you progress through the slides. PowerPoint synchronizes the recording of your voice with the changes you make to the slides.

Laser Pointer and Pen Tools: Employ the laser pointer and pen tools during the recording process to emphasize particular sections or elements on your slides.

Annotations: During the recording, you can also add annotations, such as text or shapes, to provide further clarification or emphasis.

Reviewing and Saving the Recording

End of Recording: When you're done recording your whole presentation, PowerPoint will show you a summary screen where you can listen to it again.

Save: Press "Save" to save your recorded show as a PowerPoint Show (.ppsx) file. This format enables individuals to access the presentation without requiring the installation of PowerPoint.

Rehearse Timings: If the recording fails to meet your expectations, you have the option of either discarding it and commencing again, or rehearsing timings to refine slide transitions and narration.

Ideal Procedures

Scripting: To ensure clarity and conciseness, prepare a script or outline for your narration.

Quality Microphone: To capture professional-sounding, crystal-clear audio, use a microphone of high quality.

Practice: Before you record, go over your narration and timing a few times to make sure it goes smoothly.

Pacing: Maintain an appropriate pace and refrain from hastening through the slides. Speak with clarity and an appropriate cadence.

Rehearse Timings: To ensure effective synchronization of your narration, rehearse slide timings if necessary.

Adding narration to a PowerPoint slideshow is a way to turn a presentation into an engaging multimedia experience. By recording your voice narration and managing slide transitions, you can effectively guide your audience through your content with clarity and impact. Embracing multimedia presentation in PowerPoint makes your slides more dynamic and informative for your audience.

Chapter 8: Interactive Elements And Hyperlinks

Adding Action Buttons

In PowerPoint presentations, action buttons are like tools that help you involve your audience and guide them easily through your content. These buttons work as navigation helpers, allowing you to create interactive elements that make things happen, like going to websites or moving to other slides. Let's learn how to use action buttons in PowerPoint to make your slides more engaging and interactive.

Action Button Insertion

Insert Tab: On the PowerPoint ribbon, go to the "Insert" tab to begin.

Shapes: If you click on the "Shapes" dropdown, you'll see a list of shape options, some of which are action buttons.

Action Button: Pick one from the list to do something. These pre-designed buttons are immediately customizable.

Draw Button: Place your cursor on the slide and drag it to create the button. It can be repositioned and resized as necessary.

Personalized Action Buttons

Button Text: To add text or labels denoting the function of the action button, such as "Next" or "Home," double-click on it.

Formatting: To align the action button with the design of your presentation, modify its fill color, outline, and font style.

Action Settings: Click the action button and select "Action Settings" from the context menu to access the Action Settings dialog box.

The hyperlink to Determine which action the button should execute. This may involve executing a custom macro, navigating to a specific slide, returning to the previous slide, or opening a URL or program.

Mouse Over: You can choose whether the action should happen when the mouse pointer is over the button or when the button is clicked.

Hints for Action Button

Linking Slides: Action buttons are a great way to make your presentation easier to navigate. Implement them as hyperlinks to particular slides, enabling your audience to effortlessly navigate to distinct sections.

Menu Navigation: Employ action buttons to generate interactive menus. By allocating links to distinct sections or topics within your presentation, each button provides a menu-driven navigation experience.

External Links: Put action buttons in your presentation to give people access to websites, resources, or other content that is related to it.

Ideal Procedures

Clarity: Ensure that your audience understands the function of each action button. Employ illustrative labels or icons.

Consistency: Ensure that the design and placement of action buttons remain consistent across the entirety of your presentation.

Ensuring Accessibility: Pupils utilizing screen readers should not have difficulty locating and accessing action buttons. When required, provide alternative text for buttons.

The art of incorporating action buttons into PowerPoint presentations is to generate interactive components that improve audience engagement and facilitate smooth navigation. Through adeptly inserting and personalizing these buttons, one can effortlessly and precisely direct the audience through the content, thereby generating an engaging and interactive encounter. By integrating interactivity into PowerPoint, your slides will transform into immersive experiences that encourage audience participation and exploration.

Creating Hyperlinks: Slides, Websites, and Files

In PowerPoint, hyperlinks are like shortcuts that connect slides, websites, and files, making it easy for your audience to move around. By using hyperlinks, you can refer to other slides, guide people to websites, or open files like videos or documents.

Developing Hyperlinks to Additional Slides

Text or Object Selection: To commence, choose the desired text or object (such as a shape or image) to convert into a hyperlink.

Insert Tab: On the PowerPoint ribbon, go to the "Insert" tab.

Hyperlink: To open the Insert Hyperlink box, click on the "Hyperlink" button.

Place in This Document: Choose "Place in This Document" from the dialogue box's left side.

Slides: There will be a list of all the slides in your presentation. Choose the slide that you want a link added to.

OK: To create the hyperlink, just click the "OK" button. The specified slide will now be linked to the selected object or text.

Creating Website Hyperlinks

Choose an Object or Text: Choose the text or item for which you want to make a hyperlink.

Insert Tab: On the PowerPoint ribbon, go to the "Insert" tab.

Hyperlink: Click the "Hyperlink" button to open the Insert Hyperlink dialog box.

Address: Select "Web Page" from the left panel of the dialog box.

URL: Enter the URL of the website you want to connect to in the "Address" section.

OK: The hyperlink will be created once you click the "OK" button. The designated website will now be accessed via a hyperlink in the selected text or object.

Developing File Hyperlinks

Choose an Object or Text: Select the text or object that you wish to convert into a hyperlink as a starting point.

Tab Insertion: On the PowerPoint ribbon, locate the "Insert" tab.

Hyperlink: To open the Insert Hyperlink box, click on the "Hyperlink" button.

File: From the dialog box, choose "Existing File or Web Page" from the panel on the left.

Navigate: To locate and select the file you wish to link to on your computer or network drive, click the "Browse" button.

OK: To create the hyperlink, just click the "OK" button. The specified file will now be linked to the selected text or object.

Examination of Hyperlinks

Test your hyperlinks before delivering a presentation to ensure they function properly. By activating slideshow mode (F5) and clicking on the hyperlinked objects or texts, one can verify that they lead to the desired locations.

Ideal Procedures

Descriptive Text: When using hyperlinks, use short and clear text to show where the link will take you or what it does.

Consistency: To make your presentation look polished and professional, use the same style of hyperlinks throughout it.

Accessibility: Make sure hyperlinks work for everyone, including those who use screen readers. When possible, provide alternative text.

Creating hyperlinks in PowerPoint lets you connect external resources to your presentation, making it interactive and user-friendly. By adding and customizing these links, you can guide the audience through your material and provide easy access to additional information, creating an engaging and informative presentation. Mastering the art of connectivity in PowerPoint transforms your slides into an enlightening and informative experience for your audience.

Zoom and Morph Transition Features

In PowerPoint, Zoom and Morph are powerful tools that add visual sophistication to your slides. Using these transitions lets you create presentations that are smooth, captivating, and dynamic, keeping your audience engaged.

Zoom Transition

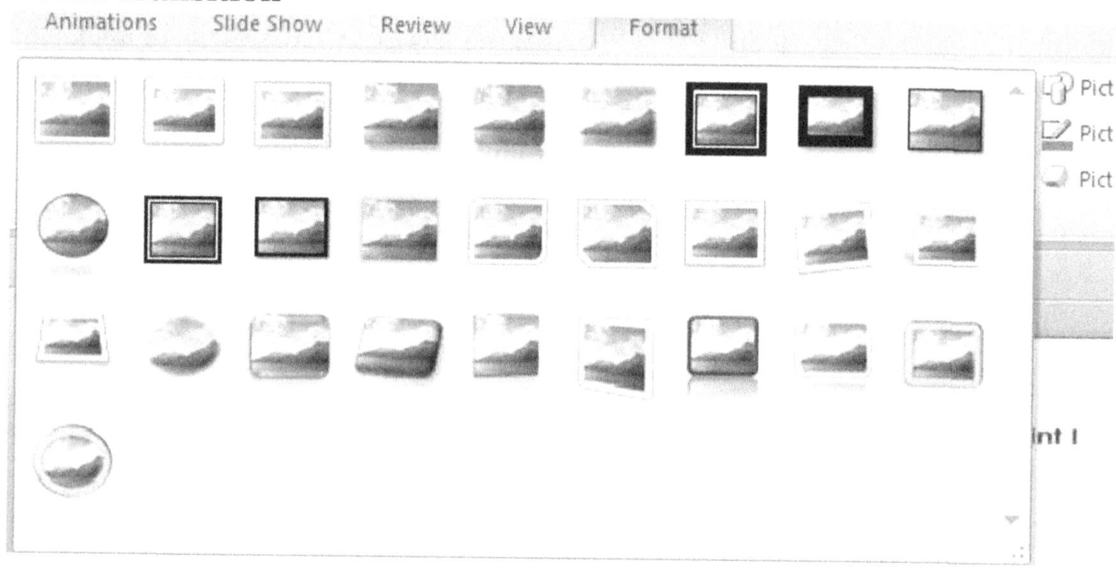

By utilizing the Zoom transition, one can effortlessly transition between slides by manipulating the size of particular objects or sections.

Instructions for using it:

Tab for Transitions: To begin, select the "Transitions" tab from the ribbon of PowerPoint.

Transition to Zoom: To apply the "Zoom" transition effect to a slide, simply click on it.

Effect Options: Utilize the "Effect Options" drop-down menu on the Transitions tab to modify the Zoom transition. By zooming in on a particular element, such as text or an image, or out to reveal the entire slide, you have the option to do so.

Duration: To regulate the speed of the zoom effect, modify the duration of the transition.

Morph Transition

By automatically tracking changes in objects, the Morph transition generates seamless animations between slides, giving the impression that the objects are effortlessly transforming and moving.

Instructions for using it:

Transitions Tab: In the PowerPoint ribbon, navigate to the "Transitions" tab.

Morph Transition: Import a slide containing the "Morph" transition effect.

Objects and Text: Modify objects or text on the duplicated slide after the intended transition slide.

Duration: Control the rate of the morphing effect by modifying the duration of the transition in the Transitions tab.

Advantages of Morph and Zoom Transitions

Visual Appeal: Both transitions enhance the presentation's visual appeal and engagement, increasing its dynamism and captivation.

Storytelling: These transitions facilitate a seamless progression between scenes or concepts, which is ideal for storytelling.

Simplifying Complex Animations: The utilization of the Morph transition enables the attainment of refined effects without the need to generate bespoke animations.

Professionalism: By incorporating morph and zoom transitions into your slides, you exhibit your meticulousness and impart a polished and expert appearance.

Ideal Procedures

Employ Slightly: Although these transitions have the potential to elevate your presentation, it is advisable to refrain from overusing them. Employ them deliberately and judiciously.

Consistency: To establish a unified visual narrative, ensure that the transitions utilized in your presentation are consistent.

Relevance of Content: Guarantee that transitions complement and harmonize with your message. They ought not to detract from the material.

Preview: Ensure that the transitions function as intended by always previewing your presentation.

In PowerPoint, zoom and morph transitions add sophistication and elegance to your slides, creating visually appealing narratives that captivate and motivate your audience. Using these transitions skillfully enhances your storytelling ability and keeps the audience engaged. Mastering the art of visual storytelling in PowerPoint transforms your slides into dynamic canvases that educate and inspire.

Chapter 9: Master Slides and Consistent Design

Understanding Slide Master Views

In PowerPoint, Slide Master Views are backstage tools to make your slides look consistent and professional. By using them, you can ensure all your slides have the same layouts, fonts, colors, and spaces for content. Explore how to use Slide Master Views in PowerPoint to give your slides a polished and unified look for your content.

Master Slide Views Access

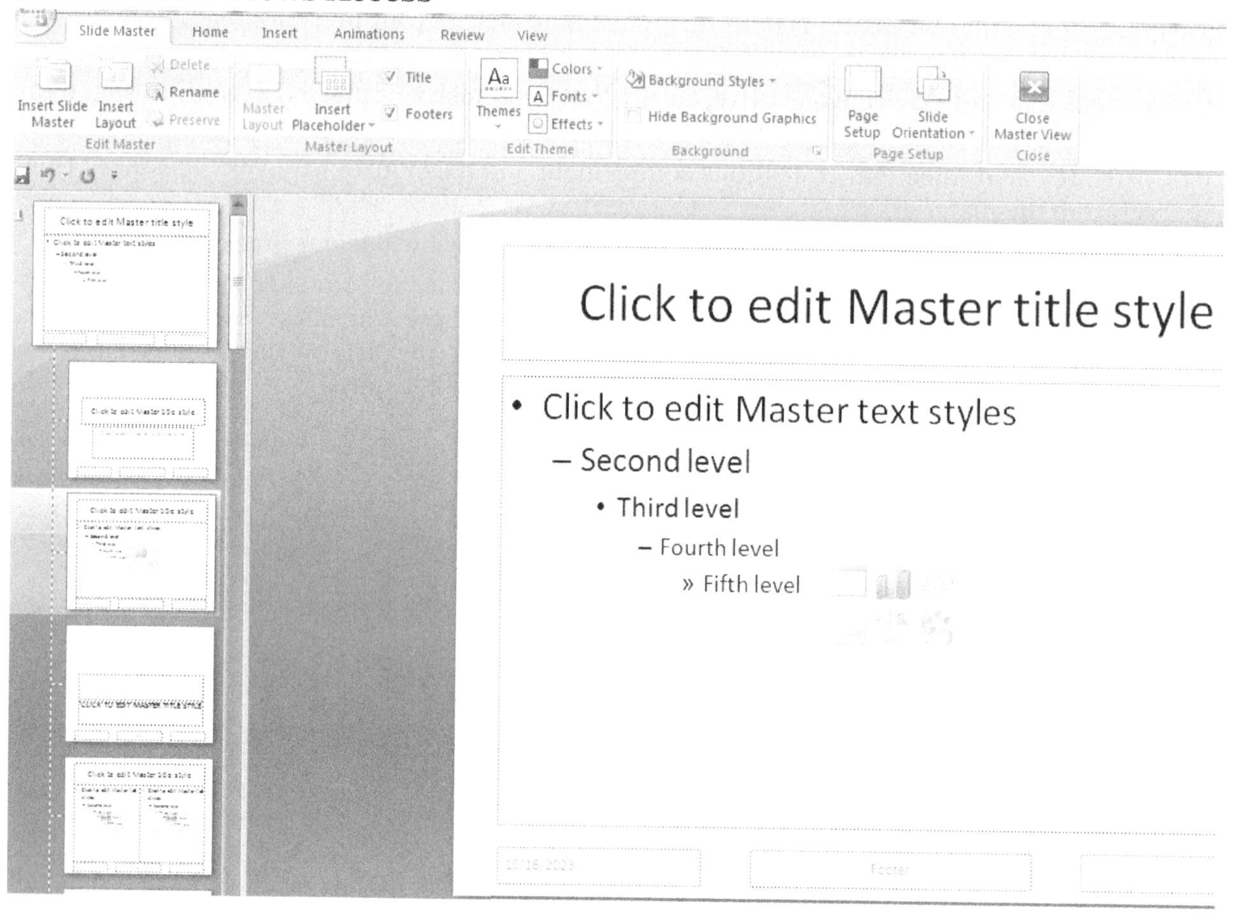

View Tab: On the PowerPoint ribbon, go to the "View" tab to begin.

Slide Master: Click the "Slide Master" button to open the Slide Master View. This view presents the design and layout of your slides in their entirety.

Comprehending the Elements of Slide Master

Slide Layouts: On the left side of the Slide Master View is a list of slide layouts. The various slide types in your presentation are represented by these layouts, including section headers, content slides, and title slides.

Slide Master: The master layout for all slides in your presentation is displayed on the top slide of the Slide Master View. Any modifications implemented here will have an impact on all slides.

Styles for Placeholders: To ensure a uniform appearance across all slides, you can modify the fonts, colors, and styles of placeholders, including title and content boxes.

Personalization of Master Slide Elements

Fonts and Colors: Navigate to the "Fonts" and "Colors" drop-down menus in the Slide Master View and choose the desired options to modify the fonts and colors for all slides.

Background: Select "Format Background" from the Slide Master menu when right-clicking to modify the background of your slides. You can specify a solid color, gradient, image, or pattern in this location.

Including Elements: Logos, footers, the date and time, and additional components that need to be present on every slide can be included. Generally, these components are incorporated into the Slide Master or particular layouts.

Hierarchy: Define the hierarchy of slide elements using the Slide Master View. One way to ensure consistency is by placing titles above the content on every slide.

Saving Changes

Exit Slide Master: To return to the standard slide view after modifying your Slide Master, click the "Close Master View" button.

Save Theme: When you make changes to the presentation's theme, PowerPoint will ask you to save those changes. Select "Yes" to incorporate the newly added theme into your presentation.

Advantages of Master Slide Views

Consistency: Slide Master Views let you keep the design of your presentation the same throughout, which makes it look more professional.

Efficiency: By modifying designs in bulk through the Slide Master View as opposed to individually modifying slides, one can effectively conserve time.

Standardization: Ensure that fonts, colors, and placeholders conform to the branding and design guidelines of your organization.

Adaptability: Modify designs to suit various slide categories while maintaining a unified aesthetic.

Ideal Procedures

Strategic Preparation: Establish a comprehensive outline of your design preferences and brand guidelines before accessing Slide Master View.

Simplify: To improve legibility and aesthetics, maintain a design that is uncluttered and clean.

Test: Ensure that your custom designs display correctly by testing them in the Slide Master View on various slide types.

Backup: Make a copy of your presentation before making any big changes in the Slide Master View to avoid making changes you didn't mean to make.

Mastering the utilization of Slide Master Views in PowerPoint is crucial for crafting a presentation that is both visually appealing and cohesive. Through adeptly modifying layouts, fonts, colors, and placeholders, you can generate slides that not only impart knowledge but also astound the audience with their consistency and professionalism.

10.2 Customizing Slide Templates

Customizing slide templates in PowerPoint allows you to create visually appealing slides that match your branding and messaging. By customizing your presentation templates, you can make your content stand out and impress your audience.

Choose a Slide Template

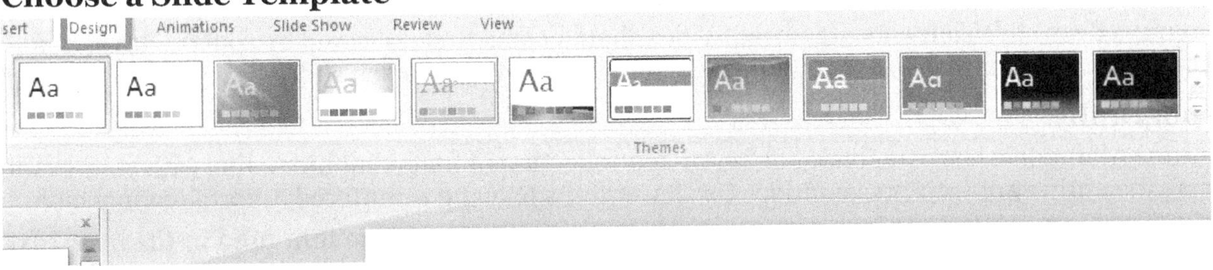

Design Tab: Select "Design" from the PowerPoint ribbon.

Themes: Under the "Themes" tab, you can access a variety of premade slide layouts. Mouse over each template to preview it with your content.

Choose a Template: Select your presentation template. PowerPoint will design your slides using the template.

Customizing Slide Templates

Slide Master: Select "Slide Master." from the "View" tab to make major slide template changes. This view lets you change master slide layouts, fonts, colors, and placeholders.

Fonts and Colors: Use the Slide Master View "Fonts" and "Colors" dropdowns to select branding-appropriate fonts and color schemes.

Background: To change your slides' backgrounds, right-click on the Slide Master and select "Format Background." Set a solid color, gradient, image, or pattern.

Placeholder Styles: Change the font, size, and style of placeholders like title and content boxes to make sure that all of your slides have the same look.

Inserting Elements: You can add logos, footers, the date and time, and other things that should show up on all slides. These elements are usually added to Slide Master or layouts.

Save Custom Templates

File Menu: Select "File" after customizing slide templates.

Save as: Click "Save As" and choose "PowerPoint Template". Save your custom template for future presentations.

Benefits of Slide Template Customization

Branding: Custom templates strengthen branding with consistent fonts, colors, and logos.

Efficiency: Reusing customized templates for future presentations saves time.

Visual Appeal: Customizing templates makes slides more appealing and engaging.

Best Practices

Branding: Match your customized templates to your company's branding.

Simplicity: Clean designs improve readability and appearance.

Testing: Always test custom templates with different content to ensure proper display.

Backup: Before making major changes, backup your template so you can revert.

You may alter PowerPoint slide templates to fit the tone and content of your presentation. Carefully modifying layouts, fonts, colors, and placeholders can create slides that inform and impress your audience with their professionalism and customization. Personalized PowerPoint templates make your slides unique and enhance your content.

Preserving Consistency Across Slides

Presentations need consistency across slides to look professional. A well-organized presentation improves audience comprehension and engagement as well as visual appeal.

Slide Layouts

Use consistent slide layouts: Place titles, content, images, and other elements in a standard slide layout for your presentation. Make sure all slides use this layout.

Slide hierarchy: Keep slide elements organized. Titles should come first, followed by content, images, and other elements. This lets your audience know where to find information on each slide.

Fonts, Typography

Font selection: Maintain a consistent use of a restricted collection of fonts that are in line with your brand identity during the entirety of your presentation. Use fewer fonts to avoid a cluttered, unprofessional look.

Font size and style: Ensure consistency in the proportions and design of the font used in the body text, titles, and headings. A consistent font size and style improve readability and visual coherence.

Color Scheme

Set a color palette: Match your branding or presentation theme. Keep text, backgrounds, shapes, and other elements in these colors.

Color contrast: Ensure there is a good contrast between the text and background colors. For an inclusive presentation, follow accessibility guidelines.

Images and graphics

Image styles: Use consistent borders, shadows, and filters. Make sure all presentation images use these styles.

Image dimensions: Maintain consistent image dimensions, particularly for logos and recurring graphics. This keeps you looking professional and balanced.

Slide Animations and Transitions

Slide transitions should be used sparingly. Overuse of transitions can detract from the content. Use one or two subtle transitions throughout the presentation.

Animation effects: Use animations consistently. For continuity, use the same animation effect for bulleted lists or images on multiple slides.

Headers/Footers and Slide Numbering

Slide numbering: Place and style slide numbers consistently. This helps viewers track progress.

Headers and Footers: For presentation title, date, and author information, use headers and footers consistently. The same information should appear on every slide.

Test/Proofread

Review and edit: Check each slide for content, formatting, and alignment before completing your presentation.

Testing: Check your presentation in slide show mode for proper elements, transitions, and animations.

Templates/Master Slides

Use templates: Use custom templates or themes to standardize slide design. Make templates that fit your branding and content.

Slide Master: Use Slide Master View to standardize fonts, colors, and layouts across your presentation slides.

To create a cohesive and appealing PowerPoint presentation, maintain slide consistency. Following design principles and best practices will ensure that your slides convey a professional and cohesive message that leaves a lasting impression.

Slide Layout and Composition

When it comes to PowerPoint presentations, the arrangement and composition of the slides are critical factors that dictate the success of the message transmission and the level of audience involvement. The strategic integration of text, images, and content on individual slides is crucial for engaging the audience and guaranteeing that the intended message is clear and concise.

Establish a Layout Consistency

Design consistency: Use the same slide layout throughout your presentation. Incorporate placeholders for titles, content, images, and other elements into a template or theme.

Slide hierarchy: It is essential to maintain a consistent slide hierarchy by placing titles at the top, followed by subheadings and content. This facilitates the audience's navigation through the presentation.

Balance visuals and text

Visual appeal: To enhance the visual appeal of your slides, integrate visuals such as images, charts, and graphics. The utilization of visual elements has the potential to augment comprehension and engagement.

Avoid clutter: Balance text and images. Do not overcrowd your slides with visuals or information, as this may become overwhelming for your audience.

Employ Efficient Typography

Fonts selection: For titles and body text, select professional and legible fonts. Ensure that the fonts you select complement your brand and theme.

Font sizes: Use consistent font sizes for titles, headings, and body text for readability and visual hierarchy.

Color Harmony

Color palette: Match your branding or theme with a harmonious palette. Consistently incorporate these hues into text, backgrounds, and accent components.

Contrast: To improve legibility, ensure adequate contrast between the colors of the text and the background. Observe accessibility standards to accommodate all viewers.

White Space and Alignment

White space: Use empty slides to create a clean look. White space improves legibility and concentration.

Alignment: For a polished and organized appearance, ensure that text and images are consistently aligned. Guides and grids should be utilized to maintain alignment.

Visual Narrative

Visual hierarchy: Use size, color, and placement to draw attention to key points and messages.

Narratives accompanied by visuals: Support your narrative with visuals and tell a story. Text alone is incapable of conveying emotions, information, and concepts with the same efficacy as images.

Emphasize Key Points

Employ contrast: Use size, color, or visual effects to emphasize important points or elements so that they stand out and attract the audience's attention.

Annotations and callouts: To emphasize and clarify vital information, utilize callout boxes, arrows, or other visual aids.

Transitional and Animated Consistency

Transitions between slides: Use the same transitions between slides all through your presentation. Excessive use of transitions can be disruptive.

Animation effects: If you use animations, make sure you use them consistently. To maintain coherence, apply the same animation effect to similar elements across multiple slides.

PowerPoint slide composition and layout are the craft of creating persuasive and effective presentations. By adhering to these recommended guidelines and adeptly organizing text, images, and content, you can generate slides that not only captivate the interest of the audience but also effectively communicate the intended message with precision and influence.

Color Theory and Font Choices

Choosing colors and fonts is important for making your PowerPoint slides look good and easy to read. Following some basic rules and knowing how colors and fonts work together helps you create presentations that share your message well and keep your audience interested.

Color Theory

Color Wheel: Become acquainted with the color wheel, which comprises tertiary colors (combinations of primary and secondary hues), secondary hues (e.g., green, orange, purple), and primary and secondary hues (red, blue, yellow).

Color Harmony: Choose analogous, complementary, or evenly spaced colors on the color wheel to create harmonious palettes. The use of harmonious color schemes improves aesthetic appeal.

Emotional Resonance: It is important to acknowledge that colors can elicit feelings. Red, for example, is energizing and attention-getting, whereas blue is calming and professional. Align the color scheme with the ambiance and significance of the presentation.

Contrast: Ensure there is a good contrast between the text and background colors. Conversely, lighter text should be placed on a dark background.

Font Selections

Typography Fundamentals: Understand words like sans-serif (simple and plain) and serif (decorative with strokes). For main text, use sans-serif fonts, and for titles and headings, go for serif fonts.

Combinations of Fonts: Effectively pair fonts. Utilizing sans-serif fonts for headings and serif fonts for body text is a frequent pairing. Explore various font pairings to identify a visually pleasing combination that complements the tone of your presentation.

Font Size and Hierarchy: Use different font sizes to show importance in your text. Headings should be bigger than regular text, and titles should be even bigger than headings. Make sure font sizes are the same for each level.

Whitespace: Use line spacing and margins to improve readability and unclutter. Enough white space improves reading and aesthetic appeal.

Considerations for Access

Accessibility Guidelines: Follow accessibility guidelines to make your presentation accessible to all viewers, including visually impaired ones. Instead of images, provide alternative text and select color combinations that satisfy contrast specifications.

Ideal Procedures

Consistency: To make your presentation look like a whole, use the same colors and fonts throughout.

Branding Alignment: Match your company's color palette and fonts.

Testing: Make sure your color and font choices look good on different screens and devices.

Simplicity: Maintain a design that is uncomplicated and basic. It is advisable to limit the number of fonts and colors used, as this can be distracting.

The skill of designing aesthetically pleasing and easily comprehensible presentations in PowerPoint is measured in color theory and font selection. You can create slides that not only captivate your audience but also effectively communicate your message by acquiring knowledge of color theory principles, choosing suitable fonts, and adhering to established guidelines. By fully embracing the principles of design in PowerPoint, your presentations will become visually captivating that effectively convey your ideas and content.

Enhancing Readability and Engagement

To ensure your audience understands and stays engaged in your PowerPoint presentation, improve readability and engagement. Design, content organization, and delivery are crucial to this goal. Let's learn how to improve PowerPoint readability and engagement to make your slides captivating and informative.

Well-organized Content

Create a clear hierarchy in your presentation by making use of headers, subheaders, and bullet points. Make key information stand out.

Logical Flow: Sequence your content to easily guide your audience through your presentation. Connect topics with transitions and summaries.

Visuals

Images: Use high-quality, content-related images and graphics. Visuals should enhance your message and show emotions or information.

Charts and graphs: Use clear and simple charts and graphs to present data. Name axes, use legends, and choose chart types to improve comprehension.

Bullet/List Points

Bullet points: Simplify complex information with bullet points. Limit bullet points per slide to avoid overwhelming your audience.

Consistency: Structure your lists and bullet points consistently throughout the presentation. All lists should be indented and formatted similarly.

Fonts and Typography

Text legibility: Use the right font size. Titles should be larger than headings and headings than body text.

Font Choice: Choose legible fonts that match your presentation's tone and branding. Avoid decorative fonts that impair reading.

Color and Contrast

Contrast: To improve readability, ensure that there is sufficient contrast between the colors of the text and the background. Dark text on light backgrounds works well.

Color: Match your branding or theme with a harmonious color palette. Maintain color consistency for headings, text, and accents.

Simplistic Design

Simplicity: Keep slides simple by removing clutter. Clean design enhances focus and comprehension.

Engaging Delivery

Body Language: Make eye contact and present confidently. Instead of reading slides, interact with your audience.

Interactivity: Use questions, polls, and discussions to engage your audience.

Practice

Practice: Give your presentation more than once so you get used to the content and the way it flows. It will boost your confidence and delivery.

Timing: You'll want to pay close attention to the timing of your presentation. Avoid rushing slides or going over time.

Accessibility Issues

Alt Text: To ensure that individuals with visual impairments can access your presentation, include alternative text for images and graphics.

Transcripts: Provide transcripts or captions for multimedia viewers.

Creating informative, captivating, and easily understandable PowerPoint content improves readability and engagement. You can make memorable presentations by focusing on content organization, visuals, typography, and delivery.

Conclusion

Throughout our in-depth look at PowerPoint, we've explored its inner workings, revealing numerous opportunities for crafting visually captivating narratives. Assembling presentations that enlighten, motivate, and enthrall audiences has become a reality with the insights and abilities imparted in each chapter..

PowerPoint enables the transformation of concepts into persuasive presentations, and has become an indispensable tool in classrooms and boardrooms alike. It requires these fundamental abilities to function efficiently and effectively, even though navigating the interface and configuring preferences may appear mundane. A comprehensive understanding of the interface enables us to concentrate on the innovative elements of our presentations, as opposed to slavishly navigating the software.

Key tasks that form the basis of our creative work involve creating, starting, and saving presentations. With these basic skills, we can begin making content confidently, knowing that our work is safe and organized.

As we learned more about PowerPoint, we discovered how to use design elements like slide styles, themes, transitions, and animations. These tools can help breathe life into our presentations, turning them from still slides into dynamic stories. We also figured out how to choose and adjust themes to match our brand and message, making our presentations look good and unified.

To create visually appealing and easily comprehensible slides, we can rely on typography, color theory, and font selection. It becomes apparent that fonts and colors serve as potent instruments for communicating emotions and messages, and not merely as aesthetic preferences. In this way, our presentations not only convey information effectively but also exhibit aesthetic appeal by attaining proficiency in these components.

It is important to find the right balance between text and images. By using images, charts, and graphs strategically, we could improve our content without overwhelming it. This approach allows us to create slides that are visually appealing and informative by keeping a delicate balance between words and visuals.

We also learned the value of transitions and custom animations when studying how to make our presentations more dynamic. These techniques can add depth and interest, captivating the audiences with the smooth flow.

Creating good-looking and interesting presentations is the responsibility of those who know how to use PowerPoint well. We need to make sure our slides are easy for everyone to use, engaging, and well-organized to leave a lasting impression on our audience.

By gaining these skills to create presentations that teach, inspire, and engage, we can become really good at using PowerPoint. It started as a simple program, but now it's a tool for us to share our ideas and stories beautifully. As we share our stories, knowledge, and progress with people around the world, let's keep using PowerPoint's amazing features to make a big impact.

Microsoft Outlook

Introduction

In today's digital world, staying on top of your organization's game is crucial for success, and Microsoft's suite pack is synonymous with productivity. More than an email client, Microsoft Outlook is a versatile communication and scheduling platform that brings a world of possibilities to your fingertips. Outlook offers a simple yet cohesive approach to seamless emailing, appointment management, and contact database maintenance with several customization and integration options.

Whether you are an executive juggling multiple appointments, a student with overlapping deadlines, or simply an individual looking to streamline daily life, Outlook is an indispensable, free tool for everyone. It offers comprehensive features to manage your digital communications and pending tasks efficiently.

Over the years, Outlook has evolved from a simple email client (known as Hotmail) to an all-in-one personal information manager. It integrates email, schedules, to-do lists, and contacts for a unified solution, simplifying day-to-day tasks. For example, you can set up a meeting, invite relevant team members, collect RSVPs, and synchronize calendars through Outlook rather than carrying out each step manually or using different software.

Microsoft Outlook is available to users for free regardless of location through its web-based version, mobile apps, or PC client. You can sign up for an account or log in using Microsoft 365 credentials provided by your school or workplace. What's more, you can consolidate all your email accounts, including major providers like Gmail, iCloud, and Yahoo.

This eBook outlines everything you need to know about Outlook, from its basic to advanced features, to get the most out of the iconic platform.

Chapter 1: Getting Started with Outlook

The first step to get started with MS Outlook involves configuring your email accounts. Since Outlook can coordinate multiple inboxes, you can save significant time rather than switching between various platforms by adding them all to the Outlook app.

Configuring Email Accounts

The setup process involves several common steps. Begin by downloading and installing MS Outlook.

Launch Outlook. If this is your first time using the app, you might be prompted to add your credentials. If not, go to File (Windows) or the Microsoft Outlook (Mac) tab at the top of your screen and select "Add account."

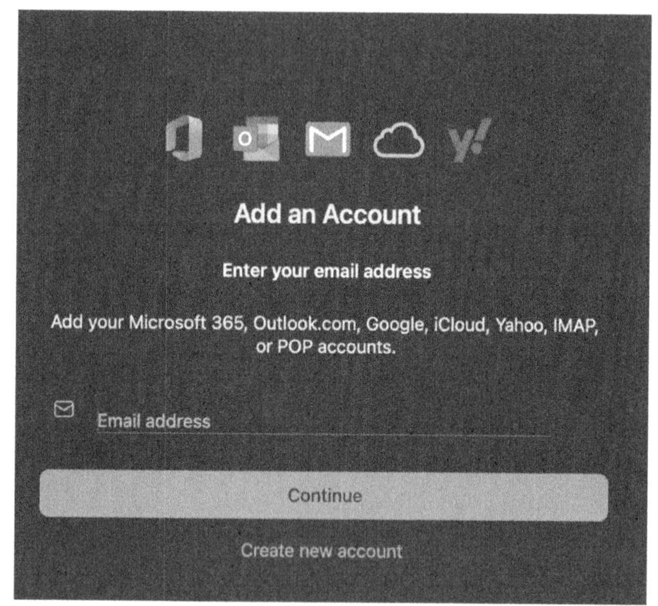

Follow the on-screen prompts and add your email address and password. Then hit "continue."

Outlook will try to configure your account automatically. If this doesn't work, you may be required to enter the server settings manually. Select "Manual Setup" or "Additional Server Types," and choose the type of email you want to configure (IMAP/ POP/ Office). For POP/ IMAP accounts, you'll require incoming and outgoing mail server details. Your hosting service provider will provide you with this information. Using the steps above as a guideline, you can also set up the Outlook mobile app to follow up on emails on the go.

Navigating the Outlook Interface

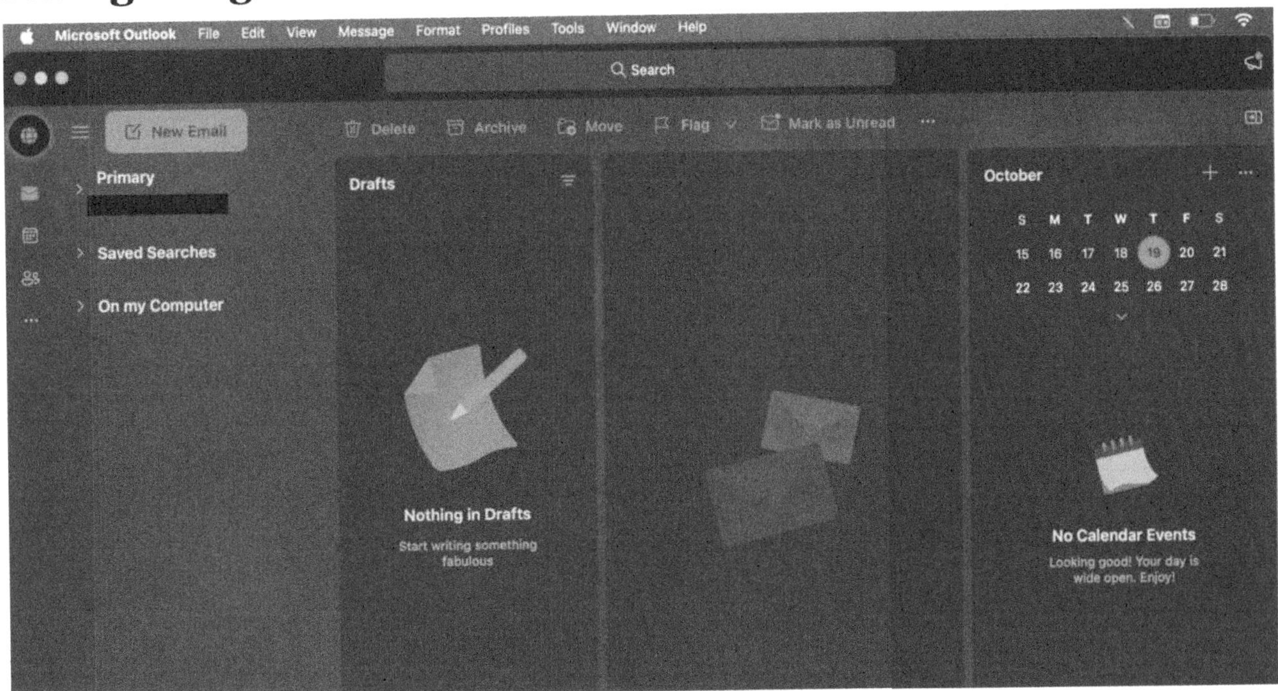

Finding your way around Outlook isn't tricky at all. At the very top of your window, you can find the Title Bar, which contains groups of commands like “File,” “Edit,” “View,” “Message,” et[illegible] Ribbon Toolbar up the settings, previews, and other configurations here. The search bar is located right und[illegible] se this to locate specific emails, contacts, or other items within your Outlook files.

Below the search bar is the Ribbon Toolbar, which changes contextually based on your actions. For instance, in the screenshot above, we h[illegible] Inbox open, so it displays tabs related to messages within that folder, like "delete" and "archive. This would change if we were composing an email or performing any other task.

The rea[illegible] always in the center of your window Reading Pane lick on an email, calendar appointment, or cont[illegible] Folder Pane layed here. In some versions of Outlook, the calendar is displayed on the right side of the window. It shows upcoming appointments and tasks. Calendar/To-Do Bar

Mail, Calendar, Contacts and Tasks

Navigation Pane

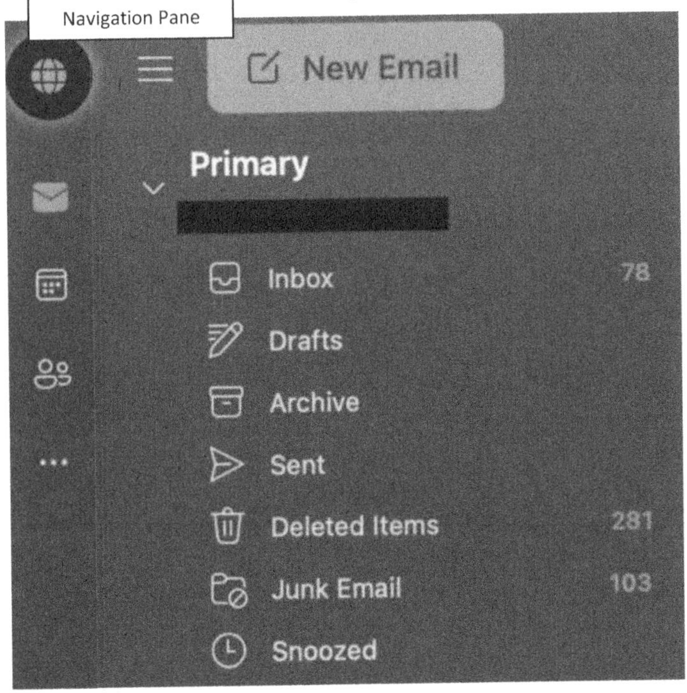

The navigation bar on the left of your screen gives you quick access to all available views. You can switch between mail, calendar, people, and more options. Outlook displays your mail by default, but you can click on a different section name or the arrow beside it to view other information like your contacts or events. Switching to another active view makes it blue.

Besides the navigation pane, you can find the folder pane. As the name suggests, it shows you available email accounts and their respective folders like "Inbox," "Junk," "Drafts," and more. This is a customizable area; you can rename files, add favorites, and more.

Every view has its own set of options. In the Mail tab, you can access your Inbox, read emails, compose new ones with attachments, and more. Outlook also has tools like folders, categories, and rules to help you organize your mailbox.

Outlook's calendar helps you manage events and appointments so you stay on top of your schedule. You can create events, receive automated reminders, and share calendars with others for optimized coordination.

The People or Contacts tab allows you to store and manage professional or personal contacts. You can manually enter their information or import contacts from social media and email accounts. Outlook also has contact categories and groups to find specific people easily.

The three dots at the bottom include "To-Do" lists and "Notes," which open in your browser as they are not built-in features yet. Through the "To-Do" list, users can add tasks with details like due dates and priority levels. These tasks can then be separated into lists with reminders.

Remember that the layout of your Outlook interface might differ slightly because of a different version or OS.

Chapter 2: Managing Email

Thanks to the numerous tools Outlook offers, emailing is a breeze. Email management is an essential aspect of the platform, packed with numerous tools and features for inbox organization and maintenance.

Composing and Sending Emails

To compose a new email, ensure you are in the central pane and then select the blue "New Email" button. A new blank message will open in your reading pane. If you'd like to open your email in a new window, double-click it in your "Drafts" inbox.

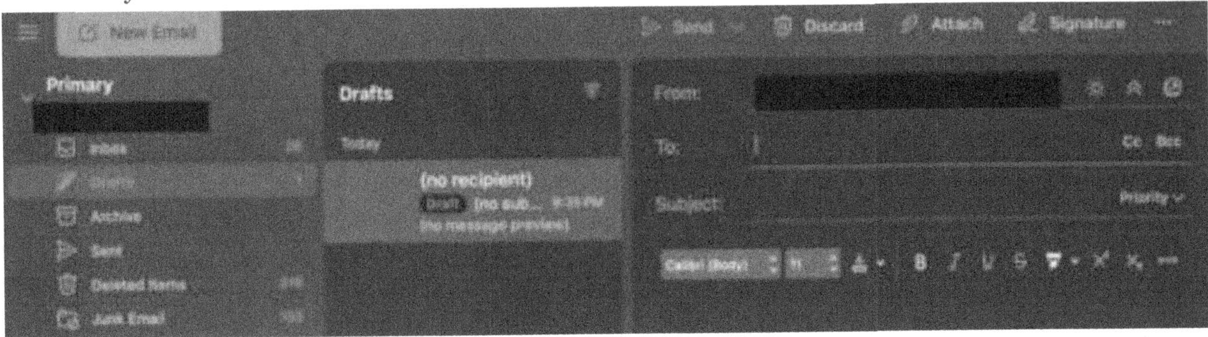

First and foremost, fill out the email header information, including the "To" and "Subject" fields. If multiple email addresses are connected to your Outlook, double-check the "From" section and select the correct email by clicking the arrow beside it.

Next, you want to identify the receiver of your email. You can either type out emails with a comma to separate each one or use the "To" field to search your email contacts. Begin typing in your contact's name, and they will appear in a drop-down dialogue box below the field.

MS Outlook also allows you to copy or blind copy extra contacts. Cc stands for carbon copied – these are recipients others can see. Typically, they are sent copies of the email for informational purposes rather than to respond. For example, copying your team leader on an important reminder. Bcc means blind carbon copied. These recipients aren't visible to others who receive your email. BCC is primarily used for privacy when emailing a large group of people, like a newsletter or announcement.

Filling in the Subject line before sending your email is highly recommended. This field serves as a concise preview of the email's contents so the recipient can assess its importance. A well-crafted subject line is essential – it encourages people to open and read your email, especially in busy inboxes where your message might get overlooked or mistaken for spam.

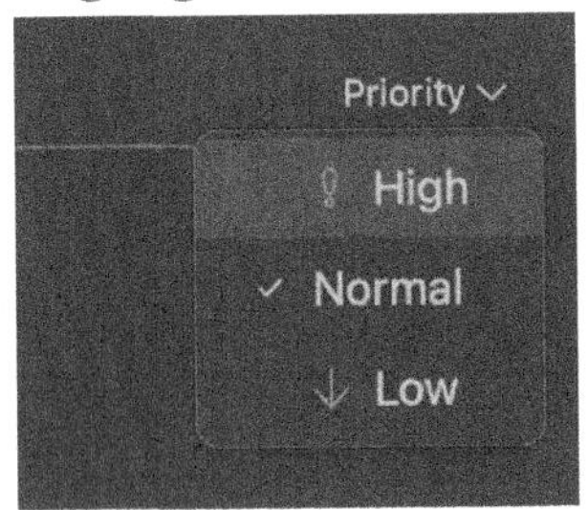

Within the subject line, you can find the "Priority" feature, which allows users to designate the importance of an email. Use the "High" importance option to flag the email as urgent or critical. If your email is not time-sensitive and doesn't require immediate attention, select the "low" importance arrow or leave it as "Normal."

Formatting Options

Even after typing out your message, you're not entirely done. Formatting your email enhances its clarity, making it easier to read and understand. Well-formatted emails convey professionalism and attention to detail. You can highlight key points, create visual distinctions, and gauge the reader's attention to the most essential parts of your message.

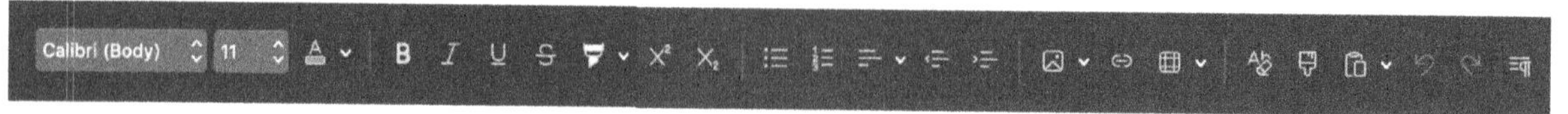

Whether it's through the use of colors, images, or other elements, formatting makes your email more visually appealing and engaging. MS Outlook has several text formatting options, like other Microsoft software. You can find them in the Format Text Ribbon under your email's subject line. Your options include:

- Font style
- Font size and color
- Bold/ Italics/ Underline/Strike-through
- Highlight
- Superscript and Subscript
- Bulleted or Numbered Lists
- Alignment
- Indentation
- Insert Picture/ Hyperlink (to a website) / Table
- Clear Formatting
- Copy Formatting
- Show Formatting Marks

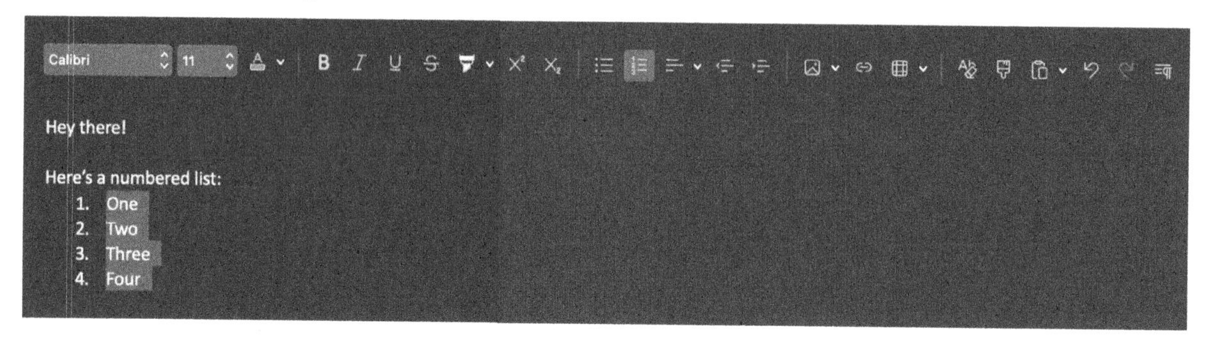

Highlight the text you want to format with your cursor and then select the formatting option you want to apply to it from the ribbon.

MS Outlook also includes quick formatting tools so you can adjust text instantly. The eraser icon clears all settings, like font style, size, colors, etc., from selected text and reverts it to default formatting. The paintbrush icon copies formatting from one section of text and applies it to another.

Attachments and Hyperlinks

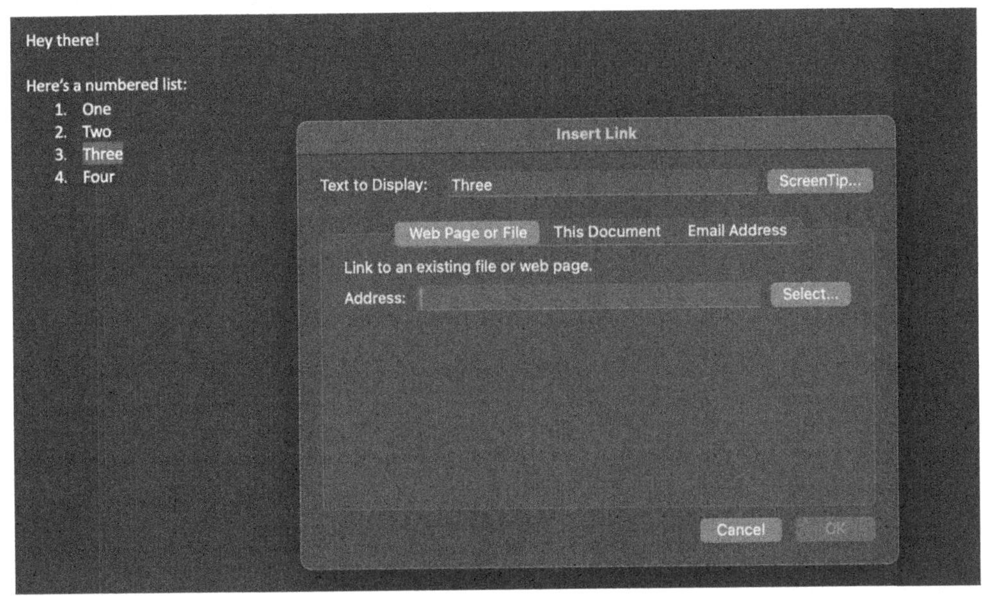

Hyperlinks are handy to make your emails more interactive. You can link text to web pages, different sections of your email contents, or other email addresses. Hyperlinks make accessing external references or related content easier without confusing your reader with additional text. Type a URL in the Address field, select a header in the "This Document" tab, or browse through your contacts to add clickable hyperlinks.

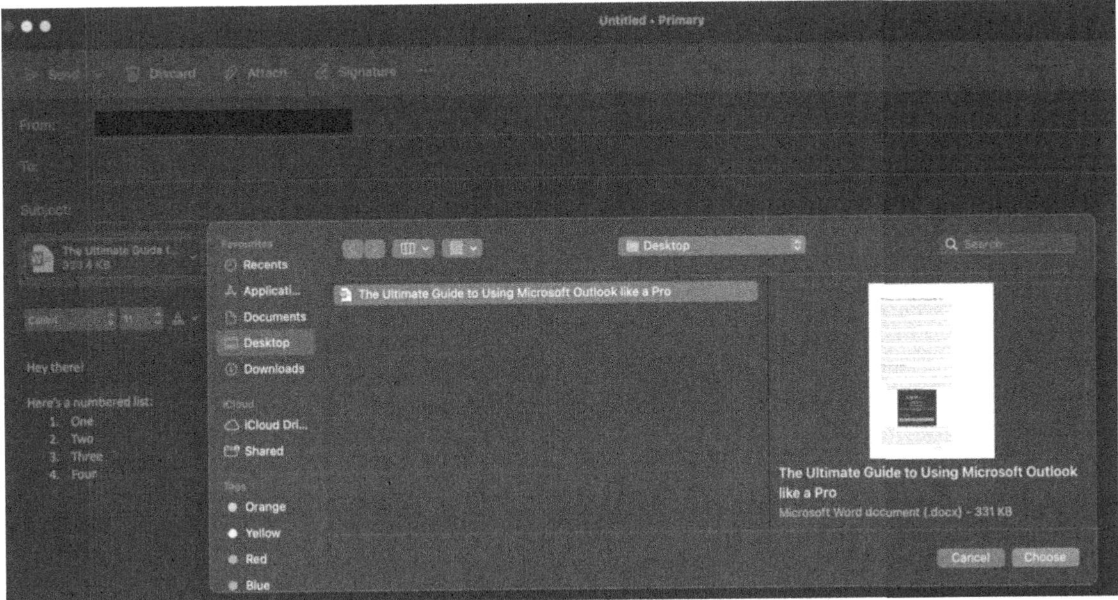

To attach a file, click the paperclip icon in the ribbon menu at the top of your window. You can attach files, documents, images, and any other resources from here if they are smaller than 25 MB. The larger the attachment, the longer it takes to upload and download. Some versions of Outlook also allow you to drag and drop files into the email composition area.

Organizing Emails

Maintaining a clutter-free inbox becomes crucial with the plethora of emails received every day. Effective email organization streamlines communication by ensuring you don't miss important messages. Outlook allows you to create folders, categories, rules, and even flags to label and categorize your emails.

Folders and Categories

Folders are a primary organization tool for all email clients. By default, MS Outlook includes Inbox, Drafts, Junk Email, Sent, Archive, and Deleted Items folders. You can create as many new folders as required to separate work projects, personal emails, and more to keep your inbox clutter-free. To create a new folder, right-click on your mailbox or locate the "New" tab in your title bar and select "New folder."

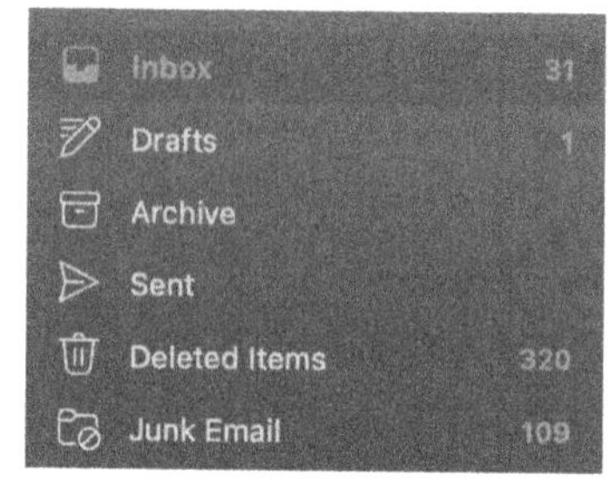

Like folders, Categories can help you organize emails through color-coded labels. Assign categories to your email by right-clicking the email or navigating to "Message" in the title bar and selecting "Categorize." MS Outlook and your operating system have built-in categories, but you can add new ones by choosing "New Category" or "Manage." A dialogue box will open from where you can enter the name and color code for the new category.

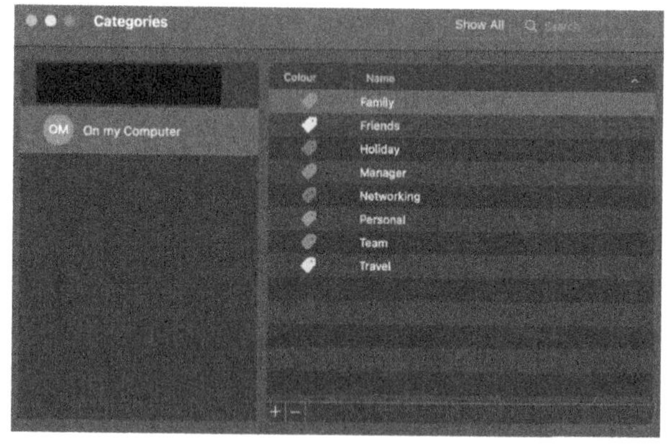

Rules and Filters

MS Outlook includes Rules to perform preset actions on incoming or outgoing emails to automate your Inbox further. Within the "Message" or "Home" tab, you can find and manage these "Rules." Specific versions include a Rules Wizard with templates you can use as a starting point. Define your conditions, like moving emails from a particular sender or including specific keywords in a designated folder. You can also select exceptions to exclude emails that meet the condition. Once configured, Outlook will automatically process all incoming and outgoing emails accordingly.

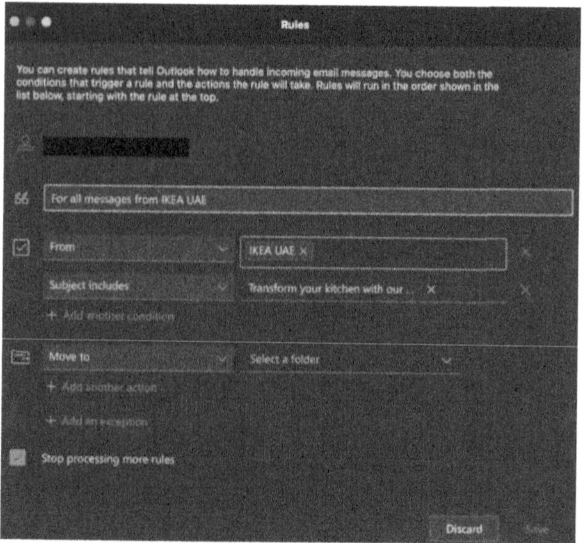

Flags and Follow-ups

Using flags, you can mark emails that require follow-ups. This includes setting due dates and reminders to turn your inbox into a task management resource.

Efficient Email Searching and Filtering

Even if you decide not to organize your Inbox, MS Outlook's efficient filtering and search features let you locate specific emails promptly. Filtering involves applying specific criteria to sort and view emails.

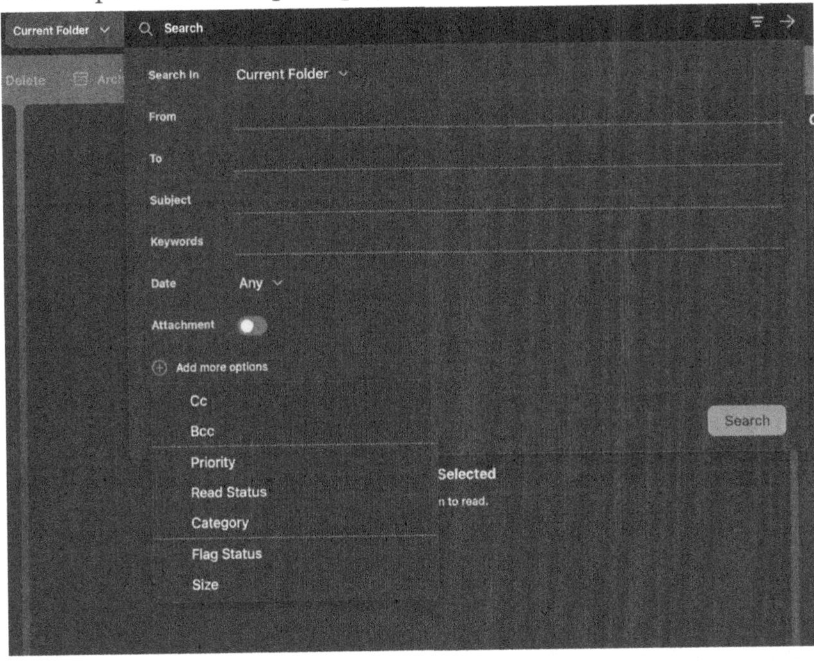

Typically, results can be filtered according to:

- Sender/ Recipient
- Subject
- Keywords
- Dates
- Folder
- Flagged or Unread
- Size
- Category
- Attachments

Outlook also keeps a list of recent searches to revisit previous queries.

Chapter 3: Mastering The Calendar

Your calendar is the heartbeat of the day-to-day organization. A well-organized calendar makes managing your workflow, team communications, and meeting schedules more straightforward. Regarding collaboration, Outlook's Calendar outshines because of its simplicity. It fosters effective communication and teamwork by ensuring everyone is on the same page.

To access the calendar, look for its icon on the left hand of your interface screen in the navigation pane.

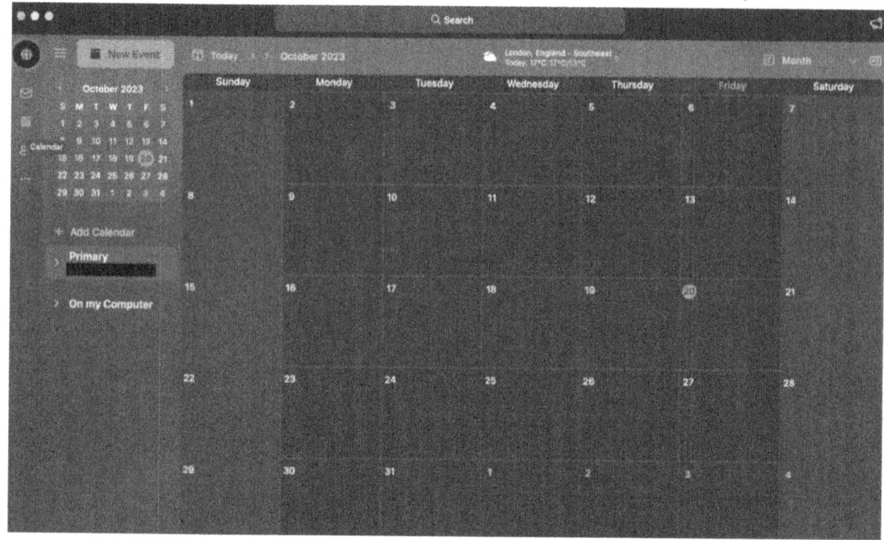

Logging in automatically synchs any upcoming events associated with the account. Basic settings for your calendar from the main menu include setting a working week, the first day of the week, default reminders, time zones, and weather displays.

Creating and Editing Calendar Events

To create an event, tap the blue "New Event" tab or double-click on the data and time in the calendar where you want to create the event.

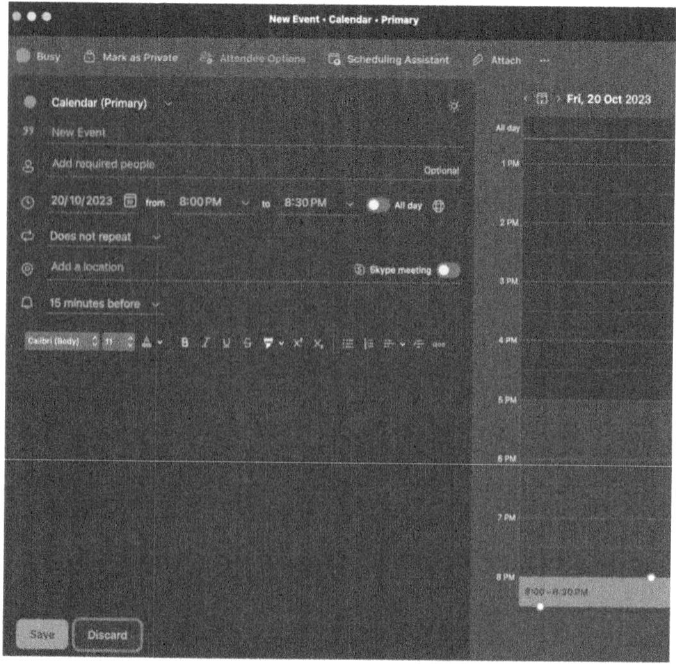

This will open up the event settings pop-up where you can add details like the location, start and end times, availability, color codes, attachments, and notes and even trigger the option of including a Skype meeting link. You can also add attendees via their email address in this window.

Alternatively, you can use the Scheduling Assistant, an excellent tool for events involving multiple attendees. Through this window, users can add attendees and view their availability to find a suitable time slot for the event.

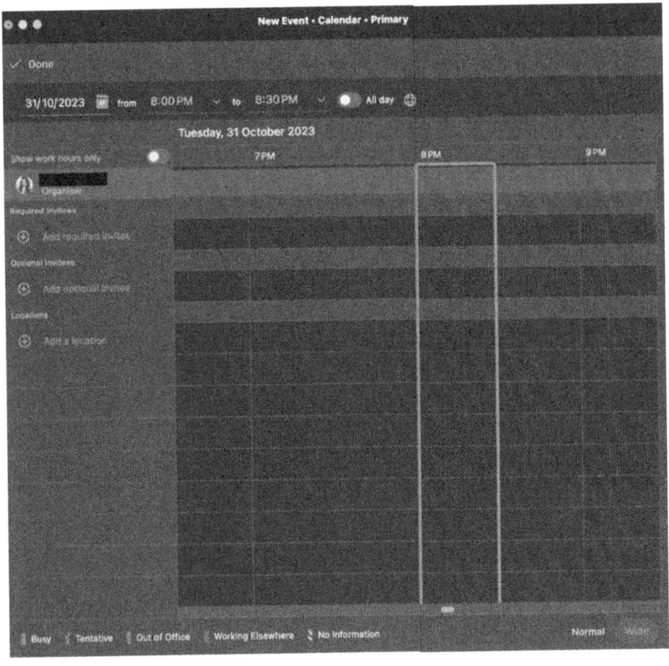

Although the Assistant doesn't reveal specific schedule details, it does indicate each participant's availability, including existing appointments. This is an excellent way to identify scheduling conflicts and overlapping events so you can quickly reschedule to a time that works for all participants. As you change the meeting details or invite more participants, everyone's calendars are automatically updated to have up-to-date information.

To edit or delete an existing event in Outlook, locate the relevant event on your calendar and double-click it. You can modify its details as needed or delete it entirely. Don't forget to click "Save" before closing the window to update attendees.

Appointments, Meetings and Events

Different versions of MS Outlook label your calendar with appointments, meetings, and events depending on their specific purpose. Meetings are used for scheduling events that involve more than one participant. Essentially, they are the same as appointments but include the added functionality of inviting others and managing their RSVPs. When creating a meeting, you can add other people who will receive invitations detailing the meeting date, time, and location. Attendees can accept, decline, or propose an alternative time for the meeting, and organizers can track their responses.

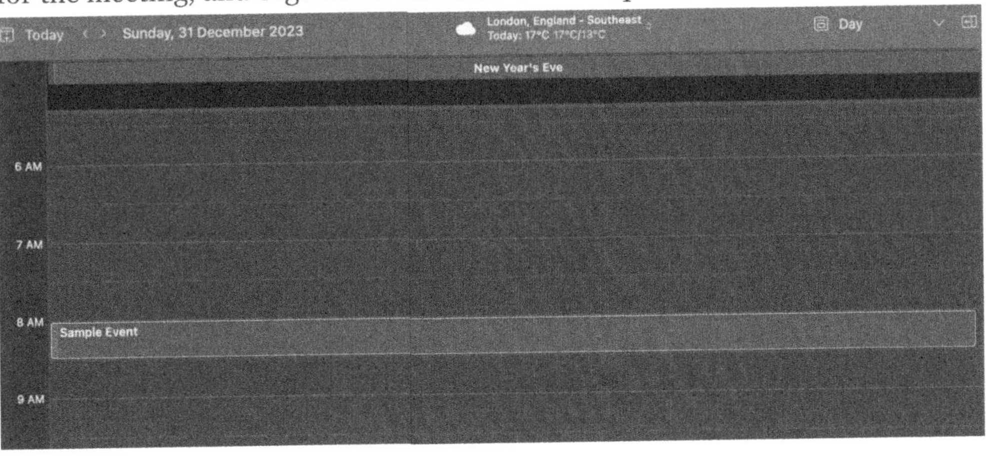

Appointments are individual time blocks that can be set to complete personal activities or events. You can set your availability as "Free," "Busy," "Tentative," or "Out of Office" to indicate your status. You can also schedule block-off times, meetings, and breaks to set aside dedicated time for work and breaks. They are private and don't involve others, but you can add reminders and locations.

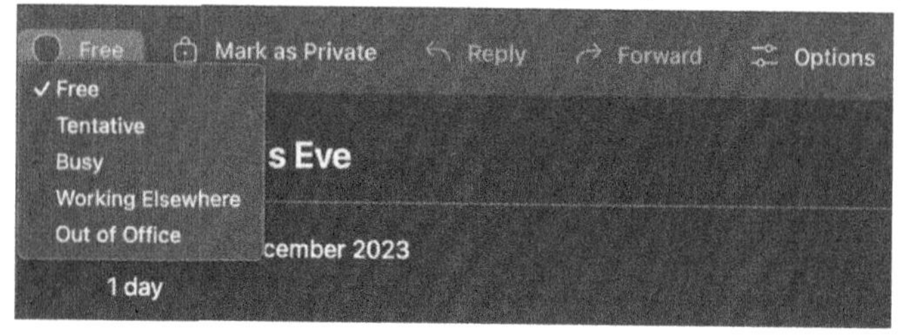

Events are typically used for more extensive or public activities that do not involve specific people. They are often used for holidays, birthdays, conferences, and seminars, focusing less on individual interactions and more on general planning.

Recurring events are a useful feature that allows you to schedule and manage regular, repetitive appointments or meetings. Instead of creating separate events, you can automatically set a scheduled event to repeat at defined intervals. You can specify how often it repeats, when the event should stop repeating, or the number of times it should recur. You can also edit one event without affecting future consolidated events. In addition to saving time, recurring events ensure consistency and reduce errors involved with manual scheduling.

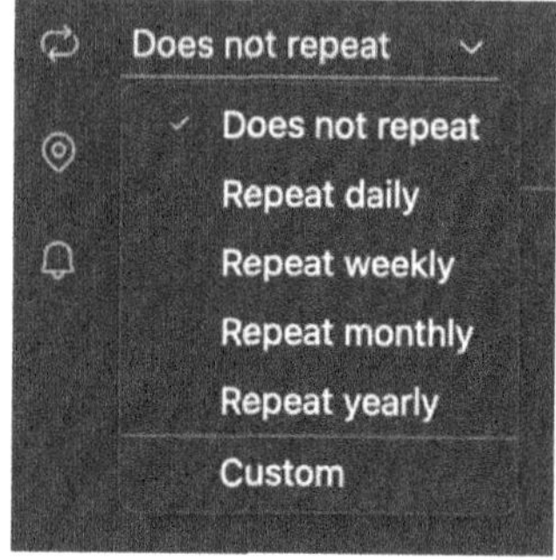

Calendar Views and Layouts

Microsoft Outlook offers various views to help you see your schedule per your preference.

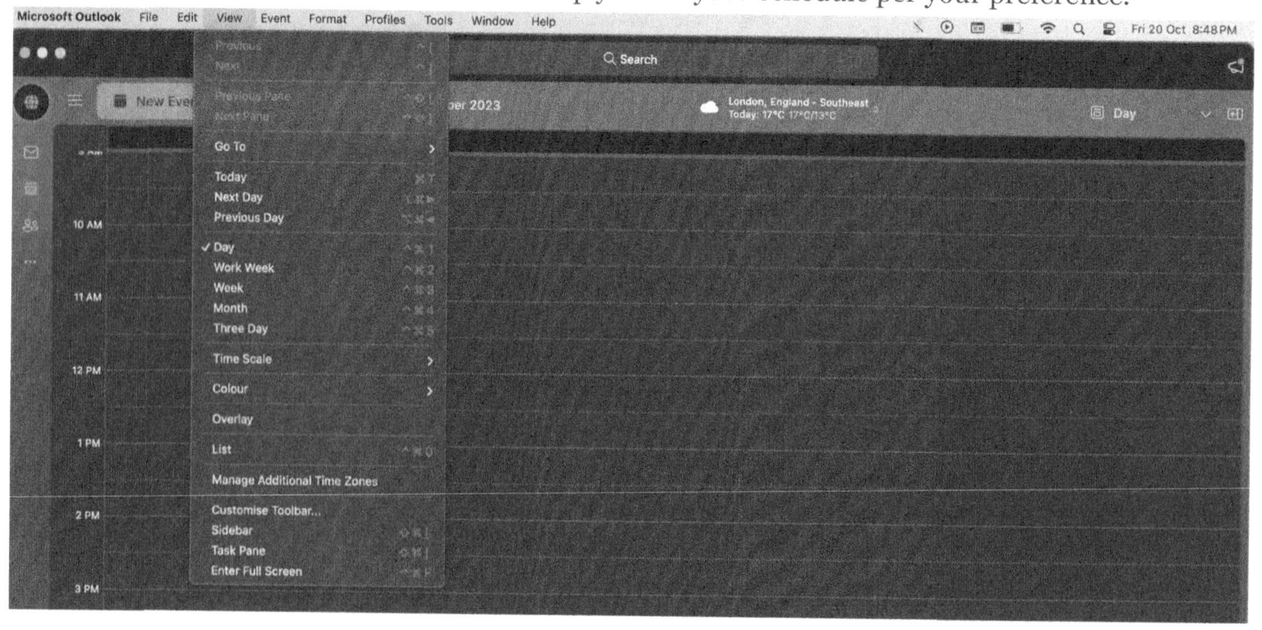

You can view calendar events in day, work week (Monday to Friday), week, month, or three-day views for a custom overview of your appointments. The daily view offers a more detailed, granular perspective of your schedule for managing tasks within a short period, while more extended views are helpful for long-term planning. Some versions also include a Schedule view that combines the above views in a scrollable timeline.

Outlook Calendar also offers different layouts. The Reading Pane previews all calendar items when you click on them, while the To-Do Bar includes all upcoming calendar items, flagged emails, and tasks so you can manage your schedule in one spot. These layouts are helpful in quickly checking event details without accessing the calendar window.

To visually organize events, like emails, you can use color-coded categories. Categories help you visually distinguish and group events based on their nature and importance. With categories, you can prioritize your time, promote consistency, and visually organize events to identify them at first glance.

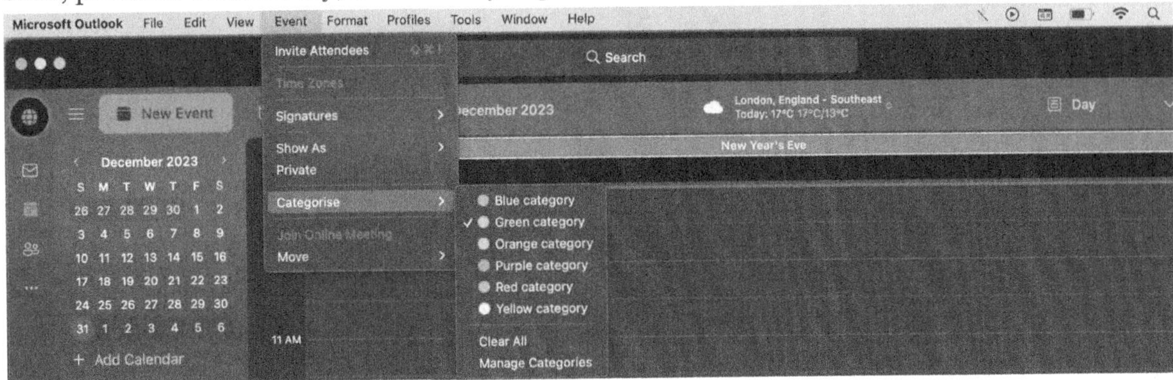

Sharing and Collaborating

You can share your calendar with other Outlook users when you want team members to have access to your schedule for coordination. To do this, right-click or locate the three dots beside your calendar and select "Share" or "Sharing Permissions."

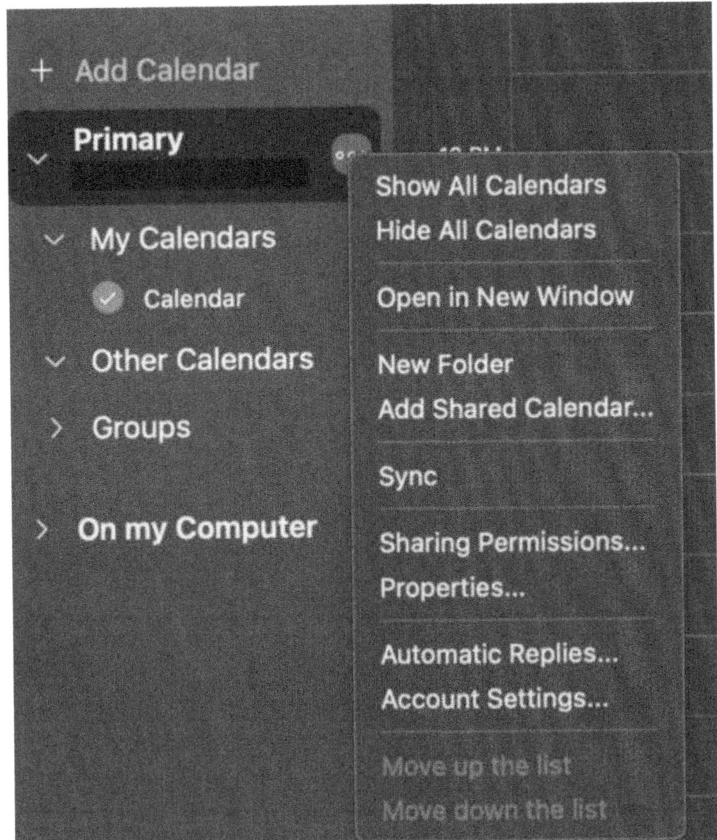

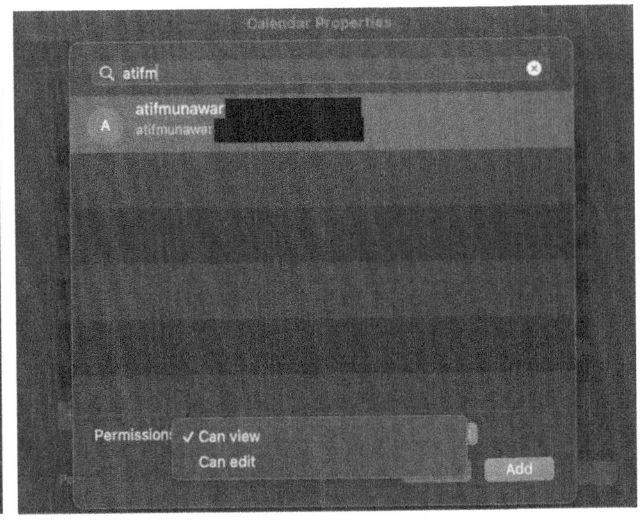

You can add as many people as you'd like to your calendar from the pop-up window with specific permissions like view-only or editor access. Adjusting calendar permissions is essential for data security and privacy when collaborating.

When creating an event, you can invite others to specific meetings or events by adding their email addresses in the "Add Required People" or "Attendees" field. Outlook will send them an email invitation, which they can accept, decline, or request another time.

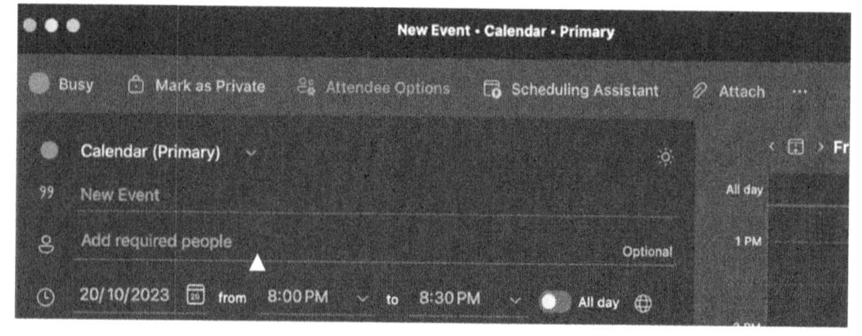

Calendar groups are an alternative way to synchronize calendars. Instead of adding multiple calendars to your view, you can create a group that combines multiple calendars for a unified view. Right-click "My Calendars" from your navigation pane or select the calendars you want to group. Then, select "New Calendar Group" from the context menu to consolidate them.

Chapter 4: Contacts And People

MS Outlook is also a robust personal information manager, helping you connect with people more efficiently. Whether you want to organize your address book, create contact groups, or link to other platforms, Outlook can help you out.

Managing Contacts

Managing your contacts in MS Outlook involves adding, editing, categorizing, or importing/exporting contact data. Importing and exporting contacts between different devices or platforms is convenient by connecting numerous email accounts or adding CSV files. If you use Outlook on multiple devices, your contacts will be automatically synchronized across them all. This includes different services like Google and more.

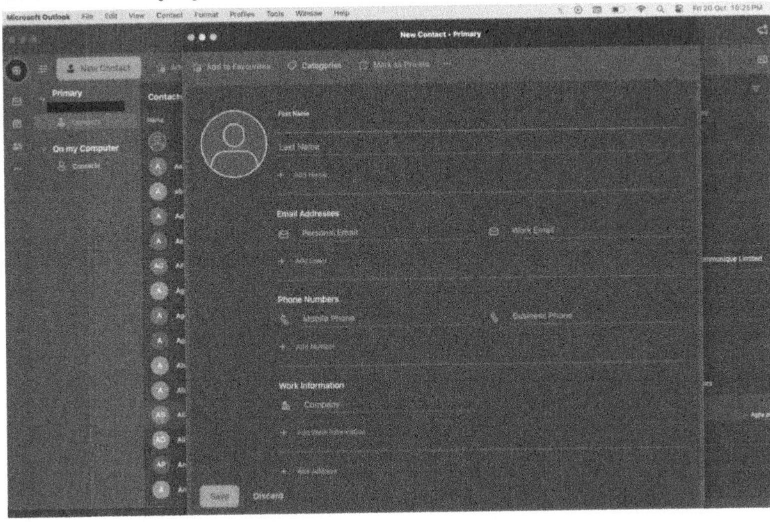

Adding and Editing Contacts

You might notice all your email contacts have already been added to your Outlook address book. In case you don't, you can add a contact manually by:

Go to the "People" or "Contacts" tab in the navigation pane.

2. Tap on "New Contact."
3. Fill in contact details, including names, email addresses, phone numbers, designation, etc. Like emails and calendar events, you can also categorize your contacts based on criteria like work, personal, family, or custom options.

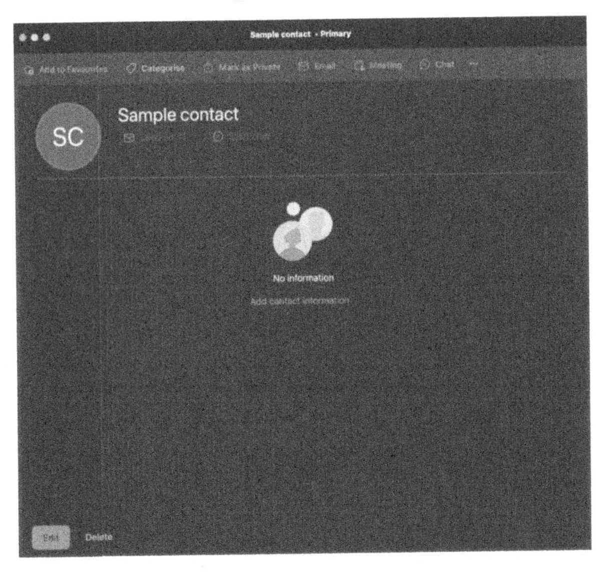

Outlook also allows you to link contacts with their social media profiles. Locate the contact whose social media profile you want to link, and select "Add" and "Linked Social Network" at the bottom end of your screen. Select the social media platform corresponding to the contact profile and add their URL or username.

You can edit your contacts by double-clicking them, opening their details, and making the necessary changes before saving the updated information. From the same window, you can also delete contacts.

Contact Groups

Specific versions of Outlook allow you to create contact groups or distribution lists. These are ideal for mass emailing or event scheduling. To create a contact group:

1. Select "New Contact Group" in the "People" or "Contacts" tab.
2. Name the group.
3. Add contacts by typing their names or emails in the "Add Members field."

When composing an email, instead of individually adding contacts from the group, you can type the group name in the "To" field. All members of the group will automatically receive your email.

Users can customize how their contacts are displayed in Outlook. You can choose from views like "Business Card" or "List." Customize the fields in your contact list to view the most relevant details. Outlook also offers search and filtering options to search by name, email address, or any other criteria.

It's important to note that Outlook for Mac devices has limited capabilities compared to its Windows version.

Linking Contacts with Social Media

Outlook has no built-in feature to link contacts with their social media profiles directly. However, using the Outlook Social Connector, you can manually add links to their social profiles. Ensure you are using a version of Outlook that supports the feature, then install it as an add-on from the Microsoft website. Then, configure and enable it following the prompts. Once the Social Connector is activated, you are good to go. Open a contact for whom you want to link a social media account. You should see an option for the People Pane or Social Connector within the contact window. Click the "Connect to Social Network" option to authorize Outlook access. You should then be able to view additional information like social media updates and profile pictures within the contact window.

Unfortunately, some versions of Outlook do not support the Social Media Connector. You can manually add social media links through the contact's "web page" field for easy access.

Integrations with Microsoft 365 and LinkedIn

Microsoft owns LinkedIn, and as a result, you can synch your LinkedIn contacts using its integration. The LinkedIn Connector lets you view profile information, photos, and shared connections within Outlook. When you receive an email from a LinkedIn connection, this integration helps you put a face to their name by displaying their profile photo from the network. By enabling LinkedIn contact synch, your Outlook contacts are automatically updated with their up-to-date profile information. The LinkedIn Connector further lets you view their LinkedIn activity updates from connections so you stay informed.

Microsoft 365 links Outlook with Microsoft Teams, SharePoint, OneDrive, and all other Microsoft Apps for accessibility. This includes instant contact sharing with others within your organization. Contacts in Outlook are closely integrated across all its various add-ons, including the Calendar app. With Microsoft 365, Outlook can become a centralized workplace for you and your connections across different platforms.

Chapter 5: Tasks And To-Do

Outlook Tasks and To-Do lists are indispensable resources for project management. They help you stay organized and focused on your goals. Tasks are a great way to track progress on work items, assignments, and other activities. They are part of a broader productivity ecosystem that helps you keep yourself in check. These tasks also sync across all your devices so that you can manage tasks from anywhere. Flagged emails appear as tasks, so you return to them on time.

Creating and Managing Tasks

Adding and managing tasks is the first step to keeping track of assignments, tasks, and other activities.

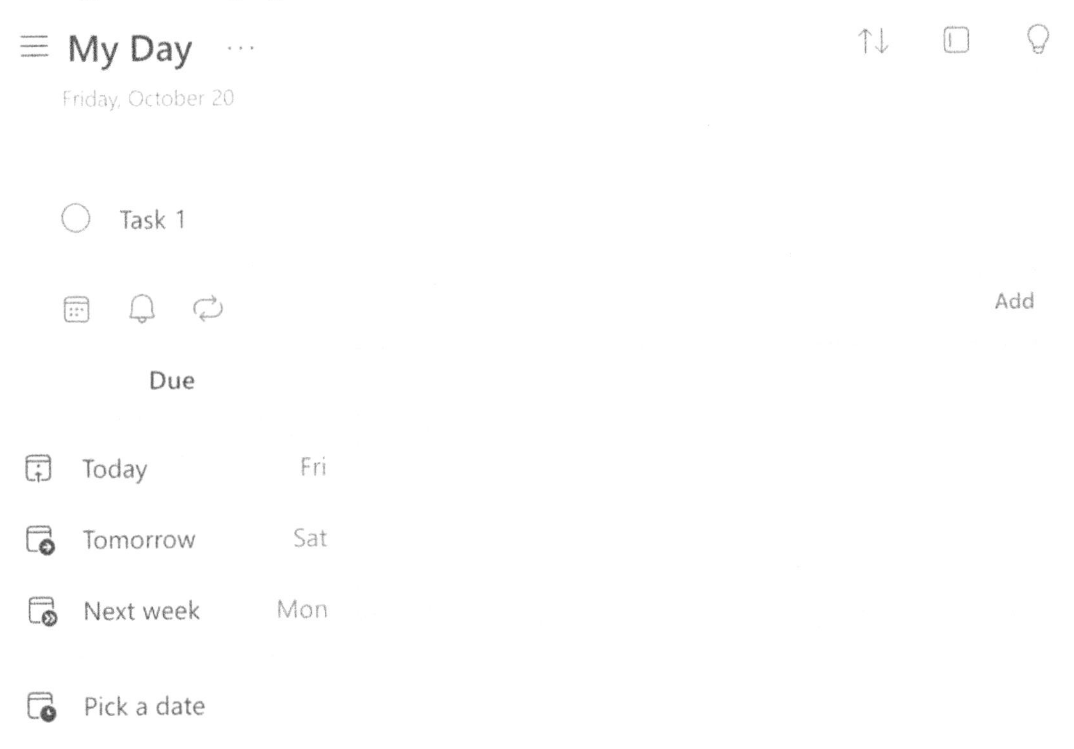

To create a task:

1. Locate and Launch the Tasks tab, typically found in the navigation bar on the bottom left.
2. Click "Add a Task" or "New Task" and enter the task's subject. Enter details like due dates and notes using the options under the task tab.

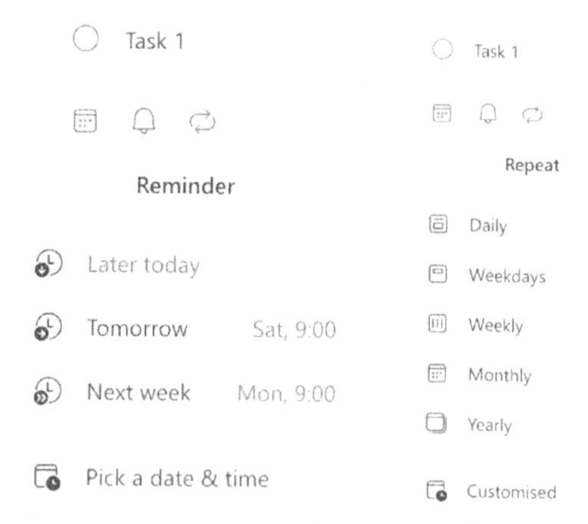

3. You can also create recurring tasks and set up reminders that synch across other Outlook apps.

You can view tasks in the same window as a to-do list, detailed list, or calendar view. When you complete a task, update its status by clicking the checkbox beside it. To edit tasks, double-click them to view their details and make changes as required. Outlook also includes tools to set reminders, add recurring tasks, or search for specific assignments.

Users can also organize tasks using color-coded categories for different projects or custom criteria for quick identification. Tasks can be classified into separate lists or folders to group related tasks.

Task Details and Due Dates

In Outlook, various detail fields help you manage your to-do lists. In addition to the subject field and title, you can add further information related to your task by mentioning its:

- Due date
- Start date
- Priority (High, Normal, Low)
- Status (Not Started, In Progress, Completed, Waiting on Someone Else)
- Category
- Notes
- Attachments
- Custom Fields (included in some versions of Outlook to include information not included in default fields)

These details give you flexibility to align your needs and workflows. They help you stay organized, prioritize work, and track the progress of various tasks.

Due dates are particularly important as they serve as a deadline or target date for completing a task. When you set a due date, you can add reminder notifications, sort and filter by the deadline, and prioritize time-sensitive tasks.

Task Assignments

Through Outlook, you can assign tasks to others and vice-versa. Go to the Assign Task option in your Task window and enter the email address of the individual you want to assign the task. They will receive the task as an email, which can be accepted or declined. Once accepted, you can track its progress in your task list.

Using the To-Do List

All tasks from various folders are displayed in your To-Do list. You can also use the "My Day" feature to select tasks from your list and add them to your daily plan. You can mark tasks as complete, sort and filter your assignments, and delegate items from here. The to-do list is a convenient way to see an overview of all upcoming deadlines so you can use time and resources effectively.

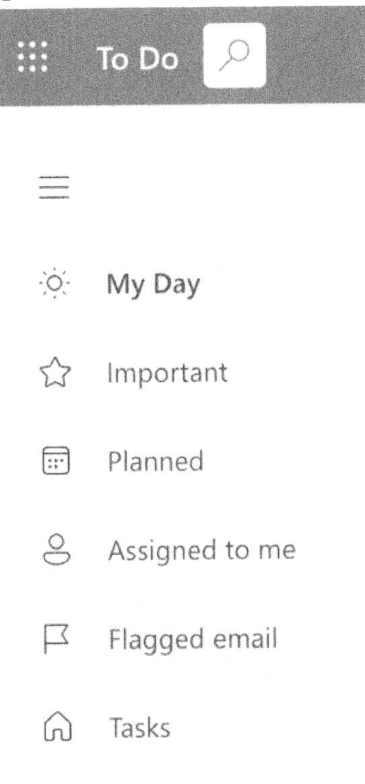

Syncing Tasks with Calendar and Email

Tasks can be synchronized seamlessly with your calendar and email apps. You can set up tasks to appear in your calendar as appointments by dragging and dropping them into the Outlook calendar. If a task has a due date, it will appear in your calendar.

Emails can be turned into tasks by flagging them or setting up follow-up reminders so you remember to address important messages. Tasks with reminders will trigger notifications across all your Outlook devices. This minimizes the risk of missed deadlines, so you're always on top of your game!

Chapter 6: Advanced Features And Customization

In addition to its basic features, Outlook is packed with advanced features that allow you to customize the app to your needs. These features are designed to boost productivity and eliminate repetitive, time-consuming tasks while reducing the risk of human error.

Outlook Rules and Automation

You can automate everything on Outlook from Email management to your to-do list. Using Outlook, you can create email templates, schedule emails, and automatically move older emails into an archive folder.

But rules are an excellent way to take things one step further. Rules are automated instructions or conditions that manage your emails, tasks, and other items. By creating rules, you can sort, filter, move, and categorize your emails without lifting a finger. Access the folder settings where you want to create the rule and locate the "Rules and Alerts" option. Then, follow the on-screen prompts and enter the relevant information. Rules can be used to flag, categorize, forward, or flag emails automatically. You can further customize rules with exceptions to fine-tune how they operate.

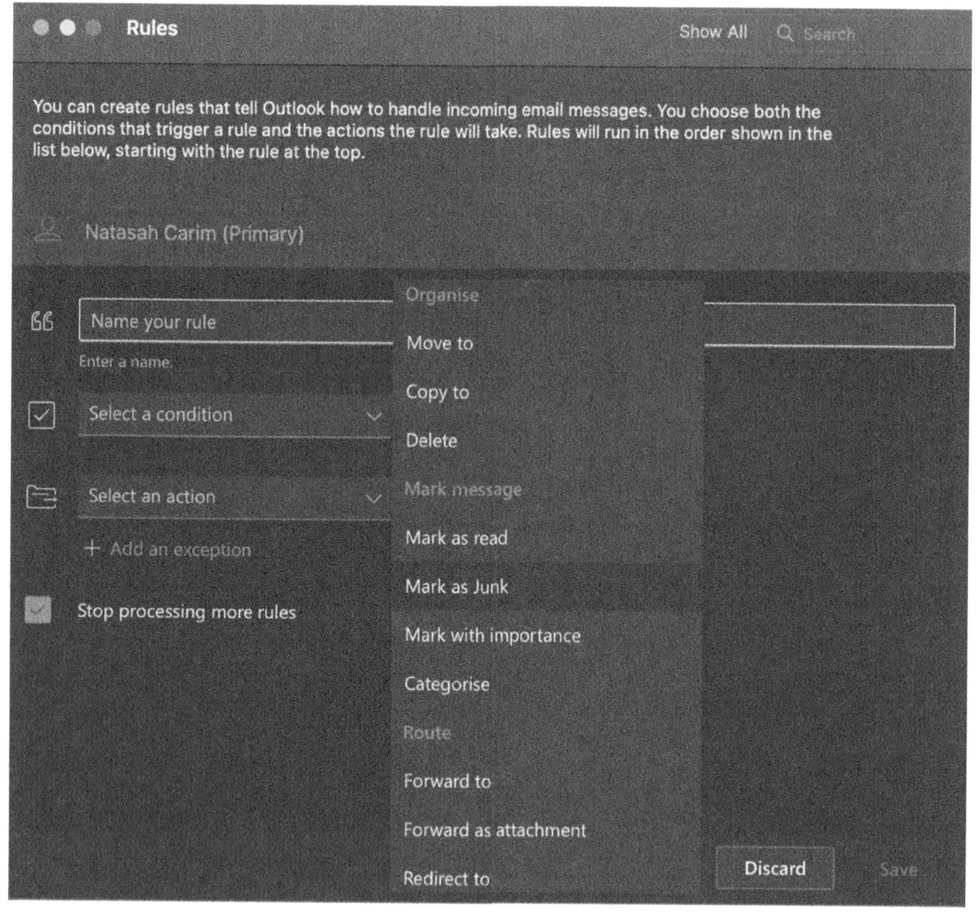

Automated Responses

Automation options also include setting up automatic email responses. In the "File" tab of your Outlook Window or from the gear tab, select "Settings" and locate the "Automatic Replies" option. Toggle it on and create the message you wish to send. You can specify different messages for senders inside and outside your organization and a time frame for these responses. Your automatic responses are not active – these are a great option to let people know when you are out of the office or on vacation for a specified time.

Conditional Formatting

Windows Outlook offers conditional formatting. When you want to apply font formatting conditions based on set criteria, you can use this option to spot emails easily in your Inbox. Start by opening Outlook, choose "View Settings," and select "Conditional Formatting." In the pop-up window, you are presented with preconfigured rules. Unread messages are highlighted in blue, and expired emails can be marked with a strike-through, depending on which options you check.

To add a new rule, select "Add.: Insert a name and adjust the font style, size, color, strike-throughs, and underlines. To specify the requirements for your rule, click "Condition." You'll see various tabs, from basic to advanced options. Go to the "Messages" tab to set up universal criteria. This includes keywords in subject lines, senders, CCs, and time periods. To set up a custom condition, tap the "Advanced" button. Use the drop-down menu to select a "Field" like "Most Used," "Mail," and "Contact." Then, adjust the values to the right and click "OK" to save. Return to the main window and ensure your rules have a checkmark next to them.

Outlook Add-ins and Integrations

Outlook also has various add-ins and integrations to extend its functionality. Built-in integrations include Microsoft Teams without additional setup requirements. Boomerang allows you to schedule emails, send reminders for follow-ups, and track email opens. You can install it from Microsoft's AppSource.

Another useful add-in is Grammarly, which helps you check and improve spelling and grammar. Zoom for Outlook allows you to schedule and start Zoom meetings from your Outlook Calendar. A few Third-Party email add-ins include:

- Salesforce (CRM)
- HubSpot
- MailChimp
- Trello
- Mimecast encryption
- LinkedIn Sales Navigator
- Calendly

To set up these integrations, access the "Add-ins" or "Integrations" section and follow the on-screen instructions when you select the apps you want to use.

You can also add multiple signatures with personalized blocks of text and images that are added to the end of your email message. Access the "Signature" settings from the "File" or "Preferences" tab and create a new signature. You can choose a default signature for each email account linked to the Outlook interface.

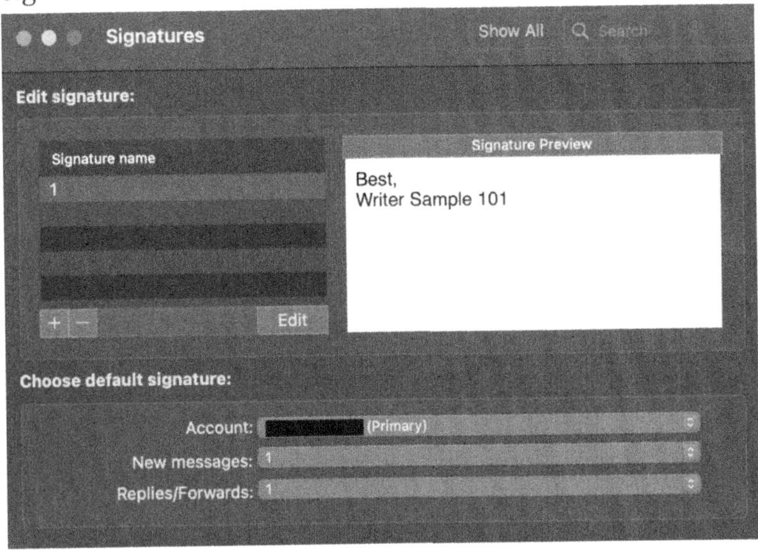

Customizing the Outlook Interface

Customizing your Outlook interface can make it more user-friendly. Options include changing the theme, customizing your ribbon, fonts, the quick access toolbar, and the navigation pane. These settings are available in the "Options" tab or "Preferences" under General settings. To customize the ribbon, right-click the toolbar with tabs like Home, Send/ Receive, and select "Customize the Ribbon" or "Customize the Toolbar." This will allow you to add, remove, and rearrange Ribbon commands.

You can create custom folders, notifications, languages, and time zones. Remember, customization depends on your Outlook version, so explore the settings or preferences menu to find all available options.

Conclusion

Mastering Outlook brings you one step closer to experiencing productivity unlike ever before. Set up your Outlook account and configure your preferences, like email signatures, themes, and other basic settings. Once you've laid the foundation, the heart of your Outlook journey lies in email and calendar management. Learn to efficiently organize and format emails leveraging rules, filters, and categories for quick access. With Outlook's integrated calendar, you can effortlessly schedule your day and collaborate with colleagues and peers.

Contact management is also more intuitive with Outlook's options. You can organize your address book, sync contacts cross-device, and use the People pane to view more details. Outlook is also known for managing tasks and to-do lists through which you can set deadlines and categorize tasks for project management. Beyond the fundamentals, Outlook's advanced features include add-ins and third-party applications for expanded functionality.

Outlook lets users create a tailored experience that meets all their professional and personal needs. That being said, the features highlighted in this guide vary depending on the version of Outlook and the operating system you use. We recommend looking over specific guides and using the search bar in the settings tab to discover what options are available for your unique use case.

Microsoft Teams

Overview of Microsoft Teams

In today's hyper-connected, remote-friendly work environment, the demand for unified communication platforms is stronger than ever. That is why Microsoft Teams, a collaboration hub has become an essential part of the modern workspace. Bundled within Microsoft 365 but powerful enough to stand alone, Teams has redefined the way businesses, educational institutions, and even casual users interact and collaborate.

This digital powerhouse is more than just a Skype replacement or an upgrade to your typical Slack channel. What sets Teams apart is its deep integration with a suite of Microsoft tools like Word, Excel, and SharePoint, as well as a plethora of third-party applications. This means you can co-author a document, share critical project updates, and even integrate complex data analytics without ever having to leave the platform. From chat threads and video meetings to shared files and professional networks, everything is nestled within a seamless interface designed for productivity.

So why should you invest your time in learning about Microsoft Teams? Whether you're an enterprise decision-maker, an educator adapting to online teaching, or someone just looking for efficient ways to collaborate, Teams has something for everyone. Its versatility extends from simple chat functionalities to complex project management workflows. And let's not forget the increased security features, a critical concern in our age of frequent cyber threats.

As you navigate through this eBook, you'll uncover tips, tricks, and in-depth insights into making the most out of Microsoft Teams. We'll explore everything from basic setups and features to advanced customization and integration.

Chapter 1:Getting Started with Microsoft Teams

Getting started with Microsoft Teams involves setting up your Teams and Channels, familiarizing yourself with the interface, and understanding key features like the Activity Feed and Notifications. These initial steps lay the foundation for seamless collaboration and effective communication.

Setting Up Teams and Channels

1. Download and Install Microsoft Teams

The first step in your journey is to download and install the Microsoft Teams application. You can download it from the official Microsoft website or from the app store of your respective operating system.

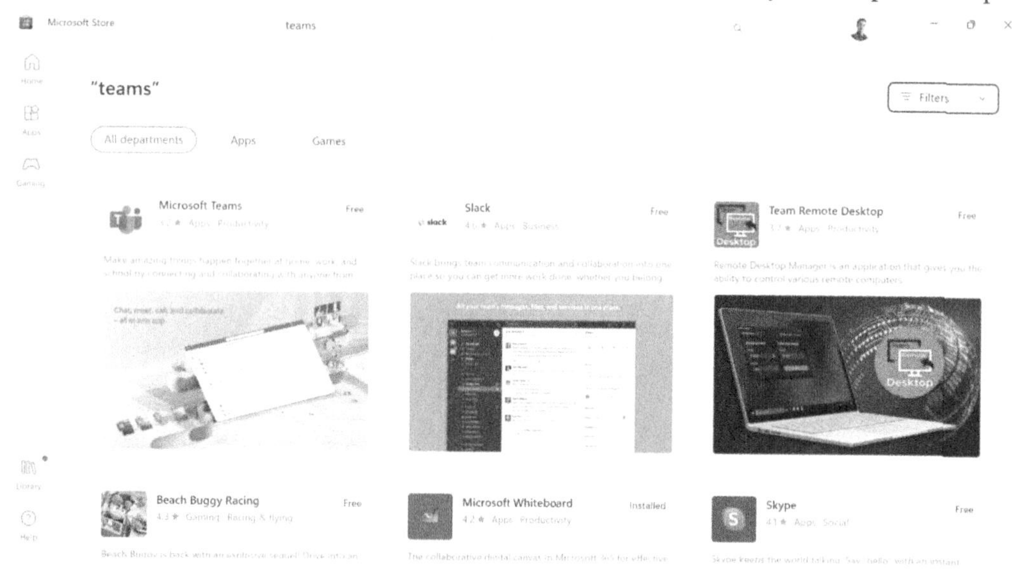

2. Log in or Sign Up

Launch the application and sign in with your Microsoft 365 account. If you don't have an account, you can create one.

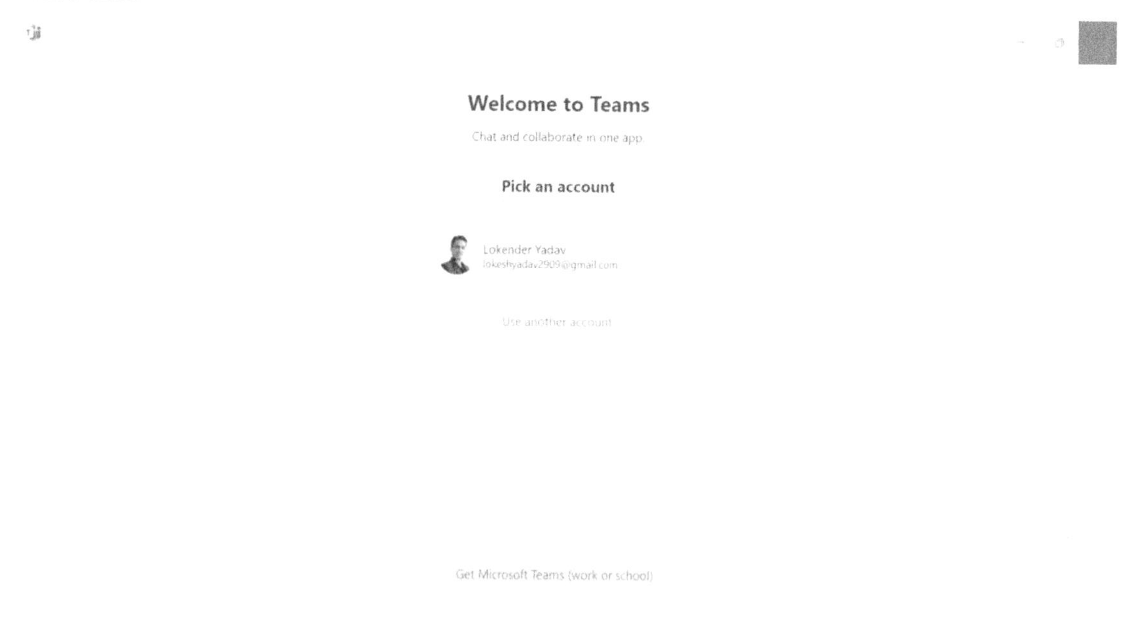

3. Create a New Team

Once logged in, click on the "Teams" icon on the left sidebar and then click on "Join or create a team" at the bottom. You will then have the option to create a team from scratch or use existing templates.

4. Adding Channels

After your Team is created, you can add Channels to categorize different aspects or departments of your team. Click the ellipsis (three dots) next to your Team's name and select "Add Channel".

Navigating the Teams Interface

1. Left Sidebar

The left sidebar contains primary navigation options like Activity, Chat, Teams, Calendar, and Files.It is your main navigational hub within Microsoft Teams. It's where you'll find icons for key functionalities like:

- Activity: This is your notification center, keeping you updated on all interactions involving you or your teams.
- Chat: Individual and group conversations can be accessed here.
- Teams: A listing of all the Teams you are part of. Clicking on a Team reveals its channels.
- Calendar: Your schedule, meeting invites, and other calendar events are displayed here.
- Files: Quick access to all your files, whether they're personal or shared within a Team.

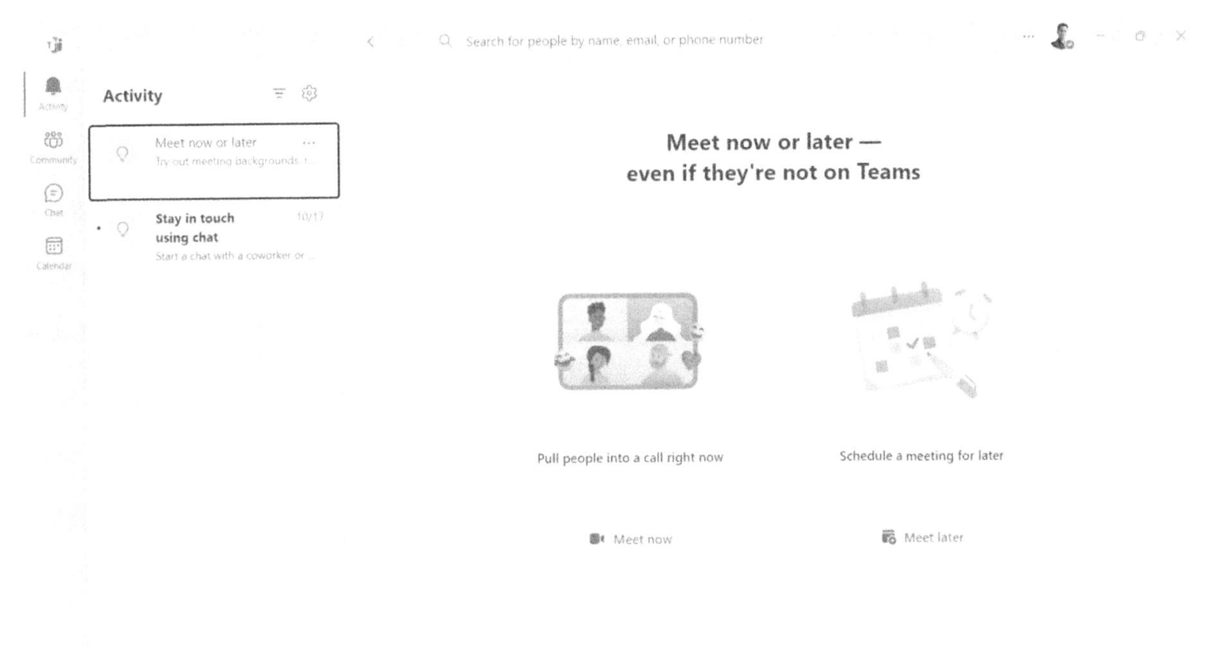

The left sidebar also includes additional options like Calls and Apps, depending on your organization's settings.

2. Main Window

The main window is where your selected channel or chat will appear. It includes the chat window, along with tabs for Posts, Files, and other added apps.

- Chat Window: The core area where messages are displayed and sent.
- Posts Tab: This tab is essentially the channel's conversation thread and it's where all the interactions occur.
- Files Tab: Shows all the files shared within the current channel or chat.
- Additional Tabs: Teams allows for the integration of apps as tabs. These could range from a Planner board for task tracking to a Power BI dashboard for data visualization.

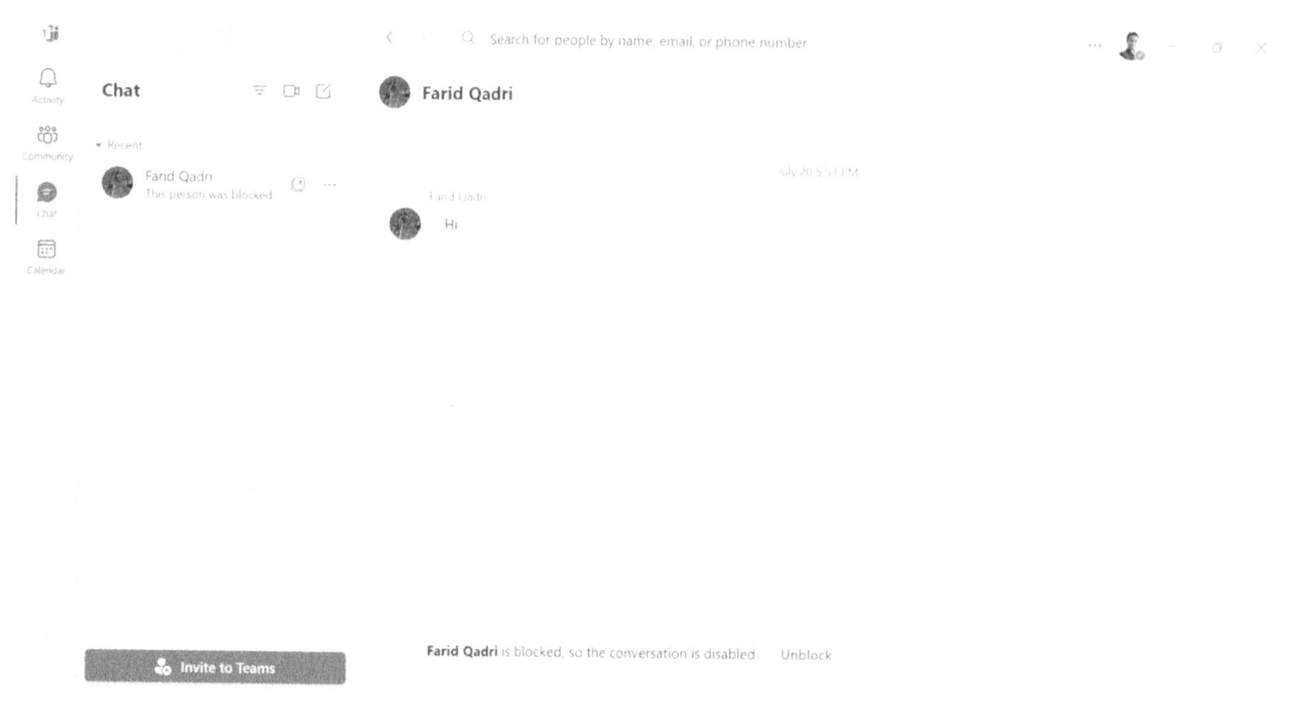

Teams, Channels, and Tabs

1. Teams

These are essentially large groups where you can organize your workforce. Each Team can have multiple Channels. Think of them as large organizational groups where you can assemble your workforce or a project's stakeholders. A Team can be an entire department or just a project squad. What makes Teams particularly efficient is their ability to host multiple Channels. So, under the umbrella of a single Team, you can have various sub-groups, each dedicated to a different topic or project. This means you could have a Team for Marketing and within that Team, Channels for Social Media, Content Creation, and SEO, thereby neatly organizing your workforce.

2. Channels

Subsections of a Team, these are used to segregate conversations and files by department or project. For instance, within a 'Product Development' Team, you might find Channels like 'UI/UX Design', 'Backend Development', and 'User Testing'. Each channel allows team members to communicate and collaborate on specific aspects without overwhelming the larger Team with irrelevant information.

3. Tabs

Within a Channel, you can add tabs. Tabs can be added for Microsoft Planner, Microsoft Forms, and other third-party services. Whether it's Microsoft Planner for task management, Microsoft Forms for collecting feedback, or even third-party services like Trello or GitHub, tabs enable you to centralize these resources. This eliminates the need to switch between different platforms, thus streamlining your project management and enhancing productivity.

Activity Feed and Notifications

1. Activity Feed: Located at the top-left corner, the activity feed consolidates all your notifications and mentions. You can filter this feed to show only unread messages, @mentions, replies, and more.

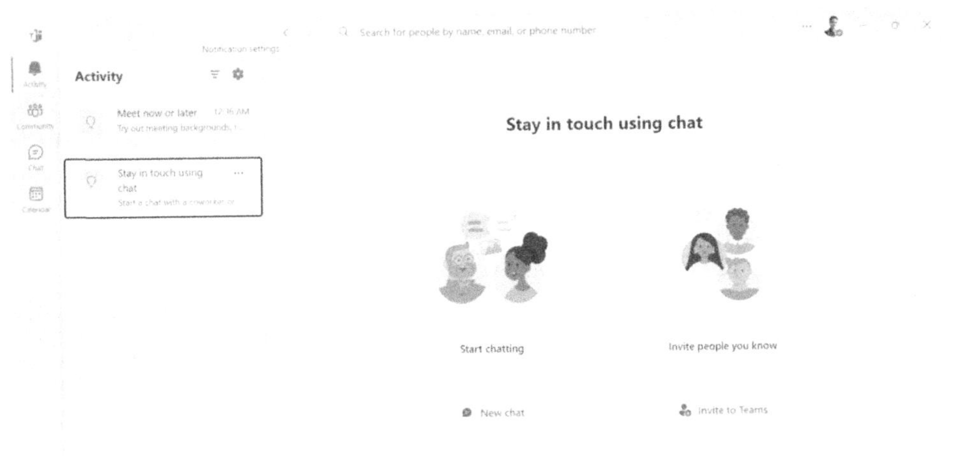

2. Setting Notifications: To customize your notification settings, click on three dots near your profile picture at the top right and choose "Settings". Navigate to "Notifications and Activity" and adjust according to your preference.

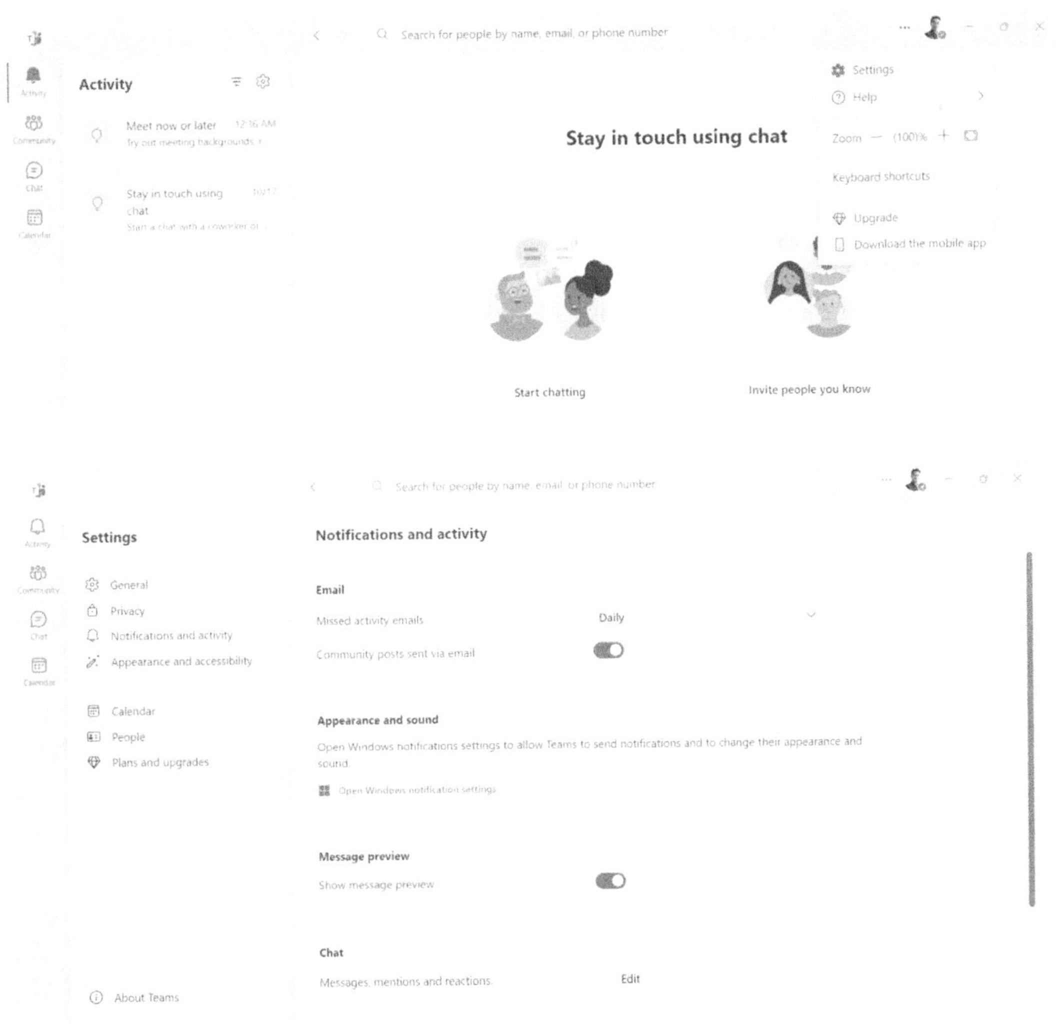

As you move forward, you'll find that the platform offers far more than just basic chatting and video conferencing; it is a platform designed to enhance productivity.

Chapter 2: Managing Teams And Channels

Managing Teams and Channels in Microsoft Teams is essential for effective collaboration. It involves setting up Teams, creating Channels for specific projects or departments, and configuring settings and permissions to control member access and maintain workflow. This organization ensures efficient communication and project execution.

Creating and Customizing Teams

1. Team Creation

If you are the administrator or have sufficient privileges, you can create a new Team by navigating to the "Teams" section on the left sidebar and clicking on "Join or create a team." Choose "Create Team" and select whether you want to build from scratch or use an existing team as a template.

2. Customization

Once the team is created, you can customize its appearance and settings. You can add a logo, change the team description, and more by clicking the ellipsis (three dots) next to the team's name and selecting "Manage Team."

3. Privacy Settings

You have the option to make the team either Private, where people need permission to join, or Public, where anyone within your organization can join.

Team Settings and Permissions

1. Access Team Settings: Navigate to "Manage Team," and then click on "Settings." Here you can configure an array of options like member permissions, @mentions, and guest permissions.
2. Member Permissions: Under this setting, you can determine what actions members can perform. For example, you can allow or disallow members from creating and updating channels, tabs, and apps.
3. Guest Permissions: Similar to member permissions but specific to guests, these settings allow you to control what actions guests can perform within your team.

Adding Members and Guests

1. Adding Members: In "Manage Team," you can add members by clicking on "Add Member." Type the email addresses of the individuals you wish to add, and they will receive an invitation to join the team.
2. Adding Guests: Adding a guest is similar to adding a member, but you will need to specify that the email belongs to a guest by choosing the "Guest" option.

Organizing Channels

1. Creating Channels: Channels can be created by clicking the ellipsis next to the team's name and selecting "Add Channel." You can specify the channel's name, description, and privacy settings here.
2. Organizing with Folders: If your organization requires more in-depth categorization, you can organize channels into folders. This is especially useful for large teams with multiple projects.

Channel Tabs and Connectors

1. Adding Tabs: In each channel, tabs can be added to integrate third-party apps or services like Microsoft Planner, Forms, or even websites. Click on the "+" symbol at the top of the channel to add a tab.
2. Connectors: These are more advanced than tabs and allow you to pull data from external services directly into a channel. You can add connectors via the ellipsis next to the channel's name, selecting "Connectors."

Managing Channel Settings

1. Moderation: You can set specific moderation policies for a channel. This includes who can start new posts and who can reply to posts.
2. Pinning: Important messages or documents can be pinned to the top of a channel for easy access by all members.
3. Archiving and Deletion: Channels that are no longer active can be archived for record-keeping, or deleted entirely if they are no longer needed.

By gaining proficiency in these features, you enhance your ability to manage your team's collaboration environment effectively. Microsoft Teams offers a depth of customization and control that makes it adaptable to various organizational needs. Therefore, understanding how to manipulate these settings is crucial for an optimized experience.

Chapter 3: Communication In Teams

In today's modern business world, effective communication is not merely an advantage; it is a necessity. Microsoft Teams goes beyond basic chat and video call features; it provides an integrated environment where text, audio, and visual communication coalesce to facilitate efficient teamwork. This section delves into the multifaceted communication tools within Microsoft Teams, detailing how each one contributes to a productive collaborative experience.

Sending Messages and Posts

1. Message Composition

Located at the bottom of each channel or chat is the message composition box. Simply type your message and hit Enter to send it. To send a message, simply type your text into the box and press Enter. The interface is designed for easy use, providing a straightforward way for users to engage in conversations, ask questions, or share updates. Messages can be as simple as a single line of text or as complex as a multi-paragraph update with bullet points.

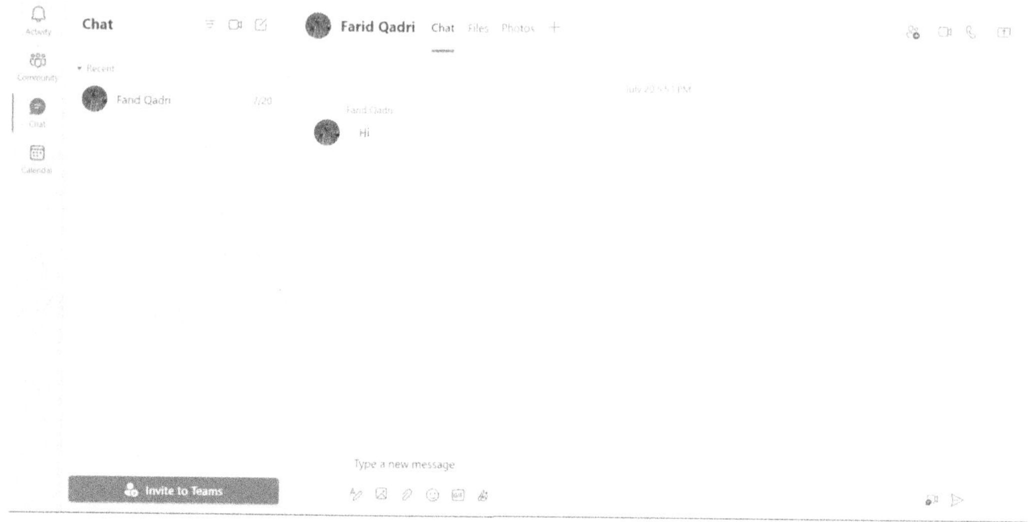

2. Attachments and Files

Beyond just text, Microsoft Teams enables you to share files and attachments directly in the chat or channel. A paperclip icon is conveniently located near the message composition box for this very purpose. By clicking on it, you can upload files. Be it documents, spreadsheets, or any other type of file, they are accessible to all members in that specific channel or chat. This integrated feature eliminates the need to rely on external storage solutions.

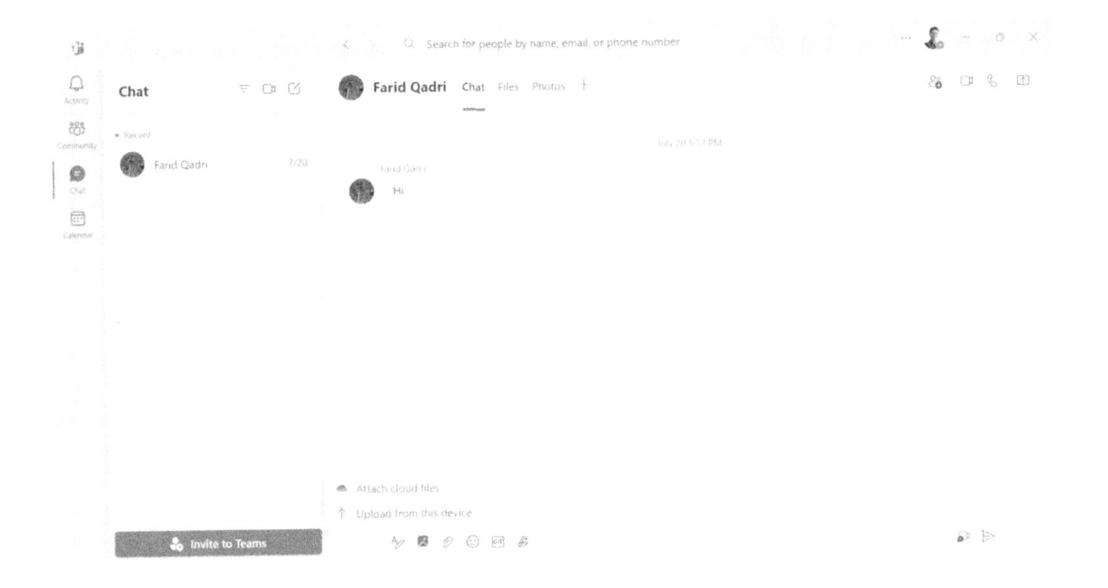

Formatting Options

1. Rich Text Editor: Click on the "Format" icon (represented by an 'A') below the composition box to access the rich text editor. This allows you to add headers, bullets, and other text formatting elements like bold, italics, and underlining. This feature is particularly useful when you need to send detailed updates, create organized notes, or draft messages that require a layer of sophistication and clarity.

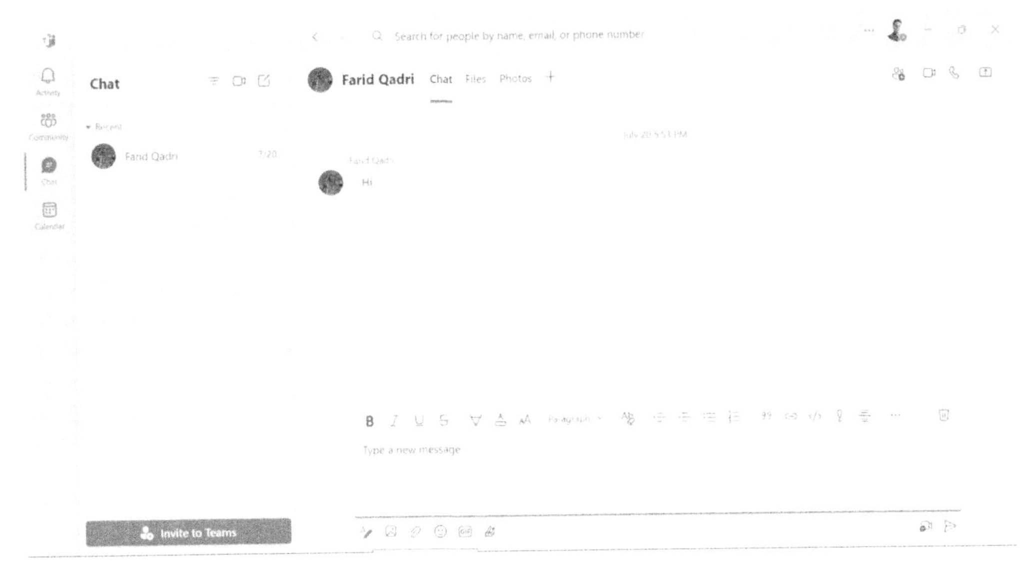

2. Hyperlinks and Code Snippets: Beyond basic text formatting, the rich text editor also allows for the insertion of hyperlinks and code snippets. With just a couple of clicks, you can make a piece of text clickable, directing team members to a relevant website, or even include snippets of code for discussion. This feature elevates the level of your messages by making them more interactive and resourceful.

Using Emoji and GIFs

While Microsoft Teams is a professional platform, a touch of personalization and emotion can enhance communication. Emojis and GIFs can be added by clicking on the respective icons in the composition box. Located right within the composition box, you'll find specific icons for adding these elements to your messages. Emojis can effectively convey feelings or reactions that may be difficult to express through text alone, such as celebration, urgency, or questioning. Similarly, GIFs can be used to add a dynamic element to the conversation, capturing a range of emotions or reactions in a fun and engaging way. The inclusion of these elements not only makes interactions more relatable but also helps in setting the tone of a message.

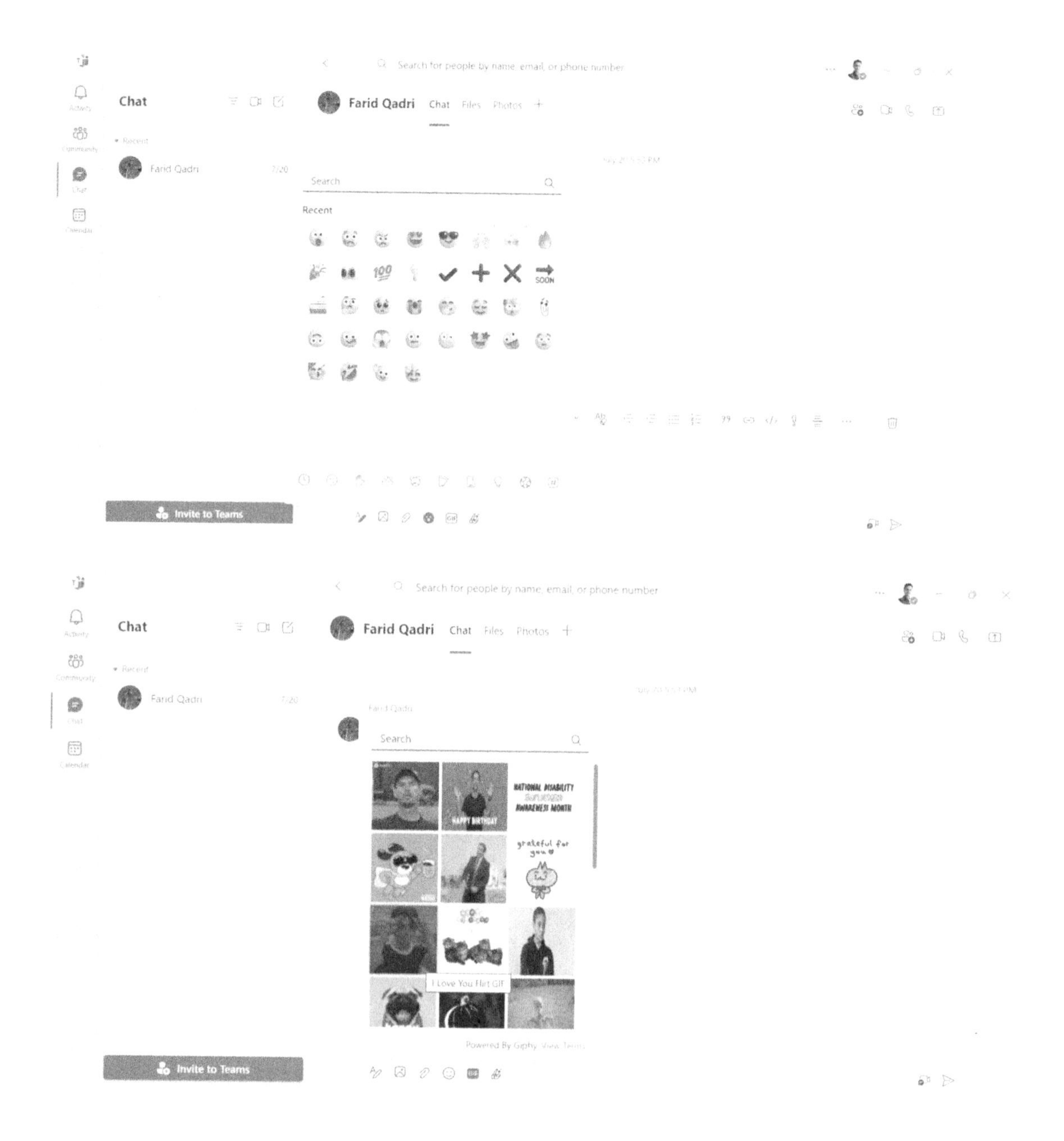

Meetings and Calls in Teams

1. Video and Audio Calls

Microsoft Teams makes it incredibly simple to connect with colleagues via video or audio calls. To initiate a video or audio call, click on the video camera or phone icon at the top-right corner of your chat or channel. This feature is especially beneficial for complex discussions that are better handled face-to-face rather than through text.

2. Group Calls

You can add multiple participants to a call, making it a group meeting. When a one-on-one conversation isn't sufficient, you can easily add more participants to the call, essentially converting it into a group meeting. This feature is particularly handy for impromptu team discussions or urgent project updates that require immediate attention from multiple stakeholders.

Scheduling and Joining Meetings

1. Calendar Integration

Microsoft Teams offers seamless integration with Microsoft Outlook. You can schedule meetings via the "Calendar" tab and invite participants, who will receive an email notification with a link to join the meeting.

2. Joining Meetings

Clicking the meeting link will redirect you to the meeting interface, where you have the option to join with video or just audio.

Meeting Options and Controls

1. Mute/Unmute and Camera Control: During the meeting, you have the option to mute/unmute your microphone and turn your camera on/off.
2. Screen Sharing: One of the most useful features is the ability to share your screen, which is instrumental for presentations and collaborative work.

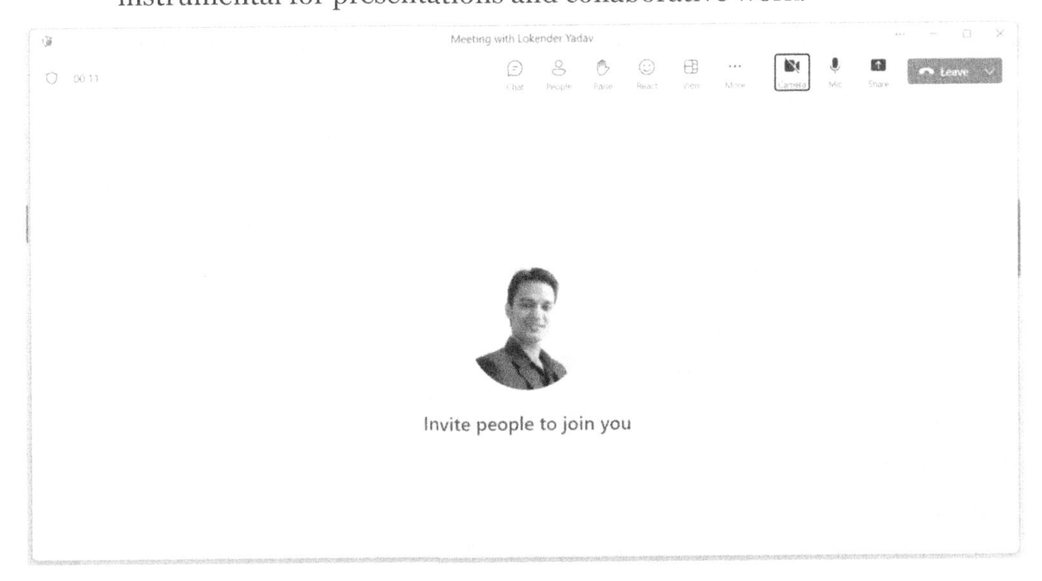

3. Recording: Meetings can be recorded for future reference or for those who were unable to attend.

Using Chat and Private Messages

1. One-to-One Chat: Microsoft Teams provides a dedicated chat feature for one-to-one conversations, allowing you to engage in private dialogues separate from the public channels. This feature is particularly useful for direct communication with a colleague, where the discussion doesn't need to be broadcast to an entire team.

2. Group Chat: Apart from one-to-one interactions, Teams also offers the functionality to create group chats. This is beneficial when you need to confer with a select subset of team members about specific issues or projects. Unlike public channels, these group chats are only accessible to invited members, ensuring that the conversation remains exclusive and private.

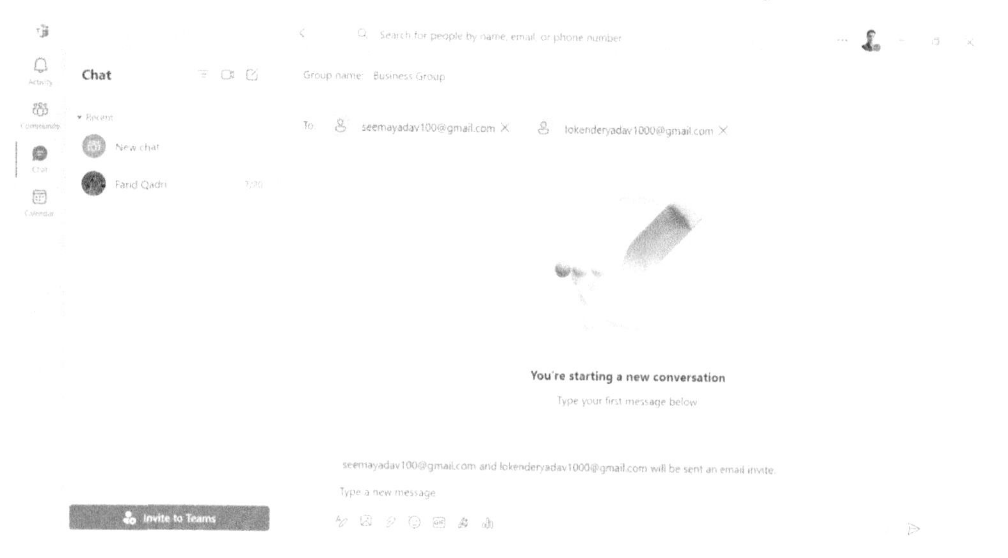

3. Confidentiality: For sensitive conversations, Microsoft Teams offers various security features to ensure that your private chats remain confidential. Security is a major consideration, especially when dealing with sensitive information. Microsoft Teams comes equipped with robust security features to ensure that your private and group chats remain confidential. From end-to-end encryption to compliance certifications, Teams put a premium on safeguarding your private communications.

Chapter 4: Collaboration And File Sharing

Collaboration and file sharing are critical components of modern team dynamics. Microsoft Teams provides a unified platform for both synchronous and asynchronous collaboration, streamlining the sharing of files and documents within team channels and chats. Unlike traditional email attachments or using disparate storage solutions, Microsoft Teams ensures that everyone has real-time access to the latest version of shared files. By consolidating communication and file-sharing capabilities into one interface, Microsoft Teams encourages productivity and efficient teamwork.

Uploading and Sharing Files

Uploading and sharing files in Microsoft Teams is designed to be straightforward. Within a chat or channel, users can click on the paperclip icon in the message box to attach a file. This file can be uploaded from your local machine, OneDrive, or directly from other channels and tabs. Once uploaded, the file is immediately accessible to all members of the chat or channel. Sharing permissions are also manageable, allowing for restricted access when necessary. The ease with which files can be shared removes the friction often associated with file-sharing through other means like email, thereby speeding up project timelines and improving team cohesiveness.

- Step 1: Open the channel or chat where you want to share the file.
- Step 2: Look for the paperclip icon below the message composition box to attach files.
- Step 3: Select the file source and the specific file. Choose the file from your local storage, OneDrive, or other channels.
- Step 4: Click 'Upload'.

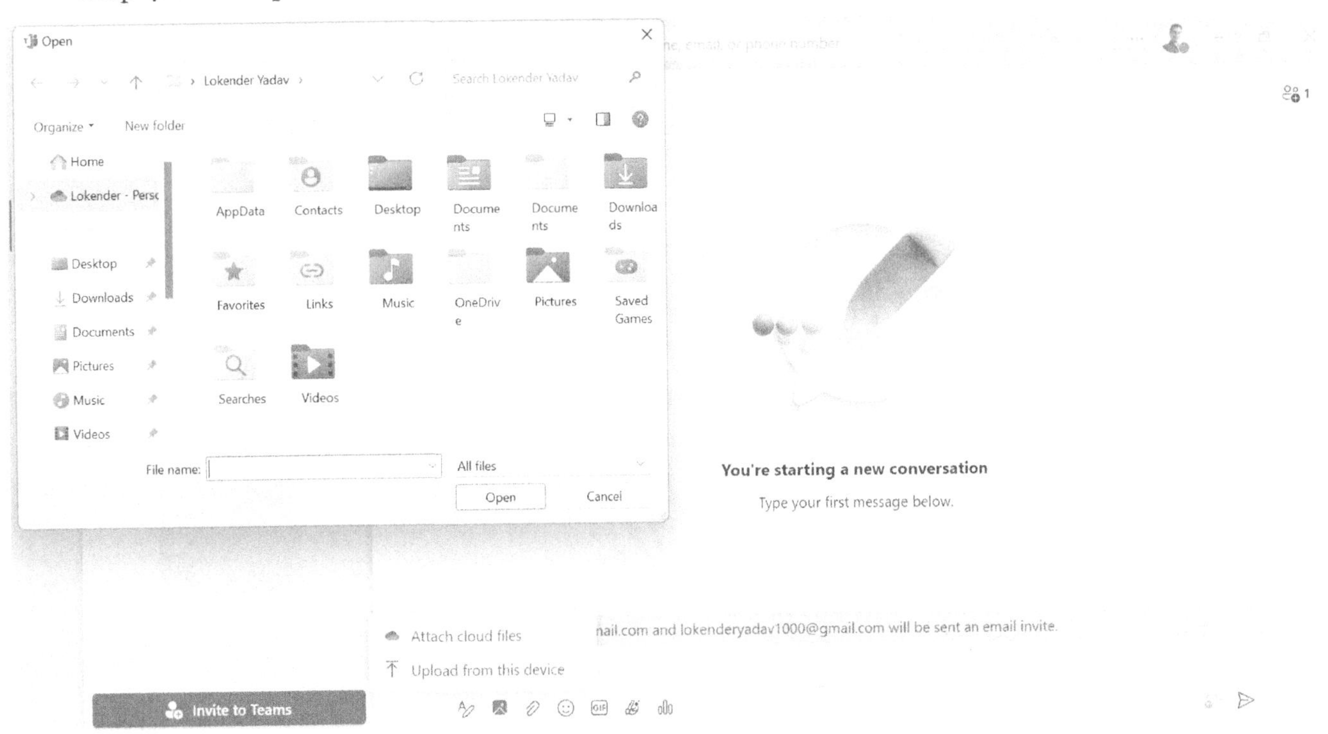

File Storage and OneDrive Integration

Microsoft Teams benefits greatly from its integration with OneDrive, Microsoft's cloud storage service. Files shared within a team are stored in a SharePoint Online site, whereas files shared during a private chat are stored in the sender's OneDrive for Business folder. This means that files are stored securely and can be accessed anytime from any device. The integration with OneDrive also allows for additional file storage capabilities, such as the ability to access files offline. This seamless combination of communication and cloud storage functionality ensures that you have all the resources you need to collaborate effectively, all within a single platform.

- Step 1: To access stored files, click on the 'Files' tab within your chat or channel.
- Step 2: You'll see options for OneDrive and SharePoint; select as per your requirement.

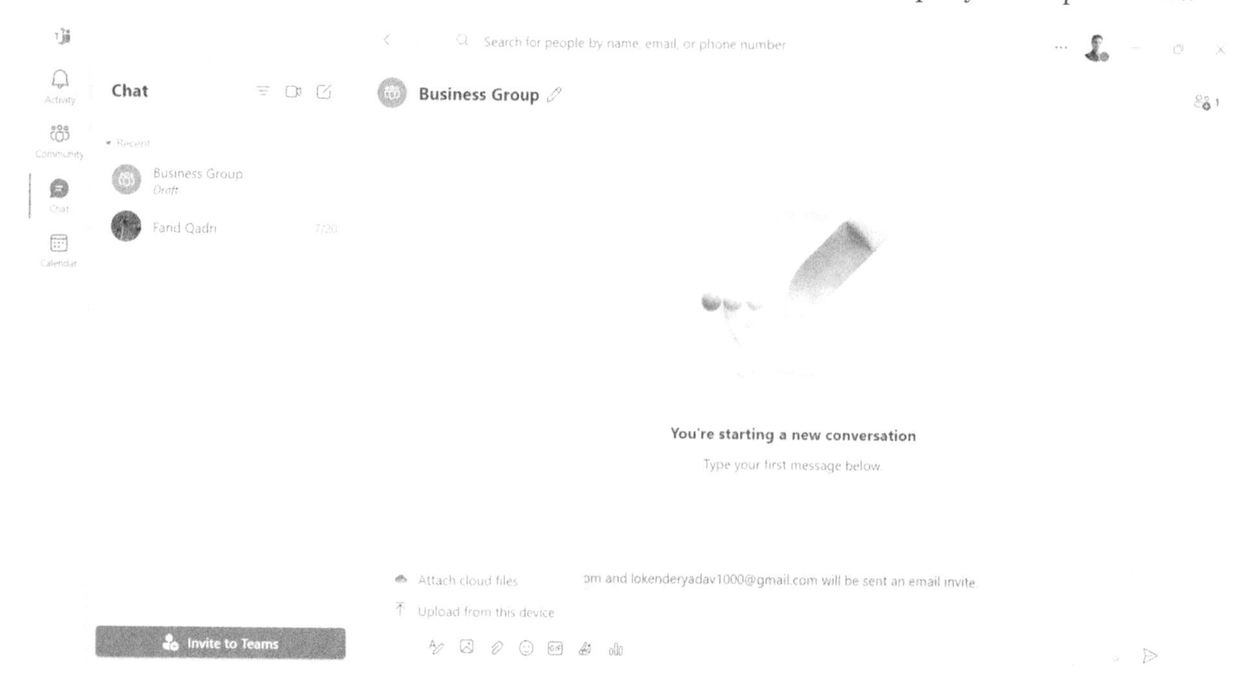

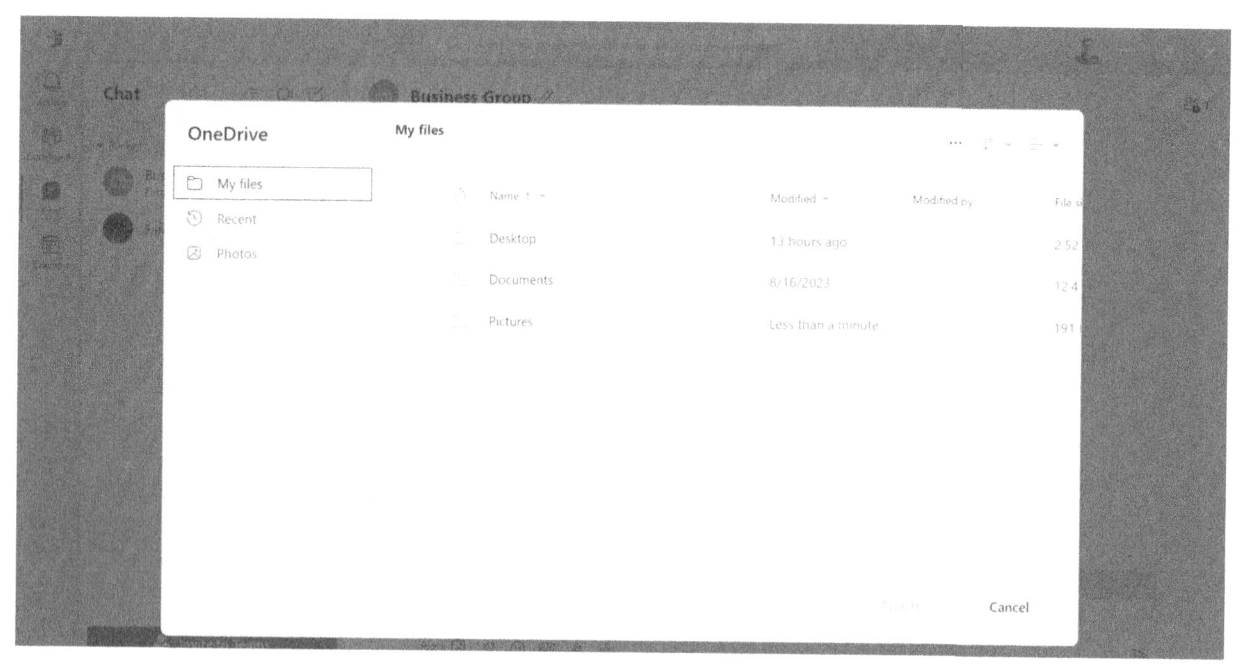

Co-authoring Documents

One of the standout features of Microsoft Teams is its ability to allow co-authoring of documents. Whether it's a Word document, a PowerPoint presentation, or an Excel spreadsheet, multiple team members can edit the document simultaneously. Real-time changes are displayed, and each author's presence is indicated by a cursor or flag with their name, fostering a sense of live collaboration. This is a game-changer for projects that require inputs from various team members, as it eliminates the need for tedious sequential editing and the confusion that comes with multiple document versions.

- Step 1: Navigate to the 'Files' tab and open the document you want to co-author.
- Step 2: Click on 'Edit in Teams' for collaborative editing.
- Step 3: Notice real-time edits by looking for cursors with team member names.

Collaborating on Documents in Teams

Collaborating on documents within Microsoft Teams negates the need for external tools or software. Directly from within a channel, you can click on a file to view it in Teams. A panel will appear that not only displays the file but also includes a chat sidebar where team members can discuss the file's contents. This chat is specific to the file, allowing for focused discussions and making it easier to refer back to these conversations later. This feature streamlines the review process, making it simpler and more efficient to incorporate feedback and make real-time edits.

- Step 1: Go to the 'Files' tab and click on the desired document.
- Step 2: A panel will appear, showing the file and a chat sidebar.
- Step 3: Use the chat sidebar for discussions related to the document.

Editing in Teams vs. Desktop Apps

Microsoft Teams offers the option to edit files either within the Teams interface or by opening the file in its respective desktop application, such as Word or Excel. Editing within Teams provides the convenience of not having to leave the platform, ideal for quick edits or collaborative sessions. However, the desktop applications offer more extensive formatting and editing features. Teams make it seamless to switch between these modes. You can start editing in Teams and then click to open the file in the desktop app, all while keeping the file stored centrally within the Teams environment.

- Step 1: Open the file within Teams.
- Step 2: Choose either 'Edit in Teams' for quick edits or 'Open in Desktop App' for more advanced editing.
- Step 3: After editing, all changes will be saved automatically to the same file within Teams.

Version History and Comments

An essential feature for collaborative work is the ability to track changes and comments, and Microsoft Teams delivers on this front with its version history capability. Any time a change is made to a shared file, Teams stores a version of that file. You can access this history to see what changes were made, who made them, and when they were made. This feature is invaluable for maintaining the integrity of collaborative projects. Comments can also be added to shared files, either as general comments or as specific annotations to particular content, providing context for changes or reviews. This functionality ensures a structured and accountable collaborative workflow.

- Step 1: Navigate to the 'Files' tab and select the document in question.
- Step 2: Click on the three-dot menu ('...') next to the file.
- Step 3: Select 'Version History' to view past versions.
- Step 4: For comments, navigate to the appropriate section in the document and add your comment.

Chapter 5: Integration And Apps

Microsoft Teams serves as an integration hub that brings together various apps and services to provide a comprehensive workspace. Below are some key components where integration is particularly beneficial.

Microsoft 365 Apps Integration

The seamless integration of Microsoft 365 apps with Teams creates a unified, all-in-one workspace. This integration allows you to not only collaborate on documents but also schedule meetings and manage tasks, all without having to leave the Teams interface. It essentially becomes a centralized hub for productivity, bringing together various tools like Word, Excel, Outlook, and Planner into one cohesive platform. This enhances workflow efficiency and ensures that all your resources and efforts are streamlined.

Steps to Integrate Microsoft 365 Apps:

- Step 1: Open Microsoft Teams and navigate to the channel where you want the app to be available.
- Step 2: Click on the '+' icon on the top bar next to the other channel tabs.
- Step 3: A menu will appear; select the Microsoft 365 app you wish to integrate, such as Planner or Outlook.

Word, Excel, PowerPoint in Teams

Microsoft Teams revolutionizes document handling by allowing you to create, edit, and collaborate on Word, Excel, and PowerPoint files directly within the application. This functionality eliminates the need to switch between different software, thus streamlining your workflow. Whether it's drafting a report in Word, crunching numbers in Excel, or preparing a presentation in PowerPoint, you can do it all without leaving the Teams environment.

Steps to Use Word, Excel, PowerPoint:

- Step 1: Go to the 'Files' tab within your Teams channel.
- Step 2: Click 'New' and select either Word, Excel, or PowerPoint.
- Step 3: Edit the document; your changes are saved automatically and are visible to team members.

SharePoint and OneNote Integration

The integration of SharePoint and OneNote into Microsoft Teams streamlines access to shared resources and notes directly within the platform. This feature simplifies collaboration by centralizing important documents and team notebooks, ensuring that all team members are aligned and have the information they need at their fingertips.

Steps for SharePoint and OneNote Integration:

- Step 1: Navigate to the desired channel.
- Step 2: Click on the '+' icon near the channel tabs.
- Step 3: Choose either SharePoint or OneNote from the dropdown list and follow the on-screen instructions.

Installing and Managing Apps in Teams

Microsoft Teams offers a streamlined process for installing and managing apps, enabling users to tailor the platform according to their specific needs. With just a few clicks, you can add a variety of functionalities ranging from project management tools to third-party integrations. This flexibility allows for a more customized experience, enhancing productivity and collaboration within your team.

Steps to Install and Manage Apps:

- Step 1: Click on the 'Apps' icon on the left sidebar.
- Step 2: Browse or search for the app you want.
- Step 3: Click 'Install' and follow any further instructions.

App Store and Third-Party Apps

Microsoft Teams comes equipped with its own App Store, a marketplace that offers a range of third-party apps designed to extend the platform's functionalities. Whether you need advanced project management capabilities, CRM integration, or specialized communication tools, the App Store likely has a solution tailored to your needs. By leveraging these third-party apps, you can enhance your team's workflow, improve communication, and achieve a higher level of customization and functionality within the Teams environment.

Steps to Use App Store:

- Step 1: Click the 'Apps' icon on the left sidebar.
- Step 2: Browse through categories or use the search bar to find apps.
- Step 3: Click 'Install' to add the app to Teams.

Custom Apps and Bots

Microsoft Teams goes beyond off-the-shelf solutions by enabling the integration of custom apps and bots, tailored to meet your team's unique needs. These custom solutions can automate repetitive tasks, streamline workflows, and bring specialized functionalities right into your Teams workspace. Whether you're looking to develop a bot for automated customer service or a custom app for project management, Teams provides the flexibility and framework to create a more efficient and personalized collaborative environment.

Steps to Integrate Custom Apps and Bots:

- Step 1: Navigate to the 'Apps' section.
- Step 2: Click on 'Upload a custom app'.
- Step 3: Browse to locate your custom app or bot and click 'Open'.

By following these step-by-step guides, users can make the most out of the integration capabilities that Microsoft Teams offers.

Chapter 6: Advanced Features And Settings

As you become more familiar with Microsoft Teams, you'll find that it's more than just a basic collaboration platform. It offers an array of advanced features and customizable settings to enhance productivity and user experience. Whether you're an administrator aiming to define how Teams is used within your organization, or an end-user looking to personalize your workspace, Teams is an excellent choice.

Customizing Teams Settings

Microsoft Teams allows users and administrators to fine-tune settings to match their requirements. These range from notification preferences to privacy controls and even team-wide settings for administrators. Customizing your Teams settings ensures that you are working in an environment tailored to your needs.

Steps to Customize Settings:

Step 1: Click on three dots near your profile picture in the top-right corner.

Step 2: Select 'Settings' from the dropdown menu.

Step 3: Navigate through the various tabs like 'General', 'Privacy', and 'Notifications' to make your preferred changes.

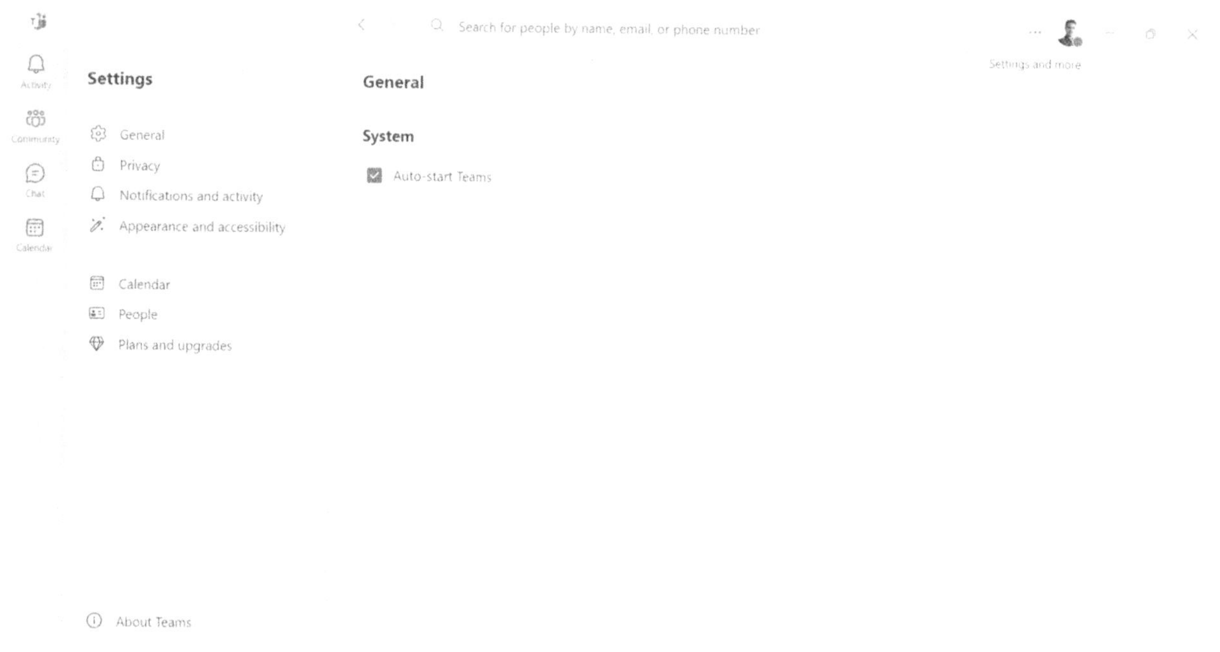

Advanced Teams Features

Microsoft Teams offers a suite of advanced features like task automation, workflow integration, and advanced meeting controls. These functionalities allow for streamlined processes, making project management and team collaboration highly efficient.

Steps to Access Advanced Features:

- Step 1: Go to the channel where you wish to implement an advanced feature.
- Step 2: Click the '+' icon next to the channel tabs to add a new tab.
- Step 3: Select the feature or app you want to integrate, like 'Planner' for task automation or 'Power Automate' for workflow integration.

Live Events

Live Events in Teams is a feature designed for hosting interactive sessions, webinars, or live broadcasts. It supports multiple presenters and allows up to 10,000 attendees in a single session. This is especially useful for large-scale corporate announcements, training, or seminars.

Steps to Set Up Live Events:

- Step 1: Navigate to the calendar tab on the left sidebar.
- Step 2: Click 'New Meeting' and select 'Live Event'.
- Step 3: Fill in the details like event name, date, and participants, then click 'Save/Schedule'.

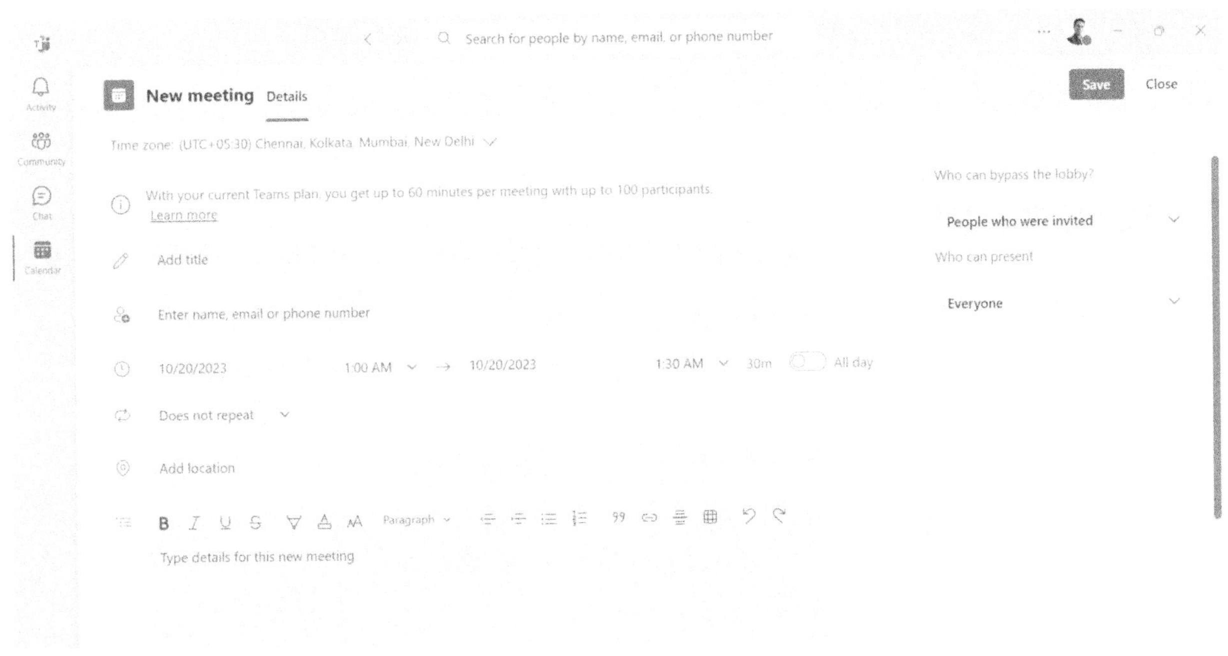

Teams Templates

Teams Templates are pre-defined structures that help you create new teams with specific channels, settings, and installed apps. This can be invaluable when you need to set up multiple teams with similar requirements.

Steps to Use Teams Templates:

- Step 1: Click the 'Teams' icon on the left sidebar.
- Step 2: At the bottom, click 'Join or create a team'.
- Step 3: Select 'Create a Team' and then choose from a list of available templates, or create your own.

Microsoft Teams' advanced features and settings are instrumental in elevating your team's productivity and collaboration. Once you start utilizing these advanced functionalities, you'll find that Teams becomes an even more powerful tool for your organization.

Conclusion

As we reach the end of this eBook, let's take a moment to revisit some of the key concepts and functionalities that make Microsoft Teams a powerful tool for collaboration and productivity. We began with an introduction to Teams, emphasizing its robust architecture that supports chat, video meetings, file storage, and integration of numerous applications, making it a one-stop hub for all your professional needs.

We explored the basics of setting up and navigating Teams, detailing how to initiate Teams and Channels, and how to make the most of the interface features like the Activity Feed and Notifications. This was followed by an in-depth look at managing these channels, highlighting crucial aspects like Team Settings, Permissions, and member management.

Our focus then shifted to the various communication options within Teams, covering everything from text-based messaging to intricate meeting setups. We learned how to format messages, integrate emojis and GIFs for expressive communication, and handle meetings and private chats with ease.

The eBook also dived deep into the collaborative aspect of Teams, especially in terms of file sharing and document editing. We discussed how Teams interacts seamlessly with Microsoft 365 applications, simplifying real-time co-authoring of documents and facilitating smooth file-sharing workflows.

The integration capabilities of Teams were another major highlight, as we walked through the process of adding various Microsoft and third-party apps to enhance functionality. This was coupled with a guide on advanced features and settings, which can significantly enhance your Teams experience.

Microsoft Teams is more than just a communication platform; it's a comprehensive workspace designed to optimize collaboration and enhance productivity. As Teams continues to evolve, the set of features and integrations will undoubtedly expand, providing even more ways to work together efficiently. Whether you are new to Teams or looking to expand your current usage, this eBook serves as a comprehensive guide to make your Teams experience as productive as possible. Thank you for reading.

Microsoft OneNote

Chapter 1:Getting Started With OneNote

Installing Microsoft OneNote:

Before getting started with OneNote, install it on your system. If you have Windows 10 and Windows 11, then it must have been already installed. You can look for it in the Start menu. To install the OneNote on Windows 7 and 8, go to the Microsoft OneNote website. Download the installation file for your Windows version. Run that file and follow the steps. For macOS, go to the Mac App Store. Search for "Microsoft OneNote." Click on the "Get" button next to the app to download and install it.

Exploring OneNote Interface

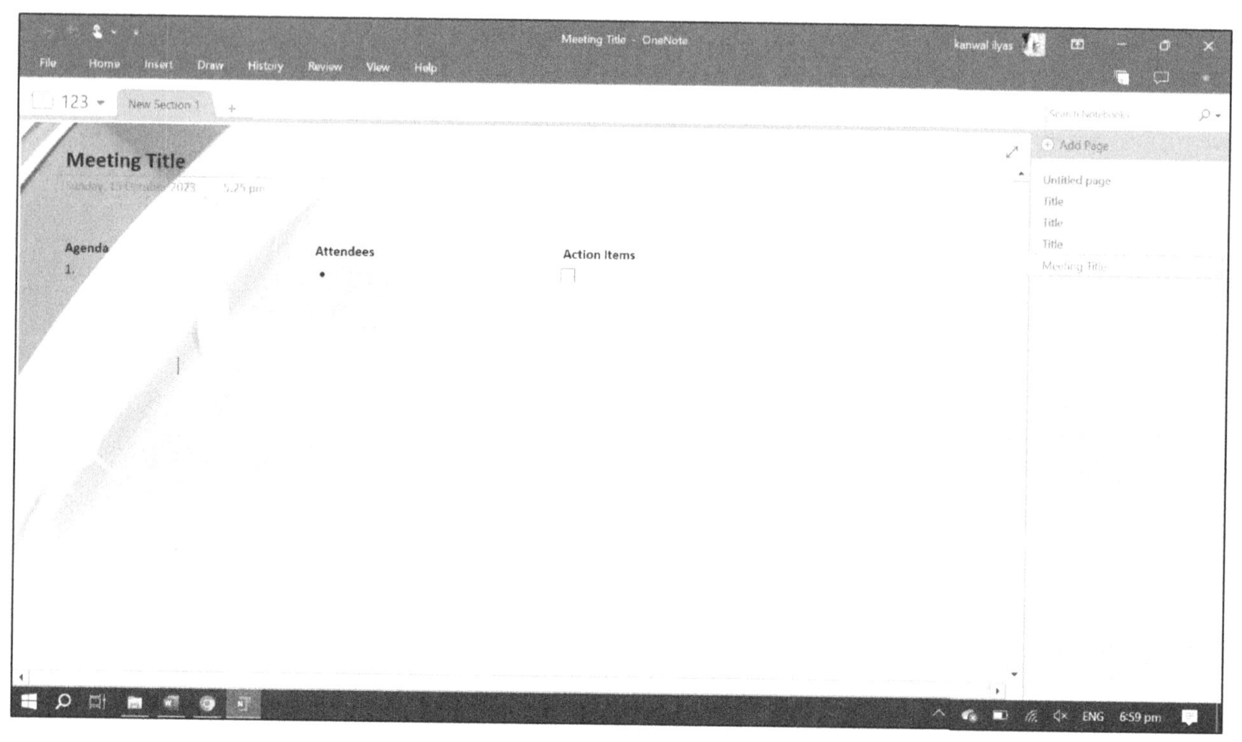

Before we dive deep into OneNote and the various ways to use all its features, let me first explain the complete interface of this application. When you know what options are there and how to access them, it becomes much easier to put them to the right use. The most amazing thing about its interface is that it is designed to be intuitive and user-friendly, which lets us to easily capture and organize notes, ideas and information. This interface meets the needs of all, from students to business professionals. Here's an overview of the main components of the OneNote interface:

Ribbon Menu:

When you open the OneNote application, you see a window! And on top of this window, there is a Ribbon menu. This menu offers a comprehensive set of tools to improve your note-taking experience. On this menu, you can see various tabs:

Home Tab:

The Home tab has basic formatting options, which let you to change font styles, text sizes and alignment to suit your preferences.

Clipboard: Inside the home tab, there are multiple options and the first few options are clubbed into a clipboard section, which has the following features:

- Cut, Copy, Paste: Standard clipboard operations for text and objects.
- Format Painter: Copies formatting from one part of the text to another.
- Clipboard History: This lets you to see and paste options from the history of your clipboard.

Font: There are options to adjust the fonts according to your needs.

- Font: Change the font family.
- Font Size: Modify the size of the text.
- Increase/Decrease Indent: Adjust text indentation.
- Bold, Italic, Underline: Apply basic text formatting.
- Text Highlight Color: Highlight selected text.
- Font Color: Change the color of the text.

Paragraph: You can adjust the paragraph settings using the following options:

- Bullets, Numbering: Create bulleted or numbered lists.
- Increase/Decrease List Level: Change the hierarchy of list items.
- Align Left, Center, right: Align text within the note container.
- Line Spacing: With this option, you can select the spacing between lines of text.
- Paragraph Spacing: With this option, you can adjust the space before and after each paragraph.

Styles: If you want to adjust the text style and add tags, then the following options will help you out:

- Headings: Apply Heading 1, 2, & 3 and different heading styles to text.
- Normal: With this option, you can reset text to the default style.
- Tags: With this option, you can apply tags to mark important points or to-do items.

Insert Tab:

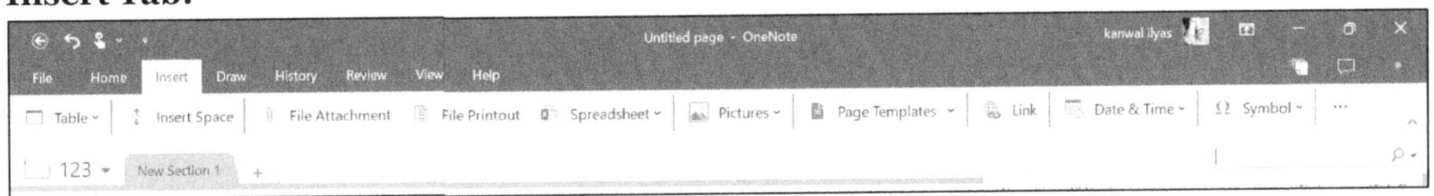

The Insert tab is where you can add additional elements to your notes by adding tables, pictures, links and attachments, enhancing the content and making it more interactive.

Tables: Using this option, you can insert text into your notes

- Table: You can draw a table of any size on your page with varying numbers of rows and columns.
- Insert Table: It provides you the option to add a table with required dimensions.
- Excel Spreadsheet: You can also add a spreadsheet from excel to your page.

Files: This is the section from where you can access other files and add them to your notes in the form of:

- Attachment: Let you attach files to your OneNote page.
- Printout: With this option you can insert a PDF file as a printout.

Pictures: If you want to add images to your notes, then through these options, you can do the same:

- Pictures: It lets you add images from your computer or other sources into your notes.
- Online Pictures: It lets you to search for images over the web and add to your notes.

- Page templates: There are several pre-made templates available, like Academic, business, blank, decorative and planner templates.

Link: If you want to add external links to your notes, then you can select any of the following information:

- Link: Adds hyperlinks to websites or external files.
- File Link: Creates a link to a file, which lets you to quickly add it to your notes.

Recording: There are more options that let you to add audio and videos to your notes:

- Audio: It lets you record audio notes directly into your page.
- Video: It lets you to record video and add it to your notes.

Symbols: Do you want to add special symbols or equations to your notes, go to the edit tab and click on these options:

- Equation: Let you insert mathematical equations.
- Symbol: Lets you to insert special symbols and characters.

Draw Tab:

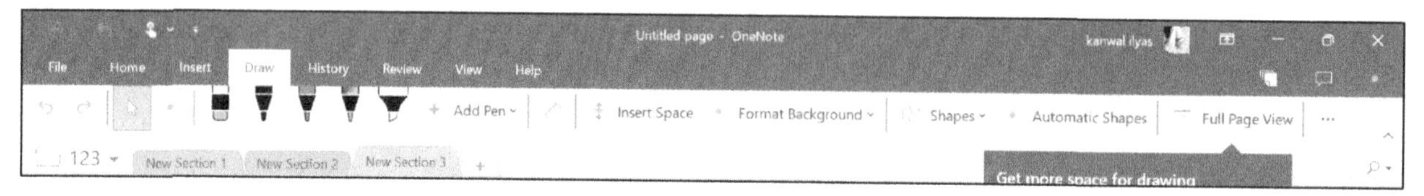

Next to the Insert tab is the Draw tab, which has a range of drawing tools for touch-enabled devices to create sketches or handwritten notes directly onto the digital canvas. There are pen options you can choose from. Then, there are options for inserting space, formatting the background, adding shapes and automatic shapes to the notes.

History Tab:

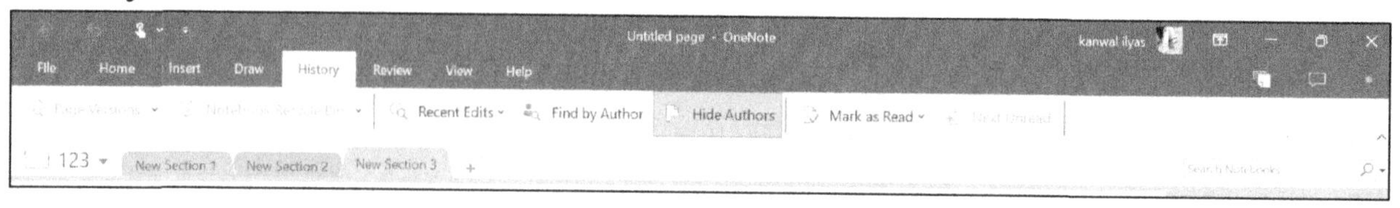

Through this tab, you can have access to previous page versions, recycle bin, recent edits, find by author, hide authors and mark as read.

Review Tab:

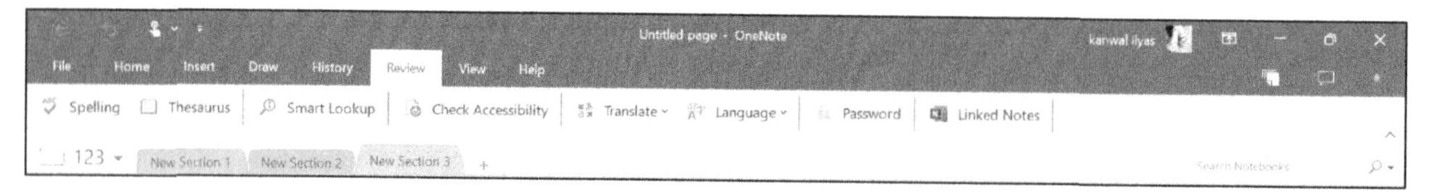

This tab has all the options to check the spellings, replace words through a thesaurus, smart lookup, check accessibility, translate, password and use linked notes. These options can be used to select the language, translate text, check the grammatical errors or replace words using thesaurus.

View Tab:

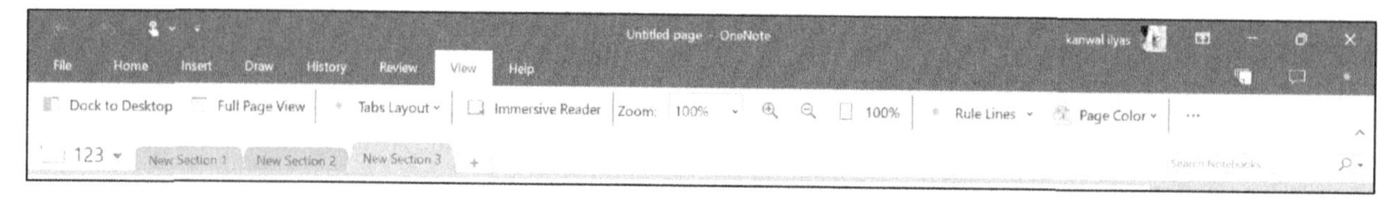

The View tab lets you customize your viewing experience, which lets you to adjust zoom levels, page colors and rule lines and ensure your notes are presented exactly as you prefer.

Note-Taking Area:

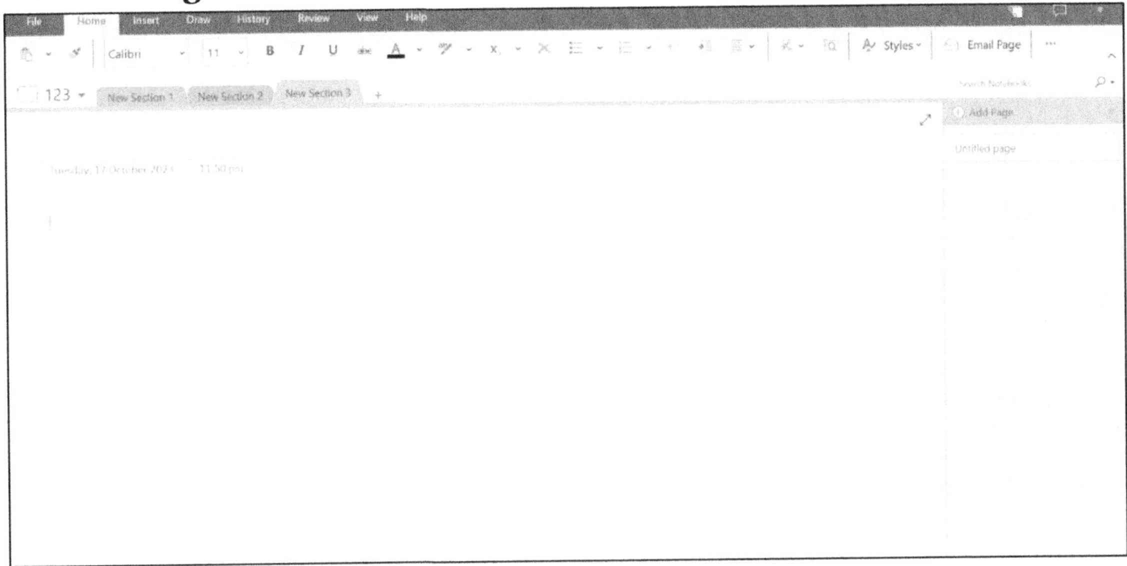

Below the ribbon menu is the note-taking area, which is the central space where you can add your notes. Here, you can type anywhere on your page. You can insert several elements such as text boxes, images, audio recordings and more, giving you the complete freedom to add and organize information in the way that best suits your needs.

Search Bar:

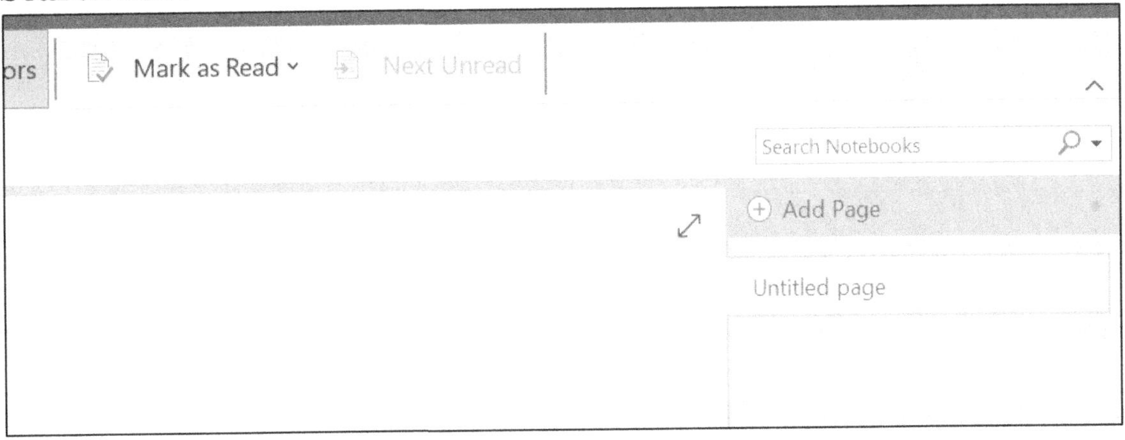

There is also a search bar on top of the note-taking space, which simplifies the process of finding specific notes or information within your notebooks. You can enter any keyword or phrase and OneNote will quickly search for relevant notes, sections, or even entire notebooks, helping you quickly retrieve the information you need.

Sharing and Collaboration:

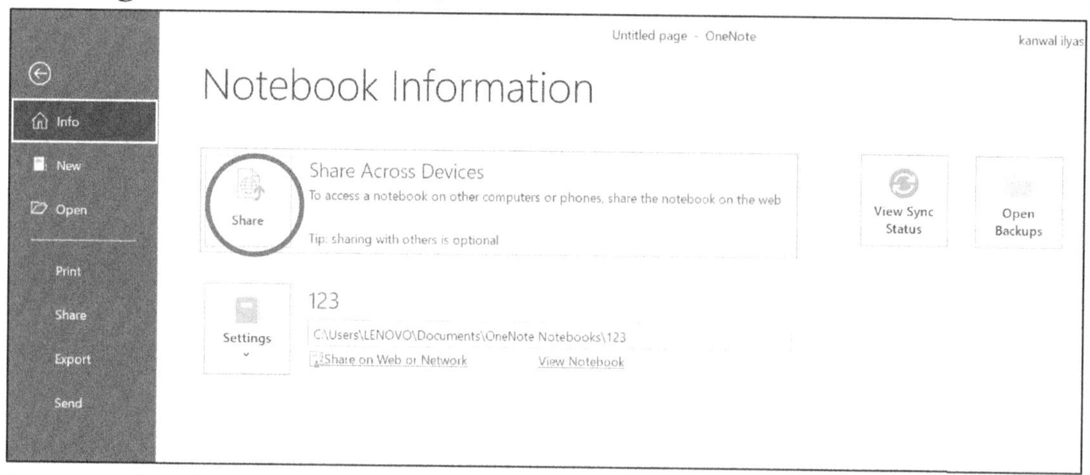

OneNote also facilitates the sharing and collaboration process by letting you to share your notebooks with others. This feature has a real-time collaboration option, which enables you and your colleagues to work on shared notebooks simultaneously.

Notebook, Sections and Pages:

The software has a hierarchical structure, which is much like physical notebooks and binders. At the top level, there are Notebooks, which are like the main containers for all your notes. Each notebook can be named after a specific topic, project, or category. Within these notebooks, you can create sections, which can be used to divide the notes into sections, much like dividers. You can label the section according to the content they have, providing a clear organizational structure. Inside each section, you have pages and on each page, you add, edit and store your notes. Think of pages as the digital equivalent of physical pages in notebooks, where you write down your ideas and information.

Chapter 2: Organizing And Managing Notes

On OneNote, you can swiftly categorize your notes, assignments, ideas and clippings by creating different sections for each topic or project within a notebook. The drag-and-drop functionality lets you to rearrange the content to ensure that the required information is always easily accessible. OneNote's powerful search feature further streamlines organization, so you can quickly locate specific notes or keywords within your vast collection of information.

Creating and Managing Notebooks

Now that you know the complete interface of your OneNote application, it's time to create your first notebook on it. To do this, open File menu on the top left corner and in that menu, you will find options like:

1. "New": After selecting new, you will have to enter the name of the notebook you would want to create and then click "create a notebook."
2. "Open": With this option, you can load and open your existing notebook.

There are other options like "print, share, export and send" as well, which we will discuss in the later sections of this chapter.

Choose a Storage Location (if applicable):

While creating a new notebook, you can select the storage location for the file according to your requirements. The "new" notebook option lets you to select OneDrive, Sharepoint, your PC, or its folders as the storage location.

Sections and Section Groups

Now that your notebook is created, the software will take you to the new notebook's writing space. On top of this space and under the ribbon menu, there is a tab that mentions the section of your notebook. By clicking the "+," you can add more sections to your notebook. You can right-click on the section tab to find options to rename the section.

To add pages to each section, there is a page pane on the right hand of the screen, which gives you the option to add more pages. Just like the sections, you can also rename the pages by right-clicking on any particular page.

Using Section Groups: You can combine relevant sections into one group as well. It's like having folders within folders, making sure that even the most extensive collection of notes remains neatly organized. Section groups provide a hierarchical structure, making navigation effortless and intuitive.

Color Coding Sections: Colors have a way of making everything better. Apply colors to your sections like a digital paintbrush. Assign a unique color to each section, turning your notebook into a vibrant canvas. Imagine having a rainbow of sections, each representing a different aspect of your life or work. It's not just visually appealing; it's functional and efficient!

Adjusting the Sections and Pages:

You can also rearrange the added sections and pages by dragging and dropping them within the Notebook Pane. Click and hold the section or page tab, then drag it to the location you want to. You can also add subpages under the main pages. To do that, right-click on a page tab and from the menu, select "Make Subpage" to create a hierarchy within your notes.

Creating and Formatting Text Notes

Your keyboard is your quill and OneNote is your canvas. Now that you know how to create notebooks, sections and pages and sync them all across devices, it's time to get down to the most important piece of the puzzle- the Notes! To create the notes, you don't have to do anything; just start typing on the page you have created.

Tables and Text Boxes:

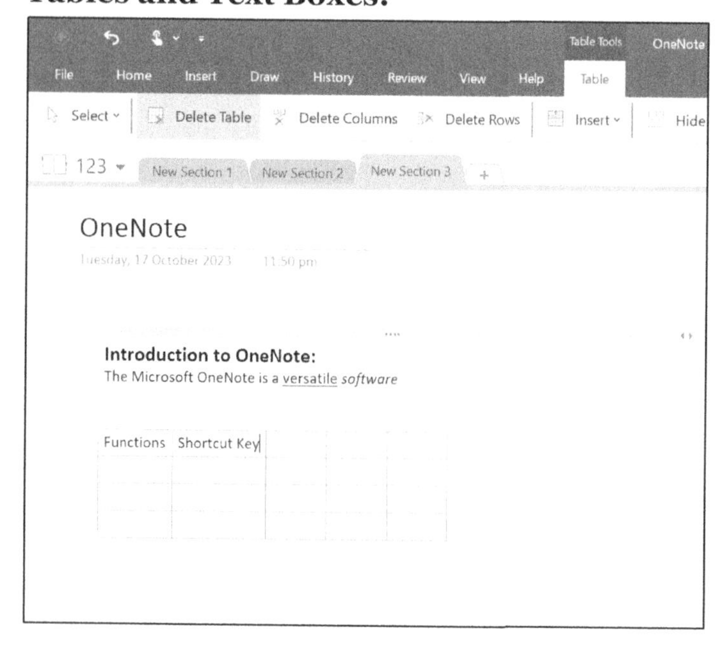

Use the Insert tab to add tables or text boxes. Tables are useful for organizing information in rows and columns, while text boxes let you to position text anywhere on the page.

Tags:

OneNote has pre-defined tags that can be used to categorize and label your text. Use the Tags button in the Ribbon to apply tags such as "To-Do," "Important," or custom tags you create.

Drawing and Handwriting:

If you are using a touchscreen device, you can switch to drawing mode and write or draw directly on the page.

Page Templates, Tags and Labels

Using templates in Microsoft OneNote can significantly enhance your note-taking efficiency by providing structured formats for various types of content. OneNote comes with built-in templates and lets you to create custom templates. Here's how you can use templates for efficient note-taking in OneNote:

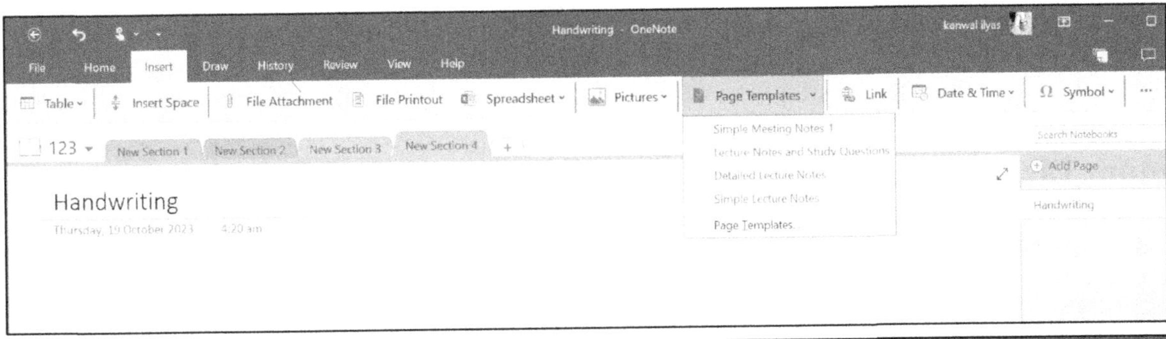

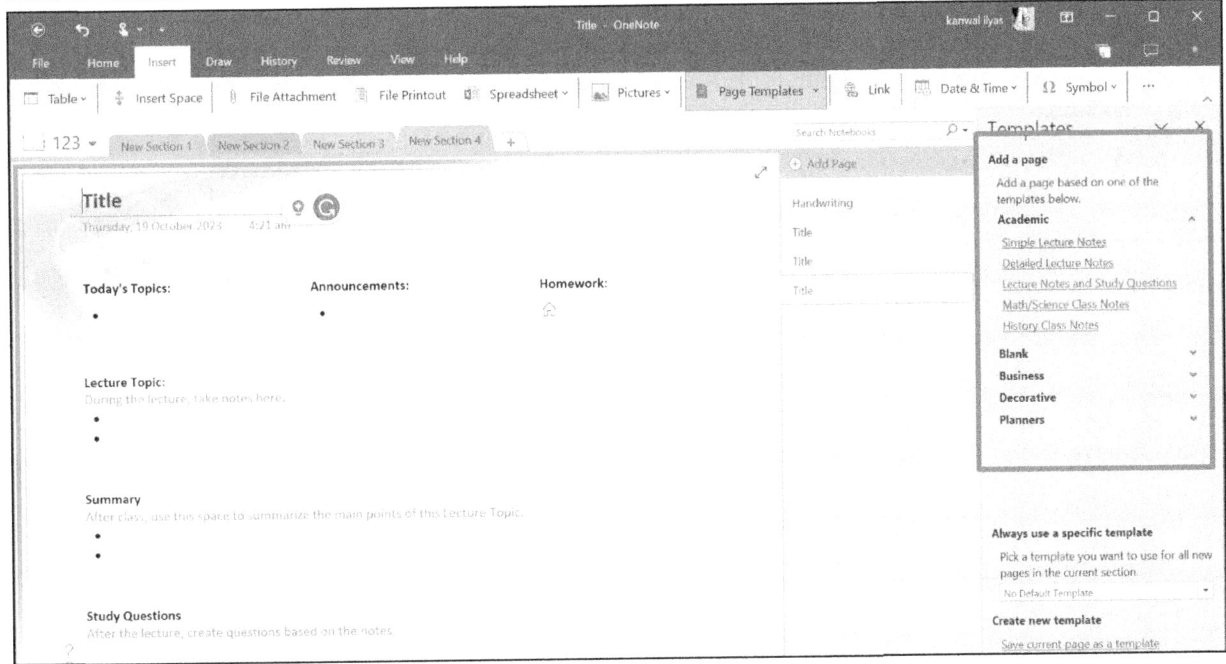

Start a new page where you want to apply a template. Use the "+" (New Page) button to create a new page in your selected section. To access the templates, click on the "Insert" tab in the Ribbon.

To choose a template, click on "Page Templates" in the Insert tab. OneNote offers a variety of pre-designed templates, such as planners, to-do lists, meeting notes and more.

Select the template you want to use. OneNote will insert the template onto your page, providing you a pre-structured canvas to add content. You can customize it as well to fit your needs. Add text, images, or drawings to the template elements. Modify as required to suit your note-taking style.

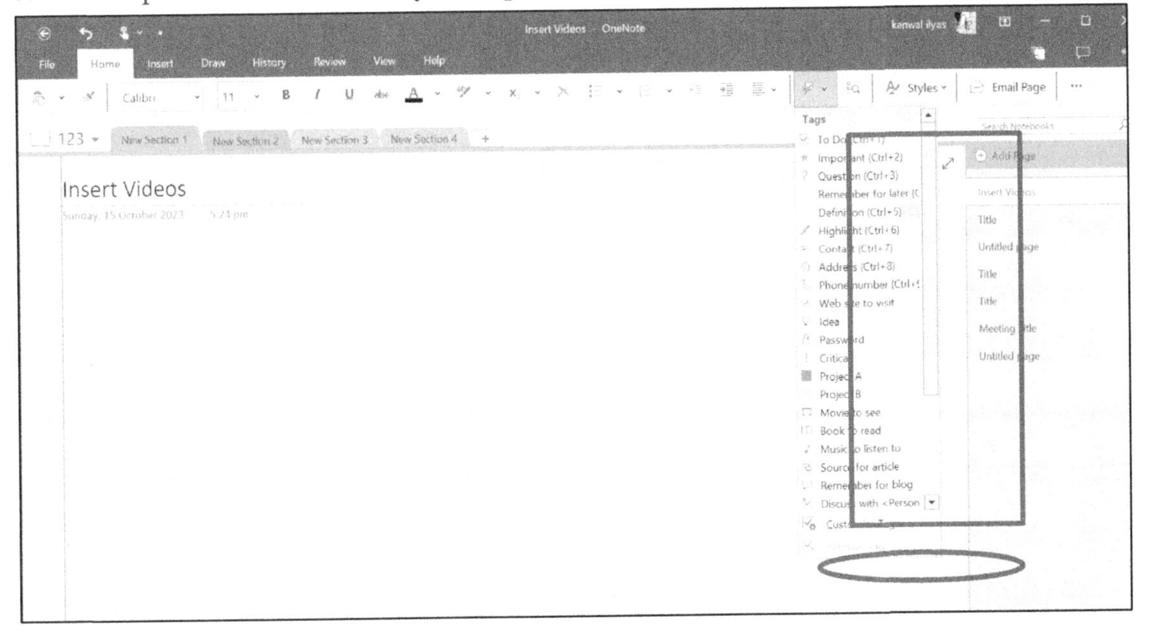

OneNote understands that not all notes are created equal. Default tags, like 'Important' or 'To-Do,' help you quickly identify and categorize your notes. Think of them as colorful sticky notes but even smarter. They highlight the essence of your content, making it easier to find and manage specific information within your vast notebook.

Creating Custom Tags:

Do you want to add a personal touch to your notes? Create custom tags! Whether it's a research idea, a recipe, or a quote that inspires you, custom tags let you to tailor your categorization. It’s like creating your own customized filing system, where each tag represents a unique aspect of your digital world. In the Tags pane, look for an option that lets you to create a new tag. This might be represented by a "+" or "New Tag" button. Use this button to create a new tag. You can give your tag a name. For example, if you want a tag for "Project Ideas," you can name it accordingly. Choose an icon for your tag. OneNote lets you to associate an icon with your custom tag for easy visual identification. Optionally, you can assign a shortcut key for quick tagging.

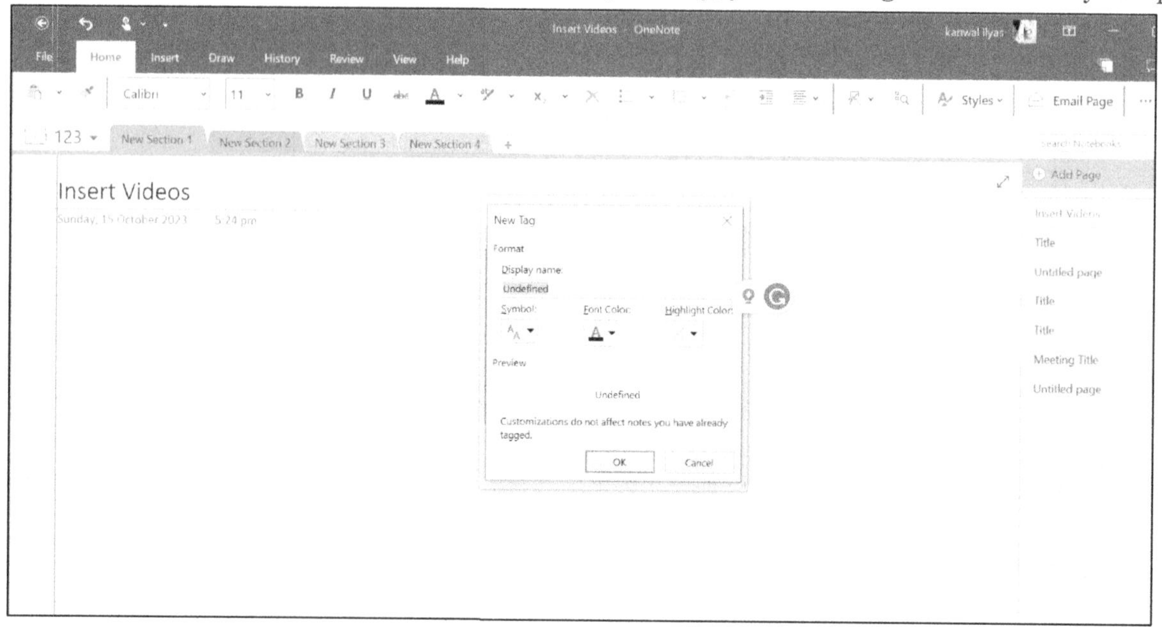

Once you have created your custom tag or chosen any other from the list, you can go back to your notes and use it. Select any part of the content you would want to tag and click/tap on your tag in the menu.

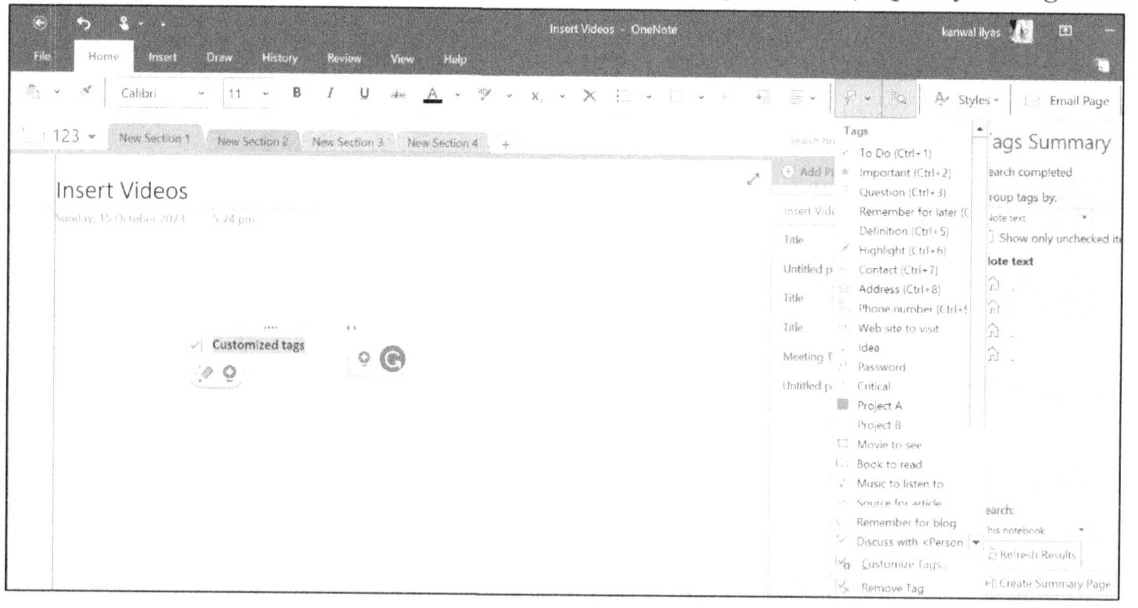

Searching and Sorting Notes

OneNote's search functionality is your trusty guide. Basic search helps you find specific words or phrases, but that's just the beginning. You can also use its advanced search options, where you can search by date, author, or even specific tags.

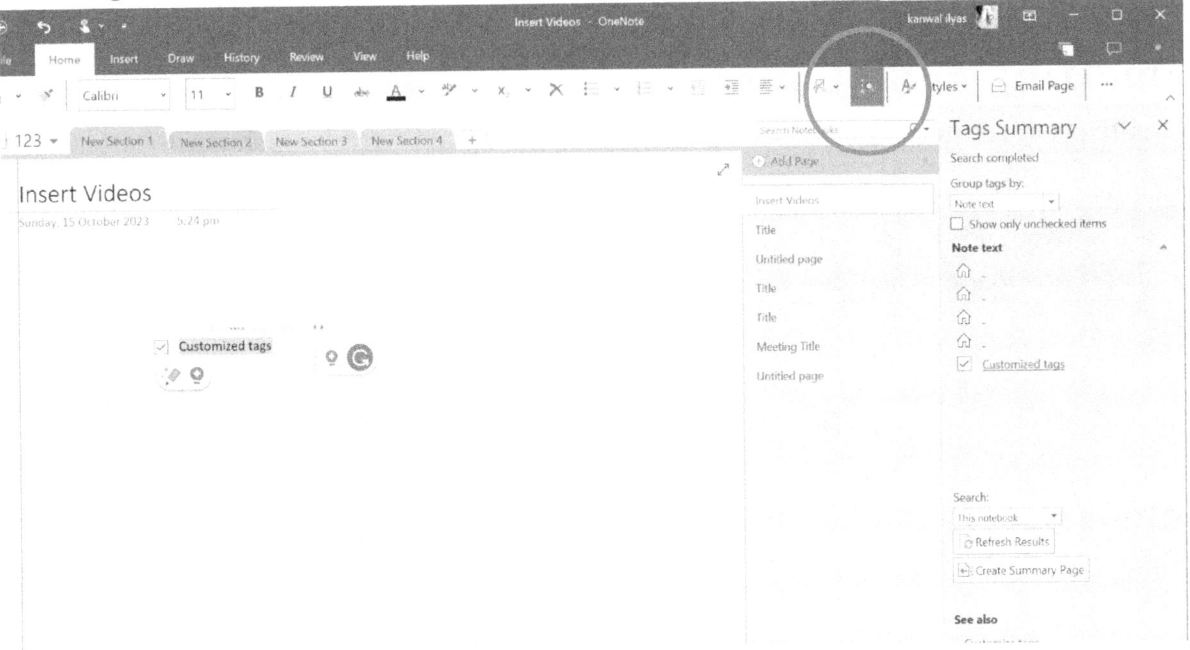

Sorting and Filtering Notes: Have you ever had a notebook flooded with information and struggled to find a specific note? Fear not! OneNote lets you to sort notes chronologically, alphabetically, or by tags. If that's not enough, filtering notes by author or content type refines your search even further.

Version History and Backup Options

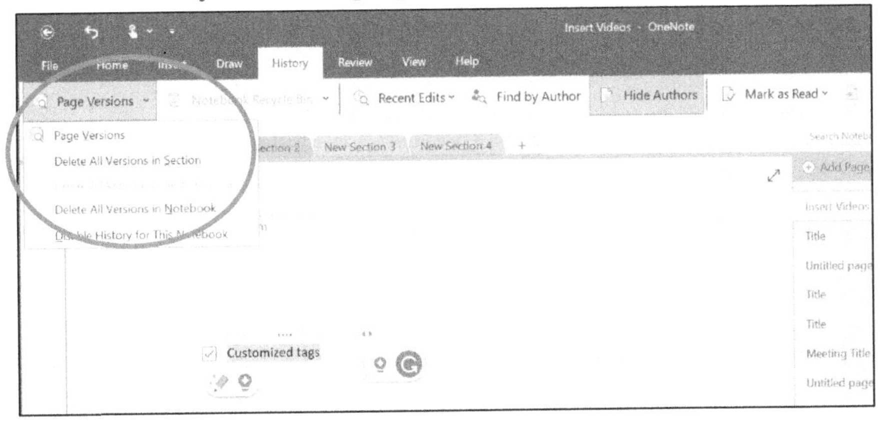

Mistakes happen and that's okay. OneNote understands. Version history lets you to revisit past iterations of your notes. Did you accidentally delete something important? Need to undo recent changes? OneNote's version history lets you step back in time and restore previous versions of your notes. It's your digital time machine, ensuring your notes are always safe and retrievable.

OneNote takes data security seriously. While it automatically syncs your notes with the cloud. You can manually back up your notebooks at location where they could be secured. Plus, having a backup lets you to restore your notes in case of unforeseen circumstances, ensuring your precious ideas are never lost.

Chapter 3: Taking Notes Effectively

Text Formatting and Styles

Once you have written your text, you can adjust the format using the option given in the home menu.

Font Styles:

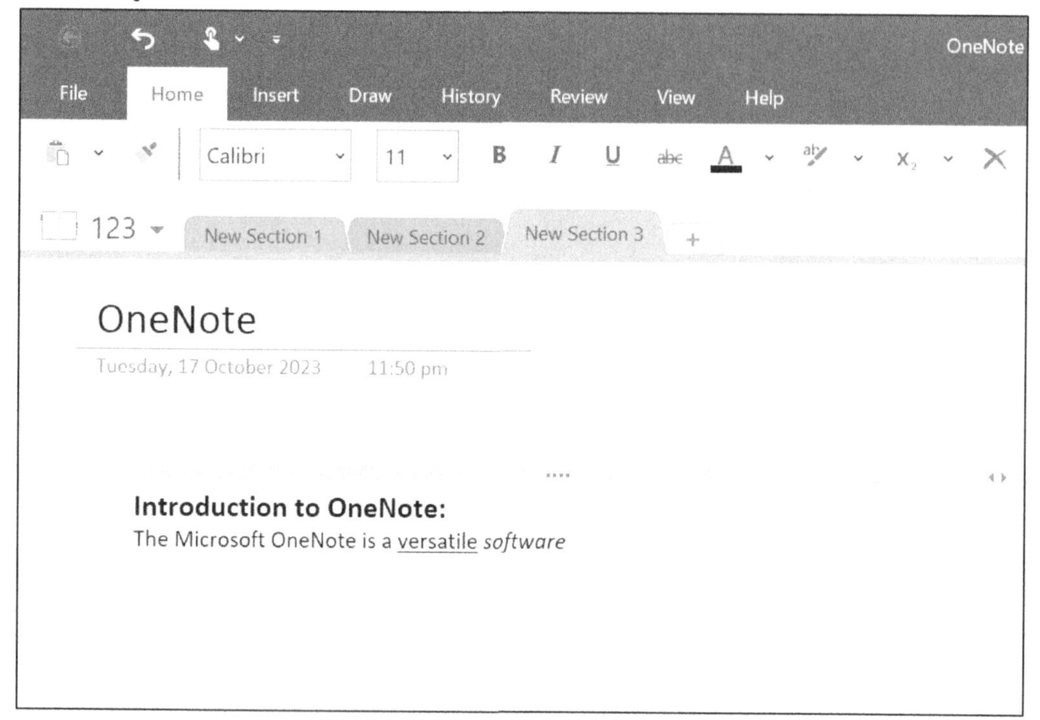

You can change font styles, text sizes and colors from the home tab in the ribbon menu. Select the text you want to format, then choose your desired font, size and color from the options provided.

- Bold, Italics and Underline: Use the B, I and U buttons in the Ribbon (or their respective keyboard shortcuts: Ctrl + B for bold, Ctrl + I for italics and Ctrl + U for underline) to apply these formatting styles to selected text.
- Bullet Points and Numbered Lists: Use the Bullet or Numbering buttons in the Ribbon to insert bullets and numbers. Click the button, then start typing. Press Enter to create the lists.
  Text Alignment: Use the Align Left, Center and Align Right buttons in the Ribbon to align your text as you desire.
- Highlight Text: Use the Text Highlight Color button in the Ribbon to highlight selected text. Click the button, then choose a highlight color from the palette.
- Hyperlinks: Select the text you want to add hyperlink to, then go to the Insert tab. Choose the Link and enter the URL. You can also link to other pages or sections within your notebook.
- Copy Formatting (Format Painter): OneNote has a Format Painter tool that lets you to copy formatting from one piece of text to another. Click this button in the Ribbon, then select the text you want to format.

Inserting Images and Files

A picture is worth a thousand words, they say. In OneNote, it's worth even more. You can insert any image or multimedia file into your notes to make your notes look more interesting.

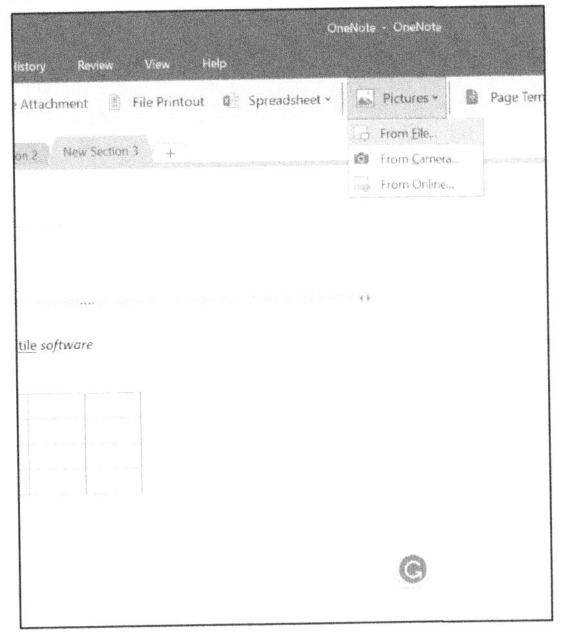

To insert the images, click on the Insert tab in the Ribbon. Select "Pictures" if you want to add your desired image from your device. Look for the image file you want to insert. Alternatively, select "Online Pictures" to search and insert images directly from the web. You can search using Bing or insert images from your OneDrive account.

Add Videos:

Besides images, you can also add videos to your notes. To do that, go to the Insert tab in the Ribbon. Select "Online Video" to search and insert videos directly from different websites like YouTube. Paste the video URL and OneNote will embed the video into your notes.

Formatting Images and Multimedia:

All the images and multimedia files can be edited. There are multiple ways to do that! Select the image. Use the handles to resize the image. Right-click on the image and select "Crop" to trim unwanted parts of the image. Right-click on the image and select "Edit Alt Text." Add descriptive alt text to make your content accessible to people with disabilities. In OneNote, you can click on an image and access the formatting options at the top of the page. These options let you to change image alignment, text wrapping and add borders.

Link Multimedia Elements:

Right-click on a multimedia element (image, video, etc.). Select "Link" to add a hyperlink to the multimedia element, directing users to a website, document, or another page within your notes.

Collapsible and Docked Multimedia Elements:

In OneNote, you can make multimedia elements collapsible. Right-click on the multimedia element and select "Collapse" to minimize it, saving space on your page. You can also dock multimedia elements to the side of your OneNote window. Right-click on the multimedia element and select "Dock to OneNote" to pin it to the side, leting you to view your content while working on other parts of your notes.

Handwriting and Drawing Tools

There is another option on OneNote which lets you to write directly in the notebook using handwriting and drawing tools. It lets you to create handwritten notes, sketches, diagrams and annotations directly on your digital canvas. It works well for the touchscreen devices which are attached to an external stylus.

Inking Tools

These are tools that let you write or draw directly on the screen which includes pen, highlighter, marker etc. To use these inking tools. Open OneNote, then select the drawing mode. Click on the Draw tab in the Ribbon at the top of the window. Choose a Pen or Pencil. OneNote offers various pen and pencil options with different colors and thicknesses.

Click on the pen or pencil icon to select your preferred writing tool. Use your stylus or touch-enabled device to start writing or drawing on the digital canvas. If you are using a mouse, you can also draw, but it might be easier with a stylus or touchpad. To change the color or thickness of your pen or pencil, click on the corresponding color and thickness icons in the Drawing Tools menu. This lets you to create colorful and varied lines.

If you write something by mistake, you can use the eraser tool to correct it. Click on the eraser icon, then rub it with your finger or the connected stylus. OneNote lets you to undo or redo your actions. Use the Undo and Redo arrows in the Ribbon or the corresponding keyboard shortcuts (usually Ctrl + Z for Undo and Ctrl + Y for Redo) to control your editing history.

Shapes and Lines

In OneNote, shapes and lines include the tools that let you to draw various geometric shapes and straight lines directly on your digital canvas. These are helpful for making diagrams, flowcharts, sketches, or any other elements in your notes. Here's how you can use shapes and lines in OneNote:

- **Click on the "Draw" Tab**: In OneNote, go to the "Draw" tab, usually located in the ribbon menu at the top of the application window.
- **Select Shapes or Lines**: In the "Shapes" group, you'll find options for basic shapes, arrows, flowchart symbols and callouts. In the "Pens" group, you can choose to draw straight lines or scribble lines.
- **Now Draw Your Shape or Line**: Click on the desired shape or line tool, then use your stylus, mouse, or touchscreen to draw the shape or line directly onto your OneNote page.

Chapter 4: Advanced Features And Tips

Now that you have mastered the basics of OneNote. It's time to step into the advanced territory where you can elevate your note-taking and organizational skills to a whole new level.

Advanced Formatting Techniques

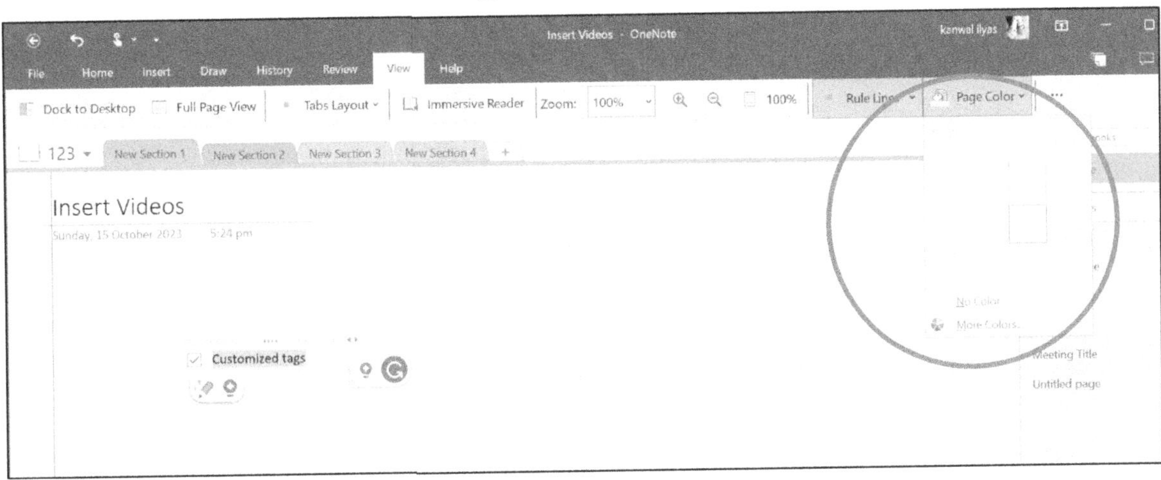

In Microsoft OneNote, you can change the page color and rule lines to customize the appearance of your notes. On the desktop version of OneNote, click on the "View" tab in the ribbon. Look for the "Page Setup" option. Within this option, you will discover the "Page Color" option. Click on "Page Color" to see the dropdown menu with options for colors. You can select any desired color from this menu, or use the "More Colors" option to create a shade of your choice. Click on the color you want to apply and the page background will change immediately.

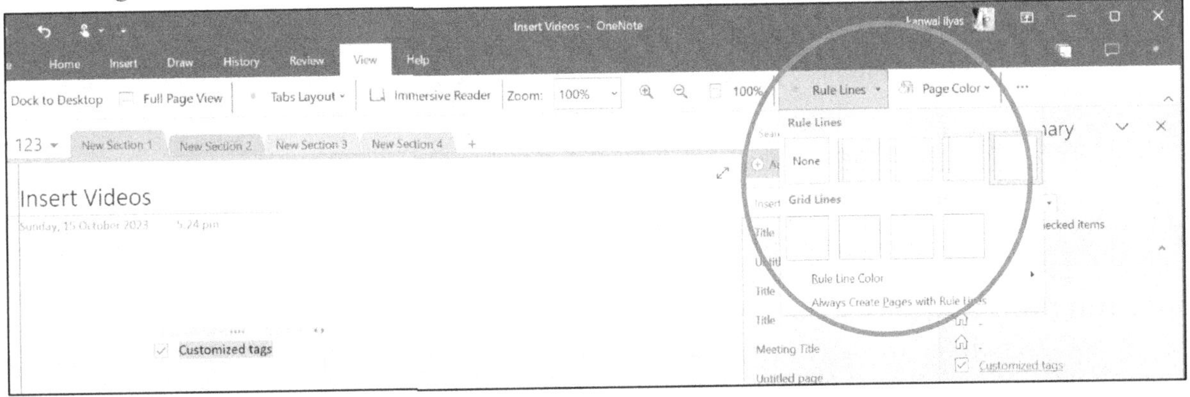

And to change the rule lines click on "Rule Lines" to reveal a dropdown menu with different types of rule lines. Select the type of rule lines you want to use, such as narrow lines, wide lines, or a grid. Click on the type you prefer and the rule lines on your page will change accordingly.

Tables, Charts and Graphs:

OneNote isn't just for text; it's a canvas for data visualization, too. Create tables to organize information neatly and make your notes dynamic by embedding charts and graphs. Visual data representation enhances understanding, making difficult information easy to understand. It's like turning your notes into interactive infographics, ensuring your data speaks louder than words.

Audio or Video Notes

This amazing feature lets you record the audio and videos in real time so that you can add them to your notes right there and then. This feature is especially used for those who use OneNote to write down notes during meetings and lectures. To use this feature, click on the Insert tab in the Ribbon. Select "Record Audio" to record audio notes directly within OneNote. Alternatively, select "Record Video" to record a video using your device's camera.

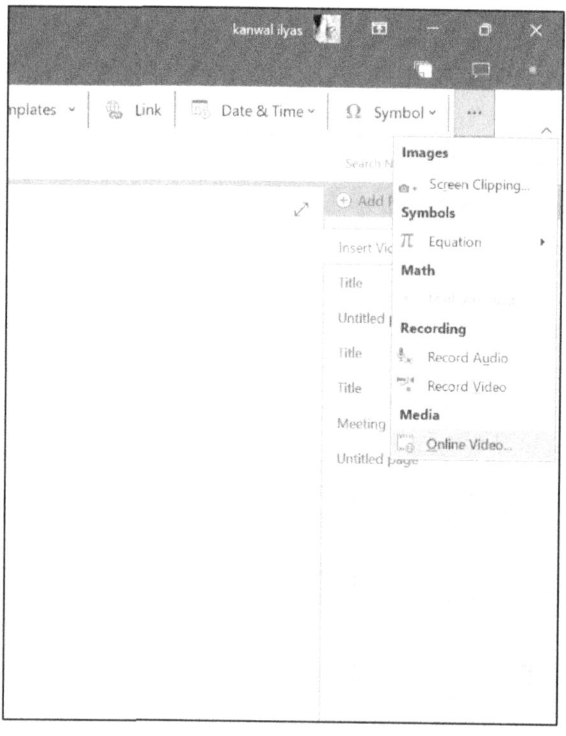

Using Templates for Efficient Note-Taking

By using templates, you can enhance the visual appeal of your notes, maintain consistency across your documents and efficiently organize information. OneNote's template feature empowers you to create professional-looking and well-organized notes without the need for extensive design skills, streamlining the note-taking process and improving overall productivity.

Custom Templates

Besides the already available templates on OneNote there is another option to create custom templates using your own personal preferences. Suppose you have created your own notes according to a set structure and then you can save this style as a template for future notes as well.

Creating And Sharing Templates:

Create a new page and design it the way you want your template to look. Add headings, text boxes, tables, or any other elements you need. Click on the "File" tab in the Ribbon. Select "Save As" and choose "OneNote Template (*.onepkg)" as the file format. Save this template in any folder of your choice on your device. Whenever you want to use your custom template, click on the "Insert" tab, then select "Page Templates" and choose "My Templates." Select your custom template and OneNote will insert it onto your new page.

Dock on Desktop

If you open the VIEW tab on your OneNote, you will see a "dock on desktop" option on the top left corner. By clicking on this option you can dock your OneNote on the desktop and then use it as a notepad while using other applications. To return to the original interface, click on the top of the dock and click on the dock on desktop option again to reverse this function.

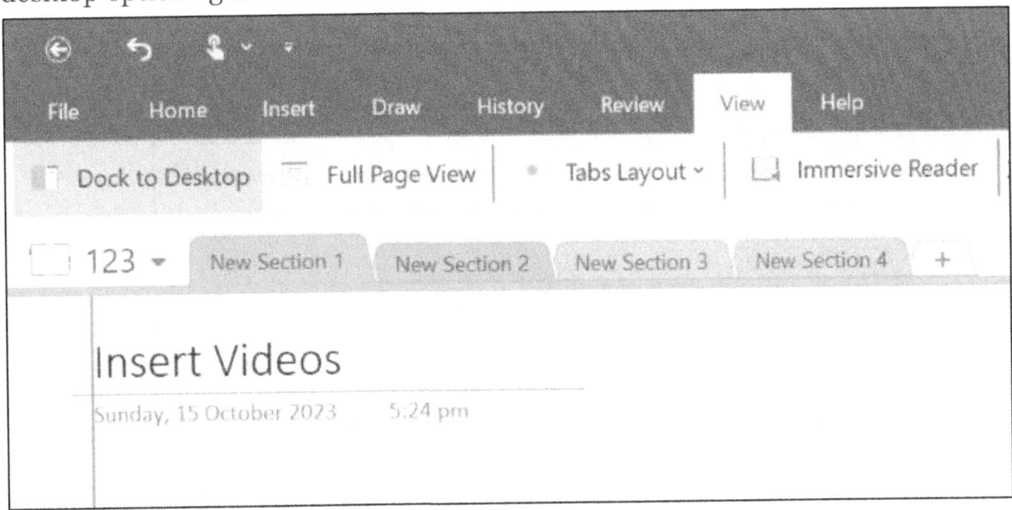

Linked Notes and Cross-Notebook Links:

Linked notes let you to connect related information within OneNote. For instance, link a meeting agenda to the minutes, creating a seamless flow of information. Cross-notebook links enable you to reference content from different notebooks, creating a network of interconnected ideas. It's like building a web of knowledge, ensuring every piece of information is interlinked and easily accessible.

Password Protection

Microsoft OneNote lets you to password protect sections of your notebooks. This feature helps you keep your sensitive information secure. On the desktop version of OneNote, click on the Review option in the ribbon. In the "Password" group, click on "Protect Section." If you are using OneNote for the web or mobile app, the process might be slightly different. Look for an option related to section protection or security in the settings or options menu.

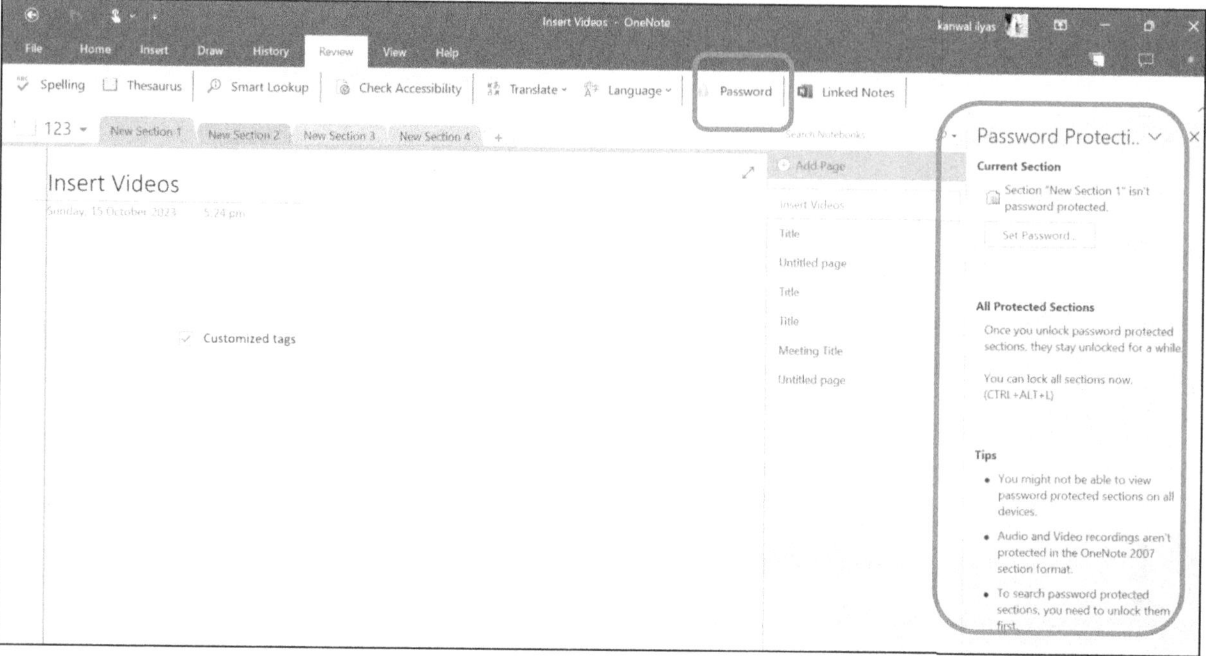

OneNote will prompt you to set a password for the section. Enter your desired password and a password hint (optional). Click "OK" or "Set Password" to confirm. OneNote will ask you to confirm your password by entering it again.

Once a section is password protected, it will be locked. After this OneNote ask for the set password to enter this section. If you forget the password, there is no way to recover it, so make sure to keep it in a secure place.

Installing and Managing Add-Ins

Add-ins are like plugins for OneNote, enhancing its functionality. Install add-ins to automate repetitive tasks, integrate with other apps, or enhance your note-taking experience. With the right add-ins, you can supercharge OneNote, customizing it to match your unique workflow.

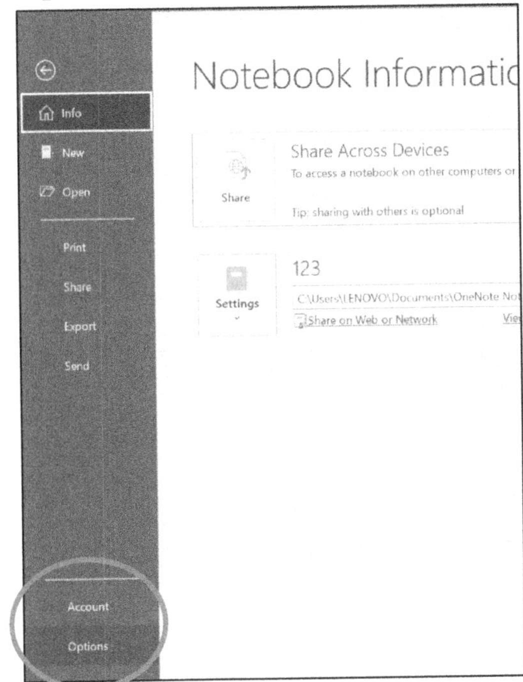

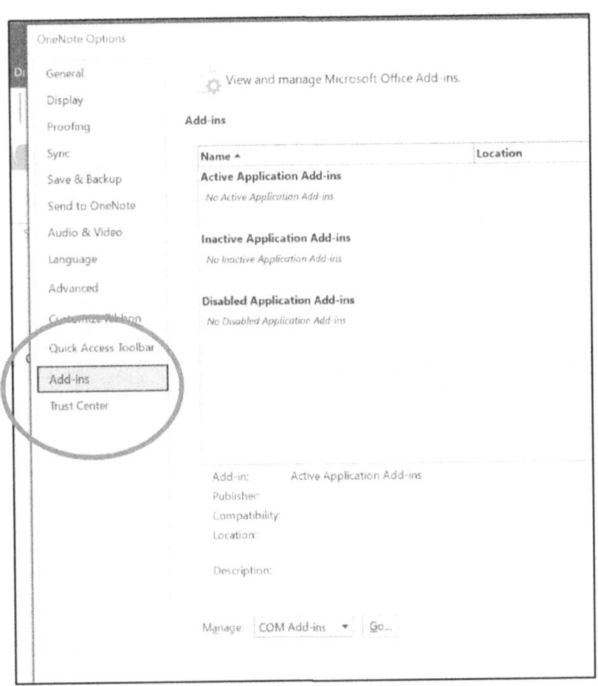

Examples of Useful Add-Ins:

Add-ins can transform OneNote into a powerhouse of productivity. For example, you could integrate a task management add-in, turning your notes into actionable to-do lists. Or perhaps a language translation add-in to break down language barriers in your notes. There are add-ins for scanning documents, creating mind maps, or even converting handwritten notes to text. The possibilities are vast, leting you to tailor OneNote precisely to your requirements. You can download the add-ins from their respective websites and then open your OneNote. Go to the file menu, then go to "options." It will open a new window that has an Add-in option on the left-hand side menu.

Keyboard Shortcuts

Time is precious and keyboard shortcuts are your best friends for saving it. Learn OneNote's keyboard shortcuts to perform tasks swiftly. From creating new pages to formatting text, these shortcuts can significantly speed up your workflow, making you a OneNote ninja in no time. Here are some useful shortcuts to try:

Ctrl + N	New Page
Ctrl + O	Open Notebook
Ctrl + S	Save
Ctrl + P	Print
Ctrl + X	Cut
Ctrl + C	Copy
Ctrl + V	Paste
Ctrl + Z	Undo
Ctrl + Y	Redo
Ctrl + B	Bold
Ctrl + I	Italics
Ctrl + U	Underline
Ctrl + 1	Apply Heading 1
Ctrl + 2	Apply Heading 2
Ctrl + 3	Apply Heading 3
Ctrl + M	New Email
Ctrl + Shift + A	Insert Audio Recording
Ctrl + Alt + D	Insert Today's Date
Ctrl + Alt + T	Insert Time
Ctrl + Alt + N	Create a New Section
Ctrl + Shift + N	Create a New Page
Ctrl + E	Start a Search
Ctrl + Alt + S	Sync Notebook
Ctrl + Alt + D	Dock to Desktop

Common Issues and Solutions

Though OneNote has a seamless interface that offers ease and convenience to every user, there still can be a few bumps on the road and you may face some difficulties or issues while using this software. There are common issues that may arise, but don't worry! Every problem has its solution:

Syncing Issues: Sometimes, changes made on one device do not reflect on other devices.

To resolve this issue, check if you are connected to the web. Try manually syncing by clicking "Sync" or "Sync This Notebook" in the toolbar; if the problem persists, close and reopen OneNote or restart your device.

Missing Sections or Pages: Sections or pages are missing from your notebook.

To resolve this issue, Check the "Recycle Bin" in OneNote; sometimes, accidentally deleted items end up there. If you find the missing sections/pages, right-click and select "Move or Copy" to put them back in the correct location.

Ink or Drawing Issues: Problems with drawing, handwriting recognition, or ink not appearing correctly. To resolve this issue, Check your device's stylus or mouse settings. Update your device drivers. If using a tablet, calibrate the pen. For ink recognition issues, try adjusting the handwriting recognition settings in OneNote options.

Error Messages During OneNote Startup: Error messages when starting OneNote.

To resolve this issue, Try repairing Microsoft Office through the Control Panel (Windows) or reinstall OneNote. Ensure your Windows or Office applications are up to date.

OneNote Crashes or Freezes: OneNote freezes or crashes frequently.

To resolve this issue, check for updates for both your operating system and Office suite. Disable unnecessary add-ins. If the issue persists, consider repairing or reinstalling Office.

Print Issues:

Unable to print from OneNote: To resolve this issue, Ensure your printer drivers are up-to-date. Try printing from other applications to check if the issue is specific to OneNote. If it is, repairing Office might help.

Chapter 5: Using OneNote Across Devices

OneNote on Desktop and Web

The installation procedure, the interface and the methods described in the previous parts of this book were all about the OneNote desktop version. You can employ those techniques to use the OneNote application on your desktop.

There is also the option to use OneNote on the web. You can access OneNote Online by visiting the OneNote website and then signing in with your Microsoft account. Unlike the desktop version, OneNote on the web offers a simplified interface, but it provides essential note-taking functionalities. You can view and edit your existing notes, create new notes, sections and notebooks directly from your web browser. It allows real-time collaboration, so at a time more than one user can work on a file. Changes made on the web version are automatically synced with the desktop application and other devices where OneNote is used, ensuring that your notes are always up-to-date.

Mobile Apps for iOS and Android

There are applications for both iOS and Android to use OneNote on your cellphones. Here's how you can access and use OneNote on your iOS and Android devices:

OneNote on iOS (iPhone and iPad)

To use this, open the App Store on your iPhone or iPad. Search for "Microsoft OneNote" using the search bar. Download and install the app developed by Microsoft Corporation. Launch the OneNote app. Sign in using your Microsoft Account (Outlook.com, Hotmail, Live, Xbox, etc.) or your work/school account associated with Office 365. Once logged in, you are then allowed to create notebooks, sections and pages. Use the touch interface to type, draw and insert images or audio recordings into your notes. Your notes will automatically sync with your OneDrive account, ensuring that your data is accessible across all devices. The iOS app supports features like drawing with your finger or a stylus, creating to-do lists, attaching files and inserting tables.

OneNote on Android

To use this, go to the Google Play Store on your cellphone. Look for "Microsoft OneNote" using the search bar. Download and install the app developed by Microsoft Corporation. Launch the OneNote app. Sign in with your Microsoft Account or your work/school account associated with Office 365. Once logged in, you can create and manage your notebooks, sections and pages. Use the touch interface to type, draw and insert various elements into your notes, just like on the iOS app. Your notes will sync with your OneDrive account, ensuring accessibility across devices. The Android app supports features such as voice dictation, document scanning and integration with other Microsoft apps.

Syncing and Cloud Storage

The best thing about OneNote is that you can sync it across various devices, which ensures that your notes are up-to-date and accessible from any device you use. It is carried out through cloud synchronization; here's how you can use the sync feature across different devices:

Sign in with a Microsoft Account:

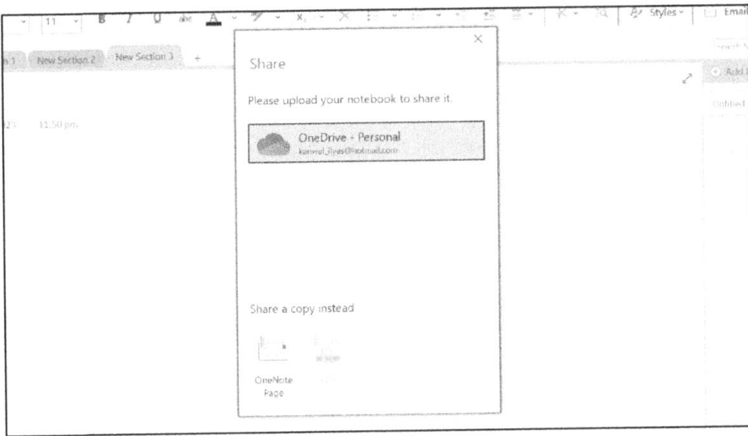

To get started, first sign in to OneNote with the same Microsoft account on all devices where you want to sync your notes.

Use OneDrive

OneNote syncs your notebooks using OneDrive, Microsoft's cloud storage service. So make sure that your notebooks are stored in OneDrive to let synchronization.

Save Your Notebooks to OneDrive

When creating a new notebook or moving an existing notebook, choose OneDrive as the storage location. If you are using OneNote 2016, click on the File menu, then go to the new option on your OneDrive and create your notebook there.

Check Sync Settings

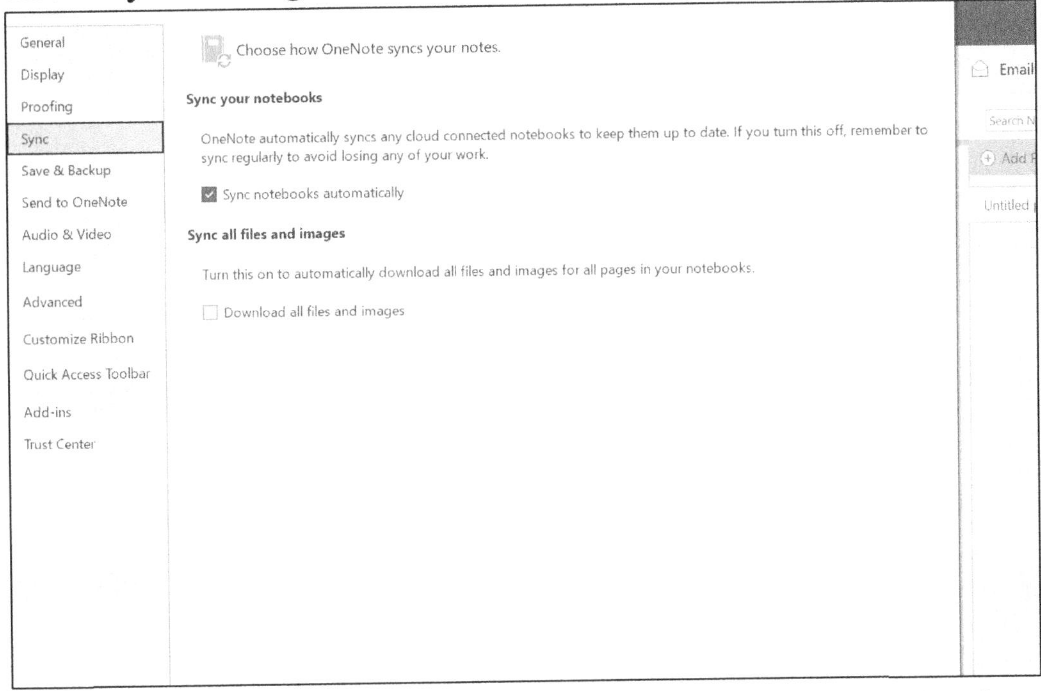

Click on your profile picture or initials in the top right corner. Select Settings from the drop-down menu. Go to the "Sync" section, and make sure that the "Sync notebooks automatically" option is turned on.

Access Notes on Other Devices

Once your notebooks are stored in OneDrive and sync is enabled, your notes will automatically update across all devices where you have signed in with your Microsoft account. Open OneNote on any other device where you are signed in and your notebooks and changes should be synchronized.

Sync on Mobile Devices

On mobile devices (iOS or Android), download the OneNote app from the respective app store.

Sign in with the Microsoft account you use for OneNote on your pc. Your notebooks will automatically appear in the app and any changes made will sync across your devices.

Collaboration and Sharing

OneNote isn't just your personal digital notebook; it's a powerful tool for collaboration and sharing ideas with others. Let's explore how you can seamlessly work together with colleagues, friends, or family members using OneNote.

Sharing Notebooks with Others

With OneNote, you can share your notebooks with others, granting specific permissions. You can select who can open, edit, or co-author your notes. These privacy settings ensure that your information remains secure while leting others to collaborate based on the level of access you provide. It's like having a guest list for your digital party, where you control who gets in and what they can do.

Collaborative Editing and Comments

Collaboration comes to life with collaborative editing. Multiple users can work on the same notebook simultaneously, making it perfect for group projects or team brainstorming sessions. Additionally, you can leave comments on specific notes, offer feedback, or ask questions. It's akin to having a virtual discussion right within your notebook, enriching your ideas through diverse perspectives.

Integrating OneNote with Other Microsoft Apps

Another amazing feature of OneNote is that it lets you to integrate other Microsoft applications as well, such as:

Outlook Integration

OneNote seamlessly integrates with Outlook, Microsoft's email and calendar app. You can send emails or meeting details directly to OneNote, turning important messages into actionable items within your notebook. It's like having a direct pipeline from your email to your to-do list, ensuring nothing falls through the cracks.

OneNote and Microsoft Teams

Microsoft Teams, a hub for teamwork, integrates flawlessly with OneNote. You can create shared notebooks for your teams, fostering collaborative environments for projects and discussions. Team members can access and edit these notebooks in real time, enabling smooth communication and information sharing.

Microsoft Access

Introduction

Overview of Microsoft Access

In a computer and on the internet, database management is very important. A computer and the user of a computer deal with a lot of data every day. The use of data can only be through good database management software. In computers powered by Microsoft, users can find Microsoft Access, which is a database management software to support all other functions of the computer. Microsoft Access is a part of the MS Office suite, and people use it along with other applications of the MS Office suite. The DBMS helps users to handle, analyze, store, and manipulate a humongous amount of data every day. The DBMS from Microsoft is easy to use and has a holistic approach, as it can save all kinds of data in it and deal with the different types of data in a seamless manner. The data kept in the database can be accessed very easily by an authorized user. The database management system can keep huge amounts of data inside it and create links between the data inside so that the user can put the data to good use very easily. In a way, the DBMS allows the user to see data in an organized, streamlined way so that he does not have to start from scratch or use any other application for management. MS Access is a classic DBMS that is versatile and feature-rich.

This DBMS is put to use in different professional fields and works with other apps seamlessly so that a number of actions can be taken by users on it. MS Access is an important application used by a number of high-profile organizations for storing and dealing with data related to their workflow. The initial version of this data entry and management application was launched in computers in the year 1992. Since then, the MS Access application has been updated to newer versions by Microsoft. The Microsoft Office suite keeps getting updated with time, and the same will be done to Microsoft Access in the next versions. With new updates, MS Access becomes more secure and feature-rich for users. A secure DBMS is needed to keep everything in place and keep them secure.

Along with the ability to save and organize data, there are also programming capabilities in MS Access, which allow the user to program with the data already stored. A graphical user interface and relational database, as well as programming capabilities in MS Access, make it one of the best DBMSs to be used by software developers and other professionals who work on computers. There have been many modifications to MS Access in recent times that support the increasing memory capacity and features of other apps of MS Office. The new age professionals have different needs and wants in their daily work. As a robust relational database management system, MS Access fulfills these needs by being a versatile tool.

Chapter 1:Getting Started With Access

Installing Microsoft Access

To use the Microsoft Access tool, you need to install it in your Windows system. The application can be used very well on desktops and laptops. Below are the steps to take to install Microsoft Access on your computer.

Before installing the MS Access application, check your computer to see if it already has the application or not. Many Windows computers and laptops come with an already installed Microsoft Office suite, which is easy to use and install Microsoft Access with. If Microsoft Access is not already present in the computer, then check if you have a supportive OS, enough disk space, and memory to support its functioning. Once you are sure that there is enough space and a good OS in the back end to help run MS Access, you can go to the Microsoft website and start the installation process.

The steps of installation are as follows-

From the main website of Microsoft, you have to navigate to the linked page of Microsoft Access and then click on the Download button.

When you click on the Download button, the website will come up with many options related to the operating system you are using. Select the operating system for which you are downloading and follow the on-screen prompts that come up after that. After this, you need to accept the terms and conditions of installing and using the Microsoft Access application on your computer. Once you accept the related terms and conditions, the download for your PC or laptop will happen, and the MS Access files will be present on your computer. Once the files are downloaded and installed properly, the user can use the DBMS to store and access data on it.

The download process is as follows.

- Open your browser
- After this, you need to type www.microsoft.com in the address bar
- Once you go to the Microsoft page, click on the Products tab on the screen
- You can then search for the search bar and type Microsoft Access in the search bar
- Click on the download now option to initiate the download process
- Once you click on the download process, you should wait for the download to finish

Once you have downloaded the MS Access application, you can go to your computer and open the File Explorer application from the taskbar. You can then go to the downloads folder where, usually, all the files that have been downloaded are stored. You will find the MicrosoftAccessInstaller.exe in the downloads section. If you cannot find the file, then you can use the search bar in the folder, present on the bottom left corner of your screen, and type the Access word to find any Access-related keyword. Once you have found the right file, you should double-click on it to run and install it on your computer.

You will be asked to choose your language of operation before you install the files for the final run. Once you choose your language, you can click on the Next button. After that, you need to read the license agreement for the application and then agree and click on the Next button to ensure that the application is ethically installed on the computer. Your computer system has mostly the installation wizard that will help you with the installation process. If the OS of the computer is compatible with the MS Access file, it will install the application quickly, and you can use it very soon. You might have to click on the Finish button to finally install and run the application on your PC.

The installation process is as follows-

- Launch the installer of the MS Access files
- Carefully go through the terms and conditions of the license agreement
- Click on the Accept and Agree button to finalize the installation
- Click on the Next button to complete the installation

- Make customizations needed and then click on the Install or Finish buttons

You can also choose the installation location and customize the application settings to keep the application in the right location and use it as you want. The Finish setup button will ensure that the MS Access application will be ready to use on the computer.

Overview of the Access Interface

The user interface of any application matters a lot in terms of the usability and comfort that any ordinary user can experience. The user interface is linked strongly with the user experience that arises from the application. MS Access is a well-organized application with good navigation, which helps professionals access different features and use the application for different purposes.

The interface of MS Access is created in such a way that you can use it to create and manage databases in one place. The user interface of MS Access is a drag-and-drop kind, which is very useful in getting the files easily and creating new files.

According to the creator company, MS Access has three main components in its user interface that make the UI very smooth for the user. The UI includes a ribbon, which is a thin strip of the screen that displays all the tabs across the top of the program window, which contains groups of commands. MS Access app also has a unique Backstage view, which is a collection of the commands that you see on the File tab on the ribbon. Another important feature that the UI has is the navigation pane. The navigation pane makes it easier for the user to navigate to different sections of the same application, switching between different task screens easily. These three elements together create the user environment in which all tasks and actions can be taken.

The ribbon is an integrated component for different icons and shortcut commands that is a good replacement for the menu bar and toolbar. The use of the ribbon creates a simplified but highly efficient workspace for the user. The ribbon has all the tabs related to what you are currently doing and also offers access to the Quick Access Tool Bar, which is where you can easily access the most commonly used tools and commands for MS Access. The ribbon allows you to control what you do in the Access Workspace and also allows you to take decisive actions so that your workflow is very smooth and efficient.

Other features and actions of the UI in the MS Access application are described in the next section.

Backstage View and Quick Access Toolbar

Let's now understand the novelty of the Backstage view and the QAT or the Quick Access Toolbar. It is the space where you can launch commands and common tools with just one click. The default set of commands that you can access on the QAT include the Undo, Redo, and Save buttons because they are the most frequently used commands. These commands will help you avoid any kind of mistakes and save the file quickly. However, once the user is acquainted with the user interface of the application, he can also customize the Quick Access Toolbar. The QAT can include other commands that the user uses frequently when handling the databases. This creates a quick and efficient workflow and an organized workspace for the user. The user can also alter the position of the QAT to ensure that the toolbar is very accessible. The QAT can also be modified in size with customization. The size can be small or large. When the Quick Access Toolbar is present on the screen in its small size, it only appears as an icon. When it is in its large size, it is just adjacent to the ribbon and expands to its full size to show all the tools and commands.

The steps to customize the QAT are as follows

- You need to click on the right-most drop-down arrow in the toolbar
- Click on the More Commands option and proceed to the next step
- The Access Options dialog box appears, where you can select the commands to include and click on the Add button.
- You can also remove commands from the customization list by highlighting the changes and then clicking on the Remove button.
- Click on the OK button when done.

The customization of the Quick Access Toolbar can help you create a workspace that is highly productive and compatible with your work style.

Now, Let's learn about the Backstage view feature of MS Access, which is unique to this particular application.

The Backstage view is close to the File tab on the ribbon and has many features that are useful for the user. It contains many commands that can be executed on the database the user works on. There are many commands that can be applied to the entire database so that the changes can easily be reflected and the whole database is streamlined. The Backstage view exists by default for any user who opens the MS Access application but has not yet opened a database to work with. Using the Backstage view, the user creates a new database; you can also open an existing database and use different files and information stored in the database. The Backstage view allows you to quickly organize and maintain a database so you can work on it.

There are also a number of templates present in the Backstage View, which helps you create databases very easily and also helps you manage the database. You can either create a database by default format or choose an existing template.

Whether it is the QAT or the Backstage view, these features of the user interface are designed to increase the accessibility and efficiency of the application for the user. MS Access is a highly efficient and versatile application that can handle complex databases and mega data sets. To use the DBMS, the user has to not only understand the user interface but also get in touch with the most basic commands and actions. Creating a new file, opening an existing file, streamlining the database, and locating data are all basic actions that a new user should learn. In the next section, you will learn about creating a new database using the commands of MS Access.

Creating a New Database

When you go to the Access main screen, you can see the Backstage View, which shows the New button. With the help of the New button, you can create a blank database or create a new file using the Template designed already in MS Access. The user can also find new templates from Office.com, download them, and use them to create new databases.

To create a blank database

There are certain steps that you need to follow to create a blank database from MS Access.

- When you go to the File tab, you need to click on New and then click the Blank Database option.
- Give the existing file a new file name in the File Name box.
- You can also change the location of the created file by clicking on Browse for a location to put your database and then click on OK.
- Once you are done, click on the Create button.
- This creates the database with an empty table, Table, and then you can Click to Add option to add more Tables to the database.

Chapter 2: Tables And Relationships

Designing and Creating Tables

You can create tables with good design and layout when you use the Table Design option in MS Access. There are many actions about the table design that you can take with the Table Design option.

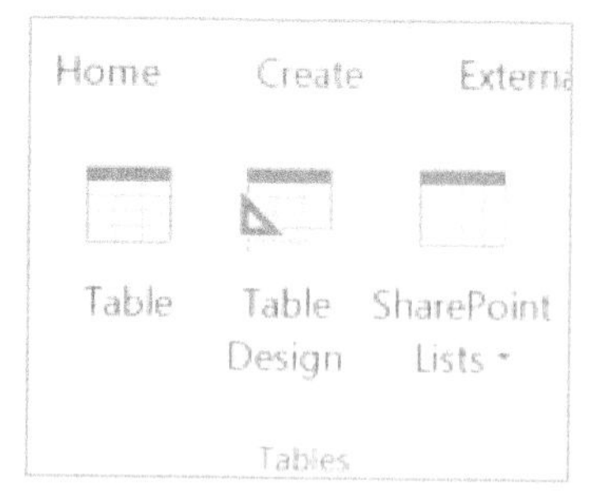

- Select Create >Table Design.
- In the new table, in the first field, you can enter the field name and a data type to specify

- You can select the primary key for the table and then select the Field Name cell for the field you want.
- After that, you can select the Primary Key.
- You can then go to the File tab and select the Save option to name the file and save it.

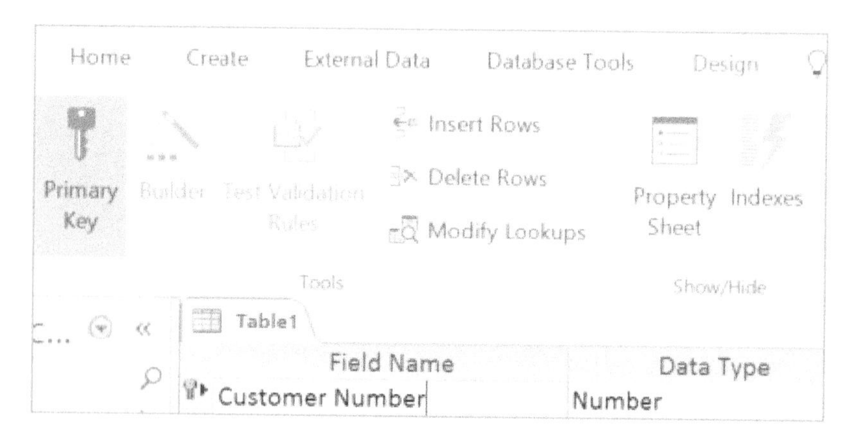

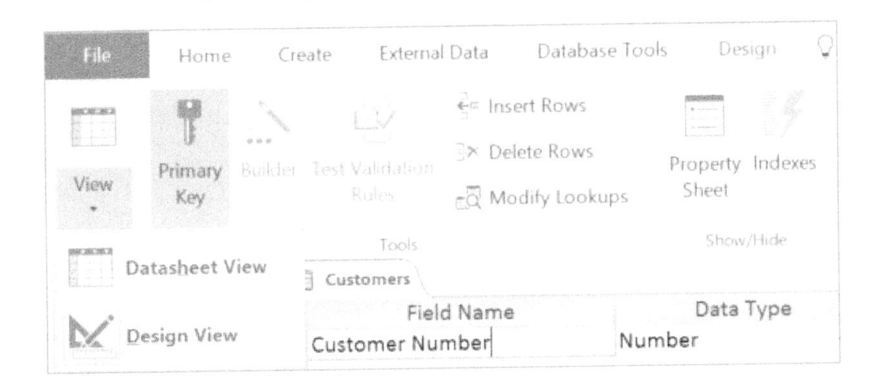

You can also do a lot of designing with tables in the Design option. For instance, you will be able to opt between Design View and Datasheet View. You can also text validation rules to the table. You can also insert and delete cells from the created table using the Design tab. You can create new elements of the table using the Design option. The Design option can be used to define relationships between the elements of the table.

Field Types and Properties

Every table created in the MS Access suite has fields; the characteristics of the data in a field are defined with the help of the properties of the field. The data type that is defined in a particular field is the main characteristic to focus on, as the data stored in it depends on it.

The data type of a field is used to define many characteristics of the field. The data type can determine the formats to be used in the field, as well as the maximum size of the field and the data that can be stored in it. The field data type also decides how the field can be used in expressions. The indexing of the field also depends on the field data type. The field data type might be predetermined in the program, or you can define the data type when creating the field.

The field data type has certain qualities, and the qualities determine the time at which the data types are used. The different data types are as follows.

Short text data type for names and alphanumeric values.

- Number data types for numeric values
- Currency data type for money values
- Yes/No data types for specification of one value from a set
- Date/ Time data types for years and time period

There are many more field data types, but these are the basic ones. When the user creates the fields and assigns data types, he can also add more properties to the fields to define them. The other properties that are specified depend on the data type that has been specified already.

Indexing and Validation Rules

The indexing and validation rules are the rules that help in defining the data so that bad data types and invalid data are not saved in the database table. The user can easily create the validation rules for fields and tables of the database to check the validity of the data present in them.

When you select the field in a table, you will see the validation rule in the lower pane.

The validation rules are applied when data is entered into the field selected.

The user can also set the validation rules for an entire table. The data table validation rules can be set through the Properties box, where you can see the validation rule for the table. The specified validation rule is applied to the entire table and all of its fields. The validity of the database and its usability depends completely on the data types stored in its fields. To ensure that there is accuracy and concurrency of data in the fields and to maintain the integrity of the table, you need to follow the validation rules.

Establishing Relationships Between Tables

The user can use different commands in MS Access to establish relationships between Tables in MS Access. A relationship can be established between two tables to create a combination of data between the data present in their fields. There are many steps that you have to follow to create relationships.

Create relationships between Tables.

- From the Database Tools tab, in the Relationship tab, you click on the Relationship option.
- From the Design tab, you need to select the Relationship group and then click on the Show Tables option.
- You can then select the table or queries from the list and then click on the Add tab. Once the selected tables or queries are added, you can click on the Close tab.
- You can drag one field from one table to the common field of another table. To add multiple fields, you can use the CTRL key and dragging of multiple fields.
- You can then see the Edit Relationships window on the screen. In the window, you can verify the field types and field names to specify the relationships. You can select the field name to edit the field name and correct it.
- You can click on the Enforce Referential Integrity to maintain the integrity of the table.
- Then, finally, click on the Create option.

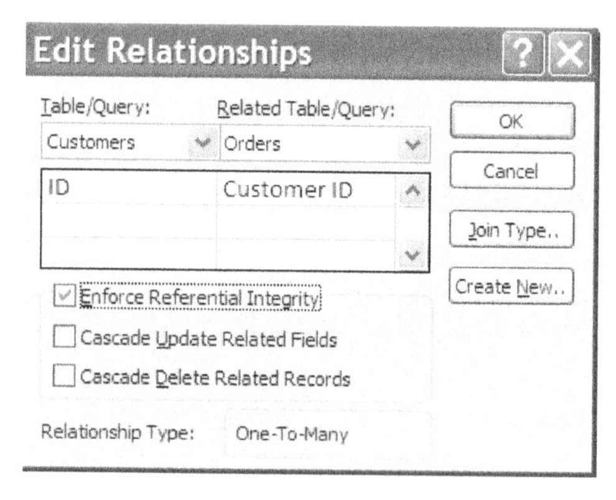

Primary and Foreign Keys

A table in MS Access can have Primary keys as well as foreign keys. The Primary key is used to define the integrity of the data in a field to ensure that the data specified inside a column is unique and true.

Under the primary key, the column cannot possess Null Values.

Most often, the foreign key of a relational database acts as a reference for the primary key of a basic table and its primary key. The foreign key is not unique and does not belong to any particular table of the database. The value of the primary key cannot face deletion from the table, but the value of the foreign key can be deleted from the relational database.

Referential Integrity

Maintaining the Referential integrity of the relational database in MS Access is very important. The referential integrity of a relational database defines the relationship between two tables of the database. The referential integrity of the database can be maintained when certain conditions are fulfilled for the tables. For example,

- From the two fields that are linked, at least one should have a primary key in it.
- Both the tables should have an identity in the tables they share.
- The linked fields of the key should have the same data type and size type.
- If a data record is already added to the primary table, the same data type can not be again added to a primary table.

When the referential integrity has been established, the user needs to maintain the primary key if the same type of data is in both tables. You cannot add or delete any kind of data from the primary table if the same records exist in both tables.

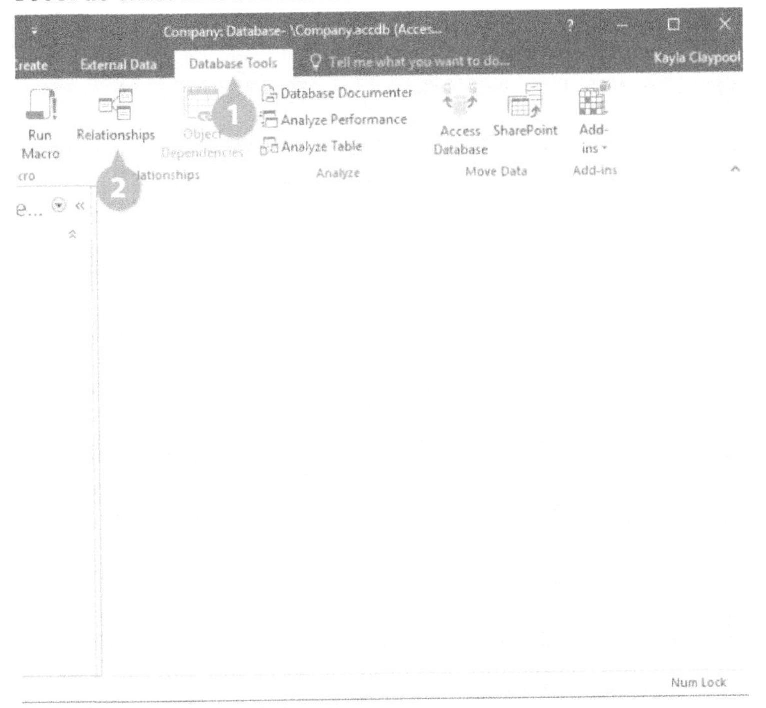

Chapter 3: Queries And Data Retrieval

Creating Select Queries

You can create select queries through the Data Retrieval method by using simple steps. The simple steps are as follows-

- You can select the specific data for which the query needs to be made.
- Select the Query button from the menu.
- Then, you select the Query Wizard option.
- You can also choose the view of the query and then click on the Finish button to create the Query.

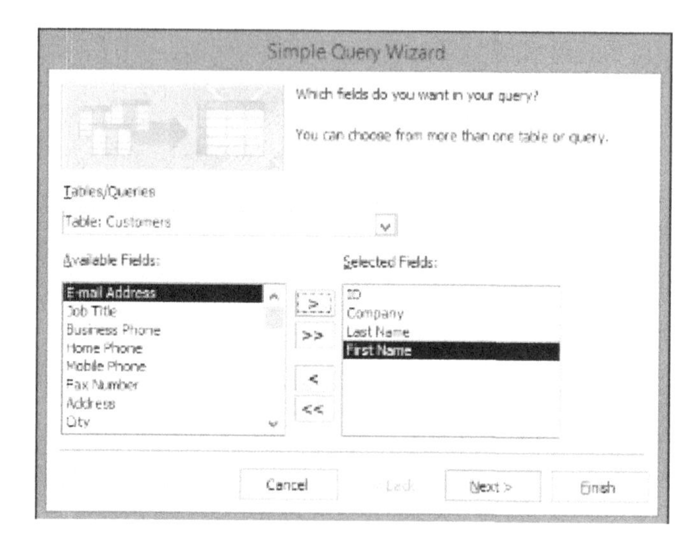

Criteria and Sorting

You can also choose to set the criteria for sorting and sort data in MS Access. If you want to sort the data of a single field, you need to follow the following steps.

- Select the column where the sorting of the data is supposed to happen.
- You can do this by clicking on the column's field name at the top of the table.
- From the ribbon, you can click on the Home tab and then find the Sort & filter option.
- You will find the Ascending and Descending options in the Sort & Filter tab.
- You can click on the Ascending A to Z tab to arrange data in an ascending manner.
- You can choose the Z to A tab to arrange in a descending manner.

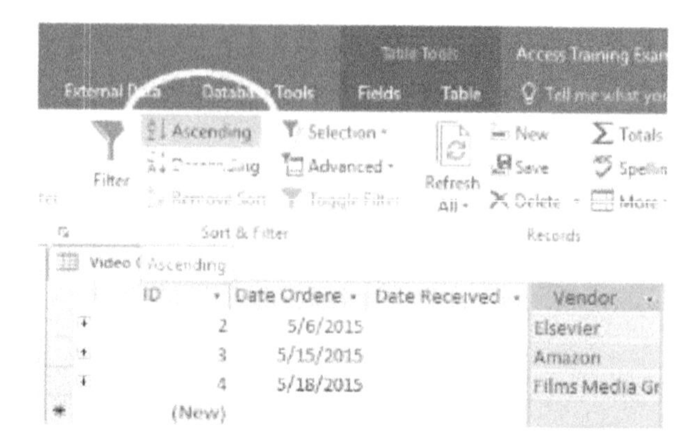

Calculated Fields

A calculated field can be created to specify some kind of arithmetic operation that has to be performed on the particular fields of a table and create another table for the outputs. Here is how to create a calculate field in the table.

- The user can navigate to the Design view tab and select the field row of a blank column
- Then, enter the field name for the field where you want the result to be displayed; then, put a colon near it.
- Enter the expression you have selected to be calculated. Ensure that you maintain proper syntax when using the expression.
- You can then select the save option and operate on the query.

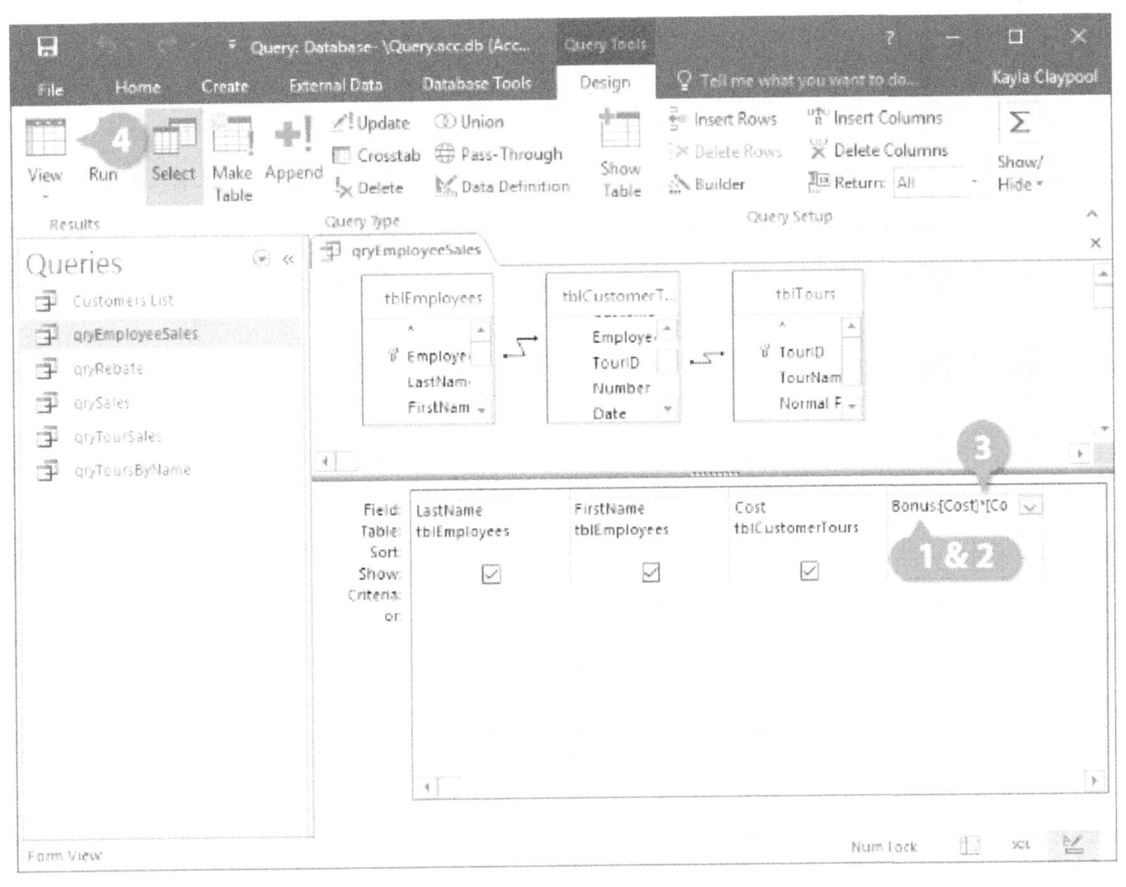

Advanced Query Techniques

The advanced query techniques of Microsoft Access are used to extract data and insights from complex data sets stored in a database. There are many types of Advanced queries that you can specify for certain operations. For example, you can create inner joins that retrieve data from multiple tables using the matching values specified in the query. You can also create Outer joins, which help you in retrieving the data from one table even if there are no matching values specified in the fields. If there are unmatched records, you can easily use the unmatched records with Outer join queries. Another type of query from the Advanced section is the subquery, which is used to filter out and aggregate data from existing queries.

Joins and Unions

You can easily create Union queries by using the SQL view in Access and using SQL syntax with the view. The Union Query can be used to create a combined record of data from two or more tables. The process to create a Union Query is as follows-

- Go to the Create Tab and then, click on the Queries group, and then click on the Query Design option.

- Then, you can double-click on the table that you want to include in the Query.
- You can also add additional criteria to the Query by typing the appropriate expressions in the Criteria row.
- Once you have finished adding the field criteria, you can go to the Design tab, and then in the Results tab, you can click on the Run option.
- Switch the query to Design View.
- Save the Select Query and then leave it open.
- You can do the same for all the select queries you want to combine for a Union Query.

Parameter Queries

The MS Access portal can also be used to create Parameter Queries for the database. The Parameter query is created to ask for criteria when another query is run. The process of creating Parameter Queries is as follows.

- If you want to create a parameter Query, create a select query form first.
- In the Criteria row of the field, the parameter to be applied should be entered as the text meant to be on display in the parameter box.
- You need to repeat the above step for each of the fields you want to add parameters to.
- Fill in the value you are looking for, and then click on the OK tab.

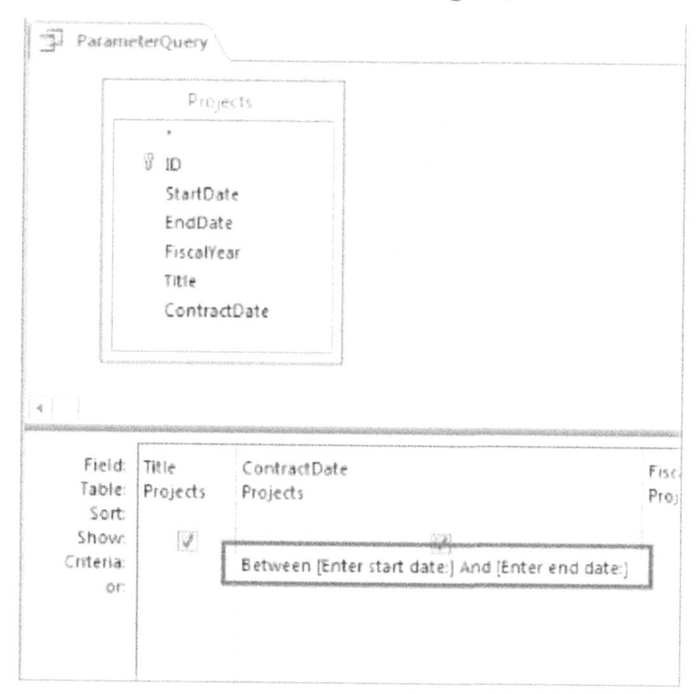

Action Queries: Update, Append, and Delete

Action queries are queries used to take action and make changes in the database you have created. You can append, delete, or update data into a database table using the Action Query option.

- At first, you need to create a regular select query and then run it.
- You then need to go to the Design View tab in the ribbon.
- Go to the Query Tools Design tab and then go to Query Type, where you can switch to the Action Query option from a Select Query Option.
- You can then go to the Query Grid and then click on the proper cell. Then you can Update to the Row Option.
- The user then writes the formula to run the query.

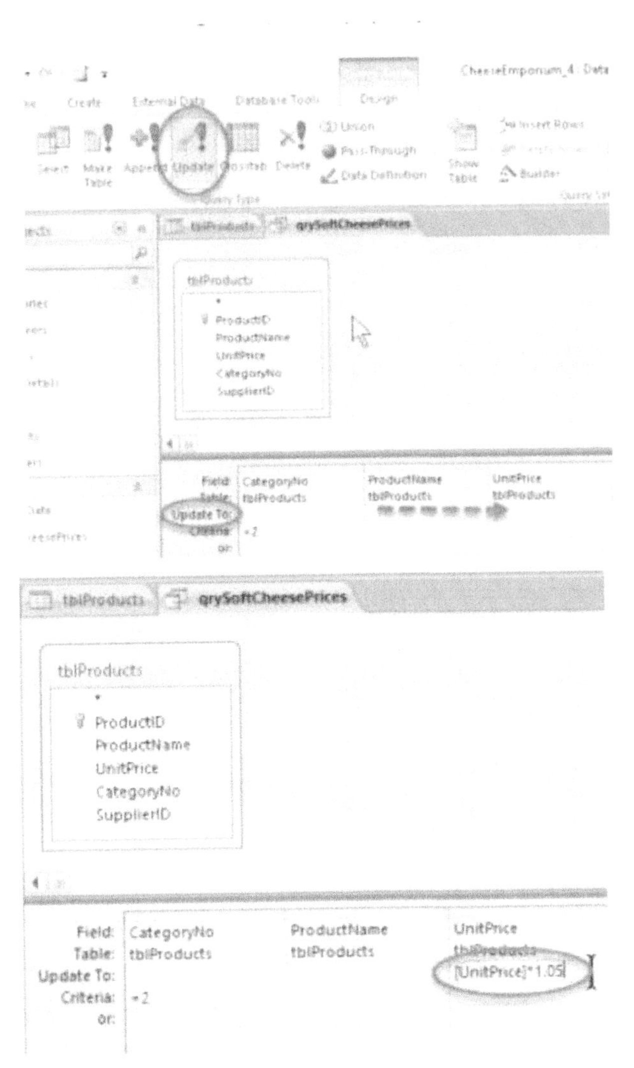

Chapter 4: Forms For Data Entry And Display

Designing Forms

Forms in MS Access are created to make the entering of data easy for the user. There are some easy instructions that you can follow to create the form in Access. The steps are as follows-

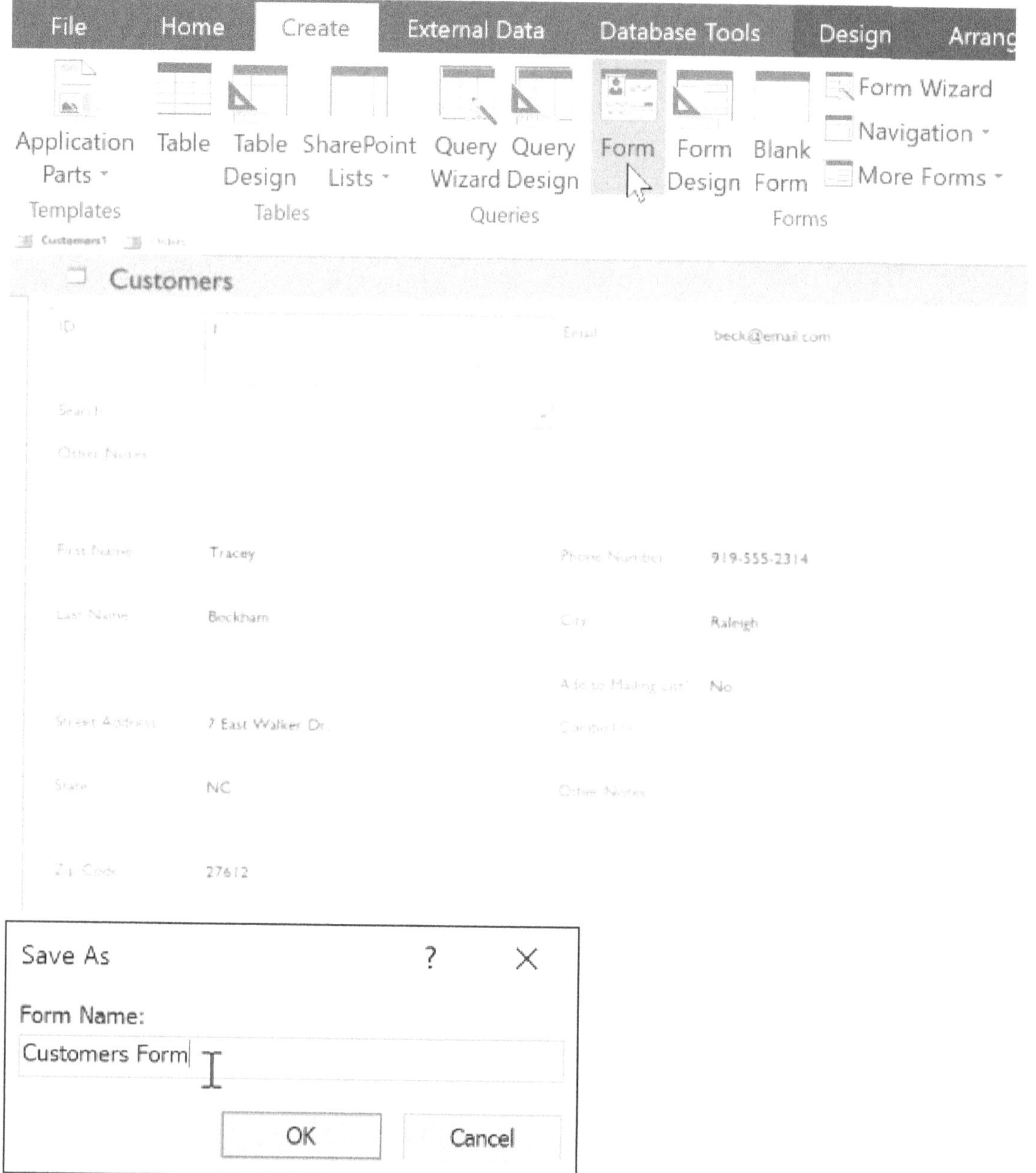

- Go to the Navigation pane and select the table of the database you want to create the form for.
- After this, you select the Create tab and locate the Forms tab. From the menu, select the Forms option to create one.
- The form will be created, and it will appear in Layout View
- The form can be saved in its design by clicking on the Save option from QAT, and then you can type the

name of the form and click on OK to save.

Form Controls and Layout

In the Layout view, the form controls and layouts are visible after you create it. You can modify the Form Controls and Layout by taking action on the form. Modifying controls can also be the removal of one or more controls from the Layout. The steps to remove one or more controls are as follows-

- Right-click on the Form you want to Modify from the Navigation Pane. Then, you can click on Design View.
- After this, you can select the control you want to remove from the Layout.
- You can also select multiple controls to remove from the Layout by pressing down on the Shift Key and then clicking on many controls.
- You can then go to the Arrange tab and then click on Table group, and select the Remove Layout option to remove the controls selected.
- You can also select one of the controls by right-clicking on them, and from Layout, you can select the Remove Layout option.
- You can take other actions like splitting the control into two or moving one control from one place to another by the same process and going to the Layout option from the Controls.

Form Properties

The forms have different properties that can be changed to manage the look and use of forms in Access. You can change the Form properties through simple steps like-

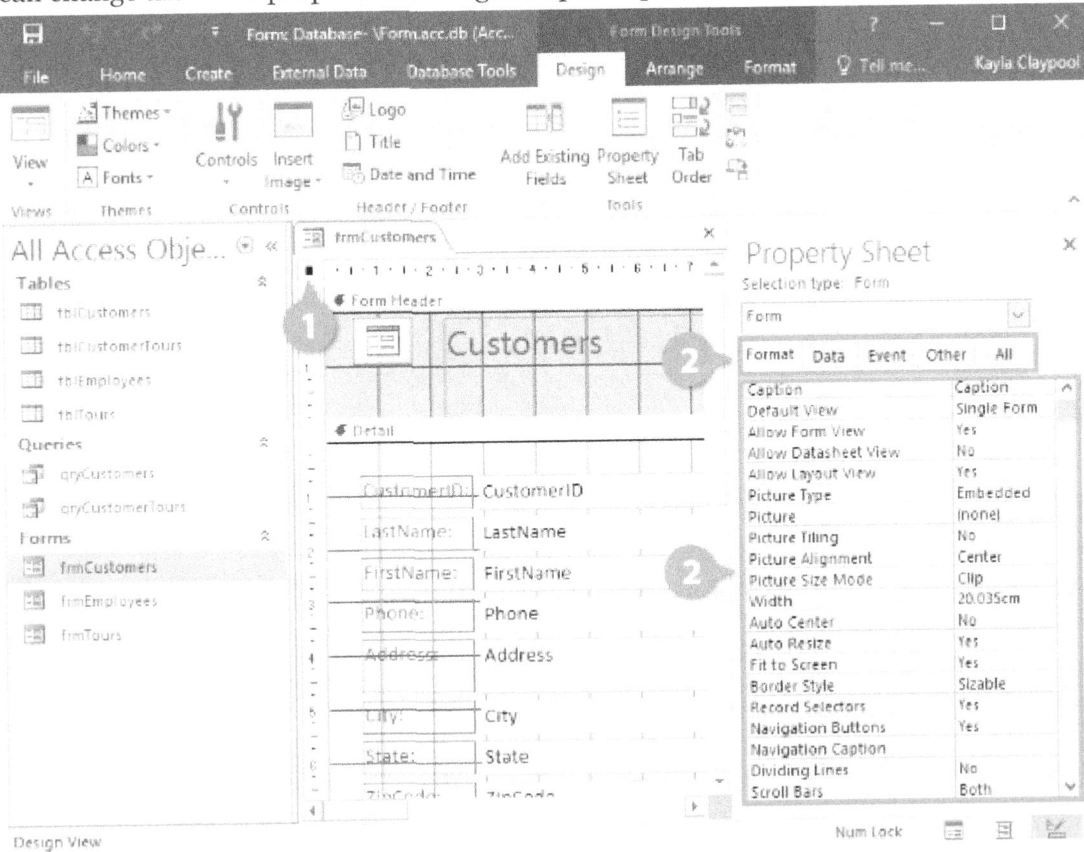

- In Design View, you can go to the Form Selector and double-click on it.
- The Form Properties are also visible from the Layout View option.
- Click on the property tab you want to modify, and then you can go to the Property box to make the needed changes.
- For example, you can go to the Default View option from the Property Sheet.

- You can select the Default List Arrow and then select the view option you want to change to as the form property.
- You have many view options like Single Form, Continuous Form, and Datasheet View to choose from.

Data Entry and Modification in Forms

You can enter and modify data in forms with the help of certain steps and commands. The forms in access are used to easily enter data. Data modification is also equally easy.

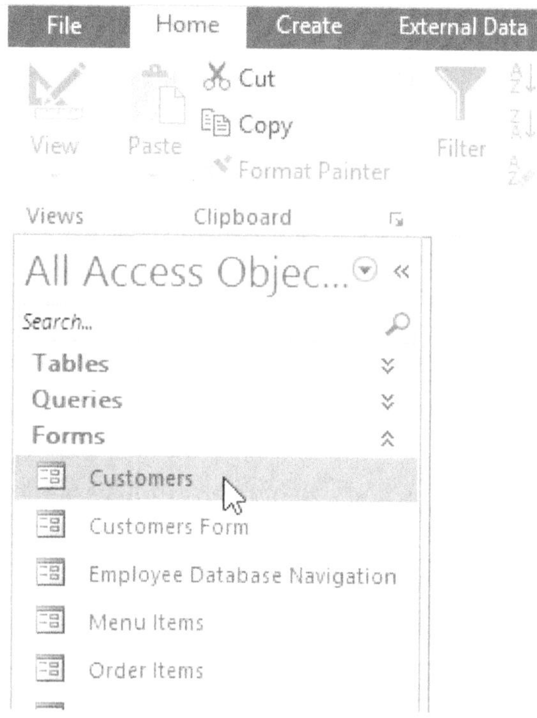

You can add a new record.

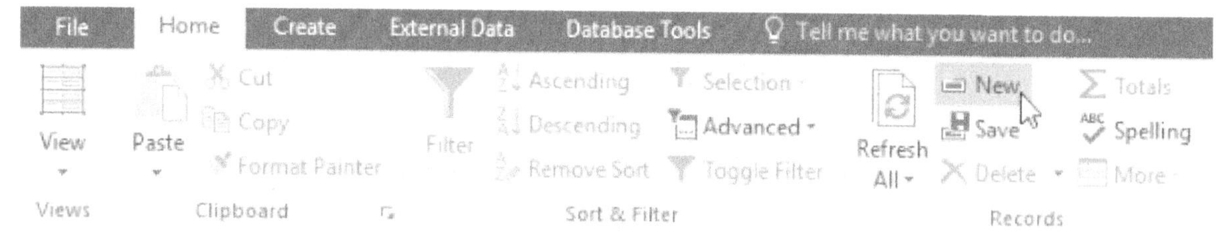

A new record can be added to make data entry into the forms. The steps are as follows-

- Go to the Home tab from the ribbon and then select the Records option.
- The Record Navigation Bar will come up at the bottom of the window. You can easily select New Record by clicking on it.
- You can also select a record to view or edit through the Navigation Pane. You can go to the Navigation Bar and use the navigation arrows to move from one record to another.

- You can also search for certain records by typing the name or word saved in that particular record in the Navigation search box.

- You can also save a record, once it is modified finally.
- You can select the Home tab and then go to the Record group. Select the Save option to take a saving action on record.

Form Views (Datasheet, Design, and Layout)

There are different form views in which the forms can be viewed and changed. There are three main types of views, which are Datasheet view, Design View, and Layout View.

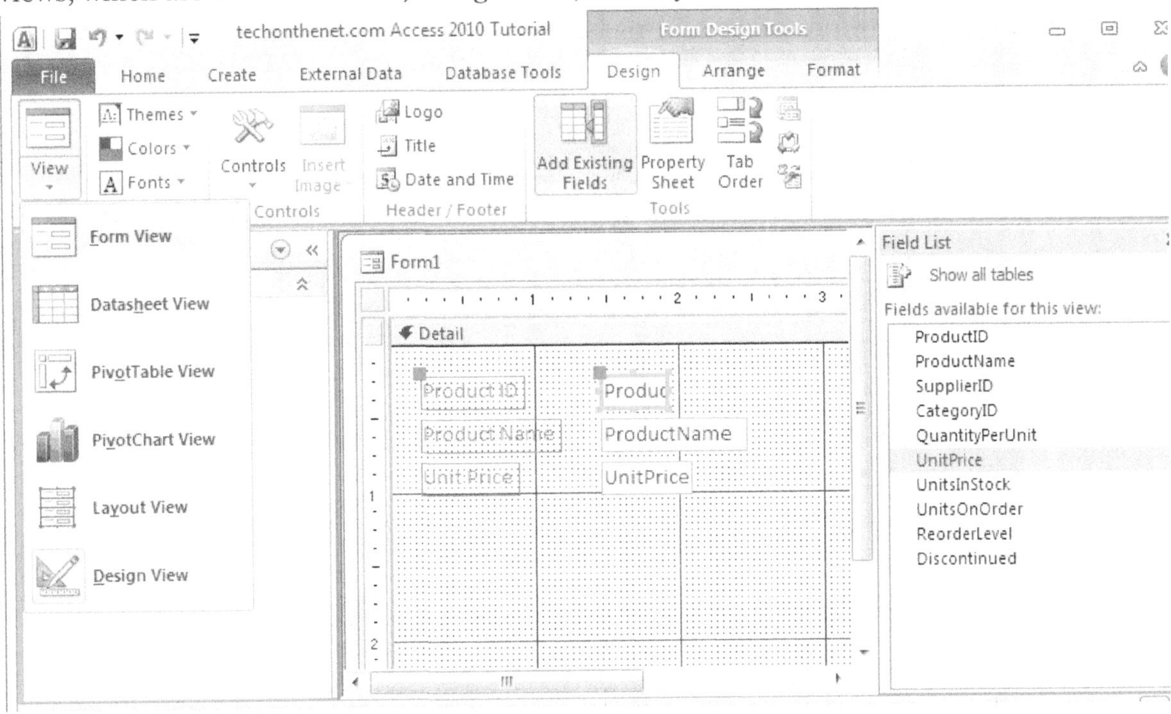

The Datasheet View is where you can only view the form as a datasheet and cannot make any major changes.

The values can be edited in the Datasheet view, but they cannot be completely changed, or the design of the form cannot be changed in the Datasheet view.

The Datasheet view is a compact view that allows the user to view multiple tables at the same time.

The Design view is where you can see and modify the design of an existing form. You can make new tables and forms in Design View.

You can also make or edit a database in Design View.

The Layout View shows the layout of the form and shows its visual orientation. The Layout View is much like the Design View option. However, in Layout View, you can change the controls of the form, but in Design View, all the aspects of the form can be edited.

In both Layout View and Design View, you can go to the property sheet to modify the properties and look of the form. The property sheet will appear after you press the F4 key.

Subforms

Access allows you to create subforms within forms in the table. The subforms are created when you want to arrange data in a table with a one-to-many relationship.

To create a subform,

- You go to the Design View section of the workspace and then resize the form as necessary.
- You can click on the Controls button from the ribbon and then click on the Subform button to create the subform.
- The mouse pointer changes to a plus sign, and then you can take the pointer and drag it to an area on the form to add a subform.
- Once you click and drag in a certain area, the subform will appear. The subform wizard will appear and

ask if you want to create a new subform or change an existing form into a subform.

- On tapping on the Next button, the wizard box will again appear, and you have to select the tables or fields that you want to include in the subform.
- You can do this from the Tables/ Queries tab.
- After selecting the suitable fields to include in the subform, you need to click on Next.
- Then, you need to specify the parent and child fields for the form and subform linkage and then click on Next.
- Once the link is established, give the subform a name you want and click on Finish to create the subform.

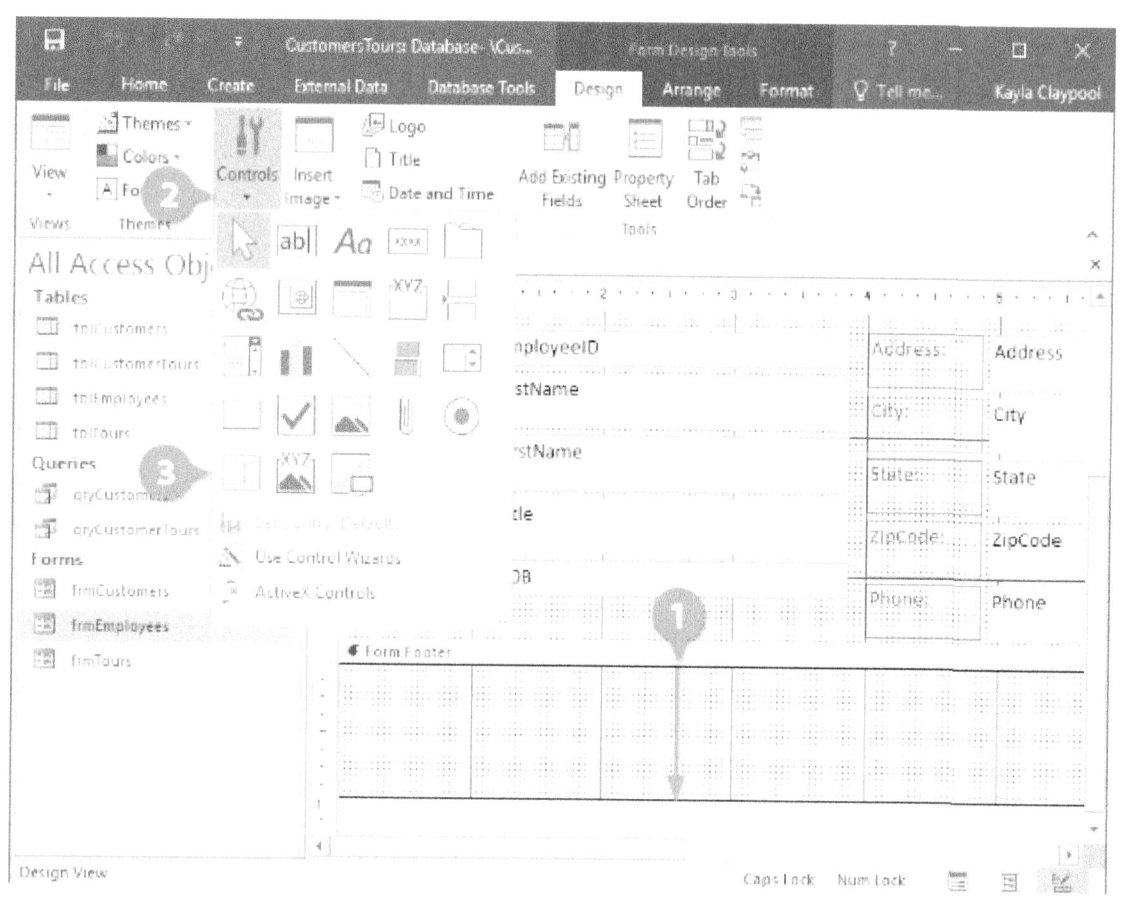

Chapter 5: Reports And Printing

Creating Basic Reports

You can easily create Basic Reports with the help of MS Access commands. For example, you can take the following steps to create a report in Access.

- If you have a table already open, you can use the Report button. You can also use the Report Wizard option to create the Report for one or two tables.
- Select the table that needs the report creation action for your work.
- After selecting the table, the Create button needs selection from the ribbon.
- From the Create options, Click on the Report Button.
- You can also select the Blank Report button or the Report Design button to decide the layout of the report.
- Click on the Save button

The report needs a name; after giving the name, click on OK to save.

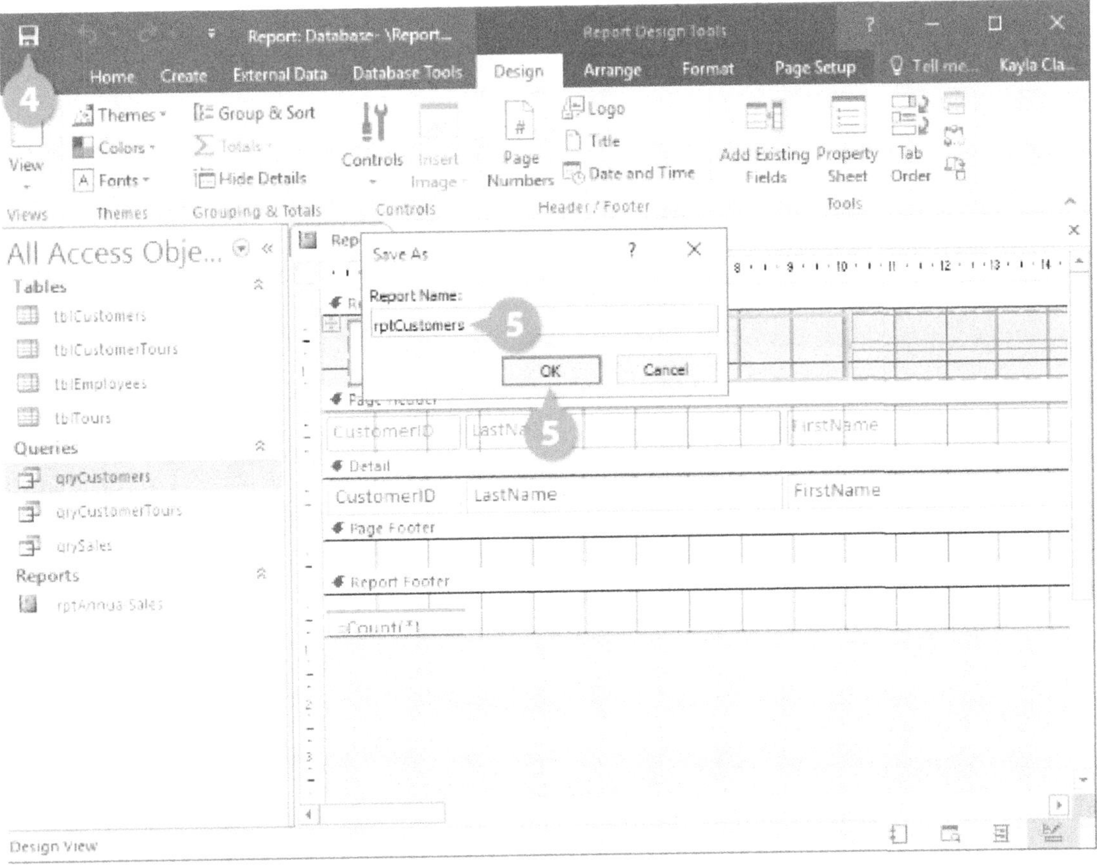

Report Design and Layout

There are many sections to the Report design and layout that one can follow. Let's know about the different sections of the report design in MS Access.

- Report Header section- It is the header at the top of the front page of the report that appears only once. It is the section that usually holds the Report title.
- Report footer- The Report Footer appears at the end of each page and holds the report totals
- Page header- The Page Header appears at the top of each page of the report. The page header usually

holds the page number. The page footer can also hold the same, but it appears at the end of each page.

- Group Header- The Group Header appears just before a group of Values. It holds the fields that are grouped.

Sorting and Grouping

You can also create a sorted or grouped report from the data present in the table.

Go to the navigation section and select the query or table that you want to create the report for.

From the Create section, click on the Report tab.

You can right-click on the specific column on which you can choose to group or sort. The user needs to select the Group button. After clicking on the Group Button, you can click on the Sort Option.

This will create the report the way you want in a grouped view.

Advanced Reporting Features

To explore advanced reporting features, you need to go to the Report Wizard option in MS Access. Here are the steps to go to Reports Wizard and create a report

- Go to the Create tab from the Ribbon of MS Access.
- Go to the reports tab. Then you can click on the Report Wizard option

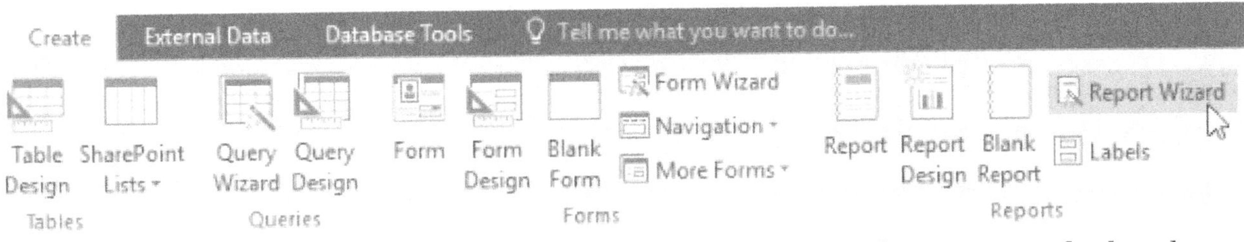

- Once the report wizard appears, you can then click on the drop-down menu and select the queries for the specific fields you want to include in the report.

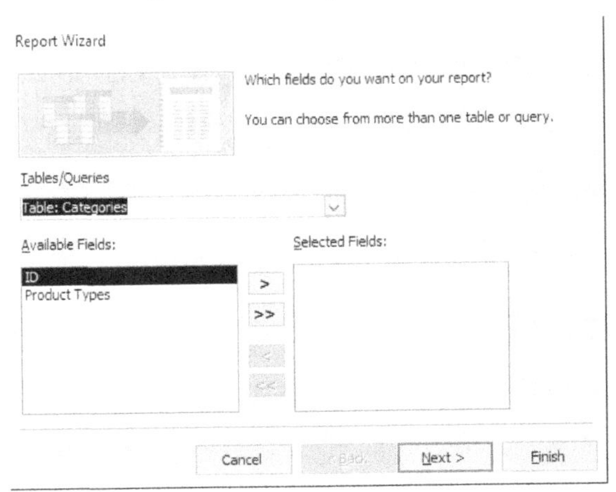

- You select a field from the list, after which you click on the right arrow to add it to the report. You can also repeat the same steps for different tables and then click on the Next button to create the final report.

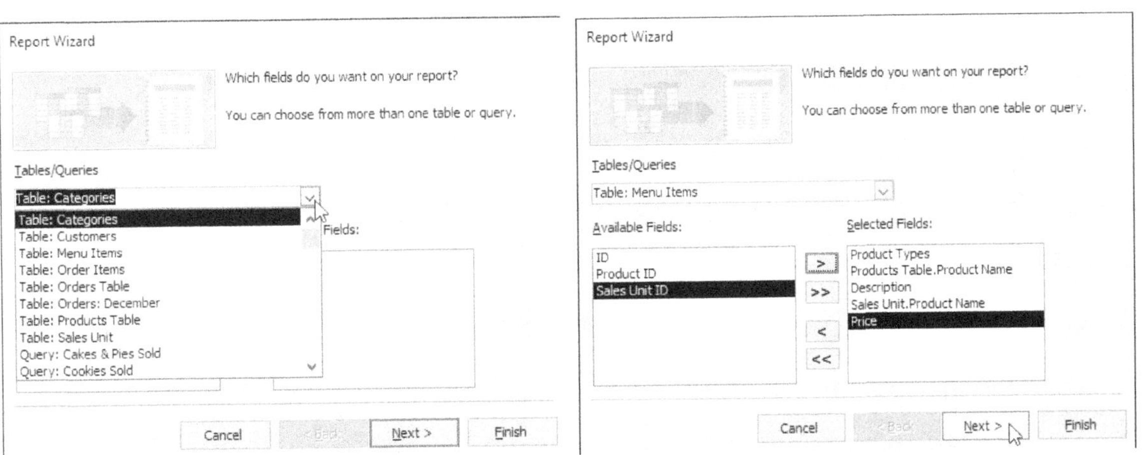

Calculations in Reports

- You can create and use Calculated Controls to calculate certain values in a report. The steps to create calculated controls for a certain report are as follows-
- To do this, you need to go to the Navigation Pane and then right-click on the report you want.
- Once done, you click on the Design View tab.
- Go to the controls group from the Design tab and then select the calculated control you want to create.
- Position the pointer on the place in the report where you want the control to be placed. Then click on the form to insert the calculated control.
- If the Control wizard starts, then click on Cancel.

The calculated control can now be used to calculate operations in the report.

Subreports

You can use the Subreport Wizard to create a subreport in the Access reports. The best way to create subreports are as follows-

- In the Navigation pane, right-click on the report you want to add a Subreport to and then go to the Design View tab.
- Go to the Design tab and then go to the Controls group.
- Once you enter the Control groups, you need to open the Controls Gallery.

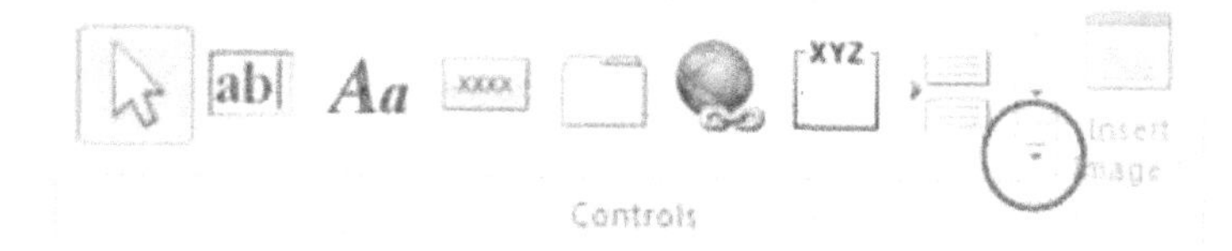

- Select the Use Controls Wizards from the menu
- Click on the Subform/ Subreport option from the Controls gallery
- On the report, you can position the pointer and click to place the subreport

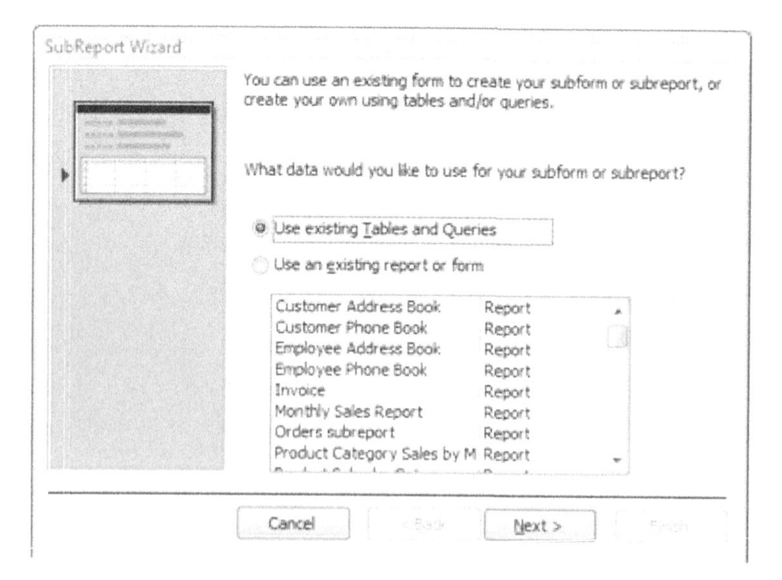

Printing and Exporting Reports

You can also print reports from the Access screen very easily. The steps to follow are as follows-

- Go to the Home tab and then go to the View command.

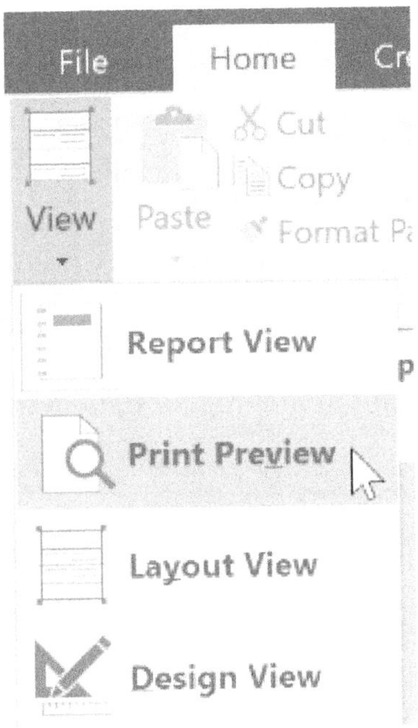

- Then click on the Print Preview option to see the preview version of the document.

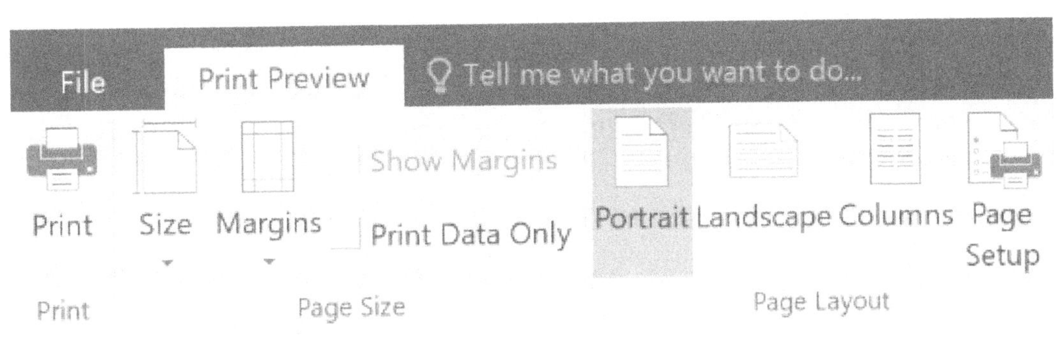

- Once the margins and layout are modified, click on the Print command.
- Once the print dialog box pops up, click on the OK option.

Chapter 6: Advanced Features And Optimization

Indexing and Optimization Techniques

You can use many techniques to optimize and index the database so that the user can access it in a better way. The indexing techniques are as follows-

- The user can define columns that can map to the primary index field.
- The user can also define secondary indexes for a table using the CREATE INDEX statement.
- The user can also use the CREATE INDEX statement to define the indexes of the table.
- The user can also define Search fields in the table to optimize the indexing and searching for data in the table.
- The user can also use the primary key to index and optimize the data of the table.

Advanced Form and Report Design

There are some advanced options that can be added to the Access Ribbon for form design and report design. The advanced options are as follows-

Design- The design option can help you change the color and the theme of the form or report in one click. The user has the ability to add more features to the design tab with this.

Arrange- You can change the layout and arrangement of the form and reports with the arrange tab.

Format- You can change the format and overall layout of the form as well as the background with the help of the format option on the ribbon.

These three options can be activated once your Forms Design View is activated and Forms Design Tools are added to the ribbon.

Tab Controls and Navigation Forms

- You can Create a Navigation form for your report or table with the Create Option from the Ribbon.
- You can then access the Forms Group, and then the Navigation menu will drop down.
- From this Navigation menu, you can see a number of form layouts and navigation modes. You can select the layout and navigation form and then drag the form to the workspace to position it in the right place.

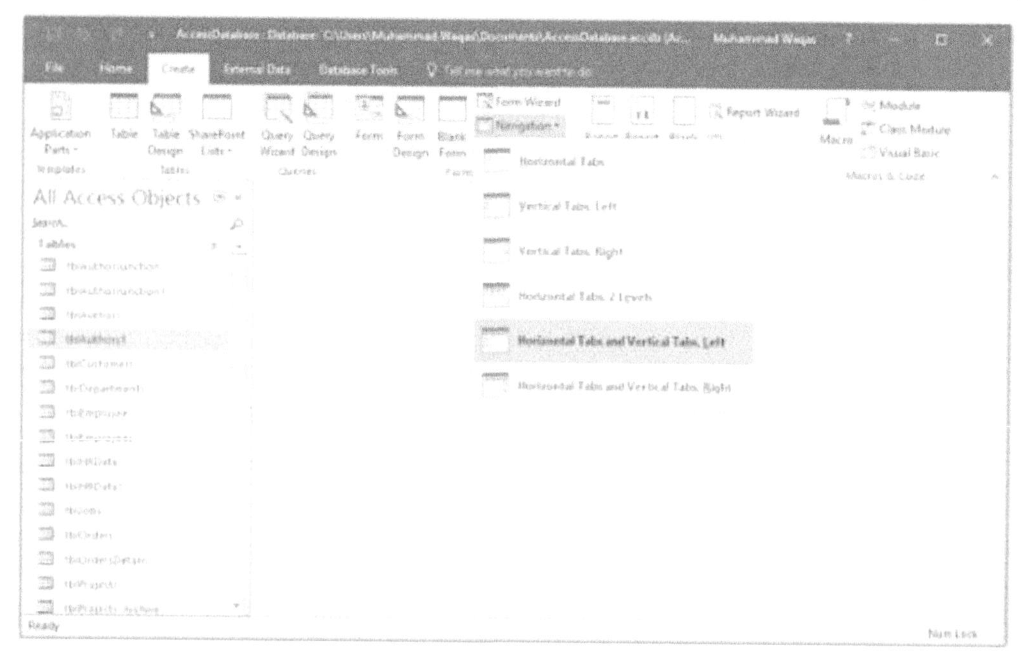

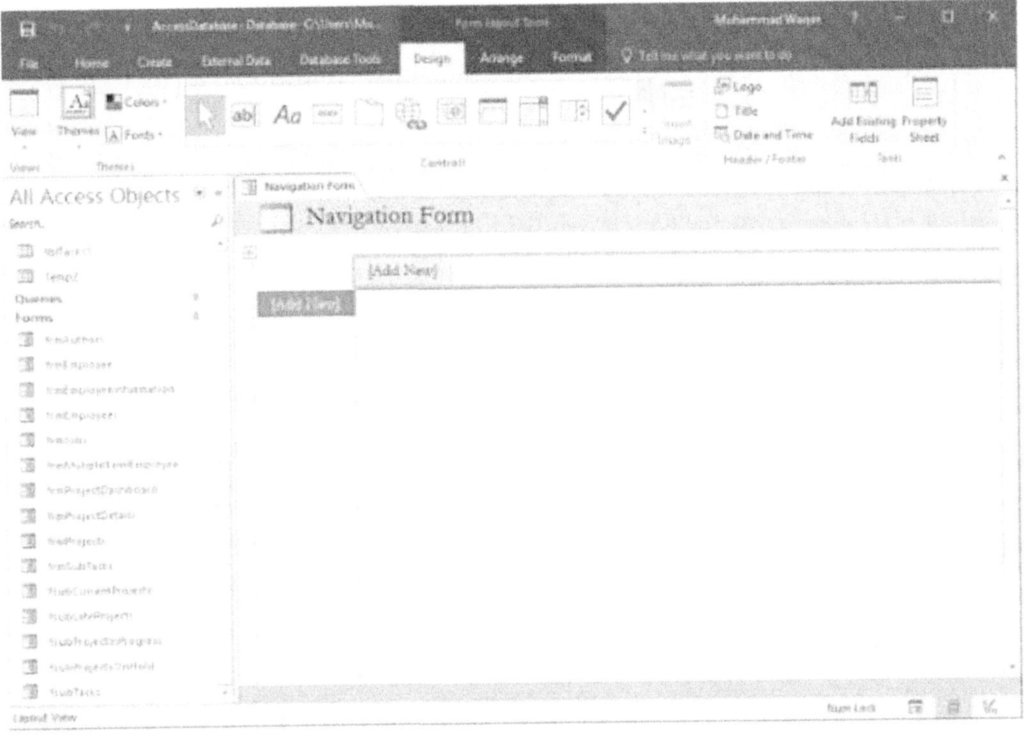
File
Home
Create
External Data
Database Tools
Design
Arrange
Format
View
Themes
Colors
Fonts
Logo
Title
Date and Time
Add Existing Fields
Property Sheet
Controls
Header / Footer
All Access Objects
Queries
Forms
Navigation Form
[Add New]
Layout View

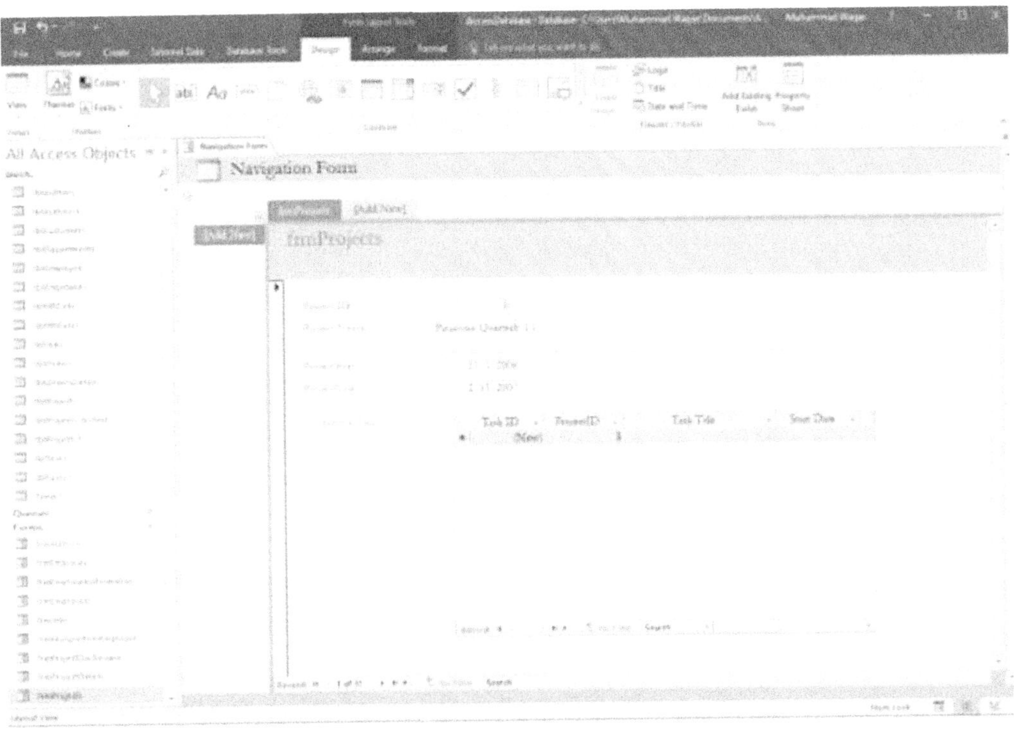
All Access Objects
Navigation Form
[Add New]
frmProjects

Conditional Formatting

The user can do conditional formatting of a report in Access. The steps to apply conditional formatting are as follows-

- You need to open the report in Layout View. Right-click on the Report button in the navigation pane and then click on the Layout View tab.
- After this, you need to select all the controls for which conditional formatting needs to be applied.
- Go to the Format Tab, then go to the Conditional Formatting Group, and then click on Conditional Formatting.
- From the many commands in the box, you can select the New Rule option.
- The New Formatting Rule box opens, in which you can select the value you want under the Select A New Rule Type tab.
- The Edit the rule description will ask you the description of the new rule you want to set.
- Click on the OK tab and then go to the Rules Manager Dialog Box and click OK again to set the conditional formatting rule you want.

These actions can set the rules for conditional formatting for your report.

Conclusion

The MS Access application is an essential application of the MS Office Suite for professionals who deal with large data sets. Since the professional world runs on data these days, learning how to create and manage databases in the DBMS from Microsoft is very necessary for your company workforce.

The commands and access points of MS Access are designed to increase the accessibility and usability of the application so one can create tables, databases, relational databases, reports, and forms.

Data can be stored and managed really well on the MS Access app. You can install the Application on your desktop or your laptop and use it if you already have MS Office.

The organization, formatting, arithmetic calculations, and other processes of data can be done easily with the MS Access Database Management System. This application has been existing for the last two decades and continues to evolve into an important application for companies and professionals. The storing, managing, and computing of data is easy with the help of MS Access. The MS Access interface can be used to deal with large-scale data that needs to be studied and arranged for better understanding. Even professional-level reports can be created with the use of this application and its command. MS Access is a very basic but useful application that can be used to strengthen the workflow of a workspace.

Microsoft OneDrive

Introduction

OneDrive is a popular file hosting service by Microsoft which offers the flexibility for accessing your files from anywhere. It was released in August 2007 and has become one of the most promising tools for document sharing alongside enjoying access to online storage. Some users require higher storage space for their files while others need to maintain backup for their documents in case of emergency. However, the lack of immediate access to storage space and the complexity of managing different portable storage devices such as flash drives can create significant setbacks for users. Microsoft OneDrive offers a promising solution to such issues of all Microsoft users.

OneDrive is the cloud storage solution of Microsoft that helps you with secure storage of all files in a specific location. It allows you to access files from anywhere with different types of devices, including iPhones, Android phones, Windows phones, Mac and Windows systems. Interestingly, users can access OneDrive on their PCs, smartphones, tablets or directly over the internet through their browsers.

You can find multiple reasons to use Microsoft OneDrive other than the advantage of accessing your files through multiple devices. Microsoft provides the assurance of data security by leveraging robust encryption techniques and best practices. OneDrive also allows users to synchronize their data easily from a local folder to the cloud. Another significant value advantage of Microsoft OneDrive is the ease of collaboration with the flexibility for sharing data with co-workers as well as friends and family. For example, you could send a file through email to multiple recipients in your project team and each member would have their own copy of the file. However, a Microsoft OneDrive link to the same file would ensure that all members would access a shared copy of the file. If any member makes changes in the file, then the other team members could view the changes.

Furthermore, OneDrive also offers the facility of data backup, which safeguards your valuable data from ransomware attacks and data loss. Most important of all, it could help you free up a lot of storage space on your device, which would ensure that it works at an optimal level.

This eBook offers you a comprehensive guide to Microsoft OneDrive and its exclusive features. You can learn how to install and set up OneDrive on your device alongside understanding the interface of OneDrive. The eBook also helps you in understanding the advanced features of OneDrive including security and privacy settings. You can use the eBook as an instruction manual for making the most out of OneDrive with detailed description of steps for uploading and managing your files. The other highlights of the eBook include versioning and file recovery in OneDrive.

Chapter 1:Getting Started with OneDrive

Microsoft OneDrive completed its 16th anniversary in August 2023 and still remains as one of the trusted cloud storage solutions. As a Microsoft user, you could get started with OneDrive right away and make the most of free storage space of 5GB. You can also increase the storage capacity with premium monthly or yearly subscription plans. However, you must learn how to set up OneDrive and create an account alongside familiarizing with the OneDrive interface before you use OneDrive.

Setting Up OneDrive

OneDrive offers you an exclusive platform for storing, sharing and synchronizing your files. It provides the flexibility for internal and external file sharing alongside real-time collaboration on MS Office documents. You can access OneDrive functionalities with a Microsoft account. If you are a Windows user, you could make the most of a powerful cloud storage solution. You can find the first step for setting up your OneDrive account from the right side of the taskbar.

You can click on the "Start OneDrive" option on the official Microsoft website.

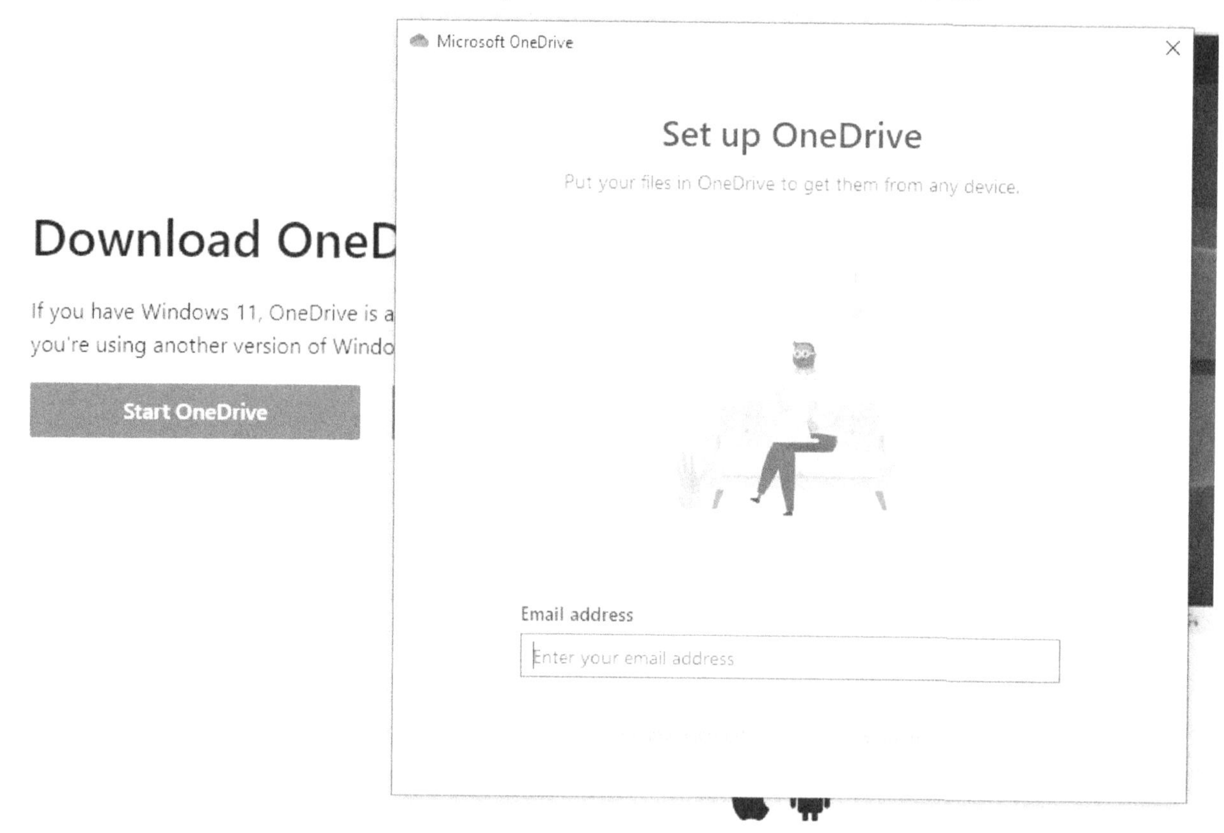

Installation and Configuration

The best thing about OneDrive is that it is already available on systems which run Windows 11. You can use the following link to access the official Microsoft website and download OneDrive.

https://www.microsoft.com/en-in/microsoft-365/OneDrive/download?ocid=cmmuspimg88&rtc=1

Microsoft | Microsoft 365 OneDrive Business Plans and pricing Features Resources Download

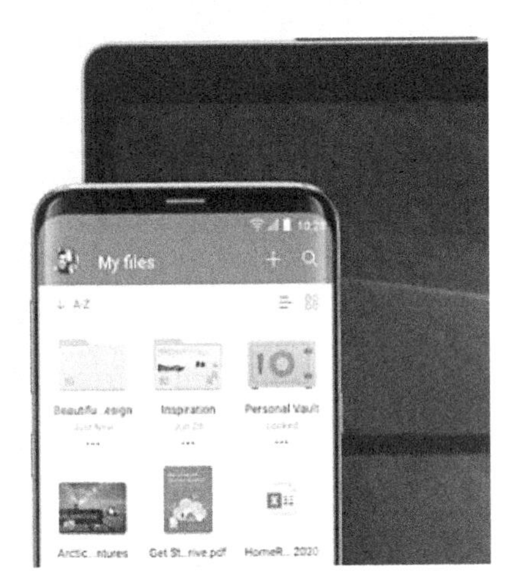

Download OneDrive

If you have Windows 11, OneDrive is already installed on your PC. If you're using another version of Windows, install OneDrive to get started.

Start OneDrive | Download

Click on the "Download" option on the official site of Microsoft OneDrive.

You would download the OneDrive setup file and you can find the file in the 'Downloads' folder.

Click on the setup file and you would find the following prompt on your screen

Once the setup is complete, OneDrive would be ready to use.

Creating a OneDrive Account

The next step in setting up OneDrive involves creating your OneDrive account. One of the trusted options for creating your OneDrive account involves clicking on the OneDrive icon in the taskbar. You can also use the following link for accessing the official Microsoft website to create an OneDrive account.

Click on the 'Create free account' button and you would be redirected to the 'Create Account' page. Here is what it would look like.

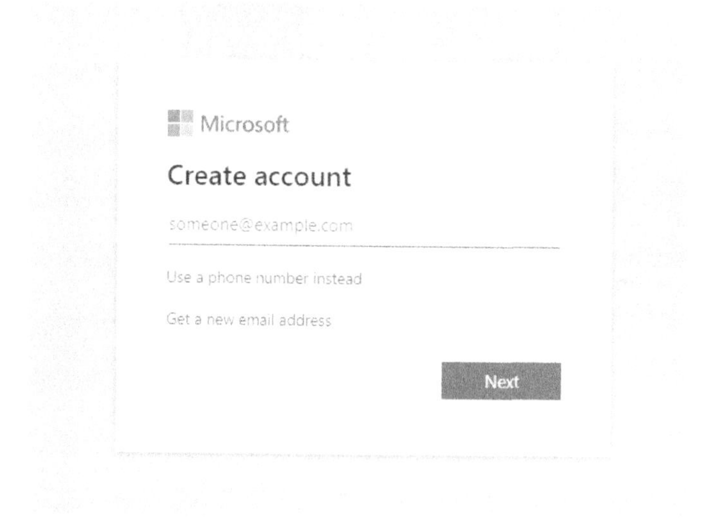

Enter the email address with which you want to create the OneDrive account and click on 'Next'. You would find the following prompt for creating a password for your OneDrive account.

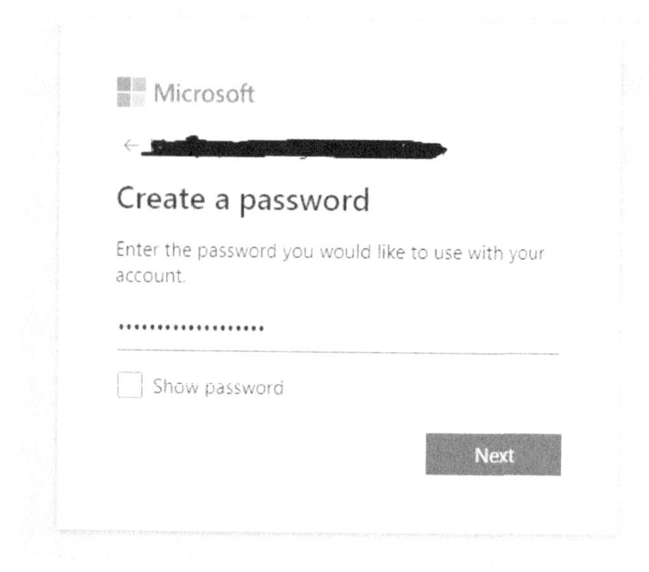

Enter a strong password and click on 'Next' to move to the next stage. Now, you have to enter your first name and last name in the required fields for setting up your account.

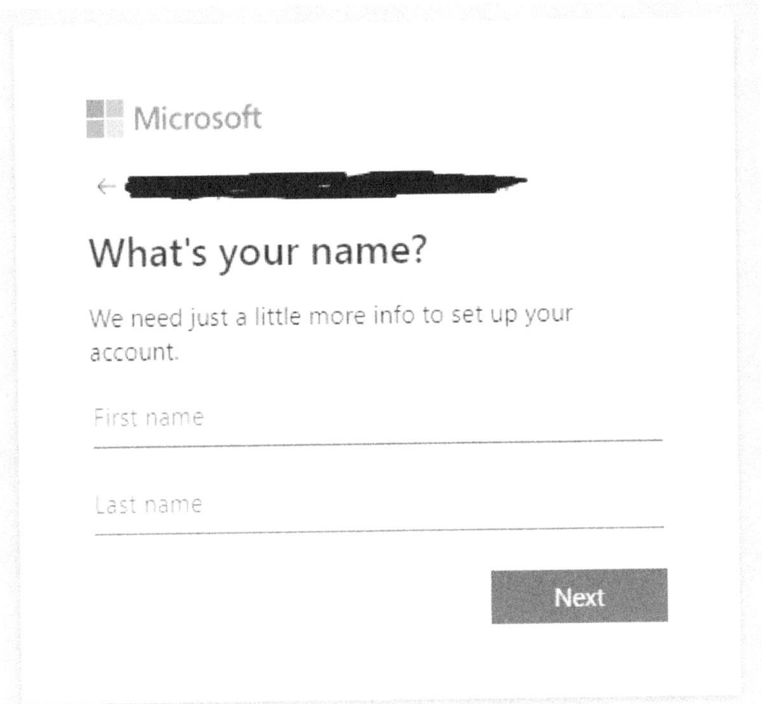

After entering your first name and last name, you can hit on "Next" to move to the next step where you have to specify your birthdate and country. Fill up the details and click on the "Next" button.

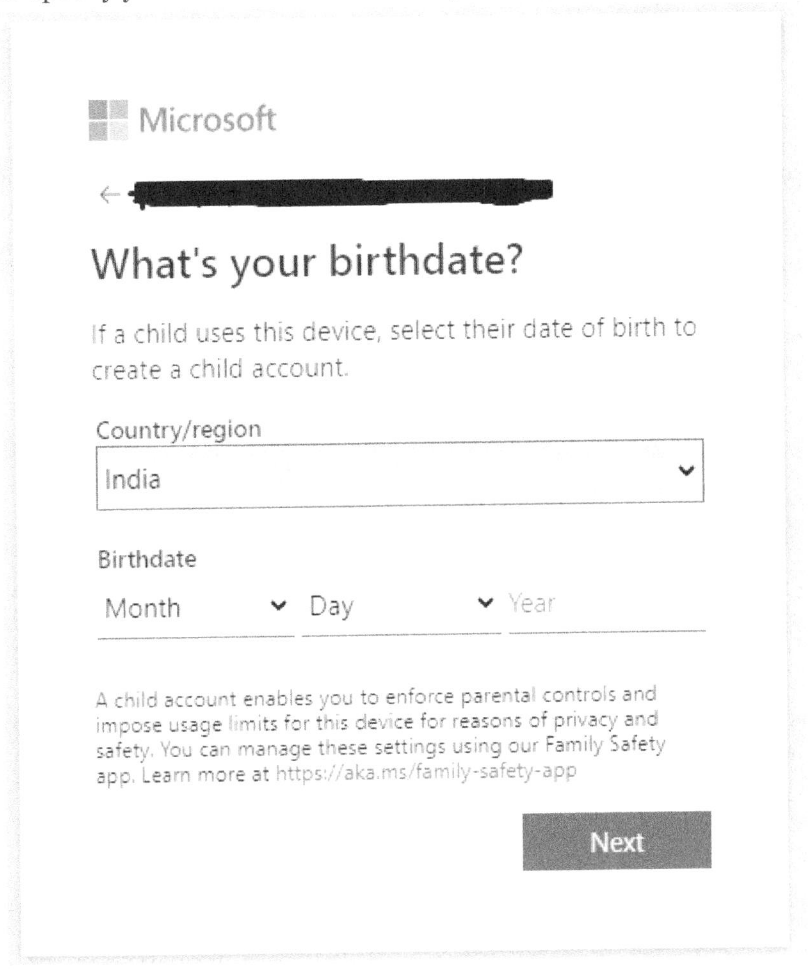

In this step, you have to enter the code sent to the email you have entered for creating the OneDrive account. Check your email for the code and click on "Next" for completing the account creation process.

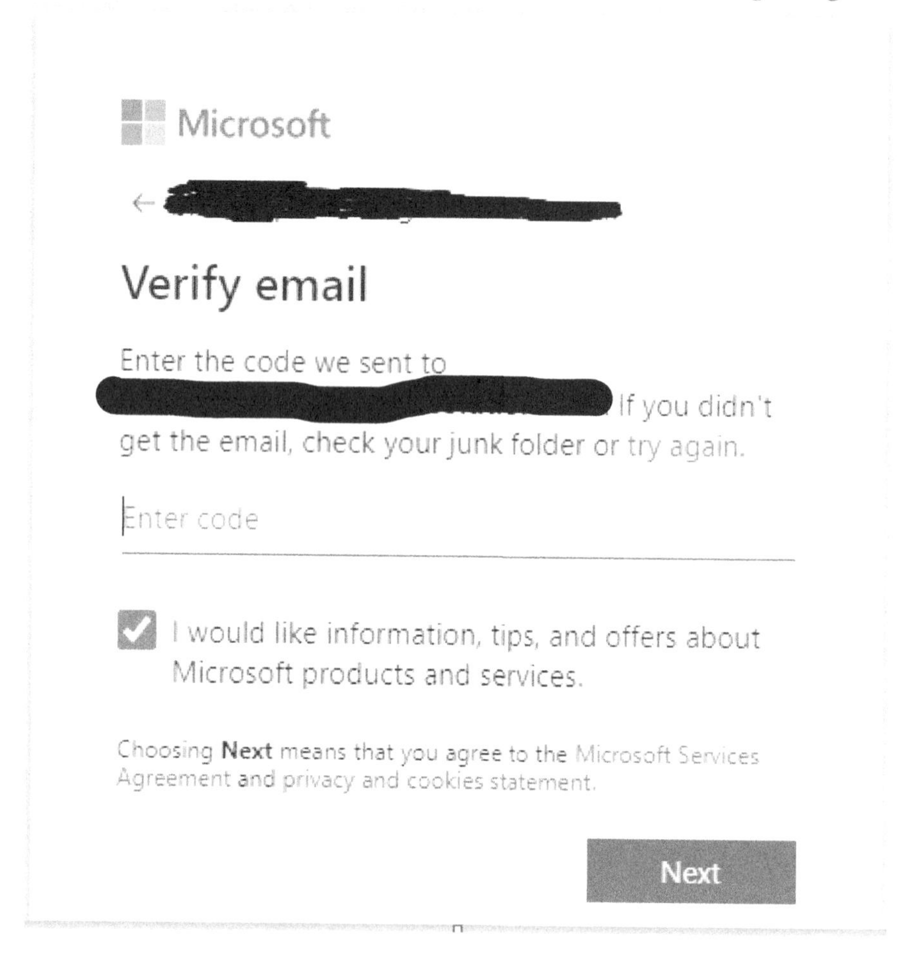

Navigating the OneDrive Interface

Once you have installed and set up your OneDrive account, you can start exploring the OneDrive interface. The interface for OneDrive looks like the following image.

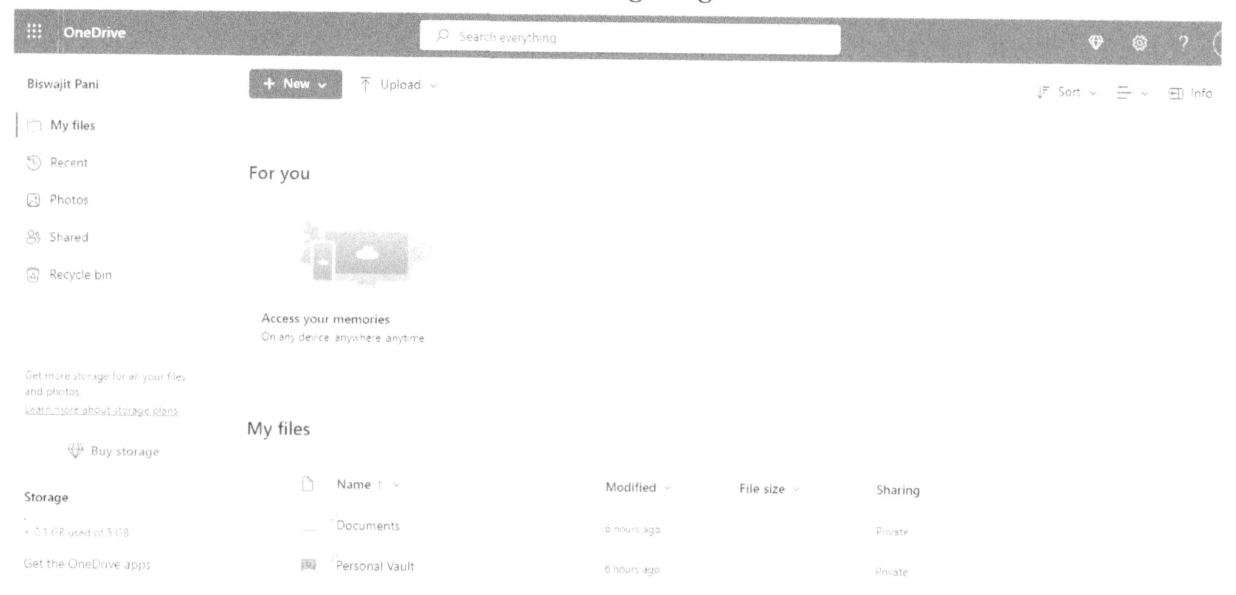

Understanding the interface of OneDrive could help you use the tool according to your desired use cases. At the same time, it also ensures that you can extract the true potential of OneDrive for storing and accessing your files. The interface shows your files in the "My files" list with details of the folder name, date of modification, file size and sharing privileges.

On the top left side of the interface, you can find different buttons such as "My Files", "Recent", "Photos", "Shared" and "Recycle Bin". Each button serves a distinct purpose as implied by their names. You can also notice the "New" button on the interface. It helps in creating a new folder, a MS Word document, an Excel workbook or a PowerPoint presentation directly in OneDrive. Users can also notice the "Upload" option near the "New" button. The "Upload" option allows you to upload files or folders according to your needs.

On the bottom left side of interface, you could find details about the storage capacity consumed by your files. The other details in the interface include the 'Sort' and 'Info' options alongside the button for modifying the type of display for the files. The interface also includes buttons for information about new upgrades and plans alongside settings and support for OneDrive users.

Web Interface

Users can access the web interface of OneDrive by using the "Sign in" option on the official website of Microsoft OneDrive. The latest OneDrive experience through the web interface works as an impressive functional and visual upgrade for accessing your files and maintaining the organization of your content. With the upgraded interface, you can access all the personal and shared files in OneDrive with ease.

Desktop & Mobile App

Another impressive factor in using OneDrive is the availability of desktop and mobile apps. You can use OneDrive on your phone, tablets or desktops for ensuring secure accessibility of files from any location. Users can download the app for OneDrive from Google Play Store. It is important to remember that you would have the OneDrive app pre-installed on Windows 10 phones. You can sign in to the OneDrive app with your work account for viewing and sharing the files on OneDrive. Users can also leverage the "Settings" for adding another account such as their personal account on OneDrive. Interestingly, you can access your OneDrive files from Microsoft Office mobile apps such as Word, PowerPoint and Excel.

Chapter 2: Uploading And Managing Files

Microsoft OneDrive is an effective solution for uploading, storing and managing your files and memories in a secure manner. At the same time, it also ensures that all your files are updated and easily accessible throughout all devices. However, storing all your files in one place could present some issues in terms of organization and management. Therefore, it is important to familiarize with the essential steps for using Microsoft OneDrive to ensure that you have everything in the right place.

Uploading Files and Folders

You can upload files and folders directly to OneDrive by using the "Upload" option in the OneDrive user interface. Click on the "Upload" button and select 'Files' or 'Folder' depending on what you want to upload.

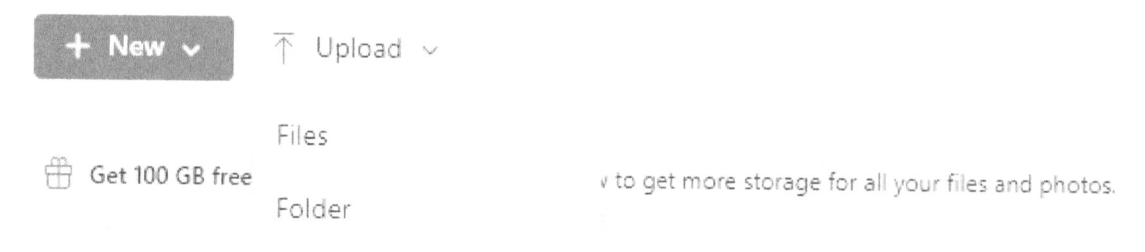

Let's assume that you select the 'Files' option. It would open up a box that allows you to select the file you want to upload. Once you select the file and click on 'Open', OneDrive would upload the file to "My files" section.

You can follow the same process for uploading folders by clicking on the "Folder" option after selecting 'Upload'. Remember that you would find a prompt asking your confirmation before uploading the content of a folder to OneDrive.

Organizing Files and Folders

The next pressing concern for any OneDrive user would be the best practices for organizing files and folders. Interestingly, you can find the ideal solution for organizing your files and folders on OneDrive directly through the "My files" section on the interface.

My files

Name ↑	Modified	File size	Sharing
Documents	7 hours ago		Private
Personal Vault	7 hours ago		Private
Pictures	2 hours ago		Private
Getting started with OneDrive.pdf	7 hours ago	1.10 MB	Private
IMG-20230331-WA0012.jpg	6 minutes ago	141 KB	Private

The "My files" section provides a comprehensive view of the details of files and folders uploaded to OneDrive. You can view the status of modification in the files in terms of time since the last modification. The "My files" section also offers a clear indication of the file size alongside the sharing privileges for the file or folder.

Creating Folders and Subfolders

The process to create folders and subfolders on Microsoft OneDrive is also an easy task. You can use the "New" button on the OneDrive interface for creating new folders and subfolders within few clicks.

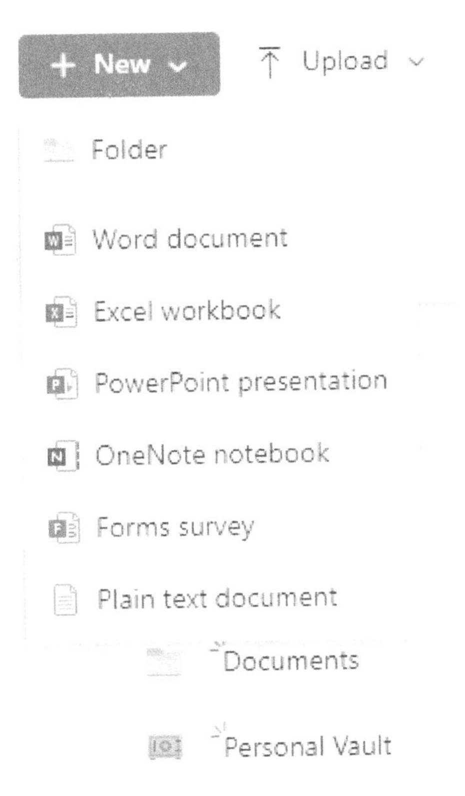

Click on the "Folder" option after selecting the "New" button on the OneDrive interface. You would find the following prompt asking you for the name of the folder.

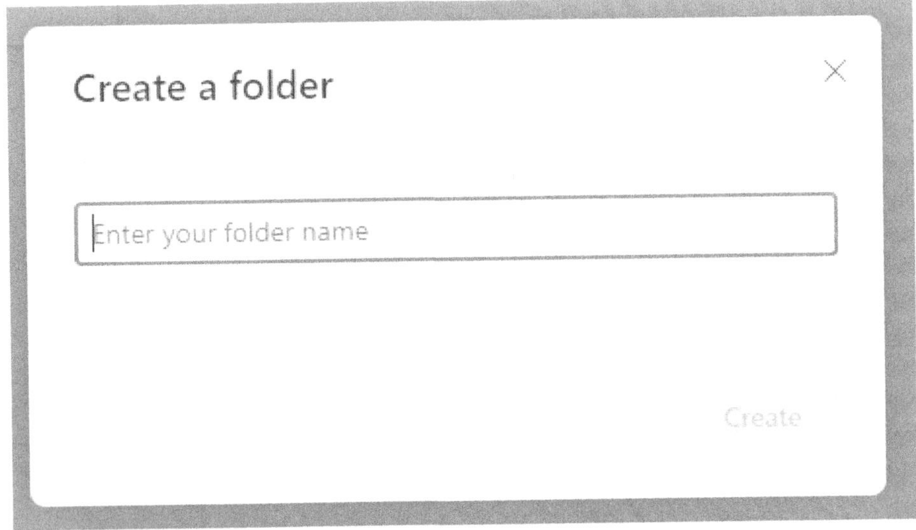

You can enter the desired folder name and click on 'Create' for creating a new folder. The same process can be repeated for creating subfolders in OneDrive.

Moving and Copying Files

The simplicity of Microsoft OneDrive is one of its foremost strengths. You can find the easiest ways for moving and copying files directly from the OneDrive interface. First of all, you have to select the file you want to move or copy in the "My files" list.

Now, you can click on the three dots next to the name of the file you want to move or copy. Upon clicking the three dots, you would find the options of "Move to" and "Copy to".

Click on the option you want to implement for your files and then follow the instructions for completing the action. You can notice that you don't need advanced technical expertise for organizing your files on OneDrive according to your requirements.

Sorting and Filtering Options

You can sort or filter the files and folders on OneDrive directly from the OneDrive interface. Look for the "Sort" button on the interface and click on it. You would find the following options in the "Sort" section.

The "Sort" option on OneDrive offers three distinct filters such as "Name", "Modified" and "File size". In addition, you can also choose to sort the files and folders in 'My files' in ascending or descending order.

Click on the filter you want to apply for your files and folders and watch how OneDrive arranges everything according to your preferences. The simple process for sorting and filtering allows anyone to use OneDrive without complaints for organization of files.

Chapter 3: Advanced Features And Settings

There are many advanced and important features in OneDrive that you should know about in order to use it properly. Some of these features and settings could be hidden and need to be explained thoroughly.

Customizing OneDrive Settings

In the OneDrive Suite, you can customize the sync settings so that the OneDrive storage is synced with local files. OneDrive does not have the capability to syncing all the cloud files to your local drive on its own. The local OneDrive folder has all the smart files or ghost files that are temporarily held by the folder. This is done to save you space as the files do not take up the entire disk space. Only the files that you need to work on are downloaded to the local drive. If you do not need to work on these files exclusively, there is no file downloaded to the local disk. Otherwise, all the files are present only in the Cloud space. However, if there is no sync, then the files will not be available when you are in offline mode. To make sure that you can access the important files at all times, you need to sync the OneDrive with your local disk. You need to open your OneDrive folder and make a right click on the given folder which needs to be used at all times. After this, you can choose the make available offline to ensure that the files are available to you on offline mode.

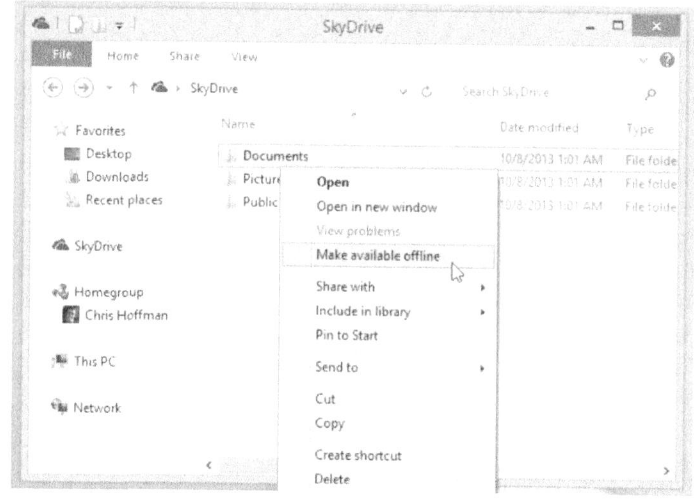

If you need the copy of all the files from the OneDrive to the local disk to access them, then you need to navigate to the OneDrive on your device and use the right hand menu that appears. After that, you need to go to the Settings menu and then click on Options. Then you can set the mode to Access All Files from the Offline to On mode.

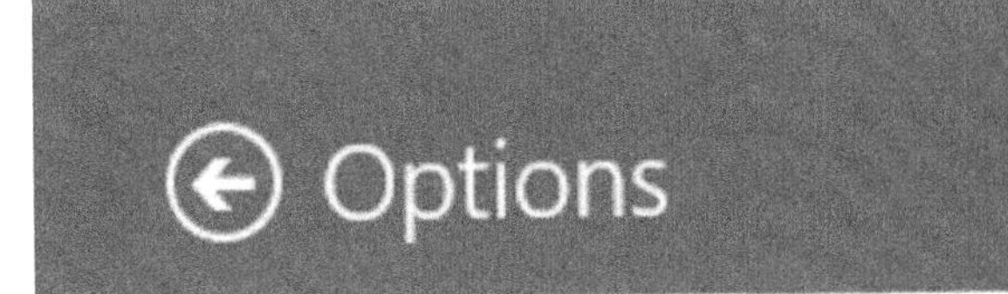

Access all files offline

Off 

Open PC settings to change other
SkyDrive options

How to select to use camera backup from OneDrive

There is another trick that you can use to make your OneDrive storage expand. OneDrive can also back up your camera pictures so that you can save your memories. Turning on the camera backup gives you an additional 3 GB space of storage too. The OneDrive suite also has a Camera Roll feature that backs up your pictures and video files. To use this feature, you need to go to the Charms bar and search for Camera roll. The uploads to the Camera roll folder are turned off under the default mode. You might also choose to go for uploading the photos in higher quality to save storage space on the particular device internal disk. You can choose to upload the photo files and choose to upload the video files differently. Once you turn on these options, the OneDrive folder will back up your Pictures and Videos libraries. The OneDrive folder can also be back up the image and video files from mobile devices. If you install and use OneDrive on your mobile phone, you can earn an extra 3 GB storage space for your local files. This trick works for Windows, iOS and android phones, but you need to install the OneDrive app and turn on the Camera Backup feature.

Upload photos and videos

If you automatically upload photos and videos from your camera roll folder to OneDrive, you can get to them from any device. Higher-quality photos will take up more space on your OneDrive.

- Don't upload photos
- Upload photos at good quality
- Upload photos at best quality

Automatically upload videos to OneDrive

Off 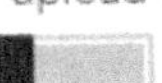

Your photos, always with you
Turn on Camera backup to automatically upload your photos to OneDrive. You'll get 3 GB of additional storage for free.
Turn on

Security and Privacy Settings

There are strong security and privacy provisions that you can control as the user of OneDrive. You can access the Account Privacy settings in the app. To access the privacy settings, you need to access the Account tab on the left pane at the bottom. Under the Account Privacy settings, you can choose the Manage Privacy settings. You can select the privacy options to customize. These privacy settings can be applied to all the Office applications like Word, Excel, PowerPoint, Outlook, OneNote etc.

You can also control your sharing settings to increase your privacy. For example, you can go to the OneDrive App and go to My files. Under the sharing tab, you can see that the files are either private or shared in nature. The private files are only accessible to you and the shared files are accessible to the people you choose.

You can also manage access to the shared folders and files by simply clicking on certain options. For example, you can right click on the shared folder and choose the Manage Access option. After you choose the Manage Access option, you can see the Direct Access option. The Direct Access option helps you review the list of everyone who has access to the particular file or folder location. Click on the pencil icon beside the access having person's name and edit the access and the view to read only access. You can also choose the stop sharing option and click on Remove to remove the person from the access list.

How to increase security of your OneDrive app

Here are some steps that you can take to actively increase the security of your OneDrive App.

You can increase the password strength of the OneDrive app. You need to create a strong password that protects your files and your information. You can also add security info like recovery phone number and other details to your particular account. You can also add security questions, and answers so that only you can access the account. You can also switch to two factor authentication to increase the security levels. The two factor authentication is done through a security code which you might get through the phone number, text, or app.

Notifications and Preferences

Get notifications when you are sharing a document on the OneDrive space and when a team member takes any actions on the file. The shared notifications help you know the changes without having to log in again and again and to spot the changes made in the shared document. You can turn the in app notifications so that you get the notifications. You can simply open a particular document and go to the title bar. Then select the

Version History option. If this is on, you will get notifications of the changes made to the document while you are not active.

Windows 10

Android

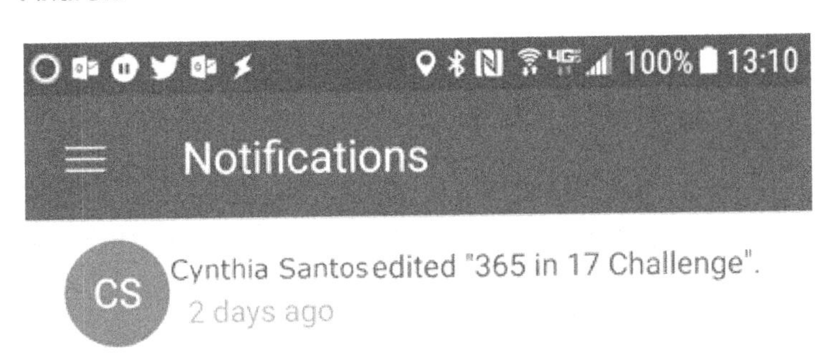

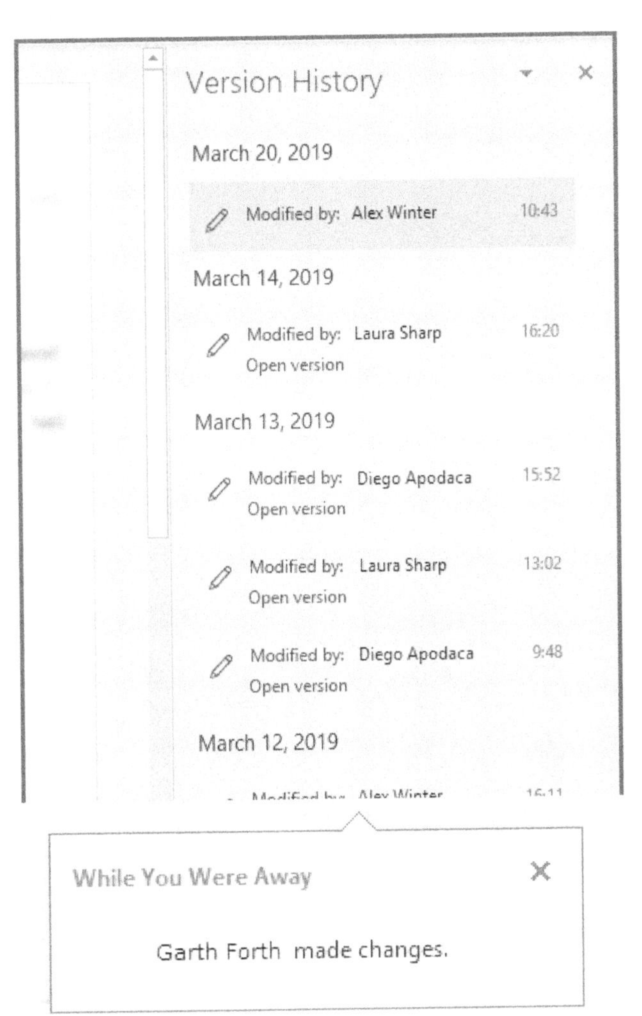

If you are using the Windows version of OneDrive, you can get notifications through the Notification center. The Notification center settings can be changed to manage the notifications. The notifications for shared files will be turned on by default and you can get the alert on screen. You can also turn the notifications on or off for all the files. You can go to the settings of the OneDrive and right click on the app icon present on the task bar. You can then go to the settings menu and then you choose the check box where you can turn on or off the notifications, This will either disable or enable the notifications.

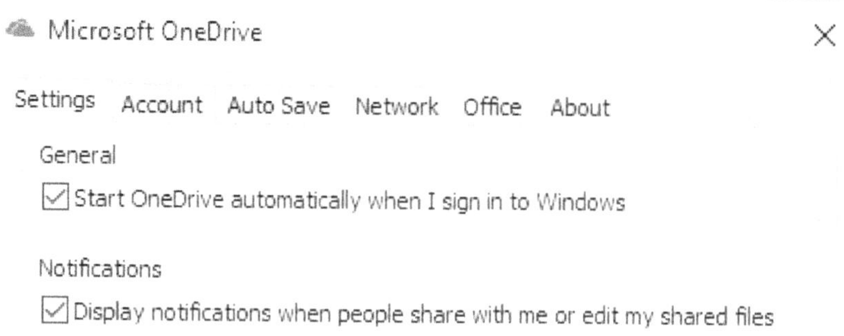

Using OneDrive with Microsoft 365

The OneDrive app can be used with Microsoft 365. The OneDrive app can be used to view your own files like My Files, you can also access shared files through the SharePoint sites. There are a multiple ways in which you can open files on the OneDrive screen. You can access the OneDrive app from the Office.com suite and launching it with the app launcher.

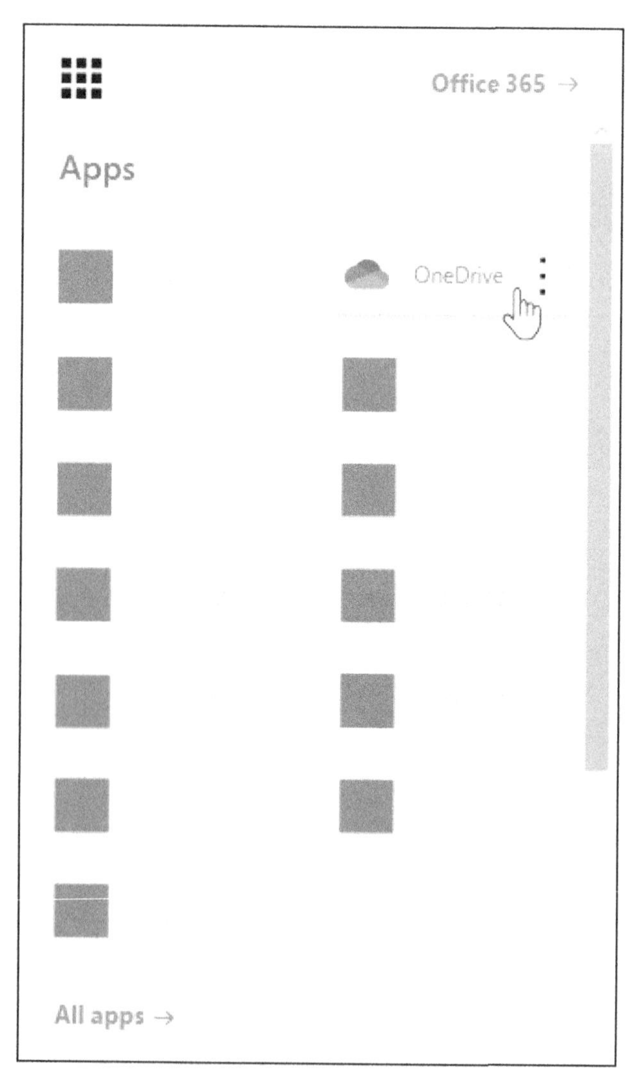

You can choose the Add Account option and create two accounts, one for your personal use and the other for work and you can also switch between them.

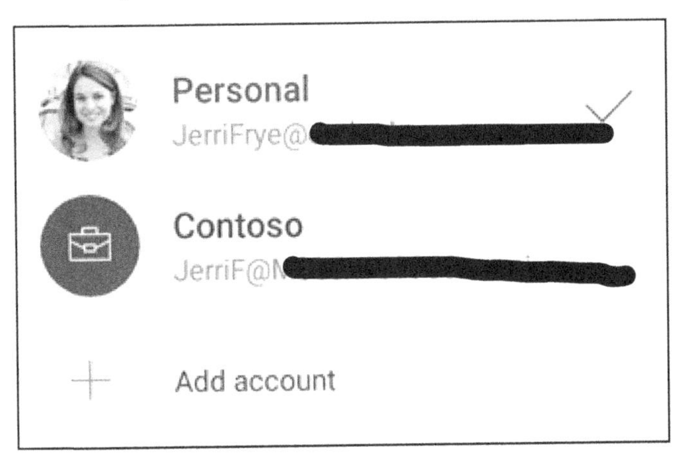

If the files are synced to a users' device, you can access the files through the File developer under OneDrive.

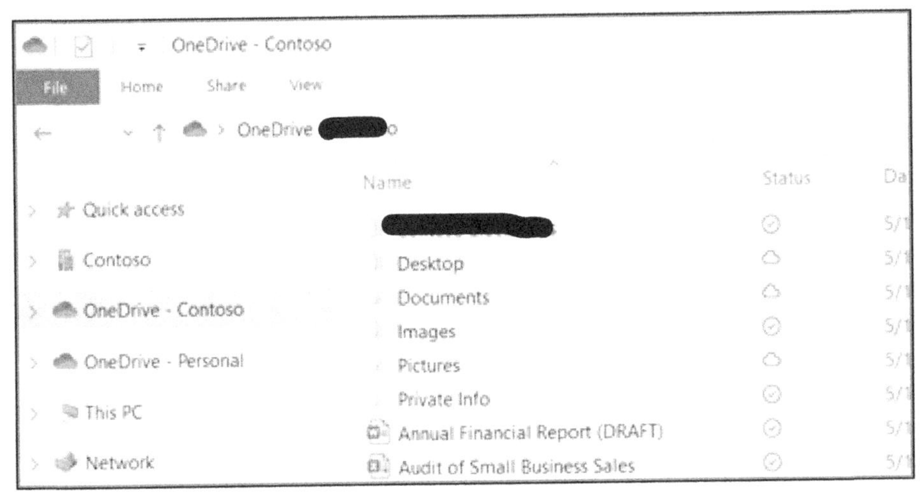

All the files that the user creates with Office Apps are automatically saved to the user's OneDrive. The uploaded files can be up to 250 GB in size so you can store almost all kinds of files. You can also upload files directly in the browser if you are signed into OneDrive.

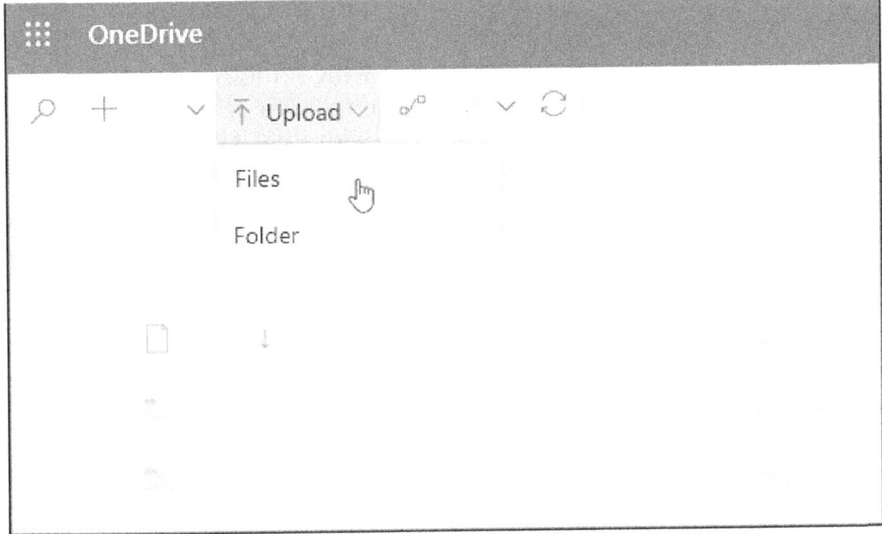

New files and folders can also be created directly from the tool bar.

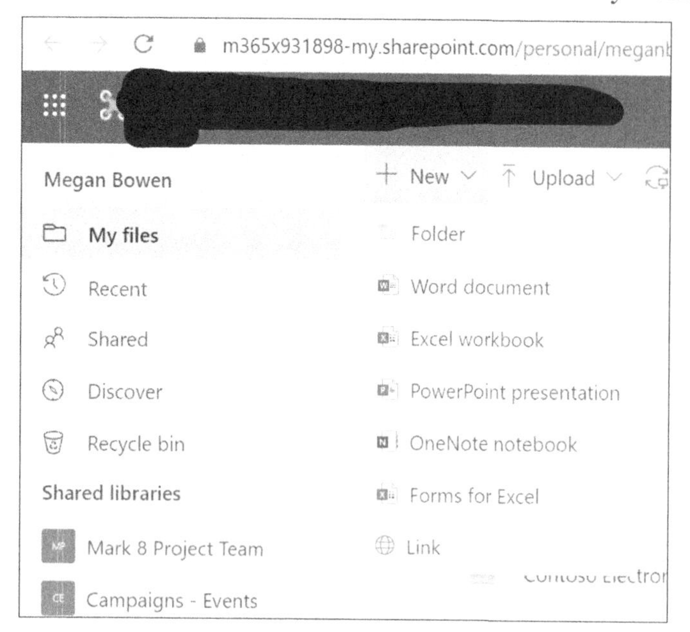

You can also save and open your Office files in OneDrive once they are in sync.

Integration with Office Apps

It is very easy to integrate your Office Apps like Excel, Word, PowerPoint, etc. In order to save the Office files to OneDrive, you need to sign into the OneDrive app when you install Office. You can do the integration from any Office App. The OneDrive and the Office app can work in sync and share document with others.

You can then open the document you want to save to OneDrive and select the File>Save As option, then choose your OneDrive as a saving option and then perform selection on the folder where you want to keep the file in saved mode. This will save the Office files and help you access the copy integrated with OneDrive space. This way you can save a lot of local disk space for your desktop.

Collaborative Features

You can easily collaborate with OneDrive as OneDrive allows you to share files and work on the files simultaneously. There are many collaborative features and settings of OneDrive. In the work environment collaboration with co workers on multiple documents is important. The OneDrive Suite helps a lot in collaboration with its advanced features.

OneDrive has many features that help in full collaboration with work colleagues. OneDrive allows the easy sharing of files between people in a shared workspace. The sharing can be internal or external to the organization with permissions. The OneDrive folders can also be integrated with Windows file explorer so that there is access of files in the offline and online mode. The OneDrive app can also be installed in tablet and other forms of devices so that you can access files from anywhere and collaborate easily.

To share a file in OneDrive, you simply have to click on an uploaded file and then click on share. Then OneDrive will ask you who you want to link with on the file so that it can be shared for work. There are many options of sharing. For example, if the OneDrive settings are turned on for anonymous sharing, you can share the file with anyone in anonymous mode. The file can also be shared with people inside the organization. This will allow the file to be accessible to anyone who has a link to the file shared in the shared space. In the collaborative environment, you can also share the file with desired recipient and only people with existing access can use the file. You can also specify the people who can access the file in your Personal OneDrive folder so that only those specific people can work with the files.

There is a shared section in the OneDrive suite where you can find the files that you have shared with the people in your organization and the files that they have shared with you. You can make this shared space public or private as per settings. For example, you can change the settings with the Manage Access menu options. You can then change the setting from view to edit or Edit to View only depending on whether you want to make it private or shareable with others.

There is also a copy link option that you can use to copy the file link and share it with others. You can click on Copy Link option to create a shareable link that can be pasted in chat or email and shared with colleagues so that they can view and collaborate on a specific file.

How to stop or change sharing mode to stop collaborating

Once you have shared the file and the work is done, it is important to keep your file private. To stop sharing, there are some simple steps that you need to take. When you own the file, keep edit permissions with you so , you can completely change the sharing permissions when needed.

You need to select the file or folder for which sharing needs to stop. After that you tap on the info icon in the upper right corner and then the details pane opens up. After that you need to select the Manage Access button and then tap on the x next to a link and then disable the access. You need to then select the can edit or can view option and then select the stop sharing button. For the same actions, you can select the change to option to change the status of the file in question.

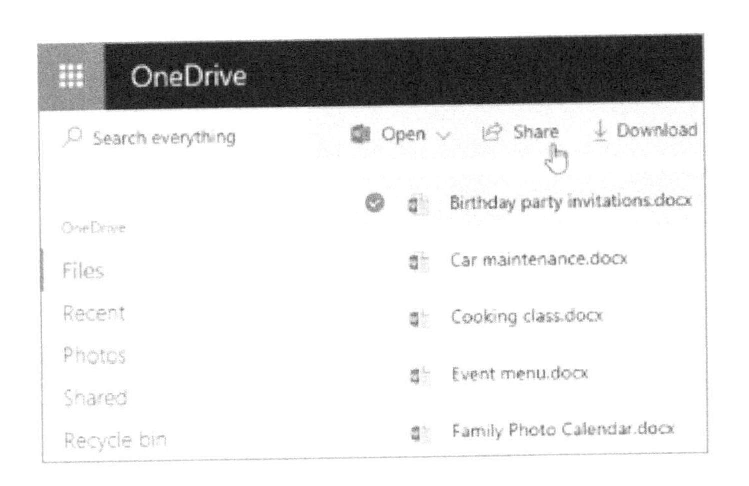

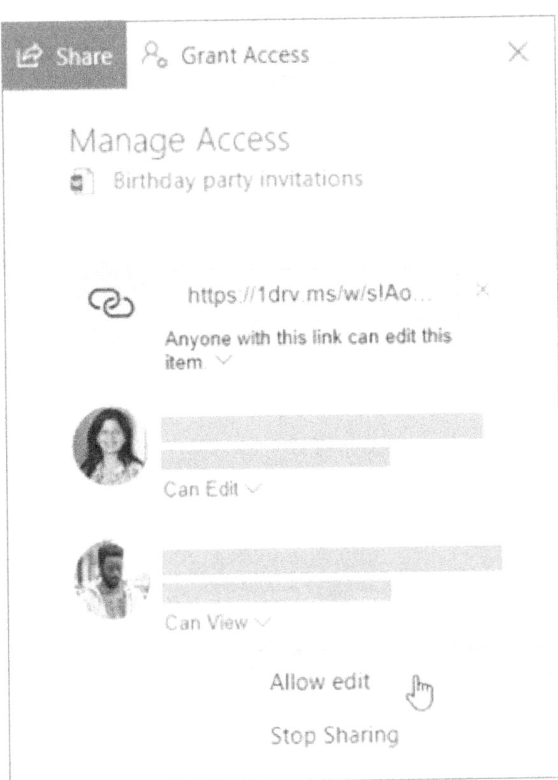

Chapter 4: Versioning And File Recovery

Version History in OneDrive

The version history of OneDrive files are very important because you want to see the different versions during collaboration or an ongoing project. Suppose you need to restore the file to a previous version, you can do the same with the version history and file recovery options. The recovery can happen if the users have not switched off the document version option. The version control is accessible through different apps of Microsoft Office or through the Microsoft 365 suite. From Microsoft Office, if there is a link between OneDrive and the Microsoft Office apps, you can see the versions when you click on the File Tab.

You need to go to the Open file section, and then click on the File tab. You can see the current version in this tab and the earlier versions are listed below them. You can click on a previous version from this list and the file will show that particular previous version. The file name and the date of saving the file will also appear at the top. There are two options that you can use, the compare option and the restore option. If you want to use the previous version as the latest version, then you can click on the restore tab. On the other hand, if the compare tab is clicked, the user monitors whole of the changes made to the document across diverse versions.

The user can also see the version history of a document from the One Drive app if you are using it to access an uploaded file.

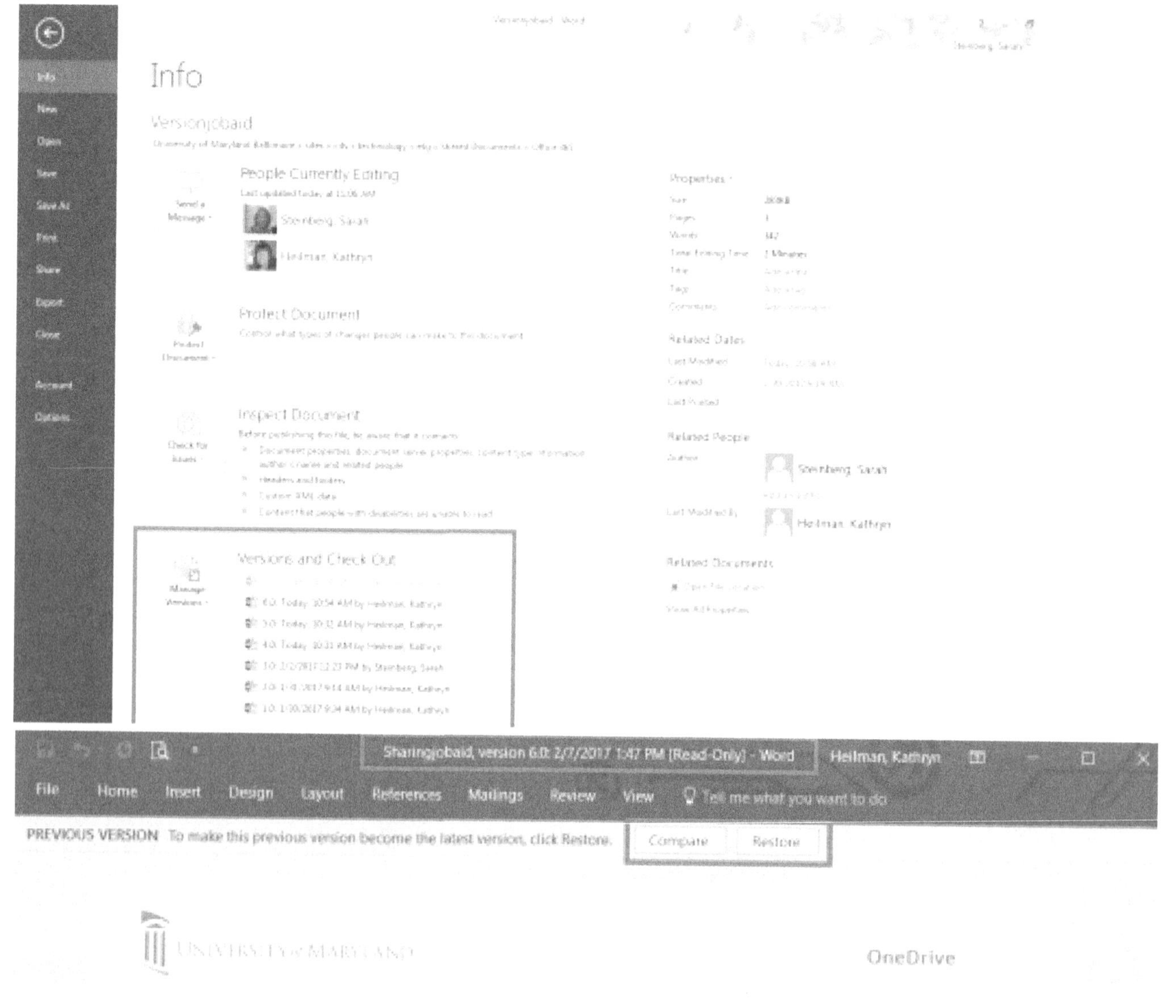

You can go to OneDrive through a portal of the web browser. From the file list stored on OneDrive, right click on the document for which you need to see the version history or restore the file version. After this, you can choose the Version History button and this will show you the history of the file in a separate section.

You can then choose the particular version of the file from the Version history dialog box to view it. The current version of the document is at the top and other versions that were created previously follow it in a top to bottom manner.

Restoring Previous Versions

You can also restore previous versions of certain files from the same window of OneDrive. If you want to work with a certain version or want to save that particular version, then there are some steps you can take. You can also restore deleted files from the OneDrive folder.

To restore a previous version of a OneDrive file,

You need to right click on the document for which you need earlier version restoration. Then you can click on the Version History tab. Once the Version History options appear, you can select the arrow just by the specific document version so that you can opt for document recovery and then you can click on Restore. Next you get a confirmation box where, you can then click on OK.

Once you have clicked on OK, that particular previous version has been restored and it works as a replacement of the current version of the file. The previous version of the specific file is not lost as it becomes the previous version for the document.

You can use the File Explorer of your PC if the File explorer is synced with the OneDrive suite. You can right click on the file for which you want to restore the earlier version. Then you can choose the Version History option from the menu. After this, you can select the ellipses and you can then click on Restore button next to the version you want to go for restoration. The document version clicked on for restoration then becomes the current version of the file.

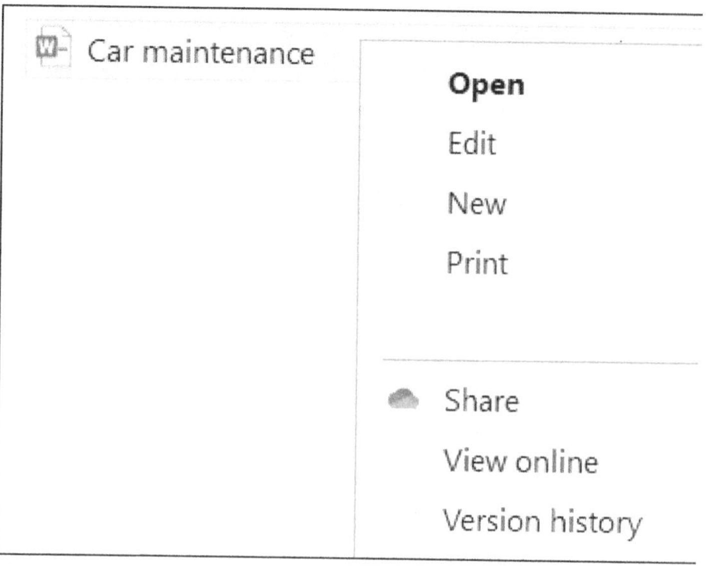

Tracking Changes

You can track changes when a document becomes shared in the OneDrive space. The document could be any Microsoft Office document like an Excel Workbook or a word document. If you have already collaborated and co edited the document, you can also track changes over a time period.

How to track and review changes to a document in OneDrive.

To track changes, you need to click on the Select Review, then click on the Track Changes option. To review a change, place the cursor on top of a red marked change and click on accept or reject the change. When you click on accept, you keep the change, when you click the Reject button, the change is rejected.

In the OneDrive suite, you can track the changes that have been made. In case of a shared document in collaborative space, you can click on Review and then on Track changes and then you can click on Highlight Changes. To see all the changes, you can go the When checklist and then click on All When from the list, while also clearing the Who and Where boxes. To view the changes that have been made after a particular date, you can choose the When check box and click on the Since Date from the list to sort according to date of change.

If as the owner of the workbook, you want to view the changes made by a particular shared user, then you can also select the Who check list and then click on the particular user for whom you want to see the changes made.

You can also see the changes in a particular manner if you like by choosing the different options of display. You can highlight the changes in the Workbook by clicking on the Highlight changes on screen checkbox. You can also display the particular changes in order in a different worksheet, by opting for the List changes on a new sheet option.

Recovering Deleted Files

By mistake, it is possible that you or one of your team members deletes a saved file from the OneDrive folder. If a file or folder from OneDrive is accidentally deleted, you can recover it from the Recycle bin section of OneDrive.

If you are signed into the OneDrive account, you can go to the navigation panel and select the Recycle bin option. You can then select the files or folders you want to put through restoration by pointing to each item and clicking on the check box given after which you click on Restore. If you use your personal account and personal OneDrive, then you also have the Restore All Items option in the Recycle bin to restore all deleted files that are in the trash.

If you deleted certain files from your OneDrive folder, you can click on the Recycle bin from your Windows home screen and see if the deleted files are still in the Recycle bin. Then you can take action to recover and restore the deleted files.

Next, open the computer Recycle Bin app and then select the files meant for document recovery. You can then right click on them and click on Restore from the pop up menu. The file or folder selected goes through restoration and return to the OneDrive folder and the deletion will be reversed. The same action can be taken on different operating systems and PC.

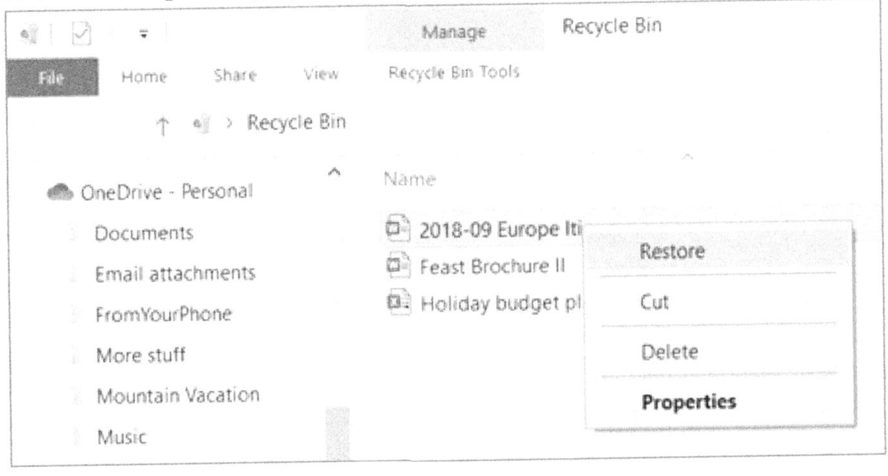

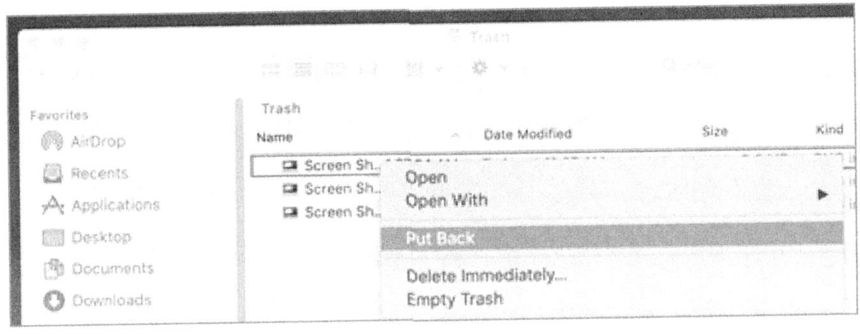

Recycle Bin in OneDrive

The Recycle bin of the OneDrive is different from the Recycle bin or trash of the PC. When you delete an item like a folder or a file from the OneDrive space, it is not immediately permanently deleted. The deleted files and folders go into the site recycle bin that the user can access through certain commands. The files and folders stay in the Recycle bin space after deletion for a period of 90 days or 3 months. The user can access the site Recycle bin and take actions on the temporarily deleted files. He can either restore the deleted files to the OneDrive Workspace or he can delete the files and folders permanently from the Recycle Bin.

To take actions, you need to access the Microsoft Portal by logging into the app through the http://portal.office.com/ link. After logging in, you can go to the OneDrive location through its icon. You can see the Recycle Bin present in the left side of navigation panel. You can then click on the Files icon where all your files and folders that have been previously deleted are present in list form.

If you want to restore a file from the Recycle bin, you can click on that particular file or folder and then the icon on the top changes to Delete or Restore. You can then select the Restore button for file restoration.

All the files in the OneDrive Recycle bin cannot be restored after 180 days of deletion because then all the files get deleted permanently. You can also take the decision to delete permanently if you want.

Permanent Deletion and Recovery

You can take actions to do permanent deletion if needed from the Recycle bin. The deletion of One Drive files can be done through the same process as recovery. You can click on the file that you want to delete, which also works for a temporarily deleted folder and then they will be selected with a tick mark appearing in blue. After this, you can click on Delete which will permanently delete the files.

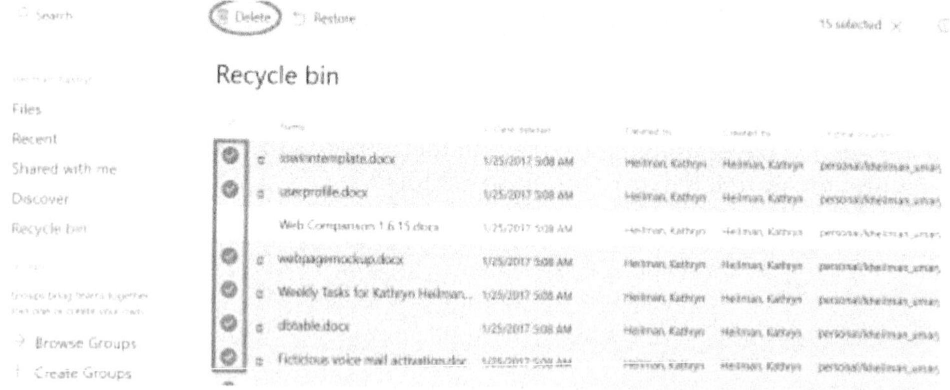

You can also take action to delete more than one files. This is done by choosing the Files option and then deleting more files. You can also choose to Empty the entire recycle bin by simply choosing the Empty Recycle Bin option.

This will remove all the files that are in the Recycle bin or Trash.

There are some points about the OneDrive Recycle bin that you should keep in mind. If you have signed into OneDrive with the help of your Microsoft Account, the temporarily deleted files present in the recycle bin go through automatic deletion after 30 days of the initial deletion from the user account. If you sign into OneDrive with a work account, the files last in the Recycle bin for almost 90 days and then get permanently deleted. However, the administrator can change the settings around these durations and change the duration for which the files are available for recovery in the Recycle bin.

If the files are deleted from the Online only mode, they will not be in the PC Recycle bin. To access the files from Online Only mode, you have to access the OneDrive Recycle bin by signing into the MS office portal with your Microsoft account.

It is also interesting to note that if you had been working on a shared folder or file, you can no longer access it or recover it from the Recycle bin when you are not the original creator. You will get an email or a notification telling you that the shared folder has been deleted, so you cannot take any particular action on it anymore. When you are the original creator and shared the folder with others, any kind of deletion happening with the file or folder is reflected in your Recycle bin. You can then restore the file contents from your Recycle bin if you want or permanently delete them.

These are some of the actions taken on files or some points taken into consideration for the files to be used. The recycle bin is there to manage any kind of accidental or intentional deletion and you can then take further action on it. If you want something permanently deleted, you can either go for deletion yourself or wait for some months for the files to be deleted permanently on their own.

Chapter 5: Accessing OneDrive Anywhere

OneDrive on Web Browsers

OneDrive is a suite of storage space that is available on multiple systems, whether it Windows, a browser, mobile operating systems or Macs. In this section, we will study how you can access and use OneDrive on Web Browsers. You can access, edit and co author documents on OneDrive even when you are doing it through a browser. Here are the steps to open OneDrive in your browser. Follow these steps to open OneDrive and use its capabilities on the internet.

You can open the site of office.com and sign into Office suite from the browser. After this, you can access OneDrive through the Office.com controls. Once you access the OneDrive suite, you can right click on a file and select a command to execute. You can also edit and use your documents on the web with the help of Microsoft 365 for the web and OneDrive. You can use Microsoft 365 through the web on any device and you will be able to use full Office capabilities for files that are uploaded and accessed through OneDrive.

To use Microsoft 365 through the web, you have to first upload files on OneDrive in the web version. For this, you need to sign in as a user to OneDrive.com. After this, you need to click on the Upload button and then pick the files from File Explorer so that you can upload and access them on OneDrive from any system or browser. Once you upload the files, the files will be visible on the OneDrive workspace. You can click on the document and the action will open up the document on the web version of Microsoft 365 even if the system you are opening it on does not have Microsoft 365 installed in it.

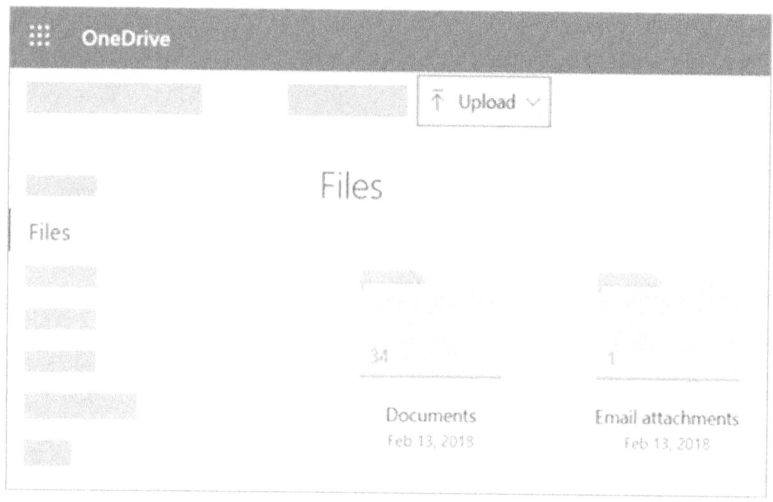

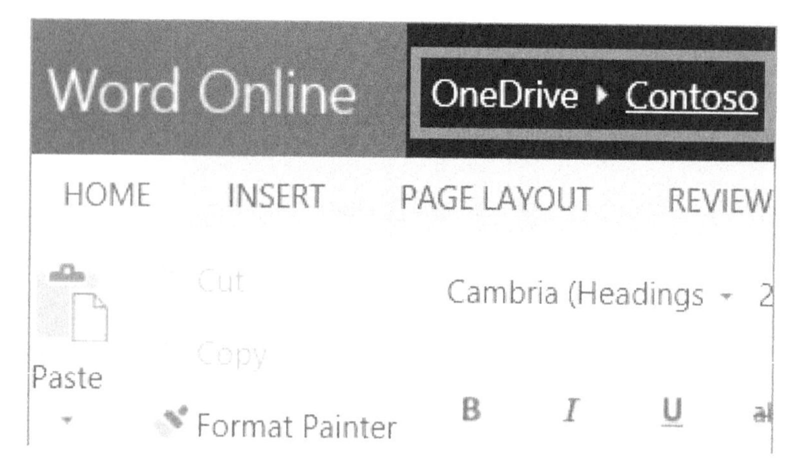

The document that opens up opens on the edit mode by default so that the user can edit and the changes are saved easily and automatically. You can then close the document and go back to the file list by clicking on one of the back links present on the top of the web page.

You can also create a OneDrive Document in the web space if necessary through the browser. You can access the suite and then click on New button to create a new document. After clicking on the New button, you will get a drop down menu of what type of documents can be created. Once you get that, you can select the type of document to create. You can also create a new folder. All these actions you can do if you have a pre existing Microsoft account.

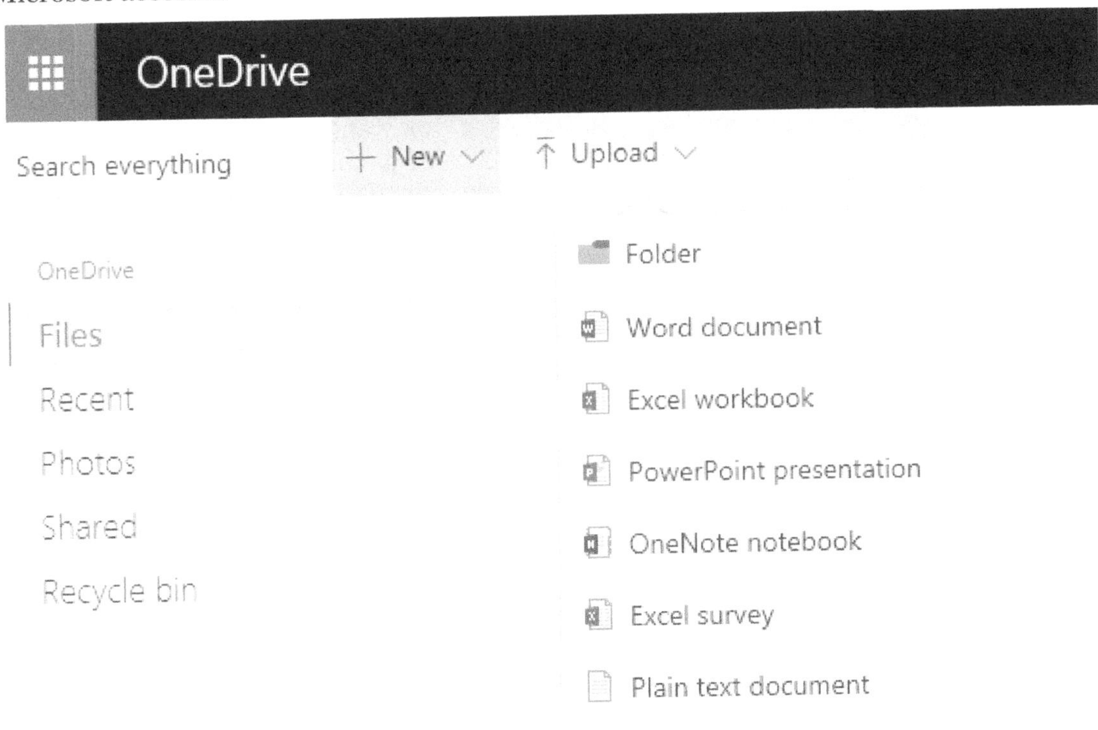

You can also save the documents to Web once you have access to OneDrive. In Office, you can directly save a document to the web if you have OneDrive integrated into it. For Office 2010, you need to open an existing document in the Office Apps, like Word, Excel or PowerPoint. Once you open and once all the work on the file is done, you can then go to File section and click on Save & Send option so that the file can be saved and sent to the web space and later accessed by a browser.

You can then click on Sign In and enter your email address and password. After entering these details, you can then click on the OK button. The file will then be sent to your pre existing Microsoft account and you can open the file using your OneDrive suite. Once you get into the OneDrive workspace through the browser and your Microsoft account, you can then select a folder in OneDrive and then click on Save As. You can then name the file directly and click on Save. This will save a copy of your document to the OneDrive space so that it can be accessed through browser or any other device at any time. Then to complete the action, you can click on File and then Close button to close the workspace.

To check if the document is accessible on the net, you can go to OneDrive.com through your PC or mobile browser and after signing in, you can click on the same folder where you had saved the file previously and then click on the appropriate file name. Once the file name is clicked, the file opens up in the OneDrive space on the browser. You can then use the Microsoft 365 through web browser controls to edit and use the document.

Thus, the browser on your PC or phone can be used to access OneDrive and Microsoft 365 so that you can take actions on your uploaded documents. The cross platform nature of OneDrive and its adaptability to browsers helps in building a collaborative environment where you can create and edit documents on the webspace and also share them with others. It is important to sync OneDrive with your Office apps and save documents to the OneDrive space to access them later on your browser. The OneDrive space opens up in any browser of your phone or PC. However, to access these capabilities, you need a pre existing Microsoft account.

The sign in process for OneDrive on Browser is not as smooth as it is for the application, but it is useful when you are working from anywhere. If you do not have an existing Microsoft Account, you can simply go to the OneDrive page and sign up on Microsoft rather than sign in. You can use your email ID to sign up for the Microsoft account.

Mobile Access with Apps

Nowadays, it is very important to keep all the files on the mobile devices so that you can gain access to them from anywhere. People sign in to their work with the help of mobile phones and handle their work through mobile apps. The OneDrive suite can also be used as a mobile app on a mobile phone operating system. The OneDrive app creates portability of files and other important details of your work so that you can turn your mobile phone into your primary work device and start working on files on the go. When you have the OneDrive mobile app on your phone, you can upload and share files as you want and you can also work on them whenever you want to. The mobile app also has all the controls same as the desktop app and you can create, rename and delete files as you want. You can also move files from the local phone memory to the OneDrive storage space when you need.

You can also capture pictures and videos with the help of the OneDrive app and create camera back up for all the important local files in different formats. The OneDrive app also comes with a Scan option that turns any physical document or card into a PDF that can be stored in a mobile device and as soft copy on the OneDrive suite. This PDF can be very easily shared with people of your team so you do not have to go the traditional way of printing documents and circulating them. On the mobile device, even when you are going to have one OneDrive app, you can sign in using multiple email accounts and create a personal account and a work account so that multiple responsibilities and areas can be handled on one app. So, all your personal and professional information can be saved and stored on the same app without taking a lot of device space. The existence of the OneDrive app on a mobile phone is beneficial because then you can manage the limited local storage space and reduce the burden on the local storage so more space can be free.

You can use the OneDrive App on multiple mobile phone operating systems like iOS, Android, and Windows. In the next sections, you will come to know about the multiple features of different versions of the OneDrive App on mobile front.

iOS App Features

The iOS OneDrive app can be installed on iPhones and iPad and other mobile offerings from Apple. Apple is a leading tech giant that specializes in creating smartphones, tablets and wearables. Apple is currently working on revolutionizing wearables and smart gadgets so that you can access multiple apps and features that help your daily life and professional responsibilities. The OneDrive app on the iOS system is a highly useful app that professionals can use during work from home and hybrid work environments. With OneDrive on the iOS system, the users can create backup for their photos, videos and important files. The security of iPhone and iPad are combined with the security provisions of OneDrive to encrypt and protect the backed up files and photos as well as videos.

The app can be used to automatically back up files, photos and videos from the iPhone and iPad storage space. The storage space available through the OneDrive app is free for 5 GB but you can also access up to 1TB space through the app if you get a Microsoft 365 subscription. The Microsoft 365 subscription comes at affordable price. Using Microsoft 365 with the OneDrive app turns your iOS system into your work system where you can store, handle and edit multiple file types. There are many useful features of the OneDrive on iOS systems and these features are fast evolving according to the new versions of iOS systems and iPad versions. Apple and OneDrive are working together to offer new features like support for iOS 15 and iPad OS 15 so that the new Apple users can get the best features according to the most updated versions of iOS systems.

In 2020, Apple launched a new iOS home screen for OneDrive iOS app. The new home screen iOS app widget allows the users to access the OneDrive space from the home screen. This way, you can easily access the important files and offline files from the home screen of the iPhone or iPad. The OneDrive App on the iOS system has three major sections that offer a unique experience. The first section is the recently accessed files so that you can easily return to working on your recent work files. On the other hand, the files downloaded section includes the files available offline that you can use after download. Once the files are downloaded and offline, you can work on the files anywhere. After working you can save the file in the local disk or turn your mobile data on to upload the final file to the OneDrive app. The OneDrive app also has an on this day section that shows the previously backed up photos that could be your memories around the same date. This way, OneDrive on new iOS systems balances out your personal files and your professional work.

You can also add a OneDrive widget to the home screen of iPhones and iPads by simply pressing and holding on your iPhone screens. After that, you can press the + button that appears on the screen and then scroll down to the OneDrive app to add the widget so that the app screen is far more accessible. If you have all your files backed up to the OneDrive suite and you use the app very often, then adding a widget helps you a lot.

There are many features of the OneDrive app that work really well with the iPhone and iPad system. For example, you can automatically back up your camera roll from your personal account on the OneDrive app. This way, your precious photos and videos are saved in cloud, well protected and available at one place for ease of access. You can then see your photos on the phone, in PC or any other device where OneDrive is installed. You can also use the Scan feature of the OneDrive mobile app to scan your personal IDs and other important identification documents so that these can be stored in a protected cloud space. The personal vault feature of the mobile app adds another layer of protection to the OneDrive files so that you can access them with proper authentication and they are well protected from privacy breaches. You can also use another cool feature of the One Drive app that helps you scan and sign physical documents in PDF formats and then send the signed PDF soft copy to people of your team through the shared space of OneDrive. This means that you can share important documents with your team and complete business formalities on the go with your iPhone or iPad. The OneDrive app in your iPhone or iPad is also useful when you have to print files from any random printer. The files that are saved on the OneDrive app can be exported to any nearby printer and printed out easily. You have to simply tap on one file to open it and then tap on the three dots icon appearing on the upper right corner of the screen and then select Print. All your files can be easily converted into digital copies with the use of OneDrive on iPhone and iPad.

Android App Features

The Microsoft OneDrive application is a multi platform cloud storage app that you can use on Android phones too. The Android version of the OneDrive app is very versatile and useful in storing files in the cloud and managing local disk space. Android is usually paired up with Google Drive but you can also install and sign into OneDrive on Android phones and tablets. The OneDrive app can be downloaded from Google Play store easily and used on Android systems. In popular Android smartphones like Samsung Galaxy phones, the Android app comes pre installed and you simply need to sign in with a Microsoft account. There are many features of the OneDrive suite that are available on Android smartphones.

The Android version of the app can be used to do basic file backup from the phone so that the internal phone storage can be freed for newer files. You can use the OneDrive app with the Microsoft 365 suite if you work with your Android phone or tablet. You can open your OneDrive app from your app list and then tap the + icon and tap on the Upload option. Once you select the Upload option you can go to the files and select the file that you want to upload.

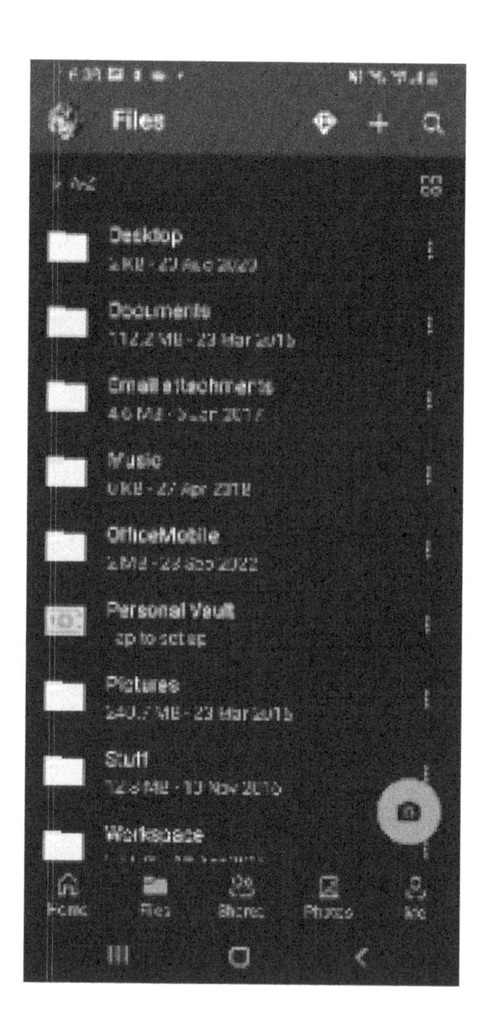

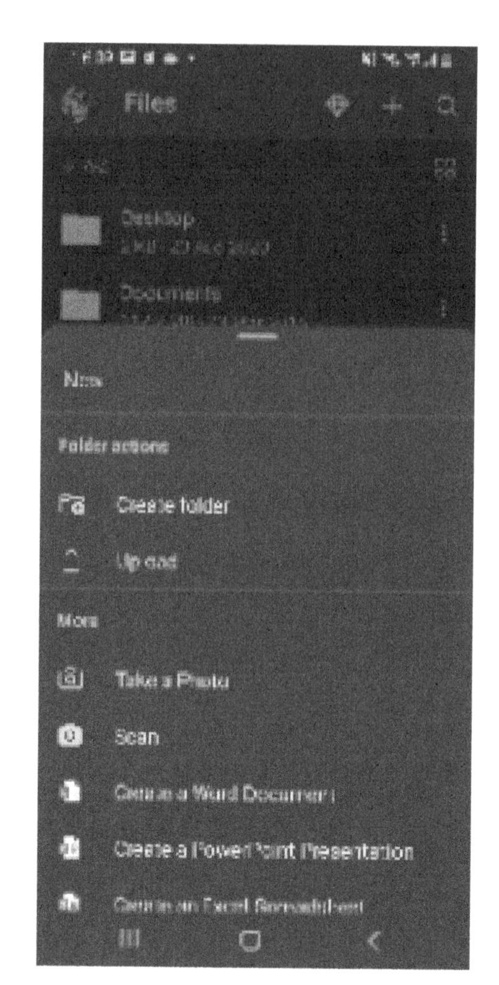

You can share your files securely once they are uploaded in OneDrive on the android phone. To share the files, you can go to the OneDrive folder and tap on the uploaded file you want to share. This will open up the file and you can then tap on the three dots on the screen. From the appearing menu, the user then chooses the share option and shares the file to your team members. When sharing, you can also manage the privacy settings by choosing to Can Edit or Can View option, so you know how people are accessing your files. If you are sharing the link to the file, you can also Set Expiration to the link so that the link will expire once the time to view is over. By choosing the Set Expiration option, you can choose to make the file available only for a limited amount of time.

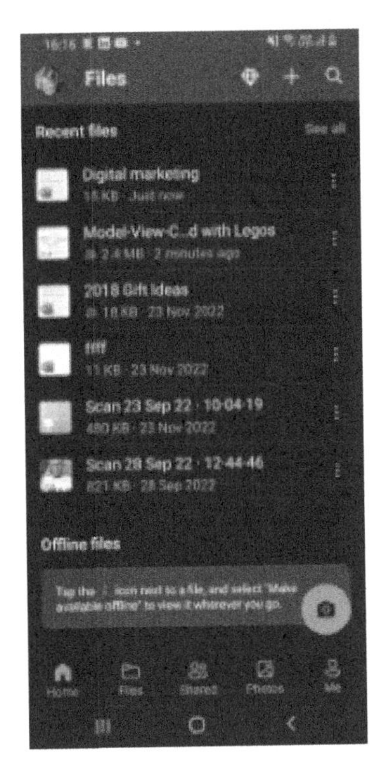

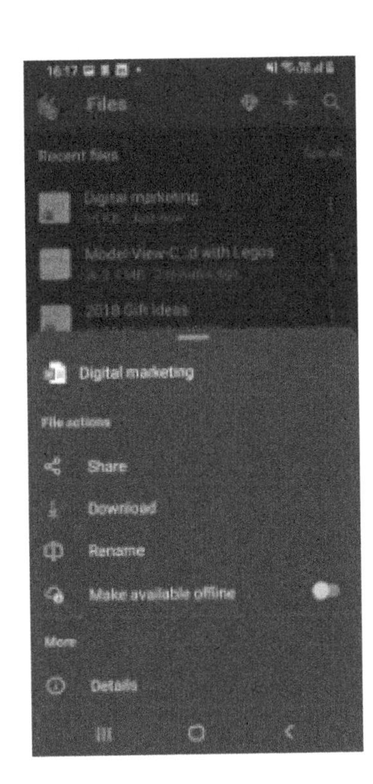

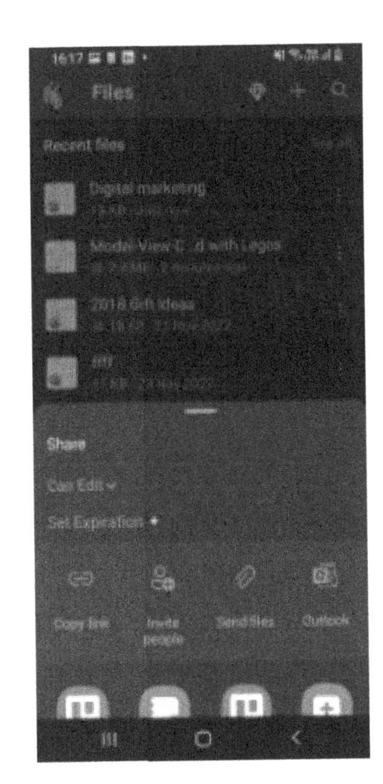

On the mobile device, you might also need to manage your private files while keeping the professional work on front. So, OneDrive on the Android device also comes with a feature that allows the user to hide private folders and files with simple actions. You can encrypt the files for sensitive information and documents like identification documents and other details. The Personal Vault feature of OneDrive is also available on the Android devices. You can launch the OneDrive app and then tap the Personal Vault option to private some selected files. Once you tap on the Personal Vault option, you have to verify your identity and for that you need to furnish your Microsoft account details. Once the identity is verified, you can then create a private six digit pin that can help you access the files later on from the Personal Vault. The security of the OneDrive App and Personal Vault can be increased by altering the security settings of the Android device. You can go to Me >Settings>App Lock to add another layer of security to the existing security of Personal Vault. This makes sure that you can encrypt and protect the files properly with Multifactor Authentication.

You can also edit your important photos in the online space with the help of your OneDrive folder. Your Personal Vault can be used to store your personal photos. You can then access the photos and edit them easily. To edit the photos, you can launch the OneDrive App and then go to Photos and then tap on Device. Then you can select the picture you want to edit and then you need to tap on Edit. After this, there are a number of actions that you can take with your OneDrive edit tools like Crop, Adjustment, Filter, etc. The photo can be edited and the edited version can be saved on the OneDrive space.

You can also open and annotate PDF files on the OneDrive Android App. By using this feature of the OneDrive app, you can simply use the app to read PDF files and do not need a different PDF reader app in your phone. OneDrive comes with a native PDF reader which allows you to read stored PDF Files and annotate them with details. Even if you want to make any changes or additions to the contents of the PDF files, you can do that with the PDF reader and other features of OneDrive.

Offline Access and Syncing

The ITB of space on OneDrive in Mobile devices can be used to sync documents and have offline access to the online files when downloaded. The files and folders that have been uploaded on the OneDrive mobile app can be marked offline to make the file available offline and for offline editing. The offline edits can then show up on the online version easily with the sync feature. The syncing happens when the Android device has web access with mobile data on again. The latest version of the file will always have the edits with the help of web access and syncing that can be selectively turned on.

You can make files available offline by going to the OneDrive app and then press and hold or tap on the three dots that appear next to the file or the folder that has to be selected for syncing. Then from the menu that appears on the screen, you opt for the Keep Offline icon which appears at the top. You can then tap on the file in the list view to open up a particular offline file so you can work on it. You can now open the file at any time, whether offline or online to work on it. The files that are available offline are also listed on the Files Available Offline view. You can tap on the Me icon on the app and then tap on the Files Available Offline to see the files that are available offline so that you can read the offline files you want to work on.

Conclusion

OneDrive is an important app to be installed in your PC or your mobile phone. At a time when we are working from anywhere and working remotely, professionals need to back up their files and access them easily through shared folders or saved ones on their laptop or phone. With the use of OneDrive, professionals and students can partition their personal files and important items from their work and assignments. OneDrive is a robust storage solution from Microsoft that protects your files and also helps you collaborate with other people.

Recap of Key Concepts

OneDrive easily integrates with a Windows 10 or 11 system and with all Office apps like Microsoft Word, Excel, PowerPoint to store the files and make them accessible on the cloud space. Microsoft users get 5 GB of free space to save their files at so that they can manage their local disk space and back up their files. You can save your camera photos and videos to the Camera back up space of OneDrive too. Thus, OneDrive is that one place where you can save information in any format. You can also save your files on OneDrive and then allow the files to be synced on different devices automatically.

OneDrive supports remote and collaborative work brilliantly because people can make files accessible from any location on the OneDrive Suite and work on the same document as a team on different locations. The sharing of files with your team members is also very easy with the use of OneDrive. In a hybrid workspace and even if you have a large team, OneDrive makes collaboration possible for you. If we talk about the integration of other apps to create an accessible workspace and easy sharing channels, then the integration of other Office apps like Word, PowerPoint, Excel and Pictures is easy through the OneDrive controls and access points. Since Microsoft is the creator of OneDrive, other Microsoft Apps easily integrate with the OneDrive suite. OneDrive comes preinstalled on Microsoft PC systems and it is easy to start using the application and sync it with other work applications. You simply need a Microsoft account to sign into the OneDrive Suite and start using it.

The OneDrive System once synced with other Office applications, allows users to simultaneously work on one file or edit a file. You can also choose to create folders and share bulk information with other team members. You can also edit files in browsers with the help of OneDrive. You can scan documents and directly save them on OneDrive. OneDrive is a versatile cloud storage that works in sync with your Meta account, your camera roll and also your email account. You can use OneDrive on your PC; you can also have OneDrive on your phone and personalize it for your personal files and memories.

OneDrive is highly flexible as it allows you to work with your files in online only mode and also in offline mode. However, if you are keen on creating a backup, you should save the files in the File Explorer and also create a backup on OneDrive. This way, you can access the files in any mode for any kind of work. OneDrive can be used with mobile phones to make files available offline and online so that you can access them in a flexible manner and at the time its most urgent.

The level of privacy and data management that OneDrive is offering is also really helpful for professionals. You can choose who you are sharing your files with and in what mode is the sharing happening. You can go for view only mode, link or edit access to others if you are working on the same project. You can easily manage access and change the settings as per your need and the requirements of the project.

OneDrive also has a section called the Personal Vault, that protects your personalized files with added protection. You can set up additional authentication and identification protection to protect your personal information in the personal vault of OneDrive. OneDrive is thus the all-in-one app that allows you to manage all your files, work and store information at the same time. Deleting and recovering data from the OneDrive suite is also very easy. The learning curve of OneDrive controls is moderately easy. From collaboration to data protection, OneDrive ticks all the right boxes. OneDrive can be found in all Windows PC and Microsoft mobile phones. You can also download the application selectively. The easy controls and actions for the OneDrive user makes this Cloud storage application a very useful and versatile PC and mobile application.

The adaptability and accessibility of OneDrive on multiple devices and browsers is a definite advantage for professionals on the go. In a remote work environment where you have to keep your files uploaded to the net and might have to access the files at any time, the browser or mobile phone version of OneDrive comes in handy. With a simple Microsoft account, you can unlock a plethora of possibilities.

This is a guide to simple actions and controls for the OneDrive User. OneDrive users can take many actions and control many aspects of the application. This guide will help you learn the basics of OneDrive and also offer you a sneak peek into advanced settings. Keep learning new things and exploring new paradigms of computer applications to make your workspace more organized and productive. Keep Reading and growing as a professional, taking the help of advanced work applications like OneDrive.

Microsoft Publisher

Introduction

Overview of Microsoft Publisher

In a world of evolving technologies, Microsoft Publisher is a flexible publishing program that allows small-scale firms, organizations, businesses, and individuals to produce professional and user-friendly publications (both print and digital publications).

As a widely accepted desktop publishing program included in the Microsoft Office program, one of Microsoft Publisher's strongest strengths is its ability to seamlessly combine text and images to create publications such as cards, brochures, newsletters, event posters, newsletters for small businesses and organizations, professional business cards, flyers and programs, postcards, and brochures and certificates.

It allows users to access a variety of elements that will assist in creating usable publications and attractive to your users.

Also, it provides a user-friendly interface and a variety of templates that make it reasonably simple for non-designers to generate publications that appear professional.

As a beginner or an expert, you can make use of templates and layouts in Microsoft Publisher that can help you get started on your creative project and serve as inspiration. Users who prefer greater control over the layout of their document over conventional word processing software will find it especially helpful.

It grants users access to carrying out simple operations within the Microsoft Publisher interface, including material in a publication, modifying text in a printed work, changing a publication's content, including and arranging images.

Microsoft Publisher allows you to save your publications in a wide range of formats, such as PNG, PDF and JPEG after the whole process if creation. Likewise, it provides easy exportation of publications as HTML web pages or PDF documents, also, it has integrated mail merge functionality, which is useful when you need to send publications to your contact list in a directly, intriguing and quite appealing manner.

Microsoft Publisher's intuitive interface facilitates the creation and editing of publications. You will produce, format, edit, and distribute publications with this publishing program.

Chapter 1:Getting Started With Publisher

Exploring the Publisher Interface

Before starting to create a publication, it is important to become acquainted with the features and tools available in the Microsoft Publisher user interface.

A startup screen displays a list of available publication templates when you first launch Publisher. For the time being, choose the default blank page option from the listing to examine the Microsoft Publisher user interface.

One of the unique features of the Microsoft Publisher interface is the task section on the right-hand side.

The Title Bar at the top of the screen, has the name of the currently published article in the center of it.

The Quick Access toolbar, to which you can add buttons for desired commands, is located at the left end of the Title Bar.

The title bar, which houses the quick access toolbar as well, the page navigation, the publication page section, the ribbon and the status bar make up the publisher interface. The page layout view bars and the zoom slider are also located in the status bar.

The Ribbon appears beneath the Title Bar. All of Microsoft Publisher's tabs, button groups, and commands are located here.

Multiple tabs labeled File, Home, Insert, Page design, Review, View, and Help is present on the ribbon.

Each tab is made up of collections of the software program's commands that are intended to accomplish various tasks or functions which enhance creativity and productivity.

Backstage View

Microsoft Publisher's "Backstage View" can be accessed through the "File" tab on the Ribbon. The most popular file management commands, such as creating, saving, and printing publications, are available in the "Backstage View."

It is employed for the management of data and files that are related to but separate from the files. Creating and saving files, modifying file preferences, and checking for hidden or private data are all covered in Backstage View.

The backstage view operates with a single mouse click, so clicking on a button or item in a list will close the backstage view and carry out the command, giving you quick access to the functionality. From Backstage view, select the Home tab or hit the ESC key on your keyboard to go back to your project.

The backstage view allows users to save current projects (Save), save the current project with your preferred title (Save As), save all recently opened projects (Save All).

Also, it allows you to preview and organize your project (Preview and Organize), select an ongoing project to launch (Open), and close an active ongoing project (Close). Before the current project is closed, you will be asked to save the changes.

Workspace and Tools

You can access the tools available on the Publisher by clicking on the "Object tab" and view the listed tools. The workspace is constructed in a way that makes it easy to navigate by both beginners and experts.

Here are few of the tools and their uses:

Layout options are a collection of rules that will assist you in aligning elements and establishing a standardized layout for your magazine. When creating a publication, users can choose from a variety of layout options offered by Microsoft Publisher.

Shapes and Graphics: You can add a variety of shapes and graphics to your publications using the Microsoft Publisher toolkit. With the help of this application, users may format and insert forms like circles, arrows, and rectangles into their publications.

Also, you can alter the forms' outline, color, and fill in addition to adding other effects like shadows and reflections.

Other tools include Images (used to insert images into a publication), Master Pages (allows you to maintain a consistent layout through the whole publication process), Text Box (allows you to add and format text), Templates, Picture placeholder, Design Checker and Backgrounds and Color Schemes.

Creating a New Publication

Choosing Publication Types

When you launch Publisher, a workspace screen opens where you can create a new publication.

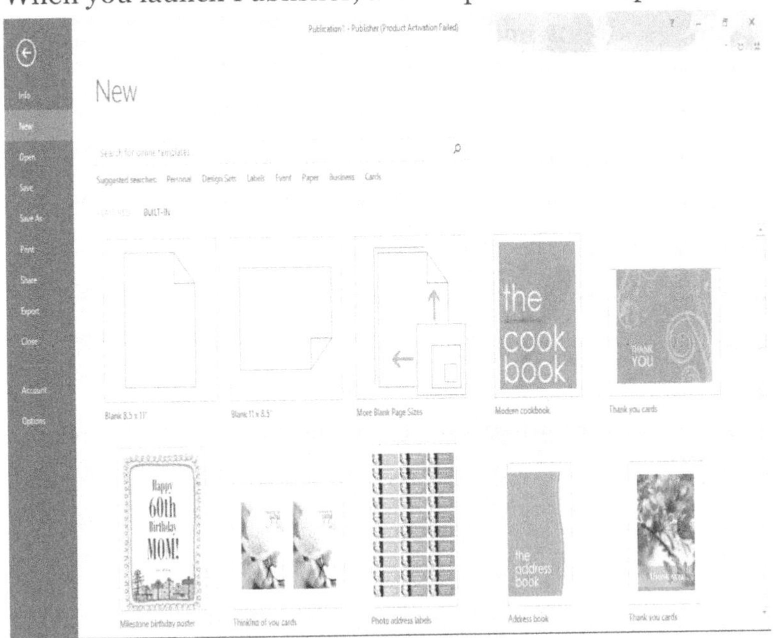

Click on the type of publication to create from the list of available templates on the right side of the workspace screen in Publisher to start a new publication.

Alternatively, click the "File" tab in the Ribbon after establishing a publication to start a new one.

Next, choose the "New" command located on the backstage view's left side. The publication design screen will then appear, allowing you to select the kind of design that best suits your project.

The pre-designed templates for each type of publication can be viewed on the right-hand side by selecting the different entries, such as newsletters, brochures, and so on. In the left column, select the publication type that you wish to create.

The pane on the right will show several templates for the selected publication type. To locate the template you wish to use, scroll through the ones in the right pane.

Next, select "Create" or "Download" from the buttons that show up to start a fresh Publisher publication using the template.

To produce a fresh, unfinished publication that is of a standard page size, select the "Blank 8.5 x 11" icon from the templates list.

You have the option to alter the publication layout regardless of whether you started from a blank page or a template. You may alter the margins, size, and orientation.

Although you can change these settings at any moment, you should exercise caution if objects such as text, images, and shapes are already present in your publication, as you will need to resize them to accommodate the new layout.

Flyers, Brochures and Newsletters

Flyers

The flyer designs and templates in Microsoft Publisher are arranged based on the intended use of the flyer. The first step in creating a flyer with the Publisher is to "Click on the New tab".

Then, select the desired template for your flyer. Next, add texts and images to the flyer. Click on the "Home Tab" to select "Draw Text tab", then, add text. You can modify your text to fit your desirable design. To add images, click on the "Pictures tab" available on the "Home tab".

Next, proceed to format the layout of the flyer. Finally, save and print the finished flyer. To save your project, click on the "Save" or "Save As" tab from the "File" tab. To print the flyer, click on the "Print" that appears on the "File" tab.

Brochures

With the brochure feature in Microsoft Publisher, you can create a personalized brochure with text and images by using Word-like commands.

Choose a design for the brochure. To open the Catalog Window, click on "File" from the home tab and then select "New". On the Wizards menu, click the "Brochures" option and choose the preferred design from the available options.

Newsletters

To access the Newsletters category, click New > Newsletters and then scroll down.

Choose a template, then select your preferred font and color scheme under "Customize". Select the desired business information set by clicking on it or make a new one.

Next, select either the "One-page spread" or the "Two-page spread" from the "Options" tab.

Select "Create." Then, modify the template to include elements such as a title and logo.

After saving your new template, select Publisher Template in the "Save" or "Save As" box and navigate to the desired location and folder using the "Save As" tab.

You can send out these attractive and well-designed newsletters to your customers or audience to create awareness, advertise goods or services and other desirable purposes.

Cards, Posters and more

Cards

Firstly, select a card category. Then, select Greeting Cards or Invitation Cards from the available templates. You can modify a wide variety of the design elements by clicking on "Customize and Options".

Select the desired business information set by clicking on it under Customize or make a new one. Click on the wanted page size from the Options menu.

Choose your preferred layout under Options. Select "Create."

Posters

To create a poster on Publisher, select the "Page Design" tab and click on the "Size Option". Then, select "More Preset Page Sizes" from the drop-down menu. Next, Select a page size.

Then, you can customize the size, font and color of the banner. Finally, save the poster using the "Save As" or "Save" button.

Setting Up Page Layout and Design

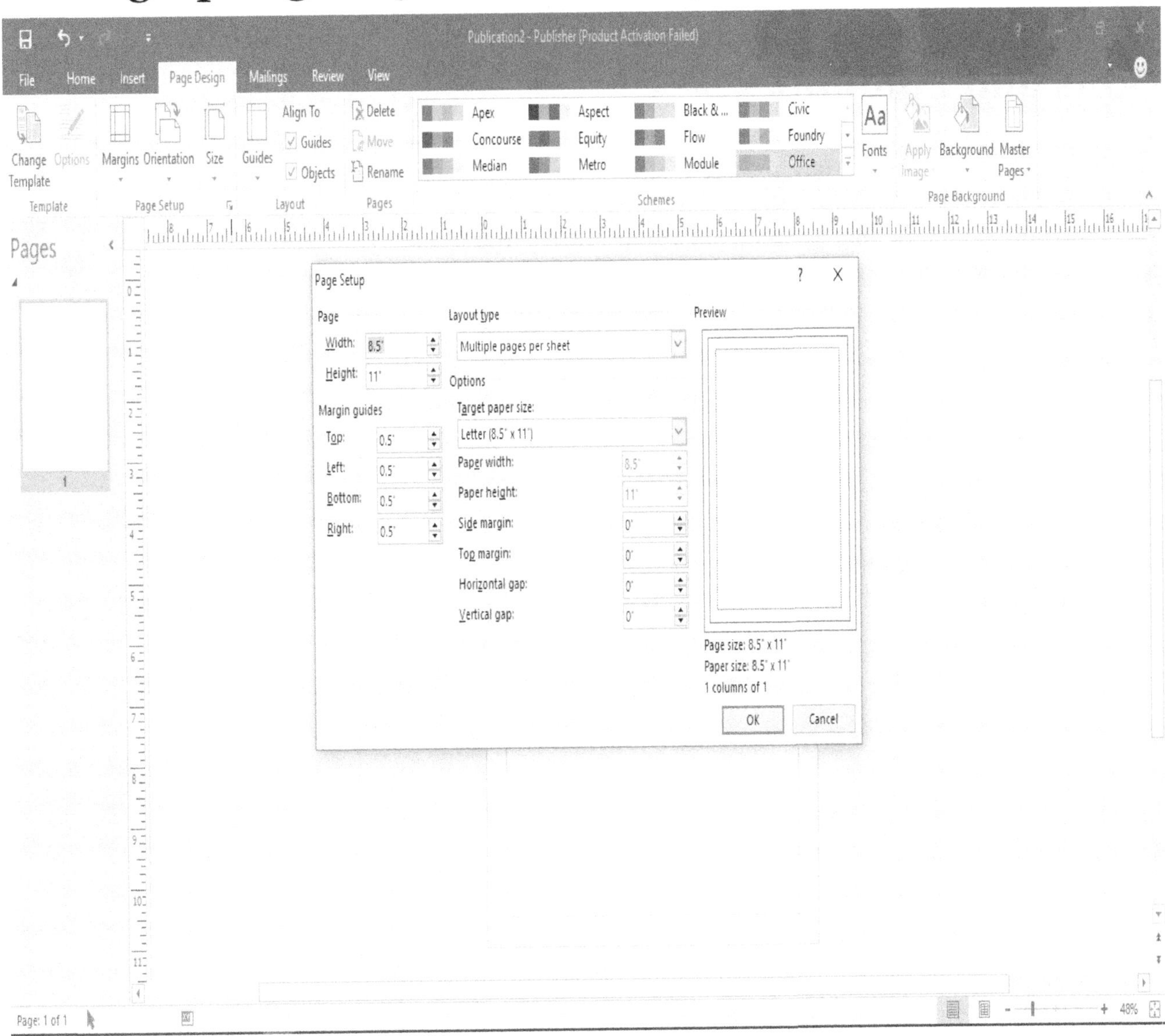

To set up the page layout and design of your publication, select "Grid and Baseline Guides" under "Page Design". Then, select the tab for Margin Guides, enter the desired amount of space for the page margins in the boxes available.

To configure the row and column guides, select "Grid and Baseline Guides" under "Page Design". Select the tab for Grid Guides. Enter the desired number of columns in the Columns box under Column Guides, and in the Spacing box, indicate the desired distance between the columns.

Enter the desired number of rows in the Rows box under Row Guides, followed by the desired amount of space.

The page design you select will determine the layout of the publication. A selection of the "Booklet" option will make your publication have a booklet design. The "email design" option will configure the email page design for your publication.

Page Size and Orientation

You can specify a custom page size or select from a list of predefined publication types to alter the size of the pages in your publication.

To change your page size, click "Page Setup" from the "File" menu. Then, Select the tab for "Layout". Choose the desired publication type under "Publication type", then enter the desired Width and Height.

Click OK.

Click "Page Setup" from the "File" menu to change your page orientation. Select the tab for Layout. For a vertical arrangement, select Portrait under Orientation; for a horizontal layout, select Landscape.

Click OK.

Margins and Columns

To add margins to a text box, click the "Text Box" tab. Enter or choose the desired margins for the Left, Right, Top, and Bottom under Text Box Margins. Click OK.

To add columns to your publication, click on columns under Text Box Tools Format. Select More Columns from the "Columns" menu. In the "Number box", enter the desired number of columns.

Use the arrow buttons in the "Spacing box" to adjust the distance between columns.

Chapter 2: Working with Text and Fonts

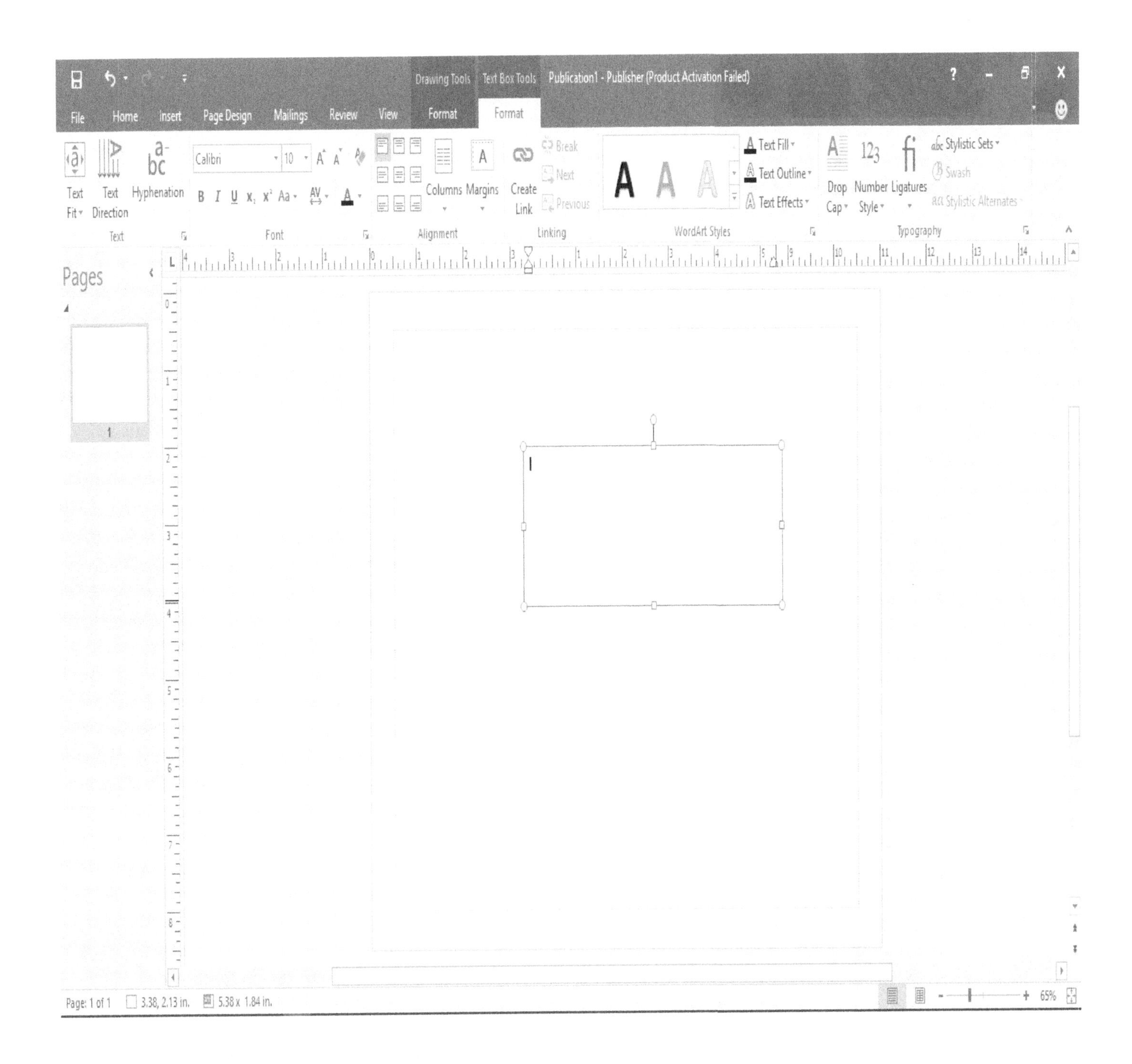

Adding and Formatting Text Boxes

Every text must always be entered into a text box when it is entered into a publication. Microsoft Publisher will occasionally generate a text box for you automatically.

A text box can be moved, resized, deleted, and stacked on top of one another.

To add a text box to your publication, click the "Home" tab on the Ribbon in Publisher. Then select the "Objects" button group's "Draw Text Box" button. Select "Draw Text Box" from the "Text" button group by clicking it next.

In the text area, type your text.

The Format contextual tab, which shows under Drawing Tools when you pick a text box, has commands that can be used to format the text box itself.

Text Box Basics

In addition to the adding and inserting of text boxes which are part of text box basics, you can also link text boxes together.

By linking the text boxes together, the text can easily flow from one box to another.

A small box with ellipses emerges in the text box's lower right corner when it contains too much content. Add a fresh text box. Your cursor changes to a pitcher when you click the overflow indicator. Finally, open the new text box.

Text Box Styles and Shapes

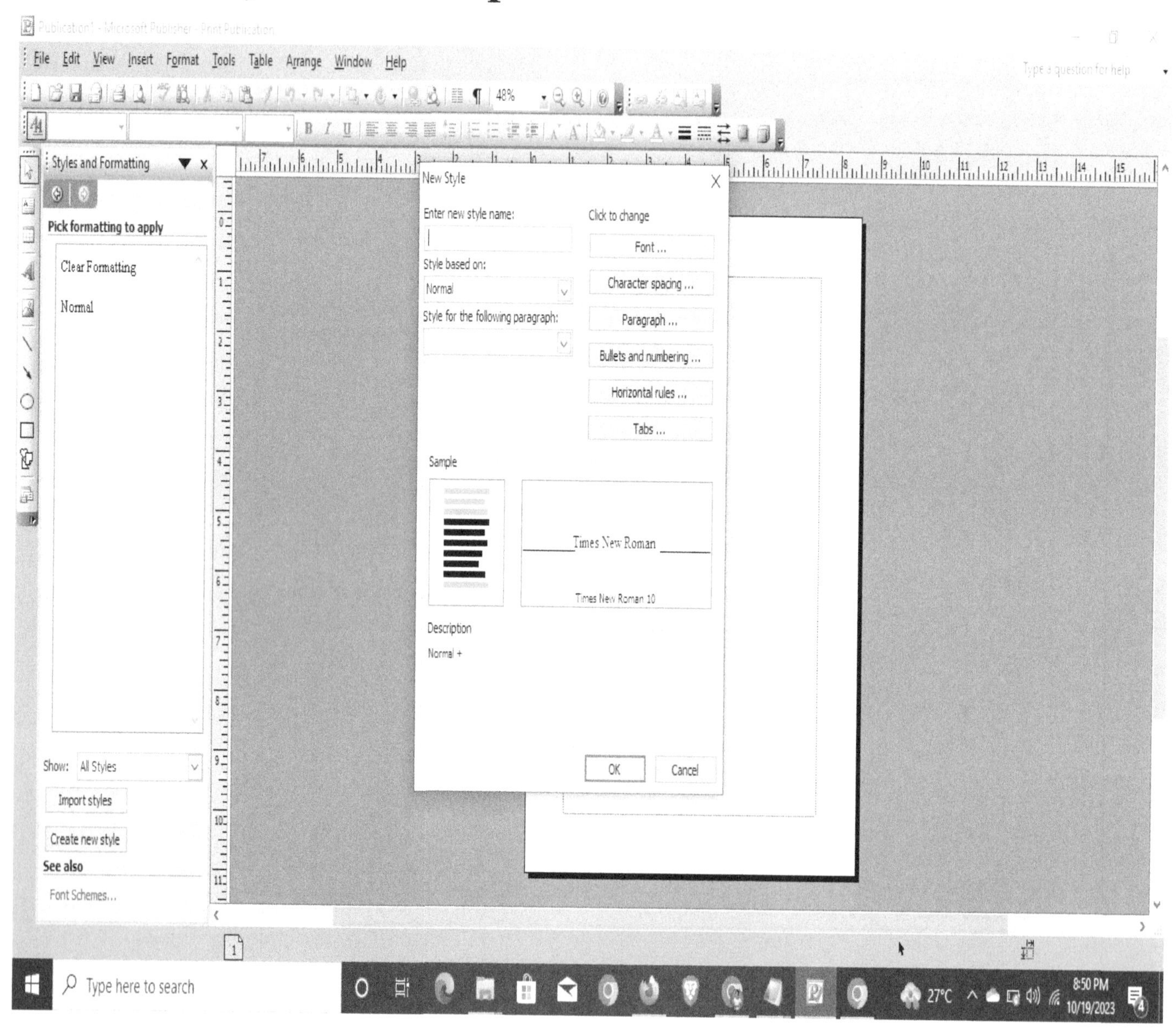

To alter the text box style: Choosing a shape style enables you to rapidly alter the look of your text box by applying pre-set colors and effects. Choose the text box that needs to be changed.

Choose the look you want to employ. The chosen style will be used shape, choose the text box that needs to be changed, then, the “Format tab” will appear.

Click the “Edit Shape” button that appears on the “Format tab”. Select the desired form from the menu that appears by hovering the cursor over Change form. The text box will display using the shape's formatting.

Typography in Publisher

Ligatures

Ligatures are links connecting characters that effectively make one character out of two. Standard ligatures will only employ the most frequent letter combinations.

Drop Cap

By employing a huge dropped initial capital letter to add attention to a newsletter or invitation, this formatting style is frequently used to mark the beginning paragraph of a publication. This option enables you to add a dropped capital letter, also known as a drop cap.

Stylistic Set

Each font might have anything between one and twenty different sets of typography styles.

Swash

If the font designer has included embellishments, which frequently take the form of large serifs, this button makes them available.

Other stylistic options

If the font designer has made alternate looks for the selected characters, this enables you to choose one of them.

Font Selection and Formatting

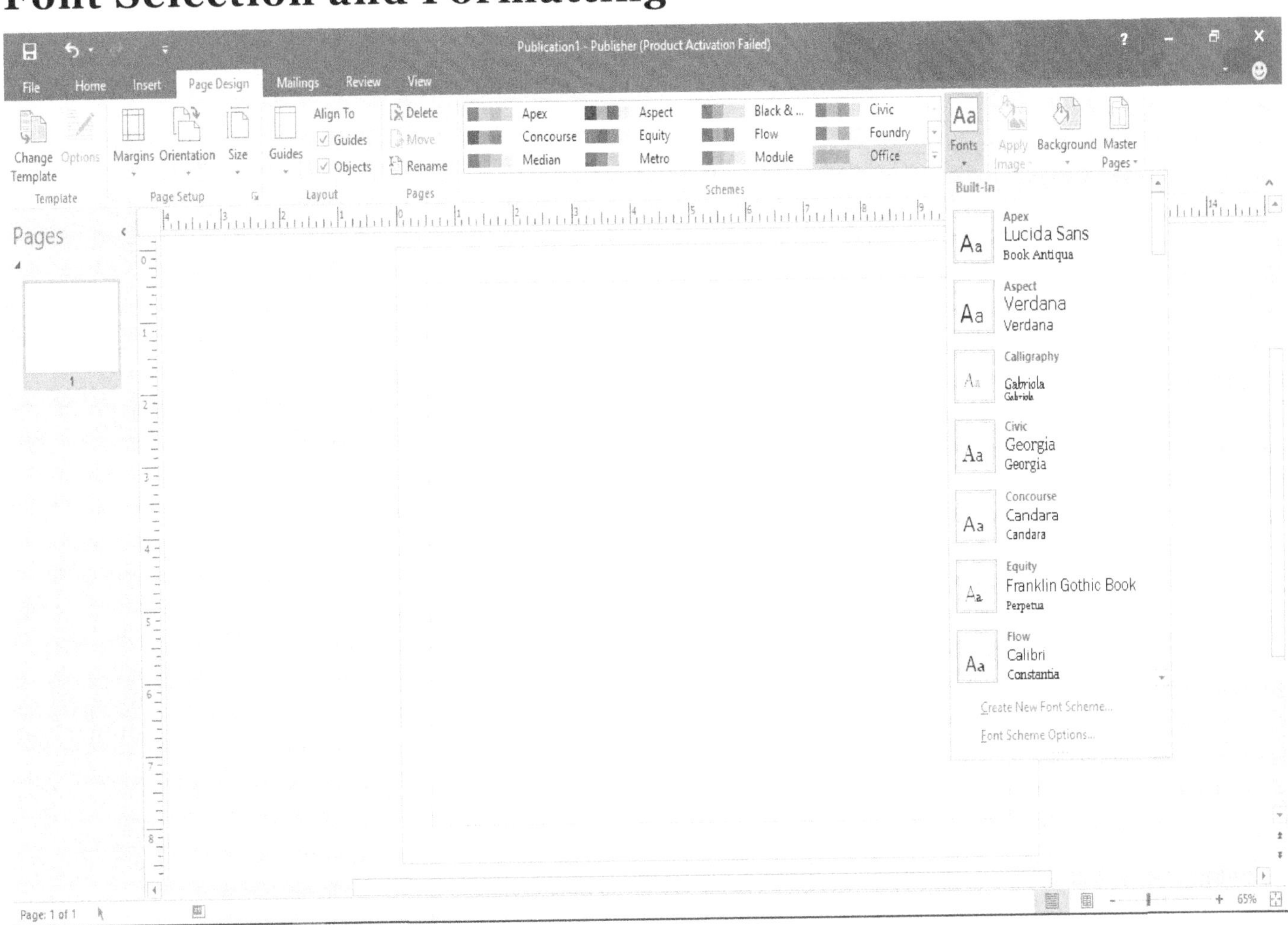

By opening a current or new publication and selecting Page Design > Fonts, Publisher offers a gallery of Built-In font combinations from which you can select.

These fonts can be easily changed using font schemes to give it a unified, polished appearance. When you use a font scheme, Publisher modifies the styles in your publication so that they no longer utilize the standard fonts for those styles and instead use one of the fonts in the font scheme.

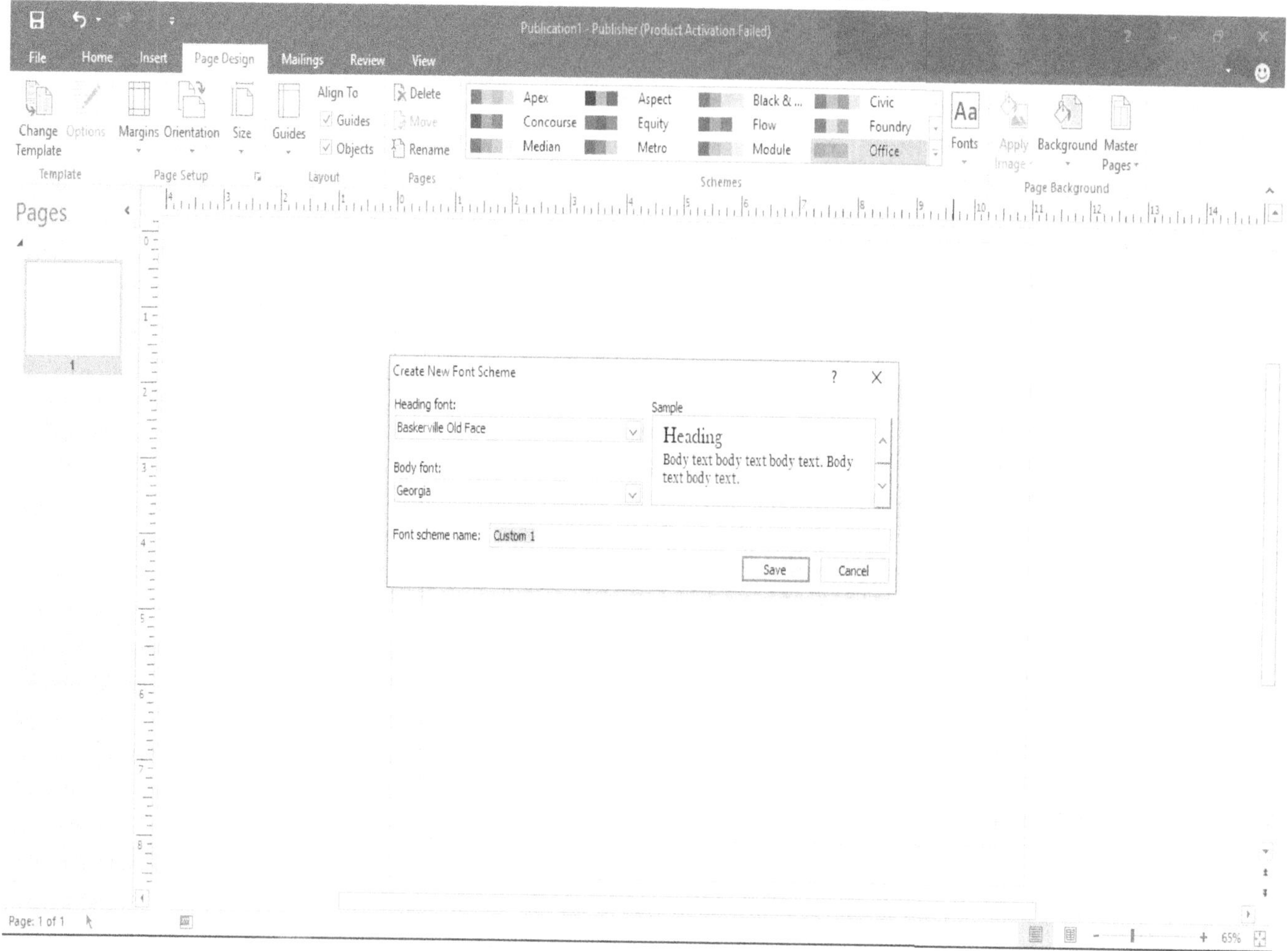

To create attractive and user-friendly publications, you can build unique font schemes in Publisher. Click on the "Page Design" tab to create unique font schemes in Publisher. After that, select "Fonts" from the "Schemes" button group's drop-down menu.

The "Create New Font Scheme" dialog box will then appear after choosing the "Create New Font Scheme" command from the drop-down menu that displays.

To choose a unique heading and body font for your unique font scheme, click the drop-down button next to the "Heading font:" and "Body font:" drop-downs in the "Create New Font Scheme" dialog box. The "Text field" is where you may give your unique font scheme a name. then press "Save" to save your customized settings.

To format your font scheme, select the "Page Design" tab from the Ribbon to use custom font schemes. Select "Fonts" from the "Schemes" button group after that. Then, from the options presented, select the unique font scheme to use.

Select the "Fonts" button from the "Schemes" button group to remove custom font schemes. The custom font scheme can then be deleted from the resulting drop-down menu by performing a right-click. Next, select "Delete Scheme" from the pop-up menu that follows. The confirmation dialog box that displays has a button labeled "Ok", click it to remove the custom font scheme.

Paragraph Styles and Alignment

Publishers makes it simple for users, whether they are experts or beginners, to apply distinctive paragraph styles and alignment.

The "Format Paragraph dialog box" in Publisher can be used to change the alignment, the line and paragraph breaks inside selected paragraphs.

To alter paragraphs in Publisher, Choose the text that needs to be changed. To display the Paragraph dialog box, click the Paragraph launcher on the "Home tab". Select the Tab for Indents and Spacing. Then, Enter or choose the amount of space you want above the paragraph in the Before or After paragraphs box.

Here are the unique paragraph styles available on Publisher:

Center paragraph style: The left and right edges of each line of text are jagged, and the middle of each line is positioned halfway between the right and left text box margins.

Right paragraph style: Each line's rightmost character is aligned with the right margin, while each line's left edge is jagged. For paragraphs with right-to-left text orientation, this is the default alignment.

Left paragraph style: Each line's leftmost character is aligned with the left margin, while each line's right edge is jagged. For paragraphs with a left-to-right text orientation, this alignment is the standard setting.

Justified paragraph style: Lines are filled by adding or removing space between and within words, and the initial and last characters of each line (except from the last) are aligned to the left and right margins.

Chapter 3: Inserting And Editing Graphics

Adding Images and Illustrations

Images have the ability to capture readers' attention and either clarify or improve your message. They assist readers understand difficult concepts and provide a succinct overview of the text's main points.

However, if the images do not directly support your message, they could also detract from it, therefore, it is important that you ensure that the images in your publication are in alignment with the message you want to communicate to your audience.

An addition of images and illustrations to your publication will help your readers in understanding your most critical points that are represented with photographs and succinct explanations because readers skim pages by reading headlines and picture captions.

There are various techniques to give images a consistent appearance. Use a limited color scheme or a single accent color, a standard graphic design, the same camera angle or point of view, or constant lighting. Additionally, you can employ the same human models in a developing plot or apply the same filter effects to every image.

Inserting Pictures

To insert a picture, you can decide to insert a picture you've saved on your computer or pick from Publisher's library of Clip Art to add a picture to your publication.

Then, select "File" and click on "Insert Picture" tab. Browse for the desired image and then choose it in the "Insert Picture" tab.

After adding images, you can then edit them to fit your desire.

Clip Art and Online Pictures

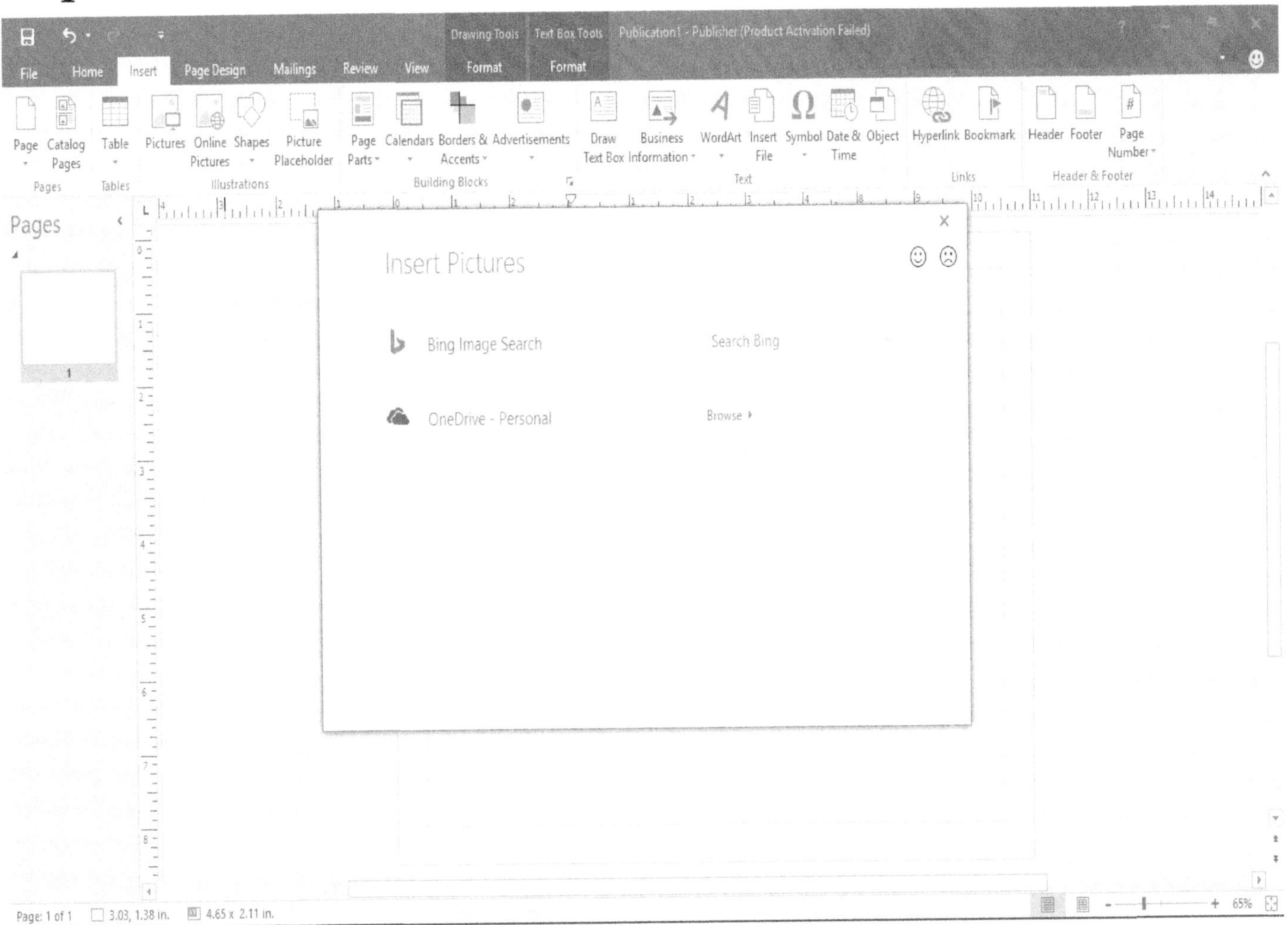

Digital images known as "clip art" are a common component of graphic design work. Clip art is used in a wide range of other print and digital items to create a uniform aesthetic that matches the tone and objectives of the content.

It is possible to employ clip art to improve a number of printed and digital projects in order to increase reader or recipient interest in the product or service you are promoting or selling.

The majority of the information you share is conveyed by text, however it is ineffective at engaging your receiver or target audience. While clip art might occasionally make up the majority of a product, it is usually added as a complement to other aspects of graphic design.

It's easy to add clip art to Microsoft Publisher by selecting the "Insert tab" and looking for an image online, on your device, or already created. Select Online Pictures under Insert > Pictures. For clipart, narrow the results by Type. Choose a photo. Click "Insert Tab".

Graphics Editing Tools in Publisher

Publisher grants users access to graphics editing tools that makes the publications appear beautiful. These include: "Select Objects" tools which is used to selects lines, shapes, graphics, and text boxes.

The attributes of selected items can be changed and they can be resized. The "Insert Table and Text Box" tool which is used to create tables and text boxes.

Cropping and Resizing

To alter the size of a picture, you can crop or resize it. While cropping reduces the size of the image by removing the vertical or horizontal boundaries, resizing alters the image's dimensions by extending or shrinking it.

Cropping is frequently used to conceal or trim undesired or distracting parts of an image.

Simply click the image you want to crop. A row of size handles in the form of white dots surrounds your image. Above the image, the floating Picture to handle becomes visible. On the "Picture" toolbar, select the "Crop" button.

The "Crop" button shows two right angles that cross each other. The cropping handles, which are a set of black dashes, appear after you click the dot-shaped scaling handles.

Once you have cropped your image to the desired size, click the "Crop" button once more to stop cropping. The scaling handle dots will replace the cropping handles once more. To crop the image, drag the cropping handle.

Depending on how you want to crop the image, you can drag any of these handles;

Drag the center cropping handle on the side you want to crop toward the center of the image to crop just that side.

Drag the mouse over a cropping handle while clicking. Your cursor will transform from a four-headed arrow to that shape when it is above a cropping handle.

Drag the corner cropping handle that is in contact with the sides you want to crop in the direction of the center of the image to crop neighboring sides.

Drag the middle handle on either of the opposing sides while continuing to hold down the CTRL key to crop the two sides evenly at the same time.

Image Effects and Corrections

To add image effect to an image, choose an image. Choose Picture Effects under Picture Tools Form. Then, select between the following effects: 3-D Rotation, Soft Edges, Glow, Shadow, and Reflection.

Rotating an image

A dynamic asymmetry can be added to a page design by rotating an image. For instance, this mask is static and predictable when oriented vertically. With a small rotation, the mask appears to move, select Arrange > Rotate.

Then, perform one of the following actions:

- To rotate the image by ninety degrees, click Rotate Left 90° or Rotate Right 90°.
- To rotate the image ninety degrees, click once. Click again and again until the clip is in the desired location. After selecting Free Rotate, move the cursor over the object's top circular green handle.
- Drag the green handle until the object appears in the circle that appears around it.

Flipping an image

A simple image flip can give the page symmetrical balance. To create this, duplicate the image on the left, then flip its pasted duplicate on the right. Choose the image. To flip horizontally or vertically, select Arrange > Rotate or Flip.

Chapter 4: Layout And Design Techniques

Arranging and Grouping Objects

By clicking on an object, holding down the CTRL key, and selecting more objects, you can group objects together. When a lot of objects need to be moved around the publication, this can be very helpful.

Similarly, you can ungroup the objects if you click on the symbol while they are grouped together. After selecting the ungrouping symbol, you can modify each individual object by clicking on it.

To make the most of Publisher's pre-designed templates, you must learn how to use the grouped object feature, which includes a lot of pictures and captions.

In addition, you can right-click on any object to bring up a dialog box with more options.

This method can occasionally be quicker than navigating the workspace's menus to find the desired option. You can alter the image, remove an object, group objects, copy, paste, alter the stacking order, and do a lot more with these options.

Working with layers

In Microsoft Publisher, every object in your publication is treated as a separate layer, whether it's a table, text box, AutoShape, image, or clip art. You can stack these layers on top of one another in order to have a visual effect.

You can make layers from the Layers panel, which you can then use to arrange objects in your design. Layer objects are presented in multiple 'stacked' layers in a logical, ordered, and managed way.

Layer Basics

Any layer that is currently selected can have a sub layer created for it. For more intricate multi-object designs, use sub layers. By keeping related objects in sub layers beneath the parent layer, you may improve object management even more. Utilize them to limit modifications and effects to the child layer alone, as opposed to a whole layer.

The layer that is currently selected is created above, or sub layers are created inside it. To add a new layer, click on "Add Layer" in the Layers menu.

In your layer stack, the layer will be positioned at the top.

Layer management

Click on the item in the stack that you wish to move up or down. A set of sizing handles will surround the selected object. In case you can't quickly select the object you want, click on any visible object and keep pressing the TAB key or SHIFT and TAB together until the object you want to move is selected.

Holding down the CTRL key while selecting each object to be repositioned allows you to select multiple objects at once. Once you've chosen the final object, release the CTRL key.

From the "Arrange" menu/ribbon, choose "Order". This group contains the four layer positioning options. Select the option that allows you to move the object within the layer stack to the desired location.

Click "Bring to Front", in order to move the chosen item to the front of the stack. It will be positioned on top of every other object if the objects are arranged to overlap. To move the selected object in front of the object it was directly behind, click "Bring Forward" (or beneath if the objects overlapped).

Select the object you want to move behind the one it was right in front of by clicking "Send Backward" (or on top of it if the objects overlapped).Press "Send to Back" to rearrange the chosen item in the stack. It will be positioned beneath every other object if the objects are arranged to overlap.

Advanced Features and Special Elements

Working with tables

A table is made up of rows and columns of grid-rearranged cells. Information can be arranged using tables in a clear, readable manner. Tables are perfect for presenting lists of related information in Publisher, such as product prices or store hours, because the text within them is simple to align and space.

Creating and Formatting Tables

Tables in Publisher are helpful for arranging and displaying data. You can alter tables in Publisher to make them blend in with the style and tone of your publication. To access the Tables group, click the Insert tab. Choose Table from the drop-down menu.

To format a table, choose the cells that you wish to modify, right-click on it and select Format Table. After selecting the desired options from the tabs at the top of the "Format Table dialog box", enter your formatting adjustments.

Importing Data Into Tables

Open the file that has the desired text or chart added to it. Choose the text. Select the text or chart with a right-click, then choose Copy. Select the table where you wish to add the chart or text. Right-click on the desired location, then, select Paste to insert the text.

The text you pasted appears in selected table in the publication. The text you paste will automatically be formatted using the publication's font scheme. The text has a different font style if the Paste Options button shows up. Click the Paste Options button, then select "Maintain Source Formatting" if you want the text to retain its original formatting.

Using Special Elements

Select "Insert" tab from the "Home menu". And this is where all of the options, such as Symbols, Math, Quotation Marks, Dashes and Hyphens, Spaces and Tabs, and Breaks, are arranged into sub-menus.

Building Blocks and Design Elements

Publisher provides you with hundreds of building blocks, such as borders, calendars, headlines, and ads, to use in your publications. On the Insert tab, click. Click a building block, such as, page Sections, timetable, accents & Borders, Commercials.

Page Parts and Master Pages

A master page is a predetermined layout that is used for all of the sections in your document. A master page with a header, a footer, and layout attributes like borders and orientation can be specified in a template.

You have the option of starting from scratch to create a new master page or duplicating an already-existing master page, which you can then edit to modify only the desired parts.

Use two-page master pages if your publication is set up to be viewed as two-page spreads. Use single-page master pages if your publication is set up to be viewed as a single page.

Additionally, you have the option to convert a one-page master page to a two-page master page or alter a two-page master page to a single-page master page or vice versa.

Click View > Master Page to view the master pages that are currently displayed in your open publication. Start editing the master page by adding headers, footers, and page numbers in the master page window. To return to publication view, click Close Master Page.

Conclusion

One of Microsoft Publisher's greatest features as a widely used desktop publishing tool that is part of the Microsoft Office suite is its ability to effortlessly combine text and images to create publications like flyers and programs, postcards, professional business cards, event posters, brochures, newsletters, and certificates.

It gives users access to a range of components that will help you create publications that are both useful and appealing to your readers.

Additionally, it offers a range of templates and an intuitive interface that make it reasonably easy for non-designers to create publications that look professional.

When you launch Publisher, a list of available publication templates appears on a startup screen. For now, select the listing's default blank page option to view the Microsoft Publisher user interface. It is used to manage files and data that are connected to but distinct from the files.

Backstage View allows you to create and save files, change file preferences, and look for hidden or private data. Publisher provides you with hundreds of building blocks, such as borders, calendars, headlines, and ads, to use in your publications.

As a beginner or an expert, you can make use of templates and layouts in Microsoft Publisher that can help you get started on your creative project and serve as inspiration.